UNDERCURRENTS OF JEWISH PRAYER

THE LITTMAN LIBRARY OF
JEWISH CIVILIZATION

Dedicated to the memory of
LOUIS THOMAS SIDNEY LITTMAN
*who founded the Littman Library for the love of God
and as an act of charity in memory of his father*
JOSEPH AARON LITTMAN
and to the memory of
ROBERT JOSEPH LITTMAN
who continued what his father Louis had begun

יהא זכרם ברוך

'*Get wisdom, get understanding:
Forsake her not and she shall preserve thee*'

PROV. 4: 5

*The Littman Library of Jewish Civilization is a registered UK charity
Registered charity no.* 1000784

Undercurrents of Jewish Prayer

JEREMY SCHONFIELD

The Littman Library of Jewish Civilization
in association with Liverpool University Press

The Littman Library of Jewish Civilization
in association with Liverpool University Press
4 Cambridge Street, Liverpool L69 7ZU, UK

www.liverpooluniversitypress.co.uk/littman

Managing Editor: Connie Webber

Distributed in North America by
Oxford University Press Inc., 198 Madison Avenue,
New York, NY 10016, USA

First published 2006
First issued in paperback 2008

Catalogue records for this book are available from the
British Library and the Library of Congress

ISBN 978-1-904113-72-0

Publishing co-ordinator: Janet Moth
Copy-editing: Lindsey Taylor-Guthartz
Proof-reading: George Tulloch
Indexing: Sarah Ereira
Designed and typeset by Pete Russell, Faringdon, Oxon.

Printed in Great Britain by
CPI Group (UK) Ltd., Croydon, CR0 4YY

In memory of

RABBI DR SOLOMON *and* JUDITH SCHONFELD

זצ״ל

&

and for

SOLOMON *and* AMOS

Preface and Acknowledgements

శ్రీ

I HAVE BEEN FASCINATED by the liturgy since, aged perhaps 4 or 5, I sat on my father's lap in the Adath Yisroel Synagogue, London, where he was rabbi, dimly aware of the emotional intensity generated by ritual words and song. This was particularly the case on Rosh Hashanah and Yom Kippur, with their mesmerizingly recurrent melodies and verbal patterns, but was also true of sabbath services and of Passover at home. I could not then begin to understand what this compellingly evocative power was, and even when I came in later years to share the narratives and values on which Jewish ceremonies are based, the liturgy seemed to contribute a voice of its own, independent of the sense of occasion or the beliefs I brought to the synagogue, with tension seeming to arise out of the very encounter with the words on the page and their public use.

I subsequently came to recognize that this had little to do with what could be understood as their obvious 'meaning'. Even with the help of translations the prayer-book seemed teasingly opaque, and the few commentaries I could find in English—including one by my grandfather, Rabbi Dr J. H. Hertz—reinforced my view that the prayer-book could not be 'read' like other works. Although at first I tried to supplement my misty impressions with hard facts, such as who wrote each prayer and where and when it was first used, I finally turned to collecting old prayer-books, relishing their feel, smell, archaic translations, and flyleaf annotations of births, deaths, and marriages, as though antiquarianism might open the door to the meaning of the liturgy.

It has taken me years to return to the texts themselves, in part because of the complexity of what appears on the page, and in part because, as I now recognize, the themes embedded there would not have occurred to the person I then was. When I was studying literature as an undergraduate, the idea that liturgy might be a literary genre seemed not to have occurred to the scholars I encountered, and this discouraged me from treating it as such myself. Even those mostly Jewish scholars who from the early 1980s spearheaded the literary analysis of biblical and aggadic texts for non-specialist readers seem to have ignored it, much as traditional commentaries in Hebrew likewise have little to say about what the prayer-book really means. This seduced me for a time into accepting that there was, in fact, very little to say about it. But literary critics are now less preoccupied than they once were with judgements of quality based on lucidity, elegance, and economy of means, and have become more inclusive in their view of what constitutes literature, and this has helped me to ask the questions anew.

I have been actively preoccupied by the issues explored in this book since the mid-1980s, when I began to teach liturgy, initially to adults and then to undergraduates and postgraduates, at first taking a broad view of the festival- and life-cycle and later using the more focused methodology adopted here. The present survey is at best a preliminary attempt to outline what I have discovered—preliminary both in the sense that it deals with only a small introductory part of the daily liturgy, so cannot achieve a comprehensive view, and because it merely scratches the surface of the subject. However, the probability that subsequent work will modify some of the conclusions, including the summary of the 'liturgical narrative' presented in Chapter 11, does not seem a good reason to refrain from documenting the findings so far. Indeed, the approach presented here must be applied to larger liturgical units, eventually encompassing the daily, annual, and life-cycle, before a clearer idea of its validity can be formed. If this book stimulates others to work in a similar direction the effort will have been worthwhile.

I have chosen to base my reading on an edition of the prayer-book published by my father, with a translation with which I helped him in a small way as a child. I now recognize that his marginal notes express his potential interest in some of the issues I raise here, although I am aware that his conclusions might have been very different from those I have reached. The Hebrew text he used as the basis of his translation was standard in western Europe from the early nineteenth century until after the Second World War, and successors to the same publishers continue to issue editions with similar fonts and layouts, some with a German translation. It is derived from the work of Wolf Heidenheim, whose commentated liturgies were printed in Rödelheim, near Frankfurt, from the early years of the nineteenth century onwards.[1] Although other translated editions have now overtaken it in popularity, it embodies what was until recently a dominant European tradition, and one whose varying type-sizes reflect a last flicker of the medieval manuscript tradition and capture the composite nature of the texts on the page.

I owe the ideas in this book to too many people to identify them all here, but it gives me great pleasure to single out a few of those who gave me special help. I owe most to my parents, Rabbi Dr Solomon and Judith Schonfeld,[2] for exposing me to religious words and music, discussing them with me, and giving me a

[1] Wolf Heidenheim's daily prayer-book, *Sefat emet*, first appeared in 1806 and has gone through some 150 editions: see Temkin, 'Wolf Heidenheim'. Editorial changes have taken place, but one edition (sometimes accompanied by a German translation) is still available from Victor Goldschmidt Verlag, Basle.

[2] Obituary, *The Times*, 8 Feb. 1984. The various spellings of the family name reflect choices made before and during the Second World War. My mother opted for 'Schonfeld' on being evacuated from London during the Blitz, hoping to avoid hostile attention in case of German invasion, and my brothers and I grew up with that spelling. My father retained the less Anglicized version (to which one of my brothers has since reverted) although it differed from that of his own father, Rabbi Dr Victor Schönfeld (1880–1930). I have retained my mother's choice as a memorial to challenging times.

copy of *Otsar hatefilot* for my bar mitzvah; so thanks are also due to Salomon Steinberger[3] for presenting them with that prayer-book—finely bound and with brass corners and studs—on their wedding in 1940; I am also grateful for the fact that, when he heard it had been passed on to me, he made me promise to use it well. He would no doubt have preferred a work of more conventional piety, but I hope he would have recognized the sincerity of my attempt to come to grips with this particularly problematic area of rabbinic writing. I am grateful to Professor Ilse Graham,[4] who, on a holiday in 1967, helped me understand the multivalence of religious writing, art, and architecture, and for showing me how these resonate with reality; to my uncle Akiba (Sir Andrew) Shonfield[5] and his wife Zuzanna[6] for encouraging me to think; to my aunt Dr Asenath Petrie[7] for daring me to do so out loud and for urging me to keep notes; to Professor Raphael Loewe for patiently helping me align my approach with traditional rabbinic thought and for commenting in detail on a first draft; to Dr Risa Domb for first suggesting that I should present this work as a doctoral thesis—that this book was begun at all owes most to her—and to her and to Professor William Horbury for supervising my work and making valuable suggestions; to Professor Philip Alexander and Professor Martin Goodman for constructively showing me how easily my approach might be misunderstood; and to the Reverend Halfon Benarroch for teaching me to lead services according to the Spanish and Portuguese tradition and inviting me to do so at Bevis Marks synagogue, London. My parents-in-law, Dr Levi-Yitzhak and Basia Rahmani, have for years provided a convivial summer home that allowed me to focus on research and reading, most of it carried out in the air-conditioned tranquillity of the library of Hebrew Union College, Jerusalem, to whose librarians I am also grateful for their patience. Marina Yedigaroff and Roger East were unfailingly generous hosts in Cambridge, where their home was my own.

Others who have commented on parts of this book or have contributed to it in various ways include David Britt,[8] Professor Claudine Dauphin, Rabbi Abraham Gubbay, Kathy Henderson, Esra Kahn, Gabriel Levin, Barry Middleton, Jane Pettit, Dr Levi-Yitzhak Rahmani, Dr Ada Rapoport-Albert, Professor Stefan Reif, Katharine Ridler, Avi Rose, Deborah Silver, Dr Judith Szekacs, Dr Mihai-Răzvan Ungureanu, Erla Zimmels, and in particular my brother, Jonathan Schonfeld. I am especially grateful to his son, Daniel Schonfeld, for his help in checking and correcting the marginal references which appear alongside the translation. The help they have given should not be assumed to represent their

---

[3] Lewin, *A Jewish Geneology*, 71–4.   [4] Obituary, *The Times*, 20 Dec. 1988.

[5] Obituaries, *The Times*, 24 Jan. and 16 Feb. 1981, *Financial Times*, 24 Jan. 1981, *Observer*, 25 Jan. 1981.   [6] Obituary, *Guardian*, 9 Mar. 2000.

[7] Obituary, *Jewish Chronicle*, 16 Feb. 2001.

[8] David Britt, who died on 23 Jan. 2002 aged 62, helped me organize the introductory chapters of this book. I and many others miss his critical sensitivity and his friendship.

agreement with the conclusions I have reached here. Those, and any errors, are entirely my own.

I am grateful also to those colleagues and students at the Spiro Institute, the Oxford Centre for Hebrew and Jewish Studies, Leo Baeck College–Centre for Jewish Education, and the London Jewish Cultural Centre, who have served as sounding boards, commentators, and critics since 1985, refining, challenging, contradicting, and contributing to the argument outlined here, mostly with kindness and forbearance.

I am most fortunate in my publisher, having been privileged to meet the late Louis Littman in connection with the paper he wrote shortly before he died, entitled 'The Littman Library of Jewish Civilization'. One can only admire the way his widow Colette and their son Roby have maintained this unique charitable enterprise, one of which Anglo-Jewry can be proud. Working with the publication team, potentially an author's nightmare, has been a pleasure. I owe a debt of gratitude to Connie Webber, managing editor, who recognized the potential of this book while it was in a raw state and made several suggestions for additions. She also suggested including illustrations and introduced me to photographer Ruthie Morris, the perfect partner in preparing the illustrations in the Appendix. Ludo Craddock has smoothed the administrative way, Pete Russell has performed design magic on intractable material, George Tulloch picked up errors everyone else had missed, John Saunders has seen the book through the printing process with unflappable good nature, and Janet Moth has overseen the editorial process, complicated by the multiplicity of languages and cultural assumptions involved. But most of all I wish to thank my editor, Lindsey Taylor-Guthartz, who has energetically edited this book, cajoling the text into readability, and lacing her editorial notes with witty asides which occasionally reduced me to tears of laughter. It was a privilege to work with such an editor.

Grants from a number of individuals and organizations enabled me to take extended leave from freelance editing and teaching while writing this book. Dr Abraham Marcus, who was the first to offer help, encouraged me to approach other donors. Rabbi Dr Sidney Brichto put me in touch with Michael Heller, Peter Levy OBE, and an anonymous donor. Isaac Zekaria suggested I approach the Lara Trust of the Spanish and Portuguese Congregation and himself communicated with other donors, including Sir David Alliance CBE and Jack Dellal. I was awarded a UJIA scholarship in 1997–2000. I have also been helped by Sir Sigmund Sternberg and Suzanne Perlman. From 2000 I was helped by Samuel Lopes-Dias through the Dias Foundation, as well as by George Weisz, both of whose kindness can be gauged by the fact that they offered help without being asked. I hope that all these feel their generosity was justified.

No one has been more constructively engaged in developing the ideas underlying this book than my wife Tamar, who coincidentally completed her psychoanalytic training on the day that the thesis on which this book is based was finished. She has made the final stages of writing, in particular, tolerable. Clearly, such a project should be dedicated to my parents, neither of whom survived to see it completed. Even though they would not have agreed with all I have said here, they would have been happy with my choice of subject. But since our sons have shown such admirable patience with an often preoccupied parent, surrendering with good grace the use of the computer for which they often had quite other plans, they also deserve a place in the dedication. I am sure they will not mind sharing this tribute of love with the grandparents they never met, but whom they would have enjoyed knowing.

J.S.

Contents

❧

Contents

APPENDIX
Photographs of Ritual Objects Used in Prayer

Note on Transliteration and Conventions Used in the Text

𒀭

THE transliteration of Hebrew in this book reflects consideration of the type of book it is, in terms of its content, purpose, and readership. The system adopted therefore reflects a broad approach to transcription, rather than the narrower approaches found in the *Encyclopaedia Judaica* or other systems developed for text-based or linguistic studies. The aim has been to reflect the pronunciation prescribed for modern Hebrew, rather than the spelling or Hebrew word structure, and to do so using conventions that are generally familiar to the English-speaking Jewish reader.

In accordance with this approach, no attempt is made to indicate the distinctions between *alef* and *ayin*, *tet* and *taf*, *kaf* and *kuf*, *sin* and *samekh*, since these are not relevant to pronunciation; likewise, the *dagesh* is not indicated except where it affects pronunciation. Following the principle of using conventions familiar to the majority of readers, however, transcriptions that are well established have been retained even when they are not fully consistent with the transliteration system adopted. On similar grounds, the *tsadi* is rendered by 'tz' in such familiar words as bar mitzvah, mitzvot, and so on. Likewise, the distinction between *ḥet* and *khaf* has been retained, using *ḥ* for the former and *kh* for the latter; the associated forms are generally familiar to readers, even if the distinction is not actually borne out in pronunciation, and for the same reason the final *heh* is indicated too. As in Hebrew, no capital letters are used, except that an initial capital has been retained in transliterating titles of published works (for example, *Shulḥan arukh*).

Since no distinction is made between *alef* and *ayin*, they are indicated by an apostrophe only in intervocalic positions where a failure to do so could lead an English-speaking reader to pronounce the vowel-cluster as a diphthong—as, for example, in *ha'ir*—or otherwise mispronounce the word.

The *sheva na* is indicated by an *e*—*perikat ol*, *reshut*—except, again, when established convention dictates otherwise.

The *yod* is represented by *i* when it occurs as a vowel (*bereshit*), by *y* when it occurs as a consonant (*yesodot*), and by *yi* when it occurs as both (*yisra'el*).

Names have generally been left in their familiar forms, even when this is inconsistent with the overall system. The transliteration of divine names follows standard Orthodox Ashkenazi convention, involving the substitution of *hashem* (the Name) for the Tetragrammaton. This was intended to avoid 'taking God's name in vain'. Following certain traditions, we have transliterated *elohim* as it is pronounced.

In citations from the books of Psalms and Daniel, I have followed the numbering system used in the Hebrew; readers using certain English translations, such as the Authorized or Revised Versions, may find that the verse number differs slightly. Similarly, in citing Mishnah *Pirkei avot*, I have followed the numbering system that appears in the Travers Herford edition in preference to alternative systems.

Thanks are due to Professor Jonathan Webber of Birmingham University's Department of Theology for his help in elucidating the principles to be adopted.

Translations of scriptural and rabbinic texts are my own.

Note on Extracts from the Liturgy

☙

The sequence of morning prayers that forms the main focus of Part II is taken from the edition by Solomon Schonfeld, *Sidur metsuyan: The Standard Siddur-Prayer Book with an Orthodox English Translation and a Lineal Set of References* (London, 1973). The selection comprises the whole of Birkhot Hashaḥar and Pesukei Dezimra, the first of which consists of blessings and meditations and the second of psalmic and other poetic texts. Jointly these units introduce the core of the morning service and, this book argues, set the scene for the liturgy as a whole. The Hebrew is unchanged from the original save the addition of line numbers. The English translations and their marginal source references have been freshly typeset to incorporate minor corrections; the source references are reproduced here in their entirety even though not all are followed up in the present discussion.

In the original these texts run continuously with only paragraph breaks. To enable them to be presented in close proximity to the discussion, they have here been divided into fifty-nine 'extracts'; reference in the text is to extract number followed by the line number of the Hebrew. This division is not intended to imply that the texts can be better understood as separate units; on the contrary, as the discussion following each extract makes clear, the emphasis throughout is on the continuity of the argument running through the liturgy. For ease of reference the extracts are listed on pages xix–xx below.

Abbreviations and Conventions Used in the Extracts

° A raised circle appears before the word or phrase to which a side note refers.
: A colon following a talmudic reference indicates that the relevant text appears on the verso of the folio referred to.

Am.	Amos	*Dn.*	Daniel
Av.	*Avot*	*Dt.*	Deuteronomy/*De'ot*
AZ	*Avodah zarah*	*Ec.*	Ecclesiastes
B'	Bavli, Babylonian Talmud	*Ed.*	*Eduyot*
BH	*Beit habeḥirah*	*Er.*	*Eruvin*
BK	*Bava kama*	*Es.*	Esther
BM	*Bava metsia*	*Ex.*	Exodus
Br.	*Berakhot*	*Ez.*	Ezekiel
Bt.	*Bekhorot*	*Fz.*	Alfazi Code
Cr.	Chronicles	*Gn.*	Genesis

Gt.	*Gitin*	*OT*	*Otsar hatefilot (sidur)*
Ha.	*Ḥagigah*	*Pe.*	*Pe'ah*
Hb.	Habakkuk	*Pm.*	*Pesaḥim*
Hs.	Hosea	*Prv.*	Proverbs
Hu.	*Ḥulin*	*Ps.*	Psalms
Ikk.	*Sefer ha'ikarim/ The 13 Tenets*	*Ra.*	Rashi
	(Maimonides)	*RH*	*Rosh hashanah*
Int.	Introduction	*RN*	Rabbi Nathan
Is.	Isaiah	*Ru.*	Ruth
Jb.	Job	*SA*	*Shulḥan arukh*
Jg.	Judges	*Sb.*	*Shabat*
Jl.	Joel	*Sf.*	*Sifrei/ Sifra/ Soferim*
Jr.	Jeremiah	*Sm.*	Samuel/ *Shema*
Js.	Joshua	*Sn.*	Sanhedrin
Kd.	*Kidushin*	*So.*	Sotah
Ki.	Kings/ *Kitsur*	*Su.*	*Sukah*
Kn.	*Kelim*	*Sv.*	*Shevuot*
Kr.	*Keritot*	*Tef.*	*Tefilah*
Krb.	*Korbanot*	*Tfn.*	*Tefilin*
Kt.	*Ketubot*	*Tm.*	*Tamid*
Ku.	*Kuzari*, by Judah Halevi	*Tn.*	*Ta'anit*
La.	Lamentations	*Trg.*	Targum
Lv.	Leviticus	*Tsf.*	Tosafot/ Tosefta
Mai.	Maimonides	*TT*	*Talmud torah/ Torah temimah*
Mal.	Malachi	*Tva.*	*Teshuvah*
Md.	*Midrash rabah/ Midot*	*Uk.*	*Uktsin*
Md.[5/7]	fifth column of seven etc.	*ult.*	end of section
Mg.	*Megilah*	*Y'*	Yerushalmi, Jerusalem
Mi.	Micah		Talmud or Targum
Mk.	*Makot*	*Yal.*	*Yalkut shimoni*
MK	*Mo'ed katan*	*YD*	*Yoreh de'ah*
Mn.	*Menaḥot*	*Yo.*	*Yomah*
Msh.	Mishnah	*YT*	*Yom tov/ Yesodei hatorah*
Mta.	*Mekhilta*	*Yv.*	*Yevamot*
Ng.	*Nega'im*	*Ze.*	Zechariah
Nh.	Nehemiah	*Zo.*	Zohar (Mantua/ Vilna
Ni.	*Nidah*		pagination)
Nu.	Numbers	*Zph.*	Zephaniah
Ob.	Obadaiah/ Bartinoro on	*Zr.*	Ezra
	Mishnah	*Zv.*	*Zevaḥim*
OH	*Oraḥ ḥayim*		

List of Extracts

&

PART I

CHAPTER ONE

❧

The Incuriousness of the Jewish Worshipper

T RADITIONAL JEWS encounter the Siddur, the Jewish prayer-book, more often than any other text, even the Bible. They repeat parts of it three or even four times a day—morning, afternoon, and evening—besides reciting blessings before and after meals and on other occasions. In contrast, the text of the Torah is read in a formal fashion only in synagogue or other communal prayer settings, when it is chanted from a scroll that has been ceremonially removed from the Ark in which it is kept. Although daily prayers can be recited almost anywhere and, in the case of blessings on special occasions, at any time, there are only four ritual readings from a Torah scroll in the course of the week: on sabbath morning, as part of the annual cyclic reading of the Pentateuch, and on sabbath afternoons and Monday and Thursday mornings, when smaller sections of the next week's portion are read. Such readings are performed only in the context of a service attended by a quorum of ten adult men.

Outside the ritual round of formal readings the Bible is indeed studied intensively by individuals and groups, usually with the help of a library of commentaries and sometimes in study programmes that extend over several years. Some of these commentaries form genres in their own right, such as the talmudic, halakhic, and midrashic literatures and the glosses that have developed around them, all of which are based more or less directly on the scriptural text. Young Orthodox men might spend a number of years in full-time study of such material, continuing to study two or more evenings a week throughout their lives, making this probably the dominant religious activity among Orthodox men, and certainly the one with the highest status.[1] Meditation and worship, in contrast, are never full-time activities but are limited to ritually prescribed occasions.[2] In addition, they confer no special social status, but are performed by all on a regular basis, with varying degrees of attention.

---

[1] Most traditional writings since the completion of the scriptural canon have consisted of its gloss, elaboration, or codification. Daniel Boyarin (*Intertextuality*, 22) describes the interpretation of Torah as 'the dominant cultural practice of rabbinic Judaism'. See Mishnah *Avot* 2: 9, BT *Kid.* 49*b*. For a sociological analysis of study-circles see Heilman, *People of the Book*, esp. pp. 24–5, 237–59.

[2] Rabbi Johanan's praise of full-time prayer in BT *Ber.* 21*a* was not intended as a practical proposal.

The intensity of contact with the prayer-book, in terms of the number of separate encounters with it in the course of each day, thus makes this the text to which traditional Jews turn most frequently, even if it does not receive the same degree of attention as the texts included in the traditional study curriculum. The hours of the day are enmeshed with the prayer-book and it is a matter of almost constant awareness. As a natural result of this daily engagement with the prayer-book and the familiarity of traditional Jews with its contents, it might have been expected to have generated at least as many commentaries as the Bible and to feature prominently in Jewish intellectual life. However, the liturgy is of negligible importance in the traditional study curriculum and is hardly ever systematically examined by groups or individuals. The prayer-book does feature in talmudic literature, but the focus there is almost exclusively on the details of performance rather than on the content or meaning of the liturgy.

What is the reason for this lack of attention in the traditional curriculum, and why are people who are used to making sense of texts as complex as the Bible and Talmud not tempted to puzzle more intensively over the meaning of the prayer-book, which they encounter far more often than any other text? Given the roles of the Bible and liturgy in Jewish thought, this inconsistency is particularly strange. The Bible clearly demands to be understood, since it is divinely revealed as a message to humanity. The liturgy, however, which is a human message to God, seems equally to demand that it be understood by the person reciting it. The speaker's comprehension is implied by the way that prayers are often addressed to 'our father, our king' and function as the human side of a human–divine dialogue. Prayer texts certainly cannot be dismissed as ephemeral, since they are based on practices traced in the rabbinic tradition to biblical times, notionally at least.[3] The neglect of meaning is therefore particularly strange.

The problem is deepened by the fact that the Jewish prayer-book—like all liturgical worship—has the effect of limiting and defining those ideas about which it is permissible to speak in prayer. Liturgy could thus be regarded as designed to prevent spontaneous outbursts, as though these might pose a danger to the social order, which rests on the decorous conduct of an official cult. Since purely personal expressions, as in the case of the biblical prophets, are regarded as disruptive and subversive and to be suppressed,[4] the words of prayer tend to be deliberately impersonal. They are commonly regarded as effective even if they are not 'meant' by the individual reciting them. If so, the formality of prayer could be interpreted as a device for suppressing feelings rather than for expressing them. However, this book aims to show how feelings that might indeed be regarded as 'unseemly' nevertheless survive their translation into the medium of a formal liturgy, and how the prayer-book might be interpreted as normalizing dissent and giving it a covert voice.

---

[3] Maimonides, *Mishneh Torah: The Book of Adoration*, 'On Prayer' 1: 4.

[4] Kraemer, *Responses to Suffering*, 217–18.

Although texts deriving from divine revelation are studied intensively, it is often tacitly assumed that prayer only needs to be spoken in order to be effective, as though it does not really address God (the issue of intention will be discussed in more detail below). The ghost of emotional immediacy does seem to survive, however, in the official assumption that a verbal relationship between speaker and hearer does indeed exist and is activated in liturgical worship. But the words that are used do not reinforce this feeling. In practice, it seems merely to be assumed that God 'hears' what is said, even though the liturgical message itself is far from transparent.

The failure of even popular curiosity about the meaning of prayer, let alone of scholarly investigation, is particularly evident among prayer-book publishers, most of whom seem to regard liturgical meaning as self-evident. In Israel, where the language of liturgy is close to the vernacular, editors and printers occasionally include a gloss of difficult words in the margins of the text, but offer little other help with wider concepts. Editions published elsewhere usually include a translation into the vernacular, facing the Hebrew original, as though the liturgy could be understood by exchanging Hebrew for another language. The approach taken by Jews in nearly all their encounters with the written word—based on the assumption that it requires meticulous attention and careful analysis—seems almost totally absent here. Aspects of the liturgical reading experience generated by the interplay of sentences, paragraphs, and entire sequences are ignored as though they were superfluous, or even, in some sense, improper subjects for investigation.

If the liturgy were indeed transparently clear and in no need of special interpretation, such a failure to elaborate on its meaning might be justified, but this is not the case. Commentaries on biblical and talmudic texts examine the resonances and the implicit meanings of each word, and are often substantially longer than the texts on which they comment. Some are so detailed that they virtually make the reader privy to the authorial or editorial process, showing how the text was assembled and leaving no element unexplained. The fact that this approach is not applied to the prayer-book, however, despite the obvious need for clarification, suggests that its obscurity is not regretted. There are very few references, either positive or negative, to liturgical obscurity in rabbinic literature.[5]

This tacit exemption of the prayer-book from exegetical curiosity is particularly surprising in view of its superficial similarity to other texts that are intensively studied. The liturgy matches or even surpasses in complexity some of the denser biblical and rabbinic writings, in part because its editors cited freely from almost every genre of biblical and rabbinic composition, juxtaposing passages or phrases in often dizzying ways, with no apparent concern for overall design. In places the prayer-book resembles a mosaic of *objets trouvés*, challenging the reader

[5] The study of liturgy is compared to the understanding of biblical texts by Levi ben Gershon in his Torah commentary, end of 'Aḥarei mot', cited in Rosenberg, 'Prayer and Jewish Thought', 81.

to recognize the contexts from which each text comes, while simultaneously accepting its place in the liturgy without comment. The reader's attention moves restlessly over the fragmented surface, engaging in a dynamic encounter rather than acknowledging an authoritative composition, other than in a formal way.

The prayer-book thus offers its users an experience so lively and unsettling that the lack of curiosity about its meaning is nothing less than astonishing. Where is the characteristic Jewish awareness that language is complex and multilayered, and can be understood only by reading between the lines? What has happened to the urge for clarity that dominates rabbinic study? The very scantiness of traditional liturgical exegesis seems not to have been noted before, or if it has, has been dismissed as insignificant. Why is incomprehension tolerated in the case of the one Hebrew text in which Jews come closest to responding to divine revelation?

This book begins with an analysis of this and related questions, and then provides a line-by-line analysis of the first part of the daily morning service. I have not attempted to discuss the entire service, both because of considerations of length and because the passages analysed illustrate points which apply to the entire liturgy, as will be argued in Chapter 11, which outlines the liturgical narrative. This reading will illustrate what emerges if rabbinic literary-critical tools are applied to liturgical interpretation, and will reveal that the prayer-book is in fact a multi-layered monologue, much of which explores the vein of dissent aroused by the divine silence following direct liturgical address. Many worshippers feel that their prayer does receive a response, and it could be argued that the worshipper's very survival at the moment of prayer is an 'answer', but the hope for a direct response is so basic to the act of addressing God that the lack of a reply cannot be ignored. The worshipper's fears concerning the outside world are the original spur to prayer, but these are joined by other anxieties deriving mostly from God's apparent silence, generating a powerful drama of doubt and uncertainty in which the worshipper is the chief player.

One reason that no book of this type has been written before, even though the analytical tools employed here could be applied by any Jewishly educated reader, is that its lack has not been noted. The neglect of liturgy has been well camouflaged, for at first sight there appears to be no lack of commentaries, glosses, or guides to its teasingly opaque Hebrew and Aramaic texts. However, the scholarly public has failed to adapt these for popular use. Traditional Jewish scholars approach most classic texts through a full range of commentaries, deployed collectively to reveal underlying difficulties and inconsistencies and to offer a range of possible solutions. Publishers have responded to this attitude by preparing editions of these works containing large numbers of commentaries, either in the margins of the main text or as appendices. Liturgical commentaries, however, are rarely compared and discussed in this way, and no edition of the liturgy that would make this possible has ever appeared—at least at the time of writing.

Not only are liturgical commentaries rarely studied, but most of those that have appeared seem to refrain from providing the kind of overview occasionally provided by scholars of other rabbinic genres, such as Nahmanides, for the Torah, or the composite commentary of Tosafot, for the Talmud. With occasional exceptions, prayer-book commentators tend to identify the scriptural and other sources from which each passage is drawn, and to neglect questions relating to the overall meaning of longer sequences or their interconnection. The result is oddly myopic and fragmentary, offering an image of the prayer-book as little more than an anthology of borrowed texts.

Why do traditional Jews—analytical acrobats in their approach to the Talmud —seem content to abandon the reading skills they have honed on other texts and, in the case of prayer alone, to behave as though these methods did not exist? Are they really content to treat the prayer-book with an uneasy blend of devotion and inattention, tacitly accepting its often almost impenetrable complexity?

The impact of this neglect of meaning on worship is well illustrated by Israel Zangwill in a passage from a novel in which he shows traditional Jews at prayer in late nineteenth-century London. His description has lost little relevance today, and will be recognized by those familiar with most varieties of traditional Judaism. He starts by describing how his worshippers

prayed metaphysics, acrostics, angelology, Cabbalah, history, exegetics, Talmudical controversies, menus, recipes, priestly prescriptions, the canonical books, psalms, love-poems, an undigested hotch-potch of exalted and questionable sentiments of communal and egoistic aspirations of the highest order. It was a wonderful liturgy, as grotesque as it was beautiful; like an old cathedral, in all styles of architecture, stored with shabby antiquities and side-shows, and overgrown with moss and lichen—a heterogeneous blend of historical strata of all periods, in which gems of poetry and pathos and spiritual fervour glittered, and pitiful records of ancient persecution lay petrified. . . . all this was known and loved, and was far more important than the meaning of it all, or its relation to their real lives; for page upon page was gabbled off at rates that could not be excelled by automata. But if they did not always know what they were saying, they always meant it. If the service had been more intelligible, it would have been less emotional and edifying. There was not a sentiment, however incomprehensible, for which they were not ready to die or to damn.[6]

Zangwill's acceptance of the situation is clear from his affectionate depiction of his characters. Like them, he does not ask himself what their liturgy might signify, and indeed he presents the prayer-book from almost every angle except that of meaning, enumerating its ingredients, listing the genres from which they are drawn, and even comparing the resulting assemblage to a building. As a guide to the liturgy, his approach is about as useful as one to a cathedral that lists its architectural parts and concludes by recommending a twilight sprint past them to enjoy them at their best.

[6] Zangwill, *Children of the Ghetto*, 142–3.

The situation seems to be that Zangwill's worshippers, perhaps like Zangwill himself and most traditional Jews since, have enough learning to recognize that the liturgy is a pot-pourri of extracts, but too little to detect any continuity of argument. Their response seems to be to accept the prayer-book as an anthology and to focus on what appeals to the ear and mind. But this amounts to treating it as a mantra—a text whose meaning is immaterial, but which generates emotions when repeated ritually. He does not ask whether such prayer might be regarded as 'effective' and, if not, what its purpose might be, for such questions clearly lie outside his field of interest. He describes only its public performance.

He does cast more light on his view of liturgy later, however, by describing how his characters were able to 'study the Law and the Prophets', but could only 'reverence the Rabbinical tradition and the chaos of commentaries expounding it', suggesting that these were beyond their comprehension. They would accordingly 'abase themselves before the "Life of Man" and Joseph Caro's "Prepared Table" [standard legal works] as though the authors had presided at the foundation of the earth', ignoring the fact that both are clearer than the prayer-book, being logically organized and simply written.[7] He does not suggest that his characters were aware of failing to understand the liturgy in the same way, however, or even that they had considered the possibility of approaching prayers as texts with a message, and in this we may detect Zangwill's own point of view. He likewise reports his admiration for the 'marvellous monument of the patience, piety and juristic genius of the race—and of the persecution which threw it back upon its sole treasure, the Law',[8] while saying nothing about the prayer-book itself. Given the synagogue setting of this scene he might well have included the prayer-book as one of the texts that can be studied. But he apparently assumed instead that the significance of prayer lies in its performance rather than in understanding it, and in this way relegated it to a non-textual limbo, reserved for writings unsuited for study.

Zangwill's depiction of the tacit acceptance of incomprehension in connection with the prayer-book is no less true of the majority of traditional Jews today, and also of users of non-Orthodox prayer-books, in which texts have been modified according to contemporary theological scruples. Even the most radical reformers have preserved some aspects of the older liturgies, and the emphasis on form over content arises wherever traditional structures are retained. Liturgies by their very nature hold the attention while simultaneously frustrating the understanding, and the liturgy will remain obscure as a result of the over-familiarity brought about by its constant use, if not because of its contents.[9]

The description given by Zangwill of the texture of the liturgy is no exaggeration, for its difficulty as a text goes well beyond a few local obscurities which could be rectified by editing or by vernacular translation. Opacity is essential to

---

[7] Zangwill, *Children of the Ghetto*, 143-4.   [8] Ibid. 145.

[9] Two sample non-Orthodox liturgies are discussed in the last chapter of this book.

the genre, as can be seen from the brief sequence examined in the present book, which covers the first third of the daily morning liturgy. This sequence begins in the early morning and accompanies the worshipper from the moment of waking in bed, through the process of dressing and leaving the house for synagogue, until the start of statutory prayer—a considerable trajectory, which shows how the worshipper regains awareness and faces the world at the start of a new day. However, instead of a straightforward sequence of blessings, scriptural quotations, or meditations relating to the experiences involved and bringing order to the process of waking, the worshipper encounters texts which are far from explicit and which teem with anomalies. The sequence discussed here includes two statements concerning waking,[10] two closely related versions of the Kaddish (following Extracts 40 and 42), an unexplained conceptual gap between petitionary prayer and the recital of sacrificial procedures (Extract 33, line 11, and Extract 34), an apparent contradiction between an expression of thanks for protection and the renewed petition that follows it (Extracts 25 and 26), and what looks like an intrusion of unrelated texts into a description of the sacrificial order (Extracts 36 and 37).

Despite this, the traditional prayer-book is inexplicably tolerated even by Jews with higher rabbinic education, including liturgical editors and exegetes. Editors have tended to regard loose links as invitations to slot in additional texts, compounding the disorder as though the authors regarded this as a virtue,[11] while commentators habitually treat structural oddities as survivals of different traditions or as attempts to resolve halakhic difficulties.[12] The introduction of *piyutim* (liturgical poems) into the prayer-book from the Byzantine period onwards may in some cases have been designed to bring order to the underlying chaos. However, Palestinian hymns in particular are often as obscure as the liturgy they supplemented or replaced, and must have been impenetrable to all but an educated elite. Such a flaunting of complexity may even have been intended to reflect the opacity of the rest of the liturgy, implicitly acknowledging that prayer is something about which it is hard to speak clearly. That it was intentional is suggested by the way poets used self-consciously archaic language in some interpolated poetic passages, as though to reflect the difficulty of expressing theological insights, but abandoned the style in parts designed for

[10] Extracts 1 and 21. These citations refer to the extracts from the edition of Solomon Schonfeld reproduced at the start of the discussion of each liturgical unit. A 'preliminary volume' containing the sabbath afternoon liturgy was published as *Pirkei Avot: The Sayings of the Fathers—Also the Sabbath Minchah Service with an Orthodox English Translation and a Lineal Set of References* (London, 1969). The full *Sidur Metsuyan: The Standard Siddur-Prayer Book with an Orthodox English Translation and a Lineal Set of References* appeared in 1973 and was reprinted in 1974 and 1976. The version used here is from the last impression.

[11] The presence of Adon Olam (Extract 15) seems to have led to the inclusion of the analogous hymn Yigdal in the present edition (Extract 14), although it does not appear in the standard edition of the Ashkenazi liturgy by Seligmann Baer, *Sidur avodat yisra'el*.

[12] See the remarks in Ch. 4 on the replacement of Extract 21 by Extract 1.

less educated readers.[13] Since the general effect of such poems is to compound the liturgy's obscurity, however, most have been allowed to lapse,[14] occasionally in response to the claim that the liturgy is sacred and should be immutable.[15] Most of the Ashkenazi liturgy's accumulation of mystical texts was pruned out by eighteenth-century editors and glossators on these grounds, ignoring the problem of opacity which arguably led to their inclusion in the first place.[16] The liturgy remains perplexing to most of its users, even though few would admit to finding it so.

The liturgy's incomprehensibility matters less as long as the prayers are able to arouse deep emotions and a feeling of mystery, which they do particularly at the penitential period of Rosh Hashanah and Yom Kippur[17] or during periods of personal crisis.[18] Indeed, the tendency to attribute such moments of coherence to theological or emotional factors, rather than to the power of the liturgy itself,[19] may help explain why traditional curricula tend to ignore the close study of liturgy.[20] This merely continues the tradition of assigning greater importance to the recital of liturgy at the correct time and with the right ritual gestures than to its comprehension.

The silence of well-educated traditional Jews about the liturgy has tended to have a corrosive effect on the life of the synagogue, however. As increasing numbers of people on the fringes of the rabbinic tradition have only a tenuous grasp of the choreography of prayer, of the theological significance of religious occasions, or of what it is like to experience regular contact with the liturgy, fewer sympathize with the idea that awed incomprehension might be an appropriate response to the prayer-book. The mantric approach to prayer permitted in many traditional communities has in many cases deteriorated into a perfunctory style of performance that can inspire in inexperienced observers little more than contempt for the liturgical genre.[21]

[13] Langer, *To Worship God Properly*, 44, 111, 113 n. 11.

[14] Ibid. 185–7.   [15] Ibid. 252–3.

[16] Such as the work of Wolf Heidenheim; see Elbogen, *Jewish Liturgy*, 283–4, 298–9. (This work was originally written in German—*Der jüdische Gottesdienst*, translated and augmented as *Hatefilah beyisra'el behitpathutah hahistorit* (Jerusalem, 1972), which was the edition translated by Raymond Scheindlin as *Jewish Liturgy*.) The consequences of liturgical reform, surveyed in Petuchowski, *Prayerbook Reform in Europe*, are discussed briefly in the final chapter of this book.

[17] Glatzer (ed.), *Franz Rosenzweig*, pp. xvi–xviii, describes how Rosenzweig abandoned his intention of being baptized after attending synagogue on these festivals in 1913. A friend described the services held as he was dying; see E. Simon, 'On the Meaning of Prayer', 108–9.

[18] Wieseltier, *Kaddish*, describes his fascination, following his father's death, with the mourners' daily recital of Kaddish in synagogue.

[19] The way in which such language may be said to 'create . . . situations' is mentioned in Langer, *To Worship God Properly*, 112. Rappaport, *Ecology, Meaning, and Religion*, 213, sees in this a source of the numinous.

[20] Fishman, *History of Jewish Education*, 44–5. He does not include it even under 'other subjects' (pp. 111–13).   [21] Hoffman, *Art of Public Prayer*, p. ix.

Texts, Translations, and Commentaries: A Survey

A brief survey of the ways in which classic Jewish texts have traditionally been printed and published will throw a stronger light on the contrast between the treatment of the prayer-book and almost every other rabbinic text.

Most classic works have hardly ever been printed without an assortment of glosses. The *editio princeps* of the Mishnah of 1492 contained Maimonides' commentary,[22] and it is unusual to find an edition of the Mishnah without annotations of some kind. The first complete edition of the Babylonian Talmud, of 1520–3, included the main text flanked by the glosses of Rashi and the Tosafot,[23] setting a precedent for almost every other edition. No traditional student would attempt to understand a talmudic text without the help at least of Rashi's commentary. Early printed editions usually included only a few commentaries, but in the nineteenth century, when inexpensive copies of rabbinic classics began to appear, publishers vied to produce versions with ever larger numbers of commentaries. The often reprinted and still standard editions printed by the Widow and Brothers Romm in Vilna exemplify the climax of this trend. Their thirteen-volume edition of the Mishnah of 1908–9 contained fifty-one glosses, 'almost all the extant commentaries',[24] while their Babylonian Talmud, published in 1880–6 with over a hundred commentaries, still represents 'the most comprehensive collection of commentaries'.[25] Their *Shulhan arukh* appeared in 1896 with 113 commentaries,[26] and the approach was extended even to an edition of the *Midrash rabah* published in 1887, despite the fact that midrashic writings have a lower status in traditional rabbinic circles than do halakhic works. The fifteen commentaries in that edition are in line with the close attention paid to the non-halakhic parts of talmudic literature by traditional commentators such as Samuel Edels (1555–1631, known by his acronym Maharsha), whose extended commentary on those elements of the Babylonian Talmud appears in the Romm edition.[27] Even pietistic works occasionally appear in folio editions designed for serious study, such as that of *Sefer hahinukh* with the commentary by Joseph Tarnipol, entitled *Minhat hahinukh*, published in Piotrków in 1902. Such publications, while not for mass consumption, were, and remain, staples of rabbinic scholarship, widely available in libraries and owned by traditional communities and many individuals.

In the case of the liturgy, however, no multi-commentary edition seems to have been issued, despite the often vigorous competition between publishing

---

[22] Stemberger, *Introduction*, 142.

[23] Ibid. 212–13.

[24] Danby, *Mishnah*, p. xxx n. 4; Stemberger, *Introduction*, 142.

[25] Stemberger, *Introduction*, 213.

[26] Rackman, Broyde, and Fishkin, 'Halakhah, Law in Judaism', 343–4.

[27] On the lower status of midrashic material, see Assaf and Urbach, 'Agadah', 353, cited and discussed in Heinemann, 'Nature of the Aggadah', 42, 50–4 n. 4.

houses to produce the most comprehensive editions of classic texts. Folio editions of the daily and festival liturgy were designed for prayer-leaders' lecterns rather than for the smaller bookrests of individual worshippers, and included usually only one relatively brief commentary. This tradition culminated in the four-volume *Sidur umahazor kol-bo* issued by Romm in 1904, in which recurring prayers are repeated in full almost every time they appear in order to avoid the need to cross-refer.[28] Since the large page size was designed to ensure that substantial passages of each liturgical sequence would appear on a single opening, it is true that adding further commentaries would have risked crowding out the liturgy and compromising the book's practical usefulness.

This does not explain, however, why an alternative folio edition designed for students, rather than prayer-leaders, was not issued, or even a smaller multi-commentary version for individual worshippers. One model might have been the so-called rabbinic bibles, known in Hebrew as *mikraot gedolot*, published in quarto size with a substantial number of commentaries, often with little more than a clause or two of the main text appearing on any one page amid a cluster of marginal commentaries. These standard publications, of which a number of editions are available, are designed for specialist use, but were presumably also intended in part for synagogue use, or they would have also been available in folio size. So the absence of even a quarto edition of the liturgy with commentaries must be assumed to reflect a lack of interest in liturgical study as such, in synagogue or elsewhere. This lack of interest cannot have resulted from a dearth of suitable commentaries, since several were available in print. Some survived in manuscript and were printed only in the later twentieth century, but even then they were not combined in larger compendia.[29]

As has been said, moreover, most commentaries do not attempt to link disparate passages in the way that talmudic commentaries do, but instead emphasize the anthological and fragmented nature of the liturgy. This is not true of David Abudarham's thorough and perceptive reading of the liturgy, however, completed around 1341.[30] This could easily have served as a key commentary in a compendium or even as the core of an entire genre, but seems almost never to have been published as a marginal text to a prayer-book and has apparently not generated supercommentaries of its own. Scholars failed to explore the field he opened up, excluding it from the curriculum of study.

Publishers nevertheless recognized the appeal of well-filled pages to a schol-

---

[28] The category is defined as *mahazor hagadol* in Goldschmidt, 'Prayer Books', 987.

[29] The first commentaries on the liturgy itself, rather than the medieval inserts, appeared in Hasidei Ashkenaz circles from 12th- and 13th-century Rhineland. These tend to compare the number of words in passages and the numerical value of letters in order to identify correspondences between liturgical or scriptural texts or to allude to theological concepts. They were used as devotional tools. See Marcus, 'Devotional Ideals', 359–60; Langer, *To Worship God Properly*, 38; and, for an example, Judah ben Samuel Hehasid, *Perushei sidur hatefilah laroke'ah*. For mystical commentaries see Scholem, *Kabbalah*, 179–80.   [30] Abudarham, *Abudarham hashalem*.

arly public and applied it to liturgy, though in a way that exposed their ambivalence about commentated prayer-books. Romm of Vilna published popular editions of a quarto-sized festival prayer-book containing the popular series of commentaries on the *piyutim* entitled *Korban aharon* by Aaron ben Yehiel Mikhel Halevi of Mikhailishok.[31] Its three marginal glosses—each covering a different aspect of the liturgy—were arranged typographically so as to suggest that they might have been written by different authors. A Yiddish translation was later added in some editions with the minimum of typographic compression, suggesting that room for more marginal commentaries could easily have been found. Yet the publishers failed to include even Aaron's commentary on the weekly prayer-book, *Nehora hashalem*, despite the fact that prayer-leaders' folio editions traditionally contained commentaries on both weekly and festival prayers.[32] The printing-house of Romm was not alone in this reluctance to juxtapose commentaries by different authors, for other prayer-books containing single-author commentaries for the festival texts appeared, such as the small-format western European classic by Wolf Heidenheim, first issued in 1800–2, which likewise lacks notes on the weekly prayers. This is surprising, since such commentaries would presumably have been well worth combining with others, such as the apparently anonymous commentary that appeared in successive editions of the *Kol-bo*.

The weekly prayer-book seems to have been no more studied than the festival liturgy, for even the commentaries of Isaiah Horowitz (1565(?)–1630) and of Jacob Emden (1697–1776), obvious candidates for parallel study, seem never to have been published together.[33] A few glosses were juxtaposed in prayer-books from various printing centres, including Vilna, throughout the nineteenth century, but all seem to have been designed for worship rather than study, since they were in formats smaller than quarto. Lack of curiosity about textual meaning is also reflected in the choice of glosses included. *Derekh hahayim*,[34] halakhic notes by Jacob Lorbeerbaum of Lissa (*c.*1760–1832), was often published with a supercommentary by Solomon Ganzfried (1804–86);[35] both works are concerned with ritual and performance rather than meaning, though they were occasionally

---

[31] Reif, *Judaism and Hebrew Prayer*, 278, 397 n. 42; editions were published in Slavuta in 1823, and in Vilna from 1835 onwards. See Benjacob, *Otsar hasefarim*, 319 para. 963. See also *Mahazor leyamim nora'im*, 59.

[32] Published in 1827, according to Goldschmidt, 'Prayer Books', 989, but in Slavuta in 1819, according to Benjacob, *Otsar hasefarim*, 663 para. 774.

[33] Goldschmidt, 'Prayer Books', 988. Horowitz's commentary, *Sha'ar hashamayim*, was printed in Amsterdam in 1717. Emden's was printed by the author in Altona in 1745–8. Both have been republished separately.

[34] First published in Żółkiew in 1828: see Benjacob, *Otsar hasefarim*, 663 para. 776; Kupfer, 'Jacob Lorbeerbaum', 492.

[35] First published in Vienna in 1839: see Benjacob, *Otsar hasefarim*, 664 para. 776; Levinger, 'Solomon Ganzfried', 314.

joined by the more textually focused *Nehora hashalem*.[36] The classic commentary on the prayer-book by Seligmann Baer, *Yakhin lashon*, published in his *Sidur avodat yisra'el*, was likewise never combined with others, although elements of it did appear in other editions.[37] Like Abudarham's work it could easily have formed the core of a fuller commentated edition.

The need for an edition that would enable worshippers to treat the weekly prayer-book with the same seriousness as other rabbinic classics was answered in a token way by Romm's publication of Gordon's *Sidur otsar hatefilot* in 1914, considerably later than other classics issued by this printing house.[38] This has been described as 'apparently the most complete prayerbook',[39] but it exemplifies the continuing failure of Jewish exegetical nerve when faced with the liturgy. The four most substantial of its ten marginal commentaries are mere digests of other material, including copious cross-references culled from a wide literature which have been invaluable in compiling the analysis offered here.[40] However, they only occasionally reproduce the original exegetical comments in full and almost never give the context in which these appear. Like most commentated prayer-books it is small enough to hold in the hand—smaller than the quarto festival prayer-books of the same publisher—so was clearly designed for prayer rather than study. In spite of this it would be virtually impossible to use it during prayer, since the pages are dominated by the commentaries, with very little liturgical text per page. The publisher's decisions clearly reflect prevailing values, since a slightly larger quarto format would have made it possible to include either more text on each page, thereby skewing the publication towards worship, or more commentary, thus emphasizing study. It seems to have been assumed that those who bought it would prefer to study during services while apparently engaged in prayer, and would thus favour a smaller volume that could be held during worship.

[36] They seem to have been published together in this way for the first time in Vienna in 1859: see Benjacob, *Otsar hasefarim*, 664 para. 776; Reif, *Judaism and Hebrew Prayer*, 278, 397 n. 41.

[37] Baer's prayer-book was published in Rödelheim in 1868, reprinted in Berlin in 1937 in quarto and in pocket format, and later in Jerusalem (n.d., *c*.1995). His notes on the Shirei Hayiḥud (pp. 133–49) are reproduced as part of a separately paginated supplement at the conclusion of *Otsar hatefilot*, 13*a*–23*a*.

[38] A precursor was *Seder rav amram hashalem*, ed. Frumkin, with two digests.

[39] Goldschmidt, 'Prayer Books', 988.

[40] It was edited by Arieh-Lev ben Solomon Gordon, said to have been born in 1845, to have moved to Jerusalem in 1891, and to have died in 1913; see Friedman, *Otsar harabanim*, 70. He also compiled five of the commentaries, and included two previously unpublished digests of midrashic and other sources by Hanokh Zundel ben Joseph (d. 1867), the midrash commentator, who claims in his preface to have based it on 200 books; see Y. Horowitz, 'Hanokh Zundel ben Joseph'. Samuel Shraga Feiginsohn, the literary director of the Romm publishing house, completed the editing following Gordon's death, and in September 1914 signed the preface on p. 8; see Slutsky, 'Romm', 255, and also Idelsohn, *Jewish Liturgy*, 64.

Publications such as this therefore imply that liturgical study is virtually an underground activity, to be conducted when it might be mistaken for devotion. But even if study were to take place outside the synagogue, the level of understanding made available by this edition would be far lower than what was expected for other texts, and would not be tolerated in the case of works designed for higher biblical or talmudic study.

The persistence of this anthological approach to liturgical study is reflected in later publications, some of which do not contain the liturgical text at all, such as Shemtob Gaguine's *Keter shem tov* (1934), which is organized thematically rather than sequentially and contains valuable footnotes discussing the differences between Sephardi and Ashkenazi practices. The author's deep knowledge of the sources is therefore harnessed to halakhic and inter-communal concerns rather than to the impulse to understand the text in its own terms. B. S. Jacobson's *Netiv binah*, a digest of a wide range of liturgical commentaries, similarly makes little attempt to link or justify the selection of views he quotes.[41] Perhaps the most ambitious traditional commentary yet attempted, in this case appearing with the text of the prayers, was begun by Jacob Werdiger in *Tselota di'avraham*, but the coverage of the sabbath liturgy is incomplete. Its two levels of commentary—again typographically distinguished as though to suggest multiple authorship—confirm that ambivalence about the propriety of liturgical study outside the synagogue still prevails, since there is too little main text on many pages for prayer and not enough material for comparative study.

The situation has been only partly rectified by the publication of *Sidur tefilah lemosheh*, a three-volume anthology of medieval commentaries on the weekday and sabbath prayer-book, typographically modelled on rabbinic bibles.[42] But although it seems to treat the prayer-book in the same way as other traditional study-texts, with fragments of the source surrounded by commentary, the table of sources makes clear that only limited selections of the sixty-three named commentaries are included. A comprehensive work, which would have to be on a far larger scale, still remains to be produced.

Even if such a work were produced, however, it would not aspire to the relentless pursuit of narrative development, authorial intention, historical background, and implicit meanings, as do commentaries on the Bible. The focus on identifying biblical and rabbinic sources apparent in most liturgical commentaries betrays their authors' low expectations of finding coherence, as though they thought the liturgy could be adequately 'understood' by tracing its component texts to their origins. Even the best of such commentaries, such as Heidenheim's festival prayer-book gloss, are principally concerned with elucidating obscurities in the *piyutim* by identifying parallels. Similarly, Baer's commentary, which

[41] Vol. i (Tel Aviv, 1964); the first thirteen introductory chapters were translated as *Meditations on the Siddur* and the commentary was translated as *The Weekday Siddur*.

[42] *Sidur tefilah lemosheh*, ed. Lupinski and Weinreb.

thoroughly examines the sources of statutory prayers, shows no interest in their structure.

If this reluctance to think about the liturgy could be attributed to scholarly disdain for a genre of merely popular interest, one would expect to see more attention being paid to it in popular and non-scholarly contexts. In Britain, however, the first translation of the liturgy, published by A. Alexander in 1770,[43] made no attempt to guide the reader through its obviously confusing content. David Levi's slightly later editions included notes on isolated passages,[44] as did D. A. De Sola's for the Sephardi liturgy.[45] But De Sola suggested that even these were unnecessary, since 'in the prayers [the liturgical editors] left us we find perspicuity of expression, united with sublimity of conception, which, while it ever maintains the dignity of the subject, may nevertheless always be easily understood by the general mass, for whose use it was designed'.[46] The attempt to explain was abandoned altogether by A. P. Mendes in his translation of the Ashkenazi weekly liturgy, issued in 1864 and designed to supplement De Sola's festival prayers of 1860; he included only halakhic notes extracted from Lorbeerbaum's *Derekh haḥayim*. Simeon Singer's translation of the Ashkenazi *Authorised Daily Prayer Book* of 1890, which went through thirty-three impressions before its radical revision in 1990, was wholly unannotated, although some copies, between the edition of 1914 and that of 1939 (at least), were bound with Israel Abrahams's *A Companion to the Authorised Daily Prayer Book*, which also appeared as a separate publication. Some copies of the earliest impression had larger margins, presumably designed for marginal notes, but this may have added too much weight to the volume and the practice was discontinued. Abrahams's notes, based on those of Baer, reflect an almost exclusive concern with textual history and sources and do not, for instance, go into detail about the opacity of what Abrahams implicitly admits is an anthology.[47] (Lewis N. Dembitz's *Jewish Services in Synagogue and Home*, an American publication which is likewise a historical rather than an analytical survey, may have been a model for his work.)

J. H. Hertz produced the first traditional-style on-the-page commentary in English in 1942, blending homily and history. The fact that it was less popular

---

[43] *Seder hatefilot*; see C. Roth, *Magna Bibliotheca Anglo-Judaica*, 303.

[44] *Seder tefilot*, for the Spanish and Portuguese rite, and *Festival Prayers*, for the German and Polish; see C. Roth, *Magna Bibliotheca Anglo-Judaica*, 306–7.

[45] *Seder hatefilot* (ed. De Sola); see C. Roth, *Magna Bibliotheca Anglo-Judaica*, 310.

[46] Introd. repr. in *Book of Prayer: Daily and Occasional Prayers*, p. xvi. But cf. his implied admission of incomprehension in his *Festival Prayers According to the Custom of the German and Polish Jews*, vol. i: *Passover*, 425–6, referring to pp. 101–3, a note that applies elsewhere throughout the six volumes of this edition.

[47] Editions appeared in 1914, 1922, and 1932 and were bound at the end of some copies of the prayer-book printed before the Second World War. Abrahams mentions his interest in history on pp. iii–iv and his debt to Baer on p. v. The way his notes on angelology, for instance (pp. xliv–xlviii), are not integrated into the rest of the discussion reflects his acceptance of the anthological view of liturgy.

than his *Pentateuch and Haftorahs* (1929–36) may reflect readers' relative indifference to liturgical meaning. His own lack of curiosity about structure is evident from his remark that the opening sequences of the daily liturgy (those analysed in the present book) are both 'a miscellany of beautiful prayers' and 'a summary of the Jewish faith'. He does not attempt to reconcile these characteristics.[48] A standard edition in the United States, Philip Birnbaum's *Daily Prayer Book*, appeared in 1949, but offers only scattered notes on history and interpretation.

A survey which tacitly acknowledges the complexity of the liturgy was published by Elie Munk in German in 1938 and translated into English as *The World of Prayer* (1954–63). This work is chiefly homiletic, but Munk does refer intermittently to the central question of how the disparate texts relate to one other. Abraham Millgram's *Jewish Worship* (1971) is a history of the prayer-book which admits the difficulty of the liturgy but does little to alleviate it. The *Complete Artscroll Siddur* (1984), edited by Nosson Scherman, includes a popular commentary that provides a wide selection of source references but neglects to discuss aspects of continuity or, in most cases, to analyse subtexts. In the centenary edition of the *Authorised Daily Prayer Book* (1990), the revision of Singer's translation, some categories of material appear even without translation,[49] although its valuable introductory notes to liturgical sequences do occasionally address the problem of continuity.

Lawrence Hoffman's *My People's Prayer Book: Traditional Prayer, Modern Commentaries*, of which eight of the nine planned volumes had appeared at the time of writing, assembles marginal annotations by a different team of writers in each volume; each commentator aims to cover a different concern, such as history, feminism, theology, halakhah, or biblical sources.[50] This approach is described editorially as an imitation of traditional study-editions, which is clearly untrue of liturgical publications. However, a larger problem is created by the fact that no author presents a view that is comprehensive and coherent in its own terms, but deals only with a limited area. Including multiple commentaries would have resulted in more repetitive and unwieldy books, but would have avoided the gaps in thinking that result from a thematic approach, exemplified by some of the tabular representations, which are based on partial analyses of the texts.[51]

Reuven Hammer's historically oriented *Or Hadash: A Commentary on Siddur Sim Shalom for Sabbath and Festivals* (2003), based on a Conservative prayer-book close to the traditional version, again includes several layers of annotation on the page, expanding on his *Entering Jewish Prayer: A Guide to Personal*

---

[48] *Authorised Daily Prayer Book* (Hertz, 1942, vol. i; 1946), pp. xxiii, 4.

[49] *Authorised Daily Prayer Book* (Jakobovits). These are the 'Hoshanot for Sukkot' (pp. 671–94), 'Torah Readings' for sabbath afternoons, Mondays, Thursdays, and festivals (pp. 833–912), and blessings over those called to read from the scroll (pp. 913–17).

[50] *My People's Prayer Book*, vol. v: *Birkhot Hashachar*, p. vii. Unsystematic provision of source references compromises the usefulness of this series.   [51] Ibid., e.g. pp. 3–4, 8, 10.

Devotion and the Worship Service (1994). Hammer provides a range of sources in his commentary but does not investigate the intertextual implications. This is also true of a general survey by the translator of the prayer-book on which Hammer bases his commentary, Jules Harlow's *Pray Tell: A Hadassah Guide to Jewish Prayer* (2003), a blend of commentary and thematic studies.

One of the most traditional of recent works is Shimon Schwab's *Rav Schwab on Prayer* (2001), containing edited transcripts of his lectures of the early 1990s. He blends homily with a concern for structure, like Munk and Jakobovits, whose background he shared, but he goes further than either of these in seeking evidence of continuity. He is only partly successful, but he does show how a traditional commentator may apply rabbinic literary-critical methods to the liturgy, and he reaches conclusions similar to those of the present study.[52] His work was incomplete at his death.

What might have been issued in the way of a commentated prayer-book in Hebrew can be seen from traditional editions of the Passover Haggadah, the one liturgical unit that is regularly studied in depth, since the Torah contains the instruction to 'tell your son' the story of the Exodus each Passover (Exod. 13: 8). Exegesis of this text is regarded as a duty and the range of editions is consequently huge. One of the most copiously annotated versions, *Migdal eder*, published by Romm of Vilna in 1892 and often reprinted, assembles 115 commentaries in a small format. Menachem Kasher's *Hagadah shelemah* summarizes early commentaries and employs non-traditional scientific approaches. A model of what might be done with the prayer-book is the *Torat ḥayim* Haggadah (1998), edited by Mordechai Katzenellenbogen and published by Mosad Harav Kook, which includes twelve early medieval commentaries, including that of Abudarham, arranged typographically like the same publisher's multi-commentary edition of the Pentateuch, also called *Torat ḥayim*. Its similarity to traditional quarto rabbinic bibles tacitly acknowledges the parallel complexity, if not status, of liturgy and Scripture, and shows how they may be approached with similar rigour. Lupinski and Weinreb's *Sidur tefilah lemosheh*, the anthology of extracts from medieval prayer-book commentaries mentioned above, falls short of the standard set here.

The edition of the standard Ashkenazi rite on which the present analysis is based, that of Solomon Schonfeld, published in 1973 and 1976, took a major step in the direction of providing an analytical tool for traditional readers in English, combining a translation with a column of marginal references, one source for each line of main text.[53] This was the first prayer-book with an English transla-

---

[52] His discussion of the Song of the Sea (Schwab, *Rav Schwab on Prayer*, 233–44), in which he addresses the problem of suffering, draws conclusions similar to those outlined here.

[53] This version, based on Wolf Heidenheim's *Sefat emet* of 1806 and related to the standard Ashkenazi edition of Baer, *Sidur avodat yisra'el*, has been selected as the source-text for the present volume not only out of filial sentiment but because its marginal references have yet to be bettered in English. The coverage of sources is not complete, because some texts are not annotated and the

tion that challenged readers to follow up their sense of curiosity about the inner workings of the weekly liturgy, and was presumably inspired by the implicit acknowledgement made in many traditional commentaries that each passage has a complex anterior and interior life of its own. The Hebrew typography, in the style established by Wolf Heidenheim in the early nineteenth century, was standard in west European Orthodox circles until the Second World War, its use of various fonts and sizes reflecting the composite nature of the liturgy and recalling manuscript traditions. Schonfeld must have been aware that non-Hebrew readers would find it hard to follow up his range of references to rabbinic sources, which appear in Latin characters beside the translation, but the tradition he was following had been designed for well-educated traditional Jews, capable of referring to Hebrew texts in the original. In keeping with the traditional approach he refrained from discussing the implications of these, thereby exemplifying the dual rabbinic approach of recognizing the layered nature of liturgical meaning and of refraining from saying what the meanings might be. His texts have been included in this book at the head of each section of the discussion. They are referred to according to the number of the extract within the overall sequence and to the line numbers that have been added to the original.

Glimpses of Structure

Schonfeld had first approached the problem of interpreting liturgy in 1943 in an educational curriculum urging teachers to ensure that children learned the texts by heart even 'without complete knowledge of the contents', as a preliminary stage to 'intelligent application of the prayers . . . to the real problems of life'. He clearly recognized the importance of ritual reading, but also that 'intelligent application' involved more than an ability to translate the texts. He even included tables defining the place of each paragraph in 'a sensible sequence . . . within the scheme of the whole day and year', but continuity and coherence as such seem to have interested him little and his homiletic remarks are brief.[54] Schonfeld may have been aware how unconventional was his suggestion that the liturgy has an underlying structural 'scheme', for even his own edition of the prayer-book thirty years later made no allusion to it and supplied only marginal references.

linear arrangement usually allows for only one citation per printed line. In addition, references may indicate sources, procedural directions, or homiletic ideas, although, since these are not distinguished, the same liturgical words may be identified in various ways. Printing errors occasionally make the references hard to use. Those for the passages analysed in this book have been checked and corrected. The prayer-book was envisaged as a strictly Orthodox alternative to the so-called 'Singer's' prayer-book issued in successive editions under the authority of the Chief Rabbi since 1890, but it has not proved popular, as reported in Reif, *Judaism and Hebrew Prayer*, 405 n. 28 (although his list of editions needs correction: see n. 10 above). See ibid. 305–8 for the development of Singer's prayer-book.

[54] Schonfeld, *Jewish Religious Education*, 67–73.

He was not alone in sensing the presence of structure, however. Immanuel Jakobovits, in the revised version of Singer's *Authorised Daily Prayer Book* of 1990, hints both at the apparent incoherence of the liturgy and at the possibility of understanding it as a continuous text, for he explains how his notes are intended 'to show the place of that section, and its design, in the structure of the relevant service'.[55] He later addresses the need to appreciate 'the sequence of themes in the ingeniously constructed building blocks which make up the majestic edifice of our liturgical texts'.[56] This architectural metaphor, recalling Zangwill's comparison of the liturgy to a cathedral, suggests the presence of a stony solidity that the words superficially lack, though the decision to resort to an architectural metaphor also confirms that as literature the liturgy is obscure.

The structural metaphor runs deep, however, for Theodor Gaster compares the revision of the liturgy to 'lopping off the spires of Chartres Cathedral because they are not in accord with modern styles of architecture'.[57] Inviting readers to view the complexity of the liturgy as one might the composite nature of a cathedral is one way of suggesting the beauty of the artefact, but it both emphasizes the liturgy's antiquity as a reason for taking it seriously and discounts its literary qualities.[58] While historical and architectural analogies do suggest the sort of deference Gaster wishes readers to feel for the liturgy, the approach exonerates anyone from engaging with its meaning, since monuments are not texts.

For some writers architecture offers mysteries of its own, as for Marcel Proust, who, after acknowledging that his local church was an incoherent jumble of tapestry, glass, and architecture, goes on to say how 'eleventh-century . . . barbarity was veiled by the graceful gothic arcade which pressed coquettishly upon it, like a row of grown-up sisters who, to hide him from the eyes of strangers, arrange themselves smilingly in front of a countrified, unmannerly and ill-dressed younger brother'.[59] Later he records how the tower appeared to his grandmother as a 'quaint old face', again using architecture to depict human qualities and relationships.[60] But this is not the approach taken either by Zangwill or Gaster, for their choice of a cathedral as a model serves to reinforce the strangeness and foreignness of the liturgy, even unconsciously suggesting that to look for liturgical meaning might be in some way 'un-Jewish'. In this way they align themselves with the traditional reluctance to seek to comprehend it in depth.

Gaster does later propose a literary approach to the liturgy, however, for he describes the prayer-book as 'more than a mere manual of devotion, it is—in a sense—Israel's personal diary, catching, as in a series of exquisite vignettes, the

---

[55] *Authorised Daily Prayer Book* (Jakobovits), p. xi.

[56] Ibid., p. xiii. It is possible that he was influenced here by Schonfeld, whom he knew well.

[57] Gaster, 'Modernizing the Jewish Prayerbook', 353.

[58] The two west towers of Chartres were built centuries apart: see Henderson, *Chartres*, 64, 160; Anderson, *Rise of the Gothic*, 34–5.

[59] Proust, *Swann's Way*, i. 80–1; id., *A la recherche du temps perdu*, i. 61.

[60] *Swann's Way*, i. 84; *A la recherche du temps perdu*, i. 64.

scenes and moments of her entire life, and recording, in a diversity of moods and styles, her deepest and most intimate emotions. Here, for those who have eyes and ears, is Sinai on the one hand, and Belsen on the other; the gleaming walls of the Temple, and the peeling walls of a Polish *klaus*; the blare of the silver trumpets, and the singsong of the Talmud student; the colonnaded walks of a Spanish town, and the narrow, winding lanes of Safed.'[61] The view that the liturgy is 'more than a mere manual of devotion' suggests that he might be addressing Jewishly uneducated readers, although even traditional worshippers, as Zangwill illustrated, are capable of a similar detachment. More problematic is the historical nature of the diary model, as though the liturgy were an archaeological tour, lacking inner coherence for individuals living in later periods. This, like the architectural metaphor, tends to ignore the literary value of the liturgy. Yet the historical metaphor may merely reflect the prevailing scholarly preference for the excavative approach to Jewish texts in general, adopted by liturgists since Zunz.[62] His works and those of his successors, such as Ismar Elbogen,[63] which only occasionally show interest in the possibility of discovering a sense of continuity,[64] were certainly familiar to Gaster and Jakobovits, and perhaps more remotely to Schonfeld.

The most creative application of the architectural model, however, is that of Jacob Emden in the eighteenth century, who reads the morning service as a progression through the Temple of Jerusalem, moving from the public area of the Court of Women through the Court of Israelites and the areas reserved for priests performing the sacrificial rituals, and into the Holy of Holies, entered only once a year by the High Priest.[65] Emden's idea is perhaps based on the model implicit in the liturgy of the Day of Atonement, in which part of the readings culminate in the High Priest's entry into the Holy of Holies.[66] But although this has the advantage of relating to a Jewish architectural model, he risks, like the others, masking the purely literary aspects of the liturgy. The details of this reading are unfortunately only inconsistently distributed, moreover, as though even he lacked faith in the inner coherence of the prayer-book.[67]

[61] Gaster, 'Modernizing the Jewish Prayerbook', 352.

[62] Zunz, *Die Ritus des synagogalen Gottesdienstes.*

[63] Elbogen, *Jewish Liturgy.*   [64] Ibid. 16 n. 5.

[65] For an outline of this plan see Emden, *Amudei shamayim* (ed. Weinfeld), i. 127, 136, 156, 166, 171, 186, where headings mark the worshipper's entry into different areas of the Temple. For an echo of this reading see Schwab, *Rav Schwab on Prayer*, pp. xxx–xxxviii, 55, 67, 80, 91, 97, 118, 127, 164, 247.

[66] This overlaps with Douglas, *Leviticus as Literature*, 218–40, whose argument that this reflects authorial intent cannot arise in the case of the liturgy, however.

[67] For architectural metaphors employed to suggest the mysteries of Torah see Talmage, 'Apples of Gold', 316–18.

CHAPTER TWO

❧

The Reticence of the Ideal Reader

T HE FACT that the liturgy is tacitly exempted from exegesis, even though it is the most familiar accompaniment to daily life, suggests that more lies behind the withdrawal of curiosity than historical accident. Although every word of classical texts is considered significant in rabbinic Judaism, in the case of the prayer-book the question of understanding seems to be raised—when it is raised at all—only in a half-hearted way. In this survey of possible causes we shall consider the most important factor last.

The Ritual Factor

The idea that worship might be a matter of ritual performance as much as of sincere petition appears as early as the Mishnah, the primary source of rabbinic law,[1] and talmudic discussions even express regret that so important an activity is commonly neglected.[2] But these texts leave it uncertain whether emotional engagement—*kavanah* (derived from a word meaning 'aim')—is essential even to the recital of the Shema, the central credal statement.[3] A similar ambivalence can be seen in the tension between the demand that the Amidah (the petitionary prayer *par excellence*) must be read regularly with complete sincerity and the implication that it might be best to avoid habitual prayer altogether since this tends to lead to inattention on the part of the worshipper.[4] Mishnaic rabbis themselves relate to this prayer as a formal composition, referring to its component blessings by titles or opening words[5] rather than focusing, even by impli-

---

[1] Mishnah *Ber.* 1: 1–3. These opening remarks on prayer emphasize formal issues over sincerity.

[2] BT *Ber.* 6*b*, where an obscure phrase from Ps. 12: 9 is interpreted as referring to prayer, leading to the conclusion that 'these are things of the greatest importance, but which people nevertheless treat with contempt'.

[3] Mishnah *Ber.* 2: 1 (on interrupting the Shema) and 3 (on reading it out of order); BT *Ber.* 13*a–b* (on intention and coherence), 16*a* (on habit), 17*b* (on intention); Elbogen, *Jewish Liturgy*, 285–6.

[4] Mishnah *Ber.* 4: 4, 5: 1; BT *Ber.* 30*b*–31*a*; Mishnah *Ta'an.* 2: 2 suggests that prayer will be sincere only if the circumstances of the worshipper make each petition of personal relevance. Mishnah *Avot* 2: 13 argues for careful reading of the Shema and Amidah as well as for inner sincerity. Later authorities assume the primacy of inner sincerity, e.g. Maimonides, *Mishneh Torah: The Book of Adoration* (trans. Hyamson), 'On Prayer' 4: 15–16, fo. 102*b*. The balance between sincerity and performance is discussed in Urbach, *Sages*, 389–98.   [5] Mishnah *Ber.* 5: 2.

cation, on their meaning.[6] Some prayers which are recorded in full in talmudic texts and have been incorporated in the liturgy are presented in their original context without interpretation,[7] as though performance, rather than understanding, is the essence of prayer.[8] This preference is also evident in the view that study, in which comprehension is all, is superior to prayer, here regarded as a performative act. This is clear from the argument that one may not interrupt study for worship, although others claim that these categories are too enmeshed to be distinguished.[9]

Post-talmudic writings reflect the continuing primacy of procedure over content by concentrating on details of performance, perhaps because commentary of a more interpretative kind was not in demand. The earliest recorded redaction of the liturgy, issued by Amram Gaon in the ninth century in response to a request for the correct form of prayer, makes no reference to its meaning, suggesting the absence of a tradition of liturgical exegesis.[10] Slightly later in the Middle Ages, Maimonides' 'Laws of Reading the Shema' and 'Laws of Prayer and of the Priestly Blessing' appear in *Sefer ahavah*, 'The Book of Adoration', a section of his codification of law (the *Mishneh torah*) which is almost uniquely concerned with procedural matters. This contains a version of the liturgy, but again no commentary.[11] Among post-Maimonidean halakhic codifiers, the opening volume of Jacob ben Asher's *Arba'ah turim*, entitled 'Oraḥ ḥayim', and the section of the same name in Joseph Caro's *Shulḥan arukh*, cover the conduct of weekday and sabbath prayer, but fail to include either full texts or analyses of their meaning. Jacob ben Asher does show an interest in the significance of liturgical texts but does not aim to provide a comprehensive guide.[12]

This at least partial indifference to meaning is of lasting influence and even appears in a positive light in hasidic tales. One of these describes how a child incapable of reading the liturgy is praised for merely reciting the Hebrew alphabet, since 'God can arrange the letters into words'. This narrative, clearly designed to comfort illiterate and uncomprehending worshippers, suggests that sincerity is acceptable even without understanding.[13] Zangwill's worshippers

---

[6] Mishnah *Ber.* 2: 2 names the paragraphs of the Shema and argues that these are in the right order, without justifying the names or analysing the paragraphs or their interaction; see also 1: 5 and 4: 3. Mishnaic comments on liturgy do occasionally show an interest in liturgical meaning and structure, most obviously in the case of the Passover Haggadah; see *Pes.* 10: 4–5.

[7] BT *Ber.* 60b has several such examples.

[8] See Tabory, 'Prayer and *Halakhah*', 62–3, and Langer, *To Worship God Properly*, 23.

[9] BT *Ber.* 7b–8a, 13b, BT *Shab.* 10a.   [10] Reif, *Judaism and Hebrew Prayer*, 186–7.

[11] Maimonides, *Mishneh Torah: The Book of Adoration* (trans. Hyamson), 94a–98a, 98a–110a; id., *Mishneh torah*, 'Sefer ahavah', ed. Rubinstein, 3–28, 29–96, 333–67.

[12] Jacob ben Asher, *Arba'ah turim*, 'Oraḥ ḥayim' 46–149.

[13] Related in Agnon, *Days of Awe*, 226–7, and endorsed by the Kotsker Rebbe in Newman, *Hasidic Anthology*, 212, and by Levi-Yitshak of Berditchev in Kahana, *Sefer haḥasidut*, 259. For a medieval variant see Marcus, 'Devotional Ideals', 363–4.

may well have been familiar with this story, and would have seen in it a justification for their mantric approach to worship, even though few would have been as unlettered as this child. An examination of the limits of inattention would require a survey of the extensive literature on the subject, but this highly simplified description is sufficient to establish the ambivalence of rabbinic writers about emotional engagement in prayer.[14]

One source of the prominence assigned to performing rather than to understanding the liturgy may lie in the sacrificial service of the Temple in Jerusalem. This was carried out by a priestly caste whose sincerity of purpose seems in general to have been less important than ritual precision; even the feelings of the non-priestly petitioner generally seem to have been immaterial. Although pentateuchal descriptions of sacrifice give precise details of the procedure, they do not mention sincerity, even in the narrative of Cain and Abel in which the plot presumably turns on this question.[15] Prophetic critics of offerings by sinners likewise criticize the general hypocrisy of those who make the offerings, without alluding to their emotions at the time of sacrifice.[16] The context of references to sincerity of feeling in the book of Psalms[17] suggests that it was frequently absent.

It thus appears that when liturgy gradually succeeded sacrifice during the Second Temple period, replacing it completely after the fall of Jerusalem,[18] emotional engagement remained inessential in the synagogue.[19] Mishnaic writers assume sincerity to be essential only in the context of petitionary prayer, such as at times of drought,[20] although its desirability is suggested in the permission given to individuals, under certain circumstances, to worship in the vernacular instead of Hebrew when praying alone.[21] The fact that communities were discouraged from doing so in public, ostensibly to ensure the uniformity of Jewish ritual throughout the diaspora, suggests that sincerity was not regarded as over-

---

[14] This is outlined in Kadish, *Kavvana*, pp. xviii, 8–9, 41, one of whose chapters is entitled 'Prayer without *Kavvana*'.

[15] See Mishnah *Zev.* 4: 6 for the primacy of the priest making the offering over the person for whom it is made. Rashi in his gloss on Gen. 4: 2, followed by David Kimhi, cites *Midrash tanḥuma* (Buber), 'Bereshit' 9 and also reflects *Gen. Rabbah* 22: 5. These imply that, since Abel is said to have brought the 'first of his flock', Cain's offering must have consisted of the least or leftovers of his produce, reflecting his disrespect and lack of emotional commitment. The way the commentators highlight the centrality of motivation in the narrative merely emphasizes its apparent absence from the biblical text.

[16] Mal. 1: 7–8. There is relatively little talmudic and later debate on the role of intention in sacrifice. Its lack of prominence is exemplified by Rashi's reflection of BT *Zev.* 46b–47a and BT *Ḥul.* 12b–13a in his remarks on Lev. 19: 5 (I am grateful to Lindsey Taylor-Guthartz for pointing out this reference to me).   [17] Ps. 51: 19.

[18] Liturgical worship is assumed to have supplanted sacrifice, and the thrice-daily services recall the sacrificial timetable of the Temple; see *Authorised Daily Prayer Book* (Jakobovits), p. xvi, and Langer, *To Worship God Properly*, 1–14. For the move from sacrifice to liturgy see ibid. 114–15.

[19] Hirsch, *Horeb*, ii. 505–6.

[20] Mishnah *Ta'an.* 2: 2.   [21] See Langer, *To Worship God Properly*, 22–3, 246.

ridingly important, however,[22] and was certainly less essential than maintaining the use of Hebrew by Jews, which the liturgy has indeed arguably helped achieve.[23] In general, therefore, the talmudic view seems to have been that it is better to pray without comprehension—or at least with reduced sincerity—than to depart from ritual performance.[24]

This preference for uniformity of practice over comprehension has led indirectly to a pattern of permitted inattention in some traditional synagogues. Sociologically speaking, these tend to be not only places of worship but of 'periodic study and frequent assembly',[25] and even their central point, the reading platform, may become a 'gathering place for interaction and sociability . . . profane rather than sacred' during weekday prayers.[26] Under such circumstances, the liturgy seems to be little more than a backdrop to social interaction or study, and shifts between these activities and prayer take place during services so smoothly that they 'appear to be almost simultaneous'.[27] Sociability may intensify during certain parts of the service, especially on weekdays, to the extent that overt study or even talk are regarded as inoffensive.[28] The existence of commentated prayer-books which can be used during worship, as noted above, reinforces the assumption that study is tolerated during worship and that the liturgy therefore does not demand exclusive attention in order to be 'effective'.

Another factor discouraging liturgical comprehension is the way synagogue worship emphasizes ritual aspects of prayer. When a *minyan*—a quorum of ten or more adult males—is present, one participant will be chosen to act as prayer-leader, variously known as a *ḥazan*, *shaliaḥ tsibur*, or *ba'al tefilah*,[29] transforming the liturgy into a public rather than a private act of devotion by each of those present. The leader chants the opening and closing clauses of most liturgical paragraphs, pacing the recitation of the other members of the group, who may themselves participate out loud,[30] although in some Sephardi synagogues the reader recites each word of the liturgy, except for the silent reading of the Amidah and certain texts and responses set aside for the congregation or choir.[31] The *minyan* remains valid irrespective (in most cases) of whether each member is attending to the liturgy, demonstrating the formal value attributed to the presence of each of the ten individuals. The prayer-leader will in any case recite each blessing formula aloud and leave time for participants to respond with the words *barukh hu uvarukh shemo*, 'blessed be he and blessed be his name', after the name

---

[22] See the impossible proviso that the Shema may be read in translation provided that this reflects its full meaning, Caro, *Shulḥan arukh*, 'Oraḥ ḥayim' 62: 2. Langer (*To Worship God Properly*, 22–3, 246) suggests rabbinic tolerance of the vernacular in public prayer, while Hirsch, *Horeb*, ii. 544, based on BT *Ber.* 13*a*, identifies the limits of their flexibility in this matter. See R. Loewe, 'Hebrew Linguistics', 104.   [23] Kadish, *Kavvana*, 345–8.

[24] Jacobs, *Jewish Prayer*, 41–3.   [25] Heilman, *Synagogue Life*, p. x.   [26] Ibid. 34.

[27] Ibid. 133.   [28] Ibid. 141–9.

[29] The mishnaic term *ha'over lifnei hateivah* (Mishnah *Ber.* 5: 3) has lapsed from informal use.

[30] Heilman, *Synagogue Life*, 87–98.   [31] Ibid. 273 n. 16.

of God is pronounced, and *amen* at the conclusion of the blessing. These responses are so well known that they are not represented in most versions of the liturgy, and are made automatically by anyone within hearing.[32] Again, the *minyan* remains valid even if the responses are not made.

The formality of worship may also derive in part from the association of parts of the liturgy with everyday actions such as waking (Extracts 1 and 21), washing (Extract 16), dressing (Extract 24, line 2), leaving home for synagogue (Extracts 11–13), or putting on *talit* and *tefilin*, the ritual garments (Extracts 2–10). The involvement of objects in worship here and their juxtaposition with texts tend to emphasize the gestural quality of the words and therefore to detract from the primacy of verbal meaning. The meditations related to these symbolic objects[33] emphasize the impression that words are secondary to gestures,[34] echoing one anthropologist's view that it is logical to involve the whole body in worship, since 'actions speak louder than words'.[35]

Even though these factors help explain why traditional Jews regard punctilious performance as more important than the meaning of texts,[36] this does not clarify why the liturgy is traditionally bypassed as a text to be studied and is frequently treated as though it were incidental to ceremonies.

The Multiple-Version Factor

Another obstacle to the study of liturgy is the argument that, because it exists in various versions and has been augmented intermittently, it must have a poor pedigree from a scholarly point of view and be unworthy of close examination (a problem which survives in the high degree of variation between prayer-books published even in modern times, especially in the case of the sequences examined in this volume). Much of the prayer-book is indeed post-talmudic, since even when early rabbinic texts mention specific prayers, they are silent about their wording; it seems that individual worshippers or prayer-leaders initially improvised around conventional themes.[37] The existence of a variety of regional and other versions may well have inhibited a coherent tradition of interpretation from emerging. Several historians argue that prayer was standardized only when Jews became less familiar with Hebrew and could no longer innovate liturgically, for instance by composing cycles of *piyutim* (liturgical poems) for each Torah reading

---

[32] An explanatory note describing these responses was added in the 1958 edition of *Book of Prayer: Daily and Occasional Prayers*, p. xii, but is absent from the Schonfeld edition, for instance.

[33] Introductory meditations suggest the primacy and eloquence of ritual acts and objects. Elbogen, *Jewish Liturgy*, 293, gives a negative view; see also Reif, *Judaism and Hebrew Prayer*, 246.

[34] Examples are the kissing of the *talit* fringes each time they are mentioned in the Shema, or the positioning of the feet in the Amidah and Kedushah, noted in the *Complete Artscroll Siddur*, 94, 98, 100.   [35] Rappaport, *Ecology, Meaning, and Religion*, 199–200.

[36] Understanding the commandments is encouraged, although no rationale may be sought for *ḥukim*, 'statutes', as Rashi remarks on Num. 19: 2.   [37] Mishnah *Ber.* 5: 2–3.

of the year, as was done in the Holy Land during the Byzantine period, before the completion of the Babylonian Talmud.[38] As a result of this fluidity in the liturgy, generally accepted liturgical texts were established only in the gaonic period (late sixth to eleventh centuries CE),[39] but by then, the lack of an existing tradition of interpretation reinforced the impression, discussed in the previous section, that liturgical meaning is of less significance than performance. The lack of exegetical curiosity about liturgy may have become enshrined as a norm, the absence of a tradition of commentary giving rise to the assumption that this silence was deliberate. The results of improvisation survived in the form of a variety of liturgical rites, each claiming primacy in its own community, but this very variability discouraged the development of a single tradition of commentary.

Rites tended to converge after the invention of printing, as the availability of relatively inexpensive texts squeezed out the more varied manuscript traditions. Even in earlier periods, the liturgies of larger centres had enjoyed greater prestige than those of less influential communities, eclipsing them and thus leading to regional uniformity. Some liturgies survived largely, or in some cases solely, in manuscript even after printing became available, such as the Yemenite rite or that of the proudly independent community of Carpentras.[40] Just as manuscript prayer-books tended to contain only one rite and to make few allowances for regional variants,[41] so printers continued to produce editions that could influence worship far from the place of publication.[42] This caused some local rituals to disappear and others to survive in only restricted use.[43] In order to attract purchasers, publishers did occasionally include a number of local variants in a single edition, but they usually failed to distinguish between them, thereby promoting the accumulation of similar or overlapping texts.[44] Rites with larger followings had stronger identities and were not conflated in this way, but an awareness of the existence of choice did discourage commentators. Medieval scholars were certainly wary of basing readings on uncertain texts and are known to have had strong reservations about variations in rite.[45]

[38] Heinemann, 'The Fixed and the Fluid', 50.   [39] Reif, *Judaism and Hebrew Prayer*, 131.

[40] These rare liturgies were transmitted in manuscript until printed in the early 18th century; see Calman, *The Carrière of Carpentras*, 155.

[41] The Ashkenazi evening inserts of *piyutim* were added to one Sephardi medieval manuscript in order to accommodate the local usage of new owners; see Malachi Beit-Arie in Schonfield (ed.), *Barcelona Haggadah*, 9*b*–*16b*, companion volume, p. 16. Another Spanish manuscript contained them from the outset; see R. Loewe (ed.), *Rylands Haggadah*, 8*a*–*10b*, 30–1.

[42] Beit-Arie, 'Affinity between Early Hebrew Printing and Manuscripts'.

[43] The old French rite represented by *Maḥzor vitry*, for instance, has lapsed from use. That of Carpentras survived until modern times.

[44] An example is the inclusion of both the Sephardi and Ashkenazi prologues to the sanctification over wine on sabbath morning in the *Complete Artscroll Siddur*, 492–3. See the survey of this edition in the last chapter of the present book for remarks on the inclusion of the Akedah and the first paragraph of the Shema.   [45] Kadish, *Kavvana*, 278–98; Marcus, 'Devotional Ideals', 359–60.

Uncertainty need not have had this effect, however, for it is encountered in other areas that are indeed studied and written about. The talmudic commentaries on the Mishnah are incomplete in both versions of the Talmud, either because they were never written or because they have been lost,[46] and the text of the Mishnah survives in more than one version.[47] In addition, the goal of rabbinic study is in general to identify and understand gaps in traditions and to reconcile apparent contradictions both in biblical texts and in the traditional statements of rabbinic commentators. Not only is the recording of these major sources uncertain, therefore, but a lack of clarity is built into the texture of rabbinic thinking about texts as such. If uncertainty on its own is unlikely to be a reason for the neglect of liturgical commentary, other reasons should be sought. Why, for example, did commentators not focus on refining existing traditions in the hope of producing a definitive version, as they did in the case of other texts? Perhaps they were discouraged from doing this by an awareness that their own regional or family liturgical traditions might be found wanting. One could therefore attribute the neglect of liturgical analysis to deference for—and even to some embarrassment about—established traditions.

The wish not to draw attention to the discrepancies between liturgies was not the only reason for failing to issue multiple-rite prayer-books, however. Another possible factor, it could be argued, was their increased bulk. Once again, this cannot have been the sole factor. Romm issued two different versions of the *Otsar hatefilot* prayer-book, one for *nusaḥ ashkenaz* (the eastern Ashkenazi rite, sometimes called *minhag polin*) and another for *nusaḥ sefarad* (the Sephardi-based hasidic rite), even though the chief differences between these lie in only forty out of the 1,500 pages, mainly in the morning service.[48] The decision to issue separate versions may therefore have been designed merely to save the printer from the embarrassing problem of deciding to which to give precedence. *Nusaḥ sefarad* was, and is, widely used, but only among hasidim, and giving it precedence would have alienated *mitnagedim*, those opposed to the hasidic movment. Even Baer's *Sidur avodat yisra'el* appeared in two editions: in this case, the alternatives on offer were those relevant to western European Jews rather than those of eastern Europe, where hasidism was popular. One version covered the eastern *minhag polin* and the other the western *minhag ashkenaz*.[49] Here, however, the differences did not affect daily services, so combining them would be less likely to lead to confusion. Again, a major consideration must have been the question of precedence.[50]

[46] Stemberger, *Introduction*, 166–8, 191.   [47] Ibid. 140.

[48] The sequence most affected is Pesukei Dezimra; see *Otsar hatefilot*, 86b–108b.

[49] Baer's parallel editions, identified in the Berlin reprint of 1937 by a red title-label on the spine for the western rite and a blue one for the eastern, differ on pp. 589–804 and 589–740 respectively.

[50] A recent edition of Isaiah Horowitz, *Sidur hashelah hashalem: sha'ar hashamayim*, i. 715–860, exceptionally includes both versions of the *seliḥot*, the rarer western *minhag ashkenaz* first and then the eastern *minhag polin*.

Regional differences are nevertheless not ignored in the halakhic literature and are compared, for instance, in the 'Tikun tefilah' gloss in *Otsar hatefilot*[51] and by Baer, who records variants such as the sixth verse of the Hanukah hymn Ma'oz Tsur, which has recently returned to popular use after centuries of apologetic suppression, apparently by Jews themselves.[52] Even though only one liturgical version is usually included in the main text of each prayer-book, therefore, variant readings are freely provided or discussed in the notes.

In this way scholars focusing exclusively on the major rites have generated enough commentaries to form the basis for serious study. Nevertheless, publishers have failed to issue an adequately commented edition. The twin factors of variability and belated crystallization have definitely contributed to the lack of critical engagement with liturgy on the part of scholars and their audiences, but this cannot fully explain the tendency among commentators and others to neglect what is, after all, the single most popular genre in Jewish writing.

The Difficulty Factor

It has so far been suggested that a tradition of study of the prayer-book failed to develop either because of the way in which the liturgy was used or because of the lack of a definitive text. However, it may be that rabbinic readers in general found its highly composite nature so insuperably 'difficult' and unapproachable that they simply could not cope with its meaning.

In some ways even the books of Psalms and Isaiah, which do appear with classic commentaries in rabbinic bibles, are less dauntingly opaque than the liturgy, mainly because there is no assumption that their passages or chapters are linked or continuous. There are also few variants, since it was popularly believed, in the face of evidence to the contrary, that the Masoretic text exists in only a single version, albeit with alternative 'read' and 'written' versions of some words.[53] Wherever discontinuity was too evident to be ignored, however, biblical commentators did seek to identify authorship and dates, information rarely given in the texts themselves,[54] and to speculate if necessary.[55] However, where this failed, the fragmentary nature of the writings was simply accepted and meaning invested in individual passages rather than entire books, although rabbinic commentators often succeeded in identifying unifying themes. Talmudic writers even applied such techniques to liturgical passages, accounting for inconsistencies and gaps by means of midrashic narratives.[56]

[51] Such as the version of Extract 24, line 11–Extract 25, given by Maimonides; see *Otsar hatefilot*, 64*a–b*. For the halakhic aspect, see Zimmels, *Ashkenazim and Sephardim*, 99–123, 324–32.

[52] *Sidur avodat yisra'el*, 440; the verse appears in the *Complete Artscroll Siddur*, 784–5 and *Authorised Daily Prayer Book* (Jakobovits), 709–10.   [53] See B. Levy, *Fixing God's Torah*.

[54] e.g. Ps. 34.   [55] e.g. Ps. 30.

[56] An example is the discussion of Grace after Meals in BT *Ber.* 48*b*.

Some portions were recognized as being beyond understanding in certain respects, such as the Shema, which was regarded by early rabbinic writers as so ancient that no date was offered for its origin.[57] Despite their fondness for narrative sense, therefore, rabbinic writers had to accept the apparent disorder. Other scriptural or later study-texts fall into the same category of accepted obscurity,[58] as do occasional prayers without obvious links to their context.[59] Medieval liturgical commentators, recognizing that many liturgical sequences and petitions seem to defy attempts at continuous reading, had no alternative but to accept the anthological nature of the liturgy, and regarded it as a patchwork with little overall coherence.

There is, nevertheless, evidence of editorial intervention which suggests that the meaning of at least parts of the prayer-book was apparent to some scholars and that they had little compunction in changing it. The blessings recited on arising in the morning, which are derived from various talmudic texts,[60] were modified in several ways, as will be seen in my discussion. Yet the 'intention' of often anonymous authors and editors, working over an extended period,[61] can seldom be identified now, which is one reason that 'meaning' has been seen to reside in the age and authorship of different texts rather than in their words. Liturgical historians, who predominate among scholars of this genre, encourage the view that the circumstances under which the texts were included in the prayer-book constitute their 'meaning',[62] but dismissing variants as no more than reflections of printers' desires for maximum sales may miss the point, as will be seen.[63]

The anthological view of the liturgy certainly justifies the idea that the prayer-book is incoherent and needs to be recited only formally, but to regard this as the sole reason that the liturgy is not studied would be to ignore the rabbinic fondness for overcoming incoherence, however intractable, and for maximizing every sign of continuity.

The Detachment Factor

The relative inattention of traditional Jews to the prayer-book may derive in part from the difficulty of focusing on texts that in some cases are recited three times daily, as discussed in the context of the 'ritual factor' above.[64] Yet since ritual

[57] Mishnah *Ber.* 1: 1–2 merely states that it is to be recited.
[58] See the discussion of Extracts 34–5 and 38 in Ch. 9.
[59] Such as the three blessings over study in Extract 18, cited from BT *Ber.* 11b.
[60] See the discussion of Extracts 22–4 in Ch. 7.
[61] And still continuing, to judge by the addition of Extract 1 to the present edition.
[62] Elbogen, *Jewish Liturgy*, is an example of this trend.
[63] See the discussion of Extract 1 in Ch. 4; Reif, *Judaism and Hebrew Prayer*, 307–8, on publishers adding texts to attract sales; and Elbogen, *Jewish Liturgy*, 284.
[64] Heilman, *Synagogue Life*, 275–6 n. 13.

worship was known to be compromised by over-familiarity, it is unclear why measures were not taken to counteract inattention, such as insisting on silence and correct posture throughout, as in the case of the Amidah. No such leeway would be allowed in dietary matters or in connection with sabbath observance, yet inattention in prayer is met with a high degree of acquiescence. Immanuel Jakobovits, for example, by recommending communal worship since it generates greater devotion than private prayer, tacitly accepts the lesser level of attention of solitary worship.[65] Indeed, in practice, as could be seen from Zangwill's synagogue scene, public worship suffers from the same problem.

If devotion in formal prayer is regarded as an unattainable ideal, however, what is the point of the exercise? Sociologically speaking, prayer-meetings make possible the daily renewal of communal ties, and the fact that Jews need to live close enough to a synagogue to reach it on foot on sabbaths and festivals determines the establishment of Jewish neighbourhoods and reinforces social identification. The role of the synagogue in community-building is confirmed by the predominance of the first person plural in the liturgy,[66] supporting the view that the prayer-book may provide an aural backdrop for a social gathering and not solely a text for solitary meditation. According to this view, the individual's understanding might therefore be incidental, especially as the liturgy is collective not only in use but in authorship. 'That such prayers succeed at all is evidence of the power of their poetry; that they fail is not surprising. For . . . prayers may become the creations of everyone and the inspiration of no one', one sociologist remarks.[67] 'Success' in sociological terms, however, may be represented by mere participation, since this is what most obviously indicates involvement in society and its value systems. Participation may generate belief by inspiring numinous feelings, making this of primary importance and the comprehension of the texts secondary.[68]

Another major effect of using the liturgy as little more than a framework for private meditation, however, is that it makes possible a free-ranging 'reverie' about the texts, 'a state of calm receptiveness [in which it is possible] to take in . . . feelings and give them meaning'.[69] The liturgical texts of the early morning, examined in later chapters of this book, are superficially inexplicit, but frame and give expression to feelings experienced by the worshipper, especially at the start of the day. The most obvious feeling is that of dread of what lies ahead.[70] Such a

---

[65] *Authorised Daily Prayer Book* (Jakobovits), p. xvii. Schonfeld, *Jewish Religious Education*, 67, recognizes that worship may lead to 'exultation'. On the primacy of communal over private prayer, see Langer, *To Worship God Properly*, 20.

[66] First person singular formulations are rare and discouraged: see BT *RH* 32*b*.

[67] Heilman, *Synagogue Life*, 67.   [68] Rappaport, *Ecology, Meaning, and Religion*, 194–5, 212.

[69] Hinchelwood, *Dictionary of Kleinian Thought*, 420.

[70] For the suggestion that numinous experience may be modelled on the infant's relationship with its mother, see Rappaport, *Ecology, Meaning, and Religion*, 212. Reverie is examined from a wider range of viewpoints in Parsons, *Dove*, 198–201.

'worst-case' scenario might seem to border on the paranoid in our fairly privileged times, but for those living in a less sanitized world than our own the prayer-book offers an opportunity to 'contain' fears, much as, psychoanalytically speaking, a mother 'contains' those of a child by protecting it and providing a setting for free-ranging thought.

Incomprehension, according to this perspective, is not therefore equivalent to inattention, for opacity may be overcome by an associative state of mind, if only unconsciously. The architectural metaphors discussed above similarly implied that the prayer-book might offer containment for the mind of the worshipper, without confinement. The way in which traditional commentaries prefer the explicit and eschew continuous argument helps provide the raw materials for a reverie. If so, what has so far been taken to be the abdication of exegetical authority may in fact be an invitation to a more free-ranging level of understanding.

Yet this does not explain the permitted inattention to liturgical meaning and only partly accounts for the apparent aversion to seeking meaning identified above. The acceptance of mantric recital in prayer remains a unique example of inattention to meaning in rabbinic Judaism. The reason for this still remains to be identified.

The Philosophical Factor

Is it possible that rabbinic users, aware at some level of what the prayer-book has to offer, wished to minimize the public debate of potentially embarrassing ideological problems by neglecting exegesis? The Oral Torah was not committed to writing for similar reasons, at least in part. There remains among some traditional Jews a preference for the richness in nuance of oral learning over the reductiveness of the digest. This tendency has a long history: it inspired the rejection of Maimonides' code of law by certain medieval Jews, and it ensures the continuing insistence that a sound classical Jewish education can be acquired only by means of traditional dialectic study of talmudic texts. But this affection for the fluidity of oral tradition may have been joined by an awareness that the themes of *agadah*, the non-legal component of rabbinic literature, are notoriously equivocal. Reluctance to document such material was overcome presumably when oppression and social disruption threatened the total loss of the oral tradition. Exegetical activity around *agadah* has continued to remain relatively scanty, even though some compendia of commentaries have appeared.[71] Only the mystical and philosophical traditions have suffered neglect comparable to that of liturgy, and they are still not generally studied in yeshiva, presumably because of the unwelcome nature of what studying them might reveal.[72]

A hint at what might have been involved appears in a talmudic discussion of *iyun tefilah*, literally 'attention to prayer', which it seems surprising to find

[71] Stemberger, *Introduction*, 31–44; Heinemann, 'Nature of the Aggadah', 52–3.
[72] BT Ḥag. 14b; Fishman, *History of Jewish Education*, 112–13.

regarded on occasion as a misdeed. Commentators explained this anomaly by interpreting the term as the desire to identify which prayers have been answered, and thereby as speculation on the efficacy of prayer.[73] Yet the term *iyun* covers more than just calculation, suggesting that talmudic disapproval included thought about prayer as such.[74] There is, indeed, good reason to feel unease about attempts to reconcile spiritual with philosophical views of worship, since liturgical address appears to presuppose the possibility of 'changing the mind' of a God who is omniscient, omnipotent, and immutable.[75] Rabbinic writers frankly acknowledge that the philosophical problems regarding prayer are not for the theologically squeamish, although they rarely say so explicitly.[76] One talmudic writer states that, since the fall of the Temple, the gates of prayer have been locked and only the gates of tears remain open,[77] implying that although prayer is effective if it is sincere, purely formal worship is not.[78] Another states more radically that we cannot understand 'the peace of the wicked and the suffering of the good', implying that even sincere prayer may not work—a view which has gained wide currency since it is expressed in these terms in a text recited on sabbath afternoons during the summer months.[79] Withdrawing support from the supernatural view of prayer in this way shows intellectual integrity, but risks undermining the very activity of prayer.

Medieval philosophers nevertheless accepted, at least in their less popular works, that formal liturgical prayer cannot be expected to persuade God to follow a certain course of action. Judah Halevi, writing in a philosophical rather than a poetic mode, defines prayer as a means for worshippers to draw near to God, rather than as an address to God.[80] This view of prayer as self-addressed—a characteristic suggested by the very prefix of the verb *lehitpalel*, 'to pray'—is tacitly acknowledged by the midrashic description of God praying to himself in order that his mercy might overcome his sense of strict justice.[81] The mishnaic statement that one must 'repent one day before one's death' in order to assure closeness to God similarly suggests that prayer is a spur to repentance addressed to the speaker, rather than a discourse directed at God himself.[82]

---

[73] BT *Ber.* 55*a*, BT *BB* 164*b*; Montefiore and Loewe (eds.), *Rabbinic Anthology*, 407–8; Reif, *Judaism and Hebrew Prayer*, 112–13. Gordon employed this term as the title of a commentary on the prayer-book, in *Otsar hatefilot*, doubtless because of its occasional positive use, for instance in BT *Shab.* 118*b* and 127*a*, texts cited liturgically in Extract 20, line 6, and discussed in Ch. 6.

[74] See the discussion of early rabbinic views of the efficacy of prayer in Langer, *To Worship God Properly*, 14–19, 37–8.

[75] Aspects of the resulting ambivalence are discussed in Fox, 'Prayer', esp. pp. 121–2, 139–40.

[76] The traditional view is discussed in Marmorstein, *Old Rabbinic Doctrine of God*, i. 166–74.

[77] BT *Ber.* 32*b*.   [78] This is discussed above in the context of the 'ritual factor'.

[79] Mishnah *Avot* 4: 15.   [80] Halevi, *Sefer hakuzari*, 3: 5; Kadish, *Kavvana*, 134–7.

[81] BT *Ber.* 7*a*.

[82] The doctrine of daily repentance in Mishnah *Avot* 2: 10 is discussed in Urbach, *Sages*, 283, 467–9.

Maimonides went as far as to describe the Temple service as a means for weaning Israelites from pagan ways, thus assigning the level at which prayer is effective entirely to those who perform it. He likewise viewed prayer as a tool for helping people to return to God,[83] and attempted to decode the symbolic language of sacrifice[84] in order to define its effect on humans.[85] However, such dismay was inspired by these ideas among more traditionally minded leaders that Maimonides' philosophical writings were regarded as unsuitable for a general readership. The Maimonidean controversies, at the climax of which his works were burned by Jews, were sparked off by fears that excessive public access to philosophical works would confirm lay readers in their dislike of certain pious beliefs. A ban on philosophical reading for the halakhically unaware was announced by Solomon Ibn Adret of Barcelona in 1305. This is a move with which Maimonides himself might have agreed, since he expressed some misgivings about the wisdom of his own project. The mainly northern European preference for faith over the southern predilection for philosophy thus gained primacy, and arguably still prevails, to judge from the lack of exegetical interest in the liturgy.[86]

Elements of this view of liturgy as self-addressed led Judah Loew ben Bezalel of Prague,[87] after acknowledging that God could grant even unexpressed wishes since he 'knows the thoughts of mankind', to locate the purpose of prayer in the need 'to make a person whole'. He described how 'a person is considered a human being because he has recourse to speech, and without this he cannot be considered human in the fullest sense of the word. . . . Therefore a person should make good his deficiency through speech, and in this way he prays for that in which he is lacking precisely through that which makes him a human being, lacking wholeness.'[88] In this way he tacitly appreciated that a liturgy written in Hebrew enables the speaker to engage in the divine scheme of history, since Hebrew is the language of revelation. Recognition of its special role acknowledges that petitionary address is not the sole purpose of prayer. A similar idea is echoed by the hasidic master who recognized that, although God knows what is in the speaker's mind, liturgical worship has the power to 'free divine speech within man'.[89]

Another hasidic leader, Nahman of Bratzlav, considered the experience of the

[83] Maimonides, *Guide of the Perplexed*, 3: 32, 36, 44, 51, and Sirat, *History of Jewish Philosophy*, 182. The classic mishnaic statement is Mishnah *Ta'an.* 2: 1.

[84] *Guide of the Perplexed*, 3: 45–6.   [85] Kadish, *Kavvana*, 142.

[86] Silver, *Maimonidean Criticism*, 34–5, 41, 136–7; Maimonides, *Guide of the Perplexed*, introd. and 1: 34.   [87] Known by his acronym as the Maharal, *c.*1512–1609.

[88] Judah Loew ben Bezalel, *Netivot olam*, 'Netiv ha'avodah', ch. 2, p. 81; the chapter is translated in Kadish, *Kavvana*, 536, and discussed by Wright in 'Speech'. This extends the idea that prayer is a tool for approaching God outlined in Sherwin, *Mystical Theology*, 133.

[89] Uffenheimer, *Hasidism as Mysticism*, 190–1, citing Jacob Joseph of Polonnoye, *Toledot ya'akov yosef*, 'Mishpatim' 62*b*.

absence of God and concluded that those who fail to experience God directly are correctly perceiving his withdrawal from creation—an act of retraction known in Lurianic thought as *tsimtsum*, performed in order to 'make room' for that which was not God. Indeed, if 'only in seeing the absence of God from the world can one truly find him', the perceived absence of God both represents his presence and thereby ensures survival. Nahman's view that one can transcend these intellectual challenges only by knowing them to be insoluble is tantamount to inviting the worshipper to enter into a mood of reverie of the kind induced by the mantric approaches to prayer discussed above. Indeed, he comments that Israel are called *ivrim* (meaning 'Hebrews', but more literally 'those who pass over') because their faith leads them to transcend all intellectuality.[90]

A contemporary writer aware of hasidic thought similarly describes both the self-addressed nature of prayer and its capacity to establish a framework for intuitive thought. Liturgy is used within 'the modality of "doubt", unclarity and contingency . . . in the characteristic posture of prayer, alert, attentive to all intimations from within and without. . . . In a situation of unclarity, such as obtains in this world, any human act requires great courage, a motive force to appropriate and transform experience into the making of a world. Prayer is the quintessential act of this kind.'[91] This too comes close to defining the state of reverie.

The difference between the supernatural and the philosophical views of prayer can be summarized as follows. According to the first view, the liturgy is a persuasive tool operating mysteriously on God's decision-making and designed for him to interpret. In such a case its meaning would be of secondary importance to the worshipper.[92] Indeed, as in Zangwill's synagogue, it would have a quasi-magical status, needing to be pronounced even by those incapable of understanding its words, as in the hasidic tale in which God organizes the alphabet recited by a child into the requisite prayers. But if the liturgy is viewed philosophically it will be regarded as acting dynamically not on God but on the worshipper. The need to understand will then come to the fore, for the onus of interpretation is not on God, but on the worshipper.[93] The liturgy will then be seen as a counterpart to revelation, a role to which it is suited by its quasi-scriptural biblical language and disturbing obscurity. Because of this it shares the 'omnisignificance' of Scripture, as a result of which the 'slightest details of the biblical text have a meaning that is both comprehensible and significant'.[94]

The philosophical view ignores, however, the fact that much of the liturgy directly addresses God, and this approach threatens to undermine the practice of worship. A mid-thirteenth-century mystic, Jacob ben Sheshet Gerondi,

---

[90] Green, *Tormented Master*, 292, 312–15, based on Nahman of Bratzlav, *Likutei moharan*, ch. 64.

[91] Zornberg, *Beginning of Desire*, 282. [92] Elbogen, *Jewish Liturgy*, 285, 305.

[93] Apparent liturgical incoherence has been regretted, particularly by Progressive thinkers; see the remarks on introducing contemporary ideas by the editors of the recent Liberal *Siddur Lev Chadash*, pp. xvi–xvii. [94] Kugel, *Idea of Biblical Poetry*, 104.

lampooned philosophical approaches to prayer for this reason.[95] Nevertheless, they survive in the normative early fifteenth-century philosophical work of Joseph Albo, who concluded that prayer cannot be expected to produce change in God, but is an appropriate way of drawing worshippers closer to one 'who needs no one's service'.[96] Albo reapplied the midrashic view that God cannot need sacrifice as food[97] and that offerings must therefore be for the benefit of the worshipper.[98] Rabbinic commentators similarly assume that Moses' raised hands helped win the battle against the Amalekites because they caused the Israelites to lift their eyes to heaven,[99] much as did the brazen serpent under different circumstances.[100] Similar uncertainties about the function of liturgical worship are reflected in the writings of contemporary thinkers such as Yeshayahu Leibowitz, who regards prayer as a matter of canon law to which the speaker is bound, irrespective of the meaning of the liturgy,[101] though few others divorce worship from the meaning of the liturgy in such absolute terms.

The recognition that the worshipper is at once the speaker and the audience blurs the boundaries between the human and divine spheres in a way that clearly requires philosophical and theological sophistication to sustain. However, since the liturgy is at once a popular and a learned genre, it must engage support irrespective of the worshippers' intellectual capacity and maturity, and the philosophical competence of the general worshipping public cannot be taken for granted.[102] In view of the complexity of the concepts involved, the slowness of the less learned to pick up such underlying ideas might even be desirable.[103] But for those more sensitive to such issues, the full implications of liturgical prayer, once glimpsed, cannot be wholly suppressed. Worshippers who understand the philosophical issues will be haunted by the thought that God cannot be reached by force of will or words, and even if it is suppressed, the idea will survive in the

---

[95] See Gottlieb, 'Gerondi, Jacob ben Sheshet', quoted in Tishby, *Wisdom of the Zohar*, iii. 950–1. On God's transcendence and the need for prayer, see Langer, *To Worship God Properly*, 36–40, 165 n. 220.

[96] Albo, *Sefer ha'ikarim* 4: 18–20. See Rosenberg, 'Prayer and Jewish Thought', 81–98. For hasidic echoes see Lamm (ed.), *Religious Thought of Hasidism*, 189–91. The theme continues in 19th-century Germany: see Hirsch, *Horeb*, ii. 472–8, followed by Jacobson, *Meditations on the Siddur*, 17–23, and *Authorised Daily Prayer Book* (Jakobovits), pp. xvi–xvii. The last three may have been influenced, directly or otherwise, by Kant, *Religion within the Limits of Reason Alone*, 183, 185, and Schleiermacher, *Predigten*, 32–3, the latter quoted in Meyer, '"How Awesome Is this Place!"', 55–6.

[97] *Pesikta rabati* 48: 3; *Num. Rabbah* 21: 16. See other sources cited in Montefiore and Loewe (eds.), *Rabbinic Anthology*, 414, and the discussion in Schechter, *Some Aspects of Rabbinic Theology*, 198 n. 3.   [98] Implied in BT *Meg.* 31b; *Pesikta derav kahana* 6: 3.

[99] BT *RH* 29a, and see Rashi on Exod. 17: 11.   [100] BT *RH* 29a, and see Rashi on Num. 21: 8.

[101] Leibowitz, *Judaism, Human Values, and the Jewish State*, 30–6; D. Hartman, 'Prayer and Religious Consciousness'.

[102] This view may be implicit in Judah Halevi's insistence on communal prayer, discussed in Schweid, 'Prayer in the Thought of Yehudah Halevi', 112, 116.

[103] Kraemer, *Responses to Suffering*, 218 n. 11, presents a different view.

unconscious and will re-emerge, however unwelcome, at moments of close attention to prayer, perhaps precisely those described talmudically as *iyun tefilah*. If the matter could be resolved it would not re-emerge as a constant undercurrent in the way that it does, of course, and the very silence surrounding doubts about prayer ensures they are one of the liturgy's major themes.

It is therefore probable that the liturgy remains unstudied because of a fear of publicly airing the ambiguities of its philosophical underpinning. Indeed, since the principal function of liturgy from an anthropological viewpoint is to stabilize social order,[104] or at least to minimize the disruptive effects of natural change by making smooth transitions possible between different age-groups or social structures (as with puberty or marriage rites), the discovery of subversive meanings could strike at the heart of popular loyalty. Such a fear might even account for the traditional tendency to augment liturgical opacity by adding new texts, rather than to clarify it, and also explain why the present book is the first to examine the subtext of a substantial liturgical sequence with some thoroughness.

What is attempted here is new, in fact, only in that it undertakes an analysis of the undercurrents of the liturgy. Most of the scaffolding for the analysis has been provided by traditional commentators who have identified the network of scriptural and rabbinic allusions of which the liturgy is composed; this book builds on their work to reveal the subtext concealed between the lines.[105] This network of undercurrents amounts to a counter-narrative, distinct from the meaning of the words on the page, both levels generating additional meanings which are essential elements of the text. Many traditional readers might disapprove of bringing such underlying ideas into the public domain, but readers who are more intellectually active are impatient of equivocation. This book suggests that participation in synagogue services demands not only philosophical competence but emotional integrity and a capacity to participate with intellectual honesty in the sacred narrative of the Jews. The synagogue, often assumed to be a place of conventional piety, can now be seen to demand of participants in its ceremonies a readiness to engage with universal issues in novel ways. Some of these emerge in Chapter 3, in which themes such as the challenge to God to keep the covenant are examined. Others, such as the analysis of Extract 7, will look at the threatening implications of the *tefilin* texts; while the discussion of Extract 20 will examine the impossibility of study; that of Extract 28 will point out the irony of references to God's mercy; and that of Extract 39 will examine the elusiveness of this mercy. These ideas, well concealed beneath the surface, overturn the superficial impression that the liturgy is based on the possibility of dialogue, and instead show how it gives voice to a powerful strain of dissent. They are summarized in Chapter 11. If it is indeed true that the daily repetition of prayer implies a critique of its own effectiveness, and that liturgical formality comments critically on the nature of

---

[104] Langer, *To Worship God Properly*, 42–5.

[105] The desirability of such an approach is noted in Blank, 'Some Considerations', 15 n. 10.

God's own promises, the absence of a tradition of liturgical exegesis becomes less surprising.

The Ideal Reader

As will be seen, liturgical opacity can be penetrated with the help of reading skills familiar to those with experience of rabbinic textual analysis and aware of the traditional works referred to here. Non-rabbinic texts will also be cited in support of rabbinic ideas, but will be used to confirm the validity of the suggested readings of the liturgy's concealed messages rather than as primary tools of interpretation.

The term 'ideal reader' does not fully describe the audience for which this book is intended. It is used here to refer to an individual who has the intellectual equipment to understand a given text, which, in the case of the liturgy, will be someone with an advanced training and wide experience in rabbinic learning. As we have seen, however, the liturgy is not systematically studied or discussed in such circles, which is why the present book is of potential interest precisely in settings of that kind. The readership for which this book is designed is far wider than that, however. It is also addressed to readers of any background who wish to understand more about rabbinic views of the world, irrespective of their training or education. The book provides the kind of data to which only specialists usually have access, and explores the liturgy in ways which traditional scholars would find natural, tracing each stage of the process by which meaning is extracted and making available to a wider readership the experiences otherwise confined to 'ideal readers'.

For the benefit of those who are unfamiliar with the kind of 'ideal reader' of the liturgy envisaged here and the place such a person occupies in the Jewish community, it will be helpful to outline his background—and it will usually be a 'he', since it is still relatively unusual for women to have such a training—and to describe some of the interpretative processes employed in traditional circles for reading non-legal texts such as the liturgy. Like Schonfeld himself, a person of this kind would ideally have studied for some years in a yeshiva and be able to approach rabbinic texts in the original languages.[106] He would have become familiar with substantial parts of the Talmud in yeshiva, and would continue to study it with the help of the standard commentaries in adult life, alone or in groups. Biblical and midrashic texts would be familiar mainly from the pentateuchal commentaries by Rashi and his successors. In thinking about the liturgy this reader's first priority, like that of the members of Zangwill's community, might be its correct performance, but he would have access to Hebrew commentaries (all untranslated, like many of the original texts to which they refer), and

---

[106] Solomon Schonfeld studied in Tyrnau (Slovakian Trnava, 1927–9), Neutra (Slovakian Nitra, 1930–*c*.1932), and Slobodka (near Kovno, *c*.1932–3).

would be able to examine their original contexts. He would do so in the first instance, perhaps, to make homiletic points at celebrations such as weddings, circumcisions, or bar mitzvahs. He would also be aware of Sephardi practice, if he is from an Ashkenazi background, or, if he is Sephardi, would have experience of Ashkenazi worship. The differences between these traditions would stimulate his curiosity about the origins and meaning of prayer. Although he might find the homiletic aspects of his discoveries interesting in themselves, his curiosity would be chiefly aroused by what lies behind the *peshat*, the 'authorized interpretation'.[107]

The liturgical commentaries would lead him to the biblical and rabbinic sources of each word, and it is from here that he would start interrogating, for instance, the creational theme alluded to in one of the early morning blessings (Extract 17), the midrashic background to an otherwise obscure pentateuchal quotation (Extract 35), or the uncertain use of the verse-sequences marking the entry into synagogue (Extracts 11–13), each of which would lead him to search further afield. He would not focus in particular on kabbalah, since this tends to be discouraged in traditional yeshiva circles, and he would find the approach taken by the Hasidei Ashkenaz (German pietists of the thirteenth century) unconvincing, due to the differences between the liturgical texts analysed there and those in current editions such as that of Schonfeld. He would have access to a wide range of nineteenth- and twentieth-century Hebrew publications, as well as to some in English and German, but these he would employ more eclectically. Since anyone of that background would normally be unaware of text-historical, literary-critical, or anthropological approaches, these will not be prominent in the analysis.[108]

It should be emphasized that this profile relates not to a small elite of especially learned Jews aspiring to rabbinical status, but to large numbers of well-educated people who might, in Israel, London, or New York, for instance, form the majority of entire congregations. Some yeshiva education is fairly general in Orthodox communities, and for several decades has been almost global. In some circles this attitude to study has also been adopted by women in recent years, as part of a general blurring of gender roles, but this remains a minority phenomenon.

It will also be useful to outline the possible stages through which such an 'ideal reader' might pass in generating the interpretation presented here. Starting on such a project might be difficult because of the cloak of vagueness that traditionally veils the liturgy, but his task would be easier than it would be for readers of English only, unfamiliar with rabbinic thought and methods of reading classic texts. He might hesitate to continue when he found some of his

---

[107] R. Loewe, 'The "Plain" Meaning of Scripture'.

[108] The literary-critical, anthropological, and psychological approaches touched on here were implicitly invited by Zahavy in 'New Approach', and Reif, 'Jewish Liturgical Research', 165–6, 169, as well as in id., *Judaism and Hebrew Prayer*, 7.

theological findings rather disturbing to think through to their conclusions, although most students encounter such ideas at least briefly at yeshiva or later.[109] His training would enable him to identify the faint allusions to biblical scenes and theological ideas to be found in the liturgy and he would have no difficulty in discovering that these form a subtext that departs from the surface meaning. Comparing these layers of meaning is complex, but differs in degree rather than quality from the work of conventional commentators. Our reader would have no difficulty in matching them with the broader 'sacred narrative' shared by Jews of most levels of education, which spans creation, election, revelation, estrangement, exile, repentance, and return, and forms the common ground for all Jewish theological thought. It is unlikely that anyone has consciously correlated the textual associations precisely as they are presented here, not only because emphases vary, but because of the psychological barriers to doing so. Nevertheless, traditional readers would almost certainly recognize the features identified here, even if their readings of details vary.[110]

Such a reader must operate at three levels, more or less sequentially.[111] First, he will follow liturgical commentators in examining evidence of the date, origin, authorship, or function of texts or sequences, a traditional approach that predates the nineteenth-century Wissenschaft des Judentums.[112] Commentators traditionally use such data both to explain repetitions and structural peculiarities of the liturgy and to explore homiletic associations. One example is the treatment of the headline of Psalm 30, 'A song of the dedication of the house—of David' by the medieval biblical commentator Abraham Ibn Ezra:[113] since David did not live to dedicate the first Temple, the 'dedication' might superficially be thought to relate to David's own palace. However, because the psalm refers not to building but to illness, the 'house' must instead be taken to refer to David's body and its 'dedication' to his recovery from illness.[114] This reading allows the psalm to resonate with particular emphasis in the context of the morning liturgy, when the soul has recently been restored to the body after death-like sleep. Such insights need have little or no relation to authorial intention to be exegetically valid in the liturgical context.

The primary aim of this level of analysis is broadly diachronic, designed to

---

[109] Possible contexts include laments for the fast of Tishah Be'av, such as the one discussed in R. Loewe, 'The Bible in Medieval Hebrew Poetry', 142–5.

[110] Traditional readings occasionally merge with the approach taken here: see references in this book to Schwab, *Rav Schwab on Prayer*.

[111] The conventional rabbinic four-level description of exegesis represented by the acronym *pardes* will not be used here. The essentially dual nature of the rabbinic approach is described in R. Loewe, 'The Jewish Midrashim', (see esp. pp. 507–10), but the present discussion is based on different assumptions.

[112] Jacob Emden in the 18th century includes talmudic references to authorship, while Leopold Zunz in the 19th century was chiefly interested in historical issues.

[113] See the remarks in Ch. 9 on Extract 42.   [114] Ibn Ezra on Ps. 30: 1.

establish how and when the liturgy grew and to locate the boundaries of each textual unit. The analysis will be based on texts that form part of a general rabbinic curriculum, and assessing the evidence depends on a sensitivity to genres, schools of thought, and period, and an ability to balance an awareness of history with exegesis. However, it is important to be aware that authorial attributions may be misleading, since the historical techniques available in these classic sources are pre-scientific. Clearly, this level of analysis tends to emphasize the anthological aspects of the liturgy.

The second level of exegetical activity involves meticulously noting the sources of citations, allusions, and echoes appearing in the liturgy, an approach which emerges from the same interest in sources and authority as the previous level, but which 'atomizes' the liturgy more minutely. It is not diachronic, however, and shows no concern with historical development. In this phase the reader, aware of the continuity and 'omnisignificance' of scriptural and rabbinic writings—*torah shebikhtav* and *torah shebe'al peh* respectively—locates each liturgical fragment within them. Jews of the Middle Ages would have been more intimate with many of these texts than are contemporary scholars, because scriptural and rabbinic passages were learnt by heart before the invention of printing,[115] and the rarity of written sources made it unlikely that a source could be checked. An ability to quote or at least recognize classical Jewish sources was as usual among them as was a knowledge of the classics among educated Europeans up to the mid-twentieth century.[116]

As the availability of printed books made rote-learning less necessary, however, memorization diminished and reference works were compiled. An index to scriptural verses cited in the Babylonian Talmud, compiled by Aaron of Pesaro (d. 1563), appeared in 1583–4 as *Toledot aharon* and was reprinted in many rabbinic bibles, alongside another index listing scriptural citations in the Jerusalem Talmud, compiled by Jacob Sasportas (*c*.1610–98) and entitled *Toledot ya'akov* (1652).[117] Similar listings of the sources of liturgical allusions appeared in most prayer-book commentaries, each author setting out to identify verbal or conceptual allusions or echoes, though each differed slightly in his choice of sources according to his taste or knowledge. The variations are considerable, and this analysis, for similar reasons, makes its own selection from what is available. Indeed, the choice of which of a number of possible sources to cite, especially when they come from different contexts with distinctive associations, may well reflect a commentator's unspoken assumptions. Schonfeld's version, the only English example of this traditional genre, is handicapped by a typographical arrangement allowing (for the most part) only one source to be quoted per line,

---

[115] Scheindlin, *The Gazelle*, 20; Kugel, 'Two Introductions to Midrash', 94–5; Mishnah *Ber.* 5: 3 suggests the need to memorize texts.

[116] R. Loewe, 'The Bible in Medieval Hebrew Poetry', 137–8.

[117] Carlebach, 'Aaron of Pesaro'.

but it has been used as the basis of this analysis nonetheless.[118] Even had a different selection been made, however, the conclusions would remain broadly similar.

The third level of reading, which emerges from the state of mind previously described as 'reverie', has not previously been documented in a liturgical context. It consists of integrating the atomized scriptural and rabbinic texts into a continuous reading, a process which can perhaps be carried out only by means of the repetition made possible by regular worship. Although the sources are mostly well known and capable of only a limited range of interpretations, unexpected links may be generated in this way, an approach exemplified by midrashic texts. This phase of liturgical reading is wholly synchronic—indifferent to historical development—but the style of association, which appears to be free, is in fact constrained by the limitations of traditional rabbinic reading. Its effect is to transform the liturgy from an anthology into a narrative, albeit of an unconventional kind.

This transformation can be described as follows. Each decontextualized citation in the liturgy is at once a component of a new liturgical text and part of its original context. Although liturgical commentators have tended to examine only the new discourse on its own terms and to have ignored the implications of its sources, the effects of these juxtapositions are fundamental to the meaning. Medieval Hebrew poems similarly developed a style based on elaborate mosaics of citation, relying for their effect on the reader's ability to identify each source. Commentators have listed the sources to which they allude, but have shown a marked reluctance to explain the literary impact of this style in explicit terms.[119] An example of this approach is the use made of the Song of Songs each sabbath eve in the poem Lekhah Dodi. Its refrain opens by citing the words 'go, my friend', from the Song,[120] inviting a male companion to meet a 'bride', identifiable in the poem as the worshipper, Israel, sabbath, Jerusalem, or the messiah, since the Song is read rabbinically as a description of the love between God and Israel. The male speaker is successively God, a fellow worshipper, Israel, or, again, the messiah. But since the couple in the Song are also potentially human, all relationships are both eroticized and aligned with the sacred narrative, although the multiple referents ensure that the poem remains a richly indeterminate survey of Jewish history from Sinai to exile, relying for its basic theme— love between God and Israel—on the associations of the Song of Songs rather than what appears on the page.[121] In a simpler example, the poem Berah

[118] Extracts appear at the head of passages in which they are discussed.

[119] Modern editions of such poetry include Yannai, *Liturgical Poems*, from 7th-century Palestine (whose allusive style influenced the work of later Ashkenazi poets), and Ibn Gabirol, *Shirei hakodesh*, a rich source of Arabic-inspired Iberian poetry of the 11th century, which had many imitators.   [120] S. of S. 7: 12.

[121] For a survey of the undercurrents of this poem see Kimelman, 'Prolegomena'.

Dodi,[122] intended for the intermediate sabbath of Passover, God is the lover, while the bower in which he meets Israel is Jerusalem. Countless other symbolic uses of biblical literature could be cited, although only some would be as transparent as these uses of the Song of Songs. Tracing some of the more abstruse allusions would pose problems for the less educated, and certain poets vied to outshine each other's erudition, but the more obvious would be clear even to lay readers.

The way in which such poetry depends for its impact on the reader's ability to recognize the origins of scriptural citations instantly and to grasp their connotations in rabbinic thought is a model for the analysis offered in this book. It depends for its effectiveness on the reader's tolerance of a high degree of indeterminacy of meaning and readiness to defer the need to establish the precise 'meaning' of the text. Indeed, any one citation might be illuminated only by others appearing later on, demanding that the reader constantly reserve judgement. It is striking that the implications of such echoes were not spelled out by commentators; one must assume that they expected rabbinic readers to take such allusions in their stride and that no explanation was considered necessary. A result of this exegetical silence is that each reader remains free to evolve an independent understanding (even though the range of possibilities is narrow) and can experience some of the pride of composition and creation in doing so. The silence equally acknowledges that the message of the poem could be expressed in no other way.

The expectation that readers would understand such allusions is not confined to poetry, but is also found in midrash, a prose genre which similarly depends for its effectiveness on a comprehensive knowledge of biblical sources. One such text points out the consonantal match between God's challenge to Adam in the Garden of Eden, *ayekah*, 'Where are you?', and the first word of the book of Lamentations, *eikhah*, 'How [the city sits solitary]', leaving the reader to draw the intended conclusion that Adam's expulsion from Eden prefigures the exile from which Jews still await rescue.[123] Other midrashic juxtapositions are still more fluid, such as the inventory of references to 'saddling up' an animal that appears in the discussion of the Binding of Isaac narrative in the book of Genesis (known as the Akedah, literally 'binding'), challenging the reader to link otherwise disconnected scenes.[124] The fact that neither liturgical commentators nor midrashic writers spell out such effects suggests that they knew their readers could understand them without help. It may therefore be assumed that traditionally educated liturgical users would likewise be undaunted by densely textured writing and would naturally employ suitable methods to understand whatever texts they encountered.

---

[122] S. of S. 8: 14, discussed in Petuchowski, *Theology and Poetry*, 56–62.

[123] *Gen. Rabbah* 19: 9, relating Gen. 3: 9 to Lam. 1: 1. [124] *Gen. Rabbah* 55: 8.

Another reason for leaving matters vague in midrash is that gap-filling is occasionally not fully effective. For instance, rabbinic readers assume that the Garden of Eden narrative took place during the sixth day of Creation and offers a close-up of the making of Adam and Eve,[125] but this involves the introduction of a chronological assumption that is not evident from the text and that fails to iron out all the difficulties.[126] This solution to the problem of how the Creation narratives interrelate is regarded as normative in standard commentaries. But the popularity of this reading, despite its drawbacks, may be due to the way it expands the relevance of the Eden story and of the expulsion with which it ends by relating these closely to the eve of sabbath and the end of the working week. The unified account which results is clearly to be read without paying close attention to inner logic or to the literal meaning of the sources, and might therefore be informally described as 'poetic' in style.

Yet another reason for failing to spell out the implications of juxtapositions is that these might be theologically compromising—although rabbinic readers would naturally pick up such meanings whether or not they were spelled out and however unwelcome they might be. If this is a factor behind the exegetical boycott of liturgy, however, it is not a matter for public debate in Orthodox circles. One traditional Jew to whom I observed that there is no comprehensively commentated edition of the prayer-book confirmed without explanation that 'We never learn [i.e. study] Siddur', while another said that 'Siddur is not a *sefer* [lit. 'a book', in the sense of a classic text]', as though it were sufficient to state, as an explanation, that it is a text that it is not customary to study.[127] Yet, as will be seen, lack of study need not imply the absence either of meaning or of understanding. It should be added, however, that making underlying ideas explicit, as in this work, lends them an appearance of everyday currency that they certainly do not have—or not to anything like the extent that their daily appearance in the liturgy might suggest. The delicate balance between faith and philosophy must be maintained for prayer to function at a social and emotional level, and it is necessary to recall that exegetical silence surrounding the liturgy has the function not only of leaving individuals free to investigate liturgy in their own ways, but of protecting public conventions from private doubts.

[125] Rashi on Gen. 2: 5, 7.

[126] Alter, *Art of Biblical Narrative*, 140–7, points out how the chaotic human relations depicted in the Garden narrative subvert the orderliness of the account of Creation in six days. In this Genesis anticipates successive liturgical texts.

[127] The first was said by a young man with seven years of yeshiva training (who said he was not surprised at my explanation for the neglect of liturgy) and the second by a mature scholar. U. Simon, 'Teaching *Siddur*', 192, deplores the failure to teach the prayer-book to Israeli children beyond their fifth school year.

The Role of Women

Even though the 'ideal reader' has been assumed so far to be a man, the traditional and almost total exclusion of women from study and their complete absence from ceremonial roles in synagogue has been eroded in some Modern Orthodox circles and entirely ended in many non-Orthodox settings. As a result, it is relevant to ask here whether there is, or could be, specifically female responses to the liturgy. In conventional terms it is assumed that prayer is one of the activities from which women are exempt under the terms of the rabbinic ruling that binds them only to those legal provisions expressed in a negative form and not bound to time.[128] However, it is clear from a number of sources that women were involved in formal prayer before the modern period. Talmudic discussions assume at least the possibility of their engagement in worship, and medieval sources make it clear that some wore *tefilin* and were called to the reading of Torah, both of which, although now common in Progressive movements, remain controversial, to say the least, in Orthodox ones.[129] Including women in worship on an equal footing and together with men is not countenanced by traditional Jews partly because women's lack of obligation to participate in formal worship suggests that they cannot assist men, who are so obliged, to discharge their own duties by participating in their quorum.

The strongest evidence of their former involvement in the liturgical sequences examined in this book comes from the introduction of a women's variant for the blessing in Extract 23, line 4, a supplement first encountered in the fourteenth century. This suggests that women not only joined in worship, although presumably separately from men, but that they could influence what was said. There is other evidence of liturgical texts written by women.[130] The separate engagement of particularly pious Orthodox women in prayer has indeed been the norm in modern times, as is illustrated by the encouragement given by Sarah Schenirer to her pupils in Kraków to attend synagogue regularly, even though only married women usually did so in Poland between the wars. She interpreted the exclusion of women from the quorum of men as evidence of their superior status, comparing their role to that of Levites who, although they did not help construct the Tabernacle, were subsequently responsible for its maintenance.[131]

[128] Mishnah *Kid.* 1: 7.

[129] Ilan, *Jewish Women*, 182–4; ead., *Mine and Yours Are Hers*, 59–63, 186–9; Reif, *Judaism and Hebrew Prayer*, 11–12 n. 36, 115 n. 71, 222–5 nn. 33–9; Grossman, *Pious and Rebellious*, 51–4, 309–26; Safrai, 'Women and the Ancient Synagogue'; Taitz, 'Women's Voices, Women's Prayers', 59–71; Haut, 'Are Women Obligated to Pray?'; Golinkin, 'May Women Wear Tefillin?'; Weiss, *Women at Prayer*. I am grateful to Lindsey Taylor-Guthartz for advice on this discussion.

[130] Levine, 'Women who Composed Prayers'.

[131] Benisch, *Carry Me in Your Heart*, 129–30, 151–4; the levitical comparison is based on Rashi on Num. 8: 2. I am grateful to Connie Webber for pointing this reference out to me.

Although women play no role in the traditional synagogue, therefore, the liturgy cannot be regarded as exclusively designed for the use of men, not only because of women's involvement at varying levels over many centuries, but because terms such as the 'Children [literally 'sons'] of Israel' naturally include women.[132] This is also clear from the way biblical and rabbinic texts refer to Jews as the female partner of God. Female gendering of Israel is particularly clear in the verses recited while winding the *tefilin* straps onto the hand (Extract 9), suggesting the potential applicability of *talit* and *tefilin* to Jews in general.[133] Even though women have good reason to feel outsiders to synagogue rituals, therefore, the liturgy itself relates equally to men and women, its themes including issues which transcend gender barriers, such as the desire for safety, survival, and comprehension of the nature of the world.

One legacy of women's optional involvement in public prayer is the contemporary adoption of ritual garments in Progressive circles. As will be seen from the discussion in Chapter 5 below, however, it can be argued that these should ideally be employed together (including head-covering), rather than selectively, on the grounds that they form a cluster of symbols that it would be subversive to disrupt.[134] Since the *talit* is worn by men on sabbaths and festivals without *tefilin*, it has coherence even on its own. But the meaning of *tefilin* is altered if they are worn on a weekday without a *talit* (or *arba kanfot*, worn as an undergarment); and if *tefilin* are worn, head-covering also seems essential, if only because *tefilin* make the head a central point of attention, even though it would otherwise be optional, at least for unmarried women. These remarks clearly do not address the halakhic dimensions of the question, but are designed to confirm that worship is no more an exclusively male activity than study, and that its rituals have a collective coherence which prohibits their separation.[135]

[132] Rashi argues in the context of Deut. 6: 7 that 'sons' need not necessarily include women, but it is unlikely that he would have taken the same view of the phrase 'sons of Israel'.

[133] Such as Jer. 2: 2 for a female Israel and Hos. 1–3 for the source of a similar coloration in the case of *tefilin*.   [134] Krauss, 'Jewish Rite'.   [135] See Sarah, 'Meditations for *Tallit* and *T'fillin*'.

CHAPTER THREE

ॐ

The Liturgical Narrative: Modern and Traditional Views

T HIS CHAPTER is designed for two kinds of reader: it will outline traditional rabbinic reading strategies for readers unused to them and will provide an introduction to contemporary literary criticism for those to whom it is unfamiliar. The two approaches—traditional and modern—have been aligned before, since some contemporary critics have paid close attention to midrashic texts and the features they happen to share with liturgy, including multiple or unknown authorship, fragmented surface textures, and submerged narrative themes. A discussion of the way a narrative sequence may emerge from a text such as the liturgy will also make it possible to outline what this particular narrative has to say about the world as seen through rabbinic eyes. Since contemporary literary-critical approaches have also contributed to the method adopted in this analysis, outlining them here is an acknowledgement of influence.

The Case for a Liturgical Genre

The question of genre barely arises in rabbinic thought and has become less relevant in other contexts too, as blends between prose and poetry, for instance, no longer cause surprise. However, the subject needs to be discussed here since liturgy retains closer links with everyday life than perhaps any other Western literary category, so much so that the sort of text analysed in this book might deserve to be regarded as a genre in its own right. There are other characteristics which make it stand out. The prayer-book is unusual in that it is neither read in solitude nor listened to by an audience, but is 'realized' when 'acts are performed and . . . utterances voiced' by an individual or a congregation.[1] Ritual objects and gestures, as well as the location—home or synagogue—in which these are used, play central roles in the liturgy and are essential to its meaning. So, for example, the liturgical sequences discussed here span the time from when the worshipper wakes in bed, then washes, dresses, and finally either leaves for synagogue or worships at home, and are recited partly while standing and partly while sitting. On weekday mornings adult men (and in some circles increasingly women too) wear *talit* and *tefilin*, the ritual garments. Liturgy cannot be understood without

---

[1] Rappaport, *Ecology, Meaning, and Religion*, 192.

an awareness of the significance of these objects and locations and the transitions between them, because these physical settings and objects are as much part of the genre as the words on the page. Liturgy is more than a purely linguistic gesture or 'speech act', partly because it relies on physical props and performance in real time for its effectiveness.[2]

There is little evidence of this in most prayer-books, however, since gestural and contextual elements are generally omitted, presumably because they are assumed to be familiar to participants, and/or because a comprehensive discussion would be too unwieldy to include on the page. It is true that procedural matters are summarized in some detail in liturgical commentaries such as those of Lorbeerbaum and Ganzfried, mentioned above, but popular editions, such as the *Complete Artscroll Siddur*, include only general guidelines, and it is more usual to find them ignored. In the case of locations this silence reflects the way prayer has occasionally become detached from ideal settings, such as the home, reducing options and making discussion unnecessary. But objects such as *talit* and *tefilin* remain as relevant as the words on the page, as is confirmed by the meditations that precede their use.[3] The liturgical silence surrounding these seems less justifiable.

The theatre offers an obvious parallel to such literary incursions into reality, but the comparison is a deceptive one, as will be seen. It is true that scenery is depicted in general rather than in particular ways in conventional theatrical writing, like ritual objects in liturgy. Terms such as 'bed' or 'home' are shared commonplaces, usually requiring no further description, although there are exceptions, such as the 'platform' in the opening scene of *Hamlet*, an element of medieval military architecture that might need explanation. However, while stage scenery may vary according to production and may even be only virtual, the ritual paraphernalia of worship must be physically there, even if the worshipper's 'home' happens to be a tent or an inner-city doorway. This analysis will ignore such variations of detail, as also those due to local ritual custom, including divergences in style of performance, worshipper participation, or the way the *talit* is worn.

Variables of this kind might seem more significant to an outsider than to a participant, in fact, for formal prayer is possible in almost any setting, indoors or out, provided that ten men are present. Indeed a non-participating 'theatre critic' would see, not a spectacle designed to impress, but people reading, some of them apparently inattentively, a few out loud and others in an undertone, engaged in what seems to be a raggedly performed private ceremony. However, liturgical realism is reinforced by its being enacted in real time in a way that performance art is not: services take place according to the clock and calendar and

---

[2] See the valuable article by Schaller, 'Performative Language Theory'.

[3] Knowledge of the design of the *talit* is assumed in Extract 3, while the *tefilin* are described in some detail in Extract 7.

are tied to the movements of the sun, moon, seasons, and the life-cycle. Festival prayers may be somewhat more 'theatrical' and be performed with greater apparent feeling, but traditional Jews usually perform the daily liturgy without gestures of attention. The occasional bow and ritual swaying, particularly of hasidic congregations, do indicate involvement in worship, but these are often accompanied by a preparedness to break off for conversation. Such interruptions are usually confined to points in the service in which they are technically permitted, but the fact that they are allowed at all is indicative of an informality that outsiders might find incongruous. There are traditional synagogues in which demonstrative prayerfulness is the norm, but in most the social functions of the synagogue keep breaking through.

This apparent detachment, one of the most striking aspects of Jewish liturgical practice, gives synagogue worship a perfunctory appearance that tends to disappoint—or merely mystify—a spectator approaching it with expectations based on the performance of worship in other religions or even on the theatre.

The analogy between theatre and liturgy looks weaker still when one considers that, unlike theatrical performers, the worshipper is neither actor nor spectator—a distinction occasionally blurred in the contemporary theatre—but both.[4] Even though liturgical action is orchestrated by the prayer-leader, who might be compared to the 'chorus' (the leading narrator) in Greek tragedy, he (for women do not officiate in traditional prayer gatherings) will be an equal member of the prayer quorum rather than a sacramental figure, and will usually be selected by common agreement from those present, especially for weekday services. On more formal occasions a professional or well-practised prayer-leader might be involved, but his status will not differ qualitatively from that of other worshippers.

In another respect the liturgy differs not only from theatre, but from other literary genres such as novels, poems, or plays. The latter invite readers to participate in the lives and relationships of fictional characters, while the liturgy is self-addressed, at least from the philosophical viewpoint discussed in the previous chapter. The present analysis differs from conventional theatre criticism, therefore, in being based on the point of view not of a spectator or a reader, but of a participant. This is why the worshipper or reader is referred to as the 'speaker', in this way taking into account the relationship between the reader and the subject, or the view that the liturgy is self-addressed. This term also avoids the detachment of the term 'user'.

Besides being both a performer and a spectator, the worshipper is also the subject of the liturgy, since its themes focus on matters affecting each individual, as this analysis will show; it juxtaposes these with central Jewish ideas that it illuminates in complex ways.[5] Since the liturgy expresses the concerns of communities more than those of private individuals, moreover, the worshipper tends

---

[4] Rappaport, *Ecology, Meaning, and Religion*, 176–7.   [5] Ibid. 182–3, 187, 204.

to be included in the larger group, and in this way is related to the broader sweep of history.

Underlying the differences between theatre and liturgy—at least in traditional communities—is the assumption that 'dramas have audiences, rituals have congregations'.[6] While the former is a voluntary, occasional, and normally a commercial arrangement, the latter is religiously obligatory, regularly repeated, and ritually time-bound. The differences between these are characterized by Thomas Hardy, who described how 'A traditional pastime is to be distinguished from a mere revival in no more striking feature than in this, that while in the revival all is excitement and fervour, the survival is carried on with a stolidity and absence of stir which sets one wondering why a thing that is done so perfunctorily should be kept up at all. Like Balaam and other unwilling prophets, the agents seem moved by an inner compulsion to say and do their allotted parts whether they will or no.'[7] Actor detachment was even regarded as a token of authenticity by Bertolt Brecht, who in his stage directions asked actors to generate an unspectacle-like impression, asking for a staging 'that . . . seems to *quote* gestures and attitudes rather than imitate them. Actors are directed to speak their lines as if "playing from memory", and to foreground, rather than conceal, the play's artificiality.'[8] This technique of 'defamiliarization', designed to rouse spectators from their habitual patterns of response and sensitize them to what is being said, is not a conscious factor behind traditional Jewish inattention to liturgical texts. But apparent detachment and formality do coexist with a similarly disorienting surface impression of juxtaposed fragments,[9] and these convey greater complexity and depth than would be possible through theatricality.

The apparent similarities between liturgy and theatre do have some basis, however, in the remote link between them in the origins of Greek drama. That tradition began as an enactment of sacred narratives and became progressively more personal as individuals and their relationships came to be depicted as fully rounded 'characters'.[10] Rabbinic liturgy occupies an intermediate position between ritual and drama, since, although it is rooted in the formality of Temple ritual, it achieves quasi-dramatic expression thanks to its association with events in everyday life. Rabbis resisted the temptation to individualize and dramatize the sacred narrative, both because liturgy must express collective rather than private experience, and because the ideas involved are arguably too complex to be presented dramatically. Certain Jewish liturgical sequences, such as the blessings that frame the Shema in the morning and evening, could form the basis for

---

[6] Rappaport, *Ecology, Meaning, and Religion*, 177.   [7] Hardy, *The Return of the Native*, 143.

[8] Sherwood, *The Prostitute and the Prophet*, 105, quoting Willett, *Theatre of Bertolt Brecht*, 168.

[9] Hoffman, *Art of Public Prayer*, 185–95, distinguishes between the distancing effect of theatricalization in liturgy and the power of theatre to engage.

[10] Burn, *History of Greece*, 125, 204, and E. F. Watling in Sophocles, *The Theban Plays*, 8–12, comparing Greek tragedy to a 'modern oratorio', based on its origins in a blend of ritual and the performance of familiar narrative (Raphael Loewe, pers. comm.).

drama, while the Binding of Isaac, the Torah reading for the second day of Rosh Hashanah, is given collective rather than private importance by being talked about rather than dramatized. This insistence on the privacy of experience resembles the biblical prohibition on depicting God, as a result of which each individual retains a dynamic idea of God rather than having to internalize one imposed by others. The sacred narrative must remain impersonal if it is to engage each individual.[11]

The disadvantages of dramatizing the sacred narrative may be conceptualized by imagining the different experiences produced by reading Aeschylus' *Prometheus Bound*, performing in it, and watching it being performed. The reader must generate inner images in response to the text, while acting in it will heighten the experience by giving these physical expression, at least for the actors. In comparison to either of these a spectator will remain an outsider. The liturgical 'speaker' thus occupies multiple 'acting roles', functioning as a performer more than a reader, and certainly not as a spectator. The example of this Greek play happens to be a fortunate one, since not only are its central themes human suffering and the need for God's mercy, but it is roughly contemporary with the fifth-century BCE date traditionally given to the origins of the liturgy under Ezra and the Great Assembly.

Links between liturgy and drama can also be seen in the similarity between the polyphonic variety of Roman Catholic liturgy, which has been described as blending 'narrative, dialogue, antiphon, monologue, apostrophe, doxology, oration, invocation, citation, supplementation, and entreaty', and the original function of the 'satire'. The latter began as a textual form whose 'diversity of genres . . . had possible magical and incantatory functions'.[12] The epic 'which liturgy anticipates' would be represented by the recitation of sacred texts,[13] which in a Jewish context would correspond to scriptural readings and their liturgical frame.

The Absent Author, Citations, Allusions, and Echoes

Although most rabbinic writers on the liturgy are preoccupied with questions of authorship and authority, the prayer-book consists largely of texts borrowed, without the sources being identified, from other genres. It is therefore almost entirely lacking in authorial or editorial data. As has been noted, this characteristic helped deter traditional commentators from investing in the genre. In addition, liturgical editors often worked at odds with each other, further undermining authorial status. Such a lack of authority on the part of the author is unsurprising to contemporary criticism, however, especially since W. K. Wimsatt and Monroe Beardsley asserted the irrelevance of authorial intention to the reading experience.[14]

---

[11] Schonfield, 'Zion'.   [12] Pickstock, *After Writing*, 213.   [13] Ibid. 214.

[14] The 'intentional fallacy' is discussed in Wimsatt and Beardsley, *The Verbal Icon*, 3, 5.

For readers expecting clarity of expression and argument, a sense of shape and direction, and, at the close of a service, a feeling that a declaration has been cogently delivered, parts of the liturgy are in danger of appearing little more than an opaque and fragmentary draft of an anthology whose compiler inadvertently dropped his notes and neglected to re-order them before publication. But readers reach beyond this view of liturgy in two ways. First, the rabbinic concept of the omnisignificance of divine teachings suggests that all opinions that are not manifestly heterodox 'are the word of the living God'.[15] Since Torah is elevated in some texts to a near-equivalence with God—knowledge of the one approaching intimacy with the other—the lack of clarity of language in the liturgy does not undermine its authority but invites the worshipper to confront a theological mystery.[16] Secondly, while anthological compositions based on revelation may communicate a sense of literary incoherence rather than of divine mercy, undermining the text's potential revelatory or salvific power, in practice, lack of clarity is counteracted by daily contact, by dint of which the fragmentary texture is metamorphosed into narrative. The argument that force of habit and the mind's natural intolerance of incomprehension generate coherence overlaps with the rabbinic tradition of interpreting scriptural language not only according to its lexical meanings, but in terms of the coloration that each term carries into its new setting from its original context. Liturgical words have intertextual connotations derived both from their meaning and their previous contexts, whether scriptural or rabbinic, and these generate counter-texts that overlay the superficial chaos with a home-grown coherence.

The potential for borrowed texts to mean more than they appear to say has been examined by Richard Hays in his analysis of fragments of the Hebrew Bible embedded in the New Testament. He distinguishes between 'citations' and 'allusions', which for him are the result of authorial intention, and 'echoes', which he sees as more incidental, arguing that all will be read intertextually—that is, as counterpoints to the main text—by the attentive or 'ideal' reader.[17] It is possible to read without attending to intertexts. But singing William Blake's 'Jerusalem', for instance, without reference to its original appearance at the end of 'To the Jews', the prose introduction to an epic poem entitled *Milton: A Poem in Two Books to Justify the Ways of God to Men*, ignores an important dimension of its meaning to the author.[18] As has been seen, Zangwill's worshippers similarly had only the vaguest grasp of the liturgy's wider meaning, although an 'ideal' reader of the kind discussed in the previous chapter would indeed recognize the prayer-

[15] See the discussions in Bruns, 'The Hermeneutics of Midrash', 193, and id., 'Midrash and Allegory', 630–3. See also BT *Git. 6b*, cited in Boyarin, *Intertextuality*, 141 n. 23.

[16] Stern, *Midrash and Theory*, 28–9, 31. A parallel may be noted with an anthropological view of scriptural origins: 'if there are going to be any words at all it may be necessary to establish *The Word*', this being 'implicit in . . . liturgical orders': Rappaport, *Ecology, Meaning, and Religion*, 202, 210.

[17] Hays, *Echoes of Scripture*, 23.   [18] Blake, *Complete Poems*, 588–9.

book as a mosaic of intertexts or as a *bricolage*, 'bodging together', of found objects.[19]

Hays compares the *bricolage* of T. S. Eliot's *The Waste Land*, where a taste for cultural continuity is reflected in the poet's notes on his sources, with Harold Bloom's remark that 'Every poem is a misinterpretation of a parent poem', in which the relationship with the past is one of conflict. Bloom argues that 'poetic influence . . . always proceeds by a misreading of the prior poet, an act of creative correction that is actually and necessarily a misinterpretation'.[20] Hays adds that not only is every poet an interpreter, but that each interpreter is a poet, since the identification of sources forms part of the reading experience. In this way, the liturgy can be seen not as a deferential homage to learning, but as an act of reinterpretation based on the manipulation of decontextualized fragments.

Hays warns against free association in understanding these texts, however, insisting that authorial intention be identified where possible. He argues that, in proposing a reading, it is necessary to take account of its plausibility (whether it was available to the author or editor), its repeatability (the likelihood that other readers would reach the same conclusion), and its theological relevance (whether it is related to the rest of the text).[21] In the case of Jewish liturgy, where most authors and editors are unknown, plausibility and repeatability are satisfied by the fact that most sources have been identified by previous rabbinic commentators. Their theological relevance is demonstrated if the implications, however unwelcome, make sense in terms of Jewish belief.

The precise mechanism by which the original context of a citation is carried into new settings is discussed by John Hollander, who describes echoes that bring with them elements of their original context as 'metalepsis'.[22] 'Allusive echo functions to suggest to the reader that text B should be understood in light of a broad interplay with text A, encompassing aspects of A beyond those explicitly echoed. . . . Metalepsis . . . places the reader within a field of whispered or unstated correspondences.'[23] Even an echo that is the 'merest cadence in the ear' suggests more than it asserts, and the process of unpacking its impact transforms the reader into a writer.[24] Free association must be avoided, he also argues, since the meaning must make sense within the community of interpretation,[25] an idea already outlined in the profile of the 'ideal reader' in the previous chapter and reflected in the need for repeatability mentioned above.

---

[19] For Claude Lévi-Strauss's use of this term and its literary applications see Genette, 'Structuralism and Literary Criticism', 63–5.

[20] Hays, *Echoes of Scripture*, 16–17, citing Bloom, *The Anxiety of Influence*, 94, 30.

[21] Hays, *Echoes of Scripture*, 29–32.   [22] Hollander, *The Figure of Echo*, p. ix.

[23] Hays, *Echoes of Scripture*, 20.   [24] Ibid. 24–5.

[25] Ibid. 26–7; Fish, 'Interpreting the *Variorum*', 327.

Indeterminacy

The sort of meaning that can be extracted from such tessellated texts necessarily appears fluid, and several critics have discussed how clarity can be achieved in understanding them. Frank Kermode describes how, for Bible readers, 'If there is one belief (however the facts resist it) that unites us all, from the evangelists to those who argue away inconvenient portions of their texts . . . it is this conviction that somehow, . . . if we could only detect it, everything will be found to hang together.'[26] But he also warns that historical readings may rob the text of its immediacy and even offer an escape from facing up to its message. 'When confronted by a problematical text, we find it easier to think about [it] if we imagine something *behind* it rather different from what we have in front of us.'[27] Among the readers who avoid this evasive approach to the text are recent critics who have attempted to read the 'gapped' nature of much biblical narrative not as evidence of multiple authorship and poor redaction, but as a tool for ensuring audience involvement.[28] A fragmentary narrative obliges the reader to become involved in the compositional process by intervening to construct a continuum, and this, according to some, will be based on pointers provided by the author or editor.[29]

This acceptance of the possibility that textual meaning will not be self-evident involves a paradoxical withdrawal of the expectation of finding clear and explicit messages. It resembles John Keats's demand that poets and readers should restrain their instinctive demand for clarity and learn to live with ambivalence. He describes this as the *'negative capability*, that is, when a man is capable of being in uncertainties, mysteries, doubts, without any irritable reaching after fact and reason. Coleridge, for instance, would let go by a fine verisimilitude caught from the penetralium of Mystery, from being incapable of remaining content with half-knowledge.'[30] Applying a tolerance of uncertainty to Bible or liturgy involves relying ahistorically on general impressions rather than on the coherence of each part, and on being prepared to see shifts in lexicon and style as evidence

[26] Kermode, *The Genesis of Secrecy*, 72.   [27] Ibid. 79 (emphasis in original).

[28] See Fishbane, 'Inner Biblical Exegesis', 31–4.

[29] For the 'fraught background' of biblical narrative see Auerbach, *Mimesis*, 11–12. For Frye's assumption of biblical unity, see Sherwood, *The Prostitute and the Prophet*, 325–6. For a later appeal for holistic rather than excavative and atomistic approaches to the fragmented surface of scriptural texts see Alter, *Art of Biblical Narrative*, 133. In response to Damrosch's remark that 'to do full justice to the dynamics of biblical narrative, we must often read a passage three or four ways at once' (see Damrosch, *Narrative Covenant*, 325), he calls for 'a reading that takes account of the bumpiness of the text without rushing to break the text down into a series of bumps and disjunctions': see Alter, *World of Biblical Literature*, 18. For the 'assumption that the Bible is a single, though enormously varied and complex book' see Josipovici, *Book of God*, 9.

[30] For Keats's letter of 22 Dec. 1818 to his brothers see *Letters of John Keats*, ed.Rollins, i. 193–4.

of possible authorial intention rather than of composite origin.[31] Such a 'literary' reading may seem historically arbitrary, but recent biblical scholars have similarly tended to give more weight to the 'final form' than to the tendency of the documentary hypothesis to fragment the text, and they would include the work of redactors as well as those more conventionally regarded as authors in the literary process.[32]

A similarly indirect approach to reading may be implied by Rashi's advice to 'avoid thinking about' the enigmatic description of the biblical rite of the red heifer which, as one of the 'statutes' or inexplicable biblical laws, can best be understood, he implies, by looking aside.[33] George Steiner likewise advocates 'deferring' the gratification of identifying a clear message and accepting the need to live with the potential for meaning of a richly suggestive text.[34] The midrashic tradition exemplifies this allusiveness, and has been traced by some critics to the analogous 'self-reflexivity, self-citation, and self-interpretation' of biblical writing.[35] This inspired readers to atomize texts in response to conceptual gaps and to understand the whole by attending to the parts and to their apparent dislocation. But if midrashic writing can be understood only by a 'radical intertextual reading of the canon, in which potentially every part refers to and is interpretable by every other part',[36] then it might also be said of liturgy that 'The verses . . . function . . . much as do words in ordinary speech . . . [forming] a repertoire of semiotic elements that can be recombined into new discourse, just as words are recombined constantly into new discourse.'[37]

Gaps in the biblical narrative, and therefore also in liturgy, thus need to be seen not as barriers to understanding, but as spurs to attention.[38] Although they result from authorial intention in some biblical texts, this is less clear in the case of the liturgy, unless one includes in the process every stage in its generation, including the work of printers and publishers. Can the bridging material generated by the reader be said to relate to the text itself? The literary critic Stanley Fish challenges the view that fixed points or 'stars' are provided by the author so that the reader can link them to make sense of what he is reading, and argues that the 'stars' are as relative as the interpretations that join them.[39] In his view the reader has primacy, at least within specific limits.[40] He warns against free association and insists that the reader should rely only on the tools available to the

---

[31] Polzin, *Moses and the Deuteronomist*, 17–18.

[32] See the discussion in Nicholson, *The Pentateuch in the Twentieth Century*, 249–68.

[33] Rashi on Num. 19: 2.   [34] Steiner, *Real Presences*, 122.

[35] Boyarin, 'Song of Songs', 223, 229 n. 23; Bruns, 'Midrash and Allegory', 626–7.

[36] Boyarin, *Intertextuality*, 16.

[37] Ibid. 28–9, where he also discusses the status of both Bible and citation as *parole*.

[38] Rimmon-Kenan, *Narrative Fiction*, 127–8, argues that it is not only in detective fiction that 'gaps . . . become the very pivot of the reading process' and that (quoting Wolfgang Iser) 'it is only through inevitable omissions that a story will gain its dynamism'.

[39] Discussed in Sherwood, *Biblical Text*, 211 n. 9.   [40] Barthes, 'Death of the Author', 171–2.

'interpretive community' within which the text was written. Recent critics of
midrashic texts have similarly concluded that readers of early rabbinic readings
of Scripture can proceed only if they understand the language of interpretation
that is being spoken. Such midrashic writings incorporate 'a kind of underlying
"deep structure" . . . that both produces and governs multiple interpretations
. . . "all is determined, and yet all is open"'.[41] Correct associations are anchored
in the authorial rather than in the exegetical community, and this requires of the
reader a sense of responsibility to the sources which limits free association.

   In Freudian terms such gaps are what ensures that texts are not merely uni-
dimensional images, but that they attain that complexity of 'over-determination'
characteristic of human mental processes. By requiring the reader to try out and
thereby experience several interpretations, gaps ensure multiple meanings,[42]
enriching the reading experience. This idea is examined by Wolfgang Iser, who
describes how

What is missing . . . is what stimulates the reader into filling the blanks with projections.
He is drawn into the events and made to supply what is meant by what is not said. What
is said only appears to take on significance as a reference to what is not said; it is the
implications and not the statements that give shape and weight to the meaning . . . [and]
the explicit in its turn is transformed when the implicit has been brought to light.[43]

The way in which 'blanks'[44] suspend 'good continuation' in the narrative helps
'to hinder (and at the same time to stimulate) the process of image-building'.[45]
This explains how abridgement can paradoxically reinforce a narrative. He cites
as an example the way in which a trailer for a forthcoming film will use a mon-
tage of cuts to create the impression of an exciting narrative: the expectations
thus raised, he says, are rarely fulfilled in a full viewing.[46] A story told in exhaus-
tive detail is a tedious one, mainly because it is more limiting than one which is
suggested and which therefore leaves the reader a measure of autonomy.

   When too many expectations are disappointed the reader may see a work as
'chaotic, destructive, nihilistic and simply a joke . . . [so that] everyday life [seems
to be] experienced as a history of ever-changing viewpoints'.[47] But such a style
may also be deployed as a way of reflecting the chaotic nature of experience itself.
In the case of the liturgy, this sense of disorientation achieves vertiginous effects
and exemplifies how the comfortingly familiar can be undercut by a sense of
unease and vulnerability. Gap-filling may appear to smooth the surface—both
of a text and of daily reality—but it also contains the seeds of its own failure.
Midrashic exercises often create even more gaps. Faced with the need to identify
to whom God was speaking during the Creation narrative when he said 'Let us

---

[41] Stern, *Midrash and Theory*, 25–6, quoting Roitman, 'Sacred Language and Open Text', 160.
[42] 'All behaviour is regarded as over-determined in the sense that it is possible to interpret it as
the result of simultaneous activity at several levels' (Rycroft, *Critical Dictionary*, 110); see also Iser,
The Act of Reading, 4–50.   [43] Iser, *The Act of Reading*, 168–9.
[44] Ibid. 182.   [45] Ibid. 187.   [46] Ibid. 192.   [47] Ibid. 210.

make man', midrashic writers decide it was angels, since these pre-existed Adam. They similarly identify Abraham's reaction to the order to sacrifice Isaac as gradually dawning comprehension, as he only slowly grasps what he is being asked to do.[48] But these readings merely raise further narrative possibilities and, at least to readers alive to the challenges being raised, bring into focus the problematic aspects of God's behaviour (duplicity or cruelty?) and frustrate the attempt to find a consoling, stabilizing text.[49] The way in which midrashic writers deepen the sense of 'muddle'[50] has much in common with liturgical editors' tendency to add material, as though welcoming the chaos that the petitionary parts of the liturgy explicitly challenge by requesting rescue and enlightenment.

The idea that the liturgy might be regarded as celebrating disorder rather than offering a solution is supported by the view that the suppression of links involves an act of concealment. Freud says, of a text that attempts to hide the fact that it contains an unacceptable message:

On the one hand it has been subjected to revisions which have falsified it in the sense of [its] secret aims, have mutilated and amplified it and have even changed it into its reverse; on the other hand a solicitous piety has presided over it and has sought to preserve everything as it was, no matter whether it was consistent or contradicted itself. Thus almost everywhere noticeable gaps, disturbing repetitions and obvious contradictions have come about—indications which reveal things to us which it was not intended to communicate. In its implications the distortion of a text resembles a murder: the difficulty is not in perpetrating the deed, but in getting rid of its traces.[51]

The reluctance of talmudic rabbis to finalize the liturgy and of later generations to arrange for its systematic study suggests an attempt, however unconscious, to cover up unwelcome ideas. The liturgical commentary presented here brings one face to face with the 'return of the repressed' in the prayer-book.[52]

The task of reading in this multi-layered way, taking into account not only what is present but also what is absent, cannot be undertaken by those unaware of the undercurrents of rabbinic thought. This presumably helps explain why the vogue of applying literary-critical insights to rabbinic texts, which has spawned a small library of works since the 1980s, has incongruously neglected the liturgy.[53] The lack of interest is all the more surprising in that the trend has been described as the product of an attempt by American academics to move away from 'high', 'Hellenistic', 'colonialist', and 'literary' texts, towards an apparently *echt* aspect of Jewish culture.[54] Since liturgy is both more 'popular' and less 'literary' than midrashic writings, this neglect is unjustified.[55] However, enough has been seen

---

[48] Ginzberg, *Legends*, i. 52–4, v. 69–71, i. 274, v. 249.

[49] Sherwood, *Biblical Text*, 90, 185–7.   [50] Ibid. 223–4, 229.

[51] Freud, *Moses and Monotheism*, 43.   [52] Boyarin, *Intertextuality*, 16, 104, 151 n. 5.

[53] Stern, *Midrash and Theory*, 95 n. 5.   [54] Ibid. 2–4.

[55] The resemblance between liturgical poetry and midrash is pointed out in Idel, 'Midrashic versus Other Forms of Jewish Hermeneutics', 46.

of its apparent difficulty to explain why it was set aside by these critics. Its component texts are less clearly demarcated than the clear midrashic hierarchy of source, interpretation, and prooftext, and most critics are not familiar with the ritual performances to which it is closely related. Nevertheless, if one focuses on the criterion of popularity, it would seem to be of more immediate interest than midrashic writing in that its themes are integrated into daily life and therefore provide what amounts to a scriptural and rabbinic gloss on everyday existence.[56] In terms of critical language, the liturgy is hyper-midrashic, transcending the conventional midrashic distinction between a superior main text and a subordinate prooftext or illustration, and constituting not exegesis, but a new narrative, equivalent to what Boyarin would regard as a 'perfect midrash'.[57]

Illegibility and Narrative

What can we claim the liturgical narrative to be? As has been suggested, it is not identical to scriptural narratives, but is constructed in the speaker's mind from fractured evidence. These fragments are, by the nature of things, moulded into one of the shapes provided by a repertoire of 'stories' made available by everyone's experience of narratives of all kinds. It is usual to draw on these in order to link otherwise apparently disjointed events in real life into a single sequence with a logic of its own. Like all tales, the one formed by the liturgy will itself be characterized by gaps to some extent, and human motives in it will be attributed on the basis of the writer's choice of plot or plots.[58] When a 'reading' of events emerges, it will in turn be compounded by the reader's own contributions, based on personal experience. Even social norms may play a role, as they seem to have done in excluding the liturgy from the rabbinic curriculum, a circumstance attributed here to a semi-conscious act of repression. One such suggestive gap in the narrative outlined so far suggests an idea which could not be made explicit in rabbinic thought—that in the liturgy the (philosophically speaking) non-hearing God is mirrored by the non-interpreting worshipper. Inattention to liturgical meaning could be a measure-for-measure response to God, a vengeful *imitatio dei* designed to promote his attribute of mercy, offering a variant on rabbinic anthropomorphisms in the form of *imitatio hominis*.[59] In the absence of the soothing, smoothing, controlling God of the Bible, the chaotic nature of the liturgical text reflects a world in need of mercy.[60]

The difficulty of the liturgy must therefore be seen as part of its meaning. Liturgical gaps must be filled, but still more gaps will emerge as a result of the

---

[56] Kugel, 'Two Introductions to Midrash', 91–2. The superimposition of past and present is implicit in the passage in the Passover Haggadah enjoining participants in the ceremony to regard themselves as though they themselves had departed from Egypt.

[57] Boyarin, *Intertextuality*, 137 n. 24. [58] White, *Tropics of Discourse*, 58–60.

[59] Stern, *Midrash and Theory*, 85–6. [60] Sherwood, *Biblical Text*, 219.

attempt to stop them, generating still others which will need to be explained in turn.[61] Human experience, with its unpredictability and frequent ambivalence, this implies, may be incomprehensible by nature.[62] Another level of gapping which is peculiar to liturgy is the division of daily time by the liturgical cycle, breaking up the experience of each worshipper. Repeating liturgical sequences around the day likewise suggests the ruptured and unaccountable relationship between the worshipper, the world, and God by implying that successive messages fail to 'get through' and need to be reiterated. The liturgy is unclear because the world to which it relates is inscrutable,[63] and because it reflects not social order (as was argued earlier of public worship), but its disorder.[64] Since so much of the liturgy is addressed to removing sources of confusion and difficulty, it can be argued that its chaotic inner structure echoes that of the outside world, and that this structure—or lack of it—is itself a gesture of protest at the apparent injustice of life.

The inscrutability of the world is also suggested by the barrier implied by the use of Hebrew and Aramaic, languages which have not been spoken as vernaculars since antiquity. Victor Shklovsky echoes Aristotle in arguing that 'poetic language must appear strange and wonderful; and it is often actually foreign: the Sumerian used by the Assyrians, the Latin of Europe during the Middle Ages. . . . The language of poetry is, then, a difficult, roughened, impeded language.'[65] Scriptural language transfers the worshipper from the familiar world into the environment of the biblical sacred narrative, a sphere characterized by the reader's subordinate status to God.[66] Even linguistically it is impossible to achieve complete competence in that narrative world. In liturgy the speaker employs the reflexive and multi-layered mode of midrash as a tool of insubordination, citing God's promises and contractual terms back at him and insisting that these should be binding. The silence of the divine interlocutor—or at least the lack of an explicit response—is inversely mirrored in the very surfeit of words generated in this attempt to storm the 'gates of prayer', regarded talmudically as locked since the destruction of the Temple. This silence is veiled by the fact that much of the liturgy is couched in direct address, which suggests that an answer is expected, and even defines the kinds of response that might be forthcoming. The sensation of many worshippers that their prayers have been 'answered' may therefore be seen as compatible with the philosophical view that prayer is addressed not to a transcendent being but to the self. The words of prayers, it could be argued, 'generate' a responding listener, although the worshipper is actually being helped by the liturgical experience to focus on overcoming other problems entirely. According to such a view the liturgy transcends mere wishful thinking and

---

[61] Boyarin, *Intertextuality*, 56.   [62] Ibid. 49.   [63] Sherwood, *Biblical Text*, 222–3.

[64] Rappaport, *Ecology, Meaning, and Religion*, 192.   [65] Shklovsky, 'Art as Technique', 27.

[66] This resembles the awareness in feminist literary criticism of the 'masculine' status of literary language. See Mitchell, 'Femininity, Narrative and Psychoanalysis', 427.

becomes part of a deeper mechanism for coping. This argument would enable rabbinic supporters of the philosophical approach to prayer to validate worship as such, although in order for it to do so they would have to suspend their disbelief during prayer and to share in the narrative on which it relies for its cogency.

In the context of a discussion such as this, it is of course appropriate to emphasize the philosophical view of prayer at its most rigorous, and even to eschew the solace of the emotionally perceived response. According to this rather stark view, which is, it should be noted, only part of the overall range of experiences made available by liturgical worship, the gap-filled complexity of liturgy therefore represents the gulf of silence between the worshipper and God. This makes each liturgical performance a disappointed dialogue, revealing the speaker's vulnerability, mutability, weakness, and ineffectiveness. The failure of dialogue leads to dissent, the citing of unfulfilled promises, and repeated attempts to gain redemption by understanding revelation, making the synagogue a place of both intimacy and its absence. The speaker attempts repeatedly to study Torah and to fulfil the human side of the covenant, while awaiting a sign that God accepts the inevitability of human failure and relates to each person through mercy rather than through severity and judgement.

This version of the liturgical narrative regards it as delineating a theological impasse, but precisely this characteristic helps to identify the particular story, from the store of those available to each reader, which most closely resembles it and on which it might therefore be based. Yvonne Sherwood defines the so-called 'traditional story' as one 'that represents chaotic, insurmountable forces beyond the human protagonist', and contrasts this with 'stories that affirm the triumph of the individual and the power of human beings to change the world and purge it of evil'. The protagonists of the former 'do not seek the action thrust upon them (and in fact are often damaged by or at odds with it); and they are frequently caught in a double bind . . . a Catch Twenty-Two, pincer-like plot'. They 'would be delighted to compromise if it were an option . . . [but] the forces that oppose the protagonists are often projections of our deepest fears (*what if* God allied himself with the enemy, and not with us?)'.[67] Sherwood cites as an example of a 'traditional story' the book of Jonah, which she describes as an imposed mission that overlaps with aspects of the Jewish condition to convey truths to the world. Similarly, in the liturgy the worshipper is poised between feelings of election and of rejection. According to Sherwood, the Bible, typified by Jonah, might be 'read as an extended meditation on questions of identity and survival, marked by an exposure to the raw vacillations of life (famine, war, disease)'. It seems possible to associate the liturgy, as Sherwood does the book of Lamentations, with moments at which God becomes 'like an enemy . . . making

[67] Quoted in Sherwood, *Biblical Text*, 223–5, 280–3, 287–8, in the course of summarizing the analysis in Roemer, *Telling Stories*, of the story gaps and all as a correlative of partly apprehended reality.

us the offscouring and refuse of the peoples', or in which 'God as a gigantic and ultimately unguessable force' encapsulates the speaker's fears for the day ahead.[68] The silence underlying much human experience, according to the liturgical narrative, could take on new meaning. A large proportion of casual verbal communication is phatic—words used in formal rather than explicit ways ('It's a nice day, isn't it?')—while the emotional content of speech is conveyed in part by gesture and tone. Given such inarticulacy, the fact that communication so often breaks down is less surprising than that it is ever established in the first place. If, under certain circumstances, speech may be more for the sake of speaking than for achieving communication, the liturgy could, as has been suggested, be partly, or even wholly, self-addressed. The liturgy is an extreme illustration of this type of monologue-based communication, for no audible response is expected. Such loneliness, which might be regarded as an aspect of the human condition, has been conveyed otherwise perhaps only in the later novels of Samuel Beckett.

Like the books of Lamentations and Jonah, the liturgy has room for both dialogue and dissent, faith and the fear of disillusion, as the speaker moves between real and imagined locations, such as the home or synagogue, and the remote past or future, including heaven. Orienting the mind to these and bridging the gaps between everyday life and the Bible involves annually enacting a reconciliation with scriptural narrative—in the form of the annual reading of Torah and the festival cycle—and experiencing the problems it posits and repeats. Juxtaposing life with the sacred narrative also invites readers to examine the nature of consciousness, the ability to act, the power of language, the rights of individuals, and the existence of suffering. The liturgy's very lack of an author undermines the struggle for coherence and stability, transforming it into a cry of protest at the silence of the universe. Piety, yoked to the inattention of traditional users, may conceivably be the most appropriate response, and may be regarded as corresponding to the silence underlying much human experience.

Reading the liturgy between the lines and against the grain in this way reveals a 'narrative' that to the best of my knowledge has not previously been identified. This is summarized in Chapter 11, and its profound critique of rabbinic thought from the inside deserves to be seen alongside rabbinic world-views, both philosophical and literary. The elements of the liturgy analysed in this book explore the instinct for survival, for peaceful relations, and for achieving happiness, in terms of anxieties over God's attentiveness, his delay in fulfilling his promised rescue, and the speaker's dependence on gaining access to an apparently opaque Torah. The Torah, closeness to which will bring redemption, corresponds to a universe which one is challenged to 'read' at every level, metaphorically representing the universal ignorance of God's larger purposes and the inability to scan the world with accuracy.

[68] Ibid. 284, quoting Lam. 2: 4, 3: 45.

The liturgical view of existence is less than tragic, however, since the speaker survives the day, attempting beyond hope of success to read, reread, and eventually penetrate the meaning of the words on which survival depends. The reverberation of these ideas around the liturgical day, week, year, and lifetime lies beyond the scope of the present volume. But each section of the liturgy can be read as both an acknowledgement that understanding is possible and a protest at its apparent inaccessibility.

The Effect of Repetition

The pattern of repetition to be found in the liturgy is so unfamiliar in Western literature that non-Orthodox movements have been led to abbreviate it, discontent having been expressed even by traditional users. Nevertheless, repetition has significant effects as a literary pattern. Variations in otherwise identical texts or different formulations within a standard structure relate liturgy more closely to music than to the logic usually expected of the written word. In addition, repetition represents the uncertainty that prayer or study has yet succeeded or can ever succeed, an idea more commonly argued philosophically than enacted as it is in the liturgy. Examining this problematic area repeatedly, but each time in slightly different terms, gradually builds up an encompassing view of the issue.

These possibilities are not considered in Solomon Freehof's study of liturgical repetition, however, although he does propose a correspondence between Birkhot Hashahar and the statutory core of the liturgy, cautiously describing the former as a miniature model of the latter. He regards this as 'half-consciously' designed to prepare the speaker for the subsequent synagogue readings, identifying various components as foreshadowings of Pesukei Dezimra, Barukh She'amar, the Shema, Amidah, Tahanun, and Torah reading respectively, making the early morning liturgy 'an informal "preview" of the morning service'.[69] While acknowledging that a variety of versions exist, he argues that 'a remarkable system and order' can nonetheless be detected. Joseph Heinemann dismisses this reading on the grounds that the morning blessings vary from rite to rite, and rarely total eighteen, so cannot correspond to those in the Amidah,[70] but this is to ignore Freehof's remark that the design is semi-conscious, and that an intuitive editorial process cannot be expected to be precise. Daniel Landes has subsequently adapted Freehof's view, matching it to the version of Pesukei Dezimra most commonly used in the United States,[71] and has provided graphic representations of how the morning sequences alternate between private and communal spheres and move from death to renewal.[72] But none of these writers explores the literary

[69] Freehof, 'Structure'.

[70] Heinemann, *Prayer in the Talmud*, 9–10 n. 15, 163; Elbogen, *Jewish Liturgy*, 407 n. 21.

[71] Landes, 'Halakhah of Waking Up', 37–8, based on the version of the liturgy in the Birnbaum edition of the prayer-book. This resembles the *Complete Artscroll Siddur*, discussed in Ch. 12 below.

[72] Landes, 'Halakhah of Waking Up', 38–40.

relevance of the patterns, and by focusing on design and structure they incidentally confirm the prejudice that liturgical writing is repetitive. The larger thematic parallels between other sequences of the daily liturgy are outlined in the penultimate chapter of this book.

The present analysis therefore suggests that duplication reflects not a paucity of subject matter, or the view that the themes of prayer are strictly circumscribed; it proposes that liturgical themes are repeated because they are impossible to conclude. The speaker rehearses them not out of a sense of liturgical propriety, but because each attempt to resolve them leads to another intellectual or emotional cul-de-sac.[73]

[73] On wave-like approaches, see Pickstock, *After Writing*, 184–5.

PART II

PART II

BIRKHOT HASHAḤAR

ﬥ

CHAPTER FOUR

ﬥ

The Darkness of Waking

'and breathed into his nostrils the breath of life'
GENESIS 2: 7

T HIS CHAPTER discusses the opening statement of the day and finds in it the
seeds of the liturgy as a whole, both in its use of language—especially the
citation or echoing of scriptural texts—and in the ideas it encapsulates. These
include the notion that human beings may have expectations of God that are not
fulfilled, that there are correspondences between daily life and biblical narrative,
and that the Torah, which human beings are supposed to understand and obey, is
dangerously opaque. This is the first of several liturgical introductions to the
morning, each of which contributes to a wider understanding of the range of
Jewish views of human life, perception, and happiness, though this version sets
the scene for the others.

ﬥ

EXTRACT I. The Opening Statement of the Day

The sentence to be discussed in this chapter opens the first sequence of the
morning liturgy, entitled Birkhot Hashaḥar, 'dawn blessings', which accompanies the speaker through waking, dressing, and leaving home for synagogue, to
the point of facing the start of a new day. The range of meanings encompassed
by this series of texts reaches far beyond this framework, however, to span the
entire sacred narrative, integrating scriptural readings into daily life. The
sequence is named after the benediction formulae (*berakhot*) at its core, although
the first of these appears only in Extract 2 and the main grouping in Extracts
22–5. Numerous other texts have accumulated around this earlier core, the origins of which will be outlined in the course of the discussion. The sequence concludes in a preliminary way in Extract 40, but was later extended by an
additional psalm, forming either an appendix or a preview of what is to come.
This delays the ending until Extract 42.

°I ACKNOWLEDGE UNTO THEE, O SOVEREIGN ALIVE AND ENDURING,   *SA-OH* 4,[23]

THAT THOU HAST RESTORED MY °BREATH-SOUL WITHIN ME,   *Zo. Ex.* 214

COMPASSIONATELY—O °HOW VAST IS THY FAITHFULNESS!   *Md. La.* 3,[6/11]

1. The opening statement of the day (*Modeh ani*)

An introductory group of texts of this kind might be expected to outline a developmental process, taking the speaker from sleep to full engagement with daily life; it might perhaps relate this transition metaphorically to larger patterns of growth, such as from conception to birth or from birth to independence. Here, however, there is no resounding introductory proclamation such as might be expected of the beginning of a new day, and its absence suggests that the moment of waking is not a point of departure for the speaker at all, but part of a continuum in which communication with God has never ceased. Indeed, the nighttime prayers, which will not be examined in detail here since they lie outside the scope of this book, can be seen as the immediate prelude to this statement, with this line as their sequel. This continuity from dusk to dawn suggests that the prayer-book relates not to a single day, framed by its own beginning and end, but to a more open-ended unit of experience within which life, on some level, is continuous rather than subdivided into conscious days and unconscious nights.

This first sentence, as will be seen below, also provides a key to the liturgical relationship with scriptural writing which lies at the heart of the Jewish contract with God. Far from deferentially redeploying scriptural words to construct a dialogue with their author, the editors of the liturgy manipulate them, highlighting ambiguities to explore existential issues. The statement made on waking also, as will be seen, reflects a pre-scientific interest in the nature of sleep and in what happens when one recovers consciousness on awakening.

The liturgical editors' compositional style of textual fragmentation makes it possible to convey meanings not merely as explicit statements, but in the form of oblique allusions. The speaker must decode these by bridging the cognitive gaps in a quasi-authorial way, generating other layers of meaning. These undermine what seems to be said, threatening to turn any statement into its own contradiction. Although liturgical diction seems direct, therefore, the words are multi-faceted and multi-layered, so that behind the appearance of dialogue lurks dissent, as scriptural narratives meet and collide in multi-layered interplay.

Like the first sentences of many literary novels, the opening statement's structure, as well as its complex messages, sets the scene for the rest of the work, which in this case encompasses the liturgy as a whole.[1] The sentence, as will be

---

[1] An obvious example is the opening sentence of Proust, *A la recherche du temps perdu*, i. 1, which previews the closing section of the novel, entitled 'Time Regained'. For discussions of opening passages and their role in the development of subsequent themes see Oz, *The Story Begins*, 7–10, citing Said, *Beginnings*, 6, 13.

מוֹדֶה אֲנִי לְפָנֶיךָ, מֶלֶךְ חַי וְקַיָּם, שֶׁהֶחֱזַרְתָּ   1
בִּי נִשְׁמָתִי בְּחֶמְלָה-רַבָּה אֱמוּנָתֶךָ!   2

seen below, illustrates the possibilities opened up by departing from the plain
meaning of scriptural revelation.

To understand this example it is necessary to be aware of the original context
and meanings of each phrase, wherever these can be identified. Behind the words
on the page and the moment for which they were intended, therefore, lie the
sentences and scenes from which the words have been extracted. The other texts
designed for the opening moments of the day and subsequently submerged by
later additions will similarly be examined at relevant points in the discussion.[2]

There is clear evidence that this sentence is indeed an element of the liturgy
in its own right, and may therefore be discussed independently of its immediate
context. It first appeared in a survey of daily life published in 1599 by Moses ben
Makhir, a sixteenth-century rabbi from the Galilee writing under the influence
of Lurianic mysticism,[3] and was slow to be accepted into the liturgy. It appeared
in the prayer-book of Jacob Emden 150 years after its first publication,[4] as well
as in various subsequent prayer-books,[5] but it was relegated to the introduction
of the standard edition of the Ashkenazi liturgy by Baer in 1868[6] and has been
omitted from editions and commentaries based on his work.[7] In the prayer-book
version used here it has been added to the existing Hebrew text—typeset early in
the twentieth century in a nineteenth-century style—in a different and far later
typeface, perhaps under the increasing influence of the east European tradition
that was evident in the 1970s when Schonfeld was working, and which gathered
pace during the 1980s.[8]

The history of its inclusion usefully illustrates how the shape of the liturgy
has been modified by a blend of human need and halakhic consideration, since an
older and more widely known waking prayer, prescribed in the Talmud and still
incorporated later in the daily liturgy (see the discussion of Extract 21), was
judged unsuitable for the moment of waking because it contained the divine

---

[2] The most obvious example is Extract 21.

[3] Moses ben Makhir, *Seder hayom*, 2–3. Moses is described as the head of the yeshiva in Ein
Zeitim, north of Safed, on the title page.

[4] Emden, *Amudei shamayim*, reproduced in the Weinfeld edn., i. 81, ii. 788.

[5] Such as *Otsar hatefilot*, 42a, and *Tselota di'avraham*, i. 1; it appears in *Book of Prayer: Daily
and Occasional Prayers*, 1.   [6] *Sidur avodat yisra'el*, 1.

[7] Such as Singer's prayer-book (1890, 1990) and the commentaries of Jacobson and Munk.

[8] As seen in the *Complete Artscroll Siddur* (1984), 2–3, and the centenary edition of Singer's
prayer-book (1990), 1–2. This trend is discussed below in Ch. 12.

name, which it was considered improper to pronounce until the hands had been washed. A blessing on washing the hands (Extract 16) could have been recited first, but the present line would then no longer have served as a waking prayer. The present text was introduced mainly because it does not include the name of God.[9]

That talmudic text also begins in conversational mid-flow without a resounding opening to suggest that it begins the liturgical day, and it even lacks an opening blessing formula, although it has a closing one. The lack of an opening blessing confirms that the paragraph merely concludes the short blessing recited last thing at night: 'Blessed are you, O God, our Lord, king of the universe, who causes the bonds of sleep to fall on my eyes and drowsiness on my eyelids.' The fact that the waking blessing omits any similar opening formula confirms that the night-time and waking blessings are elements of a single text and that the speaker's relationship with God has not been interrupted by the night.[10] The lack of a finale the night before and of a grand opening now might also suggest a reluctance to face the painful issues arising from both the nature of sleep and the silence that follows prayer. Prayers are not 'answered' in a conventional sense, so suppressing the end of the day by linking it to the beginning of the next obviates the need to expect that a 'response' will be forthcoming. The comparative informality of the beginning also serves to avoid the question of God's proximity and attentiveness, another issue implicit in the structure of the sentence, as will be seen. The speaker may at this point already be discovering that liturgy is at most a monologue with pretensions.

The ambiguity of the very first Hebrew word of the opening sentence, the verb *modeh*, touches on this theme, since it is poised vertiginously between the idea of 'thanks' and of 'acknowledgement', in the sense of 'admitting', 'assenting', 'confessing', or 'testifying', and without associations with 'thanks'. These incompatible meanings underscore uncertainty about responsibility for the speaker's life and the status of the covenant between humans and God. The translation in the present version prefers 'acknowledge', but most others adopt 'thanks', a difference with far-reaching consequences.[11] If it is translated as 'acknowledgement', the speaker can be assumed to believe that God acts according to legally binding principles rather than out of kindness, and that since he was bound to wake the speaker, no special thanks need be offered. If it is translated as 'thanks', on the other hand, the speaker regards God as free to wake the speaker or not, but as bound by no agreement to do so. This ambiguity leaves the speaker vacillating between two views of human–divine relations. According to one,

[9] Moses ben Makhir, *Seder hayom*, 2.

[10] For the idea that sleep does not constitute an interruption see Abudarham, *Abudarham hashalem*, 39, and Zedekiah ben Abraham, *Shibolei haleket*, 1b.

[11] 'Acknowledge' is supported by Ben Yehuda, *Dictionary*, ii. 1053, while 'thanks' is preferred in *Book of Prayer: Daily and Occasional Prayers*, 1. The ambiguity is noted by Heinemann in *Prayer in the Talmud*, 189, 196–7 n. 6, 206, who points out that this introductory formula suggests a legal setting, confirming the present interpretation.

humans have a right to life and to benefit from the system that God administers, but in the view of the other, God is a free agent who may or may not grant kindness.

The meaning of the verb is tipped in favour of 'acknowledge' by the Hebrew verbal prefix *she-* (in the last word of line 1), which may be translated as 'who [has returned my soul]'—stated as a matter of fact—rather than as 'for [having returned my soul]', or 'that [he has returned my soul]', which would imply that God has performed a special kindness, although it still retains some coloration of the notion of 'thanks'.[12] The Hebrew thus tends to imply that the soul is not a free gift of God for which thanks would be appropriate, but that it belongs in some measure to the speaker and is not God's to retain. If the speaker has a prior claim to the soul that has been returned, then God may be regarded less as a generous donor than as contractually bound to return the soul each morning after sleep. The connotations of the verb 'acknowledge' are clear-cut in the biblical book of Job, where it suggests 'recognition', 'resignation', or even 'submission'.[13] The full weight of this last sense will come into play only later in the liturgy.

The ambiguity of these opening words also reflects rabbinic concerns about the way sleep resembles death, and the idea that the loss of autonomy in sleep shuts down the channels of communication with God. Fear of sleep and the powerlessness it brings is reflected in a psalm that describes how God 'neither slumbers nor sleeps', ensures that 'the sun shall not smite you by day, nor the moon by night', and can 'preserve your soul' and guard 'your going out and your coming in . . . for evermore'.[14] God's freedom from sleep emphasizes the sleeping human's lack of autonomy, productivity, safety, and, most relevantly at this moment, of the ability to maintain verbal communication. This loss of speech is so mistrusted that it is implicitly denied by linking the blessing on going to sleep with that on waking. The danger of divine 'sleep' led to its use as a metaphor for circumstances in which Israel's calls for rescue are ignored,[15] when it was felt that, although God had heard an appeal for help, he had not reacted,[16] analogous to the 'hiding of God's face' which results from neglecting Torah and leads to suffering.[17] The 'king' referred to in this opening statement is clearly not asleep, but may need to be reminded of a legal obligation.

The same opening formula appears in two early rabbinic prayers which may have served as models for the present text, although neither found its way into

[12] Ben Yehuda, *Dictionary*, xiv. 6779 ('who'), 6781 ('because').

[13] Job 38: 3 and 42: 4 for resignation and recognition as distinct from thanks.

[14] Ps. 121: 4, 6–8.

[15] BT *Sot.* 48a; *Midrash Psalms* 59: 5, and Blumenthal, *Facing the Abusing God*, 106, who suggests that human sleep proves God's wakefulness.

[16] This idea is made explicit in the call 'Awake, why sleepest thou?' (Ps. 44: 24, followed by a challenge to God not to 'hide his face') included in the Sephardi rite for the concluding service for the Day of Atonement: see *Book of Prayer: Day of Atonement*, 267.

[17] Deut. 31: 18 and Ps. 30: 8, explored in a hasidic tale in *My People's Prayer Book*, iii. 63.

the liturgy. One, designed for the early morning, closely resembles the present sentence and notes that the speaker has been brought 'from darkness into light', reflecting the same ambiguity as the present liturgical line.[18] The other, to be recited on leaving the *beit midrash*—literally the 'house of study' but in practice any place where study regularly takes place—seems to relate to an activity that is less a right than a privilege for the literate.[19] But the use of the same verb may suggest that access to the Torah, as a route to covenantally promised salvation, is indeed a natural right.[20] Although the return of consciousness restores the means of salvation through study, however, the success of study, even when it is undertaken, is not to be taken for granted, for the demand for both faith and intellectual honesty leads the speaker into paradox after paradox.

Such tensions are also discernible in the words that follow the opening verb. The emphatic pronoun *ani*, 'I', introduces the dominant presence of the speaker, even though God almost invariably has primacy in liturgical texts. This opening formula is a familiar one in the liturgy and without exceptional features, but is not the only one that could have been used here. Others that might have been employed which do not highlight the speaker in this way include *avinu she-bashamayim*, 'Our father in heaven', or *yehi ratson milefanekha*, 'May it be your will'. Only with the third Hebrew word, *lefanekha*, translated here as 'unto thee', is the so-far unnamed interlocutor indirectly admitted as a presence beyond the primacy of the speaker. But this form of address, which means literally 'before you', suggests that the words are addressed merely in God's presence rather than actually 'to' him, as though it cannot be taken for granted that he will hear them. The text goes on to amplify this awareness of God's remoteness by stating that he is a 'sovereign, alive and enduring', words which suggest an auditor who transcends the speaker, a remote and perhaps inattentive ruler, as distinct from the equally common liturgical term 'father'.

Ambivalence of this kind might have been part of the authorial intention, since this liturgical opening is far from typical. Most of the liturgy assumes the presence of a community (or the larger context of the Jewish people), so speakers are nearly always plural ('we', 'us', 'our'), the first person singular appearing only in a few settings. Although the singular form used here is appropriate in the context of a waking speaker far from a community, the plural is freely used elsewhere, irrespective of whether the speaker is alone or in a group, so could have been employed here. There are halakhic reasons for the substitution here of

[18] *Gen. Rabbah* 68: 9: 'I acknowledge before you, O Lord my God, that you brought me forth from darkness to light'.

[19] JT *Ber.* 4: 2: 'I acknowledge before you, O Lord my God and God of my fathers, that you gave me a portion among those who sit in the house of study and the synagogue, and did not give me a portion in theatres and circuses, for I wear myself out [in study] and they wear themselves out [in vanities].'

[20] For the idea that study is necessary before worship and must be 'perfect' see *Tana debei eliyahu*, ch. 2, p. 12 trans. Braude and Kapstein, pp. 23–4.

divine attributes for a personal name of God, but the effect of the lack of a name is likewise distancing,[21] as is the noun 'king', which suggests remoteness, mastery, and the dispensing of justice according to abstract rules rather than kindness.[22] By contrast, the frequently used term 'father', with which 'king' is often twinned, has associations of proximity, affection, and mercy.[23]

Characteristically, however, a shadow of the opposite view can be detected in the same sentence, since the lack of a personal name might be taken instead as an indication of familiarity and accessibility, reflecting the fact that the speaker is so confident of being heard that a proper name is unnecessary. This would reinforce the impression of intimacy provided by the lack of a formal opening and the first person singular form of address. But since it cannot outweigh the suggestion of remoteness created by the prepositional formula 'before you' and the title 'king', the ambiguity remains part of the meaning.

Underlying this statement, as has been said, is a proto-scientific concern with the question of personal identity and its apparent loss in sleep. Although the statement seems to be spoken by the whole individual, it is articulated only by the body to which the soul has been returned. The body is presumably capable of expressing itself only because its soul has been restored, but in this case the former has precedence. The possessive pronoun 'my' (second word, line 2) identifies the soul as the same one that was removed the evening before, but it also indicates an awareness, reading between the lines, of the possibility of a mismatch.[24] Behind this scene seems to lurk the Creation narrative—although in the case of Adam only one soul was involved so the possibility of a mismatch did not arise[25]—because God gave Adam the 'breath of life' at Creation, reflected in the translation here of *neshamah* as 'breath-soul', alluding to the association of the word with *neshimah*, 'breath'. (The compound term is designed to avoid confusion with other Hebrew terms commonly translated as 'soul', particularly *nefesh* and *ruaḥ*, distinctions which are not central to this particular text.)

Even if there seem to be few grounds for giving thanks at this point, midrashic writers describe how God disputed with angels who were enviously opposed to Adam's creation, suggesting God's special advocacy of Adam's cause.[26] But since the Garden of Eden saw Adam fail in his encounter with God's demands and become mortal, the speaker seems justified in merely 'acknowledging' God's

---

[21] It is also liturgically unusual, although it does recur in the often-repeated Kaddish, which is discussed in Ch. 9 (Extract 41).

[22] See Schechter, *Some Aspects of Rabbinic Theology*, 92–6.

[23] The complementary terms 'mercy' and 'justice' will be discussed later, in the context of Extract 2 (Ch. 5).

[24] This concern is more complex in the text on which the present one is based, Extract 21, in which the soul that is returned is never referred to as 'mine'.

[25] Gen. 2: 7 records the joining of Adam's body and soul. The association of daybreak with the shaping of clay at Creation is suggested in Job 38: 14.

[26] *Gen. Rabbah* 8: 3–10; see Ginzberg, *Legends*, i. 52–4, v. 69–71.

involvement in presenting Adam with challenges resembling those the speaker now faces.[27] The idea that God is contractually obliged to return the speaker's soul is reinforced by his description here as 'king', a term suggesting justice.

The first direct biblical citation of the day, providing a point of entry into a scriptural story integral to the liturgical narrative, appears in the two Hebrew words that follow the term 'king'. These appear in their scriptural source (Daniel 6: 27) in Aramaic rather than in Hebrew as they are here, but the context and the fact that these words appear together only here in Scripture, show them to be a direct allusion rather than an incidental echo. The first word, *ḥai*, literally means 'alive', and the second, *vekayam*, although it is translated here as 'enduring',[28] in talmudic contexts signifies the 'fulfilling' of a promise.[29] Both interpretations of the second word—'enduring' and 'fulfilling'—are operative here to some extent, although 'enduring' merely reinforces 'alive', while 'fulfilling' highlights the contractual theme detected in the opening verb of the statement. This connotation also emerges from the scriptural context in the book of Daniel, for there the words immediately follow the word 'Lord', which, like 'king', has connotations of severity. The biblical narrative moreover bears a striking resemblance to the speaker's situation. Daniel has just emerged unscathed from the lions' den into which King Darius had been tricked into having him thrown. The king's advisers had persuaded their master to declare the act of praying a capital crime, knowing that Daniel would insist on praying to God whatever the penalty. Daniel was indeed arrested and sentenced to be thrown into a lions' den, but the king, who regretted having had to sentence him to death, declared his certainty that God would save him.[30] When the king returned to the den the next morning Daniel walked out unscathed—because, as the narrator explains, he 'trusted in God'[31]—and greeted Darius as 'king who lives for ever',[32] while Darius in turn praised 'the living God . . . steadfast for ever'.[33] These words, now reapplied in the liturgy, are perhaps best translated as one 'who lives and fulfils [his promise]',[34] suggesting that Darius was attributing to God a still greater quality than that which Daniel had just applied to him as a human king.

The similarity between the speaker's experience of waking from sleep and that

---

[27] *Gen. Rabbah* 19: 8; see Ginzberg, *Legends*, i. 76, v. 98–9 n. 72.

[28] Ben Yehuda, *Dictionary*, xii. 5907–8.

[29] Ibid. 5910–15; Jastrow, *Dictionary*, 1359 (e.g. BT *Ber.* 32*a*, BT *Git.* 88*a*, BT *Shab.* 30*a*). This relates strictly to the *pi'el* rather than *kal* form, as in Hebrew, e.g. *barukh gozer umekayem*.

[30] Dan. 6: 17.   [31] Dan. 6: 24.   [32] Dan. 6: 22.

[33] Dan. 6: 27. This is the rendering of the Authorized Version, retained in the Jewish Publication Society translation (1917), but not in the New English Bible.

[34] The ambiguity is reflected also in the scriptural and commentators' use of the same term (from the root *qum*) in several contexts: Rashi argues that Darius is urged to pass the law because it would help 'establish' his kingdom (6: 8), and the law, once 'established' (6: 16), cannot be changed, but must—in the view of David and Yehiel Altschuler, *Metsudat david*—be 'fulfilled'. However, the same commentary glosses the liturgical term as 'steady'.

of Daniel emerging from the lions' den makes it clear that the scriptural echo is part of the meaning of the liturgical text. The resemblance between sleep and death is reflected in rabbinic statements that 'sleep is one half of death'[35] or, according to a different text, a sixtieth,[36] that death occurs if the organs 'go to sleep',[37] or that sleep is a prelude to death.[38] From the speaker's point of view, waking up is comparable to the sparing of Daniel.

Another level of meaning emerges from comparing the dramatis personae in the liturgy and the Daniel narrative. In this part of the liturgy it is the body that acknowledges the return of the soul, while the soul remains silent. When this is compared with the book of Daniel, however, the waking body is aligned with Darius, a worldly outsider who acknowledges God's rescue of a friend, while the soul is identified with Daniel the Jew, who might be expected to express gratitude, but is silent. The advisers are aligned with 'sleep' as the agents of death, whether in the form of mortality or of oblivion. Darius, the body, was therefore tricked into endangering his friend Daniel, the soul, with whom he was reunited after the night, in a scene which is transformed into a rabbinic metaphor for waking and resurrection. Daniel's faith, which is silent since a soul cannot speak without the body, and Darius's trust, even though he does not have the 'soul' of Daniel's faith, reunite the Jewish and non-Jewish parts of the individual. The non-Jewish part is compared to an easily duped king and the Jewish one to a well-loved but defenceless servant, in exile from its homeland and vulnerable to envy and hatred.

This rabbinic mode of analysing the composition of the personality is part of a broader attempt to understand where the soul goes at night and what it does there. Narratives about nocturnal existence and the separation of body and soul also serve as vehicles for speculation about the relationship between God and humans. During sleep, midrashic writers state, the soul returns to God, but its departure for heaven is conditional on God's agreement to restore it the next morning. God's obligation is based on two legal provisions in the Torah, the first of which prescribes that the cloak of a poor man obliged to use it to pay a debt must be returned to him at night when he needs it.[39] Rashi's gloss explains that souls are similarly given to God in payment of debt each evening and returned when their bodies need them the next day.[40] The second provision demands that a hired worker who depends on his income should be paid at the end of each day, the text saying that he 'lifts his soul to him/it' (interpreted midrashically as referring to his employer).[41] In response, a midrash comments that all humans are hirelings who 'lift their souls' to God at the end of each day, entrusting them to

---

[35] *Gen. Rabbah* 17: 5.   [36] BT *Ber.* 57*b*.   [37] BT *Ber.* 61*a–b*.

[38] *Pesikta rabati* 14: 4.   [39] Exod. 22: 25.

[40] Rashi on Exod. 22: 25, citing *Midrash tanḥuma* (Buber), 'Mishpatim' 9. Oddly, Rashi equates the cloak with the soul, even though it might be expected to symbolize the body in its role as the soul's covering.   [41] Deut. 24: 15.

him for the night, an idea reflected in the psalmic statement 'into His hand I entrust my soul'.[42] The same midrash goes on to explain how God daily matches souls to bodies, returning each 'refreshed' to its body for the next working day, and compares the daily re-entry of the soul not only to Creation but to the resurrection of the dead.[43] In these particular rabbinic readings the soul belongs absolutely neither to God nor to its body but alternates between the custody of each.

In other respects the soul is more closely associated with heaven than with earth: unborn souls live in the 'seventh heaven',[44] are made of the same stuff as God,[45] and at conception are dispatched unwillingly to inhabit a foetus. Ownership seems then to be transferred, for body and soul are only unwillingly separated at death,[46] the soul apparently being only a visitor in the body,[47] contributed to the foetus by God while the mother and father provide the physical aspects.[48] In another contractual arrangement, humans who help God by keeping a body and soul together will be repaid by themselves being kept alive by God, who remains that person's 'debtor' until the favour of having saved a life has been repaid in kind.[49] This relationship of body to soul is true of all humans, not merely Jews.[50]

Of particular relevance to the liturgical statement is a midrash which expands on the assumption that the soul is made of the same stuff as God. This describes how, when the soul returns to heaven at night, it reports on the body's behaviour during the previous day to angels, who record the information and submit it to God in a document that will be cited at the final judgement. The body, unaware of the soul's nightly trip, is surprised at this knowledge of its deeds, until it is told that a man married to the king's daughter should not be surprised if the king knows how he behaves at home: 'You ask "whence does he know?" His daughter tells him.'[51] This midrashic description of the relationship between body, soul, and God in social and familial terms may be one of the sources of the opening liturgical statement of the day, for it presents God as the male master of an obedient female soul and the 'king' of an unruly male body, identical to the conscious self—the liturgical speaker. This remoteness coincides with the way the liturgical speaker refers to God as 'king', rather than using the accompanying title of 'father', which, as we now see, is the prerogative of the soul.[52]

---

[42] Ps. 31: 6, although the Hebrew word for 'soul' is different. See also its deployment in the closing lines of Extract 15 (Ch. 6).

[43] *Midrash Psalms* 25: 1–2. A similar equation between awaking and resurrection appears in *Gen. Rabbah* 78: 1, and BT *San.* 90b.   [44] BT *Ḥag.* 12b.   [45] *Lev. Rabbah* 4: 8.

[46] For a summary see Ginzberg, *Legends*, i. 56–9, v. 75–8 n. 20, and *Midrash tanḥuma* (Warsaw edn.), 'Pekudei' 3 and the midrashic text *Yetsirat havalad* in Jellinek, *Beit hamidrash*, i. 153–5. For its later medieval handling see Tishby, *Mishnat hazohar*, ii. 125–8, 131–6, 144–6; id., *Wisdom of the Zohar*, ii. 809–12, 815–19, 827–30.   [47] *Lev. Rabbah* 34: 3.   [48] *Eccles. Rabbah* 5: 10.

[49] *Lev. Rabbah* 34: 2.   [50] *Deut. Rabbah* 5: 15.   [51] *Pesikta rabati* 8: 2.

[52] An anonymous poetic exploration of some of this midrashic material, demonstrating its currency, appears in Carmi (ed.), *Penguin Book of Hebrew Verse*, 370–1.

The passage from the book of Daniel also has implications for the role of prayer, since Daniel was characterized as a criminal because of the very activity in which the speaker is now engaged. Daniel did not pray to be saved from the lions, it should be noted, or at least is not seen doing so in the narrative, since we are informed only of Darius's declaration of certainty that he would survive. The similarity between Daniel's words to Darius and those of Darius about God suggests that the identities of God and the pagan king overlap symbolically at different levels of this narrative, perhaps because it was precisely Darius's trust in God's ability to rescue Daniel that saved his life.

Midrashic accounts emphasize how the king refused to believe the accusation against his favourite until Daniel worshipped in his very presence, leaving the king no choice but to sentence him to death.[53] The ostensible function of prayer is therefore similar in the narrative and in the liturgical act now performed by the speaker, for Daniel proclaims his Jewish identity just as his accusers knew he would, while the formulas used by the speaker suggests his re-entry into Hebraic culture, whatever the dangers of distinctiveness. The speaker is endangered precisely by stating that God's authority is superior to that of any earthly king. In both cases Hebrew prayer is therefore arguably an 'acknowledgement', in the sense of a testimony, more than an expression of thanks, since God prevents neither unjust punishment nor sleep.

The ambiguity between 'acknowledgement' and 'thanks' noted in the first word of the opening statement is also illuminated in the Daniel narrative, for Daniel uses the same verb to describe his prayer,[54] even though the royal decree forbade only the declaration of a 'petition'.[55] The way Daniel's words are aligned with the opening statement as an 'acknowledgement' also suggests the similar effects of each action, since the speaker, who is now engaged in the very behaviour that incriminated Daniel, may likewise be exposed to danger in some way. The idea that this might be due to the manipulation of scriptural language becomes dominant later in the liturgical day, the ambiguities and ambivalences of this opening sentence continuing to resonate throughout the daily liturgy.

The second clause of the opening statement of the day (Extract 1, line 2) seems to continue the same simple statement of thanks or acknowledgement, but shifts first towards and then away from the idea of God as the primary owner of the soul. The return of the soul to the body after sleep is said to have been carried out *behemlah*, 'compassionately' (or, better, 'with pity'; third word on line 2), inclining away from acknowledgement and towards thanks by implying that the soul might be the property of God and that returning it suggests a caring relationship. But the two closing Hebrew words of the line shift the balance back in the opposite direction, for *rabah emunatekha*, 'how vast is thy faithfulness' (or

[53] *Midrash Psalms* 64; Ginzberg, *Legends*, iv. 347–9, vi. 435 n. 12.

[54] Dan. 6: 11; the other references to 'prayer' in this narrative (6: 8, 13, 14) omit the word, and Rashi on 6: 8 refers only to 'petition' and not to 'thanks'.   [55] See Rashi on Dan. 6: 8.

'reliability'), suggests that the speaker has a prior claim on the soul, which was returned according to the terms of a contract.

These last words come from another scriptural source which, together with its midrashic treatment, runs counter to the surface meaning. The biblical statement reads in full, 'Surely the Lord's mercies are not consumed, surely his compassions fail not; they are new every morning; great is thy faithfulness',[56] and was spoken by a witness of the destruction of Jerusalem in 586 BCE, mourning its loss but rejoicing in survival. A midrash on this text explicitly relates it both to daily awaking and to resurrection, making it doubly relevant to the liturgical statement.[57] Comparing the associations of this and the Daniel citation shows how liturgical arguments develop by means of what seem to be merely incidental inconsistencies at first sight.

The speaker this time is not an outsider to the inner life of the soul, however, as Darius had been, but a protagonist—a Jewish survivor of the fall of Jerusalem—and therefore equivalent in identity and survivorhood to Daniel himself. In this way he is aligned with the soul ('Daniel') in the previous scriptural source, rather than with the body ('Darius'), represented here by the ruins of Jerusalem. This juxtaposition of citations, each bearing the shadow of its original context, enables the liturgical statement to generate a narrative continuity. The speaker shifts from a Darius-like identity, not fully aligned with Jewish culture yet not hostile to it, towards that of a survivor, identified with the sacred narrative from the inside. In the citation from the book of Daniel the speaker was a pagan king, but here he is a survivor of the destruction of Jerusalem. In addition, while in the previous scriptural quotation the soul ('Daniel') was silent— although the narrator notes that he 'trusted' in God, using a term with the same root as the last liturgical word[58]—here the soul is an eloquent Jewish exile, expelled from his physical home in Jerusalem. The ruins of the city, corresponding here to the 'body', are now silent, while the speaker, representing the soul, survives physical death as the speaker of the lament survived the destruction of the city. The destruction of the city, however, like the sleep from which the speaker has just awoken, is the work of God, blurring the boundaries between natural processes and punitive suffering and implying that even the pain of exile might not be the result of misdeeds, but a morally neutral event without special meaning.

Even though a systematic account of the origins of suffering is not to be found in rabbinic thought, this idea seems at first sight to step outside those views of suffering that interpret it as the wages of sin. However, other notions with deep roots in midrashic writings retain this link with lived experience and suggest the ambivalence of God's involvement. When midrashic narratives describe how Noah's Flood killed the innocent as well as the guilty, the situation is characterized by the Greek-based term *androlemusiyah*, a word originally meaning 'the

---

[56] Lam. 3: 22–3.   [57] *Lam. Rabbah* 3: 23 (8).   [58] Dan. 6: 24.

theft of individuals' and used in Hebrew in the sense of 'lawlessness', but in this context referring to a situation created by God.[59] In the broader field of rabbinic thought, this represents the way in which all suffer when civil society breaks down. But rabbinic commentators describe how the Flood arose partly because of the withdrawal of God's attention, which encouraged people to imitate his apparent indifference. Rabbinic thinkers thus implicate God himself both in the crimes committed by humans and in the cruelty (caused by their punishment) that followed. God's failure to differentiate between the innocent and guilty during the Flood merely augmented the original problem of lawlessness, making him a contributor to the suffering. But whichever party is held to be more responsible in this case, the human or the divine, the combination of the indifference of humans and of God offers a model for the kind of suffering that the waking speaker is becoming aware might lie ahead in the day now beginning.[60]

The ambiguity of God's position is increased by the way this citation from Lamentations differs slightly from the version included in the liturgy. While the survivor in Lamentations thanks God for his 'kindness' and 'mercy' in the verse before the one in which the liturgical words appear, these two terms are replaced in the liturgical text by just one, 'pity', before the scriptural words quoted. This single liturgical term suggests that God, aware that the speaker is indeed suffering, relieves the pain. The two scriptural terms it replaces describe beneficence unrelated to any experience. So although the words of the lamenter locate the speaker in the ruins of Jerusalem, their liturgical reuse suggests that the speaker regards waking from sleep as still more remarkable than Jewish survival in exile.

The biblical echo suggests yet another paradox, however. The exiled lamenter specifically refers to being awake, suggesting that regaining consciousness in the morning corresponds not to rescue but to the experience of exile itself, and that the problems associated with daily life can be resolved only by the final salvation. The liturgical model for respite from exile is the sabbath, when messianic release, or at least elements of it, are represented as having been realized. Weekday life therefore seems particularly related to the experience of exile.

The associations of sleep with death and exile, and the paradoxical implication that these continue even in waking life, are illuminated by the liturgical context of this opening statement of the day. Its immediate sequel, from which it is now

[59] See the discussion of the development of views of suffering in Kraemer, *Responses to Suffering*, esp. chs. 8 and 10.

[60] The Greek term *androlipsia*, 'theft of men', is modified in rabbinic thought and applied to 'lawlessness'. See Kraemer, *Responses to Suffering*, 125, 239 n. 19; and Rashi on Gen. 6: 13, based on *Gen. Rabbah* 26: 5. A related assumption is made in *Gen. Rabbah* 32: 8, although *Gen. Rabbah* 36: 1 sees God's turning away as a model for, or even incitement to, human cruelty. For other uses of the term see Jastrow, *Dictionary*, 81; Krauss, *Lehnwörter*, ii. 65; Kasher (ed.), *Torah shelemah*, ii. 372 n. 18 (on Gen. 6: 2). For God turning away see Deut. 31: 17–18; on the suffering of the innocent in medieval rabbinic thought see Nahmanides on Gen. 18: 23–5 and Num. 16: 22 (citing 2 Sam. 24: 17), and Levi ben Gershon on Josh. 7: 1.

separated by successive interpolations, must have been the blessing recited over the washing of the hands, which the present text immediately precedes in some rites, though not in the version under discussion here. (The blessing will be analysed in the remarks on Extract 16.) The association of hand-washing with the idea of purification after contact with death supports the suggestion that sleep, as a pale reflection of exile and near-death, elevates the homelessness of Jews to a metaphor for the universal condition of suffering and loss. This resonance is confirmed by the fact that the present statement ends with a citation from the book of Lamentations, a text dominated by the fear of loss of all kinds, culminating in the ultimate fact of death.

To summarize some of the ideas that have emerged so far, this opening statement introduces themes that later dominate the liturgy: that God's covenant with the Jews is as binding on God as on Israel; that the human condition assumes suffering and overlaps with and approximates to the Jewish experience of exile; that Jewish identity may itself be dangerous; that suffering, even martyrdom, may not be punitive but mysterious in origin; and that release can come through closeness to God achieved by intimacy with Torah. This intimacy might be attained through the use of scriptural Hebrew, suggesting that reciting the liturgy could itself be regarded as a messianic gesture. Yet the manipulation of scriptural texts may transform these into a barrier to that closeness, modifying and altering them and turning the liturgy itself into an instrument of exile. It is also possible that salvation will equally come without apparent cause, much like waking after sleep. One idea which fades in the course of this opening statement of the day is the assumption that relations between Jews and non-Jews are potentially peaceful and complementary. Darius's friendship with Daniel is replaced by the voice of an exile speaking from the ruins of Jerusalem, a victim apparently of foreign enmity. Once the speaker is awake and the body rendered fully Jewish through contact with the soul, the outside world becomes a model for hostility, a relationship transformed only later in the morning liturgy, arguably in the closing lines of the *Aleinu* prayer, which lies outside the scope of this book.

One of the most important characters in this opening statement of the day, therefore, is the scriptural language itself. While most literature depicts situations in words, here the units of language used are biblical citations with rich connotations. Scriptural citations bring with them clear associations of character and situation, transforming what appear to be simple statements into narratives fraught with background. In this way the shift in the speaker's identity, from a non-Jewish 'body' in the opening clause to a Jewish survivor-'soul' in the closing clause, is presented in a language of citation accessible only to those aware of the original context of the words and able to read and compare clusters of such citations.

CHAPTER FIVE

❧

The Bonds of Freedom

'and clothed them'
GENESIS 3: 21

THIS CHAPTER discusses *talit* and *tefilin*, the ritual garments traditionally worn by adult males for weekday morning pra yer, and the texts that surround them. The symbolism of the garments runs deeper than their appearance suggests, however, encompassing the nature of divine kindness, experienced as human contentment, and of divine judgement, experienced as suffering. The ritual garments are shown to be complementary, enabling the speaker to enact a Jewish view of the world.

EXTRACT 2. **The Blessing Over** *Arba Kanfot*

The intense attention paid to the moment of waking in the opening statement of the day is succeeded by the texts surrounding the *talit* and *tefilin*, the ritual garments worn by men (and in some congregations by women too) at morning prayer.[1] One might expect to find some liturgical accompaniment to other stages of getting up, such as dressing and washing, to which these ceremonial clothes would provide the finishing touch. Indeed, in the talmudic source from which the first of these texts is drawn,[2] they form the climax to a series of blessings designed to accompany each stage in preparing for the day, preparation-texts that were later transferred from the home setting for which they were intended to the synagogue, as will be seen in Extract 24–Extract 25, line 4. Only the blessings attached to the *talit* and *tefilin*, the coda to this series, remain in their intended setting as accompaniments to real life, while the others have been divorced from daily life and instead introduce the public liturgy. The present texts, therefore, stand in for the process of personal preparation, covering the time from waking to the departure from home for synagogue and leading the speaker towards the daily confrontation with the world.[3]

---

[1] Practice varies: in some Orthodox communities boys wear the *talit* from early childhood; in others, it is worn only after marriage. *Tefilin* are put on, while reciting the blessing or blessings, only after bar mitzvah. Non-Orthodox practice is more varied, and tends to be elective (see the end of Ch. 2 for a discussion).   [2] BT *Ber.* 60*b*.

[3] This arrangement is also found in Emden, *Amudei shamayim*, i. 110–18, ii. 791 and *Otsar hatefilot*, 42*b*–44*b*.

°Blest art thou, God our Lord, sovereign of the universe, He	*Nu.* 15,[38]
who makes us holy through His commandments, and	*SA-OH* 8,[8]
commanded us concerning the *Mizvah* of *Zizith!*	*B'Br.* 60:

2. The blessing over *arba kanfot* (*Al mitsvat tsitsit*)

Talit and *tefilin* have been divorced from their original function for proced-ural reasons. As the liturgy associated with dressing acquired new supplements and grew in length and complexity, fewer worshippers could memorize it, and most preferred to have it recited for them.[4] Worshippers who knew it by heart or who could afford a manuscript would be able to read each element of the sequence at the correct moment, while those who did not would dress in silence (perhaps reciting only the texts over the *talit* and *tefilin* in private), walk to syna-gogue wearing the ritual garments, and hear the dressing sequence recited pub-licly in synagogue, responding 'Amen' after each blessing in order to signal their participation in the recital.

Some editions of the prayer-book locate the *talit* and *tefilin* still later in the morning liturgy, distancing these further from the act of private dressing. There they introduce the public parts of the liturgy, after the preliminaries have been completed,[5] suggesting that everything preceding them was personal prayer, even though some elements are clearly public. Since such a long delay is unlikely to have been inspired by the problem of memorizing a lengthy service, especially once printed books had become available, it may have been designed to ensure that there was sufficient daylight 'to recognize a familiar acquaintance at about four cubits',[6] the time at which daily prayers may start, which in northern European winters might be some time after the usual hour when prayers begin. The present version indeed leaves the ritual garments so typographically isolated from the rest of the liturgy that they might be put on still later, although it is unlikely that this would be after the psalm in Extract 42.

At whatever point the texts related to *talit* and *tefilin* are recited, however, unless they are located in their talmudic position the speaker will have to make sense of them in a way which resembles the work of a liturgical author or editor aiming to achieve a coherent ceremony or reading. Indeed, the speaker has fre-quently to play a quasi-authorial role in seeking to make sense of the dislocated texts. The arrangement used in the prayer-book analysed here heightens the link between symbolic and real dressing, since the ritual garments are put on soon

---

[4] Maimonides, *Mishneh Torah: The Book of Adoration*, 'On Prayer' 7: 9, insists the blessings should be recited while dressing, but the *Shulhan arukh*, 'Orah hayim' 46: 2, several centuries later, recognizes that few know the texts by heart and that consequently there is a need to separate the blessings from the dressing.

[5] *Sidur avodat yisra'el*, 55–7, or before Extract 43 in the present edition.

[6] *Shulhan arukh*, 'Orah hayim' 30: 1.

בָּרוּךְ אַתָּה יְיָ, אֱלֹהֵינוּ מֶלֶךְ הָעוֹלָם, אֲשֶׁר   1
קִדְּשָׁנוּ בְּמִצְוֹתָיו, וְצִוָּנוּ עַל מִצְוַת צִיצִת: 2

after waking. It also echoes the opening statement, in which the body clothed the returning soul, by showing how the body is now cloaked and bound with cultural clothes. *Tefilin* in particular, with Hebrew letters within and without, encode the speaker's experience of re-acquiring the use of Hebrew each morning, transforming the individual into a cultural entity clad in language and engaged in its manipulation.

Since ritual objects are traditionally assumed to be less 'eloquent' than texts, *talit* and *tefilin* were equipped with meditations to verbalize their symbolism. But even more of their meaning can be brought out by 'reading' their background, although repeated talmudic references to features of *tefilin* as 'laws [given] to Moses at Sinai'[7] acknowledge their non-scriptural and mysterious origins,[8] seeming to warn against interpretation and to imply that their importance lies more in their punctilious use than in understanding their 'message'. The emphasis on formal performance rather than intellectual engagement, left implicit in the case of the liturgy, is here transformed into near-explicit praise of the acceptance of impenetrability.

The ritual garments outlined here are so familiar to users that they are not usually described in prayer-books. However, the fact that this discussion of their symbolism will enter areas that are not usually touched on by rabbinic students suggests that a further reason for silence about them is that they embody ideas too complex for easy expression, reticence once again serving as a defence. *Talit* and *tefilin*, working in tandem, will be seen to encode a deep ambivalence about the privileges bestowed by divine election and about the nature of the 'freedom' inaugurated at the Exodus.

שׂ

The first ritual garment to be put on is the *talit*,[9] a square or rectangular prayershawl worn in most Orthodox synagogues by adult men at each morning service, although in some only by married men. In most traditions it is also worn by prayer-leaders and by those reading from the Torah even at other times, and in

---

[7] BT *Men.* 35*a–b*.

[8] This is less stringent than the category of *ḥok* ('statute') into the purpose of which it is forbidden to enquire (see e.g. Rashi on Num. 19: 2). On the present category, see Herbert Loewe, in Montefiore and Loewe (eds.), *Rabbinic Anthology*, 711–13. This corresponds to the English legal formula 'before legal memory', i.e. before Henry II (Raphael Loewe, pers. comm.).

[9] Sephardim prefer *talet*, and although the conventional plural is *talitot*, a preferable version would be *taliyot*; see Ben Yehuda, *Dictionary*, iv. 1878–80.

the Spanish and Portuguese rite also by those involved in reading from the Torah on sabbath afternoons.[10] It is donned in the afternoon of the fast of Tisha Be'av rather than in the morning, however, and is used in the evening on the Day of Atonement, the only occasion it is worn at night. It is worn together with *tefilin* on weekday mornings, but at other times is used on its own, while *tefilin* are never worn without at least an undergarment with the required fringes. A *talit* is often worn by bridegrooms at weddings, and may also serve as a shroud for men. Its use therefore marks moments of heightened significance in the life-cycle. In non-Orthodox movements it is not unusual for women to wear a *talit*, although it is more rare for *tefilin* to be used.[11]

In traditional contexts the first encounter with a fringed garment is on getting up in the morning. Then it takes the form of the *arba kanfot*, 'four corners', a smaller version of the *talit* worn like a poncho, usually under the shirt, allowing one to wear fringes throughout the day unobtrusively, although some traditional communities prefer them to be visible. The first liturgical text here relates to this garment and the remaining ones to the larger *talit* worn over the clothes for prayer.

The main feature of the *talit* is the knotted fringes, called *tsitsit*, looped through a hole in each corner, which are derived from a biblical passage instructing the Israelites to add 'fringes to the corners of your garments'.[12] Since conventional garments no longer have corners on which to put such fringes, Jews wear four-cornered garments to accommodate them, and so important is this practice that this biblical passage was chosen as the last of the three paragraphs of the Shema, the main credal statement of the day. This text explains that the fringes are to prevent Jews 'wandering after their eyes'—a synonym for idolatry—and suggests that, if they obey the words of God, he will again save them as he did from Egypt, a rescue linked in rabbinic thought to the messianic salvation which will end all suffering.[13] This rescue is particularly relevant here because of the exile promised in the second paragraph of the Shema as a punishment for failing to remain close to God's word, a lack again identifiable as idolatry.[14] Since the Shema consists of scriptural portions, it contains the solution to the problem, however, for it enables Jews to perform daily what the Torah elsewhere calls the duty to 'confess'[15] or 'return'.[16] The fringes, since they recall the commandments, are tools for transcending the everyday and for reaching towards the pos-

[10] Gaguine, *Keter shem tov*, i–ii. 5.

[11] BT *Men.* 43*a* and *Sifrei*, Num. 115 record statements in favour of women wearing fringes on their garments. Moses Isserles (Rema) accepts the practice but discourages it: see *Shulḥan arukh*, 'Oraḥ ḥayim' 17: 2.   [12] Num. 15: 37–40.

[13] Rabbinic thought on the messiah is inconclusive because of the variety of scriptural sources, but Maimonides relates it to the universal end of enmity and the restoration of the Jews to peace and freedom: see *Mishneh torah*, 'Hilkhot melakhim' xvii. 412–20; *Code of Maimonides, Book 14*, treatise 5, chs. 11–12, pp. 238–42, and the censored passage, pp. xxiii–xxiv.

[14] See also Mishnah *Avot* 5: 11.   [15] Lev. 26: 40.   [16] Deut. 30: 2.

sibility of salvation. They concretize the act of study, making it possible to 'wear' learning even without constant awareness.

The initial text related to the fringed garment (lines 1–2) introduces the blessing formula in the present prayer-book and is the first of Birkhot Hashaḥar, the 'dawn blessings'.[17] Its opening words are a formula so sacred that at least a hundred other blessings are recited in the course of the day.[18] Blessings (*berakhot*)—liturgical texts beginning with the words 'Blessed are you, God our Lord, king of the universe'—are the most common formula in Jewish prayer and gave their name to the opening tractate of the Mishnah, devoted to worship. These words are therefore the most common in the liturgy, introducing a variety of concluding texts. The present one is talmudic in origin, dating from the earliest period at which liturgical texts were recorded, and exemplifies the way blessings generally accompany rituals ascribed to divine injunctions, whether based on pentateuchal texts or on rabbinic authority, representing 'Oral Torah'.[19]

Each recurrence of the formula may be seen as a renewal of the speaker's attempt to reach God, but the words themselves imply the difficulty of doing so. Although the word *barukh*, usually translated 'blessed', is suggestively interpreted by Ibn Ezra to imply 'increase' or 'more',[20] each of the three biblical sources of the opening three words implies the difficulty of benefiting from this plenty. The first, from the book of Psalms, 'Blessed are you, O God; teach me your statutes',[21] suggests that correct understanding of biblical texts cannot be discovered without help. The second is spoken by Saul while trying to deny his failure to destroy the property of the Amalekites (the Israelites' principal enemies), just before Samuel says that his failure has cost him the monarchy, again suggesting the often near-impossibility of obeying divine law.[22] The third text records the words of David as he hands over the project of building the Temple to his son Solomon, associating the beginning of daily prayer with the building of a cultic centre. The speaker is aware, however, that David did not live to see the Temple completed and knows on some level that to quote him is to accept a similar fate.[23]

Blessings come in several forms. The present one, which consists of the opening formula and a concluding clause, is regarded as a 'short' blessing. 'Long' ones include a longer central clause and a repetition of the opening formula at the end, known as the 'seal'. Such a concluding seal consists of the first three words of the opening formula: 'Blessed are you, God', followed by a summary of the main text of the blessing. In a sequence of blessings only the first will begin

---

[17] BT *Ber.* 60*b*; this is the first daily blessing only in the present text, since that accompanying the washing of the hands precedes this act of dressing in some cases.

[18] Elbogen, *Jewish Liturgy*, 5–6.

[19] The earliest example of a non-pentateuchal practice being accompanied by a blessing is the public reading of the book of Esther, based on the direction to celebrate the feast of Purim recorded in Esther 9: 27–8; referred to in L. Roth, *Judaism*, 200–1.   [20] Ibn Ezra on Gen. 49: 7.

[21] Ps. 119: 12.   [22] 1 Sam. 15: 13.   [23] 1 Chr. 29: 10, read liturgically in Extract 55.

with the formula, although each will end with the seal. Familiar examples of such groups are the first three paragraphs of the grace after meals, those of the Amidah, and the series following the Haftarah. As noted earlier, the waking blessing begins without the opening formula since it is regarded as concluding the one recited on going to sleep.[24]

The opening formula of each blessing includes a combination of divine names: 'God our Lord', the first being the Tetragrammaton and the second the plural of one of the words usually translated as 'God'. This reflects ambivalence about God's relationship with the speaker, since, according to rabbinic convention, the first name represents God in his aspect of mercy and the second in that of severity and judgement.[25] The opening formula may therefore be read as a combination of two possibilities for relating to God. The first reflects a God whom one may address directly and personally, since the first name, associated with the attribute of mercy, implies protectiveness, restraint of power, and the withholding of punishment. The second name, associated with justice, law, and clarity of larger purpose, is followed by a term suggesting remoteness: 'king of the universe'. Both groups of attributes must be blended if the world is to endure, although mercy must predominate over judgement in order to ensure survival.[26]

This bipolarity in the rabbinic understanding of God is reinforced in blessings, such as the present one, which introduce ritual actions, for here the double introductory clause in the second person, without any time reference, is followed by another clause using the third person and the so-called past tense (which actually indicates completed action): 'who made us holy through his commandments'.[27] Rabbinic writers noted this duality and described how the blessing formula defines God as 'at once the nearest and the farthest, the most plainly revealed and the most completely hidden of all'.[28] The shift allows God to be addressed simultaneously as a being who listens to what is said in the here and now and as one so remote that he may not hear prayer, and who can be described only in terms of his past actions.

[24] Elbogen, *Jewish Liturgy*, 6.

[25] This is based on the emphatic use of the Tetragrammaton in the context of the statement of God's attributes of mercy in Exod. 34: 6–7. See Urbach, *Sages*, 451–2; Marmorstein, *Old Rabbinic Doctrine of God*, i. 43–53; Montefiore and Loewe (eds.), *Rabbinic Anthology*, 5–6; and *Gen. Rabbah* 12: 15, 21: 7; *Exod. Rabbah* 3: 6.

[26] This is a basic rabbinic assumption, and concludes Rashi's comments on Gen. 1: 1, based on texts such as *Gen. Rabbah* 73: 3 and *Num. Rabbah* 17: 3. For more on the names and the shift between them see *Sidur avodat yisra'el*, 36; *Tselota di'avraham*, i. 36–8; and *Otsar hatefilot*, 56a. For a kabbalistic response, see Sed-Rajna (ed.), *Azriel de Gérone*, 25–47, particularly p. 29.

[27] The origin of this inconsistency lies outside the scope of the present discussion. See Heinemann, *Prayer in the Talmud*, 77–103.

[28] Scholem, *Major Trends*, 107–8, 374 n. 88. See also *Sidur avodat yisra'el*, 36; *Mahzor vitry*, 56; *Otsar hatefilot*, 56a; *Tselota di'avraham*, i. 36–8, and Jacobson, *Meditations on the Siddur*, 61–4.

The term usually translated as 'sanctifies' (or here as 'makes us holy') suggests another ambiguity, for an early rabbinic text defines it not in terms of 'sanctity', but as 'made separate' or 'differentiated', in the sense of 'reserved'.[29] The wedding ceremony is accordingly referred to as *kidushin*, since this 'reserves' each member of the couple for the other.[30] The association is relevant here since the *talit* is worn by bridegrooms and may be used as a wedding canopy, but performing any ritual, particularly that of putting on the *talit*, recalls that the special relationship between God and Jews can be seen as a metaphorical marriage. As will be seen in the rest of the chapter, this relationship is so problematic that it may be seen as a metaphor for human–divine relations in general.[31] Its complexity is reflected in the threefold repetition in the last line of the root translated here as 'command', although the translator has sought both to avoid monotony and to reflect the technical nature of the statement by transliterating the third occurrence of the term as *mitsvah*, rather than as 'commandment', and by using the Hebrew word *tsitsit* without translating it as 'fringes', although this may be because their precise design makes so vague a term inappropriate.

EXTRACT 3. **The Meditation on the *Talit***

The fringed *arba kanfot*, worn as an undergarment, is always put on at home, but the *talit* proper comes into play either after dressing or in synagogue. This meditation, in which *talit* is translated as '*Tallis*-cloak', reflecting the Ashkenazi pronunciation of *talit*, links the term to *Zizith* (*tsitsit*) in order to emphasize that it is these that define the ritual garment. The text is distinct in genre from the preceding blessing, for it is not addressed to God but declares that the speaker is about to perform the ritual commandment of wearing fringes,[32] exemplifying the explicitly self-addressed dimension of prayer. It also differs from the preceding blessing, which is ancient, in that it derives from an early-modern school of thought, like the opening statement of the day.[33] It has been prefixed to the blessing over *talit* rather than to that over the *arba kanfot* since these are in most cases too small to be used for 'wrapping' oneself in the way the blessing prescribes.

The meditation is an example of a genre known as a *kavanah* ('intention'), which illustrates how ritual acts, however unclear or fluid in apparent meaning,

---

[29] *Sifra*, 'Kedoshim', introd. on Lev. 19: 2.

[30] See Schweid, 'Kedushah', 866, for a discussion of the term. The ceremony most obviously 'reserves' the woman for the man, but since the seven marriage blessings (which lie outside the scope of this book) suggest mutuality it seems justifiable to assume mutuality here also.

[31] Other scriptural sources for elements of the blessing formula are identified in Berliner, *Randbemerkungen*, i. 58–9, including Ps. 119: 12; Deut. 6: 4; Jer. 10: 10; Deut. 28: 19, 26: 19, 33: 4.

[32] Num. 15: 37.

[33] It first appears, in a longer form, in the abridged version of I. Horowitz, *Shenei luḥot haberit*, first published in 1649; see Y. M. Epstein, *Kitsur shenei luḥot haberit*, fo. 33a.

I am about to °enwrap in the *Tallis*-cloak of *Ẓiẓith* in order to	*Zo. Nu.* 245:
uphold the °command of my creator, as it is writ in the	*Zo. Dt.* 265
Torah:	*B'Gt.* 60:
°'They shall make for themselves *Ẓiẓith*-fringes upon the	*Nu.* 15,[38]
wings of their °garments, for their generations.'	*Gn.* 3,[21]
And so, as I do °enwrap with the *Tallis*-cloak in this world,	*Md. Nu.* 17 *ult.*
°likewise, may my soul merit to be enwrapped in a beauteous	*Zo. Nu.* 174.
Tallis-cloak in the future world or the °Garden of Eden—	*Msh. Av.* 5,[20]
°Amen.	*Gn.* 15,[6]

3. The meditation on the *talit* (*Hineni mitatef betalit*)

may be verbalized to be made more explicit. The scriptural prooftext on which the ritual is based contains a word usually translated as 'corners' but here rendered 'wings', to highlight its literal meaning and suggest midrashic associations. This is followed by a request for the soul to wear a *talit* after death, literally 'in the Garden of Eden', a curious juxtaposition probably reflecting the scriptural instruction for Jews to wear *tsitsit* for 'all' their generations, but also glancing forward to the use of the *talit* as a shroud. In this way the garment strengthens the symbolic link between waking and resurrection noted in the discussion of the opening statement, by emphasizing connections between waking in this world and survival in the next.

The Eden reference also recalls the unification of Adam's body and soul alluded to in the opening statement of the day, although the juxtaposition of dressing and the garden also relates to God's words to Adam after the eating of the fruit: 'who told you that you were naked?'[34] In the context of Eden, clothes denote the primary human failure to obey God's instructions, which, in terms of the speaker's current concerns, points to the need to remain close to Torah.

The association between the fig leaves of estrangement and the *talit* of reconciliation (since the ritual cloak ensures closeness to God) appears in a rabbinic text that argues that Adam and Eve were not originally naked, but wore 'skins of fingernails'.[35] These vanished following their disobedience, together with the 'clouds of glory' that had protected them, exposing them to the terrors of the natural world. Midrashic texts emphasize Adam and Eve's unfamiliarity with nature and cautious reaction to each new experience, an association which ensures that the speaker now joins Adam in his first encounter with the world. One text describes how Adam feared that the first twilight, a Friday night, might herald

---

[34] Gen. 3: 11.

[35] *Pirkei derabi eli'ezer* 14: 10, trans. Friedlander, p. 98; see also Daiches, *Babylonian Oil Magic*, 31–2 n. 1. For the reading 'clothes of light' rather than 'clothes of leather' (Gen. 3: 21) see Ginzberg, *Legends*, v. 42, 97, 103–4, and Levene, *Early Syrian Fathers*, 160–2.

הִנְנִי מִתְעַטֵּף בְּטַלִּית שֶׁל־צִיצִת כְּדֵי לְקַיֵּם מִצְוַת 1

בּוֹרְאִי כַּכָּתוּב בַּתּוֹרָה וְעָשׂוּ לָהֶם צִיצִת עַל־כַּנְפֵי 2

בִגְדֵיהֶם לְדֹרֹתָם · וּכְשֵׁם שֶׁאֲנִי מִתְכַּסֶּה בְּטַלִּית 3

בָּעוֹלָם הַזֶּה כֵּן תִּזְכֶּה נִשְׁמָתִי לְהִתְלַבֵּשׁ בְּטַלִּית נָאָה 4

לָעוֹלָם הַבָּא בְּגַן עֵדֶן, אָמֵן: 5

the end of the world and how he was saved when the personified sabbath pleaded that, since no other day had experienced destruction, it was unjust that this should be permitted on the sabbath.[36] He later similarly interpreted the decline of the sun following the autumn equinox, when Creation took place, and instituted an eight-day fast to avert catastrophe which was later transformed into the feast of Sukkot.[37] Adam's fear may be reflected in the fragility of the *sukkah*, biblically defined as a symbol of Israelite survival in the wilderness, and in the penitential themes of Hoshana Rabah (the last intermediate day of Sukkot). But the protective glory lost at Eden may still be recovered, for rabbinic writers urge Jews to 'look on the *talit* as though the glory of the Presence were upon them', comparing those who wear it to angels—quintessentially sinless beings, untouched by the events of Eden.[38]

The idea that the *talit* symbolizes reparation is reinforced in a midrash that describes how God wore one when teaching Moses how to pray for forgiveness after the Israelites had worshipped the Golden Calf.[39] This episode, which shows parallels with the disobedience in Eden, is the classic example of the breakdown of the relationship between God and Israel, since it is the moment at which the extreme difficulty of grasping the reality of an invisible God and an opaque revelation was recognized. The incident occurred when, during Moses' forty days on Mount Sinai, the Israelites felt in need of a 'real' experience of God and manufactured an idol, thereby betraying the principle that God can be

---

[36] *Midrash Psalms* 92: 3.   [37] BT *AZ* 8a.

[38] *Midrash Psalms* 24: 12, 90: 18. Midrashic writers do not say that Adam wore a *talit*, perhaps because it would have seemed inappropriate to imagine Eve, who had the same garment as he, wearing one. But the similarity between the kinds of primordial light around Adam and Eve, enjoyed by angels and promised to those who wrap themselves in a *talit*, suggests that these overlap symbolically.

[39] BT *RH* 17b; *Midrash tanḥuma* (Buber), 'Vayera' 9, 46a. For other references see Ginzberg, *Legends*, iii. 138 and vi. 57–8 nn. 296–7, and, for a discussion, Reif, *Judaism and Hebrew Prayer*, 110, 359 n. 54.

> °Blest art thou, God our Lord, sovereign of the universe, He   Zo. Gn. 23:
> who makes us holy through °His commandments, and   Ku. 3,[39]
> commanded us to °enwrap with the *Ẓiẓith*-cloth!   Ki. SA 9,[1]

4. The blessing over the *talit* (*Lehitatef batsitsit*)

fully experienced only internally. God at first proposed to destroy them, much as in the midrashic account of Adam's disobedience, but Moses persuaded him to pardon the people, and at the moment of retracting the initial proposal God wore a *talit*, linking it to an act of particular mercy. Although it is here worn by God, it is relevant that in Eden something very much like it helped Adam regain his dignity. For a worshipper to put on a *talit* therefore represents not only the will to survive as a latter-day Adam, but replicates, or encourages, divine mercy.

EXTRACT 4. **The Blessing Over the** *Talit*

The blessing for putting on the *talit*, which repeats the shift from direct to third-person discourse seen earlier,[40] refers to 'wrapping', and is the text on which the earlier blessing over *arba kanfot* was based. The translation reflects the absence of the word *talit* from this blessing, and describes the garment as a '*tsitsit*-cloth' to emphasize the primacy of the fringes over the cloak.

EXTRACT 5. **Verses on Wearing the** *Talit*

The scriptural verses recited while the head is covered with the *talit*[41] are the first such verbatim citation in the liturgy and specifically link a garment designed to recall Torah with the first act of study of the day. The four verses, echoing the number of corners of the garment itself, seem to refer only obliquely to the *talit*, yet the fact that they first appear in the present role in a work strongly influenced by Lurianic thought, published slightly earlier than the previous prose meditation,[42] suggests that they were intended for close reading. As will be seen, they touch on some rarely visited parts of the sacred narrative.

The most obvious association with *talit* emerges from the word *kenafekha*, 'your wings', the penultimate Hebrew word in line 1, which matches the word for 'corner' in the biblical text concerning the 'corners' to which fringes are to be attached.[43] This ambiguity between protective wings and mere corners links the

---

[40] BT *Ber.* 60b, BT *Men.* 43a.

[41] Ps. 36: 8–11. That this wrapping is intended to cover the head is clear from its description in rabbinic writings as *atifah yishma'elit*, 'Ishmaelite [i.e. Arab] wrapping', e.g. BT *MK* 24a.

[42] Shapira, *Metsat shimurim*, 98. For the identity of its author see Azulai, *Shem hagedolim*, 66b, no. 36, and Fürst, *Bibliotheca Judaica*, iii. 373; rather than *Sidur avodat yisra'el*, 57, last note.

[43] See Rashi on Num. 15: 41; also Deut. 22: 12.

בָּרוּךְ אַתָּה יְיָ אֱלֹהֵינוּ מֶלֶךְ הָעוֹלָם אֲשֶׁר   1
קִדְּשָׁנוּ בְּמִצְוֹתָיו וְצִוָּנוּ לְהִתְעַטֵּף בַּצִּיצִת: 2

four-cornered garment to the ingathering of the dispersed exiles, whom God promises he will gather in from 'the four corners of the earth',[44] where they have been scattered by the 'four winds of heaven'.[45] The same image of ingathering appears in a passage which lies outside the scope of this book, the liturgical paragraph before the Shema, at the point when the four *tsitsit* are to be 'gathered' into one hand. This association is reinforced by the image here of God's 'wings' as instruments of rescue and protection,[46] merging with the idea of a 'house' (in the sense of 'home') precisely when the *talit* is wrapped around the head.

The image is further enriched by the idea that God's protection brings the speaker 'bliss' (line 2) and proximity to the 'fountain of life' (line 3), an idea intensified by the sexual associations of the Hebrew word for 'those who know you' (middle word of line 4). This, and the echo in the 'fountain of life' of the well-scenes (symbolizing the marital home) that often feature in biblical love-stories,[47] link the *talit* both with a bridegroom's wedding garment and with an improvised *ḥupah* (wedding canopy). The primary associations are accentuated by the fact that the word for 'bliss', *adanekha*, shares a root with 'Eden', mentioned in the meditation before putting on the *talit*, suggesting that the *talit* repairs not only the rift generated in Eden but also that caused by the episode of the Golden Calf, which is seen midrashically as a temporary breakdown in Israel's 'marriage' to God at Sinai.[48] Thus the human *talit*, like that worn by God while pardoning the Israelites, symbolizes love and reconciliation. Intimacy will be extended to the 'upright at heart', a Hebrew term containing the four consonants of the name *yisra'el*, alluding to the speaker by a quality that might be absent, and will take the form of 'right-kindness', a translation reflecting the ambiguity of the term *tsedek*, which can mean both 'charity' and 'justice'.

The *talit* therefore symbolizes both salvation and the exile resulting from estrangement, being at once a marital home and (because the noun *bayit* is commonly employed figuratively in this way in rabbinic writings) the Temple, whose restoration will be accompanied by the ingathering of the exiles. But it also embodies the continuing exile—the Jews' native habitat—represented by the four corners of the world. The *tsitsit* passage from the book of Numbers reflects the same ambiguity, since it follows shortly after God's announcement that the

[44] Isa. 11: 12; see also Ezek. 7: 2 and Job 37: 3.   [45] Zech. 2: 10.
[46] Exod. 19: 4; Deut. 32: 11.   [47] Alter, *Art of Biblical Narrative*, 52–62.
[48] Rashi on Exod. 34: 1.

°How precious is thy loving-kindness, o °Almighty!—so the	*Ps.* 36,[8–11]
children of man seek °cover under the shelter of thy wings.	*Ku.* 4,[1]
They are abundantly satiated °from the wealth of thy house—	*B'Su.* 49:
yea, thou givest them to drink from the stream of thy bliss.	*Ikk.* 2,[15]
°For indeed, with thee is the fountain of life—through thy	*B'Ha.* 12
light do we see light. °O extend thy kindness unto them that	*Zo. Lv.* 34
°recognize thee, yea, thy right-kindness unto the °upright at	*B'Sn.* 100
heart.	*Gn.* 18,[19]

5. Verses on wearing the *talit* (*Mah yakar ḥasdekha*)

generation of the Exodus will die in the wilderness and that only its children will reach the Promised Land.

The *talit* also suggests that survival is possible even without salvation because, although the speaker's head is swathed, it is possible to 'see light' (last three words of line 3), as though the primordial light withdrawn after the disobedience of Adam and Eve can be glimpsed by means of the *talit* even before the coming of the messiah, as mentioned in the midrash quoted earlier. These words also subtly reapply to the fringes the scriptural instruction not to 'wander after your eyes', perhaps drawing on the identification elsewhere of Torah with 'light', in the sense of 'teaching'.[49] The association with light equally glances at early mystic beliefs in the effulgence of God's garment at Creation, although this is not referred to as a *talit*.[50]

These psalmic verses exemplify how texts embedded in the liturgy expand in meaning and become tools for exploring the sacred narrative in new ways, provided the speaker is able to recognize allusions of the kind identified here as aspects of the message.

EXTRACT 6. Concluding Meditation on the *Talit*

The closing *talit* text, which first appeared in the same edition of the prayer-book as the meditation before the psalmic verses (Extract 3),[51] is, unlike that text, addressed to God. It also reveals a new anxiety, for the speaker asks for wearing the *talit* to be regarded as equivalent to performing each of the 613 commandments in the Torah, making it a tool for avoiding the exile threatened in the second paragraph of the Shema as the penalty for failing to apprehend the notoriously opaque Torah.[52] The term 'commandments' is in this context a metaphor for the more general concept of Torah as revelation, here symbolized

---

[49] Prov. 6: 23.   [50] Scholem, *Jewish Gnosticism*, 57–64, and 131–2 for addenda.
[51] Y. M. Epstein, *Kitsur shenei luḥot haberit*, fo. 33a.   [52] Deut. 11: 16–17.

מַה־יָּקָר חַסְדְּךָ אֱלֹהִים וּבְנֵי אָדָם בְּצֵל כְּנָפֶיךָ יֶחֱסָיוּן: 1

יִרְוְיֻן מִדֶּשֶׁן בֵּיתֶךָ וְנַחַל עֲדָנֶיךָ תַשְׁקֵם: 2

כִּי עִמְּךָ מְקוֹר חַיִּים בְּאוֹרְךָ נִרְאֶה־אוֹר: 3

מְשֹׁךְ חַסְדְּךָ לְיֹדְעֶיךָ וְצִדְקָתְךָ לְיִשְׁרֵי־לֵב: 4

by a ritual gesture of intimacy with God, of the kind recommended by the first two paragraphs of the Shema.

The scriptural description of the *tsitsit* merely suggests that one should 'see them and remember all my commandments',[53] without explaining the details of their symbolism. A talmudic text mentions that the *tsitsit* recall the commandments, without saying how this is to be done;[54] another notes the numbers symbolized by the fringes and the numerical values of the letters in the word *tsitsit*. By adding the numerical values of the letters, which total 600, to the five double knots and eight threads in each fringe, one arrives at 613, the traditional number of the commandments in the Torah.[55] Since the four fringes function as a group, however, and no account is taken of the number of loops between the knots, this seems forced, suggesting that the symbolism is in fact more general.[56]

Such details lie only in the textual background, since the *talit*, which has already been seen to reverse exile, is based on a specific pentateuchal command. This appears in the biblical narrative after the declaration that the generation of the Exodus will die in the wilderness, as though the fringes symbolize exile. However, its last line mentions the Exodus from Egypt, which in the context of the Shema is taken to predict the eventual ingathering of exiles. The Shema therefore juxtaposes passages which promise first exile and then its reversal, and embodies these in the *talit*. But rescue will come only if the Torah is adhered to, the Shema implies, and complete precision is extremely difficult to attain. This problem amounts to a principle of necessary uncertainty that affects even the Shema itself, as rabbinic texts differ on precisely what this liturgical unit comprises. Some define it as the first sentence only[57] and others as the first two

---

[53] See Rashi on Num. 15: 39.   [54] BT *Men.* 43*b*.

[55] BT *Mak.* 23*b*–24*a*, for the traditional number of commandments and *Num. Rabbah* 18: 21 on this and its relation to fringes. Other arrangements of knots and loops are less common.

[56] See other numerological coincidences in the comments by Elliot Dorff in *My People's Prayer Book*, v. 59–60 and Schwab, *Rav Schwab on Prayer*, 121.

[57] BT *Ber.* 13*b*, BT *Suk.* 42*a*; see Montefiore and Loewe (eds.), *Rabbinic Anthology*, 685–6.

The Bonds of Freedom

°May it be willed from thy presence, God Lord of us and — Ku. 1,[1]

Lord of our ancestors, that °this *Mizvah* of *Zizith* shall be — Mai. Tva. 9,[1]

considered as if I had fulfilled it with all °its details, its minutiæ and its — Ra. Gn. 32,[5]

purports, °yea, with the 613 *Mizvoth*-commandments which — B'Mk. 23:

depend thereon—*Amen.* — Msh. Kd. 1,[9]

6. Concluding meditation on the *talit* (*Yehi ratson* (*tsitsit*))

paragraphs with various additions or alternatives.[58] The subject matter of all the paragraphs suggests that the Shema was being consolidated at a time when exile, either to Babylon or following the fall of the Second Temple, was a live issue, either potentially or actually. If this is the case, the editors of the Shema must have assumed that the attempt to maintain closeness to Torah had already failed and chose its passages with a view to accounting for the exile. Anxiety over how to achieve closeness to Torah is visible in the very uncertainty about the contents of this credal statement, and is evident even in the decision to concretize what could otherwise have been taken as a metaphorical command.[59]

A mood of uncertainty is also reflected in the way in which this petition begins by asking for help in ensuring that the ritual of *talit* is performed correctly, as though to acknowledge the opacity of all words, and to recognize that only with God's help can the speaker carry out even the simplest ceremony. Perhaps for this reason the *talit* encloses the speaker in a cloak of Torah, as a symbol of the linguistic basis of Jewish culture, replacing the home the speaker is about to leave for the outside world.

In its original source this text was recommended for use on sabbaths and festivals, when *tefilin* are not worn, so was designed to stand alone. A longer meditation, not included here, is recommended for weekdays and an equivalent text is provided for *tefilin*, suggesting an awareness of the complementary nature of *talit* and *tefilin*. This idea will be clarified in the discussion below.

EXTRACT 7. **Introductory Meditation on** *Tefilin*

Tefilin are ritual garments derived from the first two paragraphs of the Shema, so are closely related to the *talit* prescribed in its third paragraph, even though the

---

[58] Mishnah *Tam.* 5: 1 and Mishnah *Ta'an.* 4: 3 for the present texts plus the Ten Commandments; BT *Ber.* 12b for the Balak narrative instead of the third paragraph; and Mishnah *Men.* 3: 7 and *Sifrei*, Deut. 34–5 (ed. Friedmann, 74a [line 20], 74b [line 15]) for four texts, with the addition of Exod. 13: 1–16, in the *tefilin*. Reif, *Judaism and Hebrew Prayer*, 57 attributes the Shema to the Second Temple period, and on p. 83 points out the uncertain dating of the inclusion of its paragraphs, especially the third.

[59] The Septuagint translates *totafot* as 'memorials', an idea echoed by Luther (*Denkmahl*), suggesting that a metaphorical reading of the term is possible.

יְהִי רָצוֹן מִלְּפָנֶיךָ יְיָ אֱלֹהֵינוּ וֵאלֹהֵי אֲבוֹתֵינוּ שֶׁתְּהִי 1

חֲשׁוּבָה מִצְוַת צִיצַת זוֹ כְּאִלּוּ קִיַּמְתִּיהָ בְּכָל־פְּרָטֶיהָ 2

וְדִקְדּוּקֶיהָ וְכַוָּנוֹתֶיהָ וְתַרְיַ"ג מִצְוֹת הַתְּלוּיִם בָּהּ· אָמֵן: 3

sources are not adjacent to each other in the Torah. They consist of two small boxes, each containing manuscript copies of four scriptural passages; one is bound to the head and the other to the left arm during weekday morning prayers by adult men (and even in some Orthodox settings by women too). They are made of stiff leather, stretched while damp onto wooden moulds, with the wider base of each box folded over to form a loop at one side and sewn closed around the edges. Both boxes and the leather straps running through the loops to attach them to head and arm are blackened with scribal ink.

The box for the head is subdivided into four compartments, each of which contains a piece of parchment bearing one of the texts, and has the Hebrew letter *shin* moulded twice in relief on the outside, on the right side (from the point of view of the wearer) with three uprights and on the left with four.[60] Faint lines indicating the subdivision into four compartments are visible on the outside of the front, top, and back. The four scrolls, arranged in the order in which they appear in the Bible, are folded and wrapped, each in a protective fold of parchment, and tied with an animal hair. The ends of the hairs protrude from a hole in the front of the box, in the angle between the base and body of the box, at the point where the right-hand compartment ends, symbolizing, according to one source, the inevitability that the 'sin of the Golden Calf' will make itself evident despite every attempt to contain it.[61] In the box for the arm the same texts are written on a single scroll, the exterior having no details.[62]

[60] Gaguine, *Keter shem tov*, i–ii. 7–8 n. 15. Possible reasons are assembled, for homiletic purposes, in M. Munk, *Wisdom in the Hebrew Alphabet*, 209–10, and Emanuel, *Tefillin*, 298–302. None seems fully focused. It is, of course, the initial letter of the Shema, and the three and four arms total seven. It might be relevant that the box in which a *mezuzah* is housed similarly displays a *shin*, conventionally regarded as an abbreviation of the divine name Shadai which is inscribed on the back of the scroll, but that name is interpreted by some as an acronym of *shomer daltot yisra'el*, 'guardian of the doors of Israel'. Both *mezuzah* and *tefilin* are contained in a *bayit*, 'box' (literally 'house'), but since the *mezuzah* is used on a real house, the term is more than symbolic. The idea that the house relates to the individual as such gains some legitimacy from the introductory verse of Ps. 30, analysed in Extract 42. More will be said about the letter *shin* later in this chapter.

[61] Shapira, *Metsat shimurim*, 236–44; Gaguine, *Keter shem tov*, i–ii. 8 n. 16; Emanuel, *Tefillin*, 303–4.

[62] The position of the *tefilin* on the head and the left arm is discussed in BT *Men*. 36b–37b, in the course of a longer discussion of *tefilin* in *Men*. 34a–37b.

Herewith I do declare my intent by °laying *Tefillin*, to uphold the	*SA-OH*25,⁵
command of my creator who °commanded us to lay *Tefillin*, as it is °writ in	*Mai.Tfn.*1,¹
the *Torah:*	*B'Gt.*60:
ᵃ'Thou shalt bind them for a sign above thy hand and they shall be for	*Dt.*6,⁸
frontlets positioned between thine eyes;' yea, °they are these four	*B'Mn.*34
sections: *Shema; V'hoyo im shamo'a; Kaddesh; °V'hoyo ki ye'vi'acho*—	*Zo.Ex.*43,119:
in which there is the °union and oneness of Him whose name is to	*Ku.*3,¹¹
be blessed; also, so that we should recall the °wonders and the miracles	*Dt.*4,³⁴
which He wrought for us when he °brought us forth from *Mizrayim*—	*Ex.*13,⁹
yea, His is power and dominion over both the °supernal and the nether	*Mai.YT*2,⁶
beings, to do with them according to His goodwill! °Yea, He	*Zo.Lv.*82
commanded us to lay °above the hand, in recollection of His outstretched	*B'Mn.*37
arm and, as it is level with °the heart, to cause the desires and intentions of	*Sf.Dt.*6,⁸
our hearts to become °subservient to the service of Him whose name is to	*Mai.Dt.*3,²
be blessed; also on the °head, level with the brain, so that the soul-power	*Mta.Ex.*13,⁹
which is in my brain, together with my °sensations and capacities should,	*Dt.*32,³⁵
all of them, become °subservient to the service of Him whose name is to be	*Mai.Dt.*1,⁶⁻⁷
blessed; thus, from the °inspiration of the *Tefillin Mizvah* may °long life,	*B'Mn.*43:
holy influences and holy thoughts be drawn towards me, free of any ˢinful	*B'Mn.*44:
or iniquitous °thought, neither shall we be seduced nor provoked by the	*B'Tn.*7
Spirit of °Mischief—let him leave us to serve God in accordance with	*Gn.*6,⁵
°our heart's desire—*Amen.*	*B'Br.*17

7. Introductory meditation on *tefilin* (*Hineni mekhaven*)

The way in which the straps are knotted and attached to the arm approximates to various Hebrew letters, especially those forming the divine name Shadai, usually associated with attributes of power;[63] the *shin* on the box for the head also carries this connotation.

The *talit* is put on before the *tefilin*, and alone on sabbaths and festivals. These days are regarded as 'signs' of closeness to God, which is said to make *tefilin* unnecessary.[64] If it is indeed held that *tefilin* are unnecessary because they echo the symbolism of sabbath and festivals, then it must have been felt that the *talit* contributes ideas other than those implicit in the special days. This chapter will suggest, however, that *tefilin* are excluded because their message is incompatible with that of holy days, and that they are not worn then because it would be unbearable to do so.

[63] See Rashi on Gen. 17: 1.
[64] BT *Men.* 36b; and Gaguine, *Keter shem tov*, i–ii. 8 n. 19, 12 n. 23.

הִנְנִי מְכַוֵּן בַּהֲנָחַת תְּפִלִּין לְקַיֵּם מִצְוַת בּוֹרְאִי שֶׁצִּוָּנוּ לְהָנִיחַ תְּפִלִּין כַּכָּתוּב 1

בַּתּוֹרָה וּקְשַׁרְתָּם לְאוֹת עַל יָדֶךָ וְהָיוּ לְטֹטָפֹת בֵּין עֵינֶיךָ וְהֵם אַרְבַּע פָּרָשׁוֹת 2

אֵלּוּ· שְׁמַע· וְהָיָה אִם שָׁמֹעַ· קַדֶּשׁ· וְהָיָה כִּי יְבִאֲךָ· שֶׁיֵּשׁ בָּהֶם יִחוּדוֹ וְאַחְדּוּתוֹ 3

יִתְבָּרַךְ שְׁמוֹ וְשֶׁנִּזְכּוֹר נִסִּים וְנִפְלָאוֹת שֶׁעָשָׂה עִמָּנוּ בְּהוֹצִיאוֹ אוֹתָנוּ מִמִּצְרַיִם 4

וַאֲשֶׁר לוֹ הַכֹּחַ וְהַמֶּמְשָׁלָה בָּעֶלְיוֹנִים וּבַתַּחְתּוֹנִים לַעֲשׂוֹת בָּהֶם כִּרְצוֹנוֹ· 5

וְצִוָּנוּ לְהָנִיחַ עַל הַיָּד לְזִכְרוֹן זְרוֹעַ הַנְּטוּיָה· וְשֶׁהִיא נֶגֶד הַלֵּב לְשַׁעְבֵּד בָּזֶה 6

תַּאֲוַת וּמַחְשְׁבוֹת לִבֵּנוּ לַעֲבוֹדָתוֹ יִתְבָּרַךְ שְׁמוֹ· וְעַל הָרֹאשׁ נֶגֶד הַמֹּחַ 7

שֶׁהַנְּשָׁמָה שֶׁבְּמוֹחִי עִם חוּשַׁי וְכֹחוֹתַי כֻּלָּם יִהְיוּ מְשֻׁעְבָּדִים לַעֲבוֹדָתוֹ 8

יִתְבָּרַךְ שְׁמוֹ· וּמִשֶּׁפַע מִצְוַת תְּפִלִּין יִתְמַשֵּׁךְ עָלַי לִהְיוֹת לִי חַיִּים אֲרֻכִּים 9

וְשֶׁפַע קֹדֶשׁ וּמַחְשָׁבוֹת קְדוֹשׁוֹת בְּלִי הִרְהוֹר חֵטְא וְעָוֹן כְּלָל וְשֶׁלֹּא יְפַתֵּנוּ 10

וְלֹא יִתְגָּרֶה בָּנוּ יֵצֶר הָרָע וְיַנִּיחֵנוּ לַעֲבוֹד אֶת יְיָ כַּאֲשֶׁר עִם לְבָבֵנוּ· אָמֵן· 11

Some primary meanings of *tefilin* emerge from the way they are worn. While the *talit* enwraps the body and symbolizes protection, *tefilin* are bound onto the head and onto the arm and hand, hampering movement while enacting literally the instruction to bear the Torah 'as a sign on your hand and as frontlets between your eyes'. They are, in other words, designed to confine. The four biblical paragraphs in which this instruction appears are inserted in the *tefilin*, including the first two paragraphs of the Shema[65] and part of the account of the smiting of the firstborn which is divided into two, each section containing one version of the same instruction.[66] The latter two texts are not read twice daily, like the Shema, but only in the annual cyclic reading of the Torah and on the first of the intermediate days of Passover, to which they are historically linked.[67] They are otherwise not read, at least in the present prayer-book, and this omission raises questions about what these, and *tefilin* in general, have to say.

One of the differences between *talit* and *tefilin* emerges from the ambiguity of the fourfold symbolism in the latter, implied by the arrangement of the texts on separate pieces of parchment in the head *tefilin*, and on a single scroll in the case of the hand *tefilin*. A talmudic writer remarks that two of the four references to 'frontlets'[68] are in the singular and one in the plural, making a total of four, suggesting the fourfold division of texts in the 'frontlets' compared with the singular 'sign' for the hand, in which the texts are written on one scroll. This argument may have been formulated to account for an existing arrangement, and was

---

[65] Deut. 6: 4–9; 11: 13–21.   [66] Exod. 13: 1–10; 13: 11–16.

[67] See *Service of the Synagogue: Passover*, 161–2.

[68] BT *Men.* 34*b*. See n. 59 above on the possibility of metaphorical interpretation.

perhaps influenced by the dominance of the number four in the case of the *talit*. The division of a single continuous passage from Exodus, thus transforming a threefold into a fourfold division, is described in the same talmudic text as a tradition passed down 'to Moses at Sinai'. A later commentator rationalizes the numbers involved by pointing out that the head includes the four organs of smell, hearing, sight, and taste, while the hand possesses only that of touch,[69] but such interpretations seem inconclusive. Uncertainty over the number of texts in the *tefilin* also emerges from the appearance of the letter *shin* once with three and once with four arms.

The idea that *tefilin* aspire to resemble the *talit* in terms of their number symbolism has implications for the way in which they are to be 'read'. If the four corners of the *talit* suggest ingathering, then the number three will imply something else and presumably less, consequently the lack of redemption. The concerns expressed in the *tefilin* texts do overlap with those in the text describing the *talit* in some respects, but in others are completely different. For instance, the first paragraph of the Shema contains the unconditional instruction to 'bind [the Torah] as a sign on your hand and as frontlets between your eyes'. In the second paragraph this becomes a precondition for remaining in the Promised Land. However, since historically the land had been lost by the time the text of the Shema was edited, physically 'binding' these texts to one's body might be seen as reflecting the anxiety of landless Jews attempting to overcome the lack of understanding that caused their exile. The immediacy of the anxiety and the need to reverse the exile explains why this instruction to bind was interpreted physically rather than merely metaphorically. It would, after all, have been possible to recite the words without performing an actual binding. But if salvation depends on maintaining constant proximity to the Torah, then 'binding' is not such an extreme measure. Since the words of Torah have dynamic power (having been active agents in Creation, for example), they might be able to activate rescue.[70] It is a rabbinic commonplace that understanding Torah gives access to the workings of heaven and knowledge of the world.[71] In the case of the Shema an implicit link is generated between Torah and the Promised Land by the fact that both are feminine nouns. Torah, which gives access to the Land, represents a substitute for a homeland for Jews. The desire to give God's words existence by performing them literally is also based on the need to activate the terms of God's covenantal promise to save the world. But the speaker's need to bind these texts to the hand, based on the view that speech will not suffice, also suggests a low estimation of the power of words. In literary terms, the binding is an act of desperation.[72]

---

[69] Gaguine, *Keter shem tov*, i–ii. 7 n. 14. The contrast might echo the dualism indicated in the first line of the Shema.   [70] This is made explicit in Extract 43, lines 1–3.

[71] Gruenwald, *Apocalyptic and Merkavah Mysticism*, 4–8, traces this equation to the book of Job.

[72] Its physical enactment might echo the obviously literal nature of the biblical text concerning the fringes on the *talit*.

One reason for despair may lie in the two texts in the *tefilin* that do not appear in the Shema. These occur earlier in the scriptural narrative than the others, and refer to the 'hand' of God liberating the Israelites from slavery. Binding the human arm, if this mirrors that of God, reflects a desire to 'bind' God in some way.[73] Although it is unlikely that a rabbinic commentator would make this point explicitly, this might refer to the attempt to bind God to his contract with the Israelites. The Exodus text contains another reason for ambivalence, since it refers to the need to explain to each generation of children the Israelite release from 'the house of slavery',[74] an idea which echoes the daily release from darkness and immobility on waking.[75] But the Hebrew word *avodah*, here translated 'slavery', may refer equally to the Israelite entry into the 'service' of God reflected in the act of binding on the *tefilin*. These texts therefore juxtapose the liberation which freed the Jews with the relationship which holds them in exile. Liberty, for Jews, is conditional on attending to Torah, the opacity of which places their salvation effectively out of reach. The binding on of *tefilin* therefore reflects both the contractual duties that confine Jews and the desire to bind God to his covenant to save them.

Further evidence of this is that both Exodus passages, which appear in the narrative after the smiting of the Egyptian firstborn, refer to God's special claim over firstborns. They are identified as God's particular property, over which he has powers of life and death. The *tefilin* texts proclaim God's proprietorship even over the firstborn of animals, and describe how that of an ass must either be redeemed by payment or have its neck broken. These passages echo the dangers faced by the Israelites, pursued by the Egyptians to the shores of the Red Sea, and resonate with those of Jews in exile; their release, the texts imply, is beyond human power to secure.

Such a reading of the Exodus texts is not traditional but finds support in the way Moses described the Israelites to Pharaoh as God's 'firstborn'.[76] The status of firstborn sons remains particularly problematic in Jewish life: they must be ritually redeemed from a priest after birth and must fast on the day before Passover in memory of the last plague. These rituals have scriptural roots which are highlighted in midrashic readings of the sale of Esau's birthright to Jacob, the biblical narrative of which seems to describe how an elder brother's privilege is lost to a greedy younger sibling. The midrashic writers emphasize Esau's willingness to be rid of his birthright, however, and, paradoxically, Jacob's positive

---

[73] Exod. 13: 1–10, 11–16. It is tempting to see an association between God's *tefilin* and the midrashic request that his right arm, associated with the attribute of mercy, should bind his left arm, associated with severity: *Mekhilta derabi yishma'el* on Exod. 15: 5–6 (Lauterbach, ii. 41–2) and *Pesikta derav kahana* 17: 5. If this association of ideas is justified, human *tefilin* would provide an exemplar for divine conduct and form part of the conflict between the attributes identified with the names of God.   [74] Exod. 13: 14; often translated 'house of bondage'.

[75] The Passover Haggadah refers to it as a passage 'from darkness into great light'.

[76] Exod. 4: 22.

motivation in relieving him of it. The birthright involved priestly duties, transferred to the Levites and to Aaron and his family at the construction of the
Tabernacle, and Esau recognized that failing to maintain ritual purity while performing his priestly duties would result in his death. His life was therefore saved
by Jacob's acquisition of what to Esau was a burden.[77] This view of the problematic nature of firstborn status is confirmed indirectly in scriptural accounts of its
reversal in the cases of Cain and Abel, Ishmael and Isaac, Esau and Jacob, Aaron
and Moses, and Ephraim and Menasseh, the last pair deliberately reversed by
Jacob apparently to disrupt the principle of the rights of primogeniture.[78] The
role of the firstborn, even when the father is God, as in the case of Israel, is so
tempered by responsibilities and penalties that the firstborn, like the priesthood
whose functions they originally fulfilled, cannot be regarded as a privileged
group. Due to this overlap in status between firstborn and priests, the declaration
that Israel is a 'kingdom of priests'[79] may be read not only as a statement of
Jewish privilege, but as a warning of the penalties they collectively face for falling
short of sacral demands. The Levites, who in the wilderness years replaced the
firstborn and became the Israelite ceremonial caste,[80] were chosen for this role
not because of their purity of conduct, but arguably for their lack of it, for they
were linked with the massacre of Shechem.[81] Their new status even brought with
it an inherent disadvantage, for they were the only tribe without territory in the
Promised Land. This landlessness gave rise to the idea that 'their [priestly] tithe
is their inheritance',[82] but it also anticipates Israel's exile. Since *tefilin*, which
contain a text expressing the dangers of primogeniture, look towards and give
physical expression to the near-inevitability of being overtaken by younger sib-
lings and of exile, it is unsurprising that the text from Exodus about the firstborn,
with its implicit promise of exile, was felt to be too painful to include in the daily
liturgy.[83]

The *tefilin* texts are not analysed in this way in rabbinic literature, however,
so the meanings outlined here must be regarded as implicit at the most. Yet con-
firmation that their significance was of concern emerges from a midrash that
describes the texts contained in God's *tefilin*. The account appears in the same
context as God's *talit*, during Moses' vision on Sinai while seeking forgiveness
for the Golden Calf, when he is said to have seen the knot at the back of the *tefilin*

---

[77] See Rashi on Gen. 25: 31–2, and Segal, *Hebrew Passover*, 183 n. 3.   [78] Gen. 48.

[79] Exod. 19: 6.   [80] Num. 3: 12.   [81] Gen. 34: 30.   [82] Num. 18: 23–4.

[83] It was included in the morning liturgy for putting on the *tefilin*, fairly late in its development,
in several major prayer-books, including those of Jacob Emden, Isaiah Horowitz, and Nata-Nathan
Hannover, and in *Otsar hatefilot*, but is omitted from *Sidur avodat yisra'el*, suggesting Baer's misgivings. The first reference to its inclusion in the morning prayers is attributed to Joel Sirkis
(1561–1640, known after his commentary on *Arba'ah turim* entitled *Bayit ḥadash*, as Baḥ) in *Tselota
de'avraham*, i. 29 (in commentary 'Vaya'as avraham'). A proposal to include it in the Shema is
discussed in *Sifrei*, Deut. 74a and 74b.

on God's head.[84] A talmudic passage, recognizing that God would be unlikely to bind the Shema and Exodus texts to himself, suggests alternatives.[85] One of these is 1 Chronicles 17: 21, in which God declares the Jews to be 'one nation on earth',[86] complementing and reciprocating the declaration of God's unity in the first paragraph of the Shema. Such mutual dependence, which appears in other pentateuchal verses where devotion to God is linked to Israel's uniqueness,[87] is derived in part from the declaration over first fruits to be made after the conquest of the land (a passage featuring in the Passover Haggadah, like the Exodus texts above). Fruitfulness and God's unity are also linked by the juxtaposition of the statement of God's oneness in the first line of the Shema with the promise of famine and exile for failing to seek closeness to revelation in the second paragraph.[88]

Other verses in God's *tefilin* are Deuteronomy 4: 6–7, in which the nations praise Israel for their closeness to God and for the wisdom of the Torah; Deuteronomy 33: 29, which praises Israel's safety under God's protection; Deuteronomy 4: 34, which declares Israel's redemption from Egypt to be unique; and Deuteronomy 26: 19, in which they are honoured as God's holy people. The Talmud also describes how these six verses are combined so as to occupy no more than the four compartments available in the *tefilin* for the head, renewing the ambivalence about the number of compartments and texts in the *tefilin* in general.

The texts in God's *tefilin* differ from those in earthly *tefilin* by suggesting that it is in God's interest to protect the Jews, while earthly *tefilin* describe how Jews may seek redemption.[89] The idea that God requires Israel to survive for the sake of his own glory is encountered in several biblical narratives, notably that which describes how Moses seeks to persuade God that he should not destroy the Israelites for disobeying him. One midrash relates how God studies the text about the red heifer, a ritual for purifying those who come into contact with the dead so that they can take part in sacred activities,[90] thereby enabling Israel to pursue her own self-interest. In this respect, Israel's interest is also God's.

Another midrash accounting for God's interest in Israel's survival describes how human prayers that earn God praise from other nations are woven by the angel Sandalfon into a diadem,[91] which a medieval *piyut* describes as being set

---

[84] See Rashi on Exod. 33: 23, citing BT *Ber.* 7a and BT *Men.* 35b.   [85] BT *Ber.* 6a–b.

[86] See the parallel text in 2 Sam. 7: 23, part of the debate between God and David about the building of a 'home' for God, now that David has a palace.   [87] Deut. 26: 16–18.

[88] The links between Israel's ingathering and God's unity will be explored more fully in the notes on the first line of the Shema: see Extract 31 below.

[89] Samuel Edels (Maharsha) suggests that God's *tefilin* express praise of Israel, corresponding to human *tefilin* that praise God. This homiletic point comes close to the present reading.

[90] *Pesikta rabati*, 58b, trans. Braude, 14: 6, n. 28.

[91] BT *Ḥag.* 13b, *Exod. Rabbah* 21: 4, and Akdamut for Shavuot: see *Sefer hakerovot: Maḥazor leḥag hashavuot*, 42a, line *kuf*, translated by Raphael Loewe, in *Service of the Synagogue: Pentecost*, 210–11. The idea that the origins of *tefilin* lie in purses for carrying valuables, before garments

over God's *tefilin*, complementing the texts they contain. The fact that human *tefilin* contain not praise of God, but texts attributing exile and suffering to the failure to fulfil duties that are beyond human ability to perform, exemplifies the ambivalence underlying the Jewish relationship to God. If the Torah can be interiorized only by external symbols such as *talit* and *tefilin*, it must be beyond human capacity to do so intellectually. Jews have no choice but to fall back on the hope that attaining closeness to God in this way will ensure the dominance of his aspect of mercy.

The liturgical texts associated with *tefilin* veil these meanings in exegetical silence, although they are alluded to. The meditation before putting on the *tefilin* (Extract 7) first appeared in Isaiah Horowitz's prayer-book at roughly the same period as those related to the *talit*.[92] It lists the texts appearing in the *tefilin*— referred to by their opening words[93]—and identifies the symbolic features of *tefilin* in what seems to be a mechanical and literal way, describing how they are to be bound to the 'arm that is next to the heart' (line 6) and the 'head level with the brain' (line 8), to ensure that these serve God. The heart, associated here with thought, is defined as the seat of physical 'desires and intentions' (lines 6–7), while the brain is the source of 'soul-power' (line 8),[94] associated with feeling and personality, thereby reversing conventional Western views of the locations of thought and emotion. The dualism implicit in the contrast between 'head' and 'hand' and 'thought' and 'action' could be compared to the other great duality in rabbinic thought, the divine attributes associated with the two names of God in the first line of the Shema.

The preoccupation with discord between these attributes points to the concern with the consequences of failing to understand Torah, seen earlier in the *talit* meditations.[95] In this case the heart, corresponding roughly to the body in the opening statement of the day, is vulnerable to the *yetser hara* (line 11), a term rendered in the present edition as 'Spirit of Mischief', but more usually as 'the evil inclination'.[96] In rabbinic thought this concept, which is in constant opposition to *yetser hatov*, 'the good inclination', made its first appearance at the temptation of Adam and Eve,[97] whose loss of closeness to God was partly repaired by

---

contained pockets, has been discussed in H. Loewe, *Mosaic Revelation*, 9–17 (references supplied by Raphael Loewe, pers. comm.). For a historical discussion of *tefilin* see Reif, 'Early Liturgy', 334 n. 22. See also Ginzberg, *Legends*, vi. 58 n. 299.

[92] I. Horowitz, *Sidur hashelah hashalem: sha'ar hashamayim*, i. 85.

[93] The opening words and their references are as follows: *shema* (Deut. 6: 4–9), *vehayah im shamo'a* (Deut. 11: 13–21), *kadesh* (Exod. 13: 1–10), *vehayah ki yeviakha* (Exod. 13: 11–16).

[94] This translation of *neshamah*, rendered 'breath-soul' in Extract 1, line 2, seems to nod towards the English term 'will-power', attributing an element of cogitation to the brain, which in Hebrew thought usually lacks it.

[95] This will be discussed in the context of the first line of the Shema, in Ch. 8, Extract 31.

[96] e.g. *Book of Prayer: Daily and Occasional Prayers*, 3.   [97] BT *Ber.* 61a.

the *talit*.[98] Even *tefilin*, which are put on after the *talit*, cannot wholly overcome this unruly desire. They only, as the meditation says, prevent it dominating the speaker. This may be symbolized by the binding of the left, 'sinister' side, by the right side of the body. Other rabbinic texts explain why the *yetser hara* should not be wholly overcome, by recognizing it as the source of the sexual drive and by observing that without it 'no one would marry or build a home'.[99] Binding on the *tefilin* may therefore reflect a wish to control the *yetser hara* without defeating it entirely, a compromise similar to the ambivalence reflected in the dual names of God in the Shema and the *tefilin*. The *tefilin* texts, it is implied, point towards messianic redemption by recollecting the rescue from Egypt (transliterated as *mitsrayim* here rather than being translated, in order to avoid confusion between the biblical and the contemporary country).

EXTRACT 8. **The Blessings Over** *Tefilin*

The two blessings for the *tefilin*, echoing in structure those for the *talit*, relate to the boxes for the hand and head respectively. Since some rabbis thought a single blessing sufficient, and that a second blessing might entail the risk of 'taking God's name in vain', a formula was introduced for cancelling the second as soon as it had been recited (line 5).[100] This response (to be discussed in Chapter 8, in the context of Extract 31, line 2) retroactively transforms it into a declaration of praise and is prescribed for use whenever a divine name has been inadvertently pronounced, even outside the context of prayer. Since the response was originally used by angels, according to a midrash which describes one of Moses' journeys to heaven,[101] it is one of several that identify Jews, here arrayed in their ritual garments, with heavenly courtiers and choristers, a theme that will recur later in the morning service, in the Yotser blessing that follows the call to prayer and precedes the full recital of the Shema. Although this gesture, as a result of which the speaker becomes almost angelic, was prompted by editorial uncertainty about the correct blessing to use with the *tefilin* ritual, it helps the speaker attain a climactic closeness to God that every other route has so far failed to achieve. The uncertainty over the number of blessings to recite over *talit* and *tefilin* also furnishes another example of ambivalence over the numbers three and four in the present context (one blessing each over the *arba kanfot* and *talit*, and either one or two over the *tefilin*).

[98] See the remarks on the *talit* above.

[99] *Gen. Rabbah* 9: 7 and *Eccles. Rabbah* 3: 11 (3). The *yetser* is discussed in Urbach, *Sages*, 472–83.

[100] *Book of Prayer: Daily and Occasional Prayers*, 2, regards only the first blessing as essential. The conceptual background is discussed in Israel Me'ir Hakohen, *Mishnah berurah*, 25: 5, n. 21.

[101] *Deut. Rabbah* 2: 36.

°Blest art thou, God our Lord, sovereign of the universe,	*B'Mn.* 36, 42:
He who makes us holy through ° His commandments, and	*Ku.* 3,[11,39]
commanded us °to lay *Tefillin!*	*SA–OH* 25,[7]
°Blest art thou, God our Lord, sovereign of the universe,	*Dt.* 17,[11]
He who °makes us holy through His commandments, and	*Msh. Mk.* 3,[16]
commanded °us concerning the *Mizvah* of *Tefillin!*	*B'Mn.* 43
°Blest is the Name—the reverence of His sovereignty and for ever and aye!	*Zo. Dt.* 264

8. The blessings over *tefilin* (*Lehaniyah tefilin* and *al mitsvat tefilin*)

EXTRACT 9. **Verses on Putting on** *Tefilin*

The three verses to be recited while the strap is bound three times onto the middle finger, yet another recurrence of the number three, first appeared in the same work that recommended the recitation of psalmic verses after putting on the *talit*, another reapplied act of study designed to draw connotations out of otherwise ineloquent rituals.[102] The strap on the hand forms a rudimentary letter *shin*, echoing those appearing elsewhere on the *tefilin* as well as the first letter of the Shema. The original context of the verses is the climax to the scriptural account of Hosea's marriage to Gomer, who, after deceiving him, was reconciled in a scene in which their reunion was compared to the healing of God's rift with Israel.[103] Hosea's assertions of marriage, clearly linked to a wedding ceremony, are applied in the biblical narrative both to the prophet's relationship with Gomer and to God's relationship with Israel.[104] The idea that Israel is 'married' to God is normative in scriptural and midrashic thought, this passage from Hosea being only one source of the image. Appropriately, the words are included in the Haftarah for the weekly Torah reading 'Bamidbar', usually recited a week before Shavuot, the festival commemorating the revelation of the Decalogue, itself regarded midrashically as Israel's marriage contract with God. The intimacy between God and the Israelites established at Sinai was ruptured by the Golden Calf and, more profoundly, by the later episode of the Spies, events now repaired by the ceremonial gesture of binding the strap of the *tefilin* around the finger, as though in a symbolic wedding rite.

The three verses can be seen as part of the larger liturgical project of overcoming the apparent remoteness of God. The first of these is a statement of fact,

---

[102] Shapira, *Metsat shimurim*, 324–7.   [103] Hos. 2: 21–2.

[104] *Avot derabi natan*, 37 (version A), p. 110 (55*b*); trans. Goldin, *Fathers According to Rabbi Nathan*, 153–4. See also Malbim's commentary on Hos. 2: 21–2.

בָּרוּךְ אַתָּה יְיָ אֱלֹהֵינוּ מֶלֶךְ הָעוֹלָם אֲשֶׁר 1

קִדְּשָׁנוּ בְּמִצְוֹתָיו וְצִוָּנוּ לְהָנִיחַ תְּפִלִּין: 2

בָּרוּךְ אַתָּה יְיָ אֱלֹהֵינוּ מֶלֶךְ הָעוֹלָם אֲשֶׁר 3

קִדְּשָׁנוּ בְּמִצְוֹתָיו וְצִוָּנוּ עַל־מִצְוַת תְּפִלִּין: 4

בָּרוּךְ שֵׁם כְּבוֹד מַלְכוּתוֹ לְעוֹלָם וָעֶד: 5

a legal pronouncement without emotional content, as though the betrothal might be accomplished unquestioningly. The second verse lists four qualities falling into two groups. The first pair, 'right and justice', reflect the more remote and kingly attributes of God, while the second pair, 'loving-kindness and mercy', relate to the attribute of mercy, creating an equilibrium in which the goal seems to be the establishment of warm and caring relations. The verse implicitly traces a movement from one pole to the other, from the remoteness of kingship to the personal relationship implied by mercy and loving-kindness, leaving kingliness behind as the speaker approaches the third and last verse which summarizes relations with God in a single term: 'faith'. This aspect of the relationship with God encompasses all the previous four, unifying the dual attributes of God. It concludes with the suggestion that intimacy will indeed be established, in words translated here as 'and thou shalt realize God', but which mean literally 'and you shall know God', the Hebrew verb understood as having clear erotic undertones. Precisely how this intimacy is to be established is not made explicit, as the liturgical editors were doubtless aware in choosing this declaration of the need for unqualified faith. The ritual gesture of binding on the *tefilin* symbolically negotiates the transition from severity to intimacy since it enables the speaker to move towards the closeness demanded by the Shema, transcending both justice and mercy. The shifts between the numbers two, three, and four implicit in these verses will be discussed later.

The identity of the speaker of these verses in the liturgical context is also unclear. It is possible that the liturgical speaker imitates God renewing his bond to a female Israel, herself 'bound' by the *tefilin* to intimacy with God. Or Israel might be addressing the female Torah and symbolically binding it to the speaker. Lastly, the speaker could be adopting the voice of the *tefilin* themselves, as representatives of the Torah, addressing the soul, which is feminine in Hebrew. The shifting and uncertain identity of the speaker here recalls the similarly rich

°Indeed, I will betroth thee unto me for ever, yea, I will	*Hs.* 2,²¹⁻²
betroth thee unto me in °right and in justice, in loving-kindness	*Ku.* 3,¹¹
and in mercy; °Yea, I will betroth thee unto me in faith and	*SA-OH* 27,⁸
thou shalt °realize God.	*Gn.* 4,¹

9. Verses on putting on *tefilin* (*Ve'erastikh li*)

°O May it be willed from thy presence, God Lord of us	*Msh. Av.* 5,²⁰
and Lord of our ancestors, °that this *Mizvah* of laying *Tefillin* shall	*B'Mn.* 43:
be accounted as if I had fulfilled it °with all its details, its minutiæ	*B'Yv.* 48:
and its purports, °yea, with the 613 *Mizvoth*-commandments which	*B'Mk.* 23:
depend thereon°—*Amen.*	*Msh. Kd.* 1,⁹

10. Concluding meditation on *tefilin* (*Yehi ratson*)

dramatis personae identified in the opening statement of the day, discussed in the previous chapter, with the symbolic clothing of the speaker resembling the body's enclosing of the soul. In this way the liturgy uses dramatic forms to present insights into the relationships between the garments and the body on the one hand, and the soul and reunified speaker on the other hand.

The speaker's encounter with Torah via the garments and their texts is just as multivalent as the relationship of soul and body represented by the location of an exile in the ruins of Jerusalem. The speaker here encounters the Torah not only as a protective home and contractual assurance of redemption, but as the source of the exile that characterizes the experience of Jews and even the human condition of delayed or denied satisfaction.

As has been mentioned, it is usually argued that *tefilin* are not worn on sabbath because both the sabbath and *tefilin* are examples of an *ot*, 'sign',[105] thus making one of these unnecessary. However, the fact that the same word is associated with circumcision might be given as a reason for men never to wear *tefilin* at all,[106] and they are not worn on festivals either, even though these are not regarded as a 'sign' in the same way as sabbath. The practice of not wearing *tefilin* on sabbath and festivals should be traced rather to the ambivalence they reveal about the relationship between God and Israel, and to the view that they comment on the role of God in both causing exile and promising to end it.

Unlike the *talit*, which features the fourfold symbols of ingathering, the *tefilin* texts number only three, if one counts the Exodus texts as a single one, and this total also appears in the three verses from Hosea; it is doubled in the six verses in

---

[105] Exod. 31: 17, Deut. 6: 8, and BT *Men.* 36*b*.   [106] Gen. 17: 11.

וְאֵרַשְׂתִּיךְ לִי לְעוֹלָם · וְאֵרַשְׂתִּיךְ לִי בְּצֶדֶק וּבְמִשְׁפָּט

וּבְחֶסֶד וּבְרַחֲמִים · וְאֵרַשְׂתִּיךְ לִי בֶּאֱמוּנָה וְיָדַעַתְּ אֶת יְיָ:

יְהִי רָצוֹן מִלְּפָנֶיךְ יְיָ אֱלֹהֵינוּ וֵאלֹהֵי אֲבוֹתֵינוּ שֶׁתְּהִי

חֲשׁוּבָה מִצְוַת הֲנָחַת תְּפִלִּין זוֹ כְּאִלּוּ קִיַּמְתִּיהָ בְּכָל־פְּרָטֶיהָ

וְדִקְדּוּקֶיהָ וְכַוָּנוֹתֶיהָ וְתַרְיַ׳׳ג מִצְוֹת הַתְּלוּיִם בָּהּ · אָמֵן:

God's *tefilin*. The number three suggests, not the ingathering implied by the number four, but the friction-laden relationship between God, Israel, and Torah which, as we have seen, is symbolized by *tefilin*.[107] The same ambivalence between the three of friction and the four of reconciliation appears in the three and four arms of the letter *shin* on the outside of the box for the head. Significantly, the three verses from Hosea are recited while binding the strap onto the finger in the form of a three-armed *shin*.[108]

The symbolic role of *tefilin* is therefore not to resolve exile, but to represent its near-inevitability. This is possibly a reason why the *talit* of ingathering may be worn without *tefilin*, but *tefilin* are never worn on their own. Together, *talit* and *tefilin* represent the idea that the privilege of election is twinned with the reality of exile.

EXTRACT 10. **Concluding Meditation on** *Tefilin*

The closing meditation over *tefilin* repeats the formula previously employed for the *talit* with minor changes, suggesting that the garments are to be viewed in tandem. By repeating the request that the ritual should overcome the opacity of

[107] Another triad, not noted in rabbinic thought, is that of the hand that is bound, the head surmounted by a sign, and the hand that binds. The roles of limiting and of accepting limitation may well represent aspects of the relationship between Jews and God (see also n. 73 above).

[108] The four/three friction might express a tension between the Tetragrammaton, associated with mercy, and a name conventionally linked to severity, in this case the three-lettered divine name *shadai*, associated with limitation and constriction, echoing the tension embodied in the opening line of the Shema, but I have found no evidence for this in the literature.

Torah, it becomes clear that this still remains. Even if the body enacts closeness to Torah, the speaker cannot overcome the incomprehension made almost inevitable by its lack of textual clarity, leaving the speaker in exile, in body and soul. Since in their talmudic context the blessings over the ritual garments co-incide with the speaker's departure from home for the outside world, the speaker now stands on the brink of an exile similar in kind, if not as dangerous, to that implied by the texts of the *tefilin*. The separation of ritual from actual dressing robs this moment of some of its dramatic force, though it still constitutes a symbolic indication of the danger of the outside world and the speaker's need for an inexplicably elusive salvation.

CHAPTER SIX

ॐ

The Silence of Language

'and he drove out the man'

GENESIS 3: 24

THIS CHAPTER discusses liturgical texts relating to leaving home and arriving at the synagogue, and examines the tensions between these locations. It
encompasses the second series of waking prayers of the morning, now recited in
the synagogue rather than the home, including an introduction to Torah study
that reveals this to be almost impossibly difficult.

EXTRACT II. Verses on Entering Synagogue

The liturgy, now in a verbal rather than a gestural mode, begins the transition
between home and synagogue. In the edition of the prayer-book used here, the
sequence opens with a printed rule across the page, indicating the end of the section devoted to the ritual garments and challenging the speaker to identify the
continuity between that and what is to come. In other, larger-format, publications, such as that of Baer, the texts related to each of the ritual garments are
introduced by headings suggesting that these form separate chapters. The separation indicated here is relatively slight in comparison with such arrangements,
but illustrates the assumption among the editors and publishers of prayer-books
that the liturgical theme has fundamentally changed now that the garments have
been put on. As a mark of special piety the speaker may wear the symbolic garments for the journey from home to synagogue, which is itself a transitional
space between private safety and the dangers of the world, but it is more usual to
put them on in synagogue, in which case the previous sequence will be delayed
until later. Baer, for whom the opening lines examined here are the first of the
morning, assumes the latter to be the case.

If the garments are indeed being worn, the theological problems identified in
the previous discussion will already be in play, including the idea of exile alluded
to in the echo of the book of Lamentations in the opening statement of the day,
followed by the dangers of primogeniture and priestly status suggested by the
tefilin. But if they have not been assumed yet, the idea of exile in the opening
statement will be concretized instead by the speaker's departure from home and
by the fact that the synagogue is a pale reflection of the Temple of Jerusalem.

°Concerning myself, in Thine abounding kindness, let	*Ps.* 5,[8]
me enter °thy house, let me bow towards thy holy temple,	*Is.* 56,[7]
°in awe of thee.	*B'Br.* 33:
°Let us proceed with emotion into the Almighty's house.	*Ps.* 55,[15]

11. Verses on entering synagogue (*Va'ani berov ḥasdekha*)

The ritual garments will later emphasize this homelessness, enacted in the meantime by the departure from home which symbolizes the 'exile' arguably made inevitable by the human inability to comprehend Torah, a failure made visible by the *tefilin*, as the texts around them imply.

The transfer of the texts relating to dressing from home to synagogue in the edition used here ensures that the blessings over *talit* and *tefilin* are those closest to the actual process of dressing which takes place at home, and therefore the closest to fulfilling the function of the sequence of blessings devoted to non-ritual dressing and to each stage of personal preparation for the day. That sequence was intended to culminate in these blessings over the ritual garments, but in this edition the climax is delayed until long after the business of dressing has been completed. The sequence can be seen in Extracts 22–4. The series of blessings over non-ritual preparations for the day has the effect of sanctifying private life, confirming the spiritual value of the speaker's own personal gestures by linking them with divine law and narrative. This group of blessings thus functions differently from those recited over the ritual garments, for while the daily blessings are an adornment of everyday routine, the symbolic garments are additional to whatever an individual would normally wear. The blessings over daily preparation elevate the speaker's daily round of personal habits to a sacred plane, while the ritual garments inject an extraneous element into that sequence, shouldering aside the purely personal for the sake of a ceremony with only minimal links to the personal. The symbolic clothes are recognizable as relevant to daily life only because they are worn on the body, much like ordinary garments. However, they differ in other ways, since *talit* and *tefilin* are signs of affiliation to the group, emphasizing the impersonal aspects of the individual's status within the collectivity rather than elevating the everyday. The speaker's individuality and voice are thus suppressed by the ritual garments and subsumed in the scheme of history, at least until the blessings recited over dressing go some way towards restoring a sense of individuality.

This loss of voice is qualified in the present sequence, however, by the fact that the biblical citations included here open with the emphatic first-person pronoun, *va'ani*, 'as for me'. The pious custom of refraining from talking in the

וַאֲנִי בְּרֹב חַסְדְּךָ אָבֹא בֵיתֶךָ 1
אֶשְׁתַּחֲוֶה אֶל־הֵיכַל קָדְשְׁךָ בְּיִרְאָתֶךָ׃ 2
בְּבֵית אֱלֹהִים נְהַלֵּךְ בְּרָגֶשׁ׃ 3

morning before prayer might be related not only to this minimization of
the characteristics of each individual but also to the metaphorical silence created
by the use of citations. Quoting words which are not one's own is a minimalist
form of expression which leaves little room for spontaneity or originality, at least
at first sight. Yet, in this case, the very freedom with which the texts have been
selected and juxtaposed invests the individual with eloquence, much as medieval
Hebrew poets used citations to generate new meanings. A mosaic of complete
verses of this kind will be less complex and engaging than one assembled out of
faint echoes, like the opening statement of the day, but the multi-layered effect
is still in evidence. Here, entire verses are deployed as though they were single
lexical items. Sentences stand for words and are to be read not only with their
surface meaning in mind, but intertextually, in terms of their original contexts.

The three sequences of scriptural verses included here (Extracts 11–13), each
of which developed separately, set up complex harmonies of meaning. The first
group (Extract 11) consists of two verses,[1] the first of which is accompanied in
the present edition by a rubric instruction to bow towards the ark, although it
may have been introduced into the morning liturgy without this having been the
editorial intention. It was perhaps employed so that, by ticking off its ten words
one by one, it would be possible to ascertain whether a quorum of ten men had
gathered.[2] Baer relates the first of the verses to arriving at the synagogue entrance
and the second to passing through it,[3] making no reference to bowing. His view
doubtless reflects the fact that, in its original context, the verse refers not to a
synagogue ark (although this is known colloquially by Sephardim as the *heikhal*,

---

[1] Pss. 5: 8, 55: 15.

[2] In medieval versions of the liturgy the first verse appears as a preliminary to the entire service.
It is referred to by Amram Gaon (*Seder rav amram hashalem*, ii. 204*a*), in *Maḥzor vitry*, 56, and in
Abudarham, *Abudarham hashalem*, 349, and it seems to have had a practical function. Censuses are
discouraged in Scripture (see the danger implied in Exod. 30: 12 and the hostile origin of the
decision in 1 Chr. 21: 1) and Jews indeed avoid counting people. Such a reluctance, found in
many societies, may derive from primary instincts, but in contemporary terms it can be viewed as
a refusal to regard people as commodities: Lieber, 'Census'. To ascertain whether a prayer quorum
is present, the ten words of this verse would be pronounced instead of numerals (Berliner,
Randbemerkungen, i. 11). [3] *Sidur avodat yisra'el*, 33.

literally 'palace', while Ashkenazim refer to it as *aron hakodesh*, 'holy ark'), but to the Temple itself.[4] The fact that no attempt is made in the version analysed here to identify what is meant by this verse, for instance by recommending that one bow to the ark while reciting the verse referring to the sanctuary, may have arisen out of a reluctance to confuse a synagogue with the Temple, the difference between them being central to the liturgy. The synagogue is built, metaphorically, on the ruins of the Temple, and the exile symbolized by the *tefilin* is made tangible by entering the synagogue, transforming this sequence—which seems to announce the speaker's arrival in the Temple—into a study of its absence. The psalm from which the verse is drawn identifies it as a morning prayer,[5] while a midrash regards all prayer as a substitute for the Temple, the loss of which is attributed to outside hostility, a dominant theme of the liturgy since the opening statement of the day.[6]

The second verse, from a psalm expressing regret for a friend's treachery[7] and preference for life in a desert, far from people,[8] is related in a midrash to Daniel and the lions' den, like the opening statement. Translating the word *beragesh*, here rendered as 'emotion' (Extract 11, line 3, last word), as 'in a company' suggests that the act of approaching a synagogue enrols the speaker in a congregation or at least a place of prayer,[9] aligning the loss of home and Temple. The departure for a desert exile is paradoxically linked to arriving in a community of fellow-exiles, but pleasure at re-entering society is diluted by mistrust of others, a theme which will later become dominant.

The idea of the Temple's physical absence is accentuated by the fact that, while the individual speaker in the first verse addresses God in the second person, the verb in the second verse is in the first person plural and addresses God in the third person, indicating increased distance in the style of the blessing formula. The verses also describe the growing proximity of the speaker to God, since the first describes formal worship and the second the emotions felt when approaching God's house. Ambivalence about the individual's ability to approach God without the benefit of the Temple as a medium, an idea first encountered here, is frequently implicit in the liturgy, and later comes to dominate it.

EXTRACT 12. **The Transition from Home to Synagogue**

The second group of biblical verses[10] likewise accompanies the speaker's transition from the home to the synagogue and is presumably an independent compilation, since it covers similar ground to the first pair. Another sign of in-

---

[4] *Otsar hatefilot*, 'Anaf yosef', 48*b*. The use of this term is analysed in R. Loewe, 'Ark, Archaicism and Misappropriation'.   [5] Ps. 5: 3–4.

[6] *Midrash Psalms* 5: 7.   [7] Ps. 55: 13–14.   [8] Ps. 55: 7, 9.

[9] Ps. 55: 17–18.   [10] Num. 24: 5; Pss. 5: 8, 26: 8, 95: 6, 69: 14.

dependence is the fact that the second of these five verses is identical to the first of the first group, a repetition unlikely to be deliberate.[11] The verses begin with the speaker outside the synagogue, even though the previous sequence assumes entry to have taken place, suggesting that the liturgy here locates the speaker both inside and outside the building.

For Baer these verses mark the moment of arriving inside the synagogue.[12] Their history shows their role to be more complex than this suggests, however, for some are referred to in medieval versions of the prayer-book, though not in an introductory role as here.[13] Their survival illustrates how liturgical compilations tolerate redundancy, preserving side by side texts designed as alternatives and refusing, or neglecting, to suppress resulting dissonances. The harmonies these verses create result from editorial decisions based less on the desire to make sense than on the need to combine multiple traditions. However, to conclude from this that no meaning may be sought is to ignore the way in which the mind inevitably transforms even an anthology into a narrative or statement, especially if it is in daily use, as is the liturgy. The historical background to the composition is irrelevant to such an understanding and will therefore not be examined here in detail.

The role of this and the following group of verses (Extract 13) seems to be determined by the first verse included here (line 1), which in some liturgies is the first of the day, as though it could be compared to the opening statement of the day (discussed in Chapter 4).[14] In its scriptural context it is spoken by an outsider, the pagan prophet Balaam, who was ordered by King Balak of Moab to curse the Israelites, but whose curses were transformed into blessings as he spoke them (Numbers 22–4). Balaam is therefore cast here as the archetypical outsider arriving at the synagogue.

This verse, which expresses praise of the Israelite camp spread out below him, opens his final attempt to curse the Israelites. It owes its place here to a number of factors, one of them being the prominence in the Balaam narrative of the verb 'to see', recalling the return of daylight and the renewed faculty of sight. His ass 'saw' an angel barring the way that was invisible to Balaam,[15] Balaam moved to another spot from which to 'see' the camp below,[16] and he described himself repeatedly as 'a man whose eyes are open'.[17] In the present context Balaam's words suggest that the speaker might be looking back at the home that has just been left, and possibly forward to the synagogue, the first being referred to as the 'tents' and the second as the 'dwellings'. One talmudic writer argues that Balaam's words refer to the way in which Israelite tents were positioned so

---

[11] The counting function would be unlikely to account for its double appearance, *pace* Berliner, *Randbermerkungen*, i. 11.   [12] *Sidur avodat yisra'el*, 33.

[13] The first is mentioned in Amram Gaon, *Seder rav amram hashalem*, ii. 204a.

[14] See *Sidur avodat yisra'el*, 33 for a liturgical opening based on the present sequences of citations.   [15] Num. 22: 23–34.

[16] Num. 23: 13, after which he goes to *tsofim*, 'Scopus'.   [17] Num. 24: 3–4, 15–16.

°How goodly are thy tents, o Jacob, thy dwellings, o Israel!	*Nu.* 24,⁵
°Concerning myself, in thine abounding kindness, let me	*Ps.* 5,⁸
enter thy °house, let me bow towards thy holy temple, °in awe	*B'Br.* 33:
of thee.	*Mai. YT* 2,²
°O God, I do love the home at thy house, yea, °the residing	*Ps.* 26,⁸
place of thy glory.	*Dt.* 12,¹¹
°Indeed, I will bow, I will bend the knee, yea, kneel before	*Ps.* 95,⁶
°God, my maker.	*Ku.* 3,¹¹
°O God, let my prayer unto thee be a moment of	*Ps.* 69,¹⁴
°goodwill—o Almighty! in thine abounding kindness, answer	*Zo. Gn.* 105:
me °with thy true salvation!	*Zo. Ex.* 156

12. The transition from home to synagogue (*Mah tovu ohaleikha*)

that their openings did not face each other, ensuring privacy and respect for others. This implies praise for the home the speaker has just left.[18]

The presence of this verse here is supported by the talmudic proposal to include the entire story of Balaam in the Shema,[19] a suggestion rejected not on theological grounds but for reasons of convenience. It is possible that in some circles the early morning Shema (Extract 31, line 1) was followed by the Balaam story, both being recited before arriving in synagogue. This practice might underlie the midrashic view that Balaam exemplifies the futility of trying to curse a people who 'rise like lions to recite the Shema', but it would not alter the fact that Balaam set out to speak with ill intent and that his intent probably remained unaltered, despite the fact that the words placed in his mouth were wholly favourable.[20]

Another talmudic passage which identifies the 'tents' praised by Balaam with synagogues points to the speaker's arrival there as an outsider.[21] But although Israel has lost every 'tent' other than her 'synagogues and study-houses', these cannot fill the role of the Temple. Another text claims that Balaam, aware that his blessing would bring destruction, pronounced it in order to harm the Tabernacle that he knew to be dangerous to pagan prophets.[22] Rashi, more positively, argued that Balaam intended to praise the ruins of the Temple because he knew its loss would earn the Jews forgiveness,[23] an argument which illustrates rabbinic uncertainty as to whether Balaam was a great prophet, wholly wicked,

[18] Rashi on Num. 24: 5, based on BT *BB* 60a.
[19] BT *Ber.* 12b; see the discussion in Falk, *Penei yehoshua*, on that text.
[20] *Midrash tanḥuma* (Buber) 'Balak', 23.   [21] BT *San.* 105b.
[22] According to *Lev. Rabbah* 1: 12 and *S. of S. Rabbah* 2: 3 (5).
[23] On Num. 24: 5, apparently based on *Midrash tanḥuma* (Buber), 'Pekudei' 5.

מַה־טֹּבוּ אֹהָלֶיךָ יַעֲקֹב מִשְׁכְּנֹתֶיךָ יִשְׂרָאֵל: וַאֲנִי בְּרֹב   1

חַסְדְּךָ אָבֹא בֵיתֶךָ אֶשְׁתַּחֲוֶה אֶל־הֵיכַל קָדְשְׁךָ בְּיִרְאָתֶךָ: יְיָ   2

אָהַבְתִּי מְעוֹן בֵּיתֶךָ וּמְקוֹם מִשְׁכַּן כְּבוֹדֶךָ: וַאֲנִי אֶשְׁתַּחֲוֶה   3

וְאֶכְרָעָה אֶבְרְכָה לִפְנֵי־יְיָ עֹשִׂי: וַאֲנִי תְפִלָּתִי־לְךָ יְיָ עֵת   4

רָצוֹן אֱלֹהִים בְּרָב־חַסְדֶּךָ עֲנֵנִי בֶּאֱמֶת יִשְׁעֶךָ:   5

or both.[24] Most obviously, it reflects the speaker's ambivalence towards the community, leading one late medieval rabbi to argue that to quote Balaam's words is to stand with him outside the synagogue as a hostile pagan, making it improper to use this verse in the liturgy altogether.[25]

This outsider's viewpoint has already been encountered in the early morning liturgy, for the voice of the waking body in the opening statement of the day (Extract 1) was identified in Chapter 4 as Darius, a non-Jew transformed into a sympathizer by being reunited with a 'soul' in the form of Daniel. In the present case, however, the speaker is an outsider in two senses, both by wearing the symbols of exile and by having left home to face the outside world, so he may be using Balaam's ambivalence to express unconscious misgivings about the covenant. On the other hand, the overriding of Balaam's intention to curse Israel reflects the speaker's ability to overcome ambivalence about being Jewish, although the frustration of this intention might suggest an awareness that the speaker's worship and study are similarly subverted by human limitations. More promisingly, if Balaam could 'see' the Tabernacle in the tents of the Israelites, the speaker may yet be able to translate the synagogue, referred to in some rabbinic texts as *mikdash me'at*, 'miniature sanctuary', into the Temple.[26] The way this verse's ambiguity demands to be understood in terms of both the real and metaphorical locations of the speaker marks a new stage in the increasing lack of explicit everyday clarity of the liturgical narrative and in the consequent power of its poetry.

[24] BT *San.* 105b: 'Out of good work misapplied in purpose there comes [the desire to do it] for its own sake. . . . Balak was privileged that Ruth should be his descendant', an argument expanded in BT *Hor.* 10b.

[25] Solomon Luria (1510(?)–1574; Maharshal or Rashal), *Teshuvah*, 64, quoted in Nulman, *Encyclopedia of Jewish Prayer*, 234 n. 4.   [26] BT *Meg.* 29a on Ezek. 11: 16.

The following verses accompany the speaker's approach and entry into the synagogue/Temple, integrating the hostile outsider into the community. All feature the first person singular, and three of them open with an emphatic first person singular pronoun. Their psalmic source associates the speaker with David, the Temple-planner (although the building was actually completed by his son Solomon) and founder of sacrificial worship in Jerusalem (by virtue of his having captured the city and brought the Ark there). This association suggests the beginning of daily worship, but also, since he did not complete the task, casts a shadow over the speaker's use of his words.

The second verse in this group, which, as has been mentioned, is identical to the first in the first group (Extract 11, lines 1–2), again marks the speaker's arrival at the Temple or synagogue, suggesting a progression from the 'tents' referred to by Balaam to God's 'house' and then to his *heikhal*, translated here as 'temple' but which more correctly is 'palace'. The possible counting function of this verse, noted on its first appearance, suggests that once the speaker is inside the synagogue it can be used to check whether a quorum is present. The third verse (lines 2–3), expressing love for God's Temple, is drawn from a psalm declaring a preference for God's house over the company of bad people. This glances at the dangers of the outside world from which the synagogue is perhaps a refuge, even though the community may also offer threats, as will be seen later.[27]

The fourth verse (lines 3–4) suggests that the speaker has now entered the Temple and is engaged in worship, the three verbs for worship sometimes being assumed to suggest the three daily services of which the present one is the first. But the scriptural source has been modified, for the first time so far, by changing the first-person verbs from plural to singular, something that will be seen to have a deep impact on the liturgy. Some commentators dismiss this as a convenient cosmetic change, bringing it into line with the first person singular of the other verses. Others are aware that a principle is at stake,[28] for manipulating a text transforms what should be a deferential act of study into a subversive one, symbolically echoing the transformation of Balaam's words before they have left his mouth. It demonstrates the difficulty of study, as do *tefilin*, and risks exile, which is the penalty for failure in study, as the Shema makes clear. The change from plural to singular also suggests the speaker's resistance to joining the collectivity, again echoing Balaam-like hostility. However, at the same time the speaker's symbolic status as an outsider might reflect the feeling that the synagogue is a representation of exile, since arriving there completes the departure from home. In practice, both readings are valid, illustrating liturgical ambiguity with particular clarity.

The fifth and last verse in this sequence again opens with the first-person pronoun, and is associated with suffering, since its scriptural context describes fear

---

[27] *Midrash Psalms* 5: 6.   [28] Jacob b. Asher, *Arba'ah turim*, 'Oraḥ ḥayim' 116.

of exile, isolation, and the hiding of God's face.[29] Its syntax is strangely fragmented, although the translation glosses over the obscurity of the original—literally 'I, my prayer [is to] you'. These words seem simultaneously to suggest and
to demonstrate how prayer, far from being simple and spontaneous, passes out of
human control as one speaks, echoing Balaam's frustration. The psalm from
which the verse is drawn is similarly concerned with the loss of the Temple and
its replacement by liturgical worship, later verses preferring praise to sacrifice.[30]
The verse confirms the need for prayer to be recited at 'a moment of goodwill',
suggesting a time of regular prayer such as the present, according to a midrashic
reading.[31] The last three words of this verse, which are the first clear petition of
the liturgy apart from those associated with the ritual garments, are again fractured and obscure, as though the arrival in synagogue brings not fluency but
ambivalence and unresponsiveness. The speaker's transition to the collectivity
seems to bring with it a Balaam-like inarticulacy, reflecting the shortcomings of
language in general and the fact that prayer is a mere substitute for sacrifice.
Instead of dialogue the speaker finds noisy incoherence, from which only the
liturgy offers the possibility of escape.

These five verses not only accompany the speaker from the outside world into
the synagogue, however, but also trace Israelite history from desert wandering,
via the age of sacrificial worship, to the here and now of exile, accompanying the
speaker and Jews in general towards the synagogue as an institution. Arrival
there reduces the speaker to a paradoxically wordy silence.

EXTRACT 13. **Other Transitional Verses**

The third sequence, including an initial sub-group of ten[32] and a subsequent one
of six verses, which will be discussed in detail below, seems to continue the
speaker's Balaam-like inarticulacy. These sub-groups of verses are printed by
Baer as continuous text and prescribed both by him and in the present text for
the moments before formal prayer begins, so they will be discussed together
despite their typographical ambiguity in the present edition, in which they fall on
separate pages. They are more loosely organized than the previous sequence, but
the first verse's echo of the previous line suggests continuity of theme. Indeed, if
the fragmentation reflects the speaker's predicament, the opacity must itself be
part of the meaning.

The number of separate verses involved is in fact far from certain, for the first
verse in the initial sub-group of Extract 13 (line 1) is the same as the penultimate
one in the subsequent sub-group (lines 12–13)—both Psalm 17: 6—thereby
potentially reducing the total number of sixteen verses in the sub-groups taken

---

[29] Ps. 69: 18.   [30] Ps. 69: 31–2.   [31] *Midrash Psalms* 69: 2; BT *Ber.* 8*a*.
[32] Pss. 17: 6, 17: 15, 31: 15, 28: 2, 30: 3, 30: 9, 31: 17, 38: 16, 39: 13, 30: 11.

°I have called thee, Lord, that thou mayest respond unto me, o	*Ps.* 17,⁶
grant thy hearing unto me and hearken to my speech. °May I have	*Ps.* 17,¹⁵
vision of thy presence through right, may I feel fulfilled as I awaken	*Y'Tn.* 2,¹
picturing thee. °As for me, in thee, God, have I trusted, I	*Ps.* 31,¹⁵
declared: 'Thou art my °Lord'.	*Ex.* 4,¹⁶
°O, hearken the sound of my pleadings, as I do clamour unto	*Ps.* 28,²
thee, as I uplift my hands towards thy holy oracle. °God my	*Ps.* 30,³
Lord, I have cried unto thee and thou hast cured me. °Unto	*Ps.* 30,⁹
thee, God, do I call, yea, unto the Lord do I supplicate. °O let	*Ps.* 31,¹⁷
thy presence enlighten thy servitor, °save me through thy loving-	*Ps.* 33,¹⁶
kindness. °For I have longed for thee, God, thou wilt respond, o	*Ps.* 38,¹⁶
God my Lord. O hearken unto °my prayer, God, give audience unto	*Ps.* 39¹³
my clamouring, do not be muted at my weeping. °O hearken,	*Ps.* 30,¹¹
God and grant my plea, o God, °be thou my helper!	*I Sm.* 7,¹²
°*A song of the stairs—of David*:—I was gladdened when they	*Ps.* 122,¹
said unto me: 'Let us go to the house of God'. °I do rejoice over	*Ps.* 119,¹⁶²
thy message, like finding a great fortune. °Attend the sound of my	*Ps.* 5,³
clamouring, °my king and my Lord, for it is unto thee that I do	*Ps.* 5,⁴
pray. °At mornings, God, wilt thou hearken to my speech, at	*B'Br.* 6:
mornings, I do lay it out before thee and expectantly I look up. °I	*Ps.* 17,⁶
have called unto thee, Lord, that thou mayest respond unto me, o	*Ikk.* 2,²³
grant °thy hearing unto me and hearken unto mine utterance. °My foot	*Ps.* 26,¹²
is planted on a level place—let me bless God within communities.	*Yal. hic ult.*

13. Other transitional verses (*Ani keratikha—Shir hama'alot*)

together from sixteen to fifteen. In addition, two of the verses cited in the subsequent sub-group (the third and fourth verses, in lines 10–12) are adjacent in the biblical source (Psalm 5: 3–4). If these are regarded as a single citation, it would reduce the number of separate citations yet further, to fourteen. Such numerical patterns are significant because the number ten is represented in Hebrew by the letter *yod*, the number five by *heh*, and the number six by *vav*, the letters of the Tetragrammaton, the divine name associated with the attribute of mercy. A common variant of the name is the biliteral term *yod* and *heh*; but the form *heh*, *vav*, a non-biblical construct, is also used in certain contexts. A common abbreviation of the Tetragrammaton is also the letter *dalet*, representing the number four and reflecting the number of letters in the name. The five verses in Extract 12, and the sixteen, fifteen, or even fourteen in Extract 13, could there-

אֲנִי קָרָאתִיךָ כִּי־תַעֲנֵנִי אֵל הַט־אָזְנְךָ לִי שְׁמַע אִמְרָתִי׃ 1

אֲנִי בְּצֶדֶק אֶחֱזֶה פָנֶיךָ אֶשְׂבְּעָה בְהָקִיץ תְּמוּנָתֶךָ׃ וַאֲנִי 2

עָלֶיךָ בָטַחְתִּי יְיָ אָמַרְתִּי אֱלֹהַי אָתָּה׃ שְׁמַע קוֹל תַּחֲנוּנַי 3

בְּשַׁוְּעִי אֵלֶיךָ בְּנָשְׂאִי יָדַי אֶל־דְּבִיר קָדְשֶׁךָ׃ יְיָ אֱלֹהַי שִׁוַּעְתִּי 4

אֵלֶיךָ וַתִּרְפָּאֵנִי׃ אֵלֶיךָ יְיָ אֶקְרָא וְאֶל־אֲדֹנָי אֶתְחַנָּן׃ הָאִירָה 5

פָנֶיךָ עַל־עַבְדֶּךָ הוֹשִׁיעֵנִי בְחַסְדֶּךָ׃ כִּי־לְךָ יְיָ הוֹחָלְתִּי אַתָּה 6

תַעֲנֶה אֲדֹנָי אֱלֹהָי׃ שִׁמְעָה תְפִלָּתִי יְיָ וְשַׁוְעָתִי הַאֲזִינָה אֶל־ 7

דִמְעָתִי אַל־תֶּחֱרַשׁ׃ שְׁמַע־יְיָ וְחָנֵּנִי יְיָ הֱיֵה־עֹזֵר לִי׃ 8

שִׁיר הַמַּעֲלוֹת לְדָוִד שָׂמַחְתִּי בְּאֹמְרִים לִי בֵּית יְיָ נֵלֵךְ׃ 9

שָׂשׂ אָנֹכִי עַל־אִמְרָתֶךָ כְּמוֹצֵא שָׁלָל רָב׃ הַקְשִׁיבָה לְקוֹל 10

שַׁוְעִי מַלְכִּי וֵאלֹהָי כִּי־אֵלֶיךָ אֶתְפַּלָּל׃ יְיָ בֹּקֶר תִּשְׁמַע קוֹלִי 11

בֹּקֶר אֶעֱרָךְ־לְךָ וַאֲצַפֶּה׃ אֲנִי קָרָאתִיךָ כִּי־תַעֲנֵנִי אֵל 12

הַט־אָזְנְךָ לִי שְׁמַע אִמְרָתִי׃ רַגְלִי עָמְדָה בְמִישׁוֹר 13

בְּמַקְהֵלִים אֲבָרֵךְ יְיָ׃ 14

fore be viewed as pointing to ambivalence over the precise composition of the name of God.[33] The divine name related to the attribute of mercy, presented in a variety of possible spellings, might thus be the speaker's only source of hope at this point.

The ambivalence reflected in this interpretation suggests the lack of clear evidence of meaning, however, which might point to the confusion of the isolated speaker before arriving in synagogue, and to the way the moment of waking is given shape by joining the community. Yet although some verses contribute

[33] For the name *heh* and *vav*, see Mishnah *Suk.* 4: 5; BT *Suk.* 45a. Such numerical correspondences appear elsewhere in the liturgy and are based on the idea that liturgical words derived from Scripture signify more than they appear to. Liturgical editors imply their mistrust of the surface meaning of language by treating form as more important than meaning, but confirm their confidence in revelation whenever literal interpretation takes precedence.

only tenuously to the progression of ideas, all relate in some way to the beginning of daily worship, to the view that liturgy is less 'authentic' than sacrificial worship, and to the fact that psalms were employed in the Temple. Since David, the traditional author of the book of Psalms and the rejected Temple-builder, is an ambivalent figure with whom to identify precisely when the speaker is about to begin formal prayers, in view of the fact that he failed to establish the formal worship to which he aspired, the speaker may be using him to allude to the difficulty of liturgical worship.

The first three sentences cited in the initial sub-group of nine/ten verses begin with emphatic first person singular pronouns, as do all but the first and the third of the previous group (Extract 12), and there are several references to direct speech with God and to his response, as might be expected of a prelude to prayer, even though no answer to prayer is actually heard. These echo or complement the closing verse of the previous sequence. In addition, several verses reveal the speaker's disquiet. The first (line 1, Ps. 17: 6) and second (line 2, Ps. 17: 15) are from a psalm read midrashically as a reference to God's desire for daily prayer,[34] but also related to the plague brought on the Israelites as a result of David's census.[35] Although midrashically this plague resulted from the people's failure to insist on building the Temple, the biblical narrative describes how David was 'provoked' into taking a census of the people, after which the plague was sent as punishment. It was halted only when Jerusalem was about to be destroyed, whereupon the punishing angel was seen standing on the threshing-floor where the Temple would later be built.[36] This problematical census may relate to Extract 11, line 1, whose words were used to check whether a quorum of ten was present, although since the present verse, Extract 13, line 1, also contains ten words, it may similarly have been used for counting (although there seems to be no evidence for this). The present sequence could therefore, like the previous one, have been drafted as an opening to daily prayer.

The second verse (line 2, Ps. 17: 15), the last in its psalm, apparently also marks the speaker's arrival at the synagogue or Temple. It is read midrashically as a prediction of closeness to God in messianic times, a reading which led to the translation here of the words which literally mean 'see your face' as 'have a vision of Thy presence', in response to biblical statements that suggest the impossibility of actually 'seeing' God, at least before the coming of the messiah.[37] This train of thought led to the translation of *tsedek*, usually rendered 'righteousness', as 'right', with the implication of overcoming the remoteness of present exile suggested in the third verse (lines 2–3, Ps. 31: 15). The psalm from which this comes is midrashically associated with Daniel, linking this verse, via the opening

---

[34] *Midrash Psalms* 17: 1, 6.   [35] Ibid. 17: 4.   [36] I Chr. 21: 1–27.

[37] Exod. 33: 20; Isa. 52: 8. Lindsey Taylor-Guthartz pointed out to me that Ps. 17: 15 also features in the Ashkenazi memorial prayer Yizkor, where it implies awakening to eternal life.

statement of the day, with the beginning of prayer.[38] The fourth verse (lines 3–4, Ps. 28: 2) is from a psalm asking God to hear from his 'holy oracle', midrashically associated with the Temple (apparently that of Solomon),[39] described as the source of God's 'speech' to humans. This activates a further aspect of the previous verse (Ps. 31: 15) and the opening words of the psalm from which it comes, which will be present in the educated speaker's mind as an association. These twice ask God not to be silent and thereby to save the speaker from 'going down into the pit', a rare allusion in the liturgy, however faint, to God's silence. It can be compared to the speaker's energetic use of language as a medium for reaching God. The fifth and sixth verses (lines 4–5, Ps. 30: 3, 9), from a psalm that will later appear in its entirety, are apparently about the dedication of the Temple (Extract 42), again alluding to the beginning of prayer. But David did not build the Temple, suggesting the speaker's awareness of the inevitability of failure, much as the last verse of the first sequence of verses (Extract 12, lines 4–5) assumed human inarticulateness. The seventh verse (lines 5–6, Ps. 31: 17), from the same psalm as the third, refers to trust and ignores the despair implied by the previous verse; but the eighth verse (lines 6–8, Ps. 38: 16), from a psalm on affliction, is midrashically related to the suffering that results from election, as are the *tefilin* texts.[40] The ninth verse (lines 7–8, Ps. 39: 13), from a psalm in which the speaker asks to be heard, accepts the dangers implied in the previous text; while the last verse (line 8, Ps. 30: 11), from the same psalm as the fifth and sixth, is midrashically linked to Esther's rescue from Haman. The closing statement in this collection of verses—which, according to the translation here, asks God to be the speaker's helper—could be understood as a statement that God has already delivered this help, especially in the light of the celebration expressed in the verses that follow it in its original context. This would allude either to the speaker's awaking from sleep or to his safe arrival in synagogue.

These verses illustrate the idea that exile is inexplicably ordained by God, symbolized here by the speaker's departure from home for a synagogue which is itself the shadow of the Temple from which Jews are exiled. There is little overlap with the previous sequence of verses (Extract 12), beyond the resonance with its closing theme and the way it explores the model of citational worship, demonstrating the painful incoherence that results. The speaker's capacity to make sense of fragmentary texts is here stretched to the limit.

The last sub-group of five/six verses, consisting of lines 9–14,[41] is no less problematic. It superficially resembles the first of the three main groups (Extract 12) both in scale and in theme, since it deals with arrival. However, it appears to form a separate assemblage because it again approaches the Temple/synagogue from the outside, and because the penultimate verse (lines 12–13) is identical to the first in the previous sub-group (line 1), suggesting a different source,

[38] *Midrash Psalms* 31: 1.
[40] Ibid. 38: 1.
[39] Ibid. 30: 1, on Ps. 28: 2.
[41] Pss. 122: 1, 119: 162, 5: 3–4, 17: 6, 26: 12.

although it may point to the circularity of the argument and the inefficacy of anthological composition. This sub-group opens (line 9, Ps. 122: 1), not with the words of an enemy describing the Israelite camp, as did the group of five verses in Extract 12, but with those of an insider, David, in which he enquires about the well-being of Jerusalem, blending the here and now of arrival in the synagogue with the dimly recollected Temple. The reference to 'the house of God' may glance back at the speaker's own 'house', since it is described as a reason for rejoicing, or at the home-like allusions associated with the *talit* in the previous chapter (Extract 5). But David's failure to build the Temple suggests the non-fulfilment of the speaker's wishes, while the synagogue poignantly alludes to Jerusalem's destruction—a blend of ideas explored in the context of Balaam's prophecy. A midrash on this psalm remarks that David preferred study to sacrifice, as though the speaker might be rejecting the Temple/synagogue at the very moment of arriving at it.

The second verse in this third sub-group (line 2, Ps. 119: 162) expresses delight in scriptural revelation, as though confirming the value of words, and verbal worship appears again in the third and fourth verses (lines 10–12, Ps. 5: 3–4), both of which are from the same psalm as Extract 11, lines 1–2. The last of these talks of speech in the morning, just as in this opening liturgical sequence. The fifth verse (lines 12–13, Ps. 17: 6), the same as the first in the previous group (Extract 13, line 1), declares the intention to pray daily; and the sixth and last verse (lines 13–14, Ps. 26: 12), the last in the psalm to which it belongs, describes the speaker arriving at a 'level place' among a 'community'. The reference to 'my foot' suggests to midrashic writers that David worshipped with his whole body, although the mention of only one limb suggests physical and perhaps emotional fragmentation. The impression of personal disintegration at a time of arrival suggests that prayer touches on issues too painful to face.

The opacity of these citations, apparently forming a random anthology, can be penetrated, however, by means of an informed reverie of the kind described in the introductory chapters. What emerges is an examination of the problem of prayer, beginning with the hopeful clarity of the opening five verses of Extract 13 and concluding with the fragmented texture of the remainder. The recurrence of the first verse of the first sub-group (Extract 13, line 1), as the penultimate citation of the last sub-group (Extract 13, lines 12–13), suggests a circular structure, defining either the physical movement of the speaker to the synagogue, completed in Extract 13, lines 13–14, or the speaker's experience of fragmented incoherence and indirection, at least until the congregation is reached. Clarity is perhaps activated by the 'ingathering' power of the *talit*, or by the personal expression attained by citing scriptural verses. However, the tenuousness of this fragmented expression shows the difficulty of the larger attempt to establish dialogue with God. The speaker is also doubly in exile, since home has been left and synagogue not yet attained, while all Jews have lost the Temple, the place of potential closeness to God, and must depend on language to relate to God. The way that these verses point to the ineffectiveness of language bodes ill for the liturgical enterprise, but they nevertheless enable the speaker to express delight, as though arriving in the congregation also offers hope for the renewal of clarity and for leaving the disorientation of exile behind.

Liturgical editors here achieve subtle effects by means of the apparently un-creative technique of scriptural citation, weaving implied meanings into patterns that must be read impressionistically rather than explicitly if their meaning is to emerge. The reading provided here may not be the only way in which they can be understood, but it arises from a close scrutiny of the scriptural and liturgical contexts. The scriptural and midrashic contexts enrich the associations of each verse, carrying the speaker back and forth in time and place to address reality in unfamiliar ways. A text containing such 'gapping'[42] will be particularly success-ful in enlisting the speaker in the effort to extract meaning, and also in commun-icating the disorientation characteristic of exile. The need to depend on verbal worship, which replaced sacrifice only following the destruction of the First Temple in 586 BCE, highlights—by means of its very medium—the difficulty of establishing a human–divine dialogue.

EXTRACT 14. **Yigdal: A Poetic Creed**

The ambiguities of the passage from home to synagogue, during which the use of scriptural texts almost silences the individual voice, are now resolved by another beginning to the liturgical day. This takes the form of a poetic statement in rhyme and metre by a single poet, rather than a mosaic of citations. It also marks the speaker's entry, both into the synagogue and into the community, as a locus of emotional, doctrinal, and legal certainty. This sense of certainty matches the regaining of mental clarity on awaking, or of sight as daylight returns.

This metrical creed, known by its opening word, *yigdal*, meaning literally 'aggrandized [by the living God]', is probably the work of Daniel ben Judah, a *dayan* (judge) in Rome during the early fourteenth century.[43] It takes the form of a verse rendition of Moses Maimonides' thirteen articles of faith, including five verses on the nature of God, four on the Torah and prophecy, and four on re-demption, employing embedded quotations from biblical and rabbinic writ-ings.[44] By outlining the sacred narrative from before Creation to the messiah as

---

[42] For a discussion of 'gapping', a term referred to in Chapter 3 above, see Iser, 'Reading Process', 214–16.

[43] For the attribution, see Davidson, *Thesaurus*, ii. 266–7, no. 195; and *Otsar hatefilot*, 'Tikun tefi-lah', 52a–54a, quoting S. D. Luzzatto. Other metrical creeds are known, including one by Immanuel of Rome: see id., *Maḥbarot*, i. 90–4 (lines 42–93). See also Berliner, *Randbermerkungen*, i. 12–13, and Elbogen, *Jewish Liturgy*, 77.

[44] For readings of this *piyut* see Petuchowski, *Theology and Poetry*, 20–30, and Jacobs, *Principles of the Jewish Faith*, 17.

°Almighty-life!—magnified and praised!—	*Ps.* 35,²⁷; *Ku.* 4,¹
°he exists, yet there is no limit to his existence.	*Mai. Ikk.* 1
°He is oneness, there is no singleness like his unity—	*Ku.* 5,¹⁸
inconceivable, also infinite in his oneness.	*Ikk.* 2,¹
°Semblance of form is not he—he is not a body—	*Is.* 40,³⁵
°beyond assessment is his holiness.	*Ps.* 40,⁶
°Before everything that was created—	*Ikk.* 2,¹⁸
°first, yet there was no starting to His beginning.	*Prv.* 8,²²
°Lo! He is world-master, unto all that is formed—	*Dt.* 10,¹⁷
°he demonstrates his grandeur and his sovereignty.	*Ex.* 15,²
°The inspiration of his prophecy he gives,	*Dt.* 33,¹⁹
unto humans of °his selection, yea, for his glory.	*Ps.* 135,⁴
°There has not again arisen in Israel one like Moses,	*Dt.* 34,¹⁰
a prophet °beholding His semblance.	*Nu.* 12,⁸
The °*Torah* of truth God gave unto his People—	*Mal.* 2,⁶
through his prophet, °the trustee of His temple.	*Ku.* 1,⁵; 2,⁵⁶
The almighty °will never change, nor substitute for his law,	*Ku.* 1,⁸³
not for worlds, unto another.	*Ps.* 89,³⁵
°He foresees, knows our secrets—	*Prv.* 15,³
he looks to the °end of a thing as from its beginning.	*Ec.* 12,¹³
He °rewards each man's piety, according to his activity;	*Jg.* 9,¹⁶
he repays °hurt to the wicked, according to his villainy.	*Zo. Gn.* 54:
He will send our Messiah at the °right end of days—	*Zo. Gn.* 54
to redeem them who °awaited his final salvation.	*Dn.* 12,¹²
Almighty, in his abounding loving-kindness, °will revive	*B'Sn.* 91:
the dead—°everlastingly blest is his praised name!	*Is.* 26,⁴

14. Yigdal: a poetic creed

the ideological framework within which the speaker functions, it broadens the liturgical horizons from the home and synagogue to the cosmic scale of history, suggesting the potential for fuller intellectual control as the speaker rejoins the congregation. Any feelings of certainty arising from joining a collective are illusory, however, for intellectual problems remain.

The poem is a relatively late arrival in the morning liturgy and may have gained acceptance, partly because of its similarity in style and content to the still more popular text that follows it and partly because of the rousing melodies to which it is sung on sabbath and festivals. In the present location it appears to be subordinate to the following text, since it is set in smaller type, and Baer includes

יִגְדַּל אֱלֹהִים חַי וְיִשְׁתַּבַּח נִמְצָא וְאֵין עֵת אֶל־מְצִיאוּתוֹ׃ 1

אֶחָד וְאֵין יָחִיד כְּיִחוּדוֹ נֶעְלָם וְגַם אֵין סוֹף לְאַחְדּוּתוֹ׃ 2

אֵין לוֹ דְמוּת הַגּוּף וְאֵינוֹ גוּף לֹא נַעֲרוֹךְ אֵלָיו קְדֻשָּׁתוֹ׃ 3

קַדְמוֹן לְכָל־דָּבָר אֲשֶׁר נִבְרָא רִאשׁוֹן וְאֵין רֵאשִׁית לְרֵאשִׁיתוֹ׃ 4

הִנּוֹ אֲדוֹן עוֹלָם וְכָל־נוֹצָר יוֹרֶה גְדֻלָּתוֹ וּמַלְכוּתוֹ׃ 5

שֶׁפַע נְבוּאָתוֹ נְתָנוֹ אֶל־ אַנְשֵׁי סְגֻלָּתוֹ וְתִפְאַרְתּוֹ׃ 6

לֹא קָם בְּיִשְׂרָאֵל כְּמֹשֶׁה עוֹד נָבִיא וּמַבִּיט אֶת־תְּמוּנָתוֹ׃ 7

תּוֹרַת אֱמֶת נָתַן לְעַמּוֹ אֵל עַל־יַד נְבִיאוֹ נֶאֱמַן בֵּיתוֹ׃ 8

לֹא יַחֲלִיף הָאֵל וְלֹא יָמִיר דָּתוֹ לְעוֹלָמִים לְזוּלָתוֹ׃ 9

צוֹפֶה וְיוֹדֵעַ סְתָרֵינוּ מַבִּיט לְסוֹף דָּבָר בְּקַדְמָתוֹ׃ 10

גּוֹמֵל לְאִישׁ חֶסֶד כְּמִפְעָלוֹ נוֹתֵן לְרָשָׁע רַע כְּרִשְׁעָתוֹ׃ 11

יִשְׁלַח לְקֵץ יָמִין מְשִׁיחֵנוּ לִפְדּוֹת מְחַכֵּי קֵץ יְשׁוּעָתוֹ׃ 12

מֵתִים יְחַיֶּה אֵל בְּרֹב חַסְדּוֹ בָּרוּךְ עֲדֵי־עַד שֵׁם תְּהִלָּתוֹ׃ 13

it only at the end of the morning service.[45] Its uncertain status at this point and the general reluctance to deploy other summaries of this kind in the liturgy reflect an undercurrent of rabbinic mistrust of creeds as such. This could be based on the view that Judaism cannot be reduced to a statement of essentials, coupled with an awareness that such inventories were mostly inspired by a desire to establish Jewish distinctiveness from other faiths.[46] This cautious approach to philosophy gave rise to occasionally violent confrontations that came to be known as the Maimonidean controversy, which centred on the authority of Maimonides' philosophical writings. These disputes, which have been characterized as a 'cold war between the authority of revelation and the authority of reason', began in the late twelfth century, when Maimonides was still alive, and

---

[45] *Sidur avodat yisra'el*, 154.

[46] See Nulman, *Encylopedia of Jewish Prayer*, 375–6 n. 5, and *Tselota di'avraham*, i. 32–3; for ambivalence about credal statements see Abrahams, *Companion*, pp. cii–cv, or his later homonym, Abrahams, 'Belief', 429–34. On the history of creeds see Schechter, 'The Dogmas of Judaism', in id., *Studies in Judaism*, 179–221; L. Roth, *Judaism*, 78–83; Jacobs, *Principles of the Jewish Faith*, 1–32; Kellner, *Must A Jew Believe Anything?*, 24–5.

continued intermittently until the early fourteenth century, a few decades before this poem is believed to have been written.[47]

The thirteen articles of faith on which this poem is based originally appeared in Maimonides' commentary on Mishnah *Sanhedrin* 10: 1; other medieval philosophers produced rival listings. None of these occurs in prayer-books, although an inaccurate prose rendition of Maimonides' creed appears as an addendum to the morning service in most traditional prayer-books. This poem reflects Maimonides' intention more closely than the prose version, but might have been admitted to the liturgy rather than any fuller rendition because metre and rhyme seem less authoritative than prose.

Its relevance at precisely this point is uncertain: although the references in the closing line to the messiah and resurrection point to the beginning of the day, the poem has also found a place at the conclusion to sabbath and festival evening services, when it is sung to a range of melodies.[48] The case for the morning setting is supported by the second and third words of line 1, usually rendered as 'living God', but here translated 'Almighty-life', which point to the Creation theme.[49] In addition, since the link in line 5 between God's name and the idea of monarchy recurs in each blessing formula, discussed in connection with Extract 2, the poem could be regarded as an introduction to the blessings at the core of this first sequence of the morning liturgy, in Extracts 22–5, which properly belong at the beginning of the day.[50] The final clause of the last line similarly 'blesses' God in a way that might relate either to blessing formulae or to the call to prayer at the beginning of the statutory liturgy immediately after the sequences examined in this book. The reference to God as *adon olam*, 'master of the universe', in line 5 matches the opening words of the poem which follows, and may have inspired the present poem's inclusion here.

EXTRACT 15. Adon Olam: An Introductory Poem

This second poem of the day, known by its opening words, *adon olam*, translated here as 'master of the universe', is probably the most familiar in the liturgy. It appears here beneath a heading, 'Morning Service', that suggests it begins the morning service, an impression confirmed by its typographical superiority to the previous text. Like that poem, however, this one recurs at the end of sabbath and festival services, Yigdal in the evening and Adon Olam in the morning,[51] although both may have arrived on this initial page of the prayer-book because it was more convenient to add them to the flyleaves than in the body of manuscripts, irrespective of where they were to be recited.

---

[47] Silver, *Maimonidean Criticism*, 20–1; see also Ben-Sasson, 'Maimonidean Controversy'.

[48] See Gaguine, *Keter shem tov*, i–ii. 196–8 n. 245.

[49] See *Book of Prayer: Daily and Occasional Prayers*, 90–1.

[50] BT *Ber.* 40b, discussed in *Tselota di'avraham*, i. 33 (in commentary 'Emek berakhah').

[51] Gaguine, *Keter shem tov*, i–ii. 446–8 n. 496.

It has been suggested that the poet in this case was Solomon Ibn Gabirol,[52] though it could have been written by someone aware of his literary and intellectual style, and was probably completed as late as the fourteenth century, since it appears neither in prayer-books from the Cairo Genizah nor in Abudarham's commentary. Although, like Yigdal, it has the appearance of a philosophical poem, its allusions and undercurrents make it far richer than that work. The first four verses focus on God's transcendence of time (the first two words could be translated 'eternal Lord')[53] and the next two on God's unity and redemptive power. The closing four verses, however, shift from anonymous philosophical abstraction to the first person singular and are personal in tone, and the last two, describing God's custody of the soul and body during sleep, recall the opening statement of the day. The transition from the philosophical to the personal is camouflaged by rhyme and metre, however, since the repeated *beli*, 'without', of line 6 sets the scene for the first-person suffix of *eli*, 'my lord', in line 7, concealing the radical shift from philosophical purity to anthropomorphism, culminating in the word *beyado*, 'into his hand', the first in the penultimate line.

These concluding lines echo the scriptural words 'into his hand I entrust my spirit',[54] associated in a midrash with resurrection and the promise to reunite body and soul on awakening,[55] themes familiar from the opening statement of the day.[56] Similarly, to 'entrust' the spirit to God is to imply a preference for the speaker's ownership, since God seems obliged to return it. The term *ruḥi*, 'my soul', implies a lower form of 'spirit' than the *neshamah* referred to in the opening statement of the day, as though God is entrusted merely with the part of the personality responsible for remaining awake, and not that element which is engaged in the search for truth.[57] The fear of its non-return is deeper here than in the opening statement of the day, however, for although the last word of the penultimate line means 'and I shall awake', it is separated syntactically from the preceding expression of trust, implying the isolation of this particular term in the poet's mind. The last two end-rhymes, the closest in the poem, link *ve'a'irah*, 'and I will awake', with *velo ira*, 'I will not fear', and reinforce the sense of fear that the sleeper may not awake.

This makes the poem perhaps more relevant to evening than morning. However, factors linking the poem specifically to the morning include the theme of Creation in the opening four lines, since the first two suggest that the speaker is located in pre-creational silence and must complete God's kingship by proclaiming it in speech.[58] The speaker watches the world take shape at daybreak

[52] Davidson, *Thesaurus*, i, no. 575.   [53] For this rendition, see Elbogen, *Jewish Liturgy*, 77.
[54] Ps. 31: 6.   [55] *Midrash Psalms* 25: 2.   [56] Discussed in Ch. 4 above.
[57] In the Aristotelian tripartite soul, the third, 'rational' quotient, which humanity and angels alone possess, is referred to in Hebrew as the *nefesh maskelet* or *nefesh dabranit* (Raphael Loewe, pers. comm.). See Ben Yehuda, *Dictionary*, viii. 3749–50, and Klatzkin, *Otsar munaḥim hafilosofi'im*, i. 131–2.   [58] Emden, *Amudei shamayim* (ed. Weinfeld), i. 126.

MORNING SERVICE

°Master of the universe, who reigned before all forms	*Ps.* 90,[2]
were created;	*Prv.* 8,[22]
Then when all was completed according to His will, his	*Gn.* 2,[4]
name was announced: Sovereign!	*Ps.* 47,[3]
And afterwards °when all is gone, he alone, awesome,	*Jr.* 4,[27]
°will reign,	*Ex.* 15,[11,18]
For °he was, he is and will be, ever in glory.	*Mai. Ikk.* 4
Yea, °he is unique and there is no second, to compare or	*Is.* 46,[5]
to join with him;	*Ikk.* 2,[10]
Without beginning, without end—power and °authority	*Is.* 9,[6]
are his;	*Ku.* 1,[1]; 5,[18]
He is my Lord, yea, my °live redeemer, rock unto my	*Jb.* 19,[23]
°life-line in time of trouble;	*Jr.* 38,[13]
He is my banner and my refuge, the °portion of my	*Ps.* 16,[5]
cup whene'er °I call;	*Ps.* 3,[5]
°Into his hand do I entrust my spirit, when I do sleep, so	*Ps.* 31,[6]
°I may awake,	*Zo. Lv.* 33
Yea, with my spirit, also my body; °I have God!—so °I	*Ps.* 118,[6]
am not afraid.	*Dt.* 1,[17]

---

15. Adon Olam: an introductory poem

like a latter-day Adam, the first user of language. The morning associations are confirmed by the reference to God in the second line as 'king', as though this poem might be introducing the expression 'king of the universe', which appears in every blessing formula, for the first time in the day. The juxtaposition of Creation and sleep relates to the view that the world is recreated daily,[59] while the idea that the world is only temporary emerges in line 3, recalling midrashic descriptions of God creating and destroying successive worlds before being satisfied with the present one.[60]

The clearest evidence for the appropriateness of this poem to morning, however, emerges from the emphatic preoccupation with the interplay between the divine names contrasted in the first two chapters of the Pentateuch, the account of Creation.[61] The first word of the poem, *adon*, 'Lord', reflects the common euphemistic pronunciation of the Tetragrammaton, *adonai*, rabbinically linked to

[59] An idea made explicit in the second sentence of the Yotser blessing.   [60] *Gen. Rabbah* 9: 2.

[61] It is possible also that the ten lines of the poem allude to the 'ten words of Creation', Mishnah *Avot* 5: 1.

תְּפִלַּת שַׁחֲרִית·

1   אֲדוֹן עוֹלָם אֲשֶׁר מָלַךְ· בְּטֶרֶם כָּל יְצִיר נִבְרָא:

2   לְעֵת נַעֲשָׂה בְחֶפְצוֹ כֹּל· אֲזַי מֶלֶךְ שְׁמוֹ נִקְרָא:

3   וְאַחֲרֵי כִּכְלוֹת הַכֹּל· לְבַדּוֹ יִמְלוֹךְ נוֹרָא:

4   וְהוּא הָיָה וְהוּא הֹוֶה· וְהוּא יִהְיֶה בְּתִפְאָרָה:

5   וְהוּא אֶחָד וְאֵין שֵׁנִי· לְהַמְשִׁיל לוֹ לְהַחְבִּירָה:

6   בְּלִי רֵאשִׁית בְּלִי תַכְלִית· וְלוֹ הָעֹז וְהַמִּשְׂרָה:

7   וְהוּא אֵלִי וְחַי גֹּאֲלִי· וְצוּר חֶבְלִי בְּעֵת צָרָה:

8   וְהוּא נִסִּי וּמָנוֹס לִי· מְנָת כּוֹסִי בְּיוֹם אֶקְרָא:

9   בְּיָדוֹ אַפְקִיד רוּחִי· בְּעֵת אִישַׁן וְאָעִירָה:

10   וְעִם־רוּחִי גְּוִיָּתִי· יְיָ לִי וְלֹא אִירָא:

the divine attribute of mercy. It is here shorn of its first person singular suffix, since before Creation no speaker could refer to God possessively.

The preoccupation with divine names does not end here. The Tetragrammaton itself, which is never pronounced by Jews in obedience to the commandment not to take God's name in vain,[62] first appears in Genesis 2 in the context of the Garden of Eden, the reason being, as commentators pointed out, that only because of events in Eden was divine mercy needed.[63] When the complex nature of relations with God became evident, the attribute of mercy needed to be brought into play. The previous account of Creation in seven days—in which the divine name *elohim* is used exclusively—describes an orderly world in which no allowance needs to be made for imperfections and which can therefore be ruled

[62] Exod. 20: 7.

[63] Rashi on Gen. 1: 1, end, and on 2: 5. Later practice, probably linked to Lurianic thought, recognized the Tetragrammaton in the initial letters of the last two words of Gen. 1: 31 and the first two of Gen. 2: 1, and included the former as a prologue to the Kiddush for sabbath eve, suggesting that the survival of Adam depended on the prior existence of the attribute of mercy.

according to strict justice. Midrashic texts describe how the attribute of mercy, which became necessary thereafter, must remain in the ascendant if the world is to survive, although both attributes are essential.[64] It appears to be less accessible to humans than justice, however, since the divine name related to mercy is unpronounceable, while fewer restrictions apply to the name associated with justice. In this poem the spoken version of the Tetragrammaton appears as the first word, although only in abbreviated form, in order to reflect the shadowy presence of mercy in the initial stages of a creation otherwise dominated by justice. Only in the last four lines, in which the speaker seems to be identified with Adam, is God referred to initially as *eli*, 'my lord', an abbreviated form of the name suggesting justice, the first attribute encountered by Adam, shifting in the final clause to the name of mercy, this time appearing with the possessive suffix missing in the pre-Adamic first line of the poem. Its abbreviated appearance there, however, suggests that divine mercy was active even then, if only in a potential form. This interplay of divine names, moving from partial mercy to justice and, finally, to perfect mercy, traces the development—or the hoped-for development—of the human relationship with God, while simultaneously following the growth of the individual from bare body and soul to a sentient being with a conscience. It also implies that the speaker's soul might be more the property of God than of the speaker, for its return seems to be more a matter of mercy than of justice.

Further evidence of this poem's preoccupation with the interplay between the divine attributes, which does not seem to have been noted before, lies in the arrangement of letters at the ends of lines. The monorhyme is spelled three times with *alef*, three times with *heh*, and then with two pairs of *heh* and *alef* at the conclusion. It can be suggested that these point to divine names of which these are the initials—the first being a common abbreviation of the Tetragrammaton and the second the first letter of *elohim*. This view is supported by the way in which they echo the order in which the names appear in the Creation narrative—first *elohim* and then the Tetragrammaton—and then blend them. If this reading is correct, then the poem may well comment both on the opening line of the Shema, another early-morning text which attempts to unify the names and the divine attributes (an idea discussed in the analysis of Extract 31, line 1), and on the blessing formula (discussed in the context of Extract 2), likewise a morning feature.

The ambiguity of divine mercy is illuminated by a talmudic text that describes how the divine name *adon* was first used by Abraham,[65] at the point at which he was about to be promised an heir of his own. He later instituted morning prayer when fleeing Sodom and Gomorrah, although the verb for 'rising

[64] *Gen. Rabbah* 12: 15.

[65] BT *Ber.* 7b, quoted in *Otsar hatefilot*, 'Ets yosef', 50b, and 'Tikun tefilah', 51a.

early' also links it to the Akedah.[66] If so, the use of the word *adon* here would imply that at this moment the speaker occupies the role not only of Adam, but of Abraham, both of whom lived through experiences that took them through death, as the closing line of the song acknowledges also of the speaker. The Akedah, a narrative through which rabbinic thinkers explore the divine attributes of justice and mercy, midrashically links this poem not only to the early morning, but to the feelings of ambivalence, helplessness, and vulnerability experienced by the speaker on waking from sleep and facing the day ahead. The presence of both divine attributes also helps account for the fear of disintegration experienced by the speaker made in 'God's image', because the theological aspiration to 'unify' God expresses a hunger not only for safety, but also for a unity of purpose that can overcome the uncertainties ahead.

This poem thus offers a highly ambivalent introduction to the morning liturgy, spanning the period from Creation to Abraham, the first Jew, and introducing the problematic nature of Jewishness and the speaker's own trials ahead. The painful implications of its attempt to accommodate contraries are sweetened by the precision of its rhyme and metre, which leads perhaps the majority of those to whom it is familiar to regard it as a charming ornament rather than a rigorous confrontation with almost insoluble theological problems.

EXTRACT 16. The Blessing Over Hand-Washing

The powerfully organized world of poetry now gives way to prose, and personal expression to formulas, as the liturgy turns to the blessings associated with the first moments of daily consciousness. These are associated in the talmudic source with home, and were transferred to synagogue in response to the needs of those without access to written texts. The present blessing over hand-washing and its sequel are presented by late medieval codes as the first ritual gestures of the day after awaking,[67] immediately following the opening statement of the day (in Extract 1, which took the place of the talmudic waking prayer later relegated to the synagogue and now appearing as Extract 21). The initial blessings are followed in the sources by texts associated with dressing, which have been shifted still further forward in the present version.

This reorganization of the liturgy is disorienting, since reverting here to getting up at home transforms the previous songs of arrival in synagogue into waking meditations. They suit this role, since the preceding analysis showed how both address the structure of the blessing formula. But since the texts appearing after those related to the ritual garments created the impression that the speaker had left home behind, the present one, by reversing that assumption, leaves the

---

[66] BT *Ber.* 26*b*, citing Gen. 19: 27, echoed at the Binding of Isaac, Gen. 22: 3.

[67] See Caro, *Shulḥan arukh*, 'Oraḥ ḥayim' 4; *Sidur avodat yisra'el*, 2–3.

> °Blest art thou, God our Lord, sovereign of the universe,   *SA-OH*4,¹; 158,⁹
>
> He who makes us holy through His commandments, and   *Msh. So. ult.*
>
> commanded us °concerning the pouring over the hands!   *B'Hu.* 107

16. The blessing over hand-washing (*Al netilat yadayim*)

speaker in both places at once, an ambiguity supported even by the talmudic source of this blessing.[68] That text mentions a number of hand-washings, not only the present one which is the first action of the day, but another to follow dressing, presumably because this involves touching footwear that has been in contact with the dirt of the street. Baer outlines the two possibilities and opts for the earlier association, seeing its recital here by the prayer-leader as a convenience for those unable to recite it for themselves. He therefore explains that the blessing should be recited here only by those who have been able to wash their hands at home and reach the synagogue without speaking, since it must be linked to the action and not be recited twice, as doing so would involve 'taking God's name in vain'. Those who do recite it at home should respond here to the reader's recital of the blessing by saying 'blessed be he and blessed be his name' after the name of God, and 'amen' after the blessing, as one does when hearing any blessing. Baer is aware of the dislocation caused by the reorganization of the liturgy, but he seems not to consider the possibility that the blessing might refer to a different hand-washing that would indeed be correctly located here, one recommended in talmudic texts before prayer.[69] The possibility might have been omitted because no blessing was included for the first washing, on waking, or since other difficulties remain which are just as intractable.

The words *netilat yadayim* are conventionally understood to mean 'washing the hands', but are here rendered 'pouring over the hands', to reflect the ritual of pouring water first over the right and then over the left hand from a vessel held in the other hand. The Hebrew verb indeed refers neither to washing nor to pouring, as will be discussed below.

Like the previous poem, hand-washing alludes to the Creation story, since the fact that Adam was made 'in God's image'[70] inspired in rabbinic thought a particular reverence for the human body. One talmudic rabbi, asked by his students why he described going to the bath-house as a religious duty, explained that he was going to show respect to the image of God.[71] Another link emerges from the resemblance between sleep and death,[72] although hand-washing on leaving a cemetery is not accompanied by a blessing.[73] The association of waking with

---

[68] BT *Ber.* 60b.   [69] BT *Ber.* 14b–15a.   [70] Gen. 1: 27.   [71] *Lev. Rabbah* 34: 3.

[72] The elaborate rituals in connection with this that are elaborated in Num. 19: 2–22 relate only to Temple times.

[73] Caro, *Shulḥan arukh*, 'Oraḥ ḥayim' 4: 18, 23, quoted in *Sidur avodat yisra'el*, 3.

בָּרוּךְ אַתָּה יְיָ אֱלֹהֵינוּ מֶלֶךְ הָעוֹלָם אֲשֶׁר   1
קִדְּשָׁנוּ בְּמִצְוֹתָיו וְצִוָּנוּ עַל נְטִילַת יָדָיִם: 2

hand-washing reflects the complexity of the speaker's position as a reunited body and soul, as discussed in the context of the opening statement of the day (Chapter 4).

Talmudic texts compare hand-washing before eating with the washing with which priests began the day in the Temple,[74] reading the term translated here as 'pouring over' (*netilah*, literally 'taking [up]') as 'lifting up',[75] in the sense both of raising the hands for water to flow over them and of elevating them to higher functions.[76] Although this hand-washing does not relate to eating, it is part of the daily preparation for prayer and is therefore even more obviously associated with priestly activities. Enacting part of the Temple ritual at this point demonstrates the speaker's nostalgia for the Temple and acknowledges that the synagogue—and the home, if the speaker is still there—are its substitutes, serving as vehicles for mourning its destruction.

This text is also the first of the Birkhot Hashaḥar, 'dawn blessings', since the blessings over the *talit* and *tefilin*, although preceding this one in the present prayer-book, appear in the talmudic source as the culmination of the series rather than its precursor. Hand-washing would be impossible anyway while wearing *tefilin*, because of the strap bound over the hand. As a consequence of these ambiguities, therefore, the speaker, who is now located both at home and in synagogue, is in neither, but in a time and place generated by the liturgy, blending the sacred narrative with the here and now. The speaker, obliged by the two preceding poems to adopt a quasi-authorial role and to engage in study, must now decode and reconstitute the symbolic hinterground of this blessing.

EXTRACT 17. The Blessing after Excretion

Since this blessing, unrelated in the talmudic source to the waking sequence, is designed to be recited after washing one's hands after performing bodily functions, it seems inappropriate in a public setting, at least at first sight.[77] It may have been included here because it appears on the same talmudic page as the waking blessings, because it shares the feature of hand-washing with the

---

[74] BT *Ḥul.* 106a–b, quoting Exod. 30: 19–20.   [75] Ben Yehuda, *Dictionary*, vii. 3634–6.
[76] See this sense in Isa. 63: 9; and the application here in *Otsar hatefilot*, 'Iyun tefilah', 56a; *Israels Gebete*, 5–6; *Olat re'iyah*, i. 57; and Landes, 'Halakhah of Waking Up', 35–6.   [77] BT *Ber.* 60b.

°Blest art thou, God our Lord, sovereign of the universe,	*B'Br.* 60:
He who fashioned °man in °wisdom and created in him many	*Zo. Lv.* 48
openings and many cavities, it is clear and known before thy	*Mai. Tef.* 7,[5]
throne of honour that if but °one of these be forced open or be	*B'Sb.* 132
blocked up, it would be impossible to exist and °to stand	*Av.* 3,[6]; *Ku.* 3,[11]
before thy presence—blest art thou, God, who makes sound	*SA-OH* 6,[1]
all flesh, yea, °performing wondrously!	*Jg.* 13,[19]

17. The blessing after excretion (*Asher yatsar*)

previous blessing, or because early morning is a common time to relieve oneself. But while it may be recited at any time during the day, the only moment it would not be recited would be while wearing *talit* and *tefilin*, when excreting and washing one's hands are neither practical nor permitted.

The blessing's separation from its origins transforms it here into a study-text, but its location where it cannot be relevant counteracts its implied integration of physicality into the sacred system. Placing it here also relates it to the transition from sleep to cultural awareness, in which wakefulness brings control. However it is read, it calls again on the speaker's ability to perform quasi-authorial manoeuvres.

The opening theme of this blessing is Creation, as in Adon Olam, but the subject is not the reunification of body and soul, as in the opening statement of the day, but the dual themes of the irresistible physical need to digest and excrete, and of the intellectual urge to throw light on the nature of thought. In this way it prepares the ground for *talit* and *tefilin*, which are located far later in the talmudic source.

Since the blessing deals with universal experience it alludes neither to Jewish election nor to any ritual commandment, though in the present context it also relates to a pre-Jewish state of mind, in the sense that the speaker has only just awoken and has not yet begun to function in a fully Jewish way. The blessing uses universal terminology: it mentions *adam*, 'human' or 'man', in line 2, and 'all flesh' in line 6, echoing the role of Darius in the opening statement of the day and the later allusion to Balaam, suggesting that the speaker now stands outside the community and must negotiate the passage between bare consciousness and Hebrew culture. But because this edition places the blessing in the synagogue rather than the home, which is where the talmudic discussion suggests it should be, the earlier texts accompanying the transfer from home to synagogue, the place of Jewish culture, tend to be universalized, transforming this private text

בָּרוּךְ אַתָּה יְיָ אֱלֹהֵינוּ מֶלֶךְ הָעוֹלָם אֲשֶׁר יָצַר 1

אֶת־הָאָדָם בְּחָכְמָה וּבָרָא בוֹ נְקָבִים נְקָבִים 2

חֲלוּלִים חֲלוּלִים גָּלוּי וְיָדוּעַ לִפְנֵי כִסֵּא כְבוֹדֶךָ 3

שֶׁאִם יִפָּתֵחַ אֶחָד מֵהֶם אוֹ יִסָּתֵם אֶחָד מֵהֶם 4

אִי אֶפְשָׁר לְהִתְקַיֵּם וְלַעֲמוֹד לְפָנֶיךָ: בָּרוּךְ 5

אַתָּה יְיָ רוֹפֵא כָל־בָּשָׂר וּמַפְלִיא לַעֲשׂוֹת: 6

into a public one in which physicality enables the speaker to investigate concerns with division, and, as will be seen, with election and the acquisition of Hebrew.

The physical helplessness described here is therefore partly cultural, the blessing implying the gradual acquisition of competence and autonomy through its use of the Creation narrative as a metaphor for waking.[78] The theme of ignorance, both cultural and physical, is suggested by the fact that the body's 'openings' and 'cavities' are so numerous that the speaker can name them only by repeating two Hebrew words, *nekavim nekavim halulim halulim*, 'openings openings, cavities cavities' (lines 2–3), in a stammering approximation of accuracy. Even if the first and second elements of each pair of terms are read as nouns and adjectives respectively, meaning 'hollow openings and vacant cavities', the effect of the words as sounds would be similar. One midrashic writer noted that the numerical value of the Hebrew for 'many cavities' (line 3) equals 124, and that doubling it to reflect the repetition produces 248, the traditional number of parts of the body and of positive commands in the Torah.[79] But the author of the blessing is unlikely to have intended this since the numerical value of the first term, 202, is not significant. A link between Torah and the human body, however, does reflect the association in rabbinic thought between well-being and knowledge.[80] God's knowledge of the body, and implicitly of Torah too, is infinitely greater than that of humans, with their stuttering attempts to describe reality, and human ignorance is a major theme of the *tefilin* texts discussed earlier.

The version of Creation on which this blessing is based is not that in Genesis, however, but in Isaiah, the same verse of which will appear in the opening blessing of the statutory morning liturgy (which lies outside the scope of this book).[81]

[78] Drawn from the Targum of Ezek. 28, according to *Otsar hatefilot*, 'Tikun tefilah', 56*b*.

[79] *Midrash tanhuma*, 'Shemini', in a version referred to in *Otsar hatefilot*, 'Iyun tefilah', 56*b*.

[80] See Gruenwald, *Apocalyptic and Merkavah Mysticism*, 4–8, which traces the idea that knowledge of the workings of heaven (and by extension Torah) is a tool for understanding the world.

[81] Isa. 45: 7.

Unlike the Genesis version, the Isaiah text speaks for the soul recently reunited with its body and takes a human point of view. It characteristically distinguishes between higher and lower orders of creation, for the verb *yatsar*, literally 'formed', used to describe the making of each human in line 1, is applied in Isaiah's account to the making of light, while the verb *bara*, literally 'created', used to describe the making of orifices in line 2, is associated by Isaiah with the making of darkness and also of 'evil'. (The liturgical application of this verse, later in the morning service, silently modifies this last word to 'everything', departing from revelation in a way seen earlier.) In Genesis the second and more general term, *bara*, is related to everything, even to humans who are said to be 'very good',[82] suggesting that humanity is not distinguished from the rest of creation. In this blessing, however, the speaker is located on the boundary between creation and acculturation and marks the passage from sleepy helplessness to wakeful control by establishing a cultural sphere in which humans are set apart from the rest of creation.

The speaker's helplessness is also reflected in the repetition of the word *ehad*, 'one', in line 4, recalling fears about unity noted in the discussion of *tefilin*. Again, although the purpose of each aperture is 'clear and known' to God (line 3), the speaker is aware only that without them it would be impossible to 'exist or stand before thy presence' (line 5). The verb 'to exist' (*lehitkayem*), however, could allude to the idea of 'fulfilling' (*lekayem*) the covenant with God, an association noted in the context of the opening statement of the day. The onus is clearly on God to make it possible for the speaker to keep the human side of the agreement.

The link between human and divine knowledge is also suggested by the way God's knowledge is described here as *hokhmah*, literally meaning 'wisdom', but with connotations of 'skill'. The fact that the way apertures are opened or closed is beyond human understanding is implied by the use of the verb *bara*, 'created', to describe the making of the orifices, a term used in the biblical account for the whole process of creation as well as the apparently random divisions between heaven and earth and the sexes.[83] However, the term translated here as 'wisdom' is also used for the 'skill' of Bezalel in building the Tabernacle,[84] suggesting that both humans and sacred artefacts are smoothly working mechanisms, and that the speaker might employ this skill in performing Temple-like ceremonies in the synagogue, such as the daily hand-washing which has been tentatively associated with the cult. Another reading of this blessing is that it refers not to God's own wisdom, but to the fact that God endowed humans with wisdom at Creation.[85] This would likewise enable the speaker to participate, like Bezalel, in

---

[82] Gen. 1: 31.   [83] Gen. 1: 1, 27; 2: 3.   [84] Exod. 36: 1–2.

[85] *Otsar hatefilot*, 'Ets yosef', 56*b*. An additional indication of commentators' struggles with this blessing is the observation in the commentary 'Anaf yosef' on the same page that the word for 'wisdom'—*hokhmah*—is numerically equivalent to 613, the traditional total for the number of pentateuchal laws. The closest approximation, however, is 60 and 13, a poor match and dependent on a quasi-midrashic reading of Arabic numerals.

a daily rebuilding of the Tabernacle, the shadowy presence behind every synagogue or home.

The implied midrashic equation between the human body and the Tabernacle —to be discussed in more detail in Chapter 10, in the context of Extract 43—has another implication, for if both Bezalel and God used 'wisdom', then the daily re-entry of the soul into the body might point to the speaker's arrival in the Temple or synagogue, universalizing both of these as symbols of creation, much as the reuniting of Jew and synagogue breathes life into the community. Equally, the fall of the Temple and its replacement by the synagogue corresponds to sleep or to exile, ideas explored in the opening statement of the day.

The link with suffering is reinforced by the closing blessing formula that describes how God 'makes sound [or 'heals'] all flesh' (line 6). Rav, in the talmudic source of this blessing, suggested that the text should conclude with 'blessed art thou who healest the sick', but Samuel argued that this would 'turn the whole world into invalids' and proposed instead 'who healest all flesh'. The present version combines those of Samuel and of Rav Sheshet, who preferred 'who doest wonderfully'.[86] But sickness remains, confirming the built-in weakness of creation and the daily need to recreate the speaker's wholeness. The multiple references to Creation at the beginning of the blessing and the shift to healing at the end suggest the editors' awareness of their simultaneous relevance, making possible the idea—rarely expressed explicitly in rabbinic Judaism—that suffering is built into the nature of life.

This blessing, far from being a mere 'grace' after excretion, represents an attempt to bring the speaker from a pre-cultural state, struggling for articulacy, towards one in which it is possible to glimpse higher knowledge, if only through the numerical coincidences between inner organs and the positive commands in the Torah. In this respect it follows on from the farewell to mortality implied by the previous blessing.

EXTRACT 18. **The Blessings Over Torah Study**

The relevance of these three talmudic blessings[87] over Torah study to the previous text seems unclear at first, but they are linked by the way they enable the speaker to transcend universal humanity and to enter the Jewish people by means of study. They do this by allowing the speaker to redress the balance between divine knowledge and human ignorance, and to explore the nature of Jewish cultural identity. Their location is closer to the time intended by their authors than the previous blessing, but the speaker is still obliged to set aside temporarily the ideas generated by the ritual garments.

---

[86] BT *Ber.* 60*b*.   [87] BT *Ber.* 11*b*.

°Blest art thou, God our Lord, sovereign of the universe,	*B'Br.* 11:
He who makes us holy through °His commandments, and	*Ku.* 3,[39]
°commanded us to engage ourselves in *Torah* matters;	*SA–OH* 47
prithee, God our Lord, do thou make °the words of thy *Torah*	*B'Br.* 5
pleasant unto our mouths and unto °the mouth of thy	*Is.* 59,[21]
People, the House of Israel, so that we and °our offspring, yea,	*Is.* 44,[3]
the °offspring of thy People, the House of Israel, may all be	*B'BM* 85
°knowledgeable of thy name and students of thy *Torah*	*Is.* 54,[13]
°(for its own sake)—blest art thou, God, who °teaches *Torah*	*B'Br.* 17
unto his People Israel!	*B'Sn.* 99:
°BLEST ART THOU, GOD OUR LORD, SOVEREIGN OF THE UNIVERSE,	*SA–OH* 139,[4]
HE °WHO SELECTED US FROM ALL PEOPLES AND GAVE UNTO US HIS	*B'Br.* 11:
Torah—BLEST ART THOU, GOD, °GIVER OF THE *Torah!*	*B'Sf.* 13,[8]

18. The blessings over Torah study (*La'asok*; *veha'arev-na*; *noten hatorah*)

The blessings are not only concerned with study, moreover, but are them-selves acts of study, especially because the speaker must interpret them or even intervene editorially in order to understand them. Their talmudic context sug-gests that they are three variant versions of a single blessing to be recited in the morning before study. Including all three of them in chronological order of authorship, as here, ensures that they form not a single coherent statement, but an opaque collection of diverse pieces. Their anthological status is clear from the fact that, in the talmudic source, the last of the three was claimed by its author, Hamnunah, to be the finest of all blessings, rendering the others superfluous. The talmudic discussion concludes that all should be read, however, although this decision is itself an act of exegesis. Since it is not stated that a compromise was reached or rulings overturned, it seems to have been decided that engaging with divergent views in this way is a suitable prelude to study.[88]

The blessings have been included here, not because they form part of the ritual of getting up in the morning, but because they refer to the pentateuchal obligation to study Torah 'when one rises',[89] this being the earliest possible opportunity for doing so. They thus introduce scriptural study in the same way

---

[88] Historical factors behind their composition, and suggestions that the first two refer to the Written and Oral Torah and the third to both, or that the first is for the Jews, the second for Torah, and the third for God, are outlined in *Otsar hatefilot*, 57*b*–60*a*. The last is preferred by Rashi (on BT *Ber.* 11*b*) because it praises both Israel and the Torah. This variety of interpretation suggests that no clear correspondence can be detected.

[89] For instance in the credal Shema, from Deut. 6: 7.

בָּרוּךְ אַתָּה יְיָ אֱלֹהֵינוּ מֶלֶךְ הָעוֹלָם אֲשֶׁר

קִדְּשָׁנוּ בְּמִצְוֹתָיו וְצִוָּנוּ לַעֲסוֹק בְּדִבְרֵי תוֹרָה:

וְהַעֲרֶב נָא יְיָ אֱלֹהֵינוּ אֶת דִּבְרֵי תוֹרָתְךָ בְּפִינוּ

וּבְפִי עַמְּךָ בֵּית יִשְׂרָאֵל וְנִהְיֶה אֲנַחְנוּ וְצֶאֱצָאֵינוּ

וְצֶאֱצָאֵי עַמְּךָ בֵּית יִשְׂרָאֵל כֻּלָּנוּ יוֹדְעֵי שְׁמֶךָ

וְלוֹמְדֵי תוֹרָתֶךָ לִשְׁמָהּ בָּרוּךְ אַתָּה יְיָ הַמְלַמֵּד

תּוֹרָה לְעַמּוֹ יִשְׂרָאֵל: בָּרוּךְ אַתָּה יְיָ אֱלֹהֵינוּ

מֶלֶךְ הָעוֹלָם אֲשֶׁר בָּחַר בָּנוּ מִכָּל הָעַמִּים וְנָתַן

לָנוּ אֶת תּוֹרָתוֹ בָּרוּךְ אַתָּה יְיָ נוֹתֵן הַתּוֹרָה:

that other blessings precede the acts to which they relate—the previous two blessings were closely associated with hand-washing, for instance—and emphasize its prominence in Jewish life.

The juxtaposition of excretion and thought results from more than the time of day, however, since bodily functions cannot be resisted any more than Jews can renounce or, indeed, complete study. In addition, Torah can be viewed as a key to understanding the self and the human condition outlined in the previous blessing. Like the body, Torah is multi-layered and fully known only to God, for it possesses, as an early rabbinic text says, 'seventy faces'.[90] Indeed, the 'Oral Torah', the interpretation of the pentateuchal 'Written Torah', is only partly available in the form of rabbinic literature, the remainder having to be recovered anew by each act of study, eventually enabling one to piece together a comprehensive picture by the use of layers of commentaries. Jacob Emden associates the first of these blessings with the Oral Torah in particular, implicitly acknowledging its inexhaustible quality. (Each, as seen above, has been understood as relating to a different genre of Jewish literature, although there is no unanimity about the correlation of blessings and genres.) This recognition of the difficulty of the central rabbinic enterprise gave rise to the early mystical idea that knowledge of Torah can be acquired, not through rabbinic debate, but only magically through a 'single act of knowledge . . . occurring all at once'. In this way the 'mystic . . . becomes lord of . . . the entire fulness of the Torah in all its details . . . a goal

[90] *Num. Rabbah* 13: 15.

which Rabbinic Judaism only expected of the messianic period'.[91] It is unsurprising that the goal of perfect study is depicted in the liturgy as almost unattainable.

Torah conventionally encompasses not merely a specific literature, moreover, but all knowledge, so this blessing also alludes to the difficulty of gaining complete access to an understanding of the world. All three blessings reflect this in their conceptual gaps, echoing the stammering in Extract 17, lines 2–3. If each version approximates to the ultimate blessing, the perfect text eludes the speaker, implying that language, although the medium of the covenant with God, is a blunt instrument for representing reality.

The physicality of the previous blessing and the spirituality of the present one therefore represent the difficulty of understanding the spheres either of body or of mind respectively. Both challenges seem to exceed the speaker's abilities, although Jews are enjoined here to ignore the barriers to comprehending Torah and to persist against all odds.

That the term *torah* ('teaching', 'instruction', 'direction') is wider than translations such as 'law' or 'study' is clear from the midrashic view that it served as God's 'plan' in creating the world.[92] Rabbinic writers saw in this a link between study, teaching, and procreation, viewing study as a form of reproduction and students as offspring.[93] The partnership between God and Israel in giving and receiving Torah is so important for the world that, according to one midrashic view, had the Israelites not accepted the Torah, creation would have reverted to chaos.[94] Studying Torah is therefore not an abstract, unworldly process, but essential to the reality of the day ahead, making the student a partner in maintaining creation and an imitator of God's attribute of mercy.[95] Study meets worship in the mystical idea that Torah consists of 'names' of God, blurring the frontiers between study and liturgical citations.[96]

The three blessings are far from uniform in their view of study. The opening formula of the first one (Extract 18, lines 1–2) asserts that Jews are 'sanctified', or better 'reserved'—in the sense of 'drawn closer [to God]'—by the command to 'engage . . . in Torah matters'. The fact that the clause translated 'Torah matters' means literally 'words of Torah' recalls the anxiety aroused by the awareness of the impossibility of taking an all-encompassing God's-eye view of Torah, or of understanding the working of the body, the subject of the previous blessing. 'Words' are problematic entities and the reference to them in this blessing is ominous.

The opacity of Torah is acknowledged by the midrashic description of how God initially pronounced all the Ten Commandments in such a way that they

---

[91] Schäfer, 'Gershom Scholem Reconsidered', 14–16.

[92] *Midrash tanḥuma* (Buber), 'Bereshit' 5, fo. 2*b*.   [93] BT *San.* 19*b*.

[94] BT *AZ* 3*a*.   [95] *Sifrei*, Deut. 48, pp. 84–5 on Deut. 11: 22.

[96] Zohar ii. 87*a* ('Yitro'), and Nahmanides' introduction to the Pentateuch.

were aurally superimposed, and then had to repeat them individually so that they could be understood.[97] This scene probably derives from the two different scriptural versions of the commandment concerning the sabbath in the Decalogue, which a sabbath-eve hymn of the Lurianic school compares in complexity to the challenge of unifying God's name.[98]

Another ambiguity derives from the previous Hebrew term, the word *la'asok*, translated here as 'engage . . . in'. Baer recognizes that it may be spelled either with a letter *samekh* or with a *sin* as it is here, and opts for the latter because he believes it to be biblically more correct. He argues for this, however, on the basis of the single scriptural appearance of the word in this form, which is derived from the description of the dispute between the herdsmen of Jacob and of Gerar. There, however, it means not to 'engage in', but to 'fight' or 'struggle with'.[99] The spelling with *samekh*, which appears in many other editions of the liturgy and would indeed mean 'to engage with' or 'to be occupied with', is rejected by Baer in favour of a spelling which implies this other meaning.[100] Baer would have been aware of the connotations of 'tussling with Torah' that emerge from the biblical spelling but was clearly ambivalent about them, since he both minimized them in his commentary and emphasized them by his choice of spelling, exemplifying the multi-layered nature of liturgical meaning.

The idea of conflict is enacted not only in Baer's mind, however, but in the very texture of the liturgy, since by including all three blessings the liturgical editors demand that each voice be heard and that the speaker engage in the resulting 'tussle'.[101] Such reverence for divergence is assumed in a midrash describing how the divergent views of teachers disagreeing in public are all equally words of Torah,[102] an assertion based on the fundamental rabbinic principle that study is endless and constantly fruitful.[103]

[97] See *Mekhilta derabi shimon bar yoḥai*, 'Yitro' 20: 1, 8, pp. 103, 107; Rashi and Hizekuni (Hezekiah ben Manoah) on Exod. 20: 1; and summaries in Kasher (ed.), *Torah shelemah*, xvi. 221–5, and Ginzberg, *Legends*, vi. 45 n. 243. The people wanted to hear God's voice, but found it unbearable, whereupon Moses offered to pass the commandments on; Ginzberg, *Legends*, iii. 94–8, vi. 38–40 nn. 209–16.

[98] Exod. 20: 8 and Deut. 5: 12, quoted in the sabbath hymn Lekhah Dodi by Solomon Alkabets.

[99] Gen. 26: 20. Rashi glosses the word with another meaning, 'objection' (in the sense of 'protest') or 'appeal against': see Ben Yehuda, *Dictionary*, ix. 4739–41, and Jastrow, *Dictionary*, 1122; although Joel Sirkis (Baḥ), in his remarks on *Tur*, 'Oraḥ ḥayim' 47: 1, and David ben Samuel Halevi (Taz, 1586–1667), *Magen david* on *Shulḥan arukh*, 'Oraḥ ḥayim' 47: 1, define it as 'labour' and 'struggle [to master]' material that resists comprehension; see *Tselota di'avraham*, i. 9–10 (in commentary 'Vaya'as avraham').

[100] Ben Yehuda, *Dictionary*, ix. 4609–13, compared to p. 4776; Jastrow, *Dictionary*, 1098–9, compared to p. 1126; Mishnah *Avot* 3: 3.

[101] The expression 'disputes [literally 'wars'] about Torah', BT *Meg.* 15*b*, and that translated by Jastrow, *Dictionary*, 552, s.v. *teri* (especially BT *Sot.* 7*b*) as 'take up and throw back (a ball, etc.)' refer to the vigour of debate over the Torah (Raphael Loewe, pers. comm.). The latter image appears in *Pesikta rabati* 3: 2.   [102] *Pesikta rabati* 3: 2.

[103] An idea explored, for instance, in BT *Eruv.* 53*a*–55*a*.

The early-morning setting of this blessing suggests that the idea of struggle might also be related to Jacob's night-time fight with an angel. His name was changed to 'Israel' when the fight ended 'at the breaking of the day', making him the earliest precursor, or prototype, of the liturgical speaker.[104] The new name, *yisra'el*, itself echoes the theme of struggle, as the verse goes on to explain with a pun: 'you have struggled [*sarita*] with God and men and have prevailed'. The image of the outsider who nonetheless gains admittance has already been encountered several times, since the speaker has moved from the outsider status of Darius in the opening statement of the day and from that of Balaam in Extract 12, line 1, suggesting a similar movement here. This text suggests that the transition towards engagement with Torah may involve danger of the kind faced that night by Jacob, the multi-layering of meaning representing the texture both of study and of human life.

Equally implicit in the idea of struggle is the midrashic notion that Torah, beyond its transcendent complexity, is withheld by God from full human comprehension in order to prevent interference in the working of the world: 'The sections of Scripture are not arranged in their proper order, since if they were . . . and any man so read them, he would be able to resurrect the dead and perform other miracles. For this reason the proper order of the sections of Scripture is hidden from mortals and known only to the Holy One, blessed be he.'[105] The struggle is an existential one, touching on transgression and ensuring the continuation of exile almost as much as helping to end it.

The second blessing in the sequence (lines 3–7) seems to complete the previous text in a formal sense, both because its talmudic author is said to have 'concluded' the first one in this way[106] and because it lacks the introductory blessing formula, suggesting that it was not designed to stand alone. Their common origin is also suggested by the way both refer to the 'words of the Torah', but this second text adjusts the perspective outlined in the first, for the words now seem less accessible than they were previously. Although study seems to be taking place in the here and now, because Torah is said to be 'in our mouths', the speaker asks for it to be made palatable, reflecting either reluctance or the inability to 'taste' it. The speaker turns to God to ensure that study is accomplished, as though this could not be achieved alone, an idea confirmed by the request for each generation to be made 'knowledgeable of [or, better, 'intimate with'] thy name'. The 'seal' of the blessing accordingly praises God as the teacher of Torah, the participle without time reference renouncing the speaker's autonomous ability to relate to revelation. In this respect the second blessing modifies the position taken in the first: while that blessing looks forward to tussling with Torah, here the student is as much subject to God's control as was the speaker's body in the previous text.

---

[104] Gen. 32: 25–32.   [105] *Midrash Psalms* 3: 2; discussed in Urbach, *Sages*, 312.
[106] See BT *Ber.* 46*a* and Tosafot, *infra*; but cf. Maimonides, *Mishneh Torah: The Book of Adoration*, 'On Prayer' 7: 10, fo. 106*a*, which regards them as three.

The first and second blessings are also linked by the idea that 'study' is equated to 'knowing' God, the verb implying a sexual degree of intimacy.[107] Torah, as God's 'name', roughly equivalent to his 'character', is the closest humans can come to experiencing the divine, so is defined here in more personal terms than as a pre-creational plan for making heaven and earth.[108] Similar intimacy emerges from the reference to future generations as *tse'etsa'einu*, 'our issue', or more literally 'those who emerge [from] our [loins]', replacing the conventional term 'children' with a description of the process of birth. Here the speaker takes the role of progenitor, a sexual being whose physical experience is linked to that of the collectivity. Notably, this is the first reference to the group since the beginning of the morning service marked by Adon Olam, a feature suggesting the formative role of study.

The emphasis on 'issue' recalls the instruction in the credal Shema to discuss Torah with one's children, although students are also rabbinically regarded as 'children'.[109] The fact that the human body is employed as a metaphor for the world (and for the Temple) in rabbinic texts links study with creation in general.[110] But sexual implications emerge from the first word, *ha'arev*, 'make pleasant' (line 3), aligning the delights of intellectual or spiritual and of sexual intimacy.[111]

The opening verb, 'make pleasant', might refer not to the experience of the speaker, however, but to God's, much as Malachi requested that God 'approve' (*ve'arevah*) the offerings of his people, or find them pleasant, a verse cited in Extract 36, lines 3–4.[112] Such a reading would confirm that God may regard study, however imperfect, as an attempt to engage with the sacred narrative, one of whose terms is that the abandonment of Torah is tantamount to exile. This activity may therefore be able to transform the speaker's fortunes.

The idea that this blessing records a movement of transformation is suggested by the distinction in the opening lines between '*our* mouths' and those of God's people, Israel, in lines 3–4, and between 'us and our issue' and that of Israel in lines 4–5. The duplicated distinction between 'us' and 'Israel' and the later word *kulanu*, literally 'all of us', in line 5 (although it is translated here as 'may all be'), record the speaker's arrival at a collective identity. The combination of 'us' and 'Israel' is confirmed in the 'seal', in which God is praised for teaching Torah to Israel as a whole. The shift of subject that takes place in this paragraph, from belonging to study, leaves it uncertain, however, whether the collectivity now

---

[107] As in prophetic imagery such as that used in association with *tefilin*; see Extract 9.

[108] Ps. 1: 2. This intimacy is glimpsed in the psalm's reference first to 'God's Torah' and then to '*his* Torah', this being understood by Rashi as referring to the 'happy man' of the opening words of the psalm, who achieves closeness to God by means of study.

[109] See Rashi on Num. 3: 1.   [110] Such as *Midrash tanḥuma* (Warsaw edn.), 'Pekudei' 3.

[111] Rashi associates this verb with sexual experience in his gloss on Prov. 20: 17.

[112] Mal. 3: 4.

studies or whether the first-person speaker has been absorbed into a group in need of teaching.

The third and last blessing in this series (lines 7–9) is not linked to either of the preceding blessings, since it refers neither to the idea of strife, as in the first blessing, nor to intimacy like the second, but focuses on election and revelation. It also concludes with a statement, expressed in the timeless participle, that God 'gives' the Torah—or is the 'giver' of Torah—suggesting a continuous process of apparently successful revelation. It thus forms a climax to the previous blessings, tentatively reaching towards study and, via closeness to Torah, to the renewal of Jewish identity. But since it is a talmudic text, and therefore part of the Oral Torah, this blessing itself has the status of revelation, which the speaker has already accepted the challenge to study, even though it has not been made clear whether the previous petition for help has been answered. If this is a study-text, which in part it may be, it would blur the distinction between these blessings which purport to introduce study and the ostensible study-texts which follow.

Unlike the previous blessing, the seal here does not specify to whom the Torah has been given, or whether it has been accepted.[113] Jews are not specified at all, although 'we' are said to have been chosen to receive Torah. Other rabbinic texts suggest that Torah is available to all,[114] however, and state that a learned non-Jew is as worthy as a High Priest.[115] While this may be true of the universally applicable Noahide laws (*sheva mitsvot shel benei no'ah*), roughly equivalent to the contemporary concept of 'natural law', the universality of the whole Torah implied by this attitude would leave the speaker poised between Jewish and universal status. This would incidentally reduce the dangers of covenantal status identified in the context of *tefilin*, but would leave the identity of the 'we' in line 8 unclear. This and the allusion to God's people reinforce the view that the speaker is to be identified with Israel, mentioned in the last line of the previous blessing, and would suggest that the blessings need to be read together to be understood, exemplifying the 'tussle' mentioned earlier. The speaker thus appears here to engage in Torah as a Jew, rather than an outsider.

The third blessing has been selected for recital by people called to participate in the cyclic reading of the Torah in synagogue, perhaps because it does not allude to the problematic features of study and therefore seems to be a hopeful prelude to it. Nevertheless, this discussion has highlighted the debate and friction at the heart of Jewish responses to Torah.

EXTRACT 19. **The Priestly Blessing**

The talmudic text from which the previous blessings are drawn identifies a number of genres from which selections should be studied, without specifying which

---

[113] E. Munk, *World of Prayer*, i. 48, quoting Emden, from an unidentified source.
[114] *Yalkut shimoni*, 275, on Exod. 19: 2.   [115] *Sifra* 13: 12 on Lev. 18: 5.

readings would be suitable. Extracts of Torah, Mishnah, and Talmud, inserted at this point to ensure that study is performed without delay (since failing to fulfil the action related to a blessing is regarded in rabbinic thought as transgressing the prohibition in the Decalogue against taking God's name in vain), are mentioned only in a different, post-talmudic source, however, making this reading into an attempt to complete an action recommended by a talmudic text which is silent on how it is to be implemented.[116] Equally disorienting is the fact that the study-blessings and portions precede the *talit* and *tefilin* in the talmudic source, so the themes of the ritual garments still need to be held in reserve here, until they can be brought into play. These texts focus on the possibility of study and on exile from a promised land, preparing the way for the ritual garments.

The idea that all these genres need to be studied is reflected in a midrashic reinterpretation of the biblical word *veshinantam*, 'and you shall repeat them [to your children]', appearing in the prooftext for Torah study included in the Shema. That word is replaced by *veshilashtem*, 'and you shall divide [your study] into three', suggesting its division into genres,[117] an unremarkable style of argument in rabbinic writing but surprising in the present context, which would seem to call for literal accuracy rather than wordplay. Its application here suggests an awareness that study involves a degree of distortion, perhaps because the genres themselves throw different light on the meanings of Torah. The passages themselves, moreover, are multivalent and complex.

The first study-text included here—the threefold priestly blessing—is pentateuchal,[118] and was chosen not only because the preceding blessing suggests the benefits of study, but because this text is a model of divinely ordained prayer. The surrounding verses, included in the Sephardi rite, instruct priests to employ these words on Israel's behalf,[119] which they did at the consecration of the desert Tabernacle. The text's association with the inauguration of centralized Israelite worship[120] equates the beginning of synagogue worship with the building of the Tabernacle. It also relates the speaker to the priesthood—an idea encountered in the *tefilin* texts, though there to Israel's disadvantage. In the biblical scene that follows the dedication of the Tabernacle the twelve tribes bring offerings that might be equated to the rest of the liturgy,[121] although in the later Temple priests recited this blessing in conjunction with the daily sacrifice (the *tamid*), again aligning the liturgy with the Temple ritual. For Sephardi rabbis these correspondences seemed so close that they feared that by reciting the priestly blessing they might be transgressing the interdiction against reproducing the Temple cult before its messianic restoration. As a result they flanked it with the adjacent verses (22–3 and 27) which, by including contextual material extraneous to the

---

[116] Alternative groups of texts recommended for inclusion here are identified in Tosafot on BT *Ber.* 11*b* and on BT *Kid.* 30*a*, both of which listings survive in the liturgy. The first is here and the second in Extracts 34–40.   [117] BT *Kid.* 30*a*.   [118] Num. 6: 24–6.
[119] Num. 6: 23, 27.   [120] Lev. 9: 22.   [121] Num. 7.

°*May God bless thee and protect thee; May God cause his*	*Nu.* 6,[24-6]
presence° to enlighten thee and may he favour thee; May	*Md. Nu.* 11,[9/13]
God direct his presence towards thee and lay for thee	*TT La.* 3,[33]
peace!'	*Msh. Uk. ult.*

19. The priestly blessing (Birkat Kohanim)

blessing itself, transformed it from what could be seen as a ritual enactment into a study portion. Given that it follows the three introductory blessings, this is its principal function here in any case.[122]

The meaning of the blessing itself has attracted less attention than the fact that it culminates in the word 'peace'.[123] Its sixty letters were thought to symbolize the sixty tractates of the Talmud (now redivided into sixty-three), or the warriors posted protectively around the bed of Solomon,[124] while the words in each clause were read as the three, five, and seven sections into which Torah readings are divided on weekdays, festivals, and sabbaths respectively. Such numerical readings tend to make the meaning of the words marginal or even immaterial, minimizing their wider associations which, as can be seen, relate to historical and everyday life. Less metaphorically, the three verses were taken to refer to material benefits, the illumination of Torah, and the benefits to be obtained through study, a relevant reading in the context of a study sequence.[125]

EXTRACT 20. A Rabbinic Study-Text

The second text seems more suited to study but discusses problems that make study nearly impossible, helping to explain how the exile came about. Using the usual rabbinic term 'teaching Torah' for study locates its purpose more in interaction than in intellectual processes, glancing back at the idea of 'struggle'.

The Mishnah is the source of its opening words, suggesting that this is a sequel to the preceding pentateuchal text. However, the paragraph goes on to include talmudic material, implying that this passage might constitute not the second, but the second and third elements in an anthology of three Torah genres.[126] Since the talmudic texts quoted are both *baraitot* (texts in mishnaic Hebrew embedded in the Talmud) they can easily be mistaken for Mishnah,

---

[122] *Tselota di'avraham*, i. 14 (in commentary 'Vaya'as avraham').

[123] Elliot Dorff has argued that the first line refers to general favour, the second to times of God's favour, and the third to those of disfavour; see *My People's Prayer Book*, v. 129-30.

[124] *Sidur avodat yisra'el*, 38, 575.

[125] Schwab, *Rav Schwab on Prayer*, 81, based on *Num. Rabbah* 11: 5.

[126] Mishnah *Pe'ah* 1: 1; BT *Shab.* 127a (which includes two listings); BT *Kid.* 39b. A breakdown is provided in Berliner, *Randbermerkungen*, i. 18.

יְבָרֶכְךָ יְיָ וְיִשְׁמְרֶךָ: יָאֵר יְיָ פָּנָיו אֵלֶיךָ וִיחֻנֶּךָּ: יִשָּׂא יְיָ פָּנָיו 1

אֵלֶיךָ וְיָשֵׂם לְךָ שָׁלוֹם: 2

however, and even their number has been disguised by their rearrangement into continuous prose, removing repetitions or gaps. This echoes the ambiguity about the number of blessings that preceded the study-texts: here the ambivalence extends to the integrity of the texts being studied. The multiple departures from Torah produced by the editorial intervention that unified the component texts are all the more paradoxical in that each constituent passage originally culminated in a declaration of the primacy of study.[127] As a result, although the present passage seems designed both to describe and to enact study, it actually subverts it.

The opening mishnaic text, listing activities said to have 'no limit', may be symbolically aligned with the preoccupation with 'limits' in the blessing after excretion and with Jewish election in the blessings introducing study. It also recalls the uncertainty as to whether the pentateuchal passage above was spoken by priests in the Temple or by the liturgical speaker and, since pentateuchal terms appear here too, about the boundaries between rabbinic and biblical study. Particularly problematic is the fact that, although the activities listed here are not said scripturally to be limited in any way, later rabbinic writers insist, for instance, that acts of charity should not impoverish the donor.[128] If so, perhaps study is limited too, suggesting the difficulty of reconciling Written and Oral Torah.

This problem is deepened by the silent conflation of two different talmudic inventories of deeds for which one is said to enjoy the 'interest' (literally 'eat the fruits') in this world, reserving the 'capital' for the next; the metaphorical 'eating' echoing the reference to taste in the second blessing preceding Torah study (Extract 18, lines 3–7). Most of the list is derived from the talmudic tractate *Shabat*, but two of its clauses have been omitted, even though, given the context, this act of study should be flawless. The missing clauses are those advising one to raise one's children to study Torah with diligence and to judge one's neighbours favourably. It has been suggested that these could be left out since they duplicate the general instructions to study and to perform 'acts of kindness'. However, if this were a criterion, other clauses might similarly have been removed, raising the possibility that these terms were omitted for other reasons. Indeed, teaching

[127] BT *Kid.* 40b.
[128] *Sidur avodat yisra'el*, 38; Obadiah of Bertinoro's comment on Mishnah *Pe'ah* 1: 1.

°'The following matters have no fixed limit: the Residual field-corner,	*Msh. Pe.* 1,[1]
first-fruit offerings, pilgrimage-offerings, practising kindnesses	*B'Kd.* 39:
and the study of *Torah*. °For the following does a man enjoy	*B'Sb.* 127
increments in this world, °whilst the principal is laid up for him in	*Av. RN* 1,[4]
the world to come, namely: °honouring father and mother,	*Dt.* 5,[16]
practising kindnesses, early attendance in the *Beth Hamedrash* morning	*Ku.* 3,[19]
and evening, hospitality to wayfarers, °visiting the sick, dowering	*B'Sb.* 127
a bride, attending the dead, devotion in prayer, also, °making peace	*Md. Nu.* 11 *ult.*
between a man and his fellow; but °the study of *Torah* is equal to	*Js.* 1,[8]
all of them.'	*Msh. Av.* 6,[1]

20. A rabbinic study-text (*Elu devarim she'ein lahem shiur*)

Torah is rendered almost impossible precisely by the ambiguities enacted in this passage, while the need for kindness is qualified by the need to defend oneself in the outside world, a dominant theme in Extract 25.

In addition, two other clauses, introduced from a different source, recommend the promotion of marriage and providing funerals,[129] both of them selfless acts to be performed either anonymously or without expectation of thanks. Brides, it is assumed, may not be embarrassed for their poverty and the dead cannot express gratitude. These may have been added here since they relate to events at opposite ends of the life-cycle—the formation of new couples and death—and glance at the wider timescale suggested by the liturgical treatment of daybreak as a new creation. Yet parallel talmudic texts contradict these statements, arguing that study, far from taking precedence over a funeral, should be suspended to enable one to follow a cortege,[130] while another passage advises that it should stop both for a funeral and for a bride,[131] demonstrating that study does not invariably take precedence as this paragraph seems to argue.

A secondary implication of this paragraph, in view of its juxtaposition with the priestly blessing, is that Torah study is superior to the Temple cult. The fall of the Temple generated such concern as to how the divinely commanded sacrificial cult could be maintained that one talmudic rabbi argued that study is greater than sacrifice, which might be one of the implications of the association between the number of talmudic tractates and of letters in the blessing.[132]

This passage thus carries the liturgical speaker into a labyrinth of citation, silently flouting accuracy and distorting the very act of study that the paragraph should exemplify. In addition, it qualifies the liturgy itself by implying that

---

[129] BT *Suk.* 49*b*.   [130] BT *Meg.* 3*b*.

[131] BT *Ket.* 17*a*, quoted in *Tselota di'avraham*, i. 15 (in commentary 'Emek berakhah').

[132] BT *Shab.* 30*a*; BT *Men.* 110*a*.

אֵלּוּ דְבָרִים שֶׁאֵין לָהֶם שִׁעוּר הַפֵּאָה וְהַבִּכּוּרִים 1

וְהָרֵאָיוֹן וּגְמִילוּת חֲסָדִים וְתַלְמוּד תּוֹרָה: אֵלּוּ דְבָרִים 2

שֶׁאָדָם אוֹכֵל פֵּרוֹתֵיהֶם בָּעוֹלָם הַזֶּה וְהַקֶּרֶן קַיֶּמֶת לָעוֹלָם 3

הַבָּא: וְאֵלּוּ הֵן כִּבּוּד אָב וָאֵם וּגְמִילוּת חֲסָדִים וְהַשְׁכָּמַת 4

בֵּית הַמִּדְרָשׁ שַׁחֲרִית וְעַרְבִית וְהַכְנָסַת אוֹרְחִים וּבִקּוּר 5

חוֹלִים וְהַכְנָסַת כַּלָּה וּלְוָיַת הַמֵּת וְעִיּוּן תְּפִלָּה וַהֲבָאַת 6

שָׁלוֹם בֵּין אָדָם לַחֲבֵרוֹ וְתַלְמוּד תּוֹרָה כְּנֶגֶד כֻּלָּם: 7

study is superior, although it is unclear into which category—prayer or study—the preceding blessings over Torah study and the priestly blessing might fall. Our translation states that study is 'equal to all of them' (rather than 'greater', as in other editions), implying a common foundation, but this ambiguity itself subverts the 'study' this exemplifies. Another uncertainty, mentioned previously, is the meaning of the term *iyun tefilah*, translated here as 'devotion in prayer' (line 6), which is here presented as a virtue, but which in another context is criticized as the practice of speculating on the efficacy of prayer or even thinking about the meaning of its words.[133] This suggests that prayer is compromised no less than study here, condemning both to silence.

Such a view is confirmed by a midrash that praises early-morning study, but adds that since it is prone to be inaccurate it should be performed only in private.[134] This implicitly accepts the inevitability of inaccuracy and therefore also the exile attributed to it in the context of the *talit* and *tefilin*, which are to be included in the liturgy only later. Another mishnaic text warns that errors in teaching can lead to 'death', a fear implicit in the opening statement of the day.[135]

Perhaps in order to indicate a way out of this impasse, the editors included five items in the mishnaic list and another ten in the composite talmudic one, making a total of fifteen, the numerical value of the first two letters of the Tetragrammaton, the name of God associated with the attribute of mercy. This alone can offer hope at this point in the liturgy.

---

[133] BT *BB* 164*b*, discussed in Montefiore and Loewe (eds.), *Rabbinic Anthology*, 407–8, and Reif, *Judaism and Hebrew Prayer*, 112–13, 359–60 nn. 59–63.

[134] Implied in *Tana debei eliyahu*, ch. 2, p. 12, trans. Braude and Kapstein, pp. 23–4.

[135] Mishnah *Avot* 1: 11.

CHAPTER SEVEN

※

Building in Babel

'let us build a city and a tower'
GENESIS II: 4

THIS CHAPTER examines a new attempt to begin the day, previous efforts having become embroiled in apparently insoluble problems. It includes a talmudic waking sequence and ends with a theologically compromising examination of the dangers ahead. These can be attributed in the real world to human hostility, but liturgical texts implicate God in permitting them to arise.

EXTRACT 21. A Talmudic Waking Prayer

The context makes this talmudic text acutely ambiguous.[1] Is it the third element in a study anthology encompassing the three main genres of Torah—Scripture, Mishnah, and Talmud—assuming the previous text to have been mainly mishnaic? Or does it begin the day anew, leaving the anthology behind, a view based on the fact that the previous text contained both mishnaic and talmudic material? Indeed, neither study nor prayer has emerged unscathed from the analysis of the previous sections of the liturgy. The possibility of effective prayer has been challenged from the start of the liturgical day, leading the speaker to turn to study as a medium for intervening in the working of the world. Study was likewise found to contain the seeds of its own failure, due to the virtual impossibility of acquiring a God's-eye view of Torah, as was demonstrated by Extract 20, which subverted textual accuracy when it was most needed.

This prayer—if we regard it as such—would form a stronger opening to the liturgical day than anything seen so far, and is the classic waking prayer cited in the Talmud and by Maimonides,[2] appearing in Sephardi liturgies as the first statement of the day.[3] However, as a talmudic passage it could be regarded as a continuation of the study sequence begun above, offering a route to salvation by renewing the proximity to God that was lost in sleep, and serving as a corrective to the preceding passage. While that paragraph consisted of a confection of mishnaic and talmudic fragments, this one is purely talmudic and substantially intact. Nevertheless, that textual mosaic's departure from the sources cannot be

---

[1] BT *Ber.* 60b

[2] Maimonides, *Mishneh Torah: The Book of Adoration*, 'On Prayer' 7: 3, fo. 105a.

[3] *Book of Prayer: Daily and Occasional Prayers*, 2.

unmade, subverting this one as study, while the relevance of the text to the here and now increases its prayerful quality.

This uncertainty ensures that the speaker is engaged in a still higher order of analysis than that demanded by the two previous texts following the blessings over Torah study. The speaker must again construct meaning in a quasi-authorial way, spanning the roles of worshipper and student and looking beneath the superficial meaning of the words. Combining the anthological form with prayer may therefore point to the possibility of understanding, but it also places complete clarity beyond reach. The speaker is now both an actor in and a spectator of the text's ambiguity.

The ambivalence is increased by the previous paragraph's preference for study over prayer. The present text counters this by demonstrating how study can be identical to prayer in real life, although its prayer-like character is weakened by the way in which it duplicates the opening statement of the day (Extract 1), the repetition suggesting that these words are being studied rather than spoken with inner intention. That first passage, it will be recalled, was introduced in about the sixteenth century only because the present one, which contains the name of God, could not be recited before the hands had been washed. The demotion of this prayer from the opening moment of the day reinforces its study function, although commentators note that it was included here only for those unable to recite it for themselves as a home prayer. The fact that it follows the blessings over Torah study, however, ensures that its status is richly indeterminate.

The passage still retains the freshness of its original role, nevertheless, and contributes new layers to speculation about sleep, waking, and the nature of the soul. It implicitly describes waking from sleep as a minor resurrection or even final redemption, linking the personal to the historic timescale. A similar ambiguity can be seen in the second paragraph of the Shema, included in the *tefilin*, which says that Jews will 'vanish from the land' if they depart from God, but does not explain whether 'land' refers to a national territory or the earth in general.[4]

The passage covers comparable ground to the opening statement of the day by describing the uncertain relationship of the speaker to the soul (translated here as 'breath-soul' to reflect its creational associations), which has been returned to the body after sleep.[5] The lack of clarity about the ownership of the soul is re-enacted in the very texture of the writing, for the term *modeh* (line 5, second

---

[4] The ambiguity is accentuated in the scriptural sequel to the first paragraph of the Shema, excluded from the liturgy in favour of the similar text chosen as the second paragraph, which refers to total destruction: Deut. 6: 15.

[5] The translation 'breath-soul' is an attempt to distinguish the present term, *neshamah*, from *ruaḥ*, translated as 'spirit', and *nefesh*, 'soul'. In kabbalistic thought these three words denote, in descending order, the highest (human), the intermediate, and the lowest (animal) aspects of the spirit. See E. Munk, *World of Prayer*, i. 22.

°O my Lord, the breath-soul which thou hast set within	*B'Br.* 60:
me (it) is pure; thou didst create it, thou didst fashion it,	*SA-OH* 6,³; 46,¹
thou hast breathed it into me and thou dost °preserve it within	*B'Ni.* 30:
me; °yea, in time to come, thou wilt take it from me, °to	*Ec.* 12,⁷
restore it unto me again in the future hereafter; °so long as the	*B'Sn.* 91:
breath-soul is within me, I will acknowledge before thy	*Jb.* 27,³
presence, God my Lord and °Lord of mine ancestors, overlord	*Ex.* 15,²
of all works, master of all souls—°blest art thou, God, °who	*Ku.* 1,⁹⁵,¹¹⁵; 5,²⁰⁽⁴⁾
restores souls unto dead bodies!	*Zo. Gn.* 81

21. A talmudic waking prayer (*Elohai neshamah shenatata bi*)

word), translated as 'acknowledgement' but capable of meaning 'thanks', suggests that God restores souls partly as an act of kindness and partly out of contractual obligation. The opening word of the present paragraph refers to God by the name that suggests divine justice, as distinct from mercy, bending the meaning towards 'acknowledgement'.

Following this opening word the speaker addresses God six times in the second person, as though he is listening to the speaker, but the relationship becomes more formal in line 5 with the word 'acknowledgement' and other more remote forms of address before the 'seal' in line 6. Equally impersonal are the creational associations of the two verbs for 'making' in the opening lines: *beratah*, 'you created it', and *yetsartah*, 'you fashioned it' (line 2). These were used earlier to describe the higher and lower forms of creation in the blessing after excretion (Extract 17, lines 1–2), and will recur in the first statutory blessing of the day (a passage beyond the scope of this book) dealing with daily re-creation. Both the first verb for 'creation' and that describing how God breathes the soul into the speaker (line 2) appear in the Creation narrative, clearly linking waking to daily re-creation. The verb for 'keeping' (lines 2–3) suggests that God is only 'guarding' the soul in the body temporarily, sustaining the ambiguity noted earlier about the ownership of the soul as it is transferred to and from the body of the liturgical speaker. The balance is currently in favour of God's ownership, especially as the repetition of the second person singular pronoun with each action emphasizes equally the power of God and the silent helplessness of the speaker, underlining the overlap between sleep and death.[6]

An increasing intimacy with God is implied, however, by the use of divine names. In the first line and the clause immediately before the 'seal' God is the 'Lord' both of the speaker and his ancestors (the idea of family continuity being

---

[6] This is made explicit in the translation in *Book of Prayer: Daily and Occasional Prayers*, 2.

אֱלֹהַי נְשָׁמָה שֶׁנָּתַתָּ בִּי טְהוֹרָה (הִיא) אַתָּה 1

בְּרָאתָהּ אַתָּה יְצַרְתָּהּ אַתָּה נְפַחְתָּהּ בִּי וְאַתָּה 2

מְשַׁמְּרָהּ בְּקִרְבִּי וְאַתָּה עָתִיד לִטְּלָהּ מִמֶּנִּי 3

וּלְהַחֲזִירָהּ בִּי לֶעָתִיד לָבֹא: כָּל זְמַן שֶׁהַנְּשָׁמָה 4

בְּקִרְבִּי מוֹדֶה אֲנִי לְפָנֶיךָ יְיָ אֱלֹהַי וֵאלֹהֵי אֲבוֹתַי 5

רִבּוֹן כָּל הַמַּעֲשִׂים אֲדוֹן כָּל הַנְּשָׁמוֹת בָּרוּךְ 6

אַתָּה יְיָ הַמַּחֲזִיר נְשָׁמוֹת לִפְגָרִים מֵתִים: 7

another form of survival), using the name suggesting strict justice (line 5). He is then addressed as *ribon*, 'overlord', with connotations of absolute control, and finally as *adon*, 'master', associated with the Tetragrammaton of mercy (line 6), although without the personal suffix implying the speaker's voice.[7] This suggests a progression towards greater intimacy, confirmed by the way the closing 'seal' includes only the full name denoting mercy, suggesting the transition is completed (line 7). A similar movement can be seen in the biblical narrative of Creation and was identified earlier in Adon Olam (Extract 15).

The soul undergoes a more complex development, however, for in the first line it is an indefinite 'soul' without a definite article, while in line 4 it is identified by its definite article as the specific soul within the speaker, and the last word before the 'seal' implies that God is the protective guarantor of 'souls' in general, including that of the speaker, thereby reducing the latter's specificity. In the seal itself the word 'soul' appears for the first time both in the plural and without an article, suggesting a reduction of God's individual attention, paradoxically at the point when the attribute of mercy is given greatest prominence.

In this 'seal' God 'restores souls' (a process referred to earlier in line 4, in connection with resurrection) to 'dead bodies', of which the speaker is one, foregrounding the awareness of vulnerability. This highlighting of the similarity between sleep and death and between awaking and resurrection recalls that washing the hands, the first gesture on awaking, is appropriate if the speaker is a virtual corpse and therefore metaphorically a source of impurity.[8] The debate on the question of purity can also be traced in rabbinic discussions about the parenthetical variant, *hi*, in the first line of the paragraph. The term was regarded by

[7] This term is the same as the opening word of Adon Olam, and is associated with Abraham: see the discussion of Extract 15.

[8] This is an idea emerging from the data rather than a rabbinic one.

commentators as reinforcing the assertion of purity, although it does so almost imperceptibly, adding only that 'it [the soul] is [pure]'. Omitting the variant may accordingly reduce the emphasis on purity but does not remove it. Given the context, any modification in emphasis on the continuing purity of the speaker's soul will make some difference because of its presumed contact with a 'dead' body during sleep. But the issue must have seemed insoluble, since both versions remained on the page, sustaining the ambivalence of the statement. The assertion of the soul's purity was probably designed to express dissent from the Christian doctrine of the Fall,[9] but later rabbis, thinking it unlikely that the soul remained as pure as when it had first been 'breathed' by God into the body, proclaimed the word *hi* optional.[10] It is striking that in this paragraph, unlike the previous one, there seems to be some concern to respect the original talmudic source.

There are fewer underlying meanings here than in the opening statement of the day, for the passage contains only one embedded biblical text. The closing words of this text, *pegarim metim*, translated here as 'dead bodies' but literally meaning 'dead corpses', appear twice in Scripture, each time relating to the miraculous overnight destruction of Sennacherib's army in response to the prayer of King Hezekiah, one of the few Israelite kings whose prayers are recorded.[11] In both scriptural echoes, the liturgical speaker implies that survival is a night-time miracle, echoing the book of Daniel in the opening statement of the day. In this biblical source, however, the enemy is destroyed, while Daniel's lions were merely pacified; moreover, while Daniel's prayer was the source of his problems, Hezekiah's prayer is a petition for help. As in the opening statement the speaker is an outsider, in that case Darius and here, since the body of the waking speaker is itself being raised from death-like sleep, expressing the views of a fallen enemy, thus echoing the speaker's earlier citation of Balaam's foiled curse (Extract 12, line 1). Here, however, since the resurrection affects a large number of bodies, there is a possible allusion to Ezekiel's vision of the dry bones, linking waking with salvation.[12]

EXTRACT 22. The First of the Daily Blessings

This brief blessing, drawn from a talmudic source, sustains the delicate balance between worship—which is perhaps the most obvious level on which the text is to be read as the speaker engages with the here and now of waking—and study, according to which it continues the sequence of passages drawn from various

---

[9] See Petuchowski, 'Modern Misunderstandings', 47 n. 12.

[10] Purity of soul is seen as the goal of the wise in BT *Shab.* 152b, but it would be presumptuous to claim to have achieved it, according to Hayim Azulai (1724–1806; Hida), in *Kesher godel*, 5, quoted in an editorial note by Rubinstein in Maimonides, *Mishneh torah*, 'Sefer ahavah', ed. Rubinstein, iii. 68 n. 9. See also *Sidur avodat yisra'el*, 39.

[11] 2 Kgs. 19: 35; Isa. 37: 36.   [12] Ezek. 37: 1–14.

genres, introduced by the blessings over Torah.[13] A similar balance was seen in the previous text, which could likewise be seen as poised between prayer and learning. The cockerel-call that ends the night follows the previous blessing in the talmudic context and therefore presumably forms part of a continuum of waking, of which this marks a further stage. But while the first relates uniquely to inner perception, the present text displays an awareness of the outer world and employs a metaphor drawn from nature to signal a new step in the process of regaining a sense of self. The renewal of perception is here initiated by a bird (translated as 'dawn-bird' to emphasize the time of day) rather than by a human speaker. In the talmudic source this is the first of a sequence of blessings devoted to actions with which people begin the day, culminating in the *talit* and *tefilin*. In the Spanish and Portuguese liturgy the blessings, which follow the waking paragraph (Extract 21) as they do here, are almost the first of the day,[14] rather than being delayed to form part of the study sequence, after the texts associated with the speaker's passage between home and synagogue.

Blessing formulas, which enhance the everyday with the sacred narrative, were used earlier to place daily routines such as hand-washing within Jewish culture. They now continue to locate daily reality in the scriptural world, but in such an inexplicit way that the speaker must assume the role of author in order to fill the conceptual gaps between word and deed. The fact that there are fifteen blessings in the series points to the numerical value of the name of God associated with mercy, suggesting that waking goes beyond God's contractual obligation. However, his remoteness is implied by the way in which the blessing formula enacts a withdrawal from proximity, for its second-person opening shifts in the following clause to the third person, as though acknowledging the impossibility of intimacy. The withdrawal is also indicated by the way in which God is referred to first by the name associated with mercy and subsequently by that denoting judgement.

This first blessing is designed for the moment before the eyes are opened and follows directly on from the previous one, which marks the moment that consciousness is regained. However, it not only shows how the speaker's inward glance turns gradually towards an awareness of the outside world, but, in view of the previous liturgical debate on whether knowledge of Torah transcends human faculties, implies an element of envy for the cock's ability to perceive precisely when night gives way to day, suggesting its superiority over humans at least in this respect and echoing the fact that it wakes—as it was originally created —before humans. Here, in the context of a liturgical sequence in which the speaker's inability to study is regretted, mentioning the skill of the cockerel in identifying the finer shades between dark and light emphasizes another area in which human abilities fail, and indeed defines people in terms of their shortcomings.

[13] BT *Ber.* 60b.   [14] *Book of Prayer: Daily and Occasional Prayers*, 2.

°Blest art thou, God our Lord, sovereign of the universe, He	*B'Br.* 60
who °gives sense unto a dawn-bird to distinguish between	*B'Br.* 60:
day and night!	*Jb.* 38,³⁶

22. The first of the daily blessings (*Asher natan lasekhvi vinah*)

This ambiguity of the speaker's position can be seen from the scriptural source of the phrase that is often translated as 'wisdom of the cockerel'.[15] Rashi argues that the biblical word *sekhvi*, 'cockerel', indicates not animal perception but human intelligence, related to *sekhi*, 'to look out', 'hope',[16] a reading also adopted by Ibn Ezra.[17] However, in a talmudic context Rashi glosses it as a 'cockerel call', which is what it seems to mean here.[18] The ambiguity between 'human intelligence' and 'cockerel' is deepened by the fact that the dawn cockcrow is referred to mishnaically in the context of the Temple as 'the call of the *gever*', literally 'the call of the "man"',[19] which the talmudic discussion glosses as the Temple crier giving the order to clear away the ashes of the previous day's sacrifices.[20] This leaves it uncertain whether the word *sekhvi* refers to a cockerel, to human intelligence, or to the parts of humans that become aware of daybreak with the help of less-than-human senses, or even whether the Temple *gever* is a man or a cockerel.[21] The word thus glances at the limitations of human insight referred to earlier, equivocally associating them with the Temple previously encountered through the priestly blessing as a nexus of themes related to human failings.

EXTRACT 23. The Negative Blessings

The sequence of fifteen blessings of daily preparation is interrupted here by a group of three from a different talmudic context.[22] These formulas, again poised between study (since they are talmudic citations) and prayer, are the only ones in the liturgy to appear in negative form, and refer not to preparing for the day, but to existential categories.[23] Like the praise of the cockerel, they relate not to human abilities, but to deficiencies, in this case the qualities which exempt or exclude individuals from liturgical prayer or the Temple ritual. Since their

---

[15] Job 38: 36, where God challenges Job to match his wisdom and, in the next verse, refers to clouds as auguries.   [16] Jastrow, *Dictionary*, 989.

[17] A similar reading emerges from the reading of BT *Ber.* 60*b* by Asher ben Jehiel (Rosh), based on the appearance of the word in Ps. 73: 7.

[18] On BT *RH* 26*b*; Jastrow, *Dictionary*, 1571; and see *Sidur avodat yisra'el*, 40.

[19] Mishnah *Yoma* 1: 8; Mishnah *Tam.* 1: 2.   [20] BT *Yoma* 20*b*.   [21] BT *Eruv.* 100*b*.

[22] BT *Men.* 43*b*, JT *Ber.* 9:1; Tosefta *Ber.* 6: 23; and see variants noted by Eli Cashdan in the *Soncino Talmud*, *Men.* 43*b*, nn. 4 (but for 'Tosef. Ber. VII', read 'VI: 23') and 5.

[23] The Sephardi liturgy places these blessings later in the list, just before the one beginning in Extract 24, line 11, making them climactic rather than conditional.

בָּרוּךְ אַתָּה יְיָ אֱלֹהֵינוּ מֶלֶךְ הָעוֹלָם אֲשֶׁר נָתַן

לַשֶּׂכְוִי בִינָה לְהַבְחִין בֵּין יוֹם וּבֵין לָיְלָה:

1

2

talmudic context relates to idolatry—itself implicitly a failure of vision, and defined in the third paragraph of the Shema as wandering 'after your heart or after your eyes'—these formulas may be viewed as continuing the theme of perception introduced, albeit obliquely, in the previous reference to the cockerel. What is at stake here is cultural rather than natural categories, continuing the theme of the Temple, but blurring its boundaries with the home, which is where the talmudic sources assume these blessings are to be recited. Since the synagogue is occasionally referred to in rabbinic contexts as *mikdash me'at*, 'miniature sanctuary', the speaker is poised between both locations, each representing the Temple's absence.

With these blessings the waking speaker regains identity in cultural terms, no longer by exploring the boundaries between human and animal perception, but by taking stock of who the speaker is not. One commentator suggests that, once souls have been returned to bodies, the speaker's Jewishness is rediscovered and the possibility of prayer recognized, perhaps due to the association between waking and the Temple ritual.[24] Whatever the authorial intention underlying these blessings, however, their negative form has frequently been assumed to denigrate both non-Jews and women, two of the excluded categories, by aligning them with slaves, associated with Egyptian servitude.[25] The need to avoid offence in this context is reflected by the way in which talmudic writers introduced the term 'slave' only because it seemed less offensive than the earlier word *bor* ('uncultured person'),[26] which commented on people's personal qualities rather than on their legal status. In later centuries it was decided for similar reasons to emend the word *goi* (pejorative in Yiddish vernacular, but originally intended non-offensively in the sense of 'non-Jew') to the more neutral *nokhri*.[27]

Had radical contempt of these categories indeed been intended, however, they might either have been excluded altogether or more openly criticized, and one

[24] Shapira, *Metsat shimurim*, 35–6.

[25] See Tabory, 'Benedictions of Self-Identity', for a survey of some of the issues raised in this discussion. See also R. Loewe, *Position of Women in Judaism*, 43–4 nn. 33–5, and Kahn and Landes, 'On Gentiles, Slaves, and Women'. See Montefiore and Loewe (eds.), *Rabbinic Anthology*, 380, 507 n. 9 (note on pp. 656–8) and Elbogen, *Jewish Liturgy*, 78 n. 11.

[26] Ben Yehuda, *Dictionary*, i. 491; BT *Men.* 43*b*–44*a*, and Hoffman, *Canonization of the Synagogue Service*, 128–9 n. 16.

[27] See *Sidur avodat yisra'el*, 40–1, and Berliner, *Randbemerkungen*, i. 14–15.

Blest art thou, God our Lord, sovereign of the universe, °He	*SA-OH* 46,[4]
who hath not made me a °heathen!	*Ez.* 44,[7]
Blest art thou, God our Lord, sovereign of the universe, °He	*B'Mn.* 43:
who hath not made me a bondman!	*Mai. Tef.* 7,[4]
Blest art thou, God our Lord, sovereign of the universe, °He	*B'Mn.* 43:
who hath not set me the task of woman!	*Msh. Kd.* 1,[7]
Blest art thou, God our Lord, sovereign of the universe, °He who hath	*B'Kt.* 39:
made me according to his goodwill!	*Prv.* 31,[25-31]

23. The negative blessings (*Shelo asani* . . .)

might have expected them to include the term 'idolater'. The rejection of women and non-Jews was alloyed with other emotions, however, and perhaps—because of the reduction in ritual duties and consequently of the penalties for performing them wrongly—even with some of the envy implicit in the reference to the cockerel. For although non-Jews cannot participate in formal worship, they receive the same reward for fulfilling the seven Noahide laws (corresponding roughly to 'natural law') as do Jews for observing all the rituals required of them. This does constitute grounds for jealousy, at least by adult male Jews, whose duties are far greater.[28] Slaves and women are likewise exempt from certain commandments, in the case of women those expressed in positive form and needing to be performed at a particular time. The exclusion of a slave is justified by the fact that slaves have responsibilities to a master, so are not 'free' to serve God. The exemption of women is similarly based on their subjection to the authority of fathers and husbands, but the decision to extend it to all women, rather than only to dependent daughters and wives, and to define it by criteria that are difficult to apply with precision, leads in practice to the exclusion of all adult women from taking part in most public ceremonies in the Orthodox tradition. The speaker is ostensibly reciting these blessings only because he falls outside these categories, and therefore states the reason for which he is employing the liturgy. But he might well feel that there are grounds for envying those who are not obliged to do so, such are the anxieties aroused by the performance of rituals, although many women do take on the duties of prayer.[29]

The increased involvement of women in prayer must have led to their juxtaposition with slaves and non-Jews being interpreted as offensive, however, and to the introduction of the compensatory formulation in line 4.[30] It is clear that

---

[28] See *Sidur avodat yisra'el*, 41.

[29] BT *Ber.* 20*a–b* and *Midrash petirat mosheh rabenu*, in Jellinek, *Beit hamidrash*, i. 126, in which Moses asks for the people's pardon for troubling them with the commandments.

[30] Abudarham (*Abudarham hashalem*, 42) implies that this was a recent custom, and it also

בָּרוּךְ אַתָּה יְיָ אֱלֹהֵינוּ מֶלֶךְ הָעוֹלָם שֶׁלֹּא עָשַׂנִי נָכְרִי: 1

בָּרוּךְ אַתָּה יְיָ אֱלֹהֵינוּ מֶלֶךְ הָעוֹלָם שֶׁלֹּא עָשַׂנִי עָבֶד: 2

בָּרוּךְ אַתָּה יְיָ אֱלֹהֵינוּ מֶלֶךְ הָעוֹלָם שֶׁלֹּא עָשַׂנִי אִשָּׁה: 3

(Women say.)   בָּרוּךְ אַתָּה יְיָ אֱלֹהֵינוּ מֶלֶךְ הָעוֹלָם שֶׁעָשַׂנִי כִּרְצוֹנוֹ:   4

women were involved in worship when the alternative was introduced, and were sufficiently learned to understand the meaning of the prayers despite the fact that study was voluntary for them. Moreover, the retention of the version for men seemed to demand clarification even in later periods. While Jacob ben Asher's *Arba'ah turim* assumed that the Hebrew term *kirtsono*, translated 'according to his goodwill' (line 4), implies passive acceptance of an unfortunate fate, aligning a woman's fate with the way in which one might greet news of a recent death, a commentator on Joseph Caro's *Shulḥan arukh* reads this substitute for women as an indication that their fate is superior to that of men,[31] an argument perhaps based in part, although he does not say so, on the grounds for envy noted above. His observation is justified by the possibility that the term *kirtsono* usually appears in Scripture and liturgy not in the sense of passive acceptance but rather describing something 'especially acceptable'.[32] According to this reading the substitute blessing would suggest that God made women 'as he *really* wanted', an interpretation also supported in the Creation narrative. There, although Adam's superiority over the animals is indicated by his climactic position and the remark that the world was '*very* good',[33] the fact that Eve was created later suggests her superiority even to him. Samson Raphael Hirsch similarly remarked that

appears in the roughly contemporary *Arba'ah turim*, 'Oraḥ ḥayim' 46, which describes it as women's acceptance of a negative fate.

[31] David ben Samuel Halevi, *Magen david* on *Shulḥan arukh*, 'Oraḥ ḥayim' 46: 4.

[32] The word appears in Isa. 49: 8, 'an acceptable time', glossed by Rashi as a time of prayer, when Israel is close to God. In Prov. 11: 1, *retsono* (AV 'his delight') is accordingly contrasted with 'abomination'. In the seventeenth blessing of the Amidah the term is used in the sense of complete acceptance of prayer, while in the first blessing of the evening service it refers to the ordering of the stars. This association with the sources of timing may point to the independence of female body rhythms of the male time-markers of ritual and liturgy. In addition, Rabbi Meir, to whom the negative blessings are attributed in some manuscripts (see the *Soncino Talmud*, *Men.* (trans. Eli Cashdan), 264 n. 4), is presented in the rabbinic tradition as 'anything but a misogynist' (see R. Loewe, *Position of Women in Judaism*, 43–4): see BT *San.* 11a.   [33] Gen. 1: 31.

women's ceremonial obligations were fewer than men's because their gender roles made them more 'spiritual' than men and less in need of prompting to attend to sacred matters,[34] a view that happened to reflect the developing role of women in nineteenth-century European middle-class society. This view, supplemented by the partly apologetic opinion that women's functions in society are more nurturing and protective, became normative in twentieth-century Orthodox circles.[35] A radical solution, offered by Abraham Berliner, was to replace all four blessings by a single affirmative one acknowledging that God has 'made me an Israelite', a view he based on the debate by earlier commentators about the talmudic formulation proposed for women, but this was not widely accepted.[36]

Whatever the reason that the women's version was inserted, however, altering a talmudic source compounds the distortion of study-texts seen earlier and cannot have been done casually. There was even sufficient ambivalence about modifying a talmudically authorized blessing for some liturgical editors to prefer to exclude the name of God from the substitute formulation, signalling an awareness of the problems related to departing from rabbinic texts. Strikingly, however, changes were made repeatedly elsewhere without such nods to authority, as we have seen, perhaps because the implications of tampering with sources were clearer to medieval rabbis than to earlier ones.[37] As a result of this change the blessings not only interrogate the speaker's relationship to various excluded 'others', but exemplify the 'tussle with Torah' alluded to in the first Torah blessing of the morning (Extract 18, lines 1–2). Many non-Orthodox liturgies omit all these blessings or replace them with positive versions, but this involves silencing perhaps the only evidence of women's engagement in prayer to survive in the traditional liturgy, and suppressing a debate that remains relevant.

EXTRACT 24. **The Daily Blessings**

The sequence that began with the reference to cockcrow (Extract 22) now continues with blessings related to each act of preparing for the day: on opening one's eyes (line 1), dressing (line 2), stretching and sitting up (line 3, which in the Talmud appears before the previous one), straightening up (line 4), putting one's foot on the ground (line 5), fastening one's shoes (line 6),[38] walking (line 7), fastening one's clothes (line 8, which the Talmud relates specifically to a belt),

[34] Hirsch, *Pentateuch*, Lev. 23: 43, vol. iii, pt. 2, p. 712. See also E. Munk, *World of Prayer*, i. 25–30.

[35] Aaron Soloveitchik on Maimonides, *Mishneh torah*, 'Hilkhot tefilah' 7: 6, cited in *My People's Prayer Book*, v. 32–3 n. 6.   [36] Berliner, *Randbemerkungen*, i. 14–16.

[37] See Emden, *Amudei shamayim* (ed. Weinfeld), i. 133, and a discussion in *Talmudic Encyclopedia*, iv. 313.

[38] The noun in other contexts refers to excretion—*la'asot tserakhav* and *nitstarekh linkavav* (Jastrow, *Dictionary*, 1302, s.v. *tsarakh*)—an association supported by the vocalization of the noun

putting on a turban or head-dress (line 9), a post-talmudic insertion thanking God for providing strength to face the day ahead (line 10),[39] and washing one's face (lines 11–12), which in the talmudic source precedes the petition for safety to be examined in the following section.

As has been seen, the blessings for *talit*, *tefilin*, and washing the hands, which in the original source (BT *Berakhot* 60b) appear before the last of these blessings, have been removed from this context and replaced by an expression of thanks for strength. Although the insertion may have been intended to summarize the effect of the ritual garments, the earlier discussion shows this to be an over-simplification.[40] The blessing over washing the hands before prayer that appears in the same talmudic source was inserted instead in Extract 16.

The removal of this sequence, minus the ritual garments and hand-washing, from its real-life context seems to transform it from a ritualization of daily existence into an act of study. The blessings no longer play a role in ordinary dressing but have been transformed into ceremonial preparations for prayer, even though they were inserted here only so that those without access to the text could hear them recited in public.[41] Some of the blessings do continue to be associated with real life, although their original intention has been lost. Those over 'girding' and 'crowning' (lines 8 and 9) are omitted from the morning liturgy on 9 Av, when *tefilin* are not worn, as a mark of mourning, and inserted instead in the afternoon service, when they are worn.[42]

The transfer of all the blessings from home to the synagogue also aligns them with the sacralization of life seen in the Temple associations of the 'cockerel' and in the priestly texts associated with the *tefilin*, casting the speaker in the role of a Temple priest. Similar implications emerge from the psalmic echoes in lines 1, 3, 4, 5, and 7—the first three from a psalm read every morning and the fourth from one used on sabbath mornings[43]—and in an echo from the book of Isaiah in line 10 (the blessing introduced later).[44] Other, fainter biblical echoes suggest a link to the biblical narrative of Creation, repeatedly alluded to in the first moments of the liturgical day. The first blessing, on line 1, employs the same verb as that used to describe the opening of Adam's and Eve's eyes after they had eaten the forbidden fruit,[45] while the second blessing (line 2) contains the term *arumim*, 'naked',

for dual rather than plural form in some prayer-books, and by the fact that some Sephardi liturgies omit the longer blessing (e.g. *Book of Prayer: Daily and Occasional Prayers*) on the same theme (see Extract 17), probably because it was recognized as unnecessary (Raphael Loewe, pers. comm.).

[39] First recorded in *Maḥzor vitry*, 57, and omitted from Sephardi liturgies. Joel Sirkis argues, in *Bayit ḥadash* on *Arba'ah turim*, 'Oraḥ ḥayim' 46, that it must have appeared in talmudic manuscripts that have not survived.

[40] Analysed in Ch. 5 above.   [41] *Sidur avodat yisra'el*, 41.

[42] See *Authorised Kinot for the Ninth of Av*, 48 n. 3, 185–8, and see especially 188 n. 3.

[43] Pss. 146: 8, 7, 8, 136: 6, 37: 23.

[44] Isa. 40: 29, which is part of the *haftarah* (Isa. 40: 27–41: 16) for 'Lekh lekha' (Gen. 12: 1–17: 27), which opens with Abraham's departure from Ur for Canaan.   [45] Gen. 3: 7.

Blest art thou, God our Lord, sovereign of the universe, °He	*B'Br.* 60:
who enlightens the blind!	*Ps.* 146,[8]
Blest art thou, God our Lord, sovereign of the universe, °He	*Is.* 58,[7]
who clothes the °naked!	*Gn.* 3,[21]
Blest art thou, God our Lord, sovereign of the universe, °He	*Ps.* 146,[7]
who releases the °captive!	*Gn.* 39,[20]
Blest art thou, God our Lord, sovereign of the universe, °He	*Ps.* 146,[8]
who makes upright the °bent down!	*Is.* 58,[5]
Blest art thou, God our Lord, sovereign of the universe, °He	*Ps.* 24,[2]; 136,[6]
who spreads out the land above the waters!	*Gn.* 1,[10]
Blest art thou, God our Lord, sovereign of the universe, °He	*B'Br.* 60:
who makes provision for my physical needs!	*Ps.* 145,[16]
Blest art thou, God our Lord, sovereign of the universe, °He	*Ps.* 37,[23]
who prepares the foot-steps of each man!	*B'Su.* 53
Blest art thou, God our Lord, sovereign of the universe, °He	*Mai. Tef.* 7,[6]
who girds Israel with °courage!	*Jg.* 6,[12]
Blest art thou, God our Lord, sovereign of the universe, °He	*Is.* 62,[8]
who crowns Israel with glory!	*Ex.* 33,[6]
Blest art thou, God our Lord, sovereign of the universe, °He	*Is.* 40,[29]
who gives strength unto the weary!	*Msh. Kn. ult.*
°Blest art thou, God our Lord, sovereign of the universe, He	*B'Br.* 60:
who causes sleep to pass from mine eyes and °sleepiness	*Ps.* 132,[4]
from mine eyelids;	*Y'Br.* 5,[1]

24. The daily blessings (*Birkhot hashaḥar*)

recalling the same verse of the Garden of Eden narrative. However, an earlier biblical verse applies a homophone of the same root, *erom*, 'sly', to the serpent, suggesting that the speaker's dressing may re-enact an aspect of the account of the Garden unrelated to waking.[46] The third blessing, describing sleep as a prison (line 3), appears to take leave of the Creation theme, which reappears in line 5, where setting one's foot to the floor becomes a celebration of creation. Yet the first three blessings could allude to the rabbinic view that the loss of Edenic purity and innocence was less a disaster than the beginning of life as experienced in the here and now, and that the garden was a 'prison' in which Adam and Eve, who were at first 'blind', learned to see.[47] This view is reinforced by the original

[46] Gen. 3: 1, 7.

[47] This idea emerges from the juxtaposition of the first weekly reading of the year, including the narrative in Gen. 3: 4–7 mentioned above, with a *haftarah* that includes verses such as

בָּרוּךְ אַתָּה יְיָ אֱלֹהֵינוּ מֶלֶךְ הָעוֹלָם פּוֹקֵחַ עִוְרִים: 1

בָּרוּךְ אַתָּה יְיָ אֱלֹהֵינוּ מֶלֶךְ הָעוֹלָם מַלְבִּישׁ עֲרֻמִּים: 2

בָּרוּךְ אַתָּה יְיָ אֱלֹהֵינוּ מֶלֶךְ הָעוֹלָם מַתִּיר אֲסוּרִים: 3

בָּרוּךְ אַתָּה יְיָ אֱלֹהֵינוּ מֶלֶךְ הָעוֹלָם זוֹקֵף כְּפוּפִים: 4

בָּרוּךְ אַתָּה יְיָ אֱלֹהֵינוּ מֶלֶךְ הָעוֹלָם רוֹקַע הָאָרֶץ עַל־הַמָּיִם: 5

בָּרוּךְ אַתָּה יְיָ אֱלֹהֵינוּ מֶלֶךְ הָעוֹלָם שֶׁעָשָׂה לִי כָּל־צָרְכִּי: 6

בָּרוּךְ אַתָּה יְיָ אֱלֹהֵינוּ מֶלֶךְ הָעוֹלָם אֲשֶׁר הֵכִין מִצְעֲדֵי־גָבֶר: 7

בָּרוּךְ אַתָּה יְיָ אֱלֹהֵינוּ מֶלֶךְ הָעוֹלָם אוֹזֵר יִשְׂרָאֵל בִּגְבוּרָה: 8

בָּרוּךְ אַתָּה יְיָ אֱלֹהֵינוּ מֶלֶךְ הָעוֹלָם עוֹטֵר יִשְׂרָאֵל בְּתִפְאָרָה: 9

בָּרוּךְ אַתָּה יְיָ אֱלֹהֵינוּ מֶלֶךְ הָעוֹלָם הַנּוֹתֵן לַיָּעֵף כֹּחַ: 10

בָּרוּךְ אַתָּה יְיָ אֱלֹהֵינוּ מֶלֶךְ הָעוֹלָם הַמַּעֲבִיר שֵׁנָה מֵעֵינַי 11

וּתְנוּמָה מֵעַפְעַפָּי: 12

inclusion of the *talit* blessing towards the end of the sequence, an act referred to earlier as a means of restoring the lost paradisal clothing.[48] If this reading is correct, the blessings celebrate the speaker's arrival at a state of normality and describe sleep less as a haven from reality than as a failure to confront it.

The interpolation of line 10 is a first glimmer of a theme that will eventually dominate the daily liturgy: the dangers of the outside world and the speaker's fear of leaving home, or the synagogue. It may be an attempt to fill the space left at this point by the removal of the blessings over the ritual garments. Although the garments are absent from the liturgy used here, they now re-emerge as

Isa. 42: 7, 16, 18–20, in which the need to seek light and to open the eyes contrasts with the ambivalence about the opening of Adam's and Eve's eyes in the Torah reading. This implies that the expulsion from Eden might be regarded in a positive light as the discovery of perception.

[48] See the analysis of Extract 3, citing *Midrash Psalms* 24: 12, 90: 18.

relevant factors in the minds of those aware of the talmudic source. For the well-informed speaker, this is the point at which the ritual garments and their associations come into play in the liturgy. The inserted blessing might also have been designed to make up the number of the blessings to a sacred fifteen, associated with the divine name representing mercy.[49]

Both in the Talmud and here, the process of dressing closes with the blessing over washing the face (lines 11–12), which would originally have followed that over hand-washing. The present concluding blessing mirrors that recited on going to sleep ('who drops bonds of sleepiness over my eyes, yea drowsiness on my eyelids'), and emphasizes the physical over the sacral aspects of waking. Its description of sleep is drawn from a psalm devoted to seeking the Temple, suggesting that this blessing alludes to the attempt to escape the dangers of exile.[50]

EXTRACT 25. A Prayer for Protection

This long talmudic blessing sustains the balance between study and worship and intensifies the speaker's awareness of the immediate problem of facing the outside world. Since it continues the sequence above and appears as its sequel in the same talmudic source, it requires no opening formula. The *talit* and *tefilin* are now worn, activating the themes of outside enmity and the inner dangers to which Jews are exposed by their covenant with God, noted previously in the liturgical transition from home to synagogue (Extracts 11–13). But while there the speaker was looking for safety in the synagogue and the community, the focus here is on the dangers of the outside world. The speaker's passage from private to communal life is marked by the addition of the words 'Lord of our ancestors' (Extract 25, lines 1–2), which do not appear in the talmudic text. Paradoxically, the speaker is linked to the group while making changes to the source, enacting the reason for exile at the very moment of leaving home. For the source of danger, as with the ritual garments, is the failure to study, also represented here by the alteration of the talmudic text from singular to plural, even though the closing formula was always plural. This change reflects the talmudic principle that private petitions should be expressed as though they were public ones,[51] but it also exemplifies the 'tussle' that makes study almost impossible.

This paragraph also abandons the biblical echoes by which daily life has so far been sacralized and names a breathless stream of external challenges. Two re-

[49] The recurrence of the number 18 in the early-morning blessings, here formed by the present sequence and the preceding three Torah-study blessings, has been identified as a proleptic Amidah in Freehof, 'Structure', 343–6. However, variations in order and in the blessings included in the calculations suggest that the identification is weak: see Heinemann, *Prayer in the Talmud*, 9–10 n. 15.

[50] Ps. 132: 4.

[51] For examples of such prayers for times of danger and the reason they are to be in the plural—'a man should always associate himself with the congregation'—see BT *Ber.* 29b–30a.

quests for closeness to Torah (line 2)—the primary concern ever since the blessings over study—are followed by an inventory of factors distancing one from it. God is asked to lead the speaker not into 'sin . . . transgression or iniquity, nor unto temptation' (line 3), the first three items being listed in order of seriousness, literally from 'error' to 'flagrant transgression'. In asking for these to be removed, the speaker looks beyond the talmudic axiom that 'everything is in the hands of heaven except the fear of heaven',[52] and attributes to God the dangers themselves. This idea, made liturgically explicit only rarely, and mainly on Yom Kippur, holds God responsible both for the fact that sins are committed and for the punitive suffering that follows. The divine origin of suffering is also alluded to in the term *nisayon*, translated here as 'temptation' but perhaps more correctly as 'trial', the term used biblically to describe the 'test' of Abraham's faith at the Binding of Isaac.[53] In the Sephardi rite the account of the Akedah is included among the study portions that follow the three Torah blessings recited earlier, suggesting the particular relevance of that episode to the early morning.[54]

This inventory might be taken to imply, however tentatively, that God is himself one of the dangers to be removed (although this idea cannot be made explicit in rabbinic Judaism), since one of the most feared elements, because of its seditiousness, is 'any evil companion', using the word *ḥaver*, generally translated as 'friend' or 'intimate'. The outside world, a place not only of overt enmity but also of 'bad friends', corresponds to an inner world in which one is betrayed by one's own actions and criminalized by the very demand for a standard of behaviour that one cannot achieve—this being the core of the speaker's dispute with God. One model of 'bad friends' might be the Egyptians who at first invited the Israelites into Goshen and then enslaved them, a model of the trap into which the speaker has already fallen by misquoting Oral Torah.[55] As has been argued in the context of *tefilin*, each contact with Torah brings with it the near-inevitability of misreading.

---

[52] BT *Ber.* 33*b*.

[53] Gen. 22: 1 for 'trial'. This association is confirmed by the strenuous denial offered in Schwab, *Rav Schwab on Prayer*, 40–1. Raphael Loewe writes (pers. comm.): 'The translation of *lo liyedai nisayon velo liyedai bizayon* misses the point—a *ma'amin* has no right to ask to be excused proving his faith, and *Elohai netsor* [the private petition with which the Amidah concludes] makes a virtue of a humility that invites contempt by others. What is meant is to save us from putting God to the test (*lo tenasu . . . ka'asher nisitem bamasah* [Deut. 6: 16]) and from acting in contempt of him (*ki davar h' bazah* [Num. 15: 30]). The conventional interpretation of the Lord's Prayer is similarly wrong-headed.' This approach supports the view that these texts contain implicit criticisms that might well make the speaker uneasy. The urge to 'try' God by expressing them seems as irresistible as the dangers, described by Rashi as sexual, listed in similar terms in the night-time prayer (parts of which are still used) on the same talmudic folio.

[54] *Book of Prayer: Daily and Occasional Prayers*, 4–5; the implications of its inclusion at this point in the morning liturgy are discussed in more detail in Ch. 12.

[55] 'Bad friends' are included in an inventory of things to avoid in Mishnah *Avot* 2: 14.

o may it be willed from thy presence,	
God our Lord and Lord of our ancestors, °to accustom	*Mai. Dt.* 1,[7]
us to thy *Torah*, yea, to make us attached unto thy	*Mai. Tva.* 5,[8]
commandments; to °bring us not to sin, to transgression or iniquity,	*Gn.* 6,[5]
nor unto temptation or disgrace; let not the Spirit of Mischief	*Mai. Dt.* 6,[1–10]
°hold sway within us, but keep us far from any evil person and	*Msh. Av.* 2,[14]
from any evil companion, even attach us unto the Good	*Zo. Gn.* 49,165:
Inclination and unto good actions, yea, °bend our will to	*Is.* 58,[5]
subserve thee; o set us this day and every day for favour, for	*Ps.* 95,[7]
loving-kindness and mercy, °both in thy sight and in the sight	*Prv.* 3,[4]
of all who observe us, so do thou °bestow goodly kindnesses	*I Sm.* 24,[18]
upon us—blest art thou, God, °who bestows goodly kindnesses	*Is.* 63,[7]
upon his People Israel!	*Ikk.* 4,[7]

25. A prayer for protection (*Vihi ratson . . . shetargilenu betoratekha*)

Although 'evil' might be thought incompatible with the idea of God, a talmudic discussion in which well-being is attributed to human virtue comments that 'a man must bless God for evil vicissitudes as he blesses Him for the good'.[56] This is as near as rabbinic texts come to acknowledging God's responsibility for human suffering, since apparently motiveless suffering is usually interpreted as punishment for previous sins. Some texts speculate on other factors,[57] the most relevant to the present case being the suggestion that the Flood may have been caused by the apparent lack of divine engagement with wrongdoing. A midrashic text describes how 'the generation of the Flood said "he is silent towards his world; he hides his face from his world, like a judge who draws a veil over his face and does not know what happens outside"', and this silence was taken as approval of what even the perpetrators knew to be wrong.[58] Another midrashic text describes their 'sexual crimes and idolatry', punishment, or both, as *androlemusiyah*, a chaotic state of affairs in which 'the innocent are killed with the wicked'.[59] The suffering mentioned in this liturgical passage, since it does not seem to be punitive, presumably falls into the same category, which would account for the possibility that the speaker, even while appealing to God for help, is including him among the sources of suffering.

It would also explain the speaker's awareness (implied in Extract 25, lines 5–6) that only God can ensure closeness to the instinct (or potentiality) for goodness

[56] BT *Ber.* 33*b*.
[57] Discussed in Kraemer, *Responses to Suffering*, esp. chs. 8 and 10.   [58] *Gen. Rabbah* 36: 1.
[59] *Gen. Rabbah* 26: 5, and the earlier discussion of *androlemusiyah* (pp. 78–9).

וִיהִי רָצוֹן מִלְפָנֶיךָ יְיָ אֱלֹהֵינוּ וֵאלֹהֵי 1

אֲבוֹתֵינוּ שֶׁתַּרְגִּילֵנוּ בְּתוֹרָתֶךָ וְדַבְּקֵנוּ בְּמִצְוֹתֶיךָ וְאַל תְּבִיאֵנוּ 2

לֹא לִידֵי חֵטְא וְלֹא לִידֵי עֲבֵרָה וְעָוֹן וְלֹא לִידֵי נִסָּיוֹן וְלֹא לִידֵי 3

בִזָּיוֹן וְאַל תַּשְׁלֶט בָּנוּ יֵצֶר הָרָע וְהַרְחִיקֵנוּ מֵאָדָם רַע וּמֵחָבֵר 4

רַע וְדַבְּקֵנוּ בְּיֵצֶר הַטּוֹב וּבְמַעֲשִׂים טוֹבִים וְכֹף אֶת יִצְרֵנוּ 5

לְהִשְׁתַּעְבֶּד־לָךְ וּתְנֵנוּ הַיּוֹם וּבְכָל־יוֹם לְחֵן וּלְחֶסֶד 6

וּלְרַחֲמִים בְּעֵינֶיךָ וּבְעֵינֵי כָל־רוֹאֵינוּ וְתִגְמְלֵנוּ חֲסָדִים 7

טוֹבִים בָּרוּךְ אַתָּה יְיָ גּוֹמֵל חֲסָדִים טוֹבִים לְעַמּוֹ יִשְׂרָאֵל: 8

(*yetser hatov*) or bring the speaker into the service of God (*lehishtabed lakh*). Good deeds, it is implied, cannot be performed without assistance, a thought which calls into question the punishment for misdeeds. The deepening ambivalence of the speaker's feelings is clear from the use of the same Hebrew term to describe both 'service' to God and 'slavery' to an oppressor, as though the speaker can be protected from human oppression only by being 'enslaved' by God. Paradoxically, the text departs from the talmudic source at this point, since the term *lehishtabed lakh*, 'to be brought to your service', is first found in the eleventh-century talmudic digest of Isaac Alfasi.[60] The closing clause (lines 6–8) asks for favour from both God and humans, confirming that they might be equated, while the 'seal' asserts that God does indeed respond positively to his people, retreating from the implied criticisms identified here. Yet both the penultimate line and the seal refer literally to 'good kindnesses', pointing to the possibility that some kindnesses might appear otherwise in the short term, confirming the ambivalence at the heart of this paragraph.

The shift from singular to plural in the talmudic version of the seal also introduces a syntactic gap, depersonalizing the statement and transforming the speaker from an individual to a member of the group. It may simultaneously retreat from the theologically unbearable position of fear and attempt a return to the praise in the preparatory blessings. However, the praise in the seal may equally

---

[60] *Sidur avodat yisra'el*, 43. An antecedent may survive in the Christian prayer 'whose service is perfect freedom': see the Book of Common Prayer, the daily morning Second Collect for Peace, based on Romans 6: 18–22 (Raphael Loewe, pers. comm.).

°May it be willed from thy presence, God my Lord	*B'Br.* 16:
and Lord of mine ancestors, to °spare me this day and every	*B'Sb.* 30:
day from °the impudent even from impudence, from any	*Msh.Av.* 5,[20]
evil person, °evil companion or evil neighbour, and from any	*Dt.* 28,[50]
bad accident, from the °corrupting Seducer, from a harsh	*Msh.Av.* 2,[14]
verdict or a harsh litigant, whether he be a °member of the	*ICr.* 21,[1]
Covenant or be he not a member of the Covenant.	*Ku.* 3,[73]

26. A supplementary prayer for protection (*Yehi ratson . . . shetatsileni hayom*)

reflect the speaker's acknowledgement that survival is itself a wonder, avoiding the question of challenges. A similar awareness that survival is not to be taken for granted appears in the Passover Haggadah, where a declaration of the hostility of others is concluded with a statement, in the first person plural, that 'the Holy One, Blessed be He, saves us from their hands'.[61] A midrashic text on suffering accordingly suggests that, despite one's pain, 'it is sufficient that one lives'.[62]

EXTRACT 26. A Supplementary Prayer for Protection

Inner dangers now fade in the face of objective ones, as the fragile contract with God is left behind for a plea, based on law-court procedure,[63] to avert the disgrace, hostility, and plans of bad people in the outside world.[64] By repeating the previous petition for protection this passage also undermines it, implying its ineffectiveness and thus adding to the list of dangers. Denying the concluding statement of the previous text concerning God's protection proves that the subject matter is insoluble and cannot be set aside.

This text is not from the same source as the passages following Extract 21, so lies outside what must be regarded as an extended study-cum-prayer sequence. It is drawn from a discussion of mourning practices (relevant here because of the sense of loss) from elsewhere in the same tractate, thereby reintroducing textual selection to the range of editorial techniques. The talmudic debate on mourning includes an anthology of personal petitions with which various rabbis concluded the Amidah (the prayer *par excellence*), including the present example, by Judah Hanasi, the editor of the Mishnah. Its location here, after the fifteen blessings for rising and the three over Torah study, might point to its symbolic role as the last

[61] The late Sir Alan Mocatta explained to me in 1985 that at this point in the Passover ceremony he habitually added the words: 'but we are the lucky ones'. [62] *Lam. Rabbah* 3: 39.
[63] Heinemann, *Prayer in the Talmud*, ch. 8, esp. pp. 193–4. [64] BT *Ber.* 16*b*.

יְהִי רָצוֹן מִלְפָנֶיךָ יְיָ אֱלֹהַי וֵאלֹהֵי אֲבוֹתַי 1

שֶׁתַּצִּילֵנִי הַיּוֹם וּבְכָל־יוֹם מֵעַזֵּי פָנִים וּמֵעַזּוּת 2

פָנִים מֵאָדָם רַע וּמֵחָבֵר רַע וּמִשָׁכֵן רַע וּמִפֶּגַע 3

רַע וּמִשָׂטָן הַמַּשְׁחִית מִדִּין קָשֶׁה וּמִבַּעַל דִּין 4

קָשֶׁה בֵּין שֶׁהוּא בֶן־בְּרִית וּבֵין שֶׁאֵינוֹ בֶן־בְּרִית: 5

of the eighteen blessings of the Amidah.[65] But this would suggest that the entire sequence is less an informal anthology than a preview of the Amidah, itself a liturgical substitute for sacrifice and for the Temple whose absence represents the exile from which the speaker needs salvation. The status of this prayer as Torah study is subverted here, however, by its transformation from plural to singular (although not in the Sephardi liturgy),[66] paradoxically reversing the switch of the previous paragraph from singular to plural. The previous paragraph might therefore be regarded as presenting the case for the community as a whole and this one for the speaker alone, but the movement from the community to the individual at a time when the reverse might be expected suggests that this change results less from the desire to make a point than from the irresistible nature of the editorial urge to intervene, irrespective of its impact on the meaning or of the theological consequences of changing Torah.

In two respects this passage augments the previous one. First, it refers to the 'bad accident . . . [and] the corrupting seducer [or better, 'Satan the killer']', which imply unforeseen, undeserved, and apparently casual mishaps not included in the previous listing in Extract 25. Second, it is stated explicitly that danger may come from 'an evil neighbour' and that the speaker fears hostility as much from one who is 'a member of [or 'party to'] the covenant' as from one who is not (line 5). Focusing on members of the community turns the apprehension inwards and brings us up to the present moment, possibly even to the elements of the speaker's personality described in the previous paragraph as the 'evil inclination'. The inclusion of Satan, whose role in the book of Job is that of divinely sanctioned tempter, implicitly extends the range of possibilities to the

[65] E. Munk, *World of Prayer*, i. 30–1 and see the remarks above on the transfer from singular to plural of Extract 25.

[66] Part appears in the present form in BT *Shab.* 30*b*, but this would still represent it inaccurately.

author of the greatest covenant of all, God himself, although such an idea could not be made explicit in the rabbinic tradition.[67] The theologically troubling nature of this idea seems to explain why the liturgy swerves away from its trajectory at this point, as though avoiding an intolerable vein of thought. The personal nature of the outburst is likewise submerged by the sudden shift away from prayer-cum-study to pure study, the genre which dominates the opening lines of the next sequence, enabling the speaker to escape the intolerable aspects of the theme even before they become fully explicit.

[67] It appears implicitly, however, in the description of God presiding with apparent indifference over a gladiatorial contest in which one of the contestants must die: *Gen. Rabbah* 22: 9.

CHAPTER EIGHT

※

The Scattering

'confound the language'
GENESIS 11: 9

THE TEXTS discussed in this chapter focus principally on the question of suffering and whether the pain of hostility is a necessary component of human life or can be avoided by good behaviour. By asking implicitly whether God is to be criticized for failing to prevent suffering, they exemplify the liturgical critique of God's management of the world.

EXTRACT 27. The Flight into Study

This passage, which is apparently detached from the preceding material, is described in a midrashic source[1] as a formal introduction to early-morning Torah study, suggesting that it duplicates the Torah blessings in Extract 18. If so, this new attempt to study is undermined by the way in which the previous anthology was compromised by inaccuracy and finally dissolved into prayer. The morning blessings introduced with Extract 21, for instance, were transformed into prayer by their relevance to the here and now. However, they also raised issues that led to the present theological impasse, from which this passage seems to offer an escape by returning to study. The speaker is thus drawn into a pattern of repeated attempts to break out of the vicious circle of suffering and the impossibility of perfect study.

This problem has haunted the speaker since the start of the morning and there is now no alternative but to attempt to escape the paradox by means of a shift of both texture and content. The speaker can be seen here manoeuvring between genres, abandoning petitionary prayer for study for the second time in the morning. This approach is flawed, as has already been seen, however, since if the subject of study synchronizes with the speaker's preoccupations it may be transformed imperceptibly into prayer and lead to a further impasse, a tendency particularly evident in Extract 21. Here the speaker turns again towards study to avoid the painful issues raised by worship, but the fears once more prove impossible to suppress and instead become central concerns, leaving the speaker in

---

[1] *Tana debei eliyahu*, ch. 21, p. 118, trans. Braude and Kapstein, p. 256; Elbogen, *Jewish Liturgy*, 79. For its later revision see *Otsar hatefilot*, 'Tikun tefilah', 66*b*–68*a*.

°ALWAYS A PERSON SHOULD BE GOD-FEARING, EVEN IN SECLUSION;   *Mi.*6,[7]

HE SHOULD ADMIT TO THE TRUTH AND TELL THE TRUTH TO HIMSELF;   *B'Br.*8

YEA, °LET HIM RISE EARLY AND SAY: *Msh.Av.*6,[9–10]

27. The flight into study (*Le'olam yehe adam yere shamayim*)

double flight from the implications of both prayer and study, while simultaneously regarding both as places of refuge.

At first sight this text appears to be a benignly fresh opening to the daily liturgy, advising the speaker to 'rise early and say' (last two words of Extract 27,
line 2). Yet in terms of style it seems to return to the prescriptive tone of the
introductory meditations associated with the *talit* and *tefilin*, or even to the more
recently mishnaic and talmudic study passages. If it is a completely new beginning it will discount the liturgical enterprise so far, however, simultaneously
jeopardizing its own success, while if it responds to what has gone before it will
be seen to expand on the more disquieting themes raised in the previous two
paragraphs.

These themes arise from the word *vayashkem*, translated here as 'to rise early',
which alludes to two scriptural narratives in which Abraham, at moments of crisis, responds to extreme challenges by waking early. In one of these he begs for
mercy on behalf of Sodom and Gomorrah, after appeals on the basis of justice
have failed,[2] an event regarded midrashically as the time at which morning
prayer was instituted. The same scene has been mentioned as a reason that Adon
Olam (the first word of which is the name of God first used by Abraham) is
appropriate for morning prayers. In the other narrative Abraham prepares for
the Binding of Isaac, rabbinic Judaism's archetype of a divinely ordained 'trial',
of the kind from which a previous text asks for the speaker to be protected
(Extract 25, line 3).[3]

The appearance of this word here locates the liturgical speaker in scriptural
scenes in which God's attribute of mercy was not apparently active: in the first
narrative the cities were destroyed, while in the second Abraham (and Isaac)
were spared only after they had accepted a task that threatened to deny Abraham
his divinely promised descendants.[4] Morning prayer—and the speaker reciting

---

[2] Gen. 19: 27; David Kimhi points out that Abraham was praying at this moment but does not
specify for what, and adds (on the basis of BT *Ber.* 26*b*) that this action was the source both of the
practice of reciting morning prayers and of doing this in the same place each day (BT *Ber.* 6*b*).
Sforno adds that he was praying for mercy, but only once justice had failed.

[3] Gen. 22: 1 refers to the 'trial' and 22: 3 to the fact that Abraham 'rose early', but see Ch. 7
n. 53 on the idea of a trial. Similar linking of words appears in *Gen. Rabbah* 55: 8, which compares
scenes in which the words 'saddling', 'preparing', 'sword', and 'cleaving' appear.

[4] He had already been promised many descendants (Gen. 17: 4–6), but was told only before he

לְעוֹלָם יְהֵא אָדָם יְרֵא שָׁמַיִם בְּסֵתֶר וּמוֹדֶה   1
עַל־הָאֱמֶת וְדוֹבֵר אֱמֶת בִּלְבָבוֹ וַיַּשְׁכֵּם וַיֹּאמַר: 2

it—are in this way linked to attempts by the first Jew to turn aside God's power to destroy human life, emphasizing the problematic nature of the speaker's position now.[5] But in addition, since the Akedah has been rabbinically reapplied as a theological tool for elevating suffering to martyrdom, it suggests that the present moment may be reinterpreted as one of martyrdom.[6] Although there appears to be no support in rabbinic literature for the view that these liturgical words—or the paragraph that follows them—express Abraham's thoughts on founding morning prayer, or his views on the nature of suffering as he sets out for the Akedah, it is tempting to imagine that the midrashic writers were aware of such a possibility.

The midrashic source from which these opening lines are drawn quotes immediately after these words the opening clauses of the text that actually follows it in the present edition of the prayer book (Extract 28, lines 1–2), and then, without interruption, the prophetic verse that forms the climax to the group of texts discussed in this chapter (Extract 33, lines 9–11). This suggests either that the liturgical editors were aware of the midrashic source or that the midrashic writers were reflecting liturgical usage, so may confirm that the entire sequence is an act of study, even though it has been compromised, like previous ones, by changes to the original. In the Ashkenazi version used here the Hebrew word meaning 'in private' has been added to the original instruction to 'be God-fearing [or better, 'heaven-fearing']'.[7] This addition might allude to the way in which the present recital is 'private', since it takes place before the community formally gathers for prayer, in contrast to Abraham's 'trial' at the Binding of Isaac, which was implicitly necessary to demonstrate his loyalty in public. The Sephardi liturgy—echoed by a number of Ashkenazi versions—adds 'and in public', as though to exclude the possibility that one might condone open dishonesty to others by adding only 'in private'.[8] This danger is excluded in the Ashkenazi version by the inclusion of a climactic 'seal', in Extract 32, line 5,

left for Sodom that he would have a son (Gen. 18: 14). The parallel fear of childlessness, following the destruction of the cities, led Lot's daughters to commit incest (Gen. 19: 30–8).

[5] BT *Ber. 26b*. The word for 'rising earlier' appeared earlier, but without the emphasis lent it here by its isolation, in Extract 20, line 4.   [6] See Spiegel, *The Last Trial*, 13–16 and *passim*.

[7] *Tana debei eliyahu*, ch. 21, p. 118 n. 28, trans. Braude and Kapstein, p. 256 n. 22.

[8] *Book of Prayer: Daily and Occasional Prayers*, 7. Caro, *Beit yosef*, 'Oraḥ ḥayim' 46, on integrity, quotes Rashi and argues that confining one's honesty to the private sphere would be absurd.

referring to the way God is hallowed 'among the masses', making up for the exclusion of 'in public' in the opening lines.[9]

Whatever the specific implications of these changes, however, departing from the midrashic original conflicts with the aim of a study sequence, especially one introduced by lines whose last word suggests the importance of accuracy. These changes therefore set the scene for yet another failure of study, similar to that into which the speaker was led by the previous sequence, again providing a reason for the exile and suffering from which the speaker seeks relief. Particular attention is accordingly drawn here to the word 'fear', a term used in the previous paragraph to describe the speaker's response to the outside world, but here apparently to heaven or God. The liturgical argument seems to suggest the idea, impossible to express openly in rabbinic thought, that God may evoke feelings of aversion like those inspired by hostile humans.

The word 'fear' is itself ambiguous, however, for in rabbinic thought 'fear of heaven' is closely related to 'love of heaven', both approximating to the idea of 'reverence' or 'awe', or to 'fear of the consequences of a course of action'. It rarely if ever refers to 'aversion', as can be seen from a biblical description of people who 'fear' God, even though they worship both idols and God, implying that 'fear' might be a positive rather than a negative mode of relating to God.[10] The same nuance appears in a rabbinic axiom according to which it is better to serve God out of 'the fear of heaven' (clearly meaning 'love') than in the hope of receiving reward.[11] This idea also occurs in an early midrash on the opening words of the Shema, the credal statement at the climax of the present study session (Extract 31, line 1), but this first line of the Shema is associated in one rabbinic text with Rabbi Akiba's martyrdom,[12] reinforcing the view that the speaker has no alternative but to accept the dangers ahead, and suggesting that the proper response to everyday suffering is not protest, but acquiescence. This was also acknowledged by Abraham after he had appealed on behalf of Sodom and Gomorrah, first to God's justice and then to his mercy.

The term 'fear' therefore does not help the speaker identify whether the sufferings ahead are tokens of God's anger (as in the case of Sodom), trials (as with Abraham at the Akedah), or arbitrary vicissitudes which should not be chal-

[9] This 'seal' appears only in the Ashkenazi rite; the Sephardi version contains a conclusion that blesses, or congratulates, the early-rising speaker rather than God, probably because the idea of public testimony is included in the Sephardi version of the opening lines: *Book of Prayer: Daily and Occasional Prayers*, 8; but see Jacob ben Asher, *Arba'ah turim*, 'Oraḥ ḥayim' 46. The liturgical break is therefore less radical at that point. Schwab, *Rav Schwab on Prayer*, 49, points out that the entire sequence may be regarded as a study portion.

[10] 2 Kgs. 17: 33. Another example is 1 Kgs. 3: 28, where Solomon is 'feared' for his insight by those hoping to escape punishment for their crime, and 'respected' for his wisdom.

[11] Mishnah *Avot* 1: 3. *Pesikta rabati* 47: 3 compares Job unfavourably with Abraham for complaining; see the discussion in Montefiore and Loewe (eds.), *Rabbinic Anthology*, 543, 676–7.

[12] *Sifrei*, Deut., 'Va'etḥanan' 32, p. 73.

lenged, as Akiba implied at his martyrdom. The need to identify which possibility applies here places the speaker simultaneously in the role of compassionate
onlooker (like Abraham at Sodom), uncomplaining victim (like Akiba), and subject of a trial unwillingly forced into the role of perpetrator (like Abraham at the
Akedah). However, since each role might inspire aversion, this could indeed be
the meaning of 'fear' in this context.

The association with 'aversion' has led some readers to argue that these lines
were instituted at a time of persecution when the recital of the Shema had been
banned, and to see the personal reading of the credal text as a clandestine
replacement of the full reading.[13] This would suggest, however, that the aversion referred to was inspired in part by oppressors and that after the danger had
passed the text remained here for other reasons, such as editorial inertia. Such a
view, however, would fail to account for the theological danger into which the
speaker has been led and would reduce the words themselves to a mere relic of
past persecution without current relevance. Others argue that they were introduced to ensure that Torah study would be the first act 'when you rise up', as the
Shema itself says it should be,[14] but this fails to take account of the previous
study session and its three introductory blessings, and ignores the midrashic
implications of the words themselves. These implications suggest that the sequence is neither an interpolation designed to overcome a political problem nor a
procedural convenience, but a multi-layered liturgical response to the theological
impasse outlined in the paragraph above.

Other midrashic associations of these lines and of the Shema point to the
question of personal integrity, implying that honesty and transparency in the
face of hatred can deflect the dangers ahead. The words *modeh al ha'emet*, which
are translated here as 'admit to the truth' (lines 1–2), could better be rendered
'acknowledge the truth', based on the same verb as that used in the opening
statement of the day. This is a characteristic of wisdom, according to one rabbinic source of this phrase,[15] and the term 'truth' suggests a link with the Shema
itself, since although the term potentially encompasses all matters of fact, especially those that the speaker might have difficulty in acknowledging, the word is
a recurrent liturgical response to the creed.[16]

The word 'truth' appears in another scriptural context implying the need to
recognize God's reliability, confirming that the covenant will eventually be kept
despite the delay.[17] But the words 'tell the truth to himself' are explicitly associated in one midrash with the Shema and with the way Jews relate to the outside

[13] Elbogen, *Jewish Liturgy*, 79, 407 n. 19; *Otsar hatefilot*, 'Tikun tefilah', 66b–69a; Nulman,
Encyclopedia of Jewish Prayer, 227–8; *My People's Prayer Book*, v. 10–11.

[14] Deut. 6: 7, 11: 19.   [15] Mishnah *Avot* 5: 10.

[16] BT *Ber.* 33b, *infra*. The word 'true' is repeated several times in the blessing following the
recital of the entire Shema later in the morning liturgy.

[17] Ps. 71: 22 sees this as a call for special praise.

world, suggesting that the power to resolve the problem of suffering lies less with God than with the speaker. These liturgical words in fact appear in Psalm 15, which states that the ability to 'tell the truth to oneself' characterizes a person worthy of entering the Tabernacle or Temple. Much of that psalm is midrashically associated with the way Jews relate to the outside world, suggesting that the power to resolve the problem of suffering lies with the speaker, whose behaviour, as noted in the second paragraph of the Shema, determines material well-being.[18]

Integrity is talmudically associated with a certain Rav Safra, although no example of his honesty is forthcoming. Rashbam (Rashi's grandson), however, records in his gloss on a talmudic text that mentions him in this context that once, when Rav Safra was silently reciting the Shema at his market stall and was therefore unable to respond to a customer's offer, the latter interpreted his silence as a refusal and increased the offer. However, after Rav Safra had completed his recital he refused to take advantage of the misunderstanding and insisted on accepting the lower price,[19] an act of integrity in public life which the Sephardi version of the liturgy in particular suggests might deflect the hatred of outsiders.

The association of the Shema with integrity in business matters has still wider implications, for it suggests a link with the contract between the speaker and God, especially as the first line of the creed can be read as an attempt to secure the primacy of divine mercy over justice (as will be seen from the discussion of Extract 31, line 1). These words could therefore be interpreted as an attempt to encourage God to fulfil his part of the covenant openly, echoing scriptural leaders of Israel who claimed that it was in God's own interests to be seen to protect his people.[20] In their original midrashic context these liturgical lines are followed by remarks on the covenantally promised ingathering of the exiles.[21]

Although one might expect the text of the Shema to follow next, and the last word of this sentence suggests that its authors intended it to appear there, the recital of its opening line is delayed until later in the morning. More waves of preparatory texts, exploring issues already raised as well as new ones, augment the suspense and complicate the speaker's eventual response to the credal statement.

---

[18] Ps. 15: 2; *Midrash Psalms* 15. The biblical context relates to those who live in the Temple, refrain from blaming others, and show integrity in business.

[19] BT *BB* 88a; see also BT *Ḥul.* 94b. It is elevated to one of eleven fundamental principles of law in BT *Mak.* 24a and *Midrash Psalms* (addendum) 17: 19.

[20] This argument is frequently deployed by Moses to deflect God's anger: see e.g. Exod. 32: 9–14. The link with the Shema is explained in the remarks on Extract 31, line 1.

[21] *Tana debei eliyahu*, ch. 21, p. 118, trans. Braude and Kapstein, p. 256.

EXTRACT 28. **A Statement of Human Failings**

The next text is therefore not the Shema, but one that continues to explore the uncertainties noted in the previous passage. The opening words immediately follow the previous lines in the midrashic source, showing this arrangement to be ancient. The reference to God as master of *olamim*, 'worlds', the plural form of the Hebrew term *olam*, which in the previous lines meant 'always',[22] appears to refer to the present world and the afterlife. The singular form of this word in the opening clause of Adon Olam (Extract 15, line 1), read as 'Lord of the world', was taken to allude either to the Creation narrative as a model of the early morning, or as a temporal term, 'eternal'. Here it seems to mean 'always', in the sense of daily life, specifically recalling Rav Safra's integrity, Abraham's and Isaac's self-sacrifice at the Akeda, and Rabbi Akiba's martyrdom (with its particularly strong links to the Shema). Each viewed their responsibilities as extending to death, and suffering as justified by rewards in the next life. As has been seen, however, suffering can also seem to be arbitrary, especially that facing the speaker in the early morning. The view that both pleasure and pain are equally the work of God (Extracts 21–5) reaches its climax in the first line of the Shema, with its alternating use of the names of God (see the remarks on Extract 31, line 1).

The identical effect of divinely intended and arbitrary pain is explored next, starting from the fourth word of line 1. The idea that suffering is punitive is assumed by the description of the role of God's mercy. But from line 3 onwards human worthlessness is described without reference to God's role in creating the world as it is, or to the mercy needed to relieve misery resulting from human unworthiness. Mercy does not suggest guilt here, perhaps pointing to the inevitability of wrongdoing and consequently the arbitrary nature of suffering.

Two biblical quotations recommended in the Talmud for liturgical use are embedded in the passage after the opening words, referred to by their opening clauses near the end of a talmudic discussion of the Day of Atonement ritual.[23] They are still employed in the closing service of the Day of Atonement. The talmudic text, encompassing the fourth word of line 1 to the end of line 2, offers this confession from the book of Daniel as a fitting conclusion to each daily Amidah.[24] Its emphasis on God's universal power enacts the previous call to acknowledge God's rule publicly. Daniel paid a heavy price for doing so: he prayed three times a day facing Jerusalem, asking for redemption and the rebuilding of Jerusalem (like the speaker reading this prayer),[25] even though he

---

[22] The Sephardi rite adds 'Lord of lords', reinforcing the duality: *Book of Prayer: Daily and Occasional Prayers*, 7. For a discussion of the term *le'olam*, translated here as 'always', see R. Loewe, 'Jerome's Rendering of *Olam*', 300–2. [23] BT *Yoma* 87b.

[24] Dan. 9: 18. The scriptural quotation is identified not in the Talmud but by Rashi.

[25] This second theme will dominate in Ch. 9 of this analysis.

°Over-lord of all the worlds, °it is not because of our	*B'Yo.* 87:
righteousnesses that we pour our supplications before thee, but	*Dn.* 9,[18]
because of thine abounding mercies;—°What are we?—	*I Sm.* 18,[18]
What is our life?—°What, our kindness?—°What, our	*Is.* 40,[6]
rightness?—What, our saving?—What, our strength?—°What,	*Is.* 64,[5]
our courage?—°What shall we say before thee? God our Lord	*Jb.* 6,[11]
and Lord of our ancestors!—surely all the °heroes are as	*Zr.* 9,[10]
naught before thee, even, the °men of fame as though they	*Gn.* 6,[4]
had not been, the wise as if they were without intellect, and	*Jr.* 9,[22]
thinkers as though they were °devoid of comprehension, for	*Mi.* 4,[12]
their many doings are but °void, even the days of their lives	*Gn.* 1,[2]
are but a vapour before thee, °yea, the superiority of man over	*Ikk.* 3,[2]
beast is non-existent, for all is °but a vapour!	*Zo. Gn.* 146:

28. A statement of human failings (*Ribon kol ha'olamim, lo al tsidkatenu*)

knew he would be punished by being thrown into the lions' den.[26] This is the
second citation from the book of Daniel, both of which have appeared in texts
designed to open the liturgy, suggesting the centrality both of Daniel and of the
lions' den episode in rabbinic thinking about the moment of waking and of
regaining Jewish identity. Daniel, in reasserting his Jewishness, finds himself in
danger precisely because of his obedience to God, aligning him with the archetypal victim of a divine trial: Abraham at the Akedah.

If the speaker's suffering can be seen as a trial, however, then the declaration
that survival depends on divine mercy (at the end of line 2) has ironic undertones, since it was God who brought Abraham and Daniel, and now the speaker
too, into danger, making God responsible for danger as well as rescue. This also
emerges from the biblical sequel to Daniel's prayer, when the angel Gabriel
reveals the time of redemption but does so in language so obscure that it cannot
be calculated, transforming the announcement of the advent of rescue into an
explanation for its delay. The quotation from Daniel therefore implicitly
acknowledges that suffering might be a divine trial and that God's mercy is not
operative at this moment.

Equally, however, Daniel's confession of sins and petition for prayer to be
heard[27] are so similar to the prayers for the Day of Atonement, and to the longer
penitential Taḥanun prayers recited on Mondays and Thursdays throughout the
year, that a punitive explanation for suffering seems to be implied. Just as
Sodom's suffering results from a lack of integrity in daily life, so the last mishnah

---

[26] Dan. 6: 8–10, and see the remarks on Extract 1, line 1.   [27] Dan. 9: 4–19.

רִבּוֹן כָּל־הָעוֹלָמִים לֹא עַל־צִדְקוֹתֵינוּ אֲנַחְנוּ

מַפִּילִים תַּחֲנוּנֵינוּ לְפָנֶיךָ כִּי עַל רַחֲמֶיךָ הָרַבִּים ·

מָה אֲנַחְנוּ מֶה חַיֵּינוּ מֶה חַסְדֵּנוּ מַה צִּדְקֵנוּ

מַה יְשׁוּעָתֵנוּ מַה כֹּחֵנוּ מַה גְּבוּרָתֵנוּ מַה

נֹּאמַר לְפָנֶיךָ יְיָ אֱלֹהֵינוּ וֵאלֹהֵי אֲבוֹתֵינוּ הֲלֹא

כָל־הַגִּבּוֹרִים כְּאַיִן לְפָנֶיךָ וְאַנְשֵׁי הַשֵּׁם כְּלֹא

הָיוּ וַחֲכָמִים כִּבְלִי מַדָּע וּנְבוֹנִים כִּבְלִי הַשְׂכֵּל

כִּי רֹב מַעֲשֵׂיהֶם תֹּהוּ וִימֵי חַיֵּיהֶם הֶבֶל לְפָנֶיךָ ·

וּמוֹתַר הָאָדָם מִן־הַבְּהֵמָה אָיִן כִּי הַכֹּל הָבֶל :

in the talmudic tractate of *Yoma*, from which this entire liturgical passage is drawn, describes how God grants full forgiveness only if human conflicts have previously been resolved.[28] Unlike human beings, who may refuse forgiveness,[29] God, particularly if he is addressed at the end of the Day of Atonement in terms including the texts given here,[30] will forgive, thanks to his attribute of mercy, the divine characteristic promoted by the first line of the Shema. The relevance of the Day of Atonement to everyday life is clear from the rabbinic account of how 'Rabbi Eliezer said: Repent the day before you die. His disciples said, "Who knows when he will die?" All the more, then, let him repent today, for he may die tomorrow. Then all his life will be spent in repentance.'[31]

The second talmudic reworking of a biblical text in this paragraph (lines 3–9) is attributed to Mar Samuel and prescribed for the closing service of the Day of Atonement, Ne'ilah, where it still appears.[32] Its opening words, which ask the speaker's worth while appearing to assume that there is none, allude to the scriptural account of how David, when Saul offered him his daughter Merav in marriage, refused with the pretended modesty cited here.[33] David later married her sister, Michal, but they were unhappy and remained childless.[34] Although he is usually regarded as an example of heroism, David is tacitly criticized for the lack

---

[28] BT *Yoma* 85*b*.   [29] BT *Yoma* 86*b*.   [30] BT *Yoma* 87*b*.   [31] *Midrash Psalms* 90: 16.

[32] See the last Amidah of the Day of Atonement. The law-court setting of this plea is noted in Heinemann, *Prayer in the Talmud*, 196–7.

[33] 1 Sam. 18: 18, with a change from 'Who . . .?' to the present 'What . . .?'.

[34] 2 Sam. 6: 20–3.

of integrity which eventually led him to commit both adultery and murder. This quotation thus offers a preview of his dishonesty and contrasts ironically with the demand for honesty in the introductory lines.

By linking the speaker with the life of David, however, it implicitly attributes the delay of redemption to the speaker's unworthiness. Even though when David spoke these words his crime still lay in the future, it was inevitable that he should commit it, since, as this paragraph implies, it was human nature to do so. It follows that the resulting 'punishment' could be averted only by God's mercy, if his crime was indeed to be forgiven, or by his justice, if David's inability to avoid sin is acknowledged. David's role here relates not only to his sinfulness, however, but to his status as forebear of the messiah, himself an expression of mercy, since his advent will resolve all suffering, punitive or otherwise.

The theme of future crime is also implicit in the words *mah nomar*, 'What shall we say?' (lines 4–5), which echo Judah's admission of confusion when Joseph's cup is found in Benjamin's sack.[35] His statement at that moment appears in fuller form later in the morning service in Taḥanun, the penitential section, which lies outside the scope of this book. It is relevant here since Judah's situation is similar to that of David in the previous passage. Judah rightly believes himself and Benjamin to be innocent and, as the liturgical speaker is aware, has no way of knowing that Joseph had incriminated the brothers. However, the speaker is also aware that Judah had earlier been involved in the sale of Joseph and that this would set the scene for Israelite slavery in Egypt. Yet even this was part of the divine plan, since the slavery had been predicted long before to Abraham,[36] and Joseph subsequently described the deed as the work of God.[37] Since the speaker knows Judah's culpability to be necessary to the narrative development, it is possible that God has incriminated the speaker much as Joseph incriminated the brothers.[38] The liturgy at this point echoes the book of Job, therefore, since the speaker understands the action better than the central character and knows that God permits pain for reasons unrelated to the victim's actions, although the liturgical speaker also occupies the role of Job himself. In this way, rabbinic thinkers acknowledged that, if God built the capacity for evil into human character, his right to punish sin is limited.[39]

The 'abounding mercies' in the second line of this paragraph (line 2) contrast ironically with this emerging theme and also with the words *mah yeshuatenu*, 'What, our saving?' (line 4), which seem to challenge the idea of God's ultimate rescue. They probably refer to the elusive grounds for the speaker's own

---

[35] Gen. 44: 16.   [36] Gen. 15: 13–14.   [37] Gen. 45: 8.

[38] The speaker appears to be admitting the guilt of the petitioners before God as judge, but simultaneously to regard him as a litigant in the law case. See Heinemann, *Prayer in the Talmud*, 202.

[39] *Midrash tanḥuma* (Warsaw edn.), 'Bereshit' 9, describes Cain's plea of innocence on the grounds that God had given him the capacity for jealousy and had preferred Abel's offering to his own.

redemption,[40] but Baer recognized intuitively their subversive potential and included them only parenthetically. He would have removed them altogether had the liturgical commentator Isaiah Horowitz not argued that the sevenfold repetition of their interrogative form corresponds to the number of times the word 'vanity' appears in the book of Ecclesiastes and that omitting this element would disturb the symmetry. The presence of this allusion is confirmed by the last line of the text (line 9), which cites one of these occurrences.[41] The words *mah ḥasdenu*, 'What, our kindness [better, 'loyalty']?' (line 3), echo this idea, although they come from a different biblical book. The context also compares Israel's kindness to a 'cloud' or 'dew that early goes away'.[42]

Unease about God's involvement in human suffering is now briefly submerged by fresh disparagement of human worth. Heroes and scholars, listed in the distancing third person in lines 5–9, are now compared to farm animals. The fact that the term 'men of fame' (*anshei hashem*) is used scripturally to describe the children of the 'sons of God' and 'daughters of men' in Genesis,[43] whose descendants the Flood was sent to destroy, suggests that the praise may be barbed. Interest in the superhuman sphere takes centre stage in the first blessing after Barekhu, the call to prayer, when comparing humans to angels incidentally points to their lack of free will and consequent inability to sin.

The reference to *ḥakhamim*, 'the wise', and *nevonim*, 'thinkers' (line 7), suggests that it is Jewish leaders who are denigrated, although in the Ecclesiastes citation in line 9 all humans are compared to domesticated creatures.[44] It has been argued that these animals are mentioned either since human survival in a corrupt society is as precarious as that of animals raised for meat, or because human souls are as likely to survive as those of animals.[45] This double danger leaves the individual no option, according to Ecclesiastes, but 'to rejoice in his works'.[46] An ability to reflect on good fortune might be precisely what distinguishes humans from animals, however, reversing the earlier recognition of the superior senses of the cockerel (Extract 22). Its waking-call could relate to the need to tell the truth publicly, while 'rejoicing' might refer to the performance of the liturgy.

---

[40] An analogous shift of meaning may be seen in the word *zekhut*, which encompasses 'cleanliness' and 'innocence'—its original uses—and 'fitness [for merit]', leading ultimately to 'privilege'. See Ben Yehuda, *Dictionary*, iii. 1328–32, 1335; Jastrow, *Dictionary*, 397–9.

[41] *Sidur avodat yisra'el*, 44–5.   [42] Hos. 6: 4.

[43] Gen. 6: 4, *anshei hashem*.   [44] Eccles. 3: 19.

[45] Eccles. 3: 21 has been interpreted (see Rashi) as an assertion of the difference between human and animal souls, while the masoretic text—not without ambiguity—admits uncertainty: see Gordis, *Koheleth*, 238. Rabbi Johanan's prayer on concluding the book of Job (BT *Ber.* 17a) states the equivalence and specifically mentions animals raised for their meat, although that line is omitted from the version included in the conclusion to the Sephardi sabbath additional service; see *Book of Prayer: Daily and Occasional Prayers*, 120.   [46] Eccles. 3: 22.

Some have identified 'animals' not only with domesticated creatures, but with humans who inflict pain on the speaker. Yet the speaker is unlikely to be compared to a perpetrator, and the Hebrew term clearly refers to 'farm animals' rather than to carnivores, comparing humans to animals raised for their master's profit, irrespective of their fate.[47] Like the reader of the book of Job, the liturgical speaker reflects on human ignorance of God's purpose and argues that not all suffering is punitive.

The body of this paragraph therefore qualifies the mercy referred to in the second line and uncovers the speaker's horror at the human condition. But the speaker is not reduced to passivity by this train of thought, for the juxtaposition of biblical and rabbinic sources makes it possible to construct theological propositions of a complexity and precision impossible to express otherwise.

EXTRACT 29. **The Challenge of the Covenant**

The first word of this paragraph (*aval*) appears to contrast the powerlessness of humanity with the covenantal relations with God enjoyed by Jews, pointing to the difference between what has gone before and what is to come. But it could equally reinforce aspects of the previous paragraph in the sense of 'nay, indeed', and this is an uncertainty which runs through the lines that follow.[48] A contrastive 'but', which would assume that the previous paragraph refers only to non-Jews and not to the speaker, would ignore the common midrashic assumption about the decline of the generations, as well as the daily dangers faced by exiled Jews in the present. The word may therefore reflect the view implied in the previous paragraph that Jews fare no better than the rest of humanity.

A similar ambivalence emerges in the midrashic texts from which the present extracts are derived. The opening words appear in *Mekhilta*, in the context of

[47] An echo of this is found in the apparent interchangeability of the victims of the Angel of Death, chosen by their names no matter what their identity, in BT *Ḥag.* 4b–5a.

[48] Gesenius, *Handwoerterbuch*, 6, reads this word in Gen. 42: 21 and 2 Sam. 14: 5 as 'gewiss, in der Tat' (in the sense of reinforcing), and in Gen. 17: 19 as 'nein, vielmehr' (in an adversative sense). Jastrow, *Dictionary*, 6, reads it in Tosefta *Eruv.* 5: 1 as 'yes, indeed' and elsewhere as 'but, however' reflecting a similar distinction. Ben Yehuda, *Dictionary*, i. 27, divides the first meaning into two: 'truly, indeed, in der That, gewiss, en vérité, vraiement' and 'nay, indeed, gar wohl, vielmehr, de plus', distinguishing these from the adversative 'but', although some of the examples of his third usage might equally be read in the first or second. Schonfeld translates the term as 'nevertheless', which neatly captures both senses. Baer prefers the first meaning, which he gives as *be'emet*, but he then relates it to Gen. 17: 19 which suggests a distinction. It has been suggested that '*aval* is always a strong adversative (cf. *bal*, 'not'); any asseveration depends on contrast. (General awareness has led modern Hebrew > Yiddish to equate *aval* with *aber*, whereas it is nearer to *sondern*.) Baer was under the spell of the Yiddish *avol*, but corrects himself' (Raphael Loewe, pers. comm.). In the present context the term does allow at least a shadow of the possibility that a strong contrast is not being declared.

comments on the Song of the Sea, sung by the Israelites after the sea had been divided to let them through.[49] This archetypal scene of rescue is associated here with the speaker's survival of the night and, because the crossing of the Red Sea is a model of the future messianic redemption, with God's ability to save the speaker from the dangers of the day ahead. The same midrashic text and a later compilation, *Yalkut shimoni*, relate the words to the previous verse in the Song of the Sea, 'The Lord shall reign for ever and ever',[50] and point out that the imperfect tense suggests that the Israelites were implicitly denying God's present rule. Had they not done so, the writers argue, the messianic age would have begun immediately. The liturgical passage thus points both to the rescue of the Israelites at the Red Sea and to the reason that their descendants still await salvation.

The way in which the opening word reinforces the theme of the previous paragraph, however, is joined by contrastive associations that suggest precisely the opposite. The subsequent clauses suggest that the covenants with the patriarchs are the source of the speaker's continuing privilege, Abraham being referred to as 'your friend' (lines 1–2), echoing Jehoshaphat's prayer before battle[51] and a prophecy of return to the land by Isaiah.[52] Mentioning Mount Moriah (line 2), the site of the Akedah, however, points to the suffering associated with the covenant and to the way in which Abraham had to accept the role of perpetrator, much as Nebuchadnezzar is paradoxically described as God's agent in punishing Jerusalem.[53]

The speaker is also identified with the 'children of Abraham' (lines 1–2) and particularly with Isaac, 'his only son . . . who was bound' (lines 2–3), the passive participant in events over which he had no control,[54] although this scene is conventionally read as premeditated martyrdom. The biblical description of Isaac as Abraham's 'only' son—part of a longer biblical description interpreted as God's attempt to break the news about the Binding to Abraham gently[55]—reminds the speaker that Isaac is in fact not an only son. Ishmael's expulsion to safeguard Isaac's privileges, described in the biblical chapter preceding the Akedah, points to the dangers and ambiguities of the covenant.

The reference to Jacob as God's 'firstborn son' (lines 3–4) additionally alludes to the dangers of primogeniture because of the transaction with Esau.[56] The

---

[49] *Mekhilta derabi shimon bar yoḥai*, 70, on Exod. 15: 19; *Mekhilta derabi yishma'el*, ii. 80, on Exod. 15: 18. [50] *Yalkut shimoni*, Exod. 253 on Exod. 15: 18.

[51] 2 Chr. 20: 7. [52] Isa. 41: 8.

[53] *Gen. Rabbah* 56: 4 describes Abraham's awareness that the sacrifice would make him a murderer. For Nebuchadnezzar see Isa. 10: 5–6. In Jer. 25: 9 he is referred to as God's servant; see also 32: 3–5.

[54] Gen. 22: 2 for 'only'; although Zedekiah ben Abraham, *Shibolei haleket*, 3*b*, argues that Isaac was the only patriarch to have a 'single' name and that he was thus born with all the attributes required by God, unlike his father and his son, Jacob.

[55] Rashi on Gen. 22: 2. [56] Gen. 27: 32, Rashi on Gen. 25: 31–2.

Nevertheless, we are thy °People, the children of thy	*II Cr.* 19,²⁻
Covenant, the °descendants of Abraham that loved thee, to whom	*II Cr.* 20,⁷
thou didst °make oath on °Mount Moriah, the seed of Isaac,	*Gn.* 22,¹⁶
his only son, who lay bound upon the altar, the community of	*Gn.* 22,²,¹⁴
Jacob, thy °firstling son—because of the love with which thou	*Ex.* 4,²²
didst °love him and because of the joy with which thou didst	*Mal.* 1,²
rejoice over him, °thou didst call his name Israel and °*Yeshurun;*	*Gn.* 35,¹⁰; *Is.* 44,²

29. The challenge of the covenant (*Aval anaḥnu amekha benei veritekha*)

firstborn title, applied to Israel when Moses asked Pharaoh to release the Israelites,[57] is also central to two of the texts in the *tefilin*, pointing to the ambivalence of this paragraph.[58] Another allusion to uncertainty about Jewish privilege lies in the reference to Jacob's change of name (line 5). In Hebrew thought a name is linked to character, especially in the case of God, the revelation of whose 'name' is equated to understanding his behaviour[59] or his 'reputation'. When God changes the names of patriarchs he thus demonstrates his mastery over them, as Adam did over the animals by naming them. The passivity of both people and animals at such moments of naming reinforces their powerlessness.

The emphasis here on the name *yisra'el* implies the negative associations of *ya'akov*, the root of which, 'heel', is punningly used by Esau as an insult during their argument over the birthright.[60] The rabbinic view is that, since Esau could not maintain the ritual purity demanded of the firstborn, Jacob was saving his life by ridding him of his ceremonial responsibilities,[61] but this is called into question by his change of name to *yisra'el*, biblically explained as a reference to Jacob's ability to survive conflict. This suggests that the night-time struggle with the angel, like the speaker's survival of the night, transformed and strengthened Jacob for the days ahead, and may allude to the tussle with Torah in the first blessing over study (Extract 18, lines 1–2).[62] Yet the subsequent use of the name *yeshurun*, literally 'honest' or 'upright',[63] underlines in turn the negative connotations of that name too. Since no rabbinic texts explain what the shortcomings of *yisra'el* might be, one may hypothesize that the 'tussle' with Torah, possibly alluded to in the name, suggests incomprehension and therefore exile. Even the name *yeshurun* has negative associations, however, for it appears in the penta-

---

[57] Exod. 4: 22.   [58] See the discussion in Ch. 5 on Extract 7.

[59] Exod. 3: 15. See R. Loewe, 'Hebrew Linguistics', 98–9.

[60] Gen. 26: 36; and especially Nahmanides on Deut. 7: 12, where 'Yeshurun', e.g. Isa. 44: 2, is seen as a critique of Jacob's behaviour. See also Abrahams, *Companion*, p. xxii.

[61] Rashi on Gen. 25: 32.   [62] Gen. 32: 28, 35: 10.

[63] Kimhi on Isa. 44: 2, Ibn Ezra on Deut. 32: 15, and Nahmanides on Deut. 33: 5. It should be noted that both names contain a similar root, implying that the change is significant.

אֲבָל אֲנַחְנוּ עַמְּךָ בְּנֵי בְרִיתֶךָ · בְּנֵי אַבְרָהָם 1

אֹהַבְךָ שֶׁנִּשְׁבַּעְתָּ לוֹ בְּהַר הַמֹּרִיָּה · זֶרַע יִצְחָק 2

יְחִידוֹ שֶׁנֶּעֱקַד עַל גַּב־הַמִּזְבֵּחַ עֲדַת יַעֲקֹב בִּנְךָ 3

בְּכוֹרֶךָ שֶׁמֵּאַהֲבָתְךָ שֶׁאָהַבְתָּ אֹתוֹ וּמִשִּׂמְחָתְךָ 4

שֶׁשָּׂמַחְתָּ־בּוֹ קָרָאתָ אֶת־שְׁמוֹ יִשְׂרָאֵל וִישֻׁרוּן : 5

teuchal account of the inevitability of Jewish exile due to neglect of Torah. Once prosperity is secured, 'Yeshurun will kick', describing the complacency resulting from easy living.[64]

Exile is attributed in another midrashic text to the failure of parents to imitate God's loving revelation and to teach their children Torah.[65] Since some are prevented from doing so by persecution, the midrash asks for immediate redemption as a reward for those who continue to teach despite difficulties. The speaker's own act of study, flawed as it is by departing from the sources in order to generate this textual mosaic, can thus be seen as an attempt to encourage God to bring the messiah by aligning daily sufferings with the trials of the patriarchs, the primary source of merit.[66]

EXTRACT 30. On the Duty to Praise

After this survey of the sacred narrative from the patriarchs to the Exodus, the speaker's independence of voice is emphasized by a text incorporating no rabbinic sources, although it does employ scriptural and rabbinic terminology.[67] Leaving study behind, the speaker returns to a prayerfulness last seen in Extract 26, before the flight from theological impasse led to a similar change of genre.

Liturgical models for the opening word, which means 'therefore', suggest that this passage forms a climax to the entire liturgy so far,[68] and thus to the idea that

[64] The theme appears in Deut. 4: 25 and culminates in 32: 15.

[65] For the 'love' and 'joy' of God in Israel and the source of suffering see *Tana debei eliyahu*, ch. 19, p. 112, trans. Braude and Kapstein, pp. 243–4. [66] *Lev. Rabbah* 36: 6.

[67] Non-scriptural forms, such as *ḥayavim* and *hodayah*, do not detract from the scriptural core of the language used.

[68] The clause appears in the Passover Haggadah at the head of a paragraph that marks a turning point in the ceremony: it concludes the several expository sections of the Passover narrative, including lists of the plagues brought on the Egyptians, and introduces the Hallel. If this is a 'source' for the present passage it emphasizes that its origins do not lie in study. A midrashic source may have

It is, °therefore, our obligation to acknowledge unto thee,	*Ps.* 16,⁵
to praise thee, to glorify thee, to °bless, to hallow and render	*Mai. YT* 5,¹⁻⁹
praise and thanksgiving unto thy name; °well for us!—how	*Ps.* 128,²
goodly is our portion, how °pleasant our lot, how beautiful	*Prv.* 3,¹⁷
our heritage! Well for us! that we arise and retire, °at eve and	*Ps.* 55,¹⁸
at morn, declaring °twice daily:	*Mai. Sm.* 1,¹

30. On the duty to praise (*Lefikhakh anaḥnu ḥayavim lehodot lekha*)

the best response to suffering is the celebration of survival,[69] as embodied in the first statutory blessing of the morning (which lies outside the scope of this book).[70] The ambiguity of the first word of the previous paragraph, *aval*, leaves it uncertain, however, whether the present text offers thanks for Jewish distinctiveness or expresses acceptance of the universal helplessness previously compared to that of domestic animals. If the latter is preferred, this text would affirm God's responsibility for human suffering and reverse the retreat from the impasse at the beginning of this sequence in Extract 27, celebrating the refusal of troublesome ideas to be repressed. In practice, however, both meanings are relevant, since the text blends apprehension for the future with relief at survival.[71]

The seven forms of praise announced next (Extract 30, lines 1–2), matching in number the expressions of disparagement on the previous page (Extract 28, lines 3–4) and the references to 'vanity' in Ecclesiastes, are offered to God's 'name', a term relating, as previously noted, to God's nature, character, and reputation in general.[72] It also alludes to the long-expected first line of the Shema—which might have followed immediately after Extract 27, but is about to appear only now—and which, by proposing the unity of the two divine names and their distinctive associations, resolves the problem of suffering.

These seven types of praise and the seven disparaging interrogatives on the previous page are now complemented by three expressions of praise (lines 3–4), again in the form of interrogatives. The threefold form suggests a progression or

existed for this and have been lost; but the informed reader would be aware only that this is not a study text.

[69] See the similar theme discussed in the remarks on Extract 25, line 8.

[70] This sense of wonder emerges clearly in the first blessing after the call to prayer, before the Shema.

[71] This is encountered, for example, in the declaration in the Passover Haggadah that 'in every generation people stand up to destroy us, but the Holy One, blessed be He, saves us from their hand' (see p. 168, n. 61, above).   [72] Lev. 22: 32; Ezek. 36: 23, 39: 25.

לְפִיכָךְ אֲנַחְנוּ חַיָּבִים לְהוֹדוֹת לְךָ וּלְשַׁבֵּחֲךָ 1

וּלְפָאֶרְךָ וּלְבָרֶךְ וּלְקַדֵּשׁ וְלָתֶת־שֶׁבַח וְהוֹדָיָה 2

לִשְׁמֶךָ: אַשְׁרֵינוּ מַה־טּוֹב חֶלְקֵנוּ וּמַה־נָּעִים 3

גּוֹרָלֵנוּ וּמַה־יָּפָה יְרֻשָּׁתֵנוּ אַשְׁרֵינוּ שֶׁאֲנַחְנוּ 4

מַשְׁכִּימִים וּמַעֲרִיבִים עֶרֶב וָבֹקֶר וְאוֹמְרִים 5

פַּעֲמַיִם בְּכָל־יוֹם 6

at least a clear contrast between them, but commentators have had little success in decoding the allusions. It is possible that the terms are equivalent and that the superficial themes of thanks and joy are undercut with an awareness of shortcomings in each case. The first expresses thanks for *ḥelkenu*, 'our portion', a term occasionally scripturally applied to God, but which echoes the acceptance of fate in the previous paragraph by analogy with the mishnaic axiom 'Who is wealthy? He who rejoices in his portion [*ḥelko*].'[73] The second term, *goralenu*, 'our lot', is linked to the former one, 'portion', in one psalmic reference, again suggesting the positive nature of God's relationship to Jews, but it also appears in the more ambiguous biblical scene in which tribal territories in the Promised Land were chosen by lot, and the fateful moment at which the scapegoat was chosen on the Day of Atonement, a scene re-enacted verbally each year on that fast-day, alluding to the more negative aspects of the relationship.[74] The third term, *yerushatenu*, 'heritage', is closely linked to the idea of the promise of the Land, but the speaker's present exile compromises the positive nature of these associations.[75]

The adjectives 'good', 'pleasant', and 'beautiful' attached to these terms again superficially suggest intensification and progression, but have ambiguous associations. *Tov*, 'good', is a leitmotif of the Creation narrative, but is rendered ironic by the exile from Eden; *na'im*, 'pleasant', may refer to the Torah by analogy with

[73] *Sidur avodat yisra'el*, 45, states that the three clauses relate to this world, the world to come, and the messianic age, but gives no supporting evidence. For 'portion' as God, see Pss. 16: 5, 119: 57 and Lam. 3: 24. For its use suggesting resignation see Mishnah *Avot* 4: 1.

[74] See Ps. 16: 5 for the juxtaposition of both terms. For the division of land see Num. 26: 55–6, and for the scapegoat, Lev. 16: 9–10, a text recited on the morning of the Day of Atonement. The association with death is reinforced by the appearance of the word in Jonah 1: 7, recited in the afternoon of the same day.

[75] The word appears consistently in association with the Land in scriptural contexts, for instance in Exod. 6: 8 and, as a verb, in Deut. 6: 18. A near-synonym, *naḥalah*, appears in Ps. 16: 6, immediately after the psalmic verse containing the previous two terms, suggesting a relationship between that psalmic text and this liturgical one.

a scriptural verse recited by Ashkenazim at the closing of the Ark, but the opacity of revelation makes this an ambivalent association; while *yafah*, 'beautiful', a keyword for the love between God and Israel depicted, according to normative rabbinic readings, in the Song of Songs, again has ambivalent associations in view of the exile. It would be tempting to see in these adjectives an allusion to a 'creation—revelation—redemption' sequence, but the evidence is too slight to permit it.[76] These mixed messages about the benefits of the covenant, and especially of the Torah to which it is essential to achieve closeness if the speaker is to remain in the Land, neatly set the scene for the multivalence of the first line of the Shema which is shortly to follow.

The balance is tipped strongly towards the speaker's well-being, however, by the twofold assertion 'Well for us!' (lines 3 and 4), recalling the verses from Psalms 84 and 144 that form the liturgical prologue to Psalm 145, which is recited thrice daily and asserts the happiness of those who dwell in God's house.[77] For the speaker at this moment, therefore, hope lies in rising early to pray and study (line 5), precisely as this paragraph states. Nevertheless, since the verb for rising early is associated with Abraham's trials, as seen earlier in Extract 27 and Extract 20, lines 4–5, the associations with martyrdom are simultaneously renewed.

The present paragraph thus appears to provide a transition between protest at suffering and hope based on study, but the speaker is left with the ambivalent benefits both of study and of the morning worship founded by Abraham. The ambiguity established over the previous paragraphs is maintained in this way, setting the scene for the central mystery of Judaism in the next line.

EXTRACT 31. **The First Line of the Shema**

This, the first sentence of the central credal statement of rabbinic Judaism, the Shema,[78] seems to be the goal towards which the speaker has been moving since the earlier intimation, in Extract 27, that a statement of some kind was about to be made. It is also the major text contained in the *tefilin*, as discussed above, its initial letter, *shin*, appearing on the box worn on the head as well as on the back of the parchment of the *mezuzah*, the scroll bearing the first two paragraphs of the Shema which is attached to doorposts (derived from the same biblical paragraphs as the *tefilin*; the *shin* either remains visible through an aperture in the case or is indicated by an occasionally stylized letter on the case if it is entirely closed). Although only the first line of the Shema appears here, it enables the speaker to enact the instruction to discuss the Torah 'when you rise up', which

---

[76] For 'good' see Gen. 1: 4, 10, 12, 18, 21, 25, 31; for 'pleasant' see Prov. 3: 17; and for 'beautiful' in S. of S. see Mandelkern, *Veteris Testamenti Concordantiae*, 493.

[77] See Pss. 84: 5, 144: 15, and see the remarks on Extract 48, lines 1–2.   [78] Deut. 6: 4.

appears later in the first paragraph of the Shema.[79] It also provides a preview of the full text to be recited later in the morning, although this lies outside the scope of the present book. This is therefore more an illustration of what it would be like to recite the Shema than a recital in itself, even though the words are indeed recited.

The point of its presence here would be missed if this reading were to be regarded as only a procedural convenience or as a response to a ritual requirement, however. The association of the first paragraph of the Shema with the problematic nature of relating to God is clear from its rabbinic name, 'acceptance of the yoke of heaven', a deed which is performed by the act of Torah study demanded and made possible by reciting the Shema itself.[80] So central is this duty of study that this first verse of the Shema has been used as a deathbed confession and martyrs' prayer (attributed talmudically to Akiba), bearing associations with suffering referred to earlier.[81]

Most obviously, the first line of the Shema embodies the sort of 'truth' it is necessary to acknowledge in order to be 'heaven-fearing (or 'heaven-loving')', as demanded in the declaration in Extract 27, line 1. Acknowledging this truth, it is implied, will enable one to endure or understand daily dangers. But the text itself exemplifies the opacity of revelation, showing how reading must be accompanied by interpretation if sense is to emerge. Any suggestion that revelation affords privilege is undermined by the discovery that complete understanding of Torah is impossible due to the obscurity of this verse.[82]

The opening word of the Shema, a second person singular imperative meaning 'Hear', suggests that an unequivocal assertion is about to be made. However, the declaration of God's unity in this central credal statement is undermined by the way he is referred to by two names. The choice of this particular verse for such a credal role forms a climax to the liturgical theme of the Torah's opacity and demonstrates the irresistible nature of the rabbinic urge to confront precisely those parts of revelation most in need of interpretation. Underlying this declaration of unity, therefore, lies an awareness of disunity, deriving in part from the duplication of the names of God throughout the Bible. However, as discussed in Chapter 5, the two divine names also reflect an awareness of the duality of human experience, divisible into 'well-being' and 'hardship', or even 'good' and 'evil'.

---

[79] Deut. 6: 7. Some held that Deut. 6: 4 represents the entire Shema: BT *Ber.* 13b, BT *Suk.* 42a. This recital is designed to ensure that it is read near the beginning of the day; Jacob ben Asher, *Arba'ah turim*, 'Oraḥ ḥayim' 46.

[80] See Loewe in Montefiore and Loewe (eds.), *Rabbinic Anthology*, 642.　　　[81] BT *Ber.* 61b.

[82] The impossibility of completely obeying Torah, implicitly because of the difficulty of interpretation, is alluded to in the report of a debate in BT *Eruv.* 13b concerning whether it would have been better if humanity had not been created. In his comments on this passage Samuel Edels (Maharsha, 1555–1631) points out that the 365 negative commands would inevitably be kept if humans had not been created, compared with the 248 positive ones which are difficult to interpret.

°HEARKEN, O ISRAEL!—GOD OUR LORD, GOD IS ONENESS!   *B'Br.* 13:

°Blest is the Name—the reverence of His sovereignty for ever and aye!   *SA-OH* 46,⁹

31. The first line of the Shema and *Barukh shem*

Theologians have struggled to reconcile suffering with the goodness of God, most commonly by suggesting that it is punitive. But this idea, already shown by the liturgy to be untenable (by the use of arguments similar to those in the book of Job), has led rabbinic Jews to relate each divine name to a distinctive range of attributes. The Tetragrammaton, repeated twice in this line, is associated with mercy, protection, and kindness, while the name *elohim*, which appears once, flanked and outnumbered by the other, is linked to divine justice, judgement, and severity.[83] This subdivision of characteristics provides a theological framework for the division of experience into events generating experiences of well-being or of suffering.[84] Rabbinic texts explain how these attributes must be held in balance if the world is to survive, but that mercy must remain in the ascendant. The doubling here of the relevant name implies that the speaker is expected to help ensure this.[85] The scriptural use of these names may suggest that this difficulty is shared even by God, since he occasionally 'weeps' for Israel's suffering[86] or actually shares in it.[87] The tension between the attributes is dramatized in an aggadic description of how God 'prays' (i.e. seeks to ensure) that his own attribute of mercy will prevail over his attribute of justice,[88] as though he 'hopes' that punitive suffering will be averted.

These dual qualities are addressed here to *yisra'el*, the name given to Jacob after his struggle with the 'angel', in a naming scene recalling Adam's demonstration of 'dominion' over the animals,[89] alluded to in an earlier liturgical paragraph. This name is composed of *el*, a component of *elohim*, connoting severity and used in the scriptural description of the fight,[90] and of a form of *yasar*, the verb 'to struggle'. Jacob's new name thus means 'struggler with God', although this seems less of an adversarial conflict than a dispute over the proper relationship to God. In the present context the struggle referred to involves reconciling the aspects of God represented by the divine names in the Shema.

---

[83] See *Yalkut shimoni*, Deut. 835 (which describes how Israel remains loyal to God whatever the conditions) and Malbim on Deut. 6: 4 for an interpretation of this line based on the contrasting connotations of the two divine names. These and related responses are outlined in Jacobs, *Principles of the Jewish Faith*, 95–113.

[84] *Gen. Rabbah* 12: 15, 33: 3; *Exod. Rabbah* 3: 6; *Midrash tanḥuma* (Warsaw edn.), 'Shemot' 20.

[85] *Gen. Rabbah* 12: 15.   [86] Jer. 13: 17.   [87] Isa. 43: 2.

[88] BT *Ber.* 7a.   [89] Gen. 1: 26, 2: 20.

[90] Hos. 12: 4–5; although *el*, meaning 'powerful one', is indirectly linked to the rabbinic understanding of *elohim*.

שְׁמַע יִשְׂרָאֵל יְיָ אֱלֹהֵינוּ יְיָ אֶחָד׃   1

בָּרוּךְ שֵׁם כְּבוֹד מַלְכוּתוֹ לְעוֹלָם וָעֶד׃   2

The first verse of the Shema therefore challenges the speaker to recognize how the divine names—and the categories of experience that relate to them—can be reconciled as a prelude to the full 'unification' of God, which the prophets identify with the messianic resolution of all conflict.[91] The anxiety surrounding this ambition is reflected in a talmudic discussion which describes how the last word of the line should be drawn out to emphasize the last letter, a *dalet*, the numerical value of which is four. This is explained by Rashi as an attempt to unify 'up and down', meaning heaven and earth, with the four points of the compass, although it is surprising in this context to find a concern with any number other than one. The impossibility of drawing out a dental sound such as 'd'—the long 'ah' which precedes it is extended instead—further illustrates the opacity of Torah.[92]

The full implications of the division between the names of God are not explored by rabbinic texts, perhaps because they did not wish to encourage the uninitiated to contemplate them. Indeed, although an understanding of divine unity would overcome the ambivalences which have come increasingly to dominate the liturgy, this goal is no more attainable than a complete understanding of Torah. Such a realization is central to the experiences of martyrs and those on their deathbed, as noted earlier in connection with allusions to Abraham's attempt to save the cities of the plain (Extract 27, line 2) and his involvement in the Akedah (Extract 29, line 3). But even if perfect study and the unification of God's attributes are beyond human reach, the daily repetition of this verse demonstrates how Jews refuse to despair, despite the difficulty the verse exemplifies. Perhaps more than any other text, it attests to the complexity of the nature of God, which may account for its role as the central Jewish mystery.

The line that follows the Shema (line 2), which appears again later in the same location in the full liturgical reading, is invariably included here, even though it is not part of the biblical text. It is midrashically attributed to angels, who are said to proclaim it in response to Jews pronouncing the Shema,[93] and is read in an undertone to avoid imitating angelic ways. It is said aloud only on the Day of Atonement, when Jews are said to resemble angels thanks to their denial of physical needs.[94] The phrase was in regular use in the Temple as a response to each

[91] Zeph. 3: 9; Zech. 14: 9.   [92] BT *Ber.* 13*b*.

[93] *Gen. Rabbah* 65: 21 and the discussion in Gaguine, *Keter shem tov*, i–ii. 29 n. 49.

[94] *Deut. Rabbah* 2: 36.

mention of the Tetragrammaton, suggesting that its recital here is part of an attempt to recapture the prayerfulness assumed to have characterized worship there, especially when it is read out loud on the Day of Atonement in the context of a description of the Temple ritual.[95]

Another midrash relates how Jacob, on his deathbed, asked his sons whether they believed in God's unity and they answered by proclaiming the first line of the Shema. He responded by pronouncing the present line to confirm their statement,[96] and it is in this sense that it appears here. Its function is similar to the practice of reciting it after pronouncing God's name 'in vain', as in a blessing read in error. Employing the present line under such circumstances transforms the divine name into a term of praise, which is why it was included after the second blessing pronounced over the *tefilin*, in Extract 8, line 5.[97]

Including the formula at this point accordingly suggests that the first line of the Shema, recited here ostensibly as an act of study, is itself a particular 'name' of God that needs to be 'unsaid' by means of the present statement, or merely transformed into a statement of praise. The ambiguity of the first verse of the Shema suggests that it represents more than the superficial meaning of its words: the dual divine names imply that it challenges the speaker to comprehend a divine mystery on a theological level and the multiplicity of experience on an emotional level. The associations of this response with the Temple transport the speaker to a virtual setting far from the here and now, suggesting the otherworldly nature of the problem this sentence confronts.

EXTRACT 32. A Challenge to Martyrdom

While the credal statement was originally addressed by God to Israel, the present text, which opens with a second person singular pronoun, is addressed directly by the speaker to God. It focuses on God's timelessness and mastery, but soon returns to the problem of reconciling mercy and judgement, acknowledging that the challenge offered by the Shema is beyond human power to meet. It adds to this proposition, however, by challenging God to protect Jews in his own self-interest, shifting from the third to the second person to invite him to 'sanctify his name through those who sanctify your name'. This suggests that God should ensure his own reputation, but also that his people's survival might accomplish the Shema's goal of unifying the principles of life and death, combining the dual divine attributes. The closing reference to the 'sanctification of the name' in line 3 suggests that the present passage concludes not merely the Shema, but also the sequence that opened with Extract 27, rounding off the discussion of suffering that has dominated these paragraphs.

---

[95] Mishnah *Yoma* 3: 8.   [96] *Gen. Rabbah* 98: 3.

[97] It remains optional in the Sephardi rite: see *Book of Prayer: Daily and Occasional Prayers*, 2.

The passage is derived from two sources, taking leave of the near-perfect act of study that underlay the first line of the Shema.[98] Part of it appears in the *Yalkut shimoni*'s discussion of the Shema, in which God's fury with the world and his desire to destroy it are said to be provoked by idolatry,[99] more particularly by the flourishing of pagan theatres and circuses while the Temple lies in ruins. This anger is averted only when God hears the angels around him respond with this passage to Jews reciting the Shema on earth in the early morning. The Shema, this suggests, can shift the divine attributes from judgement towards mercy, though only with the help of this angelic response. It also suggests that humans could better understand the credal statement if they resembled the angels more closely, as the response to the Shema suggests the speaker is trying to do.

The context of the second source, a passage from *Tana debei eliyahu*,[100] implies that the credal statement enables the speaker to overcome the fall of the Temple that inaugurated the present exile and to introduce a Temple-rebuilding metaphor that will later dominate the liturgy. The discussion here of the first of the Ten Commandments argues that, since the Decalogue is in the first person singular, it represents a personal declaration by God to each individual. This resembles the Shema, however, especially as the last words of the third paragraph of the Shema approximate to the opening ones of the Decalogue. The *Yalkut shimoni* passage cited here goes on to describe how the creed encapsulates the teachings of the Ten Commandments. The liturgical text, however, differs from the *Tana debei eliyahu* version, which is in the first person singular, pointing not only to uncertainty about Torah, since the liturgy departs from the midrashic text, but to a lack of clarity about precisely whose voice—that of God or that of Israel—recites the present liturgical statement, an ambiguity which implicitly affects the Shema, which appears to be God's statement but is now spoken by humans.

The reference to the hallowing of a single divine 'name' in the last line of the liturgical unit suggests that this passage aspires to resolve the disparity between the divine names in the Shema. But neither name in the credal statement appears here, that of mercy in the blessing formula itself being omitted in the Sephardi version. The lack of equilibrium between the attributes associated with the names is reflected in the last line of the second midrashic context, however, which culminates in a citation of the strongest scriptural statement of the gratuitous nature of divine–human relations: 'I kill and I make alive.'[101] In the

---

[98] *Yalkut shimoni*, Deut. 836 is a late source for the text up to the first word of line 4, based on JT *Ber.* ch. 9 (*haro'eh*): see the discussion in *Tselota di'avraham*, i. 78–9 (in the commentary 'Vaya'as avraham'). *Tana debei eliyahu*, ch. 24, p. 130, trans. Braude and Kapstein, p. 282, is an earlier source for the text up to the third word of line 3, but in the first person singular voice of God.

[99] For a description of God's anger, the way he prays to himself that it should be overcome by his mercy, and how it can be exploited by Israel's enemies, see BT *Ber.* 7a.

[100] *Tana debei eliyahu*, ch. 24, p. 130, trans. Braude and Kapstein, p. 282.   [101] Deut. 32: 39.

°Thou indeed, wast before the world was created; thou art	*II Sm.* 7,[28]
the same after its creation; thou art He in °this world and	*Msh. Br.* 9,[5]
thou art He for the world to come; °hallow thy name through	*Ez.* 20,[41]
them that sanctify thy name, yea, °hallow thy name in thy	*Mai. YT*5,[11]
world, and with thy salvation uplift and °upraise our horn-	*Ps.* 89,[18]
emblem—blest art thou God, that °hallowest thy name amongst	*Ez.* 38,[23]; 36,[23]
the masses!	*Ku.* 1,[4]

32. A challenge to martyrdom (*Atah hu ad shelo nivra ha'olam*)

Sephardi version the name associated with judgement is included once, suggesting the dominance of this attribute.[102] But the reference to a single 'name' in all versions suggests that the Shema might itself be this 'name', in which both names appear, although the attribute of mercy there is dominant. The Sephardi rite emphasizes the problematic nature of God's dual identity by adding the word 'one' to the first line of the passage, to read 'You were One before you created the world',[103] specifying that the essential unity of the name has never been compromised, whatever the interplay of attributes governing the world. It also points to the salvation that would result if all were able to participate in the public 'unification' of God's name (an idea mentioned earlier in connection with the allusion to the last verse of the Song of the Sea in the paragraph beginning in Extract 29, line 1).

The final word of line 5, *barabim*, translated here as 'amongst the masses', would be better rendered 'in public', alluding to the speaker's communal setting. The rabbinic associations of the Shema implied that the speaker has accepted 'sanctification' in the sense of martyrdom (on which see more below), but since martyrdom must be faced (in certain well-defined cases) only if the desecration one is forced to perform would be witnessed by a quorum of ten adults, the recital of the Shema in a prayer-meeting in the presence of a quorum is tantamount to a declaration of preparedness to do so.[104] Between the lines one may detect an awareness of the paradox that Jewish martyrdom might be interpreted as disproving God's salvific power, although it is called 'sanctification of God's name'.

The request that God 'sanctify' his name through those who 'sanctify' it (lines 2–3) relates to the prophetic idea that the ingathering will cause non-Jews to

---

[102] *Book of Prayer: Daily and Occasional Prayers*, 8.

[103] Ibid. As has been said, in the Sephardi rite the blessing formula at the end of the present version refers to the speaker rather than God: 'Blessed be he who sanctifies your name in public' (Jacob ben Asher, *Arba'ah turim*, 'Orah hayim' 46).

[104] BT *San.* 74*a–b*. Other references to 'in public' in this context are BT *AZ* 27*b*, 54*a*.

אַתָּה הוּא עַד שֶׁלֹּא נִבְרָא הָעוֹלָם אַתָּה הוּא   1

מִשֶּׁנִּבְרָא הָעוֹלָם אַתָּה הוּא בָּעוֹלָם הַזֶּה וְאַתָּה   2

הוּא לָעוֹלָם הַבָּא קַדֵּשׁ אֶת שִׁמְךָ עַל מַקְדִּישֵׁי   3

שְׁמֶךָ וְקַדֵּשׁ אֶת שִׁמְךָ בְּעוֹלָמְךָ וּבִישׁוּעָתְךָ תָּרוּם   4

וְתַגְבִּיהַּ קַרְנֵנוּ כָּאֲ"יָ מְקַדֵּשׁ אֶת־שִׁמְךָ בָּרַבִּים׃   5

'sanctify' him, since the redemption of the Jews will demonstrate his power.[105] But making God himself responsible for ensuring that this happens effectively relieves the speaker of this responsibility, although it is still necessary to cause others to think well of God by avoiding bad behaviour. This concluding statement is ambiguous, however, because the duty to 'sanctify' God's name has become synonymous in rabbinic thought with martyrdom,[106] with which the Shema is also often associated (as mentioned in connection with Extract 27, line 2). Yet martyrdom of the kind represented by the Binding of Isaac, even though this was identified as one of the foundations of the covenant in Extract 29, line 3, could easily compromise affirmation of God's power demonstrated by his ability to protect his own people and, in addition, encourage child sacrifice.[107]

The contradiction between the kind of 'sanctification' based on God's successful protection of his people and that which emerges from his people's preparedness to sacrifice themselves in his service points to an earlier theological problem. It was implied above in Extract 32, line 3, that the demand for honesty in daily life should apply to God too, based on the view that he has neglected so far to fulfil his side of the covenant.[108] It is possible, however, that the speaker's request that God sanctify his own name alludes to an invitation to provide an opportunity for martyrdom. This can be seen from a midrashic description of Moses' and Aaron's reaction to Pharaoh's demand that they identify their God. Although they feared that he would have them killed if they answered honestly, they were consoled by the thought that their response would be a 'sanctification of God's name' and responded, according to this midrash, with a version of the present liturgical passage.[109] Their deaths would have been a 'desecration' of God's name for Jeremiah, however, who interceded during a drought by arguing that God was bringing himself into disrepute by forcing his people to live as homeless wanderers.[110]

[105] Ezek. 20: 41, 36: 20–3.   [106] Lev. 22: 32 and BT *San.* 74*a*–*b*.
[107] Lev. 18: 21.   [108] Lev. 19: 12; desecration is the cause of suffering in Mishnah *Avot* 5: 11.
[109] *Exod. Rabbah* 5: 14.   [110] Jer. 14: 9.

This shift of responsibility, from the speaker to God, for ensuring that God's name be held in honour, is illustrated by comparing the beginning of the present sequence (Extract 27) with the 'seal' (line 5). The opening lines in the liturgical version used here insisted that God be revered in private, implicitly linking this to the Shema, but failed to praise public honesty, although this has been added in the Sephardi version.[111] The conclusion, however, blesses God for ensuring that his name is publicly sanctified, and implies that this can best be done by rescuing those who face martyrdom, since the same line asks God to 'upraise our horn-emblem', a psalmic expression suggesting public success.[112] The timelessness of the blessing suggests that the liturgical speaker is among those who await rescue and that it will take place in the here and now. This sense of present reality may have been inspired by the speaker's grateful awareness of being alive, a response previously identified as characteristic of the liturgical genre.

Juxtaposing the idea that God needs to rescue the Jews for his own sake with the notion that he is best served by the praise of Jews who are prepared to die for his sake suggests a thought unlikely to be made explicit in rabbinic writing. For God to allow Jews to live irrespective of their virtue—as he must if his public glory is to be recognized—he must limit the influence of his own attribute of justice. As a result, this liturgical sequence invites him to imitate Jewish preparedness to suffer, reversing the usual expectation that humans should imitate God's virtues.

The concluding blessing formula suggests that this ends the sequence that opened with Extract 27 and that the speaker can now take exegetical breath. However, the next paragraph, which begins with the same words as the present one, echoes its subject matter and extends its implications.

EXTRACT 33. **Reminding God of the Covenant**

So similar are the opening words of this passage to those of the previous one that they might be alternative versions of the same idea, an impression the printer presumably sought to avoid by using different type-sizes. But this is far from mere duplication, following a pattern seen in other juxtapositions of similar passages, as in Extracts 25 and 26. In both cases the echoes result not from editorial negligence, but from the need to renew the liturgical attempt to reach beyond an apparent logical impasse. In the present case there is a variation on the idea that God's redemption of Israel would demonstrate his integrity, for the first two sentences (to line 3) recall the references in the earlier paragraph to God's mastery and timelessness, while the third (to line 5) asks for redemption on the grounds that this would bring glory to God's name, thereby discounting the value of mar-

---

[111] *Book of Prayer: Daily and Occasional Prayers*, 7.
[112] Pss. 89: 18, 148: 14; see Extract 51, line 12.

tyrdom. The paradox seen in the previous paragraph is sharpened by the contrast between the fourth sentence (line 7), which declares that God's will is not moved by requests, and the fifth (to line 11), which asks him to act 'for the sake of thy grand name', recalling his promise to redeem his people. These sentences juxtapose human impotence with a reapplication of the prophetic attempt to influence God by appealing to his desire for a good reputation, implying that God should rescue the speaker for his own good without having to be asked to do so.

The scriptural and other sources of these lines support and enrich this message. The first four words (line 1) echo Jeremiah's request that God ensure the honouring of his name by keeping the covenant.[113] The first word of the second sentence (line 2), 'true!', echoes the instruction at the beginning of the present sequence to acknowledge the truth (Extract 27), and looks forward to the multiple repetition of the same word in the Ge'ulah blessing, after the full reading of the Shema, an extended paragraph which begins with the same affirmative. Just as that passage follows the full Shema, this paragraph follows the recitation of the first line of the Shema. The blessing after the full recital of the Shema and the present paragraph are also similar in that they focus on rescues—the former on the Exodus and the present one on the ultimate messianic redemption.

The second sentence (line 2) continues with a fragment of Isaiah,[114] transposed from the first to the second person as though the speaker, intent on reminding God of his own promise, is prepared to risk misrepresenting scriptural writings, whatever the implications of departing from the source. As though to avoid such problems, however, the quoted words are flanked in Scripture by the assurance that Israel should 'fear not, neither be afraid'.[115]

The third sentence (lines 3–5), which focuses on the dreamed-for ingathering and rescue, contributes to a multi-layered examination of biblical accounts of redemption. It begins with a rearrangement of five words from the passage in which Isaiah describes the messianic peace between wolves and lambs. The Hebrew words *me'arba kanfot ha'arets*, translated here as 'from the four wings of the earth', are to be understood less literally as 'the four corners of the earth', the term 'wings' recollecting the redemptive associations of messianic rescue with the role of mother birds (and, incidentally, the four corners of the *talit*).[116] The translation itself thus enacts an interpretative departure from the meaning of the

---

[113] Jer. 14: 22. The Sephardi version cites 2 Kgs. 19: 15: see *Book of Prayer: Daily and Occasional Prayers*, 8, which is the text from which a later part of this same passage is drawn: see line 6.

[114] Isa. 44: 6.

[115] Isa. 44: 2, 8. A similar declaration of uniqueness appears in a later text promising redemption: Isa. 45: 21.

[116] Isa. 11: 12. The reference to *kanaf*, in the sense of 'corner', recalls its use in the sense of 'wing', particularly in the 'shadow of God's wing' (Ps. 17: 8). It also glances at the symbolism of the number 4 as related to scattering, and the ingathering symbolized by the wearing of the fringed garment described in the third paragraph of the Shema.

°Thou art God our Lord in heaven and on earth, yea, in the	*Jr.* 14,²²
supernal heavenly heavens; of truth, thou art °the first and thou	*Is.* 44,⁶
art the last and °besides thee there is no power-god; o gather them	*Is.* 45,²¹
that °hope for thee, from the °four wings of the earth; let all that	*Ps.* 25,⁸
come into the world recognize and understand that thou alone art	*Is.* 11,¹²
the Almighty, over all the states of the earth; °thou didst make	*II Ki.* 19,¹⁵
the °heavens and the earth, the ocean and all that is therein. Yea,	*Nh.* 9,⁶
°who is there amongst all thy handiworks, either the ethereal	*Jb.* 9,¹²
or the lower ones, °that could tell thee what to do, O	*Dn.* 4,³²
our °father who art in heaven, perform kindness with us for the sake	*B'So.* 49:
of thy grand name which is °invoked upon us, yea, fulfil unto us, o	*Jr.* 14,⁹
God our Lord, that which is writ: °At that time will I bring you	*Zph.* 3,²⁰
in, yea, at the time that I °gather you, I will even assign you for	*Is.* 49,¹⁸
fame and praise among all the peoples of the earth, when I	*Ps.* 126,¹
°reinstate your returning before your eyes—saith God.	*Ps.* 14,⁷

33. Reminding God of the covenant (*Atah hu hashem eloheinu bashamayim uva'arets*)

words on the page. The third sentence continues, from the seventh word of line 4 ('thou alone art the almighty') to the first word of line 6 ('the heavens and the earth'), to describe the universal recognition of God's mastery that will result from the rescue, in words from a different biblical book.[117] These words, from the only royal prayer in the book of Kings after that of Solomon, are spoken by Hezekiah before his battle with Sennacherib, a situation reflecting the speaker's awareness of vulnerability. Unlike Hezekiah, the speaker knows that the Assyrian forces were indeed destroyed,[118] suggesting the speaker's sense of identification with someone who was unaware of his fate.

This liturgical element, including the six words to the end of the sentence (seventh word of line 6), also echoes the scriptural renewal of the covenant with the returning exiles in the ruins of Jerusalem.[119] In its narrative setting it follows Ezra's reading of the Torah to the people and introduces a survey of Israel's repeated rescue by God. Here in the liturgy it suggests that the speaker, who has likewise recently engaged in an act of study by reading the Shema, will now seek to renew proximity to God by rebuilding the fallen Temple (if only metaphorically, through worship). The dangers of the coming day are equated to those

[117] 2 Kgs. 19: 15; the translation of the word *mamlekhot*, usually rendered 'kingdoms', as 'states' nods towards the modern world.

[118] This defeat was earlier alluded to in the last words of the waking prayer in Extract 21, line 7.

[119] Neh. 9: 6.

אַתָּה הוּא יְיָ אֱלֹהֵינוּ בַּשָּׁמַיִם וּבָאָרֶץ וּבִשְׁמֵי הַשָּׁמַיִם

הָעֶלְיוֹנִים. אֱמֶת אַתָּה הוּא רִאשׁוֹן וְאַתָּה הוּא אַחֲרוֹן

וּמִבַּלְעָדֶיךָ אֵין אֱלֹהִים. קַבֵּץ קֹוֶיךָ מֵאַרְבַּע כַּנְפוֹת הָאָרֶץ

יַכִּירוּ וְיֵדְעוּ כָּל־בָּאֵי עוֹלָם כִּי אַתָּה־הוּא הָאֱלֹהִים לְבַדְּךָ

לְכֹל מַמְלְכוֹת הָאָרֶץ. אַתָּה עָשִׂיתָ אֶת־הַשָּׁמַיִם וְאֶת־

הָאָרֶץ אֶת־הַיָּם וְאֶת כָּל־אֲשֶׁר בָּם. וּמִי בְּכָל־מַעֲשֵׂה יָדֶיךָ

בָּעֶלְיוֹנִים אוֹ בַתַּחְתּוֹנִים שֶׁיֹּאמַר לְךָ מַה־תַּעֲשֶׂה. אָבִינוּ

שֶׁבַּשָּׁמַיִם עֲשֵׂה עִמָּנוּ חֶסֶד בַּעֲבוּר שִׁמְךָ הַגָּדוֹל שֶׁנִּקְרָא

עָלֵינוּ וְקַיֶּם־לָנוּ יְיָ אֱלֹהֵינוּ מַה־שֶׁכָּתוּב בָּעֵת הַהִיא אָבִיא

אֶתְכֶם וּבָעֵת קַבְּצִי אֶתְכֶם כִּי־אֶתֵּן אֶתְכֶם לְשֵׁם וְלִתְהִלָּה

בְּכֹל עַמֵּי הָאָרֶץ בְּשׁוּבִי אֶת־שְׁבוּתֵיכֶם לְעֵינֵיכֶם אָמַר יְיָ:

1
2
3
4
5
6
7
8
9
10
11

faced by the returning Babylonian exiles, as the speaker recalls a ceremony marking their survival of hostility,[120] thereby aligning the beginning of the liturgical
day with the end of exile and the beginning of redemption.

The fifth sentence (lines 6–7) is a paraphrase in Hebrew of Nebuchadnezzar's
Aramaic prayer of thanks after living for a time as an animal,[121] alluding to the
conversion of enemies (previously seen in the references to Darius in the opening statement of the day, to Balaam in Extract 12, line 1, and to the similarity
between animals and humans in Extract 28, line 9). The last two words also echo
Job's recognition of God's absolute power,[122] reinforcing the idea that suffering
is inexplicable, implied earlier in the shift of tone in the paragraph before the
Shema and in the references to human impotence in the paragraph beginning in
Extract 28, line 1.[123]

The sixth and last sentence (Extract 33, lines 7–11) might be regarded as a
separate text since it begins with a vocative expression, 'our father who art in
heaven', a familiar rabbinic formula, but one that is rare in the liturgy.[124] It

---

[120] It recurs in Extract 56, lines 1–2.   [121] Dan. 4: 32 (AV 35).

[122] Job 9: 12.   [123] Eccles. 8: 4.

[124] See the discussion in Abrahams, *Companion*, p. xxiii. Other examples of the vocative use in
liturgy are in Mishnah *Sot.* 9: 15, and a group of prayers after the reading of the Torah (which lie
outside the scope of this book). God is referred to thus in Aramaic in the *kadish derabanan*, Extract
41, line 13.

should therefore be seen here not as a mere formality, but in the context of previous references to God's paternity, and particularly the duties of firstborn sons. It apparently points to the speaker's child-like status, since the aspects of paternity alluded to are associated not with the troubling themes of the *tefilin* texts, but with unconditional parental love undiluted by censoriousness. God is not a demanding or disciplining parent here but one who continues to love, despite the child's failure to live up to expectations, thus exemplifying the divine attribute of mercy.

The impression of the immediacy of parental love is contradicted, however, by the statement that God's location is 'in heaven', suggesting remoteness and a withdrawal from the proximity implied by 'father'. A similar juxtaposition in every opening blessing formula points to an awareness of God's simultaneous immanence and transcendence. The sentence continues (line 8) to specify the need for 'kindness' to be expressed unconditionally in a parental context, rather than in proportion to a child's success in keeping promises. The speaker again appeals to God to grant salvation for the sake of God's own name, although the speaker is aware that the 'name' reflected in the first line of the Shema is a blend of contrasting qualities that must be reconciled.[125] Yet, as the previous reference to the scattering of the Jews made clear (line 3), the ingathering will benefit God's 'name' (or 'reputation'). The way in which the speaker appeals here both to God's paternal feelings and to his pride implies an awareness that the other reasons for salvation—justice and integrity—cannot be assumed to motivate God, even though the speaker had previously recommended them as a tool for producing positive feelings in others (Extract 27).

The wavelike development of liturgical thought, moving fluidly between different grounds for action and parties to the debate, has tended to move away from theological ideas and towards immediate human needs. The speaker now seems to be running out of rhetorical energy, turning increasingly to deeply felt emotions as the new day approaches. The last three lines of the paragraph (lines 9–11) challenge God, more directly than previously in the liturgy, to fulfil his side of the covenant. The term used for 'fulfil', *kayem*, is based on the same root as that in the opening statement of the day, Extract 1, line 1, suggesting a return to the theme of covenant first introduced when the soul was returned to the body on awaking. Here, however, the promise involves the unification of the Jews and their homeland, repairing a rift created at the exile, an event also alluded to in the opening statement of the day by quoting from the book of Lamentations.

At this moment the liturgical text cites a prophetic promise to gather the Jews in from their dispersion, apparently not primarily for reasons of God's self-interest since no reason is given,[126] even though the context makes clear that the

---

[125] Abrahams, *Companion*, pp. xxiii–xxiv.

[126] Zeph. 3: 20. This passage from the end of the book records a reversal of fate as absolute as those in Jer. 33, Lev. 26: 42, and Deut. 30: 3–5.

rescue will reflect on him too.[127] The citation does not state the link between the ingathering of the exiles and the next scriptural subject, the re-establishment of the sacrificial offerings, emerging in the words *avi etkhem*, 'I will bring you' (lines 9–10), pointing to the speaker's ingathering towards the point from which God is speaking, which the context suggests is Jerusalem. That location is problematic, however, for it refers not only to the place of homecoming but to that which has indeed been lost and which now lies in ruins. In addition, the site of the Temple, Mount Moriah, was also the location of the central challenge to happiness in rabbinic thought, the Akedah. This theme has appeared repeatedly and recalls that the Akedah was the model for the sacrificial cult later established on Mount Moriah in Jerusalem, and also that Jews, as victims of exile, may be compared to Isaac in that they are themselves sacrifices, if only metaphorically. The speaker's growing desperation at this point derives in part from the recognition that all attempts to reach God by means of words have so far failed, even though liturgical worship is a substitute for the Temple cult, the form of worship that was explicitly requested by God. The powerlessness of the verbal medium is a major liturgical theme that will be examined in the next chapter.

The response now offered in the liturgy to the dangers of daily life is to use this very medium, although already disqualified, to point to a vision of national redemption that promises invulnerability. However, the fact that this vision of perfection is centred on Jerusalem should not be understood as evidence that the speaker ignores the wider ramifications of messianic beliefs in rabbinic Judaism. Scriptural verses cited elsewhere in the liturgy make it clear that not only Jews and the righteous of all nations will be saved,[128] but the dead too. The centrality of the restoration of Jerusalem illustrates the power of its cult and of the monarchy based there to represent the perfectibility of human life. The second part of the citation, indeed, makes it clear that the editors were not exclusively interested in the physical features of holy places.[129]

The present paragraph thus leaves the speaker at a parting of the ways. On the one hand it calls on God to honour an indeterminately timed promise to redeem the world, while on the other it employs a verbal medium, doomed to fail, for this purpose. At this moment the liturgy is thus confronted with its own silence.

꙳

The liturgical sequence described in this chapter addresses the reasons for the dangers of the outside world and reaches conclusions that overlap with those embodied in the *talit* and *tefilin*, discussed in Chapter 5. The effect of the ritual

[127] Zeph. 3: 9.
[128] *Yalkut shimoni*, Lev. 591 on Lev. 18: 4, and Maimonides, *Mishneh Torah: The Book of Knowledge*, 'Laws of Repentance' 3: 13, fo. 84*b*. For earlier, although more ambiguous, views along these lines, see e.g. Tosefta *San.* 13: 2 and the discussion in Montefiore and Loewe (eds.), *Rabbinic Anthology*, 603–6. 		[129] See Schonfield, 'Zion'.

garments would be still more powerful had these appeared later than they do in this version, ideally in their talmudic location at the conclusion of the daily blessings in Extract 24. The disruption of their message as a result of liturgical reorganization has now been repaired and augmented by liturgical editors who seem to have understood what was lost, and to have recognized how to expand the ideas expressed there. They saw no problem in duplicating material, especially when it made expansion of the concepts possible. So although the fresh material around the ritual garments confirmed the inevitability of exile, the present sequence first adds that it is in God's own interest to redeem his people and secondly points out that the speaker is entitled to protest at his failure to do so.

The speaker is enabled by these wave-like approaches to explore not only the problematic issues of daily life itself, but the consequences of failing to resolve them. The investigation of such intellectual and emotional limits, made possible by the failure of each successive attempt and the use of constantly renewed approaches to old issues, is an essential feature of the liturgical 'narrative'.

CHAPTER NINE

❦

The Imagined Temple

'Shut thy doors . . . until the fury passes'
ISAIAH 26: 20

THE BEGINNING and end of the liturgical sequence covered in this chapter imply that the Temple is actually in existence, yet the description of the sacrificial order itself and the texts inserted in it are tinged with sadness. Despite the desire to flee daily reality by any means available, the speaker is aware of the limited power of words and of the imagination to override the here and now. As a result it is acknowledged that the Temple, whose restoration would bring God's proximity and protectiveness, is irredeemably absent. This section completes the first part of the morning liturgy.

EXTRACT 34. The Daily Morning Sacrifice

The prophecy of ingathering that ended the previous chapter appeared to blend scriptural study with petition in a conventional way, but the present passage shows it to have been a turning point. It opens a subsection of the preliminary part of the morning service being analysed in this book, known as *korbanot*, 'offerings'. The previous citation at first seemed to be a polemical device for persuading God to fulfil his promise to redeem his people. However, it now becomes clear that the speaker's words had the power, if not actually to change reality, then at least to modify the worshipper's state of mind in such a way that the Temple and the sacrificial cult almost appear to be materially and actually present. At first the attention directed to the sacrifices is merely narrative in quality, as though the speaker were recounting nostalgically what had once occurred while remaining aware that this is located in the remote past. But such is the intensity of the focus generated by this depiction that, after a few paragraphs, it begins to seem less a matter of recollection than of observation, as though either the cult had never been destroyed or the promised return had finally come about. The liturgical turning point between petition and at least imaginary fulfilment seems to be the previous prophetic citation in which God promised return. This apparently carried the speaker from the here and now of the synagogue into the there and then of pre-exilic Jerusalem, if only in the mind.

°God spoke unto Moses, declaring: Command the Children of   *Nu.* 28,$^{1-8}$

Israel and say unto them:—My ration-offering for my fires, my   *Ku.* 2,^{26}

°inspirited balm, you shall °observe to bring near unto me at its   *Zo. Gn.* 89, 164:

appointed time; °So, say unto them: this by fire, you shall bring   *Zo. Gn.* 133

near unto God:—°he-lambs, yearlings, unblemished, two each day,   *Zo. Nu.* 242

a °regular Ascent-offering; One lamb for the morning, and the   *Zo. Ex.* 238:

other lamb, °do it towards twilight. Also, a tenth of an *ephah* of   *Zo. Nu.* 252:

°fine flour, as a °Gift-offering, blended with pressed oil, a quarter of   *B'Mn.* 104:

a *hin*. It is a regular Ascent-offering, as arranged on Mount Sinai,   *Ex.* 29,$^{38-46}$

for °inspirited balm, through fire unto God. Also, the Liquids-   *SA–OH* 48

offering thereof, °a quarter *hin* with each lamb; in the holy place   *Zo. Nu.* 162:

shalt thou pour out strong drink-offering unto God. As to °the   *Zo. Ex.* 21:, 239

second lamb, thou shalt offer it °towards twilight, do it with the   *Zo. Gn.* 230, 224

Gift- and its Liquids-offering as in the morning, through fire,   *B'Mg.* 31:

inspirited balm °unto God.   *Zo. Lv.* 5

34. The daily morning sacrifice (*Vayedaber hashem*)

The dominant idea in the liturgy so far—the preoccupation with everyday dangers—thus appears to be set aside at this point, replaced by the vision either of a perfected or of a pre-exilic world. But between the lines the problems of daily life still remain, temporarily suppressed, yet poised to return. The shift from the here and now to an imagined restoration has taken place precisely because the problems outlined in the previous chapter seemed to leave no alternative but textual flight.

The transition from fear of the coming day to a sense of fulfilment is also reflected in the change of tone from passionate petition to factual sacrificial description. The abruptness of the change of scene is emphasized in the present edition by a shift to smaller type and a boundary marked by a printed rule, by which the typesetter encouraged the speaker to regard this opening passage as an interpolation, distinct from what went before.

The speaker no longer forges new ideas out of a dense mosaic of scriptural and rabbinic citations but focuses on a single pentateuchal passage. This is a description of the twice-daily *tamid* offerings in the Tabernacle and Temple, lines known

וַיְדַבֵּר יְהֹוָה אֶל־מֹשֶׁה לֵּאמֹר: צַו אֶת־בְּנֵי ‎1

יִשְׂרָאֵל וְאָמַרְתָּ אֲלֵהֶם אֶת־קָרְבָּנִי לַחְמִי ‎2

לְאִשַּׁי רֵיחַ נִיחֹחִי תִּשְׁמְרוּ לְהַקְרִיב לִי ‎3

בְּמוֹעֲדוֹ: וְאָמַרְתָּ לָהֶם זֶה הָאִשֶּׁה אֲשֶׁר ‎4

תַּקְרִיבוּ לַיהֹוָה כְּבָשִׂים בְּנֵי־שָׁנָה תְמִימִם ‎5

שְׁנַיִם לַיּוֹם עֹלָה תָמִיד: אֶת־הַכֶּבֶשׂ אֶחָד ‎6

תַּעֲשֶׂה בַבֹּקֶר וְאֵת הַכֶּבֶשׂ הַשֵּׁנִי תַּעֲשֶׂה בֵּין ‎7

הָעַרְבָּיִם: וַעֲשִׂירִית הָאֵיפָה סֹלֶת לְמִנְחָה ‎8

בְּלוּלָה בְּשֶׁמֶן כָּתִית רְבִיעִת הַהִין: עֹלַת ‎9

תָּמִיד הָעֲשֻׂיָה בְּהַר סִינַי לְרֵיחַ נִיחֹחַ אִשֶּׁה ‎10

לַיהֹוָה: וְנִסְכּוֹ רְבִיעִת הַהִין לַכֶּבֶשׂ הָאֶחָד ‎11

בַּקֹּדֶשׁ הַסֵּךְ נֶסֶךְ שֵׁכָר לַיהֹוָה: וְאֵת הַכֶּבֶשׂ ‎12

הַשֵּׁנִי תַּעֲשֶׂה בֵּין הָעַרְבָּיִם כְּמִנְחַת הַבֹּקֶר ‎13

וּכְנִסְכּוֹ תַּעֲשֶׂה אִשֵּׁה רֵיחַ נִיחֹחַ לַיהֹוָה: ‎14

as *parashat hatamid*, 'the text concerning the continual offering'.[1] As the longest scriptural reading so far encountered, it leaves no room for the speaker's voice, silencing the assertiveness seen at the end of the previous sequence and reverting to the study sequence introduced by the blessings over Torah in Extract 18. There is also a shift from human speech, addressed to God, to God's instruction to Moses, informing the Israelites about the sacrificial service. As such, this description of the daily rite could be regarded as yet another opening of the liturgical day, similar in weight either to the statement with which the day began (Extract 1), the last two words of which alluded to the loss of the Temple, or to the subsequent, more poetic, beginning of personal prayer (Extract 15). It also shifts the focus from the synagogue, as a place of verbal praise, to the Temple, the location of ceremonial action, although it is accessible here only in verbal form.

As an act of study this text seems to have much in common with the talmudic waking-prayer sequence that was similarly recited as a study session (Extract 21),

[1] Num. 28: 1–8.

or with the study-text discussed at the beginning of the previous chapter (Extract 27). Yet the failure of each of these acts of study threatens to subvert the present one too, reducing it to silence before it has begun.

Since it is a pentateuchal reading, it might be expected to be the first of yet another series of texts drawn from each of the three genres of Torah study— Pentateuch, Mishnah, and Talmud—thereby re-emphasizing the token status of the actual words. But the next passage is a single pentateuchal verse from another context (Extract 35), which is followed in turn by a group of scriptural verses and, finally, by a non-scriptural poem (Extracts 36 and 37). Only thereafter do the other elements of an orderly study sequence appear: a mishnaic text (Extract 38), followed by a *baraita* (a talmudic text written not in Aramaic, but in mishnaic Hebrew characteristic of that earlier genre) in place of a midrashic or talmudic passage (starting in Extract 39).

This neglect of, or departure from, structural regularity (and, as will be seen later, indifference to accuracy of transcription) is too consistent in the liturgy to be a merely incidental feature. This is the third study sequence to be disrupted in some way. The first, introduced by a talmudic text (Extract 18), itself consisting—according to one reading—of a separate blessing formula for each of the genres of rabbinic literature,[2] continued with texts that were manipulated in various ways, as though to demonstrate the near-impossibility of accurate study. The second sequence included the first line of the Shema, which, although it was left intact, also exemplified opacity, while this third sequence, like the first, incorporates texts from the three genres of Torah study which have far-reaching implications when read between the lines.[3] This multiplication of study sequences is minimized in those rites which include the present group of three Torah texts immediately or soon after the blessings of the first of the three sequences, as though to combine them.[4] But the present arrangement should not be mistaken for mere redundancy; each sequence advances the liturgical narrative, even though the liturgical editors did not make this explicit.

The silence generated by the previous study sequences is qualified here by the emphasis on the physical dimensions of worship, aligning the Temple cult with the way in which *talit* and *tefilin* physically bind the body to ideas which transcend the human capacity for understanding. Here the action is confined to the verbal medium, however, illustrating the impossibility of escaping the silence that led the speaker to the present impasse.

The view that the Temple has now regained a degree of reality that is more than the merely symbolic or imaginary actuality acquired by any object in the

---

[2] BT *Ber.* 11*b*. The study-texts introduced in Extract 27 were less systematically arranged.

[3] BT *Kid.* 30*a*; BT *AZ* 19*a–b*; Tosafot on BT *San.* 24*a*.

[4] Amram Gaon, *Seder rav amram hashalem*, i. 38*a*; *Maḥzor vitry*, 58; Abudarham, *Abudarham hashalem*, 48; Judah ben Samuel Hehasid, *Perushei sidur hatefilah laroke'aḥ*, i. 24; Solomon of Worms, *Sidur rabenu shelomoh migarmaisa*, 10–12.

mind of a reader is based on the rabbinic view that reciting a description of sacrificial offerings is in some sense equivalent to performing them. The juxtaposition of the description with the previous prophecy of the rebuilding of the Temple suggests the potential of language to transform reality, as though the citation has itself generated salvation, if only on an imaginary level. However, the view that language may have this power contradicts the previous assumption that language is ineffective. This new belief in language may be based on the recognition that sacrifice performed according to the correct rituals is the sole divinely requested form of worship and that its verbal substitute therefore has a status that other liturgical passages do not. In reality, words—the mere substitute for actions—are unequal to the task of performing the rituals, so any attempt to pray for the actual restoration of sacrifice will be doomed to failure. Nevertheless, some attempt to relate to the Temple is essential, even though it may paradoxically be argued that this restoration can be secured only through Temple worship itself—the ideal form of divine service.

In the Sephardi liturgy the logical impossibility of this thesis stands out starkly, for there the speaker first asks for sins to be forgiven so that the Temple can be rebuilt, and then points out that it is only by means of sacrifice that forgiveness can be obtained.[5] The speaker is therefore left in a theological impasse in which the memory of the Temple is the only guide to communication with God.[6] The present passage implies that these lines of communication simultaneously exist and are absent, acknowledging that the Temple, regarded liturgically as a metaphor for a perfected world, will return not as a result of human effort, but through the unchallengeable will of God. The speaker must therefore accept exile while hoping for its eventual end, by means of a salvation presumably resulting from a spontaneous reawakening of God's mercy. Indeed the liturgy seems calculated to achieve precisely such a transformation, setting out to break through the inescapability of daily suffering by assuming that the Temple has already been restored or was never destroyed.

The centrality of the Temple in rabbinic Judaism is based on complex symbolism throughout the sacred narrative. It reverberates as a cosmic symbol from its beginning onwards, since the Tabernacle in the wilderness is compared in midrashic writings to the universe itself and its building to the creation of the world.[7] The Temple is said to have been situated at the centre of the world,[8] and its sacrificial service to have sustained existence as a whole.[9] Its presence was

---

[5] *Book of Prayer: Daily and Occasional Prayers*, 8.

[6] This paradox may be alluded to in early mystic writings: see Gruenwald, *Apocalyptic and Merkavah Mysticism*, 170–1, citing *Heikhalot rabati* 28, in Wertheimer (ed.), *Batei midrashot*, i. 112.

[7] *Midrash agadah*, 'Pekudei' 189.

[8] *Pirkei derabi eli'ezer*, ch. 35, trans. Friedlander, p. 266, and Rashi on Gen. 28: 17. See Ginzberg, *Legends*, v. 292 n. 141 and Hayman, 'Some Observations'.

[9] Mishnah *Avot* 1: 2; Maimonides, *Code of Maimonides, Book 8: Book of the Temple Service*, 'Laws Concerning Trespass' 8: 8 (pp. 441–2).

essential to the well-being of Jerusalem and rendered her impregnable to her enemies,[10] and the day it ceased to function in 586 BCE, when the city wall was breached, is commemorated by the fast of 17 Tammuz.[11] So sacred was it that some mystic texts argue that the Temple merely appears to have been destroyed and will rematerialize at the coming of the messiah.[12]

On a micro-level the Temple is equated to the human frame, to the extent that its loss diminishes each individual.[13] This emerges in the book of Lamentations, where the capital city is personified as a refugee woman,[14] an association with wider implications, since the tendency of Jewish readers to identify with the sufferer transforms everyone into a survivor of the destruction. A similar idea was implicit in earlier comparisons between the fall of the Temple and the moment of leaving the home for the outside world (see the comments on Extracts 12 and 13), and in the alignment, in the last clauses of the opening statement of the day, of the ruins of Jerusalem with the body and of the survivor with the soul. Liturgical editors saw the fall of the Temple as a metaphor for sleep and its eventual restoration as a metaphor for daily reawakening. The present text suggests that full awakening—on a cosmic rather than a personal level—must await the messianic rebuilding of the Temple, and that this ultimate redemption is in God's hands.

The symbolic importance of the Temple accordingly provides a shadowy backdrop to the liturgy throughout the year. The Additional Services for sabbath and festive days, for instance, exist primarily to provide a setting for sacrificial recitals, and each minor Torah reading on festivals (supplementary to the major readings, which generally deal with the themes of the day) is devoted to the sacrifices required for that occasion. The Temple rituals for the Day of Atonement are similarly described in detail in the liturgy for that day and its liturgical parts are re-enacted.[15] This is especially surprising because the Temple and its cult have been left behind in other respects, one rabbinic text stating that prayer has taken their place as a '[sacrificial] service of the heart'.[16] The idea that words have superseded the cult is reinforced by the practice of facing Jerusalem during prayer[17] and by the fact that the synagogue is referred to as a 'miniature Temple'.[18] Others argue that the Amidah, which some texts trace to patriarchal and therefore pre-Tabernacle times, is specifically a substitute for sacrifice, so must be recited at the times of offerings.[19] The role of sacrifice in resolving con-

---

[10] 2 Chr. 29: 5–9; BT *BK* 82b.   [11] Mishnah *Ta'an.* 4: 6.

[12] Ginzberg, *Legends*, vi. 411 n. 64.   [13] Ibid. 62–3 n. 321, 67 n. 346.   [14] Lam. 1: 1.

[15] See *Service of the Synagogue: Day of Atonement*, ii. 159–68 for the *avodah*, '[sacrificial] service'.

[16] BT *Ta'an.* 2a.

[17] See, for instance, 1 Kgs. 8: 35, 48, Dan. 6: 10, and 2 Chr. 6: 26, quoted in BT *Ber.* 30a.

[18] BT *Meg.* 29a on Ezek. 11: 16.

[19] BT *Ber.* 26b; *Gen. Rabbah* 68: 9; *Exod. Rabbah* 38: 4 (which praises verbal worship); *Num. Rabbah* 18: 21; *Midrash tanḥuma* (Warsaw edn.), 'Vayera' 1. It recurs in Jacob ben Asher, *Arba'ah turim*, 'Oraḥ ḥayim' 48, 50. This equation is discussed in Langer, *To Worship God Properly*, 6–7.

flicts with God is acknowledged in some rabbinic texts to have been taken over by prayer and repentance, although disputes between humans must be settled, as always, by compensation, requests for pardon,[20] or repentance.[21]

Other texts argue, however, that sacrifice has been replaced not by worship, but by good deeds[22] or acts of kindness,[23] implying that no liturgical substitute can be found for sacrifice, even the statutory Amidah.[24] The related view that sacrifice has been replaced by Torah study would also validate the present and other similar sequences. However, some texts argue for the superiority of study to daily sacrifice[25] and even to building the Temple, which would throw ironic light on the current readings if they were not themselves examples of study.[26]

The assumption that the loss of the Temple is not to be regretted is not typical, however, and one finds frequent expressions of sorrow at its disappearance and attempts to compensate for this.[27] One text declares that, in place of sacrifice, one now offers one's own 'fat and blood and souls' in martyrdom, recalling the martyrological associations of the first line of the Shema.[28] Indeed, the previous sequence's specific allusion to the fear of the day ahead and the present one's assumption that the Temple exists point to the idea that daily suffering is a form of martyrdom.

Ambivalence about the continuing importance of sacrifice is apparent in the works of Maimonides. In some contexts he includes the restoration of the Temple among events associated with the coming of the messiah, looking forward to the renewal of the statutory offerings (although not to the free-will ones).[29] However, elsewhere he applauds the replacement of the sacrificial cult by liturgical worship, arguing that sacrifice was introduced only to wean the Israelites from pagan ways.[30] The latter view, with its implicit rejection of the sacrificial option,

[20] BT *BK* 92a; BT *Yoma* 85b.

[21] BT *Yoma* 86a.   [22] *Pesikta derav kahana* 6: 2; *Pesikta rabati* 16: 5.

[23] *Tana debei eliyahu*, ch. 28 (end), p. 143, trans. Braude and Kapstein, pp. 311–12.

[24] This idea is taken further in a text included in *Sidur avodat yisra'el* (pp. 133–49), but not in the present edition. In the Shir Hayihud (Hymn of Unity) for Sundays (early 13th century, from the circle of the Hasidei Ashkenaz), study and humility more than compensate for the lack of the Temple: service is allegorized into an attitude of selflessness that God prefers to sacrifice. It is translated by De Sola in *Festival Prayers*, iii: *New Year*, 47–8, and by Nina Salaman in *Service of the Synagogue: New Year*, 41–2. A restoration is looked forward to in the notes to BT *Ta'an.* 27a by Samuel Edels, quoted in E. Munk, *World of Prayer*, i. 52.

[25] BT *Eruv.* 63b; *Pesikta derav kahana* 6: 3.   [26] BT *Meg.* 16b.

[27] On ambivalence concerning the loss of the Temple and its transformation into a symbolic entity, see Schonfeld, 'Zion'.   [28] Deut. 6: 4; *Num. Rabbah* 18: 21.

[29] *Code of Maimonides, Book 14: The Book of Judges*, 5: 11, 1; *Guide of the Perplexed*, 3: 26. Maimonides' attempt to analyse their possibly didactic purpose in *Guide of the Perplexed*, 3: 46, is criticized by Nahmanides in his comments on Lev. 1: 9; see I. Epstein, 'Introduction to *Seder Kodashim*', in *The Babylonian Talmud*, ed. Epstein (1978 edn.), vol. xiv, pp. xxvi–xxxii.

[30] *Guide of the Perplexed*, 3: 32, based on *Lev. Rabbah* 22: 8. See the discussion in Reif, *Judaism and Hebrew Prayer*, 100–2.

might be reflected in the talmudic interdiction against reproducing any aspect of the Temple. Yet the Temple also lives on in elements of synagogue design, such as the eternal light and the ark curtain, suggesting that the prohibition against imitating the Temple results from a refusal to settle for less than its full restoration.[31]

Arguments in favour of accepting the loss of the Temple include the view that sacrifices are of no practical use to God, and rabbis were at pains to point out that the insistent first person singular in the second verse of this text (line 2) should not be taken as suggesting that the offerings were for God's benefit. They were in fact required, it was argued, for the priestly caste, who alone of the Israelite tribes had no territory and would therefore otherwise have lacked any means of food production.[32] The rabbis also argued that the chief beneficiaries of offerings were precisely those who provided them.[33] One midrashic writer asked, 'What difference does it make to God whether one slaughters an animal from the front or the back of the neck?' and responded that the discipline itself refined the performers' lives and that it was this that God required.[34]

For rabbinic writers the Temple is thus simultaneously an obsolete symbol of proximity to God and a currently valid one of loss and of eventual return to well-being. This multivalent view, transforming the Temple from a real structure into a complex inner entity, was made possible by the rabbinic relationship to language. The use of a single Hebrew term, *davar*, to signify both 'word' and 'thing' implies an equation between the two, an idea acknowledged by the common assumption that words, once spoken, cannot be taken back.[35] This gave rise to an early recognition that sacrifice could as well be read about as performed, just such a transfer from sacrifice to prayer being endorsed by Hosea's statement that 'we will give the tribute of our prayers instead of the offering of bulls',[36] words included in the Sephardi liturgy at this point.[37] A midrash paraphrases this as meaning: 'What shall we pay in place of bullocks and in place of the scapegoat? [The utterance of] our lips.'[38]

The concerns of those who continued to believe in the need for a physical Temple were satisfied by midrashic texts which equate recitals such as the present one to rebuilding the Temple itself. For them the present liturgical passage is more than a recollection of the daily Temple sacrifice or an acknowledgement of the need for its restoration. A theory that invests language with the power to generate reality makes this reading an enactment both of prophecies of ingathering,

---

[31] Jacobson, *Meditations on the Siddur*, 120–3.

[32] *Targum Jonathan*, Num. 28: 2; and Mishnah *Zev.* 5: 5 cited below in Extract 38, line 16.

[33] Ps. 50: 7–15 lies behind *Sifrei*, Num. 143, fo. 54*a*, and see *Num. Rabbah* 21: 16, 19 and Loewe in Montefiore and Loewe (eds.), *Rabbinic Anthology*, 414.   [34] *Gen. Rabbah* 44: 1.

[35] Creation is one example and the sale of Esau's birthright another. See BT *Shab.* 119*b* for the equation.   [36] Hos. 14: 3.   [37] *Book of Prayer: Daily and Occasional Prayers*, 11.

[38] *S. of S. Rabbah* 4: 4, 9; the idea also appears in BT *Ta'an.* 27*b* and BT *Meg.* 31*b*.

such as that cited above (in Extract 33, lines 9–11), and of the promise to rebuild the Temple.[39]

It is striking, however, that it is almost uniquely in the context of the Temple that this equation between words and deeds is propounded. Such an argument would not be brought in rabbinic thought to oppose the literal performance of the biblical instructions concerning *talit* and *tefilin*, for example (discussed in Chapter 5). Nothing less than literal understanding and physical enactment would be acceptable in such a case, even though some other instructions are interpreted metaphorically in order to overcome inconsistencies. One example of this is the rabbinic assumption that the principle of an 'eye for an eye' requires compensation rather than physical enactment.[40] The Temple would thus seem to be a rare exception to the otherwise nearly general principle of literal interpretation, which may explain why the passage from Zephaniah, which appears to set the scene for the present liturgical sequence, has the ability to influence reality in the way it does.

Conceivably the usual limitations of language are overridden in this case by the sheer desperation of those who know that speech, the only remaining medium for approaching God, is not the one that God prefers in matters concerning worship. Indeed, if a similarly verbal solution could be applied to martyrdom too, daily suffering might be averted by means of liturgical formulas alone, though such a solution does not seem to be contemplated here. God's speech alone is an act in itself, as was seen at Creation. That of humans is its pale shadow.

The sequence covered in this chapter thus depicts liturgical worship both as the only way to maintain contact with God and as a form of silence in contrast to the 'reality' of sacrifice. The destroyed Temple simultaneously suggests the possibility of successful communication and of well-being and their impossibility. The juxtaposition of these incompatible views generates complex theological harmonies, especially as the loss of the Temple has already been attributed to the fact that the inaccessibility of Torah led directly to exile. However, this passage, by offering a mirage of the Temple, enables the speaker to examine the possibility that relief can be experienced by pretending that the Temple has never been absent. This denial of exile brings no relief in reality, but the speaker by now has no other means of defence against the day ahead. The sole solution at this stage is to express joy at survival, a response encountered earlier in Extract 30. This will eventually dominate the liturgy, although its delusional nature will prevent it from being the last word.

A similar balance of responses underlies the liturgical perspective on sacrifice. The present readings can be seen as atavistic appeals to a remote and—in terms

[39] BT *Men.* 110a; *Midrash tanhuma* (Warsaw edn.), 'Tsav', 14; *Lev. Rabbah* 7: 2. The relevance of the sacrifices to the entry into the Promised Land links them equally to the eventual return, according to *Pesikta derav kahana* 6: 3, *Pesikta rabati* 16: 7, and Nahmanides on Num. 28: 2.

[40] Exod. 21: 24 and Lev. 24: 18; Cohen, 'Talion'.

°So he shall slaughter it on the north side of the altar,	*SA-OH*1,[8]
before God; and the priests, the sons of Aaron, shall	*Lv.*1,[11]; *Ku.*3,[53]
sprinkle its blood upon the altar-surround.	*Md.Lv.*2,[4/5]

35. Another pentateuchal text on sacrifice (*Veshahat oto*)

of worship—pre-lingual past in which a more primary mode of communication was based on gifts and food, but they also appear to form part of a sophisticated symbolism in which it is recognized that the interposition of a priest prevents or makes redundant the worshipper's emotional engagement. The fact that sacrifice is experienced only textually here gives access to a complex experience that would have been unavailable to most people involved in the Temple and perhaps familiar only to the priests themselves. These liturgical readings are thus part of a liturgical project for returning the cult to the people, enabling the speaker to experience the complexity of the world through the intricate and apparently random nature of sacrifice. The sense of order and control that emerges from this catalogue of gestures is priestly in nature, without direct relevance to the world outside the Temple, but reflects the apparent orderliness of God's cultic relations with his people. The speaker turns to sacrifice not only as a gesture of despair at the ineffectiveness of liturgical language, therefore, but because it is a supra-lingual channel of communication with God that still recalls the problematic and inexplicable nature of existence.[41]

EXTRACT 35. **Another Pentateuchal Text on Sacrifice**

This single pentateuchal verse[42] seems to bear no relation to the previous text, even though it refers to sacrifice. If the first text initiated an anthology of genres, this one merely duplicates that first category, rather than introducing the next. In addition, on sabbaths and new moons the first pentateuchal reading simply continues after this verse, recording the sacrifices for those days as though the present verse were merely an interpolation disrupting a single reading. The present verse also destabilizes the imaginative reconstruction of the Temple begun by the previous reading by introducing a sense of geographical location that was missing from the first text. The physical dimension emphasizes the loss of the Temple site itself, since a sense of physical reality cannot be restored merely by reading about it in the way that reading about the sacrifices can 'restore' them. This intensified distancing of the sacrificial scene revives the themes of exile and

---

[41] Rabbinic beliefs in the efficacy of prayer are reviewed in Langer, *To Worship God Properly*, 14–16.   [42] Lev. 1: 11.

וְשָׁחַט אֹתוֹ עַל יֶרֶךְ הַמִּזְבֵּחַ צָפֹנָה לִפְנֵי יְהוָה 1
וְזָרְקוּ בְּנֵי אַהֲרֹן הַכֹּהֲנִים אֶת־דָּמוֹ עַל־הַמִּזְבֵּחַ סָבִיב: 2

suffering seen at the beginning of the previous text, a tendency reinforced by the two following interpolations (in Extracts 36 and 37).

The very impenetrability of the present text, however, seems to restore to the agenda the opacity of Torah that dominated the passages discussed in the previous chapter. Exegetical effort is in fact quickly rewarded, for midrashic commentators employ a play on the verse's words to identify an allusion to the merit earned by Abraham and Isaac at the Akedah. This event, which took place on the site of the Temple, recalls the theme of martyrdom seen in the previous chapter and ensures that patriarchal suffering, already linked to that of the speaker, is now related to the sacrificial cult too. The sprinkling of blood mentioned in this verse might be interpreted as adding to the vividness of the dangers facing the speaker, were it not related explicitly to sacrifice rather than martyrdom.

The midrashic transformation of the plain meaning of this text is achieved by manipulating the word *tsafonah*, literally 'on the north side', as though it meant both 'treasured up' (*tsefunah*) and 'seen' (*tsefuyah*).[43] According to this midrashic interpretation, the 'it' which is slaughtered refers not to Temple sacrifice, but to 'him'—in this case Isaac—whose suffering was 'seen' by God and whose reward, together with that of Abraham, is 'stored up' for the speaker. This characteristically rabbinic re-reading of the consonantal scriptural text, achieved by modifying the vowels, equates the speaker's suffering with the trial of Abraham and Isaac and transforms the speaker into a belated participant in the Akedah, although this can be expressed only in a literary mode by means of reciting the details of the Temple cult.[44] The sacrificial scene is also one of human suffering, at least potentially, for it is linked to the patriarchs' *self*-sacrifice, equating this with the dangers of everyday life faced by the speaker at this moment. The parallel talmudic idea that suffering transforms each individual into an altar enables this verse to accentuate the reality of the Temple and to interpret it as a symbol of human suffering.[45] If language is equivalent to action, however, reading this verse can enable the speaker to 'realize' both the sacrifice and the Akedah and to benefit as though an act of martyrdom had taken place.

---

[43] *Tana debei eliyahu*, ch. 6, p. 36, trans. Braude and Kapstein, p. 84; *Lev. Rabbah* 2: 11; *Yalkut shimoni*, Gen. 99 on Gen. 22: 4. See Spiegel, *The Last Trial*, 73–4.

[44] This pattern of symbolization happens to correspond closely to that in the Catholic Mass.

[45] BT *Ber.* 5*b*.

EXTRACT 36. **Five Interpolated Verses**

The second of three interpolations into what seemed to begin as a study session on the theme of sacrifice consists of five scriptural verses without obvious links to either the cult or the Temple. Since there are five verses, four from the Psalms and one from the book of Malachi, they might be seen as complementing the five books of the Pentateuch from which the opening reading was taken. But this would fail to explain the third interpolation, a medieval poem without scriptural associations. It is attributed to a mishnaic rabbi, but this would not transform the series of interpolations into a comprehensive study selection.

The verses appear to have been introduced into the liturgy under sixteenth-century Lurianic influence, to judge by their number symbolism. Thinking in this vein, it is possible (although no commentator seems to note it) that the three-fold occurrence of the Tetragrammaton in the first two lines alludes to the thrice-daily recital of the Amidah that midrashically replaces sacrifice. Since the first verse appears twice in the psalm from which it comes, however, there is a virtual sixth verse, which might allude to the number of times the Amidah is read and repeated by the prayer-leader each weekday.[46]

Several of the verses are found elsewhere in the liturgy. The first two—Psalm 46: 8 and Psalm 84: 13—are talmudically recommended for regular use before prayer or study[47] and appear in another Lurianic innovation, together with the third in the series—Psalm 20: 10—at the beginning of the evening service just before Barekhu, the call to prayer (which lies outside the scope of this book). Their presence here could suggest that this is yet another beginning of the daily service. In addition, the same three verses appear in the same order later in the morning service as part of a longer sequence (see Extract 45, lines 13–15), and it is perhaps from there that they have been enlisted.

When these verses are read as a series, their relevance becomes apparent, as they comprise a history of the cult-place on Mount Moriah from before the Israelite entry into the land until the present exile. An earlier collection of verses, in Extract 12, similarly traced the history of the Tabernacle and Temple and concluded with the speaker's arrival in synagogue. The present sequence confronts the deeper problem of approaching God without the Temple and considers the cost to the speaker of its continued absence. The obscurity of the message constituted by these verses echoes that of the Torah in general, although the fact that it can be decoded undermines the superficial impression of divine silence and exemplifies how the speaker may overcome exegetical challenge.

---

[46] Ps. 46: 8 and 12. The evening Amidah is not repeated in public, although liturgical echoes of such a repetition do survive, in the form of the Hashkivenu blessing and the eighteen-verse anthology that follows it, making five actual readings and one virtual reading to which these verses could correspond. This coincidence may not previously have been noted. For the substitutes for the evening Amidah see Elbogen, *Jewish Liturgy*, 87–9.　　　　[47] JT *Ber.* 5: 1.

According to some medieval interpretations, the first verse may have been spoken in the wilderness before the Tabernacle was built, since it comes from a psalm attributed to the sons of Korah, thereby locating the speaker in a narrative setting without direct links to the sacrificial theme with which this sequence began.[48] These sons were declared 'three pillars of the world' for refusing to join their father's rebellion against Aaron's priesthood, which may be why the psalm says God is 'with us' and a 'fortress' against assailants.[49] Since Korah's revolt was midrashically regarded as having been sparked off by a challenge to the design of the *tsitsit*, the speaker, who now wears a *talit* of a conventional kind, is aligned with the sons who refused to follow the uprising.[50] This midrashic association between *talit* and Korah is based on the fact that the third paragraph of the Shema, in which the *talit* is prescribed, immediately precedes the account of Korah's uprising. The way it follows soon after the account of the Spies, as a result of which the adult generation of Israelites was condemned to wander for forty years in the wilderness, recalls the suggestion made above that the *talit* resolves the problem of survival of the landless Israelites. Another midrashic comment on this episode, however, describes the continuing cries for help of Korah and his followers in Gehenna,[51] and if these are echoed in the third verse of this group, the speaker would be aligned with Korah rather than his sons. Such an identification would be ironic, however, because the speaker has not revolted but has been compelled to substitute liturgical for sacrificial worship due to the loss of the Temple. Whether the speaker is identified with Korah or with his sons, the links between the *talit*, ingathering, and the rebuilding of the 'house' of God (in Extract 5) confirm that this verse is related to survival.

The second verse,[52] again from a psalm of the sons of Korah, apparently relates to a period when the Tabernacle already existed, since it praises the 'house of God'. The psalmist is here located outside it, requesting admission, however, which is presumably why the psalm is used as a prelude to the afternoon service in the Sephardi rite,[53] introducing the description of the daily *tamid* that it follows in the present version. The way the present verse brings the speaker to the threshold of the Temple, in other versions as well as in this one, reinforces the view that the previous psalm is its prelude.

The third verse asks for rescue[54] and occurs at the end of a psalm that seems to assume the fall of the Temple, reinforcing the argument that this group of verses marks a chronological progression. A midrashic interpretation of this verse not only describes how God 'suffers' in sympathy with Israel as a result of

---

[48] Ps. 46: 8. For rabbinic views concerning the dating of these Korahides to the wilderness years or to a later period, see Rashi, Ibn Ezra, and David Kimhi on Psalm 42: 1.

[49] See *Midrash Psalms* 1: 15 for the context, and 46: 1 for their preference for virtue.

[50] See Rashi on Num. 16: 1.

[51] BT *BB* 74*a*; an earlier episode in this group of narratives relates to *tsitsit*.

[52] Ps. 84: 13. [53] *Book of Prayer: Daily and Occasional Prayers*, 63–4. [54] Ps. 20: 10.

°God of Cohorts is with us!—the Lord of Jacob is a fortress unto	*Ps.* 46,[8]
us, *Selah*. O God of Cohorts!—hale, the man that trusts in thee!	*Ps.* 84,[13]
°O God, save!—may the sovereign answer us at the time of our	*Ps.* 20,[10]
call. °Thou art covert unto me, thou wilt protect me from an	*Ps.* 32,[7]
oppressor; with singing of release °wilt thou surround me—*Selah*.	*Zo. Gn.* 178:
°The offering of Judah and Jerusalem shall be pleasing unto God	*Mal.* 3,[4]
as in days of yore, as in °years gone by.	*Is.* 43,[18]

36. Five interpolated verses (*Hashem tseva'ot imanu*)

the Temple's destruction and how his cries echo throughout the world,[55] but goes on to identify worldly suffering as a sign of the imminent arrival of the messiah.[56] Talmudic texts similarly view various forms of decadence, including ignorance of the Torah of the kind regarded so far as a cause of exile, as signs that the messiah is near.[57] It is a biblical idea that Jews will be saved when the pain of exile leads them to repentance,[58] but this is given a fresh twist by the rabbinic view that the decline of study is itself a sign of imminent salvation, an assertion that incidentally would justify the liturgical manipulation of Torah study.[59] This transformation of the opacity of revelation from a cause of exile into a sign of imminent redemption is confirmed by the threefold repetition of the Tetragrammaton, the divine name associated with the attribute of mercy, represented euphemistically here as a double *yod*, once at the beginning of each of the first three verses.

The fourth verse,[60] which carries the historical survey forward to the present exile, refers to God instead as 'covert unto me', the word *seter* ('covert') alluding to the scriptural concept of God 'hiding the face' (*hester panim*), in which, unresponsive to appeals, he permits the exile to continue out of fury at Israel's sins.[61] Other translators see the verse as a reference to protectiveness and render the same word as 'my hiding place' (in the Authorized Version of 1611), but the associations of withdrawal of favour are unmistakable and imply that no prayer can reach a God who has turned aside. If so, however, even the present recital of the sacrificial service will be ineffective, at least until God's attribute of mercy prevails. This sequence, like others before, is thus subverted almost as soon as it has begun.

In the fifth and last verse,[62] expressing the hope that the 'offering of Judah and Jerusalem' will be 'pleasing' to God, the speaker remains in exile but looks

---

[55] *Midrash Psalms* 20: 1.   [56] Ibid. 20: 4.
[57] BT *Shab.* 138*b*–139*a*.   [58] Deut. 30: 1–3; Lev. 26: 39–42.
[59] For the decline of study and the need to rely on God's mercy alone see Mishnah *Sot.* 9: 15; see also BT *Shab.* 138*b*–139*a* (quoted above) and BT *San.* 97*a*.   [60] Ps. 32: 7.
[61] Deut. 31: 18.   [62] Mal. 3: 4.

יְיָ צְבָאוֹת עִמָּנוּ מִשְׂגָּב לָנוּ אֱלֹהֵי יַעֲקֹב סֶלָה: יְיָ צְבָאוֹת 1

אַשְׁרֵי אָדָם בֹּטֵחַ בָּךְ: יְיָ הוֹשִׁיעָה הַמֶּלֶךְ יַעֲנֵנוּ בְיוֹם קָרְאֵנוּ: 2

אַתָּה סֵתֶר לִי מִצַּר תִּצְּרֵנִי רָנֵּי פַלֵּט תְּסוֹבְבֵנִי סֶלָה: וְעָרְבָה 3

לַיְיָ מִנְחַת יְהוּדָה וִירוּשָׁלָיִם כִּימֵי עוֹלָם וּכְשָׁנִים קַדְמֹנִיּוֹת: 4

forward to its end by merging the nation with its lost home, while locating the statement in the present by using the grammatical form expressing completed action.[63] Its scriptural context,[64] however, shifts ground by criticizing insincere sacrifice and praising honest speech and learning, illustrating the sometimes subtle manoeuvring of liturgical thought. But this is qualified by a description of how suffering will precede the day of judgement and how sacrificial offerings will thereafter again be acceptable, as though this too might allude to the decadence which precedes salvation. Judging from the fact that this verse concludes the sacrificial readings in the Sephardi afternoon service,[65] the speaker may also be concluding a sequence of ideas related to the Temple cult.

In these five verses the speaker spans the pre-Tabernacle period to the present exile, identifying at different times with Korah, his sons, a mourner for Jerusalem joining in God's laments, a victim of God's wrath, and one who hopes that the liturgical substitute for sacrifice will bring an end to suffering. This narrative development also marks the speaker's triumph over the difficulty of study, accomplishing this by means of the very juxtapositions that seem to subvert the purity of study. Underlying these verses, however, is the paradox that study does not give protection from suffering. Indeed, a midrashic text describing how Akiba's body was sold as carrion in a market after his martyrdom defined this as his 'reward'; since the same passage recounts how Akiba had apparently departed from the revelation delivered to Moses on Sinai,[66] his fate could be interpreted as a 'punishment' for distorting Torah, even though, as has been seen, complete adherence may be impossible.

This demonstration of how independent-minded departure from the literal meaning of scriptural texts can help recover non-literal messages restores faith in the possibility of gaining understanding through study. But it remains true that this can be done only by departing from the literal meaning, and the cost of this may be the very suffering that the sacrificial texts seemed designed to avert.

---

[63] The potentially sexual connotations of the verb 'make pleasant' have been noted in connection with the first word in Extract 18, line 3.   [64] Mal. 2: 6–7.

[65] *Book of Prayer: Daily and Occasional Prayers*, 65.   [66] BT *Men.* 29*b*.

These interpolations may therefore be read as a critical footnote to the sacrificial passages, accounting for the way in which the speaker's hopes are about to be dashed.

EXTRACT 37. **A Poetic Call for Rescue**

This poetic request for rescue, the third and last interpolation in the sacrificial sequence, marks a change of genre and tone, as though recognizing the failure of the previous sacrificial readings and abandoning the medium of scriptural quotation for mystic meditation.[67] The first line personifies the people of Israel—including the speaker—as a female captive (as does the first verse of the book of Lamentations) and requests release from exile. In view of the context, the captivity referred to here might also relate to the impasse created by the simultaneous impossibility of sacrifice and limited power of its verbal substitute. The verb *tatir*, 'release', suggests the possibility of resolving the imponderable relationship with Torah, an idea supported by the fact that a related term is employed in contexts associated with being 'tongue-tied', one aspect of the problem faced by the speaker.[68] Paradoxically, however, the poem demonstrates a particular freedom of expression and strength of emotion, even though the speaker's ignorance is one reason for the continuing exile. The speaker's inability to make words effective is implicitly regretted in the last line by referring to God as 'perceiver of hidden things', implying his knowledge both of the speaker's thoughts and of that which cannot be understood or said, including such mysteries as the reason for suffering and the time of redemption. God's invisibility, mentioned in the fourth verse above (Extract 36, line 3), even serves as a metaphor for the hopelessness from which the speaker begs for release in line 7 of the present extract, the speaker's incomprehension of the inscrutable nature of existence symbolizing exile.

The 'hidden things' might also be the preceding scriptural verses and even the words of this poem, characterized by heightened meaning and magical design. For if the verses in Extract 36 indeed number six instead of five, the present text (if regarded as a single statement and combined with them) would form a seventh, harmonizing with a poem that contains seven names of God and seven lines of six words each, making a total of forty-two words. The initial letters of these words were assumed by some mystical commentators to represent the forty-two-letter name of God referred to in the Talmud,[69] which is why the poem is followed by the same response as the first line of the Shema (line 8).[70]

---

[67] It does include scriptural fragments and echoes, such as 'thy right [hand]' (Exod. 15: 16) or 'eye-pupil' (Ps. 17: 8).

[68] I am grateful to Raphael Loewe for pointing out the relationship between the term *ilem*, 'dumb', for instance in Exod. 4: 11, and *me'alemim alumim*, 'binding sheaves', in Gen. 37: 7, an association between the ideas of speechlessness and of being bound which is supported by the fact that the next line of the poem relates to prayer.

[69] BT *Kid.* 71a.   [70] Gaguine, *Keter shem tov*, i–ii. 29–30 n. 50.

If this poem is simultaneously a name of God and a petition for redemption, it is aligned with the first line of the Shema, likewise a name of God, enabling the speaker to unify the dual names of God and therefore the divergent human experiences of the world.

In the light of the talmudic description cited earlier of how God himself 'prays' that his compassion may overcome his anger and that the attribute of mercy will become dominant,[71] this poem might even represent God's prayer to himself.[72] This reading is supported by the allusion to the Binding of Isaac (Extract 35), previously referred to in the debate on suffering (Extract 29, lines 1–2), which apparently identifies exiled Jews as a 'sacrifice'. The speaker hopes to be spared by the divine attribute of mercy just as Isaac was replaced by a ram, and, in the later sacrificial cult, the scapegoat, described in the liturgy for the Day of Atonement and regarded as atoning for the sins of the nation.[73] The similarity noted between humans and domestic animals in Extract 28, line 9, supports the idea that the liturgy compares sacrifices and Jews, especially as the liturgical sequence in which this poem is set suggests that the speaker's release can be secured by substituting martyrdom for the descriptions of animal sacrifice in the Temple.

This poem is occasionally deployed elsewhere in the liturgy at moments of heightened significance, such as after counting the Omer, in the edition used here, and in other versions of the Ashkenazi rite also on each sabbath eve. Its attribution to Nehunya ben Hakanah, a second-century tannaitic rabbi, apparently on the grounds of its power, could explain why it has been located here in a position suited to a mishnaic text, though it is included elsewhere in non-study contexts. This authorship is fictional, however, since its rhyme-scheme and the acrostic in the second line that reads *kara satan*, 'rend Satan', suggest that it is a thirteenth-century kabbalistic *reshut* (a prayer-leader's petition for public prayer to be heard) either from Spain or from Franco-Germany.[74]

This series of three interpolations in the sacrificial sequence, consisting of one pentateuchal verse, five scriptural verses, and a poem, seem suited to the conclusion of the sacrificial sequence, and would indeed be in tune with the concluding petition for redemption in Extract 40. The texts were inserted here, however, presumably because they relate to the verse from Leviticus rather than to later texts in the sequence. Whatever the reason, the present location suggests an awareness that the sacrificial readings simultaneously do and do not have an effect on reality, a paradox which runs deep in rabbinic thought. The recognition

---

[71] BT *Ber.* 7*a*.

[72] No evidence has been found to support this hypothesis, which is derived from the context.

[73] Mishnah *Yoma* 6: 2–8.

[74] The attribution to Nehunya ben Hakanah may have been inspired by his interest in servitude and release, suggested by Mishnah *Avot* 3: 6. The alternative provenances are given in Weinberger, *Jewish Hymnography*, 169, and anon., 'Ana bekho'aḥ'.

Prithee, with the °great might of Thy right, do thou release	*Ex.* 15,⁶
the °captive one;	*Nu.* 33,⁵⁵
Yea, accept the °chanting of thy People, uphold and purify	*B'Br.* 31
us, o °awesome one!	*Dt.* 7,²¹
O almighty, do thou °guard as eye-pupil, them that search	*Ps.* 17,⁸
for °thy union;	*Ki. SA* 148,¹
Yea, bless, °purify and pity them, ever bestowing thy °right-	*Mal.* 3,⁸
kindness upon them;	*B'Kt.* 50
°O vast-holy one, in thine abounding goodness, guide thy	*Ps.* 89,⁹
community; single triumphant one, o °turn towards thy	*Lv.* 26,⁹
People, they that are °mindful of thy holiness;	*Nu.* 15,³⁹
Yea, °receive our clamour and hearken to our crying, o	*Jb.* 2,¹⁰
perceiver of °hidden things!	*Ps.* 44,²²
°Blest is the Name—the reverence of His sovereignty for ever and aye!	*Msh. Yo.* 6,²

37. A poetic call for rescue (*Ana bekho'ah gedulat yeminkha*)

that the sacrificial readings are both an enactment and a recollection argues for the indissoluble nature of the paradox offered here. Sacrificial worship nevertheless has a continuing value in the minds of the liturgical editors, if only as a verbal gesture suggesting the impossibility of realization.

EXTRACT 38. A Mishnaic Chapter on Sacrifice

Following these three interpolations in the sacrificial readings the speaker comes to the longest study passage encountered so far. This is a mishnaic sequel to the pentateuchal paragraph with which the sequence began,[75] apparently setting aside the doubts implied by the interpolations and renewing the sense of reality conveyed by the opening sacrificial description. A nostalgia for the lost locations of the Temple runs through this sequence, and its talmudic elaboration (which does not appear here) even includes outliness of physical details of the Temple and the sacrificial service, as an informed reader would be aware.[76] A similar preoccupation with location appears in the verse from Leviticus in Extract 35, but although those words are cited in the first mishnah (lines 1–2), the midrashic interpretation of the word *tsafon* as an allusion to the Akedah appears neither here nor in the talmudic expansion.[77]

   This text forms a sequel to the pentateuchal texts with which the sacrificial sequence began also in the sense that it comes from the Mishnah, and the study

[75] Mishnah *Zev.* 5: 1–8.   [76] BT *Zev.* 54*a–b*.   [77] BT *Zev.* 48*a–b*.

אָנָּא בְּכֹחַ גְּדֻלַּת יְמִינְךָ תַּתִּיר צְרוּרָה ׃ 1

קַבֵּל רִנַּת עַמְּךָ שַׂגְּבֵנוּ טַהֲרֵנוּ נוֹרָא ׃ 2

נָא גִבּוֹר דּוֹרְשֵׁי יִחוּדְךָ כְּבָבַת שָׁמְרֵם ׃ 3

בָּרְכֵם טַהֲרֵם רַחֲמֵם צִדְקָתְךָ תָּמִיד גָּמְלֵם ׃ 4

חֲסִין קָדוֹשׁ בְּרֹב טוּבְךָ נַהֵל עֲדָתֶךָ ׃ 5

יָחִיד גֵּאֶה לְעַמְּךָ פְּנֵה זוֹכְרֵי קְדֻשָּׁתֶךָ ׃ 6

שַׁוְעָתֵנוּ קַבֵּל וּשְׁמַע צַעֲקָתֵנוּ יוֹדֵעַ תַּעֲלֻמוֹת ׃ 7

בָּרוּךְ שֵׁם כְּבוֹד מַלְכוּתוֹ לְעוֹלָם וָעֶד ׃ 8

anthology will conclude with another text from a quasi-talmudic source.[78] This emphasis on the different genres comprising Torah both renews the trust in textual study interrupted by the insertions in Extracts 36 and 37 and reduces them to token status, in so far as their significance lies here more in their source than in what they appear to say. The prominence of genre also minimizes the extent to which these descriptions might be held to approximate to sacrificial enactments, and in this way counteracts the suggestion, implicit in the various interpolations, that something approaching an act of worship is being performed by means of this reading. The idea that study has indeed returned to the agenda is confirmed by the fact that this mishnaic passage is reproduced unmodified, like the opening pentateuchal text, as though belatedly accepting the absence of the Temple and ignoring the earlier recognition that the ideal of study has been tried and found wanting.

Traditional commentators attribute the choice of this passage less to its link to what has gone before, however, than to the fact that it is virtually the only mishnaic chapter recording no rival views or procedural mishaps. This seems to reflect an awareness of the talmudic advice to study Torah as a prelude to prayer, while ensuring that the subject is concluded, so that one is not distracted from worship by thinking about legal problems. The talmudic discussion in which this is recommended then gives examples of closed debates of this kind, but these turn out to be complex matters illustrating the need to read beyond the obvious

---

[78] Jacob ben Asher, *Arba'ah turim*, 'Oraḥ ḥayim' 50; Caro, *Shulḥan arukh*, 'Oraḥ ḥayim' 50.

1. °Which are the proper locations for the sacrifices? The more   *Msh. Zv.* 5,[1–8]
holy were slaughtered °on the northern side; the bull and he-goat   *Lv.* 1,[11]
of the °Day of Atonements were slaughtered at the north, and their   *Lv.* 16,[3,9]
blood was received in a °vessel of ministration, at the north; their   *Ex.* 24,[6]
blood required °sprinkling between the Ark-staves, towards the   *Lv.* 16,[14]
Sanctum-°curtain and on the Golden altar; the omission of any of   *Msh. Yo.* 5,[8]
these sprinklings °invalidated the whole; the residual blood he   *B'Zv.* 36:
poured upon the western °base of the outer altar, but if he did not do   *Lv.* 4,[7]
this, he has °not invalidated it. 2. The bulls and the he-goats which   *B'Zv.* 40
had to be °burnt were slaughtered at the north, and their blood   *Msh. Zv.* 4,[4]
was received in a vessel of ministration, °at the north; their blood   *Sf. Lv.* 1,[67]
required °sprinkling towards the Sanctum-curtain and on the   *Sf. Lv.* 16,[37]
Golden altar; the omission of any of these °sprinklings invalidated   *Mai. Krb.* 7,[2]
the whole; the residual blood he poured upon the western base of   *Ku.* 1,[99]
the outer altar; but °if he omitted to do so, he has not invalidated   *Y'Yo.* 5,[6]
it; both of the above were burnt °in the repository of ashes. 3. As   *Lv.* 4,[12,21]
to the °Error-offerings of the congregation and of the individual—   *Mai. Krb.* 1,[16]
the following are the Error-offerings of the congregation: °the   *Ku.* 3,[11]
he-goats of the °New-moon days and of Festivals—these were   *Nu.* 28,[15,22]
slaughtered at the north, and their blood was received °in a vessel   *Msh. Ng.* 14,[8]
of ministration at the north; their blood required °four sprinklings   *B'Zv.* 53:
on the four altar-corners. How was this done?—°The priest went   *Mai. Krb.* 5,[6]
up on the ramp, and, °turning along the ledge, he reached the   *Mai. BH* 2,[7]
south-east, north-east, north-west and south-west corners; °The   *Msh. Ob. hic*
residual blood he poured upon the southern base; °the meats thereof   *B'Zv.* 52
had to be eaten °within the Precincts, by males of the priesthood,   *Lv.* 6,[9]
in any cuisine, within the same day and the following night, °until   *Msh. Br.* 1,[1]
midnight. 4. °The Ascent-offering, among the more holy, had to   *Zo. Lv.* 26
be slaughtered at the north and its °blood was received in a °vessel   *Lv.* 1,[5]
of ministration, °at the north; its blood required two sprinklings,   *B'Tm.* 30:
branching into four; the offering had to be °flayed, cut up and   *Lv.* 1,[6]
entirely °consumed by fire. 5. As to the sacrifices of °Peace-offerings   *I Sm.* 7,[9]
by the congregation, and Trespass-offerings; the following   *Lv.* 23,[19]
are the °Trespass-offerings: the Trespass-offerings for robbery,   *Lv.* 5,[18–26]
for appropriating sanctified objects, °in regard to a betrothed   *Lv.* 19,[21]

38. A mishnaic chapter on sacrifice (*Eizehu mekoman shel zevaḥim*)

א אֵיזֶהוּ מְקוֹמָן שֶׁל זְבָחִים קָדָשֵׁי קָדָשִׁים שְׁחִיטָתָן בַּצָּפוֹן

פָּר וְשָׂעִיר שֶׁל־יוֹם הַכִּפּוּרִים שְׁחִיטָתָן בַּצָּפוֹן וְקִבּוּל דָּמָן

בִּכְלִי שָׁרֵת בַּצָּפוֹן וְדָמָן טָעוּן הַזָּיָה עַל־בֵּין הַבַּדִּים וְעַל

הַפָּרֹכֶת וְעַל־מִזְבַּח הַזָּהָב מַתָּנָה אַחַת מֵהֶן מְעַכָּבֶת שְׁיָרֵי

הַדָּם הָיָה שׁוֹפֵךְ עַל יְסוֹד מַעֲרָבִי שֶׁלַּמִּזְבֵּחַ הַחִיצוֹן אִם־

לֹא נָתַן לֹא עִכֵּב : ב פָּרִים הַנִּשְׂרָפִים וּשְׂעִירִים הַנִּשְׂרָפִים

שְׁחִיטָתָן בַּצָּפוֹן וְקִבּוּל דָּמָן בִּכְלִי שָׁרֵת בַּצָּפוֹן וְדָמָן טָעוּן

הַזָּיָה עַל־הַפָּרֹכֶת וְעַל־מִזְבַּח הַזָּהָב מַתָּנָה אַחַת מֵהֶן

מְעַכָּבֶת שְׁיָרֵי הַדָּם הָיָה שׁוֹפֵךְ עַל יְסוֹד מַעֲרָבִי שֶׁלַּמִּזְבֵּחַ

הַחִיצוֹן אִם־לֹא נָתַן לֹא־עִכֵּב אֵלּוּ וָאֵלּוּ נִשְׂרָפִין בְּבֵית

הַדָּשֶׁן : ג חַטֹּאת הַצִּבּוּר וְהַיָּחִיד אֵלּוּ הֵן חַטֹּאת הַצִּבּוּר

שְׂעִירֵי רָאשֵׁי חֳדָשִׁים וְשֶׁל־מוֹעֲדוֹת שְׁחִיטָתָן בַּצָּפוֹן וְקִבּוּל

דָּמָן בִּכְלִי שָׁרֵת בַּצָּפוֹן וְדָמָן טָעוּן אַרְבַּע מַתָּנוֹת עַל אַרְבַּע

קְרָנוֹת : כֵּיצַד. עָלָה בַכֶּבֶשׁ וּפָנָה לַסּוֹבֵב וּבָא־לוֹ לַקֶּרֶן

דְּרוֹמִית מִזְרָחִית · מִזְרָחִית צְפוֹנִית · צְפוֹנִית מַעֲרָבִית ·

מַעֲרָבִית דְּרוֹמִית·שְׁיָרֵי הַדָּם הָיָה שׁוֹפֵךְ עַל יְסוֹד דְּרוֹמִי·

וְנֶאֱכָלִין לִפְנִים מִן־הַקְּלָעִים לְזִכְרֵי כְהֻנָּה בְּכָל־מַאֲכָל

לְיוֹם וָלַיְלָה עַד־חֲצוֹת : ד הָעוֹלָה קָדֶשׁ קָדָשִׁים שְׁחִיטָתָהּ

בַּצָּפוֹן וְקִבּוּל דָּמָהּ בִּכְלִי שָׁרֵת בַּצָּפוֹן וְדָמָהּ טָעוּן שְׁתֵּי

handmaid, of a Nazirite, °of a leper, and for a trespass pending; all	*Lv.* 14,[12]
these were °slaughtered at the north and their blood was received in a	*Mai. Krb.* 9,[1-9]
vessel of ministration, °at the north; their blood required two	*Ex.* 40,[22]
sprinklings, branching into four; °they had to be eaten within the	*B'Zv.* 55
Precincts, by males of the priesthood, in any cuisine, within the	*Mai. Msh. Zv.* 5,[6]
same day and the following night, until midnight. 6. °The Thanks-	*Yal. Ps.* 854
offering and the ram offered by a Nazirite were of a °lesser	*Zo. Nu.* 255
holiness: they might be slaughtered in any part of the Court, and	*Nu.* 6,[17]
their blood required two sprinklings, branching into four; they	*B'Zv.* 53:
were eaten in any part of the City and by °any person, in any	*Lv.* 10,[10]
cuisine, °within the same day and the following night, until	*Lv.* 7,[17]
midnight; the same applied to the portions °raised therefrom, except	*B'Zv.* 55
that these might be eaten °only by the priests, their wives, their	*Lv.* 10,[14]
children and their servitors. 7. °Peace-offerings were also of a lesser	*Zo. Lv.* 11
holiness, °they might be slaughtered in any part of the Court, and	*B'Zv.* 4
their blood required two °sprinklings branching into four; they	*Lv.* 3,[2]
were eaten in any part of the City and by °any person, in any	*Lv.* 19,[6]
cuisine, °within two days and one night; the same applied to the	*B'Zv.* 56:
portions °raised therefrom, except that they might be eaten only by	*Sf. Lv.* 3,[5-6]
the °priests, their wives, their children and their servitors. 8. A	*Lv.* 10,[15]
Firstling, also °tithes of live-stock and the Paschal lamb were of	*Lv.* 27,[32]
lesser holiness, they were slaughtered °in any part of the Court and	*Tsf. YT Zv.* 5,[7]
their blood required °one sprinkling only, the priest had to direct it	*Nu.* 18,[17]
°towards the base of the altar. The difference in their consumption	*B'Zv.* 57
was that °the Firstling might be eaten only by the priests, but the	*Nu.* 18,[18]
Tithe °by any person. They could both be eaten in any part of the	*Dt.* 12,[6-7]
City, in any cuisine, within two days and one night. °The Paschal	*Mai. Krb.* 18,[12]
offering, however, could be eaten only °that night, only up till	*Pm.* 8,[1]
midnight, °only by those pre-counted for it, and only roast.	*Ex.* 12,[4]

38 (*cont.*)

meaning of the text, in a way that happens to resemble the thinking in this analysis. In one case the authors even seem to delight in revealing the failure to
close a legal loophole, thereby emphasizing the attraction of dissent rather than
the ability to overcome that inclination. These examples thus contradict the way
in which the present passage (according to traditional commentators) exemplifies
the defeat of the urge to disagree, to which the exile is attributed, and the elusive-

מַתָּנוֹת שֶׁהֵן אַרְבַּע וּטְעוּנָה הַפֶּשֶׁט וְנִתְּוַחַוְכָלִיל לָאִשִּׁים: 20

ה זִבְחֵי שַׁלְמֵי צִבּוּר וַאֲשָׁמוֹת· אֵלּוּהֶן אֲשָׁמוֹת אֲשַׁם גְּזֵלוֹת 21

אֲשַׁם מְעִילוֹת אֲשַׁם שִׁפְחָה חֲרוּפָה אֲשַׁם נָזִיר אֲשַׁם 22

מְצוֹרָע אֲשַׁם תָּלוּי·שְׁחִיטָתָן בַּצָּפוֹן וְקִבּוּל דָּמָן בִּכְלִי שָׁרֵת 23

בַּצָּפוֹן וְדָמָן טָעוּן שְׁתֵּי מַתָּנוֹת שֶׁהֵן אַרְבַּע·וְנֶאֱכָלִין לִפְנִים 24

מִזֶהַקְּלָעִים לְזִכְרֵי כְהֻנָּה בְּכָל־מַאֲכָל לְיוֹם וָלַיְלָה עַד חֲצֹת: 25

ו הַתּוֹדָה וְאֵיל נָזִיר קָדָשִׁים קַלִּים שְׁחִיטָתָן בְּכָל־מָקוֹם 26

בָּעֲזָרָה וְדָמָן טָעוּן שְׁתֵּי מַתָּנוֹת שֶׁהֵן אַרְבַּע·וְנֶאֱכָלִין בְּכָל 27

הָעִיר לְכָל־אָדָם בְּכָל מַאֲכָל לְיוֹם וָלַיְלָה עַד חֲצוֹת:הַמּוּרָם 28

מֵהֶם כַּיּוֹצֵא בָהֶם אֶלָּא שֶׁהַמּוּרָם נֶאֱכָל לַכֹּהֲנִים לִנְשֵׁיהֶם 29

וְלִבְנֵיהֶם וּלְעַבְדֵיהֶם: ז וּשְׁלָמִים קָדָשִׁים קַלִּים שְׁחִיטָתָן 30

בְּכָל־מָקוֹם בָּעֲזָרָה וְדָמָן טָעוּן שְׁתֵּי מַתָּנוֹת שֶׁהֵן אַרְבַּע 31

וְנֶאֱכָלִין בְּכָל־הָעִיר לְכָל־אָדָם בְּכָל־מַאֲכָל לִשְׁנֵי יָמִים 32

וְלַיְלָה אֶחָד: הַמּוּרָם מֵהֶם כַּיּוֹצֵא בָהֶם אֶלָּא שֶׁהַמּוּרָם 33

נֶאֱכָל לַכֹּהֲנִים לִנְשֵׁיהֶם וְלִבְנֵיהֶם וּלְעַבְדֵיהֶם: ח הַבְּכוֹר 34

וְהַמַּעֲשֵׂר וְהַפֶּסַח קָדָשִׁים קַלִּים שְׁחִיטָתָן בְּכָל־מָקוֹם 35

בָּעֲזָרָה וְדָמָן טָעוּן מַתָּנָה אֶחָת·וּבִלְבַד שֶׁיִּתֵּן כְּנֶגֶד הַיְסוֹד: 36

שִׁנָּה בַּאֲכִילָתָן הַבְּכוֹר נֶאֱכָל לַכֹּהֲנִים וְהַמַּעֲשֵׂר לְכָל־אָדָם 37

וְנֶאֱכָלִין בְּכָל־הָעִיר בְּכָל־מַאֲכָל לִשְׁנֵי יָמִים וְלַיְלָה אֶחָד· 38

הַפֶּסַח אֵינוֹ נֶאֱכָל אֶלָּא בַלַּיְלָה וְאֵינוֹ נֶאֱכָל אֶלָּא עַד־חֲצוֹת 39

וְאֵינוֹ נֶאֱכָל אֶלָּא לִמְנוּיָיו וְאֵינוֹ נֶאֱכָל אֶלָּא צָלִי: 40

ness of the peaceful unanimity promised for the messianic age.[79] Nevertheless, however precious that unanimity, liturgical editors seem to have been unable to resist interrupting the sequence of which it forms part with dissident interpolations, thereby reflecting the unavoidable nature of dissent, uncertainty, and misunderstanding.

[79] BT *Ber.* 30*b*–31*a*; Caro, *Beit yosef*, 'Oraḥ ḥayim' 50.

°Rabbi Ishmael declared: the *Torah* can be expounded on thirteen rules:	B'Sn. 86
	Lv. Sf. Int.
(1) °Proof from a major instance to a minor one; or from	B'BK 25
(2) °An identical expression;	SA-YD 334,⁴⁴
(3) °A principle built up from one or two texts;	Mta. Ex. 12,⁵⁹
(4/5) °A generalization followed by particulars or vice versa;	Sf. Lv. 1,⁸¹⁸
(6) °A generalization, then particulars and a further generalization—	B'BM 57:
°one can only include items similar to the particulars;	B'Sv. 43
(7) °A wider expression that requires the specification, also, from a	B'MK 3
specification that requires the wider °expression;	B'Mn. 55:
(8) °Any item which is included in a general rule, but which is	Zo. Nu. 149
then detached therefrom—it is detached °not only concerning that	Ps. 145,¹⁸
specified case but °also concerning the whole rule;	Js. 2,¹
(9) Any item which is included in a general rule, °but which is then	B'Sb. 70
detached therefrom, °still being in accordance with the general	B'Kr. 2:
rule—it is specified °in order to make it easier, not stricter;	Dt. 19,⁵
(10) Any item which is °included in a general rule, but which is	Lv. 22,¹¹⁻
then detached therefrom, to elucidate °something different and not	Ex. 21,²
in harmony with the general rule °—it is specified in order to make	B'Kd. 16
it °partly easier and partly stricter;	Ex. 21,¹¹
(11) °Any item which is included in a general rule but is then	Sf. Nu. 6,¹³⁴
detached therefrom, to declaring °something new, must not be	B'Yv. 7
restored to the general rule °until the text itself distinctly restores it;	Lv. 22,¹⁸
(12) °A passage that is explained by its context, and a passage that	B'Sn. 86
is °understood from its concluding terms;	B'Hu. 115:
(13) Similarly, °two texts may contradict each other until a third	Sfr. Lv. 1,⁵
text is found that will °resolve the difference between them.	B'Sn. 7

39. The inventory of exegetical principles (*Rabi yishma'el omer*)

EXTRACT 39. **The Inventory of Exegetical Principles**

The last text in this sequence seems out of place here, since it relates not to sacrifice but to study.⁸⁰ But this is merely an impression, because the rabbinic view that words may, under certain circumstances, represent actions so strongly

⁸⁰ The *Baraita derabi yishma'el*, *Sifra* 1, is not strictly a talmudic text, but Abudarham argues that midrash is the generic equivalent of Talmud in *Abudarham hashalem*, 48, and see Caro, *Shulḥan arukh*, 'Oraḥ ḥayim' 50.

רַבִּי יִשְׁמָעֵאל אוֹמֵר, בִּשְׁלֹשׁ עֶשְׂרֵה מִדּוֹת הַתּוֹרָה

נִדְרֶשֶׁת: מִקַּל וָחֹמֶר. וּמִגְּזֵרָה שָׁוָה. מִבִּנְיָן אָב מִכָּתוּב

אֶחָד וּמִבִּנְיָן אָב מִשְּׁנֵי כְתוּבִים. מִכְּלָל וּפְרָט. וּמִפְּרָט

וּכְלָל. בִּכְלָל וּפְרָטוּכְלָל אִי אַתָּהדָן אֶלָּא כְּעֵיןהַפְּרָט.מִכְּלָל

שֶׁהוּא צָרִיךְ לִפְרָט וּמִפְּרָט שֶׁהוּא צָרִיךְ לִכְלָל. כָּלדָּבָר

שֶׁהָיָה בִּכְלָל וְיָצָא מִןהַכְּלָל לְלַמֵּד לֹא לְלַמֵּד עַלעַצְמוֹ

יָצָא אֶלָּא לְלַמֵּד עַלהַכְּלָל כֻּלּוֹ יָצָא. כָּלדָּבָר שֶׁהָיָהבַּכְּלָל

וְיָצָא לִטְעוֹן טְעַן אֶחָד שֶׁהוּא כְעִנְיָנוֹ יָצָא לְהָקֵל וְלֹא

לְהַחֲמִיר. כָּלדָּבָר שֶׁהָיָה בִּכְלָל וְיָצָא לִטְעוֹן טְעַן אַחֵר

שֶׁלֹּא כְעִנְיָנוֹ יָצָא לְהָקֵל וּלְהַחֲמִיר. כָּלדָּבָר שֶׁהָיָה בִּכְלָל

וְיָצָא לִדּוֹן בַּדָּבָר הֶחָדָשׁ אִי אַתָּה יָכוֹל לְהַחֲזִירוֹ לִכְלָלוֹ עַד

שֶׁיַּחֲזִירֶנּוּ הַכָּתוּב לִכְלָלוֹ בְּפֵרוּשׁ. דָּבָר הַלָּמֵד מֵעִנְיָנוֹ.

וְדָבָר הַלָּמֵד מִסּוֹפוֹ. וְכֵן שְׁנֵי כְתוּבִים הַמַּכְחִישִׁים זֶה

אֶתזֶה עַד שֶׁיָּבוֹא הַכָּתוּב הַשְּׁלִישִׁי וְיַכְרִיעַ בֵּינֵיהֶם:

that recitals amount to deeds relates in this case to sacrifice. Human language lacks creative power, but in a legal context at least can be regarded as binding. The link to the Temple is clear here since this text is a preface to *Sifra*, an early midrash on Leviticus, and thus marks the beginning of the major scriptural treatment of the Tabernacle and its service. It simultaneously suggests that sacrifice cannot be understood without literary exegesis; the techniques listed here are analysed in more detail following this introduction, in passages not cited here. Yet even in this abbreviated inventory informed readers would recognize a toolbox of reading skills analogous to those employed in the present analysis.[81] Indeed, the same theme appears in the talmudic discussion of the previous mishnaic passage,[82] suggesting that early rabbis habitually associated the sacrificial theme with the question of the status of words.

In addition to the redemptive effect of both study and the cult, intellectual agreement would avoid 'needless hatred', one of the causes of the fall of the

---

[81] The fuller version is translated by Daniel Landes in *My People's Prayer Book*, v. 175, 182–5.
[82] BT *Zev.* 49*b*–51*a*.

Second Temple and a reason for the delaying of redemption.[83] The last sentence in particular offers a metaphor for conflict resolution, by describing how 'two texts that contradict each other' can be reconciled by 'a third text . . . that will resolve the difference between them' (lines 13–14). A hermeneutic approach capable of decoding the real world, parallel to the one recommended here for deciphering Torah, would itself obviate conflict and secure peace. However, the fact that the Torah has already been found almost impenetrably complex suggests that the world is just as opaque, undermining the effort from the start. The hermeneutic approaches listed here may number thirteen because this, according to normative rabbinic views, is the number of attributes of divine mercy, the only remaining source of redemption in an imperfect world.[84]

The tragic undertone of this passage is emphasized by its attribution to Rabbi Ishmael, who had once debated the nature of martyrdom and whose murder under Roman rule, like that of Rabbi Akiba, who died while reciting the Shema,[85] demonstrates that Torah study, however profound, may not avert suffering. Rabbi Ishmael, the son of a high priest who had officiated in the Temple, must also have known how to pronounce the Tetragrammaton—the divine name of mercy—and presumably made use of it in seeking clarification of the origin of suffering.[86] His authorship of this passage thus links it to the discussion of the relationship between suffering and martyrdom encountered earlier in Extract 35, further enmeshing the themes of Temple, study, and redemption introduced by the first sacrificial reading of this sequence.

EXTRACT 40. Closing Petition for the Rebuilding of the Temple

This petition, which fittingly concludes the sacrificial sequence by asking for the Temple to be rebuilt, is also a study-text since it once concluded the mishnaic tractate of *Pirkei avot*, although it has now been submerged in that context by the addition of later supplementary material.[87] It could thus be seen as a coda to the entire liturgy up to this point, in so far as this has been an extended study sequence. However, emphasizing study, as in the previous paragraph, would reinforce the doubts about the efficacy of prayer outlined in the introductory chapter. The present paragraph, being both study and prayer, would thus resolve the dissonance between God's demand for Torah study and the speaker's instinct to engage in prayer. Indeed, this study petition is for the rebuilding of

---

[83] BT *Yoma* 9b; Ginzberg, *Legends*, vi. 388 n. 16.   [84] See Rashi on Exod. 34: 6–7.

[85] BT *Ber.* 61b.

[86] S. Safrai, 'Ishmael ben Elisha', 86, and the liturgical poem Eleh Ezkerah in *Service of the Synagogue: Day of Atonement*, ii. 179.

[87] Mishnah *Avot* 5: 23. See Herford, *Pirke Aboth*, 143–4; *Maḥzor vitry*, 562–3; Heinemann, *Prayer in the Talmud*, 267–8.

the Temple, without which prayer will not work, deepening the sense of paradox. Since it is the concluding text of a tractate it also implies that an act of study has been successfully completed. For similar reasons the same words reappear at the end of each Amidah, a prayer midrashically regarded as a substitute for the cult.

The mishnaic context of this passage asserts, however, that even without the Temple and a comprehensive understanding of Torah, God's will can be performed with the energy of a leopard, eagle, hart, or lion, implying, as did the first blessing of the morning in Extract 22, that intellectual understanding is less important than obedience.[88] Both in the liturgy and in the mishnaic source there follows a request for a 'part' in the Torah, alluding to the need for divine help in engaging with it, or perhaps the realization that only a small fragment can be comprehended at a time. This text is then followed by one paragraph (not included in the liturgy) that specifies the ages at which one should begin each branch of Torah study, and another stating the inexhaustible wealth of Torah and of the need to scrutinize it from every angle, underlining precisely what renders it opaque.[89] The chapter then concludes with a statement that study is rewarded according to the effort invested and, implicitly, not according to the student's success in understanding what has been read, a view which the speaker will find encouraging.[90] It is thus clear that study must continue, whatever the obstacles, and that the discovery of deep paradoxes does not alter rabbinic devotion to the task of understanding Torah.

The last line of this liturgical statement (line 3) adds a request for the restoration of the Temple, returning to the form of worship that can best ensure God's attention. The first three words echo a psalm offering protection if one 'serves' God,[91] the context suggesting that 'service' is equated with correct behaviour.[92] The last four words—*kiymei olam ukhshanim kadmoniyot*—echo the quotation from Malachi encountered in Extract 36, line 4,[93] in which the prophet looks forward to the renewal of sacrificial 'service' once the exile is over, and asks God to accept honesty and patience in the meantime as substitutes for sacrifice. The earlier demands for energetic study and ceremonial correctness are expanded here to include personal virtue.

On each repetition the implications of this quotation from Malachi change slightly in response to the context. On its first appearance the 'offering' seemed to consist of liturgical words, while here the second part of the line refers to the sacrificial cult and requests its renewal. The same biblical verse appears in the

[88] Gaguine, *Keter shem tov*, i–ii. 31 n. 52 suggests that the opening sentence of this *mishnah* (*Avot* 5: 23) describes the promptness and purity of purpose of a judge, making it a logical sequel to the listing of Rabbi Ishmael's hermeneutic rules.

[89] Mishnah *Avot* 5: 23–5.   [90] Mishnah *Avot* 5: 26.

[91] Ps. 2: 11. If Deut. 6: 13 is the source, the problem of study is deeper, since the words follow closely on the first paragraph of the Shema, which demands study.

[92] This idea occurs in Tosefta *Edu.* 1: 1.   [93] Mal. 3: 4.

°May it be willed before thee, o God our Lord and Lord of	*Msh. Av.* 5,²³
our ancestors, that the Sanctuary-temple be rebuilt soon, within	*Zo. Gn.* 100
our days, and do thou grant us °a part in thy *Torah*; Yea, may we	*Ku.* 3,⁴⁹
there serve thee in awe, °as in days of yore, as in years gone by.	*Mal.* 3,⁴

40. Closing petition for the rebuilding of the Temple (*Yehi ratson . . . sheyibaneh beit hamikdash*)

brief prayer before the priestly blessing on festivals, comparing liturgical texts to Temple offerings as though renewing the speaker's trust in the effectiveness of words.[94] But although the effect of contexts on meaning demonstrates the contingent nature of every act of study, each repetition offers the hope that a comprehensive series of connotations could eventually be covered.

The sacrificial sequence as a whole echoes the commonplace midrashic view that complete study will be possible only in the setting of a restored Temple,[95] however, so the speaker is spared the need to comprehend immediately the multiplicity of meanings, and thus avoids the theological impasse into which this would lead. A compromise is struck instead, whereby study must continue and the Temple be allowed as much existence as language permits. In this way the speaker can imagine that the dangers of everyday life have been diverted or overcome and can re-enact former happiness in verbal gestures of remembrance. This literary response to danger can claim triumph neither in recreating the Temple nor in achieving perfect study, but it does engage the speaker in the study that is the sole route to intimacy with God. Imagining the Temple in existence may only represent the overcoming of problems, rather than overcoming them in reality, but this is perhaps preferable to despair.

EXTRACT 41. Kaddish: The Rabbinical Kaddish (lines 1–13, 16–18)

Each major liturgical sequence concludes with Kaddish, a passage of praise largely in Aramaic, marking a change of genre and even of language. In this case its appearance is only indicated by a rubric, for reasons that will be explained below. This doxology ('declaration of praise') concludes Birkhot Hashaḥar, the first liturgical section of the day, of which the sacrificial readings are only the last of several parts. Its end is delayed after this Kaddish by another addition, requiring yet another Kaddish to bring it to a close.

Kaddish appears at different points in the liturgy in five versions, each

---

[94] This text lies outside the scope of the present book.
[95] This idea is also implied in Lam. 2: 9.

יְהִי רָצוֹן לְפָנֶיךָ יְיָ אֱלֹהֵינוּ וֵאלֹהֵי אֲבוֹתֵינוּ שֶׁיִּבָּנֶה   1

בֵּית הַמִּקְדָּשׁ בִּמְהֵרָה בְיָמֵינוּ וְתֵן חֶלְקֵנוּ בְּתוֹרָתֶךָ:   2

וְשָׁם נַעֲבָדְךָ בְּיִרְאָה כִּימֵי עוֹלָם וּכְשָׁנִים קַדְמוֹנִיּוֹת: 3

קדיש דרבנן

designed to fulfil a different function.[96] The present one—*kadish derabanan*, 'rabbinical Kaddish'—appears in lines 1–13 and 16–18 and fulfils the original function of the Kaddish of concluding a study session. Its inclusion here reinforces the view, implied by the previous paragraph, that the entire liturgy so far has been a study-text. Statutory prayer has indeed not yet begun.[97] The origins of Kaddish in the *beit midrash* (house of study) rather than the synagogue are reflected in the fact that it refers to God indirectly rather than by name, since the house of study, although sanctified by its purpose, did not share the particular quality of the synagogue as a [*beit*] *mikdash* [*me'at*], 'miniature sanctuary'.[98] The fact that it is predominantly in Aramaic, the vernacular rather than the sacred language of early Jewish communities, also testifies to its origins outside the synagogue. Its core was drafted while the Temple still stood, since it includes no petition for its restoration, a poignant feature after a sequence hinting at the simultaneous presence and absence of the Temple.

The need to recite Kaddish at this point is indicated only by a rubric in many prayer-books because printers traditionally do not repeat Kaddish on each of its many appearances, and because there is some uncertainty about the need for it here. The liturgy has so far been a private rather than a communal matter, even if it is recited in synagogue, since a *minyan*, a quorum of ten adult males, which is essential for the recital of Kaddish, may not yet have gathered.[99] As a result, it is possible that Kaddish is in practice recited neither here nor after Extract 42, thereby reducing the staccato quality of this stage in the liturgy and blurring the distinctions between the sequences that end and begin around here. The absence of Kaddish at this point will also modify the concluding function of the previous paragraph.

A quorum is required for all prayers talmudically regarded as involving 'sanctification', a category defined rabbinically as the present text, Barekhu,

[96] Most of these appear in the course of the liturgical day. One is reserved for funerals and for the occasion of completing the study of a talmudic tractate. [97] Elbogen, *Jewish Liturgy*, 82.

[98] Heinemann, *Prayer in the Talmud*, 266–7; Reif, *Judaism and Hebrew Prayer*, 210.

[99] Baer, for instance, does not even refer to its inclusion at this point, assuming this part of the liturgy to be private.

°Aggrandized and sanctified be His grand name!—   *Ex.* 38,[23]

throughout the universe which he created °according to his   *Dn.* 2,[20]

purpose; yea, °may he manifest his kingship within your   *B'Pm.* 119:

lifetime and °in your days, even within the lifetime of all   *Jb.* 1,[2]

the House of Israel, speedily and soon—°and say ye: *B'Su.* 39

°*Amen!*   *Md. Dt.* 7,[1]

°*Let his grand name be blessed for ever, yea, for worlds of eternities.*   *SA-OH* 56,[1]

°Be he blessed, praised and glorified—yea, exalted, and   *Zo. Ex.* 105

venerated, even, adored, upraised and lauded, be the name   *Zo. Gn.* 232:

of the Holy One, Blest is He, °above all benedictions and   *Nh.* 9,[5]

hymns, praises and °mutations that are recited in the world—   *Ze.* 1,[13]

and say ye: °*Amen.*   *Nu.* 5,[22]

(°O receive our prayers with mercy and with goodwill!)   *Is.* 49,[8]

Unto Israel, yea, unto °the rabbins, also, unto their pupils and unto   *Trg. Ps.* 68,[28]

all the °students of their pupils, even unto all who engage with the   *Tsf. Ed. ult.*

Torah—they of this locality or °they that are of any place else—unto   *SA-YD* 244,[1]

them (also, unto ye) let there arise abounding peace, °grace, loving-   *Es.* 2,[17]

kindness, mercy, long-living and ample sustenance, °yea, deliverance   *Trg. Ps.* 118,[15]

emanating from the presence of °the father who is in heaven (and on   *Msh. RH* 3,[8]

earth)—and say ye: *Amen.*

O may the °prayers and requests of the whole of Israel   *Dn.* 6,[11]

be accepted, in the presence of their father who is in   *Ku.* 2,[50]

°heaven—and say ye: *Amen.*   *I Ki.* 8,[30]

(°May the name of God be blessed henceforth and for evermore!)   *Ps.* 113,[2]

°O may there arise from heaven abounding peace, also,   *Ps.* 85,[9]

life, upon us and upon all Israel—and say ye: °*Amen.*   *Dt.* 27,[15]

(°My help is from the nearness of God, maker of heaven and earth.)   *Ps.* 121,[2]

°He who establishes harmony in his high regions, may He   *Jb.* 25,[2]

establish peace for us and for all Israel—and say ye: °*Amen.*   *SA-OH* 55,[1]

41. Kaddish

יִתְגַּדַּל וְיִתְקַדַּשׁ שְׁמֵהּ רַבָּא בְּעָלְמָא דִּי־בְרָא כִרְעוּתֵהּ

וְיַמְלִיךְ מַלְכוּתֵהּ בְּחַיֵּיכוֹן וּבְיוֹמֵיכוֹן וּבְחַיֵּי דְכָל־בֵּית־

יִשְׂרָאֵל בַּעֲגָלָא וּבִזְמַן קָרִיב, וְאִמְרוּ אָמֵן ·

יְהֵא שְׁמֵהּ רַבָּא מְבָרַךְ לְעָלַם וּלְעָלְמֵי עָלְמַיָּא ·

יִתְבָּרַךְ וְיִשְׁתַּבַּח וְיִתְפָּאַר וְיִתְרוֹמַם וְיִתְנַשֵּׂא וְיִתְהַדָּר

וְיִתְעַלֶּה וְיִתְהַלָּל שְׁמֵהּ דְּקֻדְשָׁא בְּרִיךְ הוּא לְעֵלָּא

מִן־כָּל־בִּרְכָתָא וְשִׁירָתָא תֻּשְׁבְּחָתָא וְנֶחֱמָתָא דַּאֲמִירָן

בְּעָלְמָא וְאִמְרוּ אָמֵן : Cong. קַבֵּל בְּרַחֲמִים וּבְרָצוֹן אֶת תְּפִלָּתֵנוּ :

עַל יִשְׂרָאֵל וְעַל רַבָּנָן וְעַל תַּלְמִידֵיהוֹן וְעַל כָּל־תַּלְמִידֵי

תַלְמִידֵיהוֹן וְעַל כָּל־מָן דְּעָסְקִין בְּאוֹרַיְתָא דִּי בְאַתְרָא הָדֵן

וְדִי בְּכָל־אֲתַר וַאֲתַר יְהֵא לְהוֹן (ולכון) שְׁלָמָא רַבָּא חִנָּא

וְחִסְדָּא וְרַחֲמִין וְחַיִּין אֲרִיכִין וּמְזוֹנָא רְוִיחָא וּפֻרְקָנָא מִן

קֳדָם אֲבוּהוֹן דִּי בִשְׁמַיָּא (וְאַרְעָא), וְאִמְרוּ אָמֵן : יהא שלם וכו׳

תִּתְקַבַּל צְלוֹתְהוֹן וּבָעוּתְהוֹן דְּכָל־יִשְׂרָאֵל קֳדָם אֲבוּהוֹן

דִּי בִשְׁמַיָּא, וְאִמְרוּ אָמֵן : Cong. יְהִי שֵׁם יְיָ מְבֹרָךְ מֵעַתָּה וְעַד עוֹלָם :

יְהֵא שְׁלָמָא רַבָּא מִן־שְׁמַיָּא וְחַיִּים עָלֵינוּ וְעַל־כָּל־

יִשְׂרָאֵל וְאִמְרוּ אָמֵן : Cong. עֶזְרִי מֵעִם יְיָ עֹשֵׂה שָׁמַיִם וָאָרֶץ :

עֹשֶׂה שָׁלוֹם בִּמְרוֹמָיו הוּא יַעֲשֶׂה שָׁלוֹם עָלֵינוּ וְעַל כָּל־יִשְׂרָאֵל, וְאִמְרוּ אָמֵן:

1
2
3

4

5
6
7
8

9
10
11
12
13

14
15
16
17
18

Kedushah, and the reading of the Torah.[100] Kaddish, whose name means 'hallowing', may be read only in the presence of a quorum symbolizing the 'Children of Israel', because God is said scripturally to be 'hallowed among the Children of Israel'. The terms *betokh* or *mitokh*, 'among', do not define how many must be present for the nation to be adequately represented, however. The number ten—the conventional number of the quorum known as a *minyan*—is derived from another verse linking the same word to the term *edah*, 'congregation'.[101] The context of that verse relates to the number of spies who reported negatively on the Promised Land, discouraging the Israelites from completing their journey. It was for believing their reports that the entire generation of Israelites released from Egypt was condemned to wander for forty years and die in the wilderness.[102] The appearance here of the number ten therefore aligns the speaker both with the failure to reach the Promised Land and with the need to invest hopes in the next generation. But whether the *minyan* is identified with the spies themselves or recalls the need to rebel against their failure of nerve and of understanding, the Israelites' delayed arrival parallels the speaker's own exile, which cannot end without perfect study of the kind demanded by the Shema.

Positive associations of the number ten emerge, however, in midrashic comments on the ten good people for whose sake God agreed not to destroy Sodom, and in the idea that had Noah's family numbered ten rather than eight, the Flood might have been prevented.[103] But whether its connotations are positive or negative, the fact that a *minyan* is assigned such power gives a higher status to prayers such as Kaddish which cannot be recited in the absence of a quorum. The formal posture prescribed for Kaddish—standing with feet together while facing the Ark—and the associated congregational responses heighten its solemnity. The fact that these associations are brought out by exegetical methods like those described above, moreover, raises the Kaddish from a formal concluding statement to part of the developing liturgical narrative.

Scriptural phrases embedded in the text echo the more redemptive associations of the *minyan*.[104] The first two words, *yitgadal veyitkadash*, 'aggrandized and sanctified' (line 1), are related by a medieval commentator to the biblical description of the war with Gog and the land of Magog, described in the book of

---

[100] The last three fall outside the scope this book. *Soferim* 10: 7, elaborated in Aboab, *Menorat hamaor*, 3: 3: 1: 5, pp. 213–16.

[101] Mishnah *San.* 1: 6; BT *Meg.* 23*b* on Lev. 22: 32 and Num. 16: 21 and 14: 27; BT *Ber.* 21*b*; BT *Ket.* 7*b*.

[102] Num. 14: 28–33. Another association is with Joseph's ten brothers, whose crime is emphasized in *Midrash asarah harugei malkhut*: see *Otsar midrashim*, 444, and the supplement on p. 448. Joseph's brothers are linked to the *minyan* by Bahya ben Asher in his commentary on the Pentateuch, 'Mikets' 42. Another possible model is the ten companions of Ishmael, the assassin of Gedaliah, whose death is commemorated by a fast on 3 Tishrei. See 2 Kgs 25: 25; Jer. 41: 1.

[103] *Gen. Rabbah* 49: 13 on Gen. 18: 32.

[104] For a fuller analysis of its history and composition see Weitzman, 'Origin of the "Qaddish"'.

Ezekiel shortly after the messianic vision of the dry bones,[105] just before the description of the restored Temple.[106] The context, which suggests the violence of the messianic advent, consolingly views danger as a portent of redemption and supports the idea that God must rescue his people to save his name from defamation.[107] The third and fourth words, *shemeh raba*, 'his great name', echo the prophetic promise that only in messianic times will God's name be single and great,[108] reflecting the idea that the Shema enacts a precondition for the coming of the messiah. The Sephardi version of this paragraph reinforces the messianic theme by adding the petition that God 'cause his salvation to spring forth and hasten the coming of his anointed', after the first two words of line 2.[109] It also adds, on the first day of Rosh Hashanah, the request that he 'complete [*vishakhlel*, i.e. 'restore'] his Temple and redeem his people'.[110] Both ideas are implicit in the version examined here, and are presumably editorial additions to a text which pre-dated the destruction of the Temple.

The last four words of line 1 apparently recommend resignation, however, since *be'alma di-vera khirutei*, 'in the world which he created according to his will', suggests the need to accept existence as it is, whatever its imperfections, since this is the will of God.[111] But the first two words of line 2 return to the petitionary mode, for *veyamlikh malkhutei*, literally 'and his kingship will be rendered kingly',[112] alludes to the completion of God's reign by means of the redemption.[113] The speaker implicitly acknowledges the imperfection of the world again in lines 2–3 by urging its transformation. Indeed, the study sequences that this prayer concludes aim to overcome the barrier to redemption represented by the opacity of Torah.[114]

The speaker's hope of redemption emerges in the congregational response in line 4—*yehe shemeh raba mevarakh le'alam ul'almei almaya*, 'Let his grand name be blessed for ever, yea, for worlds of eternities'—based on Daniel's words when he saved himself and the royal magicians from death by successfully interpreting Nebuchadnezzar's dream;[115] his powers of interpretation suggest that insight

---

[105] Ezek. 38–9.   [106] Ezek. 40–8.

[107] Abudarham, *Abudarham hashalem*, 66, on Ezek. 38: 23; Jacob ben Asher, *Arba'ah turim*, 'Orah hayim' 56.

[108] Ezek. 36: 23 echoes the phrase, part of the prelude to the vision of the dry bones; Obad. 1: 21; Zech. 14: 9 (which will be encountered at the conclusion of the next sequence of the liturgy in Extract 58, lines 1–2). See Jacob ben Asher, *Arba'ah turim*, 'Orah hayim' 56, which adds that God's name will be complete when Amalek is finally defeated.

[109] *Book of Prayer: Daily and Occasional Prayers*, 14.

[110] *Book of Prayer: New Year Service*, 27; Gaguine, *Keter shem tov*, i–ii. 169–71.

[111] *Otsar hatefilot*, 'Iyun tefilah', 218a, suggests that it might have been this praise that this text says he created, and that the world is merely where it is located.

[112] Translated here 'may he manifest his kingship'.

[113] Cf. Zech. 14: 9.   [114] BT *Sot.* 49a–b.

[115] Dan. 2: 20. It resembles Pss. 41: 14 and 113: 2, and Neh. 9: 5, all in Hebrew.

into Torah, on which redemption depends, might be miraculous in origin. The present line is consequently regarded as so sacred that everyone present must join in reciting it, even if this involves interrupting mystic meditation.[116] The response is said to support the world,[117] to cause evil decrees to be torn up in heaven,[118] and to bring as much honour to God as did the Exodus.[119] By offering a solution to the opacity of Torah, and by extension ensuring the continuation of existence itself, the response resolves an issue that has resisted every attempt to overcome it since the opening statement of the day.

In role and content this line resembles the response to the first sentence of the Shema (Extract 31, line 2), acting out the speaker's acceptance of the challenge to unify God's name, the accomplishment of which is a feature of the messianic age. It is also analogous to the call to prayer at the beginning of statutory worship, which follows the introductory sequences examined in this book. One of its scriptural sources is David's prayer on handing over the Temple-building project to his son Solomon, a text included later in the liturgy (and discussed in the context of Extract 55, lines 1–2), which reinforces the speaker's sense of reconciliation to failure. It also suggests the need to persist with both study and prayer, and to pass the task of prayer to others who are more able, or merely longer-lived. Another source is a psalm attributed to David in which he looks forward to rescue because God helps the downcast.[120] A midrashic description of God as an unwilling participant in exile reports that, when these words are heard in heaven, 'the Holy One, blessed be He, shakes his head and says: Happy is the king who is praised thus in his house. Woe to the father who had to banish his children, and woe to the children who had to be banished from the table of their father.'[121] The speaker's acceptance of exile is thus part of the covenant between God and Israel, despite the potentially negative effect on God's reputation of the punitive side of his agreement with Israel. The view that suffering results from God's neglect fades, as it can now be accepted that God 'suffers' from the exile. This midrashic description of cosmic loss may have helped inspire the later association of Kaddish with bereavement.

The second paragraph of Kaddish (lines 5–6) opens with eight exhortations to praise God. These, together with the two at the beginning of the first paragraph, make a total of ten, the number of commands by which the world was created and also of the commandments received at Sinai,[122] both alluding to God's power. However, the association with laws suggests that the speaker's suffering

---

[116] BT *Ber.* 21*b*.   [117] BT *Sot.* 49*a*.

[118] BT *Shab.* 119*b* and *Midrash mishlei* 10: 16, fo. 33*b*.

[119] *Sifrei*, Deut., 306, fo. 132*b* on Deut. 32: 3 (which resembles Barekhu, the call to prayer); see also Rashi on Exod. 14: 4.   [120] 1 Chr. 29: 10; Ps. 113: 2.   [121] BT *Ber.* 3*a*.

[122] Judah ben Samuel Hehasid, *Perushei sidur hatefilah laroke'aḥ*, i. 240, for this and other numerological interpretations. See also Jacob ben Asher, *Arba'ah turim*, 'Oraḥ ḥayim' 56, and Zedekiah ben Abraham, *Shibolei haleket*, 4*a*.

might be punitive, in contrast with the number thirteen, for example, which is commonly aligned with the attribute of mercy. An awareness of the kingly associations of the number ten—as of the number eight, which completes the seven days of Creation with the additional one of divine unity—may have led to the practice of shifting the first term, *yitbarakh*, 'blessed', back to the end of the previous congregational response, making a total of three in the opening lines and of seven—a number suggesting completeness and new beginnings—in the body of the text.[123]

Unease about divine mercy is not disposed of, however, since the inventory culminates in a declaration of God's blessedness in line 6, emphatically echoing the opening word of David's blessing over the Temple and the early-morning blessing formulas (in Extracts 22, 23, and 24). This resembles the way blessings juxtapose an awareness of God's simultaneous immanence and transcendence, although in that case the immediacy of the name associated with mercy gives way to that of judgement as the formula shifts from the second to the third person.

The theme of ambivalence is completed by the admission in line 7 that the human voice cannot adequately express praise,[124] however, returning to the idea of the impossibility of effective prayer and the consequent dependence on divine mercy. This encapsulates more clearly than any previous statement the speaker's logical impasse in having to depend on a verbal medium to communicate with God, even though this is known to be ineffective. The recurrence of this idea at the conclusion of each section of the liturgy undermines the very medium in which it is expressed, although the impact is limited by the fact that these are not the last words of the Kaddish. It is one of the mysteries of the liturgy that language can continue to be used after such a statement. Despite the declaration that God is above all blessing, the liturgical project is not reduced to silence but returns to ideas raised by the previous sacrificial sequence. The theological courage to continue or will to survive is perhaps related to Maimonides' scripturally based view that silence is itself a form of worship,[125] a source for the awareness of the philosophically sophisticated worshipper that the liturgy only appears to be a dialogue and is in fact at least partly self-addressed. If prayer operates on the speaker, as in the imagining of the Temple and the reading of Torah, the problem of the efficacy of worship does not arise.

The scope of this attempt to persist despite the apparent impossibility of success can be seen from the next paragraph, lines 9–13, the only one specific to this rabbinic form of the Kaddish. The petition for the welfare of all those who study Torah, clearly including the speaker, does not claim that students have special merit or that study ensures their safety. It suggests instead that they are

---

[123] Hoffman, *Canonization of the Synagogue Service*, 56–8. For the view that these seven names correspond to the seven heavens, see Amram Gaon, *Seder rav amram hashalem*, i. 93*b*.

[124] This echoes Neh. 9: 5, which describes, however, the rebuilding of the Temple after the exile.   [125] Maimonides, *Guide of the Perplexed*, i: 59.

in special need of 'grace, loving-kindness, mercy . . . and ample sustenance' (lines 11–12), perhaps because they devote time to study instead of gainful employment, as though each act of study were a minor martyrdom. Prayer was similarly regarded in the opening statement of the day, since the speaker re-enacts the very deed by which Daniel was entrapped by his enemies.

The Kaddish ends with two requests for peace, the first in Aramaic (lines 16–17) and the second its approximate translation in Hebrew (line 18). This later Hebrew version also appears after the concluding blessing of the Amidah, which is itself a blessing for peace.[126] On saying these words, both in the Kaddish and in the Amidah, the speaker or prayer-leader takes three steps back before saying the first three words of the last line, bowing left and right, as though taking leave of a king, before returning after a short pause. The theme of peace at the end of the Amidah is related to the threefold priestly blessing (encountered earlier in Extract 19) and to the scriptural verses recited at the closing of the Ark on sabbaths.[127] But since the present words were spoken to Job by Bildad, in a speech that Job then proceeds to disprove, they suggest error, mystery, and the revelation of God's unchallengeable power, rather than his kindness or blessing.[128] The Aramaic version of this paragraph may have been designed to complete a study session with words of comfort for the exile (also reflected in the word *nehamata*, 'comfortings', in line 7), providing another reason for the medieval transfer of the Kaddish to the home of a mourner.[129] The reasons for this association of Kaddish with mourning and the practice of reserving the recital of some forms of Kaddish for mourners is discussed below.

The congregation responds 'Amen' after this and each paragraph, but the present version includes other minor responses in lines 8 and 17, each previewing the line that follows and introducing the divine name that Kaddish otherwise lacks. The speaker thus pre-empts the prayer-leader and reclaims the verbal initiative, introducing the theme to come by including God's name in a text from which it has otherwise been absent, removing the liturgical performance from the house of study in which it was first used, and restoring it to the synagogue where God's name can be freely spoken. In addition, these responses show how the speaker resists to the last the submission to everyday circumstances, towards which much of the liturgy seems to point.

The fact that this doxology fails to conclude even the opening segment of the liturgy, however, emphasizes the powerlessness of words and leaves the speaker

---

[126] The 'peace' in heaven is contrasted with the dissent of rival worldly monarchs in the same words in Job 25: 2.   [127] Num. 6: 24–6; Ps. 29: 11.   [128] Job 25: 2.

[129] Elbogen, *Jewish Liturgy*, 80–1, quotes *Soferim* 19: 12 and points out the similarity of line 4 to Job 25: 2, which he may have regarded as an indication of a link with mourning. The appearance of this word in the Kaddish may echo the fact that Syriac *nehemata*—and probably the related Hebrew expression *ereh benehamah* (see Ben Yehuda, *Dictionary*, vii. 3609–10)—refers to resurrection (Raphael Loewe, pers. comm.).

able neither to argue effectively, to judge by line 7, nor to refrain from speaking. A midrashic explanation relates directly to this feature, seeing the use of Aramaic in the text as an attempt to conceal from the angels, who understand only Hebrew, the power of Israel's praise of God and the fact that the 'consolations' in line 7 refer to God's 'sorrow' at his people's homelessness and at the loss of the Temple. Their suffering, shared by the speaker, reflects negatively both on God's power to compensate for the sufferings of exile and on the ability of Jews to persuade God to bring about redemption.[130] The angels, whose location around the throne of God seems to give them special privileges, are here Israel's rivals for attention, even suspected of conveying the speaker's prayers inaccurately.

This text discounts language as a channel of communication, although the word 'blessing' survives to become the opening term both of the next liturgical sequence in Extract 43, and of the morning service proper, which falls outside the scope of the present book. A meditation on the scriptural use of language which follows the next Kaddish will simultaneously endorse and override the powerlessness of words.

EXTRACT 42. **Psalm 30 on David's 'House'**

The preceding Kaddish seemed not only to conclude the liturgical unit, but to rule out the verbal medium as an option. Yet this paragraph, by its very presence, overcomes the loss of linguistic confidence. If there is no *minyan* present this text will follow directly on from the one before the Kaddish, while the second Kaddish that follows this text will likewise be omitted, emphasizing liturgical continuity. But if there is a *minyan*, the present text, flanked by the previous version of Kaddish and the one to come, will bridge the end of Birkhot Hashaḥar and the start of Pesukei Dezimra, the next sequence, which begins with Extract 43.

This psalm is one of a number of insertions made under Lurianic influence at points in the liturgy that seemed to invite additions, an earlier example being the group of verses that interrupted the sacrificial readings in Extract 36.[131] Fragmentary citations appeared earlier in Extract 13, lines 4–5 and 8, but the editors responsible for including the whole text in the early sixteenth century would have been drawn to numerological features such as its tenfold repetition of the name of God (corresponding to the number of creational commands and

---

[130] BT *Shab.* 12*b*; BT *Sot.* 33*a*; see the discussion in Judah ben Yakar, *Perush hatefilot vehaberakhot*, 19–20, and supplementary page 6, and the remarks in Abudarham, *Abudarham hashalem*, 69–70; Judah ben Samuel Hehasid, *Perushei sidur hatefilah laroke'aḥ*, i. 242–7; Solomon of Worms, *Sidur rabenu shelomoh bar shimshon migarmaisa*, 77–82, and Aboab, *Menorat hama'or*, 3: 3: 1: 5, pp. 214–16 n. 5.

[131] It is not in *Sidur avodat yisra'el*; see *Tselota di'avraham*, i. 147 (in commentary 'Vaya'as avraham') and Berliner, *Randbemerkungen*, i. 22, for background. Gaguine, *Keter shem tov*, i–ii. 35–6 n. 57, says he cannot trace the Lurianic sources for the practice.

°*Psalm song at the dedication of the house—of David:*	*Ps.* 30,[1-18]
°I extol thee, God, for thou hast drawn me up and hast not	*B'Sv.* 15:
let my foes to °rejoice over me; God my Lord, I have clam-	*La.* 2,[17]
oured unto thee, and thou didst °cure me; O God, thou	*Ex.* 15,[26]
broughtest up my being from the °abyss; thou hast given life	*Dt.* 32,[22]
unto me, so I should not °sink into the pit; Sing unto God, ye	*Is.* 38,[18-20]
his °devotees, yea, acknowledge unto the mention of his	*Dt.* 33,[8]
holiness. °Indeed, his anger is but °for a moment, life is of his	*Md. Es.* [49/52]
willing, weeping may tarry for a night, but joy comes in the	*B'Br.* 7
morning. As for me, I had said in my security: °I shall never	*Dt.* 32,[15]
founder. In °thy goodwill, God, thou hadst set me up like	*Is.* 49,[8]
a mountain range—but when °hiding thy countenance,	*Dt.* 31,[18]
I was °confounded. Unto thee, God, do I call, yea, unto the	*Gn.* 45,[8]
Lord, I make supplication: °What profit is there in my bleed-	*Ku.* 4,[3]
ing, if I sink down into the abyss?—°can dust acknowledge	*Ps.* 115,[17]
thee?—can it declare thy truth? O hearken, God, and grant my	*Ps.* 6,[6]
plea, o God, be thou °my helper! Thou hast turned for me my	*II Cr.* 18,[31]
wailing into dance-round—thou hast °loosed my sackcloth	*B'Br.* 55:
and girded me with gladness; °To the end, that thou shalt be	*Zo. Gn.* 39,71:
intoned in glory, °not in silence, yea, God my Lord, I will ever	*La.* 2,[18]
°acknowledge thee!	*I Ki.* 8,[38]

42. Psalm 30 on David's 'house' (*Mizmor shir ḥanukat habayit*)

of statements in the Decalogue), as well as the terms of praise in the Kaddish, and the quorum without which Kaddish may not be read. If there is no quorum, therefore, this psalm might constitute a symbolic substitute. Its fifteen verses similarly correspond to the numerical value of the name of God connoting mercy (*yah*), the pre-eminence of which, according to elements of the subtext identified in the discussion above, was assumed in the Kaddish even though it was not spelled out. The psalm is thus a suitable sequel to the Kaddish (or possibly a substitute for it should a quorum not yet have gathered) and a fitting prologue to what follows it in some rites. Its introduction was also inspired by the need to provide opportunities for another mourner to recite Kaddish, since in many congregations some occurrences of this text are recited by single mourners rather than in unison by all mourners present. The Kaddish which follows this psalm does indeed conclude the liturgical sequence.

The passage also looks forward to the series of psalms in the next liturgical sequence, Pesukei Dezimra (Extracts 43–59). The independence of this bridging

מִזְמוֹר שִׁיר־חֲנֻכַּת הַבַּיִת לְדָוִד: אֲרוֹמִמְךָ יְהֹוָה כִּי 1

דִלִּיתָנִי וְלֹא־שִׂמַּחְתָּ אֹיְבַי לִי: יְהֹוָה אֱלֹהָי שִׁוַּעְתִּי 2

אֵלֶיךָ וַתִּרְפָּאֵנִי: יְהֹוָה הֶעֱלִיתָ מִן־שְׁאוֹל נַפְשִׁי חִיִּיתַנִי 3

מִיָּרְדִי־בוֹר: זַמְּרוּ לַיהֹוָה חֲסִידָיו וְהוֹדוּ לְזֵכֶר קָדְשׁוֹ: 4

כִּי רֶגַע בְּאַפּוֹ חַיִּים בִּרְצוֹנוֹ בָּעֶרֶב יָלִין בֶּכִי וְלַבֹּקֶר 5

רִנָּה: וַאֲנִי אָמַרְתִּי בְשַׁלְוִי בַּל־אֶמּוֹט לְעוֹלָם: יְהֹוָה 6

בִּרְצוֹנְךָ הֶעֱמַדְתָּה לְהַרְרִי עֹז הִסְתַּרְתָּ פָנֶיךָ הָיִיתִי נִבְהָל: 7

אֵלֶיךָ יְהֹוָה אֶקְרָא וְאֶל־אֲדֹנָי אֶתְחַנָּן: מַה־בֶּצַע בְּדָמִי 8

בְּרִדְתִּי אֶל־שָׁחַת הֲיוֹדְךָ עָפָר הֲיַגִּיד אֲמִתֶּךָ: שְׁמַע 9

יְהֹוָה וְחָנֵּנִי יְהֹוָה הֱיֵה עֹזֵר לִי: הָפַכְתָּ מִסְפְּדִי לְמָחוֹל 10

לִי פִּתַּחְתָּ שַׂקִּי וַתְּאַזְּרֵנִי שִׂמְחָה: לְמַעַן יְזַמֶּרְךָ כָבוֹד 11

וְלֹא יִדֹּם יְהֹוָה אֱלֹהַי לְעוֹלָם אוֹדֶךָּ: קַדִּישׁ אַבֵּל 12

text, which fully belongs to neither liturgical unit, is emphasized by the framing Kaddish versions. Pesukei Dezimra is dominated by King David, since it consists mostly of psalms that are traditionally attributed to him, making the present one a suitable point from which to start. It also stands out as the first complete biblical text in the liturgy so far, breaking the pattern of fragmentary citation and reinforcing the theme of study.

The last line refers to the successful completion of an undefined act, referring perhaps to worship, study, or awakening but symbolized by the finishing of the 'house' mentioned in the first line; this suggests that the present psalm serves as yet another introduction to the liturgical day. Its associations explain why it has been located close to the moment at which Temple sacrifice began for the day. Not only does the remark about awaking in lines 5–6 link it to the opening statement and to beginnings in general, but it continues the Temple theme of the previous sequence, denying the finality of the petition with which that ended, as well as the role of the previous Kaddish. The beginning of the psalm suggests a resurgence of the Temple theme, while the reference to 'silence' in line 12 reflects on the insistence in the Kaddish on the powerlessness of words. The Temple's virtual presence here responds to the theological impasse in a similar way to the prophetic reading in Extract 33, lines 9–11.

The Temple associations are reinforced by a mishnaic report that this psalm was sung by Levites as the firstfruits were brought to the sanctuary each spring, linking it to the pentateuchal scene in which the speaker takes stock of the sacred narrative and celebrates the arrival in the Promised Land—a passage which was recited formally during the ceremonial presentation of the firstfruits in the Temple.[132] This allusion therefore aligns the start of the day either with the establishment of the Israelites in the Promised Land or with the end of the first agricultural cycle after their settlement, a new liturgical metaphor for awakening.[133] This psalm is thus the first actual enactment of a Temple ceremony, suggesting that the virtual building generated by the previous sequence is now being put to use, and that the psalm may not have been introduced into the liturgy by earlier editors precisely to avoid the appearance of reproducing Temple ritual.

The precise link between this psalm and the Temple is uncertain, however, for the first line, 'Psalm . . . at the dedication of the house—of David', leaves it unclear whether David is the master of the house, the author of the psalm, or merely its user. If the psalm is regarded as a symbolic dedication of the Temple it would resemble the way the Temple was brought at least virtually into the here and now by the earlier verbal 'performance' of the daily sacrifice in the previous sequence.

Rabbinic readers recognized that this could not have been a dedication hymn for the Temple, however, since David neither built the Temple nor lived to see it completed, so could not have written this psalm for its opening. A midrashic author responded by arguing that, since it had been David's plan to construct the Temple, it remained his to dedicate, and that this is the psalm he wrote for its eventual opening.[134] David's absence from the dedication makes the use of this text an admission that, for the speaker too, the Temple represents something hoped for but inaccessible.

Other commentators link the 'house' to David's own palace,[135] which complicates the text's meaning, since it was mainly because David had built his own home before that of God that he was prevented from building the Temple.[136]

---

[132] See the ritual recital in Deut. 26: 1–15, echoed in the central narrative of the Passover Haggadah.   [133] Mishnah *Bik.* 3: 4; also in BT *Shev.* 15*b*.

[134] *Midrash Psalms* 30: 2–4, 6 and Rashi on Ps. 30: 1, based on 1 Kgs. 8: 17. Other midrashic texts argue that he was indeed present, either by being raised from the dead or by being brought in his coffin: see *Pesikta rabati* 2: 5, *Eccles. Rabbah* 4: 3 (1), and other sources in Ginzberg, *Legends*, iv. 156, vi. 296 n. 65. See also the discussion in Horbury, 'Cult of Christ', esp. p. 457.

[135] Moses Mendelssohn, quoted in Jacobson, *Weekday Siddur*, 70.

[136] David's house-building is mentioned in 2 Sam. 5: 11; 1 Chr. 17: 3–12 offers no reason for forbidding him to build the Temple, but his taste for warfare is said to render him unworthy to do

But since the speaker has just left home for synagogue in symbolic exile, the use of this psalm potentially suggests both that David's error is being avoided and that every place of worship may be regarded as a 'miniature sanctuary'. David's crime in building his own home before the Temple was recalled some centuries later by the prophet Haggai, who accused the whole people of dwelling 'in your well-roofed houses, and this house lies waste'.[137] This locates the speaker in the days of Haggai and the years before the building of the Second Temple. Since at both periods the Israelites seemed reconciled to the lack of a cultic means of approaching God, the present quotation of David's psalm seems to condemn the speaker to silence and exile.

Borrowing the voice of David incriminates the speaker in another way, noted earlier in connection with allusions to David, Judah (another adulterer) in Extract 28, lines 3–5, and the sons of Korah in Extract 36. David was unworthy to build the Temple because he conspired to have Uriah killed to cover up his adultery with Uriah's wife, Bathsheba; associating the speaker implicitly even with wrongs which David had not yet committed at the time he wrote this psalm recalls previous concerns about the unavoidable nature of sin.

Other commentators argue, however, that the absence of any reference to the process of building and the fact that the text is in the first person singular suggest that the 'house' is not a building at all, but the body of the speaker, the 'home' of the soul. The idea that the psalm relates not to building, but to recovery from illness[138] would echo the symbolic equation, mentioned earlier, between the Temple and the body and would also emphasize the speaker's vulnerability to the dangers ahead, much as did the Temple allusion in the opening statement of the day. The 'illness' would in this case represent exile, and the healing correspond to successive redemptions, a reading which would explain the reference to the 'hiding' of God's face (line 7), a common metaphor for the withdrawal of divine attention at a time of danger or suffering. The argument that the speaker's silencing through death would deprive God of human praise is deployed in lines 8–9, while the speaker goes on to mirror the opening words of the Shema in lines 9–10, inviting God to 'hear' petitions for release, recalling that death would end the ability to speak.

In the context of the morning, therefore, this psalm alludes to resurrection from death-like sleep, suggested by lines 5–6, to recovery from the 'illness' of excretion mentioned in Extract 17, line 6, or to the hope of surviving those everyday dangers that dominated the early-morning liturgy. Misery is transformed into an occasion for dance in lines 10–12, pointing to the speaker's

---

so in 1 Chr. 22: 8 and 28: 3. 1 Kgs. 5: 17 suggests that war left him no time for building. 2 Sam. 12: 10 says that David will never be free of 'the sword' after the Uriah episode, an assertion that links all three explanations.

[137] Hag. 1: 4–11.

[138] Malbim on Ps. 30: 1, Ibn Ezra on Job 4: 19, and Rashi and Ibn Ezra on Eccles. 12: 3.

release from sleep and regaining of the ability to recite this psalm. A midrashic text describes how it was sung after the defeat of Haman and following several other rescues.[139] The continuing exile and David's ultimate lack of success nevertheless show that rescue is still needed, even though the speaker's survival at this moment is grounds for thanksgiving, as seen earlier in Extract 30.

This climactic psalm thus marks the meeting point of the speaker's private world and the divine scheme of history. Its blurring of the boundaries between awaking and redemption exemplifies the 'overdetermination' of liturgical texts—their ability to sustain multiple meanings and to suggest complex states of mind. It also demands that the speaker relocate liturgical elements, displaced from their dramatically relevant positions for practical reasons, but remaining nonetheless eloquent. Many editions of the Ashkenazi rite, including that of Baer, insert the texts associated with the *talit* and *tefilin* at this point, even though they were included in the present version before the speaker's departure from home for synagogue.[140] The texts associated with the ceremonial garments would certainly highlight some of the themes outlined here, but would tend to conclude rather than introduce them.

EXTRACT 41. **Kaddish: The Mourners' Kaddish (lines 1–8, 16–18)**

The rubric indicating a mourners' Kaddish (Extract 42, line 12) introduces a new voice into the liturgy, although if a mourner has been leading the service up to this point, as is the practice in some congregations, the distinction will be blurred or lost.[141] Like the previous Kaddish, this one is recited only in the presence of a *minyan*, and might have been introduced merely to provide another mourner with an opportunity to recite this text, although practice varies on whether it is recited by only one mourner, a group of mourners collectively, or the prayer-leader accompanied by any mourners present. In some traditions a mourner leading the recital comes to the front of the synagogue, while in others the individual or group remain in their places. Sephardi practice is for mourners to stand during its recital by the prayer-leader and for the rest of the congregation to remain seated. Ashkenazim invariably stand for Kaddish.[142] The involvement of mourners indicates the engaged awareness of the community of the private lives of its members, particularly at moments of vulnerability.

---

[139] *Midrash Psalms* 30: 6 sees 'thou hast drawn me up' in lines 1–2 as release from exile. 'Hiding thy countenance' (line 7) is a metaphor for exile in Deut. 31: 18. The psalm is associated specifically with the rescue of Mordecai in *Lev. Rabbah* 28: 6, *Est. Rabbah* 10: 5, and *Pesikta derav kahana* 8: 4. Ibn Ezra on Ps. 30: 1 claims that the psalm also refers to the messianically restored Temple.   [140] *Sidur avodat yisra'el*, 55–7; the present edition, Extracts 7–10.

[141] Like the previous Kaddish and the psalm, this is not in *Sidur avodat yisra'el*.

[142] For a summary of some practices, see Daniel Landes in *My People's Prayer Book*, vi. 26.

The idea that Kaddish is to be recited daily by a mourner during the eleven months after the death of a parent, sibling, child, or spouse, and thereafter on the anniversary of the death (a practice extended in some Progressive circles to include female mourners), has become so deeply rooted in popular perceptions of the prayer since the Middle Ages that it has been reductively redefined as a 'prayer for the dead'. The association with death derives from talmudic texts which refer to the fact that children can help their deceased parents by good deeds,[143] and later ones that describe how this can be achieved through prayer.[144] One of the earliest identifications of Kaddish with this prayer is in a thirteenth-century Ashkenazi work in which Rabbi Akiba ensured a dead man's release from Gehenna by teaching his son to recite this prayer, as a result of which the congregation responded with the text at line 4.[145]

Mourners may have been associated with this text since a prayer-leader who had personal access to the darker side of life would best be able to fulfil the talmudic ideal of reflecting the 'bad' as well as 'good' aspects of life.[146] The importance of accepting all experience is reflected in referring to a funeral service as *tsiduk hadin*, 'acknowledging the justice of [divine] judgement', a term derived from a talmudic account of martyrdom but implying acceptance.[147] The name 'Kaddish' itself echoes a pentateuchal text demanding the 'sanctification of God's name', a rabbinic synonym for martyrdom, as though acknowledging the suffering of the mourner.[148] The identification of bereavement with martyrdom is alluded to in the metaphorical description of the destruction of the Temple as widowhood in the opening words of the book of Lamentations and in the practice of taking leave of a mourner after a condolence visit with a statement that compares the bereaved to those who suffer the loss of the Temple. The mourner's recital of a prayer lamenting exile introduces this scene and others related to martyrdom, such as the Akedah, into the life of the speaker.

The present version of Kaddish differs from the rabbinic version discussed above in that it omits the petition for scholars and students (lines 9–13). Although on a formal level it serves to conclude the act of study represented by the intervening psalm, the way it repeats most of the previous Kaddish suggests

---

[143] BT *San.* 104a. For a *minyan* gathering to study where a person died, see BT *Shab.* 152a–b.

[144] *Tana debei eliyahu* (*zuta*) 2: 17, p. 23, trans. Braude and Kapstein, pp. 448–9. Such belief in the efficacy of prayer reflects more on the involvement of children in sacred matters than on the general question of the efficacy of prayer discussed above.

[145] Isaac b. Moses of Vienna, *Or zarua*, 'Shabat', 50 (see ii. 11: 2) quoted in Jacobson, *Weekday Siddur*, 298–300; based on *Otiyot derabi akiva* (*zayin*), in Jellinek, *Beit hamidrash*, iii. 27–9. See also Elbogen, *Jewish Liturgy*, 82.

[146] BT *Ber.* 33b, 54a. These and other ideas are explored in Wieseltier, *Kaddish*, whose spiritual and intellectual journal of a year of mourning, based on textual research, unfortunately lacks details of the sources quoted. [147] *Sidur avodat yisra'el*, 586–7, and BT *AZ* 18a.

[148] The name first appears in the post-talmudic tractate *Soferim*. For the association with Lev. 22: 32, the prooftext for martyrdom, see e.g. Zedekiah ben Abraham, *Shibolei haleket*, 4a–5a.

the ineffectiveness of the text. The reprise of the closing appeal for peace particularly highlights its elusive nature, symbolized in the previous psalm by the absence of David's 'house'.

The version known as the 'full Kaddish', which is inserted only towards the conclusion of the morning liturgy, is implicit here, especially as it likewise concludes a liturgical unit. Its defining characteristic is a request for prayers to be heard (lines 14–15), suggesting that all previous petitions, in this case the entire service, may not have been listened to. Just as the deceased person prayed in vain for death to be averted, so the mourner demonstrates reconciliation to death by echoing the same text. The paradoxical attempt to employ the disqualified verbal medium to reinforce itself echoes the central mystery of liturgical prayer.

A medieval commentator indicates that he implicitly understood the way in which Kaddish compromises language itself by identifying the second and third words of line 14—*tselotehon uva'utehon*, translated 'prayers and requests'—as 'by my sword and by my bow'. This is the targumic rendering of the same words in Jacob's farewell to Joseph, when the younger son was promised the double portion appropriate for a firstborn. But if the weapons in question correspond to the prayer and petition named in the Kaddish,[149] this text recommends force in facing the day ahead, even though violence was biblically discredited by Jacob's criticism of Levi's and Simeon's massacre of the men of Shechem,[150] a criticism reinforced by the closing petitions for peace in the Kaddish. This condemnation again leaves the speaker vulnerable to the dangers ahead, however, and armed only with the hope that the divine covenant will be activated by the intervention of God's mercy. The speaker is now a player in a drama of ideas that has become a matter of life and death.

---

[149] Judah ben Yakar, *Perush hatefilot vehaberakhot*, 19, on Targum to Gen. 48: 22. See Rashi's remarks, based on Targum and BT *BB* 123a.　　　　　　　[150] Gen. 49: 5.

PESUKEI DEZIMRA

☙

CHAPTER TEN

☙

Hope in Words

'Words without knowledge'
JOB 38: 2

THIS CHAPTER discusses the second of the two preliminary liturgical sequences of the morning, Pesukei Dezimra ('sections of songs'), leading the speaker to the brink of the statutory morning service. Its mostly poetic texts, the majority related to King David—psalms or other writings—involve the speaker in a virtual rebuilding of the Temple planned by David, but completed only by his son Solomon. They also point towards its destruction. The Temple symbolizes communication with God and the happiness resulting from this, while its absence is experienced as the transcendent difficulty of achieving such contact, leaving the exiled speaker no option but to hope for miraculous intervention.

EXTRACT 43. The Introductory Blessing of Pesukei Dezimra

The Kaddish that ended the previous sequence suggests that this passage might constitute a new liturgical opening to the day, without links to what has gone before. But the emphasis on God's blessedness in the first lines resembles phrases in the preceding Kaddish (Extract 41, lines 6–7), while the reference to 'psalms of David' (lines 8–9) glances back at the previous psalm and forward at those to come. The earlier psalm now emerges as a preview of others, the speaker quasi-authorially reconciling multi-layered significances to produce kaleidoscopic literary effects in which here and now meets there and then in repeating and constantly renewed harmonies.

Developmentally speaking, this passage is distinct from everything that has gone before. In Amram Gaon's version it begins morning prayer,[1] opening a

---

[1] *Seder rav amram hashalem*, i. 69b–72a. It is first mentioned by Alfasi as a twin of the closing paragraph in his discussion of BT *Ber.* 32b, in id., *Hilkhot rav alfas*, i. 23a. Elbogen, *Jewish Liturgy*, 15–16, records the transformation of this initially unofficial element of the liturgy into a formal and public one. For a general discussion, see ibid. 72–4.

Blest is he who but °spoke and the universe existed!	*Ps.* 33,[9]
Blest is he, blest—the °maker of Genesis, blest—who says	*Gn.* 1,[1]
and performs, blest—who decrees and °fulfils, blest—	*Ps.* 33,[6], *B'Br.* 57
°who has mercy upon the world, blest—who has mercy	*Ku.* 1,[89]
upon the creatures, blest—who °grants goodly reward	*Ikk.* 4,[18]
unto his venerators, blest—who lives °to infinity and	*Ps.* 132,[14]
endures unto the °finale, blest—who redeems and rescues;	*Ps.* 68,[17]
blest is his name!—°blest art thou, God our Lord,	*Mai. Tef.* 4,[16]
sovereign of the universe, the °almighty, °the father, the	*Dt.* 10,[17]
merciful, praised by the mouth of his People, lauded and	*Ps.* 103,[13]
glorified by the tongue of his °devotees, his servants, yea,	*Ps.* 149,[1]
with the psalms of David thy servitor we °will praise thee,	*II Cr.* 23,[18]
God our Lord, with laudation psalms we will °aggrandize	*Ps.* 95,[3]
thee, laud and glorify thee, yea, we will make mention of	*Ex.* 3,[15]
°thy name and proclaim thee king, o our sovereign, our	*Dn.* 12,[7]
Lord, single one, the °life of worlds, sovereign, lauded	*Ps.* 132,[14]
and glorified, his great name endures °unto endless infinity	*Fz. Br.* 32
—°blest art thou, God, sovereign extolled in laudations!	*Mai. Br.* 11,[1]

43. The introductory blessing of Pesukei Dezimra (*Barukh she'amar*)

sequence of psalmic and other passages which foreshadow the praise of God at the beginning of statutory prayer. However, its role as a new opening to prayer has been submerged by the transfer of Birkhot Hashaḥar from home to synagogue. This has cost it some of its power to startle, but the emphasis on creation reflects the way the world regains shape at dawn and the Adam-like reuniting of waking human bodies and souls. Its location after Kaddish also relates it to the newly gathered congregation in synagogue, emphasizing the daily rebirth of communal life. Its introductory role led to it being read in medieval Regensburg with such reverence on sabbath that it took an hour to complete,[2] and it is still recited while standing and holding the two front fringes of the *talit*, these being kissed when the recital ends.[3] Sephardim sing it on sabbaths and festivals to a

[2] Zunz, *Die Ritus des synagogalen Gottesdienstes*, 70, and Elbogen, *Jewish Liturgy*, 383.

[3] *Sidur avodat yisra'el*, 58. This might be a preview of the symbolic ingathering represented by gathering all four fringes for the reading of the Shema, but see Nulman, *Encyclopedia of Jewish Prayer*, 90 n. 5, and Schwab, *Rav Schwab on Prayer*, 121, who argues that the sixteen threads and ten double knots, totalling twenty-six, equal the numerical value of the Tetragammaton associated with divine mercy.

בָּרוּךְ שֶׁאָמַר וְהָיָה הָעוֹלָם • בָּרוּךְ הוּא • בָּרוּךְ 1

עוֹשֶׂה בְרֵאשִׁית • בָּרוּךְ אוֹמֵר וְעוֹשֶׂה • בָּרוּךְ 2

גּוֹזֵר וּמְקַיֵּם • בָּרוּךְ מְרַחֵם עַל הָאָרֶץ • בָּרוּךְ 3

מְרַחֵם עַל הַבְּרִיּוֹת • בָּרוּךְ מְשַׁלֵּם שָׂכָר טוֹב 4

לִירֵאָיו • בָּרוּךְ חַי לָעַד וְקַיָּם לָנֶצַח • בָּרוּךְ פּוֹדֶה 5

וּמַצִּיל בָּרוּךְ שְׁמוֹ • בָּרוּךְ אַתָּה יְיָ אֱלֹהֵינוּ מֶלֶךְ 6

הָעוֹלָם • הָאֵל הָאָב הָרַחֲמָן הַמְהֻלָּל בְּפִי עַמּוֹ 7

מְשֻׁבָּח וּמְפֹאָר בִּלְשׁוֹן חֲסִידָיו וַעֲבָדָיו • וּבְשִׁירֵי 8

דָוִד עַבְדֶּךָ נְהַלֶּלְךָ יְיָ אֱלֹהֵינוּ בִּשְׁבָחוֹת וּבִזְמִירוֹת 9

נְגַדֶּלְךָ וּנְשַׁבֵּחֲךָ וּנְפָאֶרְךָ וְנַזְכִּיר שִׁמְךָ וְנַמְלִיכְךָ 10

מַלְכֵּנוּ אֱלֹהֵינוּ יָחִיד חֵי הָעוֹלָמִים • מֶלֶךְ מְשֻׁבָּח 11

וּמְפֹאָר עֲדֵי עַד שְׁמוֹ הַגָּדוֹל • בָּרוּךְ אַתָּה יְיָ 12

מֶלֶךְ מְהֻלָּל בַּתִּשְׁבָּחוֹת: 13

traditional melody, shortly after *hashem melekh*, 'The Lord reigneth', the first chant of the morning.[4]

The text begins the second section of the morning liturgy, Pesukei Dezimra, which consists of poetic scriptural texts and forms the first part of the public, rather than the purely private, liturgy. The name Pesukei Dezimra is talmudic, and although its contents are not defined in early rabbinic writings, later commentators ascribe to it material that is included in the present version.[5] In the talmudic source this second sequence is referred to mainly as Hallel, 'praise', a name now more familiarly attached to Psalms 113–18 (strictly the 'Egyptian Hallel', as distinct from Psalm 136, the 'Great Hallel'), which are still recited on festivals and the New Moon as they were in the Temple. The present sequence,

[4] Gaguine, *Keter shem tov*, i–ii. 41–2; *Book of Prayer: Daily and Occasional Prayers*, 17, 18–19, 276–80.

[5] BT *Shab.* 118*b*, which Rashi defines as Pss. 148 and 150. The lack of clarity of earlier sources on the contents of the sequence is pointed out in Hoffman, *Canonization of the Synagogue Service*, 127–8. Variants are discussed in Liebreich, 'Compilation of the Pesuke de-Zimra'. Its halakhic status is discussed by Daniel Landes in *My People's Prayer Book*, iii. 24–5.

like that form of Hallel, is framed by a pair of blessings, in this case extended passages with concluding blessing formulas. The first of these is the present paragraph and the second appears as Extract 59.

The two opening sequences of the day—Birkhot Hashaḥar and the present Pesukei Dezimra sequence—appear at first sight to be poorly distinguished from each other in function. In Sephardi parlance, indeed, both sequences are jointly referred to as *zemirot*, 'songs', and in all rites the prayer-leader for this portion of the liturgy is known as a *mezamer*, minimizing the differences between these units and suggesting that they are either continuous or duplicate openings to the day.

The idea that the present passage is a new beginning, however, survives especially clearly in those versions that separate the sequences not with Kaddish (or, in the version used here, with two occurrences of Kaddish, the second after Psalm 30), but with the ceremonies of *talit* and *tefilin*, which appear in the version analysed here near the beginning of the liturgical day.[6] Inserting the ritual garments at this point associates the first sequence with the private spheres of waking and the passage between home and synagogue, and the second one with the semi-public pious practice of meditating for an hour before reciting the Amidah. This introductory period of meditation was regarded by the Mishnah as an ancient ideal.[7]

The present passage continues to resonate with previous themes, however, looking towards a resolution of the theological impasse into which the speaker has been led. The opening words of this paragraph focus on God's language and describe how his words approximate to actions or to speech-acts, continuing to explore the problem of the opacity of Torah which, in the previous sequence, was overcome by verbally re-enacting aspects of Temple life.[8] That attempt foundered on the limitations of human language suggested by the repetition of the Kaddish, however, hinting at the impossibility of verbal effectiveness.

The opening words of the present passage suggest that the speaker's language is indeed a pale reflection of God's creative power, which the biblical narrative describes as being wielded through words. One midrashic text describes how brute matter was shaped when God pronounced even the weakest aspirate, the letter *heh*, a power which highlights the speaker's incapacity even to understand the language of Torah, let alone to wield it with divine creativity.[9] A mishnaic text reports how the account of Creation was recited daily by priests who

---

[6] *Sidur avodat yisra'el*, 55–7; *Israels Gebete*, ed. Hirsch, 42–3; *Sidur avodat halevavot*, 23–6; *Authorised Daily Prayer Book* (Hertz), 44–8.

[7] BT *Ber.* 30*b*, 32*b*; study is recommended in *Tana debei eliyahu*, ch. 2, p. 12, trans. Braude and Kapstein, p. 23.

[8] For a philosophical reading of this mystic idea see Smirnov, 'Universe as a Phenomenon of Language'.

[9] Mishnah *Avot* 3: 18 mentions that the tool of Creation has been made available to Jews, but does not suggest that the act may be imitated by them. For the midrashic reading of Ps. 33: 6, sug-

remained in their villages, while others from the same locality were invited to spend a week in the sanctuary in Jerusalem.[10] The Creation recital did not survive in synagogue use, partly to avoid reproducing aspects of the Temple cult, but allusions remain embedded in the liturgy, linking the speaker to Temple practice.

The distinction between human and divine language, the central theme of the opening lines of this paragraph, is addressed by rabbinic thinkers in the following exchange: 'How do we know that speech is like action? Because it is said "By the word were the heavens made".' They go on to explain that 'he who recites on the eve of the Sabbath "the heaven and the earth were finished" [Gen. 2: 1–3] is regarded by Scripture as though he had become a partner of the Holy One, blessed be He, in the creation'.[11] The power of ordinary language at best to 'represent' God's creativity was transcended only by the Tabernacle-builder, Bezalel, who manipulated the letters of the alphabet to perform work on the wilderness sanctuary that was midrashically compared to cosmic creation.[12] The liturgical speaker has recently attempted to emulate him by reciting God's promise to Zephaniah (Extract 33, lines 9–11), but conjured the Temple only into potential re-establishment.

The sacrificial recitals that followed this 'speech-act' became obscured in linguistic opacity and embroiled in the dissonance between the Temple's status as a symbol of well-being and the suffering associated with its absence. The speaker who left home for the *mikdash me'at* in the hope of bringing redemption by means of language is still Temple-less and in exile, and is powerless to influence reality. If only God can 'decree' (lines 2–3), the act of quoting Zephaniah's prophecy will not help bring its fulfilment.[13] The fact that the Hebrew term *gozer*, 'decree', is familiarly associated with restriction and even punishment may even throw ironic light on two references to God's mercy (lines 3–4), which must therefore be read as expressions of hope that God's kindness will outweigh his justice.[14] God's contractual reliability is nevertheless praised (lines 4–5) as though eventual salvation were certain (lines 5–6), but it might be said that the

gesting that Creation was performed by God pronouncing half of the shortest form of his own name, Yah, see *Gen. Rabbah* 12: 10.

[10] BT *Ta'an.* 26*a*, 27*b*.

[11] BT *Shab.* 119*b*. God's power to create from nothing by the power of words is mentioned in *Abudarham hashalem*, 59, and Sa'adiah Gaon, *Book of Beliefs and Opinions*, 106. See the note on line 13 below for parallels to 'he who spoke and the world was' as an established surrogate for the name of the Deity.

[12] BT *Ber.* 55*a* and other examples discussed in Gruenwald, *Apocalyptic and Merkavah Mysticism*, 11.　　　　　　　　　　　　　　　　　　　　[13] Elbogen, *Jewish Liturgy*, 73–4.

[14] In the latter sense it appears in the Unetaneh Tokef prayer recited in the Additional Service on Rosh Hashanah and the Day of Atonement. See *Service of the Synagogue: New Year*, 146–7; ibid., *Day of Atonement*, ii. 149–50. In general see Jastrow, *Dictionary*, 231–2.

covenant has been kept only if the speaker's survival in the present is equated to the promised salvation.

Appreciating the present moment does not relieve the speaker's fears about the day to come, however, and the liturgy now seems propelled by its own momentum into proclamations of praise that recall Job's awe at God's power[15] or the shift from fear to praise in the paragraph before the Shema in Extract 30. The speaker celebrates God's verbal might as if its human echo were an emotional life-raft. Earthly words are no more real than the imagined Temple in the previous sequence.[16]

The present moment can thus be linked to the periods before the building of the first Temple and after the exiles' return from Babylon, before their construction of the second. Verbal echoes associate the liturgical speaker with both David, who did not live to see the Temple completed, and the returned exiles, who suffered drought and famine because of delays to work on the Temple caused by Samaritan attacks.[17] Both groups survived situations similar to the speaker's and had to engage in building the Temple without the support of its sacrificial cult; they are implicitly linked to this text by the recurrent use of the word 'blessed', already encountered in blessing formulas but here used in a greater variety of ways. The term has strong associations with the Temple because of its appearance in scriptural accounts of how David asked to be blessed by God when it was revealed to him that his son Solomon would be allowed to build the Temple, even though he himself would not.[18] It recurs in descriptions of how David blessed God on handing over the building materials to his son,[19] as did Hiram on accepting the commission to carry out the work.[20] The same word is echoed by Solomon once the work is completed.[21] This word, and the benediction formula derived from it, became so attached to the idea of liturgical worship that *Berakhot*, 'blessings', is the title of the mishnaic tractate on prayer. Its repeated appearance here, in a passage introducing psalmic and other texts by David, thus implies that the speaker is likewise preparing for worship but is aware, like David, that the task might not be completed. In addition, unlike the returned exiles, who were troubled because they 'dwell in [their] well-roofed houses . . . while this house lies waste',[22] the speaker has left home for synagogue, showing how everyday life can imitate the sacred narrative.

Reciting songs of David could therefore be seen as a literary response to the powerlessness revealed by the speaker's previous failure to recreate the Temple (see the notes on Extract 35) and as a sign of acceptance that redemption will be

---

[15] Job 42: 1–6.

[16] Hasidic tales record the view that the letters of the alphabet themselves might form 'prayers' that God may combine into words. See the jocular application in Agnon, *Days of Awe*, 226–7, its endorsement by the Kotsker Rebbe in Newman, *Hasidic Anthology*, 212, and the approval by Levi-Yitshak of Berditchev in Kahana, *Sefer haḥasidut*, 259.   [17] Hag. 1: 3–11.

[18] 2 Sam. 7: 12–13, 27–9.   [19] 1 Chr. 29: 10, 20.

[20] 1 Kgs. 5: 7.   [21] 1 Kgs. 8: 14–15, 55–6.   [22] Hag. 1: 4.

enjoyed only by the next generation. But even this expectation of delayed gratification is compromised by the fact that the monarchy fractured under Solomon's successors, transforming the references to the Temple here into indications of the need to accept ultimate failure. With nothing to celebrate but the exiled speaker's survival in the present, reflected in the Temple's successor, the *mikdash me'at*, this leaves the speaker poised between the remembrance of security and its catastrophic loss, the personal and communal spheres of home and synagogue, and the present and the past. Hope is possible only because David survives in rabbinic thought as an exemplum of prayer and a messianic figure with a role in the building of the third and final Temple, which is why the present liturgical sequence, though devoted mainly to his psalmic and other writings, has clear messianic undertones.[23]

Awareness of the inevitability of exile is also suggested by the practice of holding the two front fringes of the *talit*, the ritual garment whose associations include redemption and homecoming (see Chapter 5 above). The remoteness of rescue is suggested by the fact that only two of the four fringes are held, disrupting the ingathering symbolized by all the corners. Since the *talit*, according to talmudic texts, is essential for those wishing to discuss the wonders of creation, the underlying theme of the first lines of this paragraph,[24] its partial use here additionally suggests incomprehension of Torah.

The liturgy thus offers a way forward from the two theological dead ends encountered in the previous sequence. The first of these, the attempt to offer sacrifices verbally even when language is known to be ineffective, is paradoxically addressed by the recurrence of the word 'blessed'. The second, the need to depend for redemption on gaining an understanding of Torah that transcends the most intense intellectual approach, is alluded to by the fact that David retains a messianic role despite his personal failings. Although the liturgical texts seen so far address these ideas only implicitly, similar silences in scriptural narratives suggest that failures to express ideas explicitly might constitute a biblical literary technique that has been adopted in liturgical composition. The Israelites moved to Egypt, for example, without reference to the fact that Abraham had been told that his descendants would be enslaved.[25] Jacob may have expressed misgivings about the move, since God assured him that he would be in Egypt with them,[26] a statement that is otherwise unprompted, but even this remains implicit. The reader therefore knows more than the protagonists, the narrative silence implying unspoken or unconscious worries, much as the speaker here leaves major theological problems unaired.

The first of the two sections into which the present paragraph falls, lines 1–6, focuses, as we have seen, on the Creation theme and the effectiveness of God's words at Creation. These introductory lines are followed by a long blessing,

[23] See Menn, 'Praying King and Sanctuary of Prayer', 319–23.   [24] BT *Ḥag.* 14*b*.
[25] Gen. 15: 13–14.   [26] Gen. 46: 4.

beginning and ending with the benediction formula, which announces the psalmic texts forming the bulk of the sequence (lines 6–13). This second part of the paragraph once stood alone, forming the opening paragraph to Pesukei Dezimra,[27] and had to begin and end with a blessing formula since it is the first of a group of blessings. The second blessing of the pair associated with Pesukei Dezimra (Extract 59), which ends the sequence, closes with another such formula but does not need to begin with one. In the present passage, the introductory section preceding the blessing formula (lines 1–6) was added in antiquity, perhaps so that this text would match Barekhu, the formulaic opening of Yotser, the first element of the statutory liturgy (which lies outside the scope of this book), forming a declaration of blessing that introduces the blessing itself.[28]

The body of this blessing reflects the speaker's need to activate God's merciful and paternal aspects, which are here juxtaposed with praise of his power (line 7), as though to echo Job's solution to the problem of suffering. The reference to David (lines 8–9) recalls the speaker's unworthiness to build the Temple, but the text goes on to praise God's kingliness (line 10) and to unify his name (line 11), as though enacting the challenge implied in each blessing formula (see the discussion of Extract 2) and in the Shema. The speaker, undeterred by failure, finds hope in the idea of David's messianic role.

The 'seal' of the blessing announces the theme of *halel*, 'praise', that will dominate the sequence this passage introduces, and apparently promises uncritical worship rather than the alternation of mercy and judgement implicit in the initial blessing formula. The term 'praise' leaves behind the suffering associated with Temple-building and looks forward to the cult for which the sanctuaries were built. Since psalms were the principal texts to be recited there, the speaker no longer sees David as a builder embroiled in conflict who died without seeing his Temple completed, but as the author of psalms and the symbol of the messianic perfectibility of the world.

It is clear that liturgical writers and editors recognized that this paragraph engages with issues such as the power of words, since its language was habitually understood in quasi-magical ways. For instance, it was noted that in some medieval versions the word 'bless' appears ten times, triggering associations with the ten creational pronouncements, the Decalogue by which the world survives,[29] and the ten items created on the eve of the first sabbath,[30] all of which are metaphorically related to the Temple as the culmination of Creation and the home of the Ark containing the Tablets of the Ten Commandments. Midrashic

[27] Fleischer, *Tefilah*, 215–57: see esp. pp. 233, 238, 246.

[28] Heinemann, *Prayer in the Talmud*, 267.

[29] Mishnah *Avot* 5: 1; *Gen. Rabbah* 17: 1. See Abraham ben Isaac, *Sefer ha'eshkol*, 11; Solomon of Worms, *Sidur rabenu shelomoh migarmaisa*, 20 n. 12; Abudarham, *Abudarham hashalem*, 61–2, and Ginzberg, *Legends*, iii. 104–6, for the Decalogue corresponding to the ten 'words' of Creation.

[30] Mishnah *Avot* 5: 9.

texts additionally associate the Ten Commandments, read liturgically in early times, with the Shema, although the Decalogue was dropped to ensure that it would not rival the primacy of the central credal text.[31] Its exclusion was also a rabbinic response to Christian singling out of the Decalogue from the corpus of preceptive Judaism.[32]

In the present version the word *barukh*, 'blessed', appears eleven times before the introductory blessing formula, although the second occurrence, in 'blessed be he', might be an interpolation. It then appears twice in the blessing itself, making a total of thirteen occurrences. This number is commonly related to the thirteen attributes of God's mercy associated with the Tetragrammaton,[33] the thirteen exegetical principles of Rabbi Ishmael (by which the Torah can be read and contact be made with God),[34] and even, depending on how they are subdivided, the possibility that Pesukei Dezimra itself includes thirteen texts.[35] However, other versions of this paragraph contain the word more or less frequently, suggesting that it is more an emphatic introduction to blessing than a numerical code.[36] The fact that the entire sequence culminates in a proclamation of blessing at the beginning of statutory prayer supports this interpretation.

Commentators sought number symbolism here in particular, however, noting that certain versions of the paragraph contain eighty-seven words, corresponding to the Hebrew word *paz*, 'refined gold'. This was assumed to refer to the excellence of the prayer,[37] to the gold-work of Bezalel, whose creativity with letters of the alphabet has been mentioned,[38] or to a royal crown, described in this way in a psalm on the crowning of the messianic king.[39]

This numerological tendency suggests that language was felt to be used here in a gestural rather than a cognitive way and that it signposts ideas with something approaching the multi-layered creativity of God's language. The halakhic

---

[31] BT *Ber.* 12a.   [32] H. Loewe in Montefiore and Loewe (eds.), *Rabbinic Anthology*, 641.

[33] This appears first in Gen. 2: 4; the attributes are derived from Exod. 34: 6–7.

[34] See the remarks on Extract 39 above; and Eleazar of Worms, *Sefer haroke'ah*, 209, section 320.

[35] Only ten are included, according to Judah ben Yakar, *Perush hatefilot vehaberakhot*, 6, while Aboab, *Menorat hamaor*, 93, p. 210, illustrates the flexibility of this homiletic approach, mentioning the seven forms of praise in lines 9–10. Aggadic explanations for the inconsistency are outlined in Gaguine, *Keter shem tov*, i–ii. 38–9 n. 60. In the present version it is difficult to identify which texts might be included in such reckonings.

[36] Hoffmann, *Das Buch Leviticus*, Lev. 1: 7, analyses the liturgical paragraph as an inventory of divine attributes designed to introduce prayer conceptually. This is quoted approvingly in Elbogen, *Jewish Liturgy*, 405 n. 4, and E. Munk, *World of Prayer*, i. 61–4, but it seems forced except in its correct recognition of the division of the paragraph. They do not point out that the term 'blessed' clusters especially around themes associated with the Temple.

[37] *Sidur avodat yisra'el*, 58; Eleazar of Worms, *Sefer haroke'ah*, 209, section 320, among other commentators.

[38] This must remain a possibility only, since the word *paz* is not employed scripturally in connection with the Tabernacle.   [39] Ps. 21: 4.

prohibition against speaking informally between this passage and the end of Pesukei Dezimra can be attributed to the idea that texts flanked by blessings are regarded as a single blessing, and that it would be improper to interrupt such a reading.[40] But the ruling also draws attention to the fact that this paragraph is preoccupied with the power of speech, human or divine, thereby revising the earlier fear of the inefficacy of human speech.

This paragraph appears to address yet another major theological theme, the need for God to keep his covenantal promise, though this emerges more explicitly in fast-day laments than in weekday texts. Rabbinic writings commonly refer to God as '[the one] who but spoke and the universe existed' (line 2),[41] but in lines 1–2 these words are unusually prefixed 'Blessed be . . .'. This rare formulation appears in a midrashic text recommending that humans imitate God's patience with Israel[42] and be patient until God keeps his side of the covenant. The text goes on to attribute delay to human sin, thereby avoiding criticism of God, but it finally reverts to the view that sin need not be involved, concluding that redemption will eventually come as a result of God's goodwill rather than as a reward for virtue.

The idea that survival is itself a form of redemption emerges from the words 'maker of Creation' (line 2), which appear in a talmudic blessing for when one sees, among other things, a clear sky such as that which follows a windy night. Since the source adds that such a sky has not been seen since the Temple was destroyed, the words suggest that exile may have been left behind.[43] The words 'who says and performs . . . decrees and fulfils' (lines 2–3) appear in a prayer to be recited on seeing a place from where earth has been removed from the ruins of Babylon to make bricks,[44] likewise a sign, if not of redemption, then of the overthrow of those who destroyed the first Temple in Jerusalem. The words 'says and performs' (line 2) also appear in midrashic discussions touching on Creation, election, revelation,[45] and God's fulfilment of promises,[46] while the formula 'who has mercy on the land' (line 3) looks forward to a still fuller redemption than that represented by the speaker's survival. This forms the climax to mishnaic blessings for times of drought, implying that the speaker is now in synagogue rather than the Temple, although the drought could reflect either the agricultural failure that precedes the exile[47] or the suffering before salvation.

---

[40] Caro, *Shulḥan arukh*, 'Oraḥ ḥayim' 51.

[41] The term, based on Ps. 33: 9, appears in the Talmud—*Shab.* 139a, *San.* 76b, 105a, *Ḥul.* 63b, 84b—and in *Mekhilta derabi shimon bar yoḥai*, 'Va'era', Exod. 6: 2, p. 4, and other references listed in *Sidur avodat yisra'el*, 58. It is said to be tannaitic in Marmorstein, *Old Rabbinic Doctrine of God*, i. 89. References to the verbal nature of God's creation are a commonplace, e.g. *Gen. Rabbah* 3: 1, 31: 8, 44: 22 and *Midrash Psalms* 107: 3.

[42] *Tana debei eliyahu (zuta)*, ch. 4, p. 179, trans. Braude and Kapstein, p. 381.

[43] BT *Ber.* 59a–b.   [44] BT *Ber.* 57b.

[45] *Exod. Rabbah* 30: 9.   [46] *Midrash Psalms* 119: 35–6.

[47] Mishnah *Ta'an.* 2: 4; based on the argument in the Shema: see Deut. 11: 16–17.

Repeated references to God's mercy reflect the speaker's awareness of the midrashic statement that the world survives only because mercy was created before the attribute of strict judgement.[48] However, they might also reflect an awareness of the absence of mercy and the speaker's consequent vulnerability. The words 'he who lives to infinity and endures' (line 5) echo a talmudic description of how in prayer one stands before the King of Kings.[49] But the association of the word *kayam* with 'keeping a promise' (rather than with 'enduring', as in the present translation) has been noted in connection with the opening statement of the day. Here it also alludes to the idea that God should respect the covenant out of a sense of kingly justice rather than of paternal mercy. The words 'life of worlds' (line 11) are linked in one source to God's reward for human kindness,[50] but in another to the coming of the messiah, likewise associated with mercy.[51] The root letters of the word *melekh*, 'king', appear five times in this paragraph, but those of 'father' only occur once (line 7), implying again that the remoter aspects of God's justice are more evident here than his mercy.

The subtext generated by these associations shifts from appeals to God's mercy to acceptance of his mastery, followed by a recognition that only a gratuitous act of mercy such as sending the messiah can offer release from the dangers of the day ahead. The delay in the fulfilment of the covenant must be accepted because it is an expression of God's will, and the speaker cannot intervene in its workings. Yet precisely as the speaker accepts the inevitability of delay, joy incongruously takes over, apparently in response to the recognition of survival in the here and now. This would account for the outpouring of praise here, although such verbal excess might be tinged with fear and even doubts about the validity of the covenant (an idea no rabbinic commentator would express explicitly). A similar manoeuvre was noted in the context of Extract 30, where praise inexplicably followed the appeals for safety in Extract 25.

A sequence of five terms of praise in Extract 43, lines 9–11, has been identified by one modern commentator as a template for the authorial division of the rest of Pesukei Dezimra into distinct stages, but this idea ignores the narrative development of the liturgy. It does however reflect an awareness that the praise is repetitive and could therefore be seen as excessive.[52] Its ambiguity is even clearer in the Sephardi version of this paragraph, where God is described as one 'before whom there is neither iniquity, nor forgetfulness, nor respect of persons, nor the taking of bribes', reflecting concern of precisely the kind discussed above.[53]

---

[48] *Gen. Rabbah* 12: 15. See also Sed-Rajna (ed.), *Azriel de Gérone*, 51, in the course of an extended kabbalistic commentary on this passage (pp. 47–58).

[49] BT *Ber.* 33a.   [50] *Eccles. Rabbah* 7: 5.   [51] Dan. 12: 7.

[52] Schwab, *Rav Schwab on Prayer*, 127. His subdivision suffers from the exclusion of *nehalelkha* in line 9. The first part (*negadelkha*) ends before Ps. 145; the second (*neshabeḥekha*) is represented by Ps. 145; the third (*nefa'erkha*) begins with Ps. 146; the fourth (*venazkir shimkha*) with *vayevarekh david* (Extract 55, line 1); and the fifth (*venamlikhekha*) with Extract 58, line 1.

[53] *Book of Prayer: Daily and Occasional Prayers*, 18, quoting Mishnah *Avot* 4: 29.

EXTRACT 44. **Bringing the Ark to Jerusalem**

The Pesukei Dezimra sequence itself—the cycle of praise announced in the previous paragraph—begins with this biblical poem attributed to David, different versions of which appear in historical and poetical scriptural books. The present redaction is from a historical work, suggesting that it is not merely to be read as a poem, but that the wider span of David's career is relevant here.[54] It is associated with his arrival in Jerusalem with the Ark, after which he planned to build the Temple, and was sung as he accompanied his prize into Jerusalem, the city whose capture gave the Israelites hope of a national future. But David's project was completed only after his death, as has been seen, and the monarchy he founded ended in decadence and exile, suggesting the speaker's awareness that the sacred narrative looks beyond climactic triumph to the loss that follows.[55]

Another negative association derives from the parallel narrative of Michal, David's wife, who criticized his ecstatic dancing as he accompanied the Ark and, as a result, died childless, as implied by an authorial remark.[56] Yet David's liveliness, implicitly praised here, also led to his entanglement in wars, adultery, murder, and failure to complete the Temple, recalling the earlier petition to be spared the *yetser hara*, 'instinct to do evil'. This ambivalence about the *yetser* is echoed by rabbinic writers who accept that the sexual drive is essential for a full life (discussed in the context of Extract 7).

The next episode in David's narrative, the choosing of a site for the Temple to house the Ark after its entry into Jerusalem, also has ambivalent associations.[57] The biblical account describes how, when God was angry with the Israelites for unexplained reasons, he paradoxically first caused David to carry out a census of the Israelites and then said he would 'punish' both him and the people for doing so.[58] God next asked David what punishment he would prefer—famine, sword, or plague—and David replied that whatever it would be, he wished to receive it directly from God rather than from humans. David chose a plague because war or famine would give him and his family an unfair advantage over his subjects, thanks to the guards and extra food supplies available to the royal court.[59] The plague was halted just as an angel was about to destroy the city,[60] 'a drawn sword in his hand stretched out over Jerusalem',[61] a phrase used in the Passover

---

[54] 1 Chr. 16: 8–36. It is similar to Pss. 105: 1–15, 96: 1*b*–13, and 106: 1, 47–8.

[55] David's son will build the Temple in his stead, but will be no less subject to the conditional nature of survival than his father. See 2 Sam. 7: 12–14; 1 Kgs. 6: 11–13.

[56] 2 Sam. 6: 20–3.   [57] 2 Sam. 24: 1–25.

[58] Rashi and David Kimhi on 2 Sam. 24: 1 say they do not know what the sin was, but Joseph Kara relates it to the death of Uriah, based on *Pesikta rabati* 11: 3, while Gersonides remarks on the ethical difficulty raised by this episode.

[59] David's concern that his status would not protect him more than his people is explored in *Pesikta rabati* 11: 3.   [60] 2 Sam. 24: 16.   [61] 1 Chr. 21: 16.

Haggadah to describe the redemptive power of God's hand at the Red Sea. The fact that the hand reflects rescue there, rather than the irrational sources of suffering, shows how the disturbing implications of this narrative have been suppressed in rabbinic thought. The biblical narrative is related not only to the origins of the Temple and therefore of morning worship, however, for the threshing-floor of Araunah the Jebusite, where the angel stood, was also associated with the Akedah, a type-scene of the ambivalence of divine protection.[62] In this way the Temple is associated with suffering long before its destruction and the exile that followed.

David's crime—counting people—is still discouraged among Jews, implicitly because people are regarded not as commodities to be enumerated, but as each unique in their own right, a sensitivity derived in part from this passage. It is associated with morning prayer because it is necessary to count people in order to ensure that a quorum is present. In practice, as has been mentioned, a biblical verse containing ten words is usually recited, in which each word stands for one of the numerals from one to ten. The ten imperatives to praise God in the first five lines might have fulfilled such a need in a liturgical arrangement in which Kaddish was not recited after Birkhot Hashaḥar (since that was recited in private) or in which the present text was a prelude to Kaddish, since this represented the whole or most of Pesukei Dezimra. Kaddish itself contains the same number of terms of praise. But central to the role of this passage is the similarity between the way in which David is punished for a sin he performed on God's instruction and the speaker's awareness of the need to remain close to Torah on pain of exile, only to find that its opacity makes this impossible. The crime would therefore appear to originate with God, rather than with the speaker, and the present narrative highlights David's recognition of ethical ambiguity. This is why he does not claim total innocence of the crime of counting the people, but asks God to spare the people. 'These sheep', he asked, 'what have they done?', a question he might have asked on his own behalf.[63]

The Davidic origin of this text also serves to align the speaker's departure from home for synagogue with David's regret at having built his own home before that of God. Both biblical and rabbinic writers are ambivalent towards his sins, for these are excluded from the book of Chronicles (the very book from which this particular passage is drawn) and underplayed by later authors.[64] The *mikdash me'at* where the liturgy is now recited may therefore paradoxically symbolize either the site of the unbuilt Temple or the ruins of its destruction, and the passage from home to synagogue either the building of one of the Temples or exile from Jerusalem. The speaker is thus poised between the roles of David, the

[62] *Gen. Rabbah* 55: 7.   [63] 2 Sam. 24: 17; 1 Chr. 21: 17.

[64] The book of Chronicles alone gives this prayer and suppresses reports of David's crimes, for instance in 1 Chr. 20: 1–3, which corresponds to 2 Sam. 11: 1–27, 12: 7–24, but omits the story of Bathsheba. In 1 Chr. 23: 1 the intrigues involving Bathsheba beginning in 1 Kgs. 1: 5 are also omitted.

°O, acknowledge unto God! call upon his name, make	*I Cr.* 16,[8-36]
known his doings among peoples—°Sing unto him, intone	*Ps.* 105,[1-15]
unto him, talk over all his wonders—Glorify in his holy	*Zo. Ex.* 196
name—let the heart of them rejoice that seek God! °Seek	*Dt.* 12,[5]
God and his fortitude, °entreat his presence continually—	*Ps.* 27,[8]
Remember °his wonders which he hath performed, his	*Ps.* 111,[4]
marvels and the verdicts of his mouth; O ye °seed of Israel,	*Is.* 41,[8]
his servitor, ye children of Jacob, °his selected ones! He is	*Is.* 45,[4]
God our Lord, his judgments throughout the world—°Remember	*Ps.* 111,[5]
for ever his covenant, °the word which he ordained	*Dt.* 33,[4]
for a °thousand generations. The same which he did covenant	*Dt.* 7,[9]
with Abraham, °yea, his oath unto Isaac. Even, He	*Gn.* 26,[3-5]
confirmed it unto °Jacob as a statute, unto Israel an everlasting	*Ps.* 81,[4]
°covenant, Saying: Unto thee will I give the land of Canaan,	*Gn.* 17,[10]
°the allotment of your inheritance; When ye were but few in	*Ps.* 16,[5-6]
number, insignificant and strangers in it, °Though they went	*I Cr.* 16,[20]
from nation to nation, yea, from one kingdom to another	*Ku.* 2,[2]
people—He suffered no man to oppress them, yea, °he	*Gn.* 31,[29]
reproved kings for their sakes: °Touch ye not mine anointed and	*Ps.* 132,[17]
do ye no harm unto my prophets! °Sing unto God, o world	*Ps.* 96,[2]
entire, °send a message from one day to another concerning	*Ps.* 19,[3]
his salvation, °Tell of his glory among the nations, of his	*Is.* 66,[19]
marvels among all the peoples, °For God is grand, overall to be	*Ps.* 145,[3]
lauded, awesome is he over all °power-gods, For all the power-	*Ex.* 7,[1]
gods of the peoples are °idols, whereas God, he made the	*Lv.* 26,[1]
heavens. °Majesty and splendour are before him, fortitude and	*Ps.* 96,[6-11]
gladness are in his precinct; Render unto God, ye °races of	*Ze.* 14,[17]
peoples, render unto God °reverence, yea, enduring; O render	*Ps.* 96,[8]
unto God the reverence due to his name, °raise an offering and	*II Sm.* 8,[2]
come before him, °bow unto God in the beauty of holiness;	*Ps.* 29,[2]
°Tremble before him, world entire, verily, Thou didst secure	*I Cr.* 16,[30-6]
the globe that it will not founder. Let the °heavens rejoice,	*Ps.* 96,[11]
yea, let the earth revel and let them say °among the nations:	*Ps.* 86,[9]
°God is regnant. Let the sea roar, also the fullness thereof,	*Ps.* 93,[1]
°let the verdure-lands exult, even all that therein is, Then	*Ps.* 96,[12-13]

44. Bringing the Ark to Jerusalem (*Hodu lashem kiru vishmo*)

הוֹדוּ לַיְיָ קִרְאוּ בִשְׁמוֹ הוֹדִיעוּ בָעַמִּים עֲלִילֹתָיו: 1

שִׁירוּ לוֹ זַמְּרוּ־לוֹ שִׂיחוּ בְּכָל־נִפְלְאֹתָיו: 2

הִתְהַלְלוּ בְּשֵׁם קָדְשׁוֹ יִשְׂמַח לֵב מְבַקְשֵׁי יְיָ: 3

דִּרְשׁוּ יְיָ וְעֻזּוֹ בַּקְּשׁוּ פָנָיו תָּמִיד: זִכְרוּ נִפְלְאֹתָיו 4

אֲשֶׁר־עָשָׂה מֹפְתָיו וּמִשְׁפְּטֵי־פִיהוּ: זֶרַע יִשְׂרָאֵל 5

עַבְדּוֹ בְּנֵי יַעֲקֹב בְּחִירָיו: הוּא יְיָ אֱלֹהֵינוּ בְּכָל־ 6

הָאָרֶץ מִשְׁפָּטָיו: זִכְרוּ לְעוֹלָם בְּרִיתוֹ דָּבָר צִוָּה 7

לְאֶלֶף דּוֹר: אֲשֶׁר כָּרַת אֶת־אַבְרָהָם וּשְׁבוּעָתוֹ 8

לְיִצְחָק: וַיַּעֲמִידֶהָ לְיַעֲקֹב לְחֹק לְיִשְׂרָאֵל בְּרִית 9

עוֹלָם: לֵאמֹר לְךָ אֶתֵּן אֶת־אֶרֶץ־כְּנָעַן חֶבֶל 10

נַחֲלַתְכֶם: בִּהְיוֹתְכֶם מְתֵי מִסְפָּר כִּמְעַט וְגָרִים 11

בָּהּ: וַיִּתְהַלְּכוּ מִגּוֹי אֶל־גּוֹי וּמִמַּמְלָכָה אֶל־עַם 12

אַחֵר: לֹא־הִנִּיחַ לְאִישׁ לְעָשְׁקָם וַיּוֹכַח עֲלֵיהֶם 13

מְלָכִים: אַל־תִּגְּעוּ בִמְשִׁיחָי וּבִנְבִיאַי אַל־ 14

תָּרֵעוּ: שִׁירוּ לַיְיָ כָּל־הָאָרֶץ בַּשְּׂרוּ מִיּוֹם־אֶל־ 15

יוֹם יְשׁוּעָתוֹ: סַפְּרוּ בַגּוֹיִם אֶת־כְּבוֹדוֹ בְּכָל־ 16

הָעַמִּים נִפְלְאֹתָיו: כִּי גָדוֹל יְיָ וּמְהֻלָּל מְאֹד 17

וְנוֹרָא הוּא עַל־כָּל־אֱלֹהִים: כִּי כָּל־אֱלֹהֵי הָעַמִּים 18

אֱלִילִים וַיְיָ שָׁמַיִם עָשָׂה: הוֹד וְהָדָר לְפָנָיו עֹז 19

וְחֶדְוָה בִּמְקֹמוֹ: הָבוּ לַיְיָ מִשְׁפְּחוֹת עַמִּים הָבוּ 20

לַיְיָ כָּבוֹד וָעֹז: הָבוּ לַיְיָ כְּבוֹד שְׁמוֹ שְׂאוּ מִנְחָה 21

וּבֹאוּ לְפָנָיו הִשְׁתַּחֲווּ לַיְיָ בְּהַדְרַת־קֹדֶשׁ: חִילוּ 22

מִלְּפָנָיו כָּל־הָאָרֶץ אַף־תִּכּוֹן תֵּבֵל בַּל־תִּמּוֹט: 23

יִשְׂמְחוּ הַשָּׁמַיִם וְתָגֵל הָאָרֶץ וְיֹאמְרוּ בַגּוֹיִם יְיָ 24

מָלָךְ: יִרְעַם הַיָּם וּמְלֹאוֹ יַעֲלֹץ הַשָּׂדֶה וְכָל־ 25

shall the trees of the °forest jubilate, before God; °because	*Is.* 7,[2]
he is come to judge the world. °O acknowledge unto	*Ps.* 98,[9]
God, for he is good—indeed, his loving-kindness is forever.	*Ps.* 118,[1]
So say ye: °O save us, Lord of our salvation, gather us	*Ps.* 106,[47]
together and °rescue us from amongst the nations, °to	*Ez.* 34,[10]
acknowledge unto thy holy name and to acclaim in thy praise!	*Ps.* 145,[21]
°Blest is God, Lord of Israel, from this world unto eternity—	*I Cr.* 16,[36]
even, all the people said, *Amen*, yea, praise unto God!	

44 (*cont.*)

builders of the second Temple, and the Babylonian or contemporary exiles, awaiting the appearance of the first, second, or messianic third Temples. But the focus on David, who never achieved his dream, recalls the inevitability of failure in this case.

Equally, however, this song suggests the reality of the Temple, for one rabbinic text describes how the words were recited each day while the Temple stood. Once sacrifice had been inaugurated, after the conquest of Jerusalem, the first part was used after the morning sacrifices and the second following those of the afternoon, the sections being separated at verse 23 (line 15, second word).[65] Some editors were wary of including it in the liturgy at all since it re-enacted a Temple practice, preferring to locate it in the sacrificial sequence described in the previous chapter.[66] One rabbi even claimed that psalms in general may only be 'read' in the synagogue and not 'sung' as they were in the Temple,[67] which may be why Sephardim postpone the opening blessing of Pesukei Dezimra until the core of the sequence, which begins here in Extract 47. That arrangement defines the present text as an act of study rather than an outpouring of praise or a Temple re-enactment. This last danger is in fact remote, for both the morning and afternoon sections are included here, and they are separate from the times of Temple sacrifices. Ashkenazim as much as Sephardim therefore regard Pesukei Dezimra as a continuation of the synagogue's homage to the cult of Jerusalem, while minimizing its resemblance to the Temple ritual on which it is based.

The midrashic view that the building of the Tabernacle and Temple completed the creation of the world, and that the lighting of the candelabrum corresponded to the creation of light,[68] means that this text also continues the theme

[65] *Seder olam rabah*, ch. 14, fo. 30*b*, and nn. 2–3.　　[66] *Sidur avodat yisra'el*, 59.

[67] Sa'adiah Gaon, in U. Simon, *Four Approaches*, 23–7.

[68] Ginzberg, *Legends*, iii. 217–18, vi. 79 n. 418.

אַשְׁרֵכוֹ: אָז יְרַנְּנוּ עֲצֵי הַיָּעַר מִלִּפְנֵי יְיָ כִּי־בָא 26

לִשְׁפּוֹט אֶת־הָאָרֶץ: הוֹדוּ לַיְיָ כִּי טוֹב כִּי לְעוֹלָם 27

חַסְדוֹ: וְאִמְרוּ הוֹשִׁיעֵנוּ אֱלֹהֵי יִשְׁעֵנוּ וְקַבְּצֵנוּ 28

וְהַצִּילֵנוּ מִן־הַגּוֹיִם לְהוֹדוֹת לְשֵׁם קָדְשֶׁךָ 29

לְהִשְׁתַּבֵּחַ בִּתְהִלָּתֶךָ: בָּרוּךְ יְיָ אֱלֹהֵי יִשְׂרָאֵל 30

מִן־הָעוֹלָם וְעַד הָעֹלָם וַיֹּאמְרוּ כָל־הָעָם אָמֵן 31

וְהַלֵּל לַיְיָ: 32

of Creation from the previous passage.[69] Similar statements to the effect that the Temple was a microcosm of the individual[70] suggest that the conquest of Jerusalem was analogous to the 'rebirth' of the speaker implicit in the previous passage. The rebuilding of the Temple, implicit here, equally points towards the messianic transformation of the world.

None of these undercurrents appears on the surface of what seems to be a simple song of praise, however. The first part (Extract 44, lines 1–15; also in Psalm 105: 1–15), in its original context of the book of Chronicles, recounts the fulfilment of God's promise to give the land to the Israelites and to protect them, alluding to the victory over the Philistines and the recapture of the Ark. Describing Israel both as God's 'servants' (the same Hebrew word as 'slaves') and as his 'chosen' (implying favour) suggests the ambiguity of their position (lines 5–6). The previous study sequence ensures that the speaker is included among the 'anointed' ones and 'prophets' who are not to be touched (line 14), glossed in the Talmud as 'schoolchildren' and 'sages' occupied with Torah. One rabbi claims the whole world 'endures only for the sake of the breath of school-children', an idea which, since the introductory sequence of the morning liturgy concluded with study-texts, gives the speaker a cosmic role.[71] The opacity of Torah is not directly alluded to, but that idea, implicit in the liturgical context, is enacted here by the fact that the present text is now read outside the Temple and the land of Israel, the possession of which depends on closeness to Torah, according to the Shema.

The second part (lines 15–32, corresponding to Psalms 96: 1b–13 and 106: 1, 47–8) celebrates future judgement, redemption, ingathering, and, in its last verse,

[69] Ibid. iii. 150–1, vi. 62 n. 320.

[70] Ibid. iii. 151, vi. 62–3 n. 321. This and related ideas are integral to the symbolic system developed by Judah Loew of Prague, known as the Maharal; see Sherwin, *Mystical Theology*, 133, 147–8.

[71] BT *Shab.* 119b.

blessing (line 30). This conclusion sufficiently resembles the final verses of the five psalmic books for editors to have regarded this as a suitable psalm with which to 'complete' the daily Hallel recommended by the talmudic source.[72] Including this verse in David's victory song reinforces the association of blessings with the Temple, and highlights the Temple's role in the blessing-dominated morning liturgy.

EXTRACT 45. **A Psalmic Anthology of Twenty-Two Verses**

This passage, consisting of twenty-two psalmic verses drawn from each of the five sections of the biblical book of Psalms, follows on from the end of the previous extract on the same printed line, after a small gap.[73] It is another version of the talmudically recommended Hallel, implied in the talmudic name Pesukei Dezimra, literally 'verses of song', and perhaps represents the entire book of Psalms promised by the opening blessing of the sequence (Extract 43, lines 8–9). Because the verses also correspond in number to the letters of the Hebrew alphabet, they similarly symbolize the texture of Torah, the primary tool of Creation.[74] This idea recalls the wider symbolic equation between the book of Psalms and the Torah, both of which contain five books,[75] the 150 psalmic chapters approximating to the 154 weekly portions of the triennial cycle of Torah reading (the practice of reading the Torah ceremonially over a period of three years, rather than over one year, as has been usual since the early Middle Ages).[76]

Some commentators have sought thematic continuity in the selection,[77] but this seems to be limited to the possibly dialogic arrangement of the last five verses. The first two of these are spoken by Israel (lines 20–1), while the next is a divine response (lines 21–2) and the last two a declaration of gratitude by Israel (lines 23–5).[78] Most readers have focused on its numerological features,[79] regarding its language as gestural rather than as cognitive. But one can detect a narra-

---

[72] Rashi on BT *Shab.* 118b.

[73] Pss. 99: 5, 99: 9, 78: 38, 40: 12, 25: 6, 68: 35–6, 94: 1–2, 3: 9, 46: 8, 84: 13, 20: 10, 28: 9, 33: 20–2, 85: 8, 44: 27, 81: 11, 144: 15, 13: 6.

[74] For rabbinic sources on the symbolic dimensions of the alphabet see Ginzberg, *Legends*, i. 5, v. 5–6 n. 10, v. 64 n. 3. Ben Yehuda, *Dictionary*, iv. 2040–1 n. 1, quotes as an etymology of *kiveyakhol* ('as though one might say such a thing [of God]'), *kavyakhol* ('[only in the confines of the] twenty-two [letters of the Hebrew alphabet in which the Torah is written] can [such a thing be said]'), a definition linked to the idea of the omnipotence of letters.

[75] See Baer's introduction to the book of Psalms, at the end of *Sidur avodat yisra'el*, 6–8.

[76] Rabinowitz, 'Psalms, Book of', 1323.

[77] Elbogen, *Jewish Liturgy*, 74, 405 n. 5, outlines the history; Jacobson, *Weekday Siddur*, 82–4 and E. Munk, *World of Prayer*, i. 68–9 claim to detect an argument, but outline it unconvincingly. *Sidur avodat yisra'el*, 60, does not suggest there is a theme.   [78] Hammer, *Entering Jewish Prayer*, 115.

[79] Ps. 78: 38 discusses mercy and contains thirteen words, corresponding to the thirteen attributes of divine mercy; it is followed by Ps. 40: 12, containing ten words, corresponding to the ten trials of Abraham.

tive sequence by reading between the lines. Some of the earlier verses express gratitude for help or rescue, suggesting that God's 'footstool' (the Temple) is already in existence (lines 1–3), while others offer thanks for mercy (lines 3–7) or praise for God's vengeance on Israel's enemies (lines 7–15). There follow appeals for rescue (lines 15–17), as though the vision of a rebuilt Temple has faded, after which God responds (lines 21–2) by recollecting the Exodus (the Hebrew name of Egypt, *mitsrayim*, being transliterated here rather than translated in order to distance the biblical people from the modern state), and by noting the good fortune of those who remain close to him (line 23), encouraging the speaker to trust in the restoration of the Temple.[80] The speaker finally affirms an intention to praise God (lines 24–5), an act which is the main function of the Pesukei Dezimra sequence. But this now seems ambiguous, since midrashic readings of this last verse link human salvation with the 'well-being' of God himself, echoing the idea that the speaker must attend to God's 'home' and 'unity' if God is to secure the integrity of the speaker. The need to perform Temple ritual correctly suggests a preoccupation with formal acts analogous to the gestural undertones of these verses, the result of their Temple-based origins.[81]

The fact that three of the verses, lines 13–15, were included in Extract 36, lines 1–2, in a petition for the rebuilding of the Temple, again exemplifies how scriptural citations are treated in liturgy as though they were lexical items that can be recombined at will. If they were only verbal gestures there would be no point in studying them, but the way in which texts change coloration at each such repetition gives them more than token status. Using David's psalms in this way almost magically transforms the speaker into a precursor of a Temple-builder, therefore, using the sanctuary as a metaphor for protection from a hostile world. Midrashic texts suggest that the speaker even shares a common fate with God himself, rendered 'homeless' by the exile.

EXTRACT 46. A Psalm of Thanksgiving—Psalm 100

In contrast to the fragmentation of Scripture seen in earlier passages, this psalm appears in its entirety.[82] Its headline, a 'psalm of thanksgiving', echoes the gratitude in the last line of the previous selection[83] and suggests that it accompanied personal thanksgiving offerings in the Temple, which were presented after the morning *tamid* sacrifice and before that of the afternoon.[84] As such it is the logical sequel to the description of these sacrifices in Extract 38, lines 26–30, and to the song which accompanied them, Extract 44. The link is emphasized by the

---

[80] Ps. 144: 15 (line 23) is borrowed as a prologue to Ps. 145 (see Extract 48, line 2) and follows the praise of the Temple in the previous line.   [81] *Midrash Psalms* 13: 4 and 9: 14.

[82] Ps. 100.   [83] *Sidur avodat yisra'el*, 61.

[84] BT *Shev.* 15*b*. See the remarks on Extract 1, line 1, for the preferability of 'acknowledgement' to 'thanksgiving'. Braude, in his translation of *Midrash on Psalms* on this psalm, prefers 'avowal'.

°O exalt ye God our Lord and bow towards his °foot-stool—	*Ps.* 99,[5] *Is.* 66,[1]
holy is He! °Exalt ye God our Lord and bow towards his	*Ps.* 99,[9]
holy °mount, for holy is God our Lord!	*Ex.* 15,[17]
Yea, °He, being merciful, forgives wrong-doing and doth	*Ps.* 78,[38]
not destroy—indeed, often he turns his anger away and °doth	*Zo. Ex.* 151
not pour out all his °wrath.	*B'Kd.* 31: *Tsf.*
Thou, o God, °wilt not withhold thy mercies from me, thy	*Ps.* 40,[12]
loving-kindness and thy °truth continually preserve me. °Recall, o	*Is.* 38,[19]
God, thy mercies and thy loving-kindnesses, verily, they	*Ps.* 25,[6]
are of eternity. °Render ye triumph unto the Almighty—His	*I Sm.* 2,[10]
excellency is over Israel, even, his power is in the	*Ps.* 68,[35]
stratospheres. Almighty, awesome from thy °temples, the Lord	*Lv.* 19,[30]; 26,[2]
of Israel he grants fortitude, also, powers unto the people—	*Ps.* 68,[36]
blest is Almighty! °Lord of retributions is God, o Lord of	*Ps.* 94,[1]
retributions—appear! °Arise, thou judge of the earth, render	*Ps.* 94,[2]
unto the proud their deserts. °Triumph belongs unto God!—	*Ps.* 3,[9]
thy blessing upon thy People, *Selah*. °God of Cohorts is with	*Ps.* 46,[8]
us!—the Lord of Jacob is fortress unto us, *Selah*. °O God of	*Ps.* 84,[13]
Cohorts! hale, the man that trusts in thee! °O God, save!—	*Ps.* 20,[10]
may the sovereign answer us at the time of our call. °Save thy	*Ps.* 28,[9]
People and bless thy heritage, yea, tend them and °uplift them	*Is.* 63,[9]
unto everlasting. °Our soul hath waited for God—he is our	*Ps.* 33,[20]
help and our shield, °Indeed, our heart is gladdened in him,	*Ps.* 33,[21]
because we have relied on his holy name. °May thy loving-	*Ps.* 33,[22]
kindness, o God, be upon us, according as we have °expected of	*Ps.* 37,[7]
thee. °Show us thy loving-kindness, o God, and grant us thy	*Ps.* 85,[8]
salvation. °Arise for our help, and release us for thy kindness'	*Ps.* 44,[27]
sake. °I am God thy Lord who brought thee up from the land	*Ps.* 81,[11]
of *Miẓrayim*—open wide thy mouth, and I will fill it. °Well for	*Ps.* 17,[5]
the people that such is its lot—°well for the people unto whom	*Ps.* 144,[15]
God is Lord! °Concerning myself, I have relied upon thy	*Ps.* 13,[6]
loving-kindness—let my heart rejoice in thy salvation! I will	*Ps.* 142,[8]
sing unto God, °for he hath showered bounty upon me.	*I Sm.* 28,[18]

45. A psalmic anthology of twenty-two verses (*Romemu hashem eloheinu vehishtaḥavu*)

רוֹמְמוּ יְיָ אֱלֹהֵינוּ וְהִשְׁתַּחֲווּ
לַהֲדֹם רַגְלָיו קָדוֹשׁ הוּא: רוֹמְמוּ יְיָ אֱלֹהֵינוּ
וְהִשְׁתַּחֲווּ לְהַר קָדְשׁוֹ כִּי קָדוֹשׁ יְיָ אֱלֹהֵינוּ: וְהוּא
רַחוּם יְכַפֵּר עָוֹן וְלֹא יַשְׁחִית וְהִרְבָּה לְהָשִׁיב
אַפּוֹ וְלֹא יָעִיר כָּל חֲמָתוֹ: אַתָּה יְיָ לֹא תִכְלָא
רַחֲמֶיךָ מִמֶּנִּי חַסְדְּךָ וַאֲמִתְּךָ תָּמִיד יִצְּרוּנִי:
זְכֹר רַחֲמֶיךָ יְיָ וַחֲסָדֶיךָ כִּי מֵעוֹלָם הֵמָּה: תְּנוּ עֹז
לֵאלֹהִים עַל יִשְׂרָאֵל גַּאֲוָתוֹ וְעֻזּוֹ בַּשְּׁחָקִים:
נוֹרָא אֱלֹהִים מִמִּקְדָּשֶׁיךָ אֵל יִשְׂרָאֵל הוּא נֹתֵן
עֹז וְתַעֲצֻמוֹת לָעָם בָּרוּךְ אֱלֹהִים: אֵל נְקָמוֹת
יְיָ אֵל נְקָמוֹת הוֹפִיעַ: הִנָּשֵׂא שֹׁפֵט הָאָרֶץ
הָשֵׁב גְּמוּל עַל גֵּאִים: לַיְיָ הַיְשׁוּעָה עַל עַמְּךָ
בִרְכָתֶךָ סֶּלָה: יְיָ צְבָאוֹת עִמָּנוּ מִשְׂגָּב לָנוּ אֱלֹהֵי
יַעֲקֹב סֶלָה: יְיָ צְבָאוֹת אַשְׁרֵי אָדָם בֹּטֵחַ בָּךְ:
יְיָ הוֹשִׁיעָה הַמֶּלֶךְ יַעֲנֵנוּ בְיוֹם קָרְאֵנוּ: הוֹשִׁיעָה
אֶת עַמֶּךָ וּבָרֵךְ אֶת נַחֲלָתֶךָ וּרְעֵם וְנַשְּׂאֵם
עַד הָעוֹלָם: נַפְשֵׁנוּ חִכְּתָה לַיְיָ עֶזְרֵנוּ וּמָגִנֵּנוּ
הוּא: כִּי בוֹ יִשְׂמַח לִבֵּנוּ כִּי בְשֵׁם קָדְשׁוֹ
בָטָחְנוּ: יְהִי חַסְדְּךָ יְיָ עָלֵינוּ כַּאֲשֶׁר יִחַלְנוּ לָךְ:
הַרְאֵנוּ יְיָ חַסְדֶּךָ וְיֶשְׁעֲךָ תִּתֶּן לָנוּ: קוּמָה
עֶזְרָתָה לָּנוּ וּפְדֵנוּ לְמַעַן חַסְדֶּךָ: אָנֹכִי יְיָ אֱלֹהֶיךָ
הַמַּעַלְךָ מֵאֶרֶץ מִצְרָיִם הַרְחֶב פִּיךָ וַאֲמַלְאֵהוּ:
אַשְׁרֵי הָעָם שֶׁכָּכָה לּוֹ אַשְׁרֵי הָעָם שֶׁיְיָ אֱלֹהָיו:
וַאֲנִי בְּחַסְדְּךָ בָטַחְתִּי יָגֵל לִבִּי בִּישׁוּעָתֶךָ
אָשִׁירָה לַיְיָ כִּי גָמַל עָלָי:

°A psalm of thanksgiving:	*Ps.* 100,$^{1-5}$
°Acclaim unto God, world entire! Serve ye God in gladness—	*Zo. Gn.* 163,229
come unto his presence with jubilation; °O realize that God he is	*Ikk.* 3,^{33}
almighty, he made us and his we are, his people, yea, flock of his	*Md. Gn.* 100,^{1}
shepherding. °O enter his gates with thanksgiving, even his °courts	*Gn.* 28,^{17}
with laudation, °acknowledge unto him, bless his name, For °God is	*Dt.* 32,^{8}
good, his loving-kindness is forever, yea, °his faithfulness is	*Dt.* 32,^{4}
generation after generation.	*Is.* 34,^{17}

46. A psalm of thanksgiving—Psalm 100 (*Mizmor letodah*)

practice of reciting the psalm only on days when such offerings would have been made. It is therefore omitted on sabbaths and festivals, as well as the day before Passover and its intermediate days, when the bread included in sacrifice would be forbidden and could not be offered up.[85] Some stand while reciting this psalm, again recalling these cultic associations.

This series of texts with Temple associations reinforces the impression that the Temple is present, its actuality being underlined by the description here of entering the Temple (line 3), although the exiled speaker now has access only to a pale substitute, the synagogue. Since midrashic texts suggest that thanksgiving offerings will be among those that will continue even in the messianic era, this recital suggests that redemption might already have taken place, perhaps having been summoned into existence by the morning liturgy.[86]

EXTRACT 47. A Psalmic Anthology of Eighteen Verses

The dream of the Temple's restoration is interrupted by a reversion to the fragmented, gestural language of the psalmic collection seen in Extract 45 in another collection of verses, this time numbering eighteen.[87] The antiquity of this renewed draft of Pesukei Dezimra is clear from the fact that its opening words are referred to in rabbinic literature and appear in early liturgies.[88] It includes verses from all the five books of psalms except the second book, which is represented only in the Yemenite liturgy.[89] Unlike the verses in the earlier extract,

[85] *Sidur avodat yisra'el*, 61; see also Gaguine, *Keter shem tov*, i–ii. 43–4 n. 66.

[86] *Midrash Psalms* 100: 4, *Midrash tanḥuma* (Warsaw edn.), 'Emor' 14, and *Lev. Rabbah* 9: 7, 27: 12. The idea appears also in Caro, *Shulḥan arukh*, 'Oraḥ ḥayim' 51: 9.

[87] Pss. 104: 31, 113: 2–4, 135: 13, 103: 19; 1 Chr. 16: 31; a composite line (based on Pss. 10: 16, 93: 1 or 97: 1, and Exod. 15: 18, which first appears in *Soferim* 14: 8 (ed. Vilna, 40*b*)); Pss. 10: 16, 33: 10; Prov. 19: 21; Pss. 33: 11, 33: 9, 132: 13, 135: 4, 94: 14, 78: 38, 20: 10.

[88] *Soferim* 17: 11, 18: 2; Amram Gaon, *Seder rav amram hashalem*, i. 84*a*; Sa'adiah Gaon, *Sidur rav sa'adiah gaon*, 33.   [89] Ps. 46: 12, see Abrahams, *Companion*, p. xxxv.

מִזְמוֹר לְתוֹדָה הָרִיעוּ לַיְיָ כָּל־הָאָרֶץ: עִבְדוּ אֶת־יְיָ בְּשִׂמְחָה בֹּאוּ 1

לְפָנָיו בִּרְנָנָה: דְּעוּ כִּי יְיָ הוּא אֱלֹהִים הוּא עָשָׂנוּ וְלֹא (וְלוֹ ק) אֲנַחְנוּ 2

עַמּוֹ וְצֹאן מַרְעִיתוֹ: בֹּאוּ שְׁעָרָיו ׀ בְּתוֹדָה חֲצֵרֹתָיו בִּתְהִלָּה הוֹדוּ לוֹ 3

בָּרְכוּ שְׁמוֹ: כִּי־טוֹב יְיָ לְעוֹלָם חַסְדּוֹ וְעַד־דֹּר וָדֹר אֱמוּנָתוֹ: 4

however, the present ones are linked by common terms[90] or concepts.[91] The last two lines include a clear petition that transcends the incoherence inherent in the technique used in both this and the earlier collection.

The sequence summarizes in Davidic language the sacred narrative from Creation to election and the exile, although one verse is from Proverbs, traditionally attributed to David's son Solomon (lines 9–10), and another is composite and not even scriptural (lines 7–8).[92] Most verses contain the Tetragrammaton, the divine name associated with God's mercy, as though to confirm that salvation might have come and the Temple been rebuilt. Some do not, however, suggesting an awareness that this hope of rescue is illusory.

The opening verses of the present extract relate to Creation, echoing the opening blessing of the present liturgical sequence (Extract 43),[93] while lines 8–12 compare human weakness with divine power, another theme of that blessing. They allude to the might of enemies[94] and to the need to strive for closeness to Torah if the speaker is to avoid suffering, a goal already recognized as nearly impossible. The theme of election appears in line 12,[95] while lines 15–17 call for

[90] *Yehi, shem, shamayim, melekh/malakh, mahshevot/mahashavot, adonai, atsat, ta'amod/ya'-amod, bahar.* Elbogen, *Jewish Liturgy*, 74–5, claims incorrectly that each verse contains the Tetragrammaton.

[91] *Mevorakh-mehulal-kevodo-zikhrekha* (lines 2–4); *amar-bahar* (lines 12–13); *tsiyon-ya'akov-amo* (lines 13–14); *lo ya'azov-lo yashhit* (line 15).

[92] The first element of this composite line echoes Pss. 93: 1, 96: 10, 97: 1, and 99: 1, and 1 Chr. 16: 31; the second is reminiscent of Pss. 10: 16 and 29: 10, and the third of Exod. 15: 18, the last verse of the Song of the Sea, discussed in the context of Extract 57, line 32.

[93] The *kavod*, 'reverence', for God in the first line is said to be the motive for creating the world: see Mishnah *Avot* 6: 11. This verse (Ps. 104: 31) is spoken by 'the angel of the world' in praise of the newly created trees: see *Midrash Psalms* 104: 24 and BT *Ḥul.* 60a.

[94] Absalom (against Solomon), Haman, Pharaoh, and Egyptian children informing on Israelites, in *Midrash mishlei*, 43b, on Prov. 19: 21.

[95] *Midrash Psalms* 132: 3 (on 132: 13) associates this line with the election of the land of Israel and the dynasties of Aaron and David.

°May the reverence of God endure forever—may God be	*Ps.* 104,[31]
glad with his works. °May the name of God be blessed,	*Ikk.* 2,[15]
henceforth and °for evermore! From the rising of the sun	*Ps.* 113,[2]
unto its setting is God's name praised, °High above all nations	*Ps.* 113,[4]
is God, above the heavens is his glory. °Thy name, o God, is	*Ps.* 135,[13]
forever, thy mention, God, generation after generation. °God	*Zo. Lv.* 220
established his throne in the heavens and his sovereignty hath	*Ps.* 103,[19]
sway over all. °Let the heavens rejoice, yea, let the earth	*I Cr.* 16,[31]
revel, let them say among the nations: °God is regnant.	*Zo. Gn.* 34
God reigns, God hath reigned, °God will reign for ever and	*Ex.* 15,[18]
aye. °God, king for ever and aye, nations may disappear	*Ps.* 10,[16]
from his territory. °God upsets the plan of nations, he	*Ps.* 33,[10]
refuses the designs of peoples. °Many are the designs in a	*Prv.* 19,[21]
man's mind but the plan of God, that shall stand. The °plan	*Ps.* 33,[11]
of God shall stand forever, °the designs of his mind for generation	*Gn.* 8,[21]
after generation. °For he but spoke and it existed, he	*Ps.* 33,[9]
commanded and it stands firm. °Indeed, God hath selected Zion,	*Ps.* 132,[13]
he hath willed it as a residence unto himself. °For the Deity	*Ps.* 135,[4]
hath chosen Jacob unto himself, Israel as his select one. °For	*Ps.* 94,[14]
verily, °God will not abandon his People, neither will he forsake	*Zo. Ex.* 151
his heritage. Yea, °He, being merciful, forgives wrong-doing	*Ps.* 78,[38]
and doth not destroy—indeed, often he °turns his anger away	*B'Kd.* 31: *Tsf.*
and doth not pour out all his wrath. °O God, save!—may the	*Ps.* 20,[10]
sovereign answer us °at the time of our call.	*Gn.* 5,[1]

47. A psalmic anthology of eighteen verses (*Yehi khevod*)

mercy, ideas linked by the realization that God's demand for closeness is beyond human ability to achieve, leaving the speaker no hope but in divine mercy.[96] Since the last two verses also introduce the evening service, this sequence might be regarded as marking the beginning of morning worship.

There is also evidence of number symbolism here, much as in the verses of Extract 45. The fifteen psalmic verses correspond to the numerical value of the letters included in the divine name *yah* which, since that represents only the first half of the name denoting mercy, might imply its current incompleteness. If we add in the non-psalmic verses, which include one each from Proverbs and

[96] *Midrash Psalms* 20: 10 describes the last verse as a call for instant help; ibid. 94: 3 (on 94: 14) states that God will guard his people so long as they remain close to Torah.

יְהִי כְבוֹד יְיָ לְעוֹלָם יִשְׂמַח יְיָ בְּמַעֲשָׂיו: יְהִי שֵׁם 1

יְיָ מְבֹרָךְ מֵעַתָּה וְעַד־עוֹלָם: מִמִּזְרַח־שֶׁמֶשׁ 2

עַד־מְבוֹאוֹ מְהֻלָּל שֵׁם יְיָ: רָם עַל־כָּל־גּוֹיִם יְיָ 3

עַל הַשָּׁמַיִם כְּבוֹדוֹ: יְיָ שִׁמְךָ לְעוֹלָם יְיָ זִכְרְךָ 4

לְדֹר־וָדֹר: יְיָ בַּשָּׁמַיִם הֵכִין כִּסְאוֹ וּמַלְכוּתוֹ בַּכֹּל 5

מָשָׁלָה: יִשְׂמְחוּ הַשָּׁמַיִם וְתָגֵל הָאָרֶץ וְיֹאמְרוּ 6

בַגּוֹיִם יְיָ מָלָךְ: יְיָ מֶלֶךְ יְיָ מָלָךְ יְיָ יִמְלֹךְ לְעוֹלָם 7

וָעֶד: יְיָ מֶלֶךְ עוֹלָם וָעֶד אָבְדוּ גוֹיִם מֵאַרְצוֹ: יְיָ 8

הֵפִיר עֲצַת־גּוֹיִם הֵנִיא מַחְשְׁבוֹת עַמִּים: רַבּוֹת 9

מַחֲשָׁבוֹת בְּלֶב־אִישׁ וַעֲצַת יְיָ הִיא תָקוּם: עֲצַת 10

יְיָ לְעוֹלָם תַּעֲמֹד מַחְשְׁבוֹת לִבּוֹ לְדֹר וָדֹר: כִּי 11

הוּא אָמַר וַיֶּהִי הוּא צִוָּה וַיַּעֲמֹד: כִּי־בָחַר יְיָ 12

בְּצִיּוֹן אִוָּהּ לְמוֹשָׁב לוֹ: כִּי־יַעֲקֹב בָּחַר לוֹ יָהּ 13

יִשְׂרָאֵל לִסְגֻלָּתוֹ: כִּי־לֹא־יִטֹּשׁ יְיָ עַמּוֹ וְנַחֲלָתוֹ 14

לֹא יַעֲזֹב: וְהוּא רַחוּם יְכַפֵּר עָוֹן וְלֹא יַשְׁחִית 15

וְהִרְבָּה לְהָשִׁיב אַפּוֹ וְלֹא יָעִיר כָּל־חֲמָתוֹ: יְיָ 16

הוֹשִׁיעָה הַמֶּלֶךְ יַעֲנֵנוּ בְיוֹם־קָרְאֵנוּ: 17

Chronicles and one composite sentence, we have a total of eighteen, corresponding to the number of references to God in the Shema, the original tally of blessings in the Amidah, the numerical value of the letters of the word *ḥai*, 'life', and, in rabbinic thought, the number of human vertebrae (as noted in *Leviticus Rabbah* 1: 18). These correspondences suggest that this version of Pesukei Dezimra might have been designed to stand alone as an introduction to statutory prayer, its structure foreshadowing the Shema and Amidah (the latter conventionally referred to as *Shemoneh esrei*, 'eighteen', after the number of blessings it once contained). A different version of this sequence may have contained twenty-one references to the name of God, since a commentator says that this is the number of times it appears here, and that this equals the number of verses in

Psalm 145, the next liturgical text.[97] (This is correct if one ignores the three verses added to that psalm in liturgical use—two before it and one after it: see Extract 48, lines 1–2 and 25.[98])

Some of the verses are employed here gesturally, having already appeared in the morning liturgy. The one from Chronicles (lines 6–7) appeared in David's song at the entry of the Ark into Jerusalem (Extract 44, lines 24–5), while the penultimate verse (lines 15–16) was included in the previous anthology (Extract 45, lines 3–5) and the final one both there (line 15) and in an earlier sacrificial sequence (Extract 36, line 2). Although this collection must presumably have been intended as a complete Pesukei Dezimra, it now overlaps and interacts with others, thereby confirming the ineffectiveness of human speech in gaining access to divine language. Human powerlessness is emphasized by the unfavourable comparison of the 'designs in a man's mind' with 'the plan of God' in lines 9–10, the recollection of God's use of language at Creation in lines 11–12, and the description of the election of Israel as the result of a divine pronouncement in lines 12–15. These tend to confirm the inherent fallibility of the linguistic medium both in prayer and in study.

Yet the continuous thought achieved in this verse anthology challenges the speaker to engage with scriptural meaning, offering hope of recovering meaning from the juxtaposed verses of the first group too. It might be argued that the first group thus looks back at the power of language and its potential for building the Temple, while the second urges the speaker forward, viewing statutory worship, especially the Shema and Amidah, as a route to gaining access to the Torah and thereby to redemption.

EXTRACT 48. **Ending Hallel—Psalm 145**

The series of six psalms that opens here (145–50) is the most substantial formulation of Pesukei Dezimra and the longest scriptural reading so far, demonstrating a will to adhere closely to scriptural texts and forming the climactic core of the liturgical sequence.[99] Since it follows the previous two verse collections (Extracts 45 and 47), however, its failure is to be expected, although the pattern of liturgical repetition of which this is part employs language in wave-like movements that reflect the speaker's desperation. The gapped texture also requires the speaker to engage quasi-authorially in the work of constructing meaning from these multiple versions of the daily morning Hallel. It thus marks a new approach to the themes of human inarticulacy and the inefficacy of language, for this, the longest sequence of uninterrupted scriptural reading so far, silences the independent voice of the speaker and halts the vigorous debates implicit in the

---

[97] Moses of Premysl, *Mateh mosheh*, 49, p. 56.

[98] *Otsar hatefilot*, 'Tikun tefilah', 107*b*.

[99] Maimonides, *Mishneh Torah: The Book of Adoration*, 'On Prayer' 7: 12, fo. 106*a*.

liturgy. The paradoxical failure of human speech implicit in line 6—*veligdulato ein ḥeker*, literally 'his greatness cannot be researched'—may be resolved here by the speaker taking on David's voice, even though this involves merging with a morally ambiguous figure.

Two other groups of six psalms are included in the liturgy. One of them, introduced by Lurianic liturgists into the Friday evening service, is followed by two more psalms in honour of sabbath. The other six are recited as a series, one on each day of the week; this was performed in the Temple and is still included in the liturgy later in the weekday morning service. The fact that these psalms were related by Rabbi Akiba to the six days of Creation[100] suggests that the series of six psalms recited in the early part of the morning liturgy might likewise have a creational theme, which would echo the introductory blessing of the sequence (Extract 43). It would also confirm a medieval commentator's interpretation of Pesukei Dezimra as a re-enactment of Creation[101] and the view that the alphabetical acrostic of the first psalm of the series, Psalm 145, in which the initial word of each line begins with part of the sequence, represents the letters with which Creation was performed. Other alphabetical psalms were less suitable, Psalm 34 alluding to suffering and Psalm 136 depicting a less than perfect world.

One possible reason for including six psalmic chapters in the morning liturgy is that, by reciting this number of psalms each weekday, the biblical book of 150 psalms could be completed in a month. However, there is no evidence that such a practice lies behind the present group of psalms, which are not part of a cyclic reading of the entire book but serve rather to 'complete the Hallel', in that they consist of the concluding chapters of the entire book. Sa'adiah Gaon, in his tenth-century outline of the liturgy, states that psalms should be recited between waking and prayer, but does not define which or mention verse anthologies.[102] Abudarham in the fourteenth century recommends these concluding chapters as 'intercessors for prayer',[103] either because they introduce major liturgical themes, or because each begins and ends with the word *haleluyah* (except for the first), relating them to the root *h-l-l*, 'praise'.[104] That term, alluded to in the 'seal' of the introductory blessing of Pesukei Dezimra (Extract 43, line 13) and included in full at the end of David's song for the Ark (Extract 44, line 32), was absent from the first anthology, however, and appears only once in the second. In the first psalm of the present series it occurs only as a noun, *tehilah*, translated 'praise', appearing at the beginning of the first and last lines, this being the only chapter in the biblical book to begin in this way (Extract 48, lines 3 and 24). The entire book, nevertheless, is known as *tehilim*, 'praises', the plural form of that noun.[105]

---

[100] BT *RH* 31a. [101] Abudarham, *Abudarham hashalem*, 62–3.
[102] *Sidur rav sa'adiah gaon*, 32. [103] Abudarham, *Abudarham hashalem*, 62.
[104] BT *Shab.* 118b (but see Rashi) and *Soferim* 17: 11. For *halaluyah* see Gesenius, *Grammar*, 52–3, 182. [105] The addition of the introductory and concluding lines is discussed below.

°Well for the residers at Thy house—they can always	*Ps.* 84,[5]
laud thee, *Selah.* °Well for the People that such is its lot	*Ps.* 144,[15]
—well for the People unto whom God is Lord!	*B'Br.* 4:
°*Praise—of David*:—I extol thee, my Lord, o sovereign,	*Ps.* 145,[1-21]
yea, I do bless thy name for ever and aye—°Every day do	*Ikk.* 2,[26]
I bless thee and praise thy name for ever and aye, °Grand	*Md. Ru.* 6,[4/4]
is God and entirely to be praised, yea, °his greatness is not of	*B'Ha.* 15:
research; °Generation unto generation lauds thy doings	*Ex.* 3,[15]
and they tell of thy mightinesses,	*Zo. Nu.* 137:
°Of the beauteous honour of thy majesty, yea, words of thy	*Ps.* 124,[1-8]
wonders °do I mumble;	*Ps.* 102,[1]
While they talk of the °power of thine awe-inspiring acts, I	*Ps.* 24,[8]
relate thy grandeur; °*They* express the mention of thine	*Zo. Gn.* 7
°abounding goodness and sing of thy fair-dealing:	*Ps.* 31,[20]
God is bounteous and merciful, long-suffering and of °great	*B'Br.* 7
loving-kindness—°God is good unto all, yea, his mercies	*Gn.* 1,[31]
are over all His works. °All thy works acknowledge thee,	*B'Sn.* 39:
God, yea, °thy devotees do bless thee;	*B'Br.* 4:
They say: Honour to thy sovereignty—°they speak of thy	*Ikk.* 2,[14]
might; °To make known unto mankind his °acts of power,	*I Cr.* 29,[11]
also, the glory of his beauteous kingship;	*Ps.* 29,[2,10]
Thy royalty is sovereignty over all °worlds, yea, thy dominion	*Is.* 26,[4]; 34,[10]
is over °each and every generation;	*Zo. Dt.* 267
°Always God supports the falling and makes erect all that	*Zo. Gn.* 3
are bent down; °The eyes of all do wait upon Thee and	*B'Kt.* 67:
thou givest them their nourishment °in due season;	*Zo. Nu.* 226
°Thou dost open thy hand, satiating every living being with	*B'Tn.* 2:
goodwill; °God is right-kind in all his ways and loving-	*B'RH* 17
kind in all his acts: °God is nigh unto all that call upon him,	*Md. La.* 3,[7/11]
unto all that call upon him °in sincerity;	*Jg.* 9,[16]
°The purpose of his venerators he will perform, yea, their cry	*Md. Gn.* 78,[5/6]
he hearkens and he will save them;	*Y'Br.* 5,[1]
°God protects all that love him—but all the godless will he destroy;	*Md. Es.* 2, *ult.*
°My mouth utters the praise of God, so °all flesh shall bless his	*Ps.* 145,[1]
holy name forever and aye!	*Ze.* 2,[17]
°As to ourselves, let us bless the Deity henceforth and for	*Ps.* 115,[18]
evermore—*halleluyah* (praise ye God)!	*Yal. Ps.* 873

48. Ending Hallel—Psalm 145 (*Ashrei*)

אַשְׁרֵי יוֹשְׁבֵי בֵיתֶךָ עוֹד יְהַלְלוּךָ סֶּלָה: 1

אַשְׁרֵי הָעָם שֶׁכָּכָה לּוֹ אַשְׁרֵי הָעָם שֶׁיְיָ אֱלֹהָיו: 2

תְּהִלָּה לְדָוִד 3

אֲרוֹמִמְךָ אֱלוֹהַי הַמֶּלֶךְ וַאֲבָרְכָה שִׁמְךָ לְעוֹלָם וָעֶד: 4

בְּכָל־יוֹם אֲבָרֲכֶךָ וַאֲהַלְלָה שִׁמְךָ לְעוֹלָם וָעֶד: 5

גָּדוֹל יְהֹוָה וּמְהֻלָּל מְאֹד וְלִגְדֻלָּתוֹ אֵין חֵקֶר: 6

דּוֹר לְדוֹר יְשַׁבַּח מַעֲשֶׂיךָ וּגְבוּרֹתֶיךָ יַגִּידוּ: 7

הֲדַר כְּבוֹד הוֹדֶךָ וְדִבְרֵי נִפְלְאֹתֶיךָ אָשִׂיחָה: 8

וֶעֱזוּז נוֹרְאֹתֶיךָ יֹאמֵרוּ וּגְדֻלָּתְךָ אֲסַפְּרֶנָּה: 9

זֵכֶר רַב־טוּבְךָ יַבִּיעוּ וְצִדְקָתְךָ יְרַנֵּנוּ: 10

חַנּוּן וְרַחוּם יְהֹוָה אֶרֶךְ אַפַּיִם וּגְדָל־חָסֶד: 11

טוֹב־יְהֹוָה לַכֹּל וְרַחֲמָיו עַל־כָּל־מַעֲשָׂיו: 12

יוֹדוּךָ יְהֹוָה כָּל־מַעֲשֶׂיךָ וַחֲסִידֶיךָ יְבָרֲכוּכָה: 13

כְּבוֹד מַלְכוּתְךָ יֹאמֵרוּ וּגְבוּרָתְךָ יְדַבֵּרוּ: 14

לְהוֹדִיעַ לִבְנֵי הָאָדָם גְּבוּרֹתָיו וּכְבוֹד הֲדַר מַלְכוּתוֹ: 15

מַלְכוּתְךָ מַלְכוּת כָּל־עֹלָמִים וּמֶמְשַׁלְתְּךָ בְּכָל־דּוֹר וָדֹר: 16

סוֹמֵךְ יְהֹוָה לְכָל־הַנֹּפְלִים וְזוֹקֵף לְכָל־הַכְּפוּפִים: 17

עֵינֵי כֹל אֵלֶיךָ יְשַׂבֵּרוּ וְאַתָּה נוֹתֵן־לָהֶם אֶת־אָכְלָם בְּעִתּוֹ: 18

פּוֹתֵחַ אֶת־יָדֶךָ וּמַשְׂבִּיעַ לְכָל־חַי רָצוֹן: 19

צַדִּיק יְהֹוָה בְּכָל־דְּרָכָיו וְחָסִיד בְּכָל־מַעֲשָׂיו: 20

קָרוֹב יְהֹוָה לְכָל־קֹרְאָיו לְכֹל אֲשֶׁר יִקְרָאֻהוּ בֶאֱמֶת: 21

רְצוֹן־יְרֵאָיו יַעֲשֶׂה וְאֶת־שַׁוְעָתָם יִשְׁמַע וְיוֹשִׁיעֵם: 22

שׁוֹמֵר יְהֹוָה אֶת־כָּל־אֹהֲבָיו וְאֵת כָּל־הָרְשָׁעִים יַשְׁמִיד: 23

תְּהִלַּת יְהֹוָה יְדַבֶּר פִּי וִיבָרֵךְ כָּל־בָּשָׂר שֵׁם קָדְשׁוֹ לְעוֹלָם וָעֶד: 24

וַאֲנַחְנוּ נְבָרֵךְ יָהּ מֵעַתָּה וְעַד־עוֹלָם הַלְלוּיָהּ: 25

The first psalm here is suited to the morning liturgy because the term 'blessing', which dominated the introductory sequence of the day, appears in the first, second, and last lines (lines 4–5 and 24). Talmudic writers regarded this as the most important chapter in the book since its praise is unmingled with complaint, and it is therefore perhaps the first liturgical moment of praise untainted by ambivalence. It is also universalist, since it does not refer to Israel or the Temple. Talmudic writers recommended it for thrice-daily recital, perhaps because the reference in line 19 to the opening of God's hand alludes to three daily meals,[106] a verse highlighted by some on weekdays by touching the *tefilin* on the hand and head, and by Sephardim by spreading the open hands as though receiving a gift. Such gestures are otherwise reserved for liturgical moments such as the Shema, suggesting the symbolic weight of this psalm and of this verse in particular.[107] One midrashic text confirms this preoccupation with nourishment by stating that the ability to earn a livelihood is a miracle greater than the splitting of the Red Sea or even the messianic rescue, an idea which recalls the view that survival is itself a form of redemption.[108]

To align this psalm more fully with a sequence known as Hallel recited on festivals and New Moon, comprising texts which begin and end with *haleluyah*, additional psalmic verses were added, two at the beginning and one at the end, the first containing a form of the root *h-l-l*[109] and the last concluding with *haleluyah*,[110] thereby both restoring the speaker's independence and undermining perfect study. The additional opening lines include a threefold repetition of the word by which this psalm is conventionally known—*ashrei*, 'Well for . . .', or 'Blessed is . . .' (AV)[111]—perhaps echoing the talmudically recommended thrice-daily recital of the psalm. Since this is also the initial word of the first psalm, the present psalms, which include the first and last words of the book of Psalms, might be viewed as encompassing the whole and, for this reason, as a way of 'completing the Hallel'. The emphatic use of the letter *alef*, the first letter in the alphabet, in this repeated first word may underline the alphabetical acrostic according to which the psalm is organized.

This psalm is suited to the beginning of prayer since the supplementary opening line refers to 'the residers at [literally 'those who sit in'] Thy house', alluding

---

[106] BT *Ber.* 4*b*; see *Sidur avodat yisra'el*, 68–9, and Abrahams, *Companion*, p. xxxvi. Its threefold daily repetition is said to ensure a place in the afterlife. It is said twice in the morning liturgy and then in the afternoon only, rather than in the morning, afternoon, and evening, because the evening service was originally optional (see Gaguine, *Keter shem tov*, i–ii. 44–5 n. 67) and is recited when it is not strictly 'day'. For the repetition see *Otsar hatefilot*, 'Tikun tefilah', 108*b*–109*a*.

[107] The status of this psalm as a credal statement has been analysed in Kimelman, 'Psalm 145', but its interaction with the texts with which it is juxtaposed here is not discussed. An abridged version of his paper appears in *My People's Prayer Book*, iii. 31–9. [108] *Gen. Rabbah* 20: 9.

[109] Pss. 84: 5, 144: 15. [110] Ps. 115: 18; see Jacob ben Asher, *Arba'ah turim*, 'Orah hayim' 51. [111] BT *Ber.* 4*b* refers to it by the opening words of the psalm itself: 'Praise—of David'.

to the speaker who meditates before statutory worship.[112] The psalm from which that initial line is taken, in which the word 'house' is central, is used at the beginning of the afternoon service in the Sephardi rite, reinforcing the initial force of this series of psalms.[113] Since the word 'house' here applies to a synagogal substitute for the Temple, however, it also emphasizes exile.

The second introductory verse, apparently included because it contains the word *ashrei*, is the last verse of the psalm that precedes the present one, as though to emphasize the sequence of which Psalm 145 is part. Its last two words are forms of God's more familiar names, looking backward and forward to the messianic project of unifying God's attributes proposed by the Shema.

This psalm echoes themes seen earlier, in some cases summarizing them. The failings of human perception are implied in line 6, which notes the impossibility of understanding God's greatness and recalls previous reflections on God's inscrutability. A similar uncertainty about human expression is alluded to in the translation of the Hebrew word *asihah*, usually rendered 'I will speak', but here as 'I mumble'.[114] The allusion to the thirteen attributes of God's mercy in line 11[115] recalls the episode of the Golden Calf, in the course of which these were first proclaimed. Their initial declaration culminated in the affirmation of God's adherence to 'truth', a term omitted here as though it might be incompatible with the mercy the speaker desires.

The positive character of this text was so treasured that the absence of a line beginning with the letter *nun* in the Masoretic text[116] was talmudically attributed to the fact that it would have had to begin with a reference to the *nefilah*, 'fall', of the Temple. That the fall is very much in mind is confirmed by the fact that lines 16–17, which follow, contain the same word in the context of the relief of suffering. This attempt to deny suffering that is in fact present is supported by the way in which this psalm addresses God variably in the second or third person, as though reflecting barriers to proximity to God.[117]

Midrashic discussions of this psalm focus on the reference to God's 'mercy over all his works' (line 12), a quality about which rabbinic writers are ambivalent, as has been seen. One text states that God's mercy is greater than that of

---

[112] It is cited in BT *Ber.* 32*b* as the prooftext for the practice of sitting (although that term is translated here as 'residing') and meditating in synagogue for an hour before prayer—the original function of Pesukei Dezimra—and was taken as an indication that what follows is suitable material for such a time. Elbogen, *Liturgy*, 75.

[113] *Book of Prayer: Daily and Occasional Prayers*, 63–4. Another verse appears in Extract 36, lines 1–2 above.   [114] See *Book of Prayer: Daily and Occasional Prayers*, 20.   [115] Exod. 34: 6–7.

[116] Accounted for in BT *Ber.* 4*b* as an avoidance of a line beginning with a word based on the root *n-f-l*, 'fall', suggesting misfortune, based on Amos 5: 2. A line beginning with the letter *nun* which appears in several ancient versions, although it is of doubtful authenticity, begins *ne'eman*, 'faithful', and serves to underline the preoccupation with suffering betrayed by this rationale. See Kittel (ed.), *Biblia Hebraica*, 1021 n. 13, and Kimelman, 'Psalm 145', 49–51.

[117] See, for instance, lines 6, 11–12, 15, 17 and 20–3, the psalm ending in the more remote vein.

°*Halleluyah* (Praise ye God)!—praise God, o my soul, I	*Ps.* 146,¹⁻¹⁰
will praise God while I live, I will sing unto my Lord °through-	*Jb.* 27,³
out my existence: °Put not your trust in grandees, not in any	*Ex.* 35,²
human being, he hath not the gift of salvation; °His spirit	*Gn.* 7,²²
departs, he returns to his clay, in that very day his plans	*Ps.* 104,²⁹
perish. °Well for him that hath the Lord of Jacob for his help,	*Ps.* 17,⁵
whose expectation is in God, his Lord, Who made heaven and	*Zo. Ex.* 198
earth, the °sea and all that therein is, who guards truth for	*Gn.* 1,²¹
ever, °Who carries out justice for the oppressed, gives food to	*Ex.* 22,²⁶
the hungry—°God releases captives, God enlightens the blind,	*B'Yo.* 35:
°God makes upright the bent down, °God loves the religious,	*Zo. Gn.* 195
God protects the aliens, he encourages the °fatherless and the	*Gn.* 7,¹
widow; but, the path of the godless he despoils; °God shall	*Dt.* 10,¹⁸
reign for ever!—thy Lord, o Zion, generation after generation	*Ze.* 14,⁹
—°*halleluyah* (praise ye God!)	*B'Pm.* 117

49. Psalm 146 (*Haleluyah: Haleli nafshi*)

humans to each other,[118] while another claims that it needs to be promoted by individual acts of kindness in daily life.[119] The awareness of suffering that pervades the morning liturgy may indeed suggest that humans can relieve pain which God does not resolve. David Kimhi (*c.*1160–*c.*1265), in his commentary on verses 15–17, points out that, although God shows 'kindness to all', he paradoxically allows some of his creatures to feed on others (lines 18–19). This awareness of ambivalence might have inspired the present translation's rendition of *tsadik* and *hasid* (line 20) as 'right-kind' and 'loving-kind', rather than the more usual 'righteous' and 'merciful', as though to emphasize the inadequacy of the conventional forms of divine attributes.

EXTRACT 49. Psalm 146

The five concluding chapters of the book of Psalms, included here in full and in their correct sequence, begin and end with the word *haleluyah*, exemplifying the praise announced in the opening blessing of the sequence (Extract 43, lines 7 and 13) and alluded to in the first preliminary verse of the previous psalm (Extract 48, line 1).

Psalm 146 expands on the fear of hostility mentioned above (lines 2–3), while withdrawing from the implied universalism of the previous psalm by referring specifically to 'Jacob' (line 4). It is also the source of three of the early-morning

---

[118] *Midrash tanḥuma* (Buber), 'Vayetse' 10.   [119] *Gen. Rabbah* 33: 3.

הַלְלוּיָהּ הַלְלִי נַפְשִׁי אֶת־יְהוָה: אֲהַלְלָה יְהוָה בְּחַיָּי 1

אֲזַמְּרָה לֵאלֹהַי בְּעוֹדִי: אַל־תִּבְטְחוּ בִנְדִיבִים בְּבֶן־אָדָם שֶׁאֵין 2

לוֹ תְשׁוּעָה: תֵּצֵא רוּחוֹ יָשֻׁב לְאַדְמָתוֹ בַּיּוֹם הַהוּא אָבְדוּ 3

עֶשְׁתֹּנֹתָיו: אַשְׁרֵי שֶׁאֵל יַעֲקֹב בְּעֶזְרוֹ שִׂבְרוֹ עַל־יְהוָה אֱלֹהָיו: 4

עֹשֶׂה שָׁמַיִם וָאָרֶץ אֶת־הַיָּם וְאֶת־כָּל־אֲשֶׁר־בָּם הַשֹּׁמֵר 5

אֱמֶת לְעוֹלָם: עֹשֶׂה מִשְׁפָּט לַעֲשׁוּקִים נֹתֵן לֶחֶם לָרְעֵבִים 6

יְהוָה מַתִּיר אֲסוּרִים: יְהוָה פֹּקֵחַ עִוְרִים יְהוָה זֹקֵף כְּפוּפִים 7

יְהוָה אֹהֵב צַדִּיקִים: יְהוָה שֹׁמֵר אֶת־גֵּרִים יָתוֹם וְאַלְמָנָה 8

יְעוֹדֵד וְדֶרֶךְ רְשָׁעִים יְעַוֵּת: יִמְלֹךְ יְהוָה לְעוֹלָם אֱלֹהַיִךְ 9

צִיּוֹן לְדֹר וָדֹר הַלְלוּיָהּ: 10

blessings seen above,[120] recalling the specifically Jewish character of the liturgy and the comparison between regaining consciousness and salvation. However, it now becomes clear that the early-morning blessings omitted the reference to orphans and widows, their absence perhaps constituting a thinly veiled criticism of God since commentators identify the 'orphans and widows' as Israel and Jerusalem, and therefore the speaker, in exile. This omission is another instance of manipulation of scriptural texts, analogous to the incomprehension that leads to exile.

A similar critique of God is implied in the midrashic gloss of the Hebrew words *matir asurim*, translated here as 'releases captives' (line 7). A midrashic comment renders this as '[God] will [in messianic times] permit that which is [currently] forbidden [under the dietary laws]', thereby removing a reason for Jews to suffer punishment.[121] Such a reading is in harmony with the praise of God in line 7 for opening human eyes, which contradicts his anger at Adam and Eve's eye-opening in Eden after eating the fruit, the source of human mortality and suffering. This rabbinic ambivalence about Adam and Eve's role in the Eden episode is echoed in the juxtaposition of the first weekly Torah reading, 'Bereshit', with a Haftarah (prophetic reading) which presents enlightenment, seen in Genesis in a negative light, as a normal state.[122] The last line promises

[120] Compare line 7 with Extract 24, lines 1, 3, 4. It also contributes to the Amidah. Loeb, 'Les Dix-huit bénédictions', 34, points out that this and the next psalm contain parallels to almost all the blessings in the weekday Amidah.

[121] *Midrash Psalms* 146: 4.   [122] Gen. 3: 7; Isa. 42: 7, 16, 19–20.

°*Halleluyah* (Praise ye God)!—for it is good to sing unto	*Ps.* 147,[1-20]
our Lord, yea, it is pleasant, °praise is seemly; God is the	*Ikk.* 3,[24]
rebuilder of Jerusalem, °he will ingather the dispersed of	*B'Br.* 49
Israel; He who °heals the broken-hearted and binds up their	*Zo. Gn.* 139
hurts; °He counts by number the stars, he calls them each by	*B'Sn.* 39
name; °Grand is our Lord, yea, °of much power—there is no	*B'AZ* 4
assessing his comprehending; God encourages the meek—	*B'Mg.* 31
°he depresses the wicked down to the ground; Respond unto	*Mai.Ikk.* 11
God with °thanksgiving, intone upon the harp unto our Lord,	*Ps.* 100,[1]
°Who covers the skies with clouds, who °prepares rain for the	*Ikk.* 4,[8]
earth, who causes grass to grow upon the hill-sides—He gives	*Gn.* 2,[6]
unto beast his food, yea, °to the young ravens when they call;	*B'Kt.* 49:
It is not °horse power which He treasures, nor is he interested	*Ex.* 15,[1]
in the muscles of a man—°God approves them that revere him,	*Ikk.* 4,[37]
°them that await his loving-kindness; O Jerusalem, laud God,	*Zo. Gn.* 194:
praise thy Lord, o Zion, For He hath strengthened the battens	*Gn.* 15,[6]
of thy gates, °he hath blessed thy children in thy midst. He	*Dt.* 7,[13]
who °establishes thy borders with peace, who satiates thee	*B'BM* 59
with the richness of wheat; It is °He who sends forth his	*Ps.* 19,[3]
message to the world, yea, his word runs swiftly, He, who gives	*Md.Ex.* 20,[2/6]
°snow like wool, he scatters the hoar-frost like ashes, He casts	*Msh.Ng.* 1,[1]
abroad his ice, like crumbs—°who can stand up to his freeze?	*Zo.Nu.* 210
—If°He issues his command, he melts them, he turns his wind	*Am.* 1,[10]
and the waters do flow—°He told his message unto Jacob,	*Zo.Lv.* 42
°his statutes and his judgments unto Israel—°He did °not do	*Zo.Ex.* 18:,257
so with every nation—and as for his judgments, they have	*Ku.* 2,[56]
not heard them—*halleluyah* (praise ye God)!	

50. Psalm 147 (*Haleluyah: Ki tov*)

the restoration of God's presence in Zion, reflecting the speaker's certainty that the reconstruction of the Temple either will take place or has already occurred.

EXTRACT 50. **Psalm 147**

Psalm 147 opens with a discussion of the building of Jerusalem and the ingathering of the exiles (line 2), the concluding idea of the previous psalm. It then explores God's control of the climate, a tool of retribution in the second para-

הַלְלוּיָהּ ׀ כִּי־טוֹב זַמְּרָה אֱלֹהֵינוּ כִּי־נָעִים נָאוָה תְהִלָּה: 1

בּוֹנֵה יְרוּשָׁלִַם יְהוָה נִדְחֵי יִשְׂרָאֵל יְכַנֵּס: הָרֹפֵא לִשְׁבוּרֵי לֵב 2

וּמְחַבֵּשׁ לְעַצְּבוֹתָם: מוֹנֶה מִסְפָּר לַכּוֹכָבִים לְכֻלָּם שֵׁמוֹת 3

יִקְרָא: גָּדוֹל אֲדוֹנֵינוּ וְרַב־כֹּחַ לִתְבוּנָתוֹ אֵין מִסְפָּר: 4

מְעוֹדֵד עֲנָוִים יְהוָה מַשְׁפִּיל רְשָׁעִים עֲדֵי־אָרֶץ: עֱנוּ לַיהוָה 5

בְּתוֹדָה זַמְּרוּ לֵאלֹהֵינוּ בְכִנּוֹר: הַמְכַסֶּה שָׁמַיִם בְּעָבִים 6

הַמֵּכִין לָאָרֶץ מָטָר הַמַּצְמִיחַ הָרִים חָצִיר: נוֹתֵן לִבְהֵמָה 7

לַחְמָהּ לִבְנֵי עֹרֵב אֲשֶׁר יִקְרָאוּ: לֹא בִגְבוּרַת הַסּוּס יֶחְפָּץ 8

לֹא־בְשׁוֹקֵי הָאִישׁ יִרְצֶה: רוֹצֶה יְהוָה אֶת־יְרֵאָיו אֶת 9

הַמְיַחֲלִים לְחַסְדּוֹ: שַׁבְּחִי יְרוּשָׁלִַם אֶת־יְהוָה הַלְלִי אֱלֹהַיִךְ 10

צִיּוֹן: כִּי־חִזַּק בְּרִיחֵי שְׁעָרָיִךְ בֵּרַךְ בָּנַיִךְ בְּקִרְבֵּךְ: הַשָּׂם 11

גְּבוּלֵךְ שָׁלוֹם חֵלֶב חִטִּים יַשְׂבִּיעֵךְ: הַשֹּׁלֵחַ אִמְרָתוֹ אָרֶץ 12

עַד־מְהֵרָה יָרוּץ דְּבָרוֹ: הַנֹּתֵן שֶׁלֶג כַּצָּמֶר כְּפוֹר כָּאֵפֶר 13

יְפַזֵּר: מַשְׁלִיךְ קַרְחוֹ כְפִתִּים לִפְנֵי קָרָתוֹ מִי יַעֲמֹד: 14

יִשְׁלַח־דְּבָרוֹ וְיַמְסֵם יַשֵּׁב רוּחוֹ יִזְּלוּ־מָיִם: מַגִּיד דְּבָרָיו 15

לְיַעֲקֹב חֻקָּיו וּמִשְׁפָּטָיו לְיִשְׂרָאֵל: לֹא עָשָׂה כֵן לְכָל־גּוֹי 16

וּמִשְׁפָּטִים בַּל־יְדָעוּם הַלְלוּיָהּ: 17

graph of the Shema,[123] echoing the theme of nourishment in Psalm 145 (lines 18–20).[124] But God's punitive relations with Israel are assumed in the rabbinic association of the final verse of this psalm with God's demand that his people accept the Torah on pain of death,[125] suggesting that Torah can be seen not as the key to redemption by ensuring closeness to God, but as the source of suffering due to human inability to interpret it correctly. The idea that force of arms is

[123] Deut. 11: 17.
[124] Ibn Ezra on verse 19 suggests this coincidence. See also *Otsar hatefilot*, 'Iyun tefilah', 112a.
[125] BT *Shab*. 88a (where the theological objections to the notion are also explored).

°*Halleluyah* (Praise ye God)!—praise God from the	*Ps.* 148,¹⁻¹⁴
heavens, praise him in the celestial heights! °Praise him, all his	*Zo. Ex.* 216:, 232
angels! praise him, °all his cohorts! Praise him, sun and	*Ps.* 103,²¹
moon! °praise him, all stars of light! Praise him, heavens of	*Zo. Gn.* 231:
heavens, also, those waters that float above the skies°—Let	*Ps.* 104,³
them praise the name of God, for he °commanded, and they	*Md. Gn.* 1,³/⁸
were created! He established them °endlessly, forever, he set	*Is.* 30,⁸
them a limit—it shall not be overstepped; °Praise God from the	*B'Ha.* 14:
world, °sea-monsters and all sea-deeps, Fire and hail, snow and	*B'Ha.* 12:
vapours, °stormy wind, doing his bidding, Mountains and all	*Zo. Nu.* 175:
hills, fruit-trees as well as countless cedars; °Those beasts and	*B'Hu.* 139:
all cattle, creeping things and winged birds; World emperors	*Is.* 17,¹²⁻¹³
and all °empires, notables, yea, all judges of the world—Both	*Md. Gn.* 8,²/⁷
lads and lasses, old men together with youngsters—°Let them	*Ps.* 118,¹,²⁹
praise the name of God, for his name, alone, °is exalted, his	*Is.* 2,¹¹
majesty is over land and sky, He also hath raised a °horn-	*Ps.* 112,⁹
emblem unto his People, a praise for all his °devotees, unto	*Dt.* 32,⁸
the children of Israel, the People of his °intimacy—*halleluyah*	*Dt.* 30,¹⁴
(praise ye God)!	*Md. Lv.* 4, *penult.*

51. Psalm 148 (*Haleluyah: Halelu et-hashem*)

useless against human enemies (lines 8–10) points to the possibility, or even the certainty, that these are sent by God, although this notion is later challenged (Extract 52, lines 5–8).

The reference to the strengthening of the gates of Jerusalem (line 11) suggests a historical link with accounts of the returning Babylonian exiles who, as was seen earlier, were prevented by their neighbours from rebuilding the Temple.[126] Since the speaker's redemption may likewise be delayed by the absence of the Temple, it is unclear how rebuilding might begin. The synagogue meanwhile represents a shadow of the Temple which itself may delay the rebuilding, as did the returned exiles' homes in the Nehemiah text. This is yet another theological impasse from which the speaker can escape only by an act of God's mercy.

EXTRACT 51. **Psalm 148**

Psalm 148, which calls on all creation to praise God, including angels, planets, weather, landscapes, creatures, and humanity, seems to be set after redemption

---

[126] Neh. 3: 3, 6, 13, 14, 15. This psalm may even have been one of the songs referred to in 12: 27–47 that was used at the rededication.

הַלְלוּיָהּ ׀ הַלְלוּ אֶת־יְהֹוָה מִן־הַשָּׁמַיִם הַלְלוּהוּ ۱

בַּמְּרוֹמִים: הַלְלוּהוּ כָל־מַלְאָכָיו הַלְלוּהוּ כָּל־צְבָאָו: ۲

הַלְלוּהוּ שֶׁמֶשׁ וְיָרֵחַ הַלְלוּהוּ כָּל־כּוֹכְבֵי אוֹר: הַלְלוּהוּ שְׁמֵי ۳

הַשָּׁמָיִם וְהַמַּיִם אֲשֶׁר ׀ מֵעַל הַשָּׁמָיִם: יְהַלְלוּ אֶת־שֵׁם ۴

יְהֹוָה כִּי הוּא צִוָּה וְנִבְרָאוּ: וַיַּעֲמִידֵם לָעַד לְעוֹלָם חָק־נָתַן ۵

וְלֹא־יַעֲבוֹר: הַלְלוּ אֶת־יְהֹוָה מִן־הָאָרֶץ תַּנִּינִים וְכָל־ ۶

תְּהֹמוֹת: אֵשׁ וּבָרָד שֶׁלֶג וְקִיטוֹר רוּחַ סְעָרָה עֹשָׂה דְבָרוֹ: ۷

הֶהָרִים וְכָל־גְּבָעוֹת עֵץ פְּרִי וְכָל־אֲרָזִים: הַחַיָּה וְכָל־ ۸

בְּהֵמָה רֶמֶשׂ וְצִפּוֹר כָּנָף: מַלְכֵי־אֶרֶץ וְכָל־לְאֻמִּים שָׂרִים ۹

וְכָל־שֹׁפְטֵי אָרֶץ: בַּחוּרִים וְגַם־בְּתוּלוֹת זְקֵנִים עִם־ ۱۰

נְעָרִים: יְהַלְלוּ ׀ אֶת־שֵׁם יְהֹוָה כִּי־נִשְׂגָּב שְׁמוֹ לְבַדּוֹ הוֹדוֹ ۱۱

עַל־אֶרֶץ וְשָׁמָיִם: וַיָּרֶם קֶרֶן ׀ לְעַמּוֹ תְּהִלָּה לְכָל־חֲסִידָיו ۱۲

לִבְנֵי יִשְׂרָאֵל עַם קְרֹבוֹ הַלְלוּיָהּ: ۱۳

because Israel is referred to as God's 'intimate people' (lines 12–13).[127] This psalm, describing a perfected world, was identified by Rashi, together with the final psalm appearing below, as constituting the whole of the Pesukei Dezimra sequence.[128] The two psalms may have been selected because they represent something approaching the fulfilment of messianic hopes for the direct rule of God, which the earlier sacrificial recitals were intended to conjure into virtual existence by means of reproducing the Temple cult.

EXTRACT 52. Psalm 149

Psalm 149, the penultimate text in the sequence, suggests a new approach to the challenges of the coming day, referring to Israel's 'saviour' and proposing that he be praised with a 'new song', as though rescue had already come.[129] The speaker,

[127] The last two verses are read at the closing of the Ark. The idea of praise proclaimed by the whole of creation, on which this psalm is based, recalls the antiphonally arranged praise in the Kedushah, inserted into the repetition of the third blessing of the Amidah.

[128] See his comment on BT *Shab.* 118*b*, *pesukei dezimra*.

[129] The *ḥasidim* in Extract 51 line 12, are rejoicing here in line 8. See *Midrash Psalms* 149: 1.

°*Halleluyah* (Praise ye God)!—sing unto God a new song,	*Ps.* 149,[1-9]
his praise is in the congregation of the devout; °Let Israel be	*Zo. Nu.* 219:
glad with his maker, let the children of Zion °rejoice in their	*Jl.* 2,[23]
king; Let them praise his name in dance-round, let them	*Jg.* 11,[24]
intone unto him with lyre and harp—°For God values his	*Ikk.* 2,[24]
People, he glorifies the meek through salvation—°Let the	*Zo. Lv.* 62
devout exult in honour, singing even upon their couches,	*B'Br.* 5
°Powerful uplifts through their throats, like a many edged	*Zo. Gn.* 28:
°sword in their hand—To carry out retribution among the	*Md. Nu.* 11,[7/13]
nations, °sentence among the empires, °To confine their	*Zo. Nu.* 211:, 238
kings in chains and their notables in fetters of steel, To carry	*Jr.* 40,[1]
out prescribed justice among them—such is splendour unto all	*B'AZ* 16:
his devotees—°*halleluyah* (praise ye God)!	*Zo. Lv.* 62

52. Psalm 149 (*Haleluyah: Shiru*)

meanwhile, contemplates vengeance, although the use of force was discounted in Psalm 147 (Extract 50, lines 8–9). This text nevertheless unequivocally introduces the theme of military triumph, an idea that will resurface at several points over the coming pages.[130] Since vengeance is said to be scripturally promised (literally 'written': Extract 52, line 8), it is perhaps expected to follow the joy at survival alluded to in previous texts. Alternatively, the speaker may now despair of peaceful solutions, although the text assumes military dominance lies in God's competence, making this a theological rather than a political matter. Rashi excluded this psalm from Pesukei Dezimra, perhaps because of his misgivings about this theme.

EXTRACT 53. **Psalm 150**

Psalm 150, the last in the series, replaces the military image with an inventory of musical instruments with which God may be praised, culminating in a call for 'every breath-soul [to] praise the Deity' (line 5). Including nature in its entirety universalizes the liturgy and excludes the option of violence offered by the 'new song' of an earlier psalm. But declaring living creatures, including the speaker, to be instruments on which to play cosmic compositions minimizes the autonomy of souls. The choice of musical instruments again conjures up a vision of a

---

[130] *Midrash Psalms* 149: 5 suggests that the Israelites' swords are their words, presumably meaning those of the liturgy. The psalm may date from the time of the rebuilding of the Temple, which would account for the juxtaposition of praise and warfare.

הַלְלוּיָהּ ׀ שִׁירוּ לַיהוָה שִׁיר חָדָשׁ תְּהִלָּתוֹ בִּקְהַל 1

חֲסִידִים: יִשְׂמַח יִשְׂרָאֵל בְּעֹשָׂיו בְּנֵי־צִיּוֹן יָגִילוּ בְמַלְכָּם: 2

יְהַלְלוּ שְׁמוֹ בְמָחוֹל בְּתֹף וְכִנּוֹר יְזַמְּרוּ־לוֹ: כִּי־רוֹצֶה יְהוָה 3

בְּעַמּוֹ יְפָאֵר עֲנָוִים בִּישׁוּעָה: יַעְלְזוּ חֲסִידִים בְּכָבוֹד יְרַנְּנוּ 4

עַל־מִשְׁכְּבוֹתָם: רוֹמְמוֹת אֵל בִּגְרוֹנָם וְחֶרֶב פִּיפִיּוֹת בְּיָדָם: 5

לַעֲשׂוֹת נְקָמָה בַּגּוֹיִם תּוֹכֵחוֹת בַּלְאֻמִּים: לֶאְסֹר מַלְכֵיהֶם 6

בְּזִקִּים וְנִכְבְּדֵיהֶם בְּכַבְלֵי בַרְזֶל: לַעֲשׂוֹת בָּהֶם ׀ מִשְׁפָּט 7

כָּתוּב הָדָר הוּא לְכָל־חֲסִידָיו הַלְלוּיָהּ: 8

restored Temple in Jerusalem, transforming the synagogue from a 'minor sanctuary' into an anticipation of the messianically restored sanctuary.

The last sentence (line 5) concludes the biblical book of Psalms and the sequence begun at Extract 48, line 1, and is the only one in this passage to be composed of a single clause rather than two parallel ones, suggesting a unification of the climactic kind assumed to affect divine names in messianic times. It also echoes aspects of the last line of Psalm 145 (Extract 48, line 24), implying that that single psalm has the coherence of this entire group and can therefore stand alone. It similarly recalls the opening theme of the morning liturgy, the return of the soul to the body on waking (Extracts 1 and 21), bringing the speaker full circle and aligning awaking with victory over the forces of death and destruction. The last line is traditionally recited twice, presumably expressing reluctance to leave the biblical book behind,[131] but it may also reflect the speaker's difficulty in surrendering the complex images of redemption contained in the psalm.

The absence of the theme of vengeance from this psalm is contradicted by a midrashic writer, however, who links the very praise of God to the idea of vengeance on enemies, providing a bridge between the previous psalm and subsequent texts exploring the military option, to be examined below.[132] The theme is less prominent on sabbaths and festivals, when the statutory morning service opens with a passage echoing this last line of the book of Psalms, making it clear

[131] Jacob ben Asher, *Arba'ah turim*, 'Oraḥ ḥayim' 51; *Otsar hatefilot*, 114b, rubric.
[132] *Midrash Psalms* 150: 1.

°*Halleluyah* (Praise ye God)!—praise God for he is holy—	*Ps.* 150,$^{1-6}$
praise him in the skies of his surpassing—°Praise him for his	*Zo. Nu.* 120
mighty acts—praise him according to his vast grandeur—	*Y'Bt.* 3,^{2}
Praise him with °a fanfare of *Shofar*—praise him with lyre and	*B'RH* 32
harp—Praise him with °drum and dance-round—praise him with	*Ex.* 15,^{20}
strings and flute—°Praise him with resounding cymbals—	*Md. Gn.* 14,$^{4/5}$
praise him with alternating peals!—°Let every breath-soul	*B'Br.* 25:
praise the Deity—*halleluyah* (praise ye °God)! (*This verse is repeated.*)	*Zo. Ex.* 174

53. Psalm 150 (*Haleluyah: Halelu hel bekodsho*)

that the chorus of voices is not a coded reference to military solutions, but a song of praise by creation. This may suggest that violence is more tolerated on weekdays than on festive ones.[133]

In one respect this psalm seems to be about anything but violence, for the imperative to 'praise' God appears thirteen times, corresponding to the attributes of God's mercy, as though human enmity might be removed by kindness. Since there are also the same number of references to 'blessed' in the opening blessing of Pesukei Dezimra, this psalm, with its theme of praise, becomes a textual goal of the sequence, leading into the concluding paragraph of the sequence (Extract 59), which in turn introduces the strongest statement of blessing of the morning, with which the statutory service opens.

When it began, the sequence of psalms that ends here could have been taken as a merely formulaic tool for 'completing the praise' demanded by talmudic writers. However, its theme can now be seen to be human powerlessness in exile, which only God can resolve, whether by peaceful or by violent means. In either case the attribute of mercy will dominate, at least from the speaker's point of view, suggesting that if violence is used, it will be sufficient only to effect the rescue.

EXTRACT 54. **Concluding Psalmic Verses**

These four psalmic verses, derived mostly from the ends of the five subsections of the biblical book, are another sign of reluctance to leave the book of Psalms behind.[134] Each begins with an imperative to bless God (*barukh*), a repeated motif in the opening blessing of Pesukei Dezimra and the keyword of the call to prayer that will open the statutory service. The first and last verses end with a

[133] The passage begins *nishmat kol ḥai*, 'The soul of all that lives shall bless your name . . .'.

[134] *Pss.* 89: 53, 135: 21, 72: 18–19. They are first found in this context in Eleazar of Worms, *Sefer haroke'aḥ*, 320, p. 209. They recur in the evening liturgy.

הַלְלוּיָהּ הַלְלוּ־אֵל בְּקָדְשׁוֹ הַלְלוּהוּ בִּרְקִיעַ עֻזּוֹ׃ 1
הַלְלוּהוּ בִגְבוּרֹתָיו הַלְלוּהוּ כְּרֹב גֻּדְלוֹ׃ הַלְלוּהוּ בְּתֵקַע 2
שׁוֹפָר הַלְלוּהוּ בְּנֵבֶל וְכִנּוֹר׃ הַלְלוּהוּ בְתֹף וּמָחוֹל הַלְלוּהוּ 3
בְּמִנִּים וְעֻגָב׃ הַלְלוּהוּ בְצִלְצְלֵי־שָׁמַע הַלְלוּהוּ בְּצִלְצְלֵי 4
תְרוּעָה׃ כֹּל הַנְּשָׁמָה תְּהַלֵּל יָהּ הַלְלוּיָהּ׃ 5

double *amen*, echoing the circularity of the final group of psalms above and the repetition of the last verse of the last psalm. The word is also the formal response to formulas of blessing throughout the liturgy.

The double *amen* is additionally associated with one of the most painful legal provisions in the Pentateuch, however, for the ritual ordeal prescribed for a wife accused of unfaithfulness concludes with this repeated word, indicating her acceptance of the possibility that she may die.[135] The view that Israel is God's bride and has been exiled for her unfaithfulness is a commonplace in Jewish thought, alluded to here merely by the climactic moment of the biblical ritual for detecting guilt. But the reference suggests that the speaker's suffering might also be attributed to unfaithfulness, transforming the morning liturgy into a trial for idolatry, the punishment for which is either exile or death, though mortality is inescapable. Since the innocent are spared, the speaker's exile suggests that guilt has been proven.

These psalmic verses could equally be a study anthology, but they neither form a complete series of verses nor appear in their correct order.[136] The first verse in this group ends the third book of psalms, while the final verse of the first book does not appear at all. The verse may have been placed in this initial position because it slightly resembles the concluding verse of the first book that does not appear.[137] The second verse does not conclude a book, but may have been included since its messianic and territorial element sustains interest in the solution to suffering suggested in Psalm 149. The last two verses appear close to the end of the second book,[138] while the conclusion of the fourth book is omitted, perhaps because it resembles the last words of David's song at the arrival of the

---

[135] The double *amen* appears in the account of the ordeal in Num. 5: 22; it also appears in Neh. 8: 6, when the people renew their acceptance of Torah. Single occurrences of the word appear in Deut. 27: 15–26, 1 Kgs. 1: 36, and elsewhere. See also Mishnah *Sot.* 2: 3, 5, *Midrash Psalms* 89: 4 and 106: 9, and BT *Shev.* 29b.

[136] The books comprise, respectively, Pss. 1–41, 42–72, 73–89, 90–106, and 107–50.

[137] Ps. 41: 14. [138] The final verse is a non-poetic statement of closure, so is omitted.

BLEST IS °GOD FOREVER, *Amen* AND *Amen*; BLEST FROM ZION IS	Ps. 89,[53]
GOD, °WHO ABIDES AT JERUSALEM—*halleluyah* (PRAISE YE GOD)!	Ps. 135,[21]
°BLEST IS GOD ALMIGHTY, LORD OF ISRAEL, °WHO ALONE DOETH	Ps. 72,[18]
WONDROUS THINGS. °YEA, BLEST IS THE NAME, HIS REVERENCE,	B'Ni. 31
FOREVER, SO, LET HIS REVERENCE FILL THE WHOLE WORLD—	Ps. 72,[19]
Amen AND *Amen*.	

54. Concluding psalmic verses (*Barukh hashem le'olam*)

Ark in Jerusalem, cited earlier, and because it includes a single rather than a double *amen*, weakening the emphasis on the doubling of this word, but echoing Extract 44, lines 30–2.[139] The last verse of the fifth section of the book of Psalms appears immediately above (Extract 53, line 5), so is not repeated. Instead of ensuring that the end of each book of psalms is present, therefore, on the principle that completing a book is equivalent to reading it in its entirety, the editors seem to have included only the correct number of verses, irrespective of their source. The commentator who points out that the number of words in each line symbolizes the Barekhu, Shema, and Amidah, key parts of the statutory prayers to come, is in danger of reducing the words to counters in an abstract game of letters, ignoring the meanings that can be detected, perhaps because at least one of these is unwelcome.[140]

The emphatic and accelerated repetition of the word *barukh*, 'blessed', in these lines recalls the theme of blessing in the opening paragraph of Pesukei Dezimra and prepares for the climactic declaration at the start of statutory prayer. In addition the verses form a miniature messianic cycle, opening with God's association with Zion and his people and concluding with universal glory, again pointing towards the call to prayer to be encountered shortly, when the gathered worshippers are finally consolidated into a congregation.

They may once have concluded the Pesukei Dezimra as a whole, to judge by the medieval practice of permitting the service to be interrupted by conversation only from this point onwards, following the enforced silence since the opening blessing of the sequence.[141] However, the texts which follow it disguise its climactic position.

---

[139] See also Ps. 106: 48.
[140] Nulman, *Encyclopedia of Jewish Prayer*, 87, quoting Moses of Premysl, *Mateh mosheh*, 54, p. 58.   [141] Ibid.

בָּרוּךְ יְיָ לְעוֹלָם אָמֵן וְאָמֵן: בָּרוּךְ יְיָ מִצִיּוֹן שֹׁכֵן   1

יְרוּשָׁלַםִ הַלְלוּיָהּ: בָּרוּךְ יְיָ אֱלֹהִים אֱלֹהֵי יִשְׂרָאֵל   2

עֹשֵׂה נִפְלָאוֹת לְבַדּוֹ: וּבָרוּךְ שֵׁם כְּבוֹדוֹ לְעוֹלָם   3

וְיִמָּלֵא כְבוֹדוֹ אֶת־כָּל־הָאָרֶץ אָמֵן וְאָמֵן: 4

EXTRACT 55. David's Last Temple Prayer

Traditional commentators felt that this passage foreshadowed the vocabulary of praise in the closing blessing (Extract 59), symbolically introducing the end of the sequence rather than forming part of Pesukei Dezimra.[142] But besides generating suspense, it returns the speaker to the narrative introduced by David's prayer on bringing the Ark into Jerusalem, with which Pesukei Dezimra began in Extract 44.[143] This passage is David's last speech, consisting of his public prayer as he handed over the Temple treasures and building materials to his son, Solomon, who would complete the task he himself could not undertake.

While the opening scene of David's Temple-building, read earlier in the liturgy, seemed to introduce the virtual performance of the sacrificial service, this closing passage confirms the speaker's awareness of implication in David's misdemeanours. These are minimized in the book of Chronicles,[144] but the reasons for which David must hand over the building project are no secret. Indeed, Solomon was similarly implicated in the failure of his dynasty and the ultimate fall of the Temple, and therefore in the speaker's exile, showing how David's role in Pesukei Dezimra is to point to non-fulfilment.

The opening words of the paragraph are central to the blessing theme that has gathered pace over the previous psalmic verses. David's first statement— 'Blessed art thou, God Lord of Israel' (lines 1–2)—is one of only three scriptural instances of the word *barukh*, 'blessed be', followed by *atah*, 'you'. These words dominated the benedictions of Birkhot Hashahar, 'dawn blessings', as well as the introductory paragraph and concluding psalmic verses of Pesukei Dezimra, and set the scene for the proclamation of the blessing formula at the beginning of statutory prayer.

The narrative background to each use of the blessing formula, as has been mentioned, suggests disappointment and disillusion, however. The present

---

[142] Jacob ben Asher, *Arba'ah turim*, 'Oraḥ ḥayim' 51, and Abudarham, *Abudarham hashalem*, 63.

[143] 1 Chr. 29: 10–13. [144] 1 Chr. 28: 3; but see n. 64 above.

°Then David blessed God in the presence of the whole	*I Cr.* 29,[10–13]
congregation, and David declared—°Blest art thou, God Lord of	*Ps.* 119,[12]
Israel, our father from °everlasting unto everlasting. Thine, o	*Zo. Gn.* 34
God, is magnificence and power, also, the glory, °the final	*Zo. Ex.* 43, 117
victory and the majesty, °for all that is in heaven and on the	*Is.* 43,[7]
earth °is thine, thine is sovereignty, o God, yea, °superiority	*Ku.* 4,[4]
over every pre-eminence; Both riches and honour are from thy	*I Ki.* 1,[5]
presence, for thou °rulest over all—yea, in thy hand is power	*II Cr.* 20,[6–]
and might and in thy hand it is to °aggrandize or to give	*Js.* 3,[7]
strength unto anyone; Now therefore, our Lord, we	*Ps.* 138,[2]
acknowledge unto thee and render praise unto thy °glorious name.	*Jr.* 13,[11]

55. David's last Temple prayer (*Vayevarekh david*)

context implies David's (and the speaker's) unworthiness to inaugurate worship. The context of another phrase suggests the difficulty of obeying God's will and the need for his help in understanding Torah, a statement which accounts for the destruction of the Temple.[145] The last appearance of the phrase is linked to Samuel's discovery that Saul is not worthy to rule since he had neglected the command to kill the Amalekite king,[146] focusing on the failure of his monarchy and the replacement of his dynasty by that of David and, at the moment in which the present citation is set, of Solomon. All three sources therefore point to the failure of confidence in the human ability to approach God.

That this is not an incidental echo is made clear by the fact that other liturgical texts are derived from this speech. The opening words of the penultimate blessing of the Amidah sequence, *modim anaḥnu lakh*, 'we acknowledge unto thee', derive from this passage (line 6), while the fact that the Amidah is described midrashically as a substitute for the sacrificial order again links the speaker to the absence of the Temple. This biblical citation breaks off just before David begins his prayer for the well-being of the Temple, however, and also lacks that section's opening admission that humans are mere strangers on earth, a declaration perhaps too painfully relevant to include at this point. A later verse in the present passage glances forward to the Temple's destruction,[147] reinforcing the liturgical undercurrent of failure. Hope is sustained by David's status as eventual messianic king, and by the allusion to the promise of protection implicit in the description of God as 'our father' in line 2, but this optimistic reading is qualified by the midrashic view that Jacob, in his dream on Mount Moriah, the eventual site of the Temple, was shown its building, destruction, and ultimate reconstruction, including the tragic phases in the sacred narrative as well as the final

---

[145] Ps. 119: 12.   [146] 1 Sam. 15: 13.   [147] This is foreshadowed here by 1 Chr. 29: 15.

וַיְבָרֶךְ דָּוִיד אֶת־יְיָ לְעֵינֵי כָּל־הַקָּהָל וַיֹּאמֶר דָּוִיד בָּרוּךְ 1

אַתָּה יְיָ אֱלֹהֵי יִשְׂרָאֵל אָבִינוּ מֵעוֹלָם וְעַד־עוֹלָם: לְךָ יְיָ 2

הַגְּדֻלָּה וְהַגְּבוּרָה וְהַתִּפְאֶרֶת וְהַנֵּצַח וְהַהוֹד כִּי־כֹל בַּשָּׁמַיִם 3

וּבָאָרֶץ לְךָ יְיָ הַמַּמְלָכָה וְהַמִּתְנַשֵּׂא לְכֹל לְרֹאשׁ: וְהָעֹשֶׁר 4

וְהַכָּבוֹד מִלְּפָנֶיךָ וְאַתָּה מוֹשֵׁל בַּכֹּל וּבְיָדְךָ כֹּחַ וּגְבוּרָה 5

וּבְיָדְךָ לְגַדֵּל וּלְחַזֵּק לַכֹּל: וְעַתָּה אֱלֹהֵינוּ מוֹדִים אֲנַחְנוּ לָךְ 6

וּמְהַלְלִים לְשֵׁם תִּפְאַרְתֶּךָ: 7

salvation.[148] Yet the fact that David is praying at this moment suggests that the Temple may not be essential to intimacy with God. If everything belongs to God then the Temple is not a uniquely divine location, making homelessness essential to the human condition and exile without special significance.[149] Security lies not in locations, therefore, but in remaining close to the Torah, as though the liturgical editors wish to minimize the value of the Temple at the very moment when its physical reality seems more immediate than at any previous point in the morning.[150]

The beginning of statutory prayer therefore situates the speaker at the narrative moment at which David takes leave of the Temple he did not live to see built, thereby preparing the ground for its destruction and for the speaker's exile, all of them attributed to the failure to understand Torah. It is clear that these ideas were difficult for the liturgical editors to accept, since the passage breaks off before the principle of necessary exile is outlined in 1 Chronicles 29: 15, where it is stated that 'We are strangers before you and sojourners like all our fathers; our days on earth are like a shadow, there is no hope.' The educated speaker, however, will be able to reconstruct it. The omission must accordingly be regarded as part of the argument, enacting on a literary level the failure to remain close to Torah made inevitable by the limitations of human intellect.

The particular reverence in which this text is held, reflected in its being recited while standing, may reflect the fact that the terms used in line 3 to describe God's grandeur were included in the sefirotic tree, a symbolic representation first found in the kabbalistic *Sefer bahir*.[151] Its inclusion in the liturgy may even be related to the importance of these words.

---

[148] *Gen. Rabbah* 69: 7, on Gen. 28: 17.

[149] 1 Chr. 29: 14–16.

[150] 1 Chr. 28: 7–9.

[151] Scholem, *Origins of the Kabbalah*, 161.

°Thou indeed art God, thou alone, thou madest heaven, the	*Nh.* 9,⁶⁻¹¹
heavens of heavens, °with all their satellites, the earth and all	*Gn.* 2,¹
upon it, the seas and all that therein is, for thou °givest life	*Zo. Gn.* 37, 169
unto them all, yea, the legions of heaven °do bow before	*Ps.* 97,⁷
thee, Thou, indeed, art God the Almighty who didst °select	*Is.* 41,⁸
Abram, yea, thou didst extract him from out of °Ur of the	*Gn.* 11,²⁸
Chaldees and didst set his name °'Abraham', And thou	*Gn.* 17,⁵
didst °find his heart trustworthy before thee, yea, didst cleave	*Gn.* 15,⁶
the covenant with him °to grant unto him the land of the	*Ra. Gn.* 15,¹⁶⁻¹⁹
Canaanites, the Hittites, the Amorites and the Perizzites,	*Gn.* 15,¹⁸⁻²¹
also, the °Jebusites and the Girgashites—to give it unto his seed,	*I Cr.* 11,⁴
yea, °thou didst carry out thy promise, for thou art righteous;	*Ps.* 37,²¹
So when thou didst see the °debasement of our ancestors in	*Ex.* 2,²²
Mizrayim and didst hearken to their cry by the °*Suph* Sea, Then	*Ex.* 14,¹⁰
thou didst impose °marks and striking wonders upon Pharaoh,	*Dt.* 34,¹¹
upon all his minions and upon all the people of his country, for	*Y'So.* 5,⁶
thou didst know that they had °acted viciously against them	*Ex.* 18,¹¹
—indeed, °thou didst set for thee a name, as it is this day; Yea,	*Jr.* 32,²⁰
the sea didst thou °sunder before them, so they went °through	*Ex.* 14,²²
the midst of the sea on dry land and their pursuers thou didst	*Gn.* 1,⁹
cast into the fathoms, °like a stone into torrential waters.	*Ex.* 15,⁵

56. Announcing the second Temple (*Atah hu hashem levadekha*)

EXTRACT 56. **Announcing the Second Temple**

The scene switches rapidly, away from the building site of the first Temple towards its ruins, where exiles returning from Babylon are dedicating the second Temple.[152] This scene takes place centuries after the dedication of Solomon's Temple, when the Persian conqueror of the Babylonian empire had allowed Judaean exiles to return and rebuild their sanctuary. While this paragraph might have been designed to complement the dedication texts related to Solomon's Temple, the implications of its inclusion are more radical than might be thought at first glance.

David's voice is now absent for the first time since Pesukei Dezimra began, as the focus shifts to Temple-building. The speakers in the later period, like those of David's time, suffer delays to the building and, as is clear from the closing

---

[152] Neh. 9: 6–11.

אַתָּה הוּא יְיָ לְבַדֶּךָ אַתָּ

עָשִׂיתָ אֶת־הַשָּׁמַיִם שְׁמֵי הַשָּׁמַיִם וְכָל־צְבָאָם הָאָרֶץ וְכָל־

אֲשֶׁר עָלֶיהָ הַיַּמִּים וְכָל־אֲשֶׁר בָּהֶם וְאַתָּה מְחַיֶּה אֶת־כֻּלָּם

וּצְבָא הַשָּׁמַיִם לְךָ מִשְׁתַּחֲוִים: אַתָּה הוּא יְיָ הָאֱלֹהִים

אֲשֶׁר בָּחַרְתָּ בְּאַבְרָם וְהוֹצֵאתוֹ מֵאוּר כַּשְׂדִּים וְשַׂמְתָּ

שְׁמוֹ אַבְרָהָם: וּמָצָאתָ אֶת־לְבָבוֹ נֶאֱמָן לְפָנֶיךָ וְכָרוֹת עִמּוֹ

הַבְּרִית לָתֵת אֶת־אֶרֶץ הַכְּנַעֲנִי הַחִתִּי הָאֱמֹרִי וְהַפְּרִזִּי

וְהַיְבוּסִי וְהַגִּרְגָּשִׁי לָתֵת לְזַרְעוֹ וַתָּקֶם אֶת־דְּבָרֶיךָ כִּי צַדִּיק

אָתָּה: וַתֵּרֶא אֶת־עֳנִי אֲבֹתֵינוּ בְּמִצְרָיִם וְאֶת־זַעֲקָתָם שָׁמַעְתָּ

עַל־יַם־סוּף: וַתִּתֵּן אֹתֹת וּמֹפְתִים בְּפַרְעֹה וּבְכָל־עֲבָדָיו

וּבְכָל־עַם אַרְצוֹ כִּי יָדַעְתָּ כִּי הֵזִידוּ עֲלֵיהֶם וַתַּעַשׂ־לְךָ שֵׁם

כְּהַיּוֹם הַזֶּה: וְהַיָּם בָּקַעְתָּ לִפְנֵיהֶם וַיַּעַבְרוּ בְתוֹךְ־הַיָּם בַּיַּבָּשָׁה

וְאֶת־רֹדְפֵיהֶם הִשְׁלַכְתָּ בִמְצוֹלֹת כְּמוֹ־אֶבֶן בְּמַיִם עַזִּים:

verses of the speech from which these lines are taken, at the end of the same chapter, they fear exile, almost concealing the change of time and place. By suggesting the equivalence of the Temples and the irrelevance of the intervening years, it also loosens the chronology, potentially including the speaker in both scenes. The events could be taking place in the here and now, in which case the synagogue would represent the Temple and its worshippers the returned exiles, aligning the fall of the Temples with the present exile.

The broadening of the timescale can also be seen in the opening use of the Creation theme, echoing the introductory blessing of Pesukei Dezimra and paraphrasing an earlier liturgical statement made in the context of a challenge to God to keep his covenantal promise (Extract 33, lines 5–6). The editors of that blessing may even have had the present scriptural text in mind, since both blend creational and Temple ideas, showing how wave-like repetitions of liturgical elements reflect the development of ideas. This passage goes on to survey covenantal history (Extract 56, line 4) from Abraham to the crossing of the Red

Sea,[153] stopping short of the Temple theme perhaps because this can be assumed from the context. The liturgical version likewise omits the scriptural references to the entry into the Promised Land and to the eventual exile,[154] possibly because the exile represents the speaker's own experience. The scriptural text itself is silent on the returned exiles' attempts to restore Jerusalem in the face of enmity, as well as on the suffering that results from this failure, suggesting that these are too familiar to need describing or too painful to contemplate.

The liturgical version of this scriptural text therefore leaves the speaker at the Red Sea, waiting for it to be divided in the archetypal act of divine rescue. This scene, in terms of rabbinic thought, is located not only in the past, but in the future as a model for the messianic redemption, perhaps of the kind previewed in the 'vengeance' theme of Psalm 149 above. That idea, originally thought to have been incidental to the main liturgical argument and to have been no more than a harmonic variant, now seems to be amplified into a main melody.

The returned exiles resemble the speaker in another respect too, for this scriptural passage follows the description of how Ezra read and interpreted the Torah to the people while standing on a wooden platform, anticipating the public scriptural reading at the core of synagogue worship. That ceremony—one central to Jewish ritual and thought—in which Jews repeatedly hear, recite, and attempt to understand the Torah, can be regarded as a defining characteristic of Jewish culture. Ezra's use of Hebrew and his recitation and reapplication of Scripture make him a prototypical prayer-leader, the synagogue reader's desk being frequently referred to in rabbinic writings as the *amud*, 'pillar', the scriptural term for Ezra's platform. The importance of this particular passage in synagogue life is reflected in the number of times it is echoed in the traditional prayer-book, its structure remaining implicit in many liturgical sequences.[155]

It could have been far more integrated into the previous Davidic passage, but the liturgical editors began their extract immediately after the opening declaration of blessing addressed to God, to which the people responded with a double *amen* as in the psalmic verses above.[156] Perhaps it was feared this would repeat the Davidic theme, or pre-empt the later call to prayer,[157] but the educated reader would automatically reconstruct it, strengthening the impression that the biblical events are blurred and treated as though they were continuous. The way in which the Sephardi liturgy does include the call merely emphasizes the symmetry and the bending of the liturgical timescales.[158]

---

[153] Based on Gen. 15: 13–14. Abraham is linked to Creation by the midrashic idea that the world was made for Abraham. See Montefiore and Loewe (eds.), *Rabbinic Anthology*, 38, and *Gen. Rabbah* 12: 9.　　　　　　　　　　　　　　　　　　　　　　　　　　　　[154] Neh. 9: 12–37.

[155] Liebreich, 'Impact of Nehemiah 9: 5–37'.　　　　　　　　　　　　　　[156] Neh. 8: 1–8.

[157] The present passage, without the blessing verse, is first mentioned as an innovation in Eleazar of Worms, *Sefer haroke'aḥ*, 320, p. 209.

[158] Neh. 9: 5, which is included in the present reading in *Book of Prayer: Daily and Occasional Prayers*, 22.

The larger liturgical idea of study as a source of rescue, implicit in Ezra's Torah reading, is juxtaposed here with the notion of the Temple as a place of safety. But these themes, previously discredited, are undermined by the excisions that emphasize the problematic nature of study. The concertina-like foreshortening of time weakens the authority of scriptural narrative, leaving the speaker metaphorically on the shore of the Red Sea with the Israelites, death approaching from behind and escape barred from before.

Hope lies only in the covenant, alluded to by the special use of this passage whenever a circumcision is performed in the synagogue. Alternate phrases, from the allusion to circumcision in the reference to Abraham's covenant in Extract 56, line 7,[159] to the end of the Song of the Sea in Extract 57, line 33, are recited antiphonally by the circumciser and the *sandek* (the person appointed to hold the baby, such as the grandfather or another honoured person).[160] The midrashic report that Abraham circumcised himself suggests that the speaker may be the author of his own suffering, as though challenging God to rescue the speaker from the effects of a covenant to which the speaker is helplessly bound.[161] The idea of circumcision also aligns the speaker with Abraham's Binding of Isaac, which contains the earliest biblical reference to Moriah, regarded rabbinically as the future site of the Temple.[162]

EXTRACT 57. **The Song of the Sea**

The truncation of the previous text at the Red Sea episode apparently prompted the inclusion here of Moses' and the Israelites' song of triumph following their crossing.[163] It is possible, although less likely, that the Nehemiah passage was included in the liturgy later than the Song of the Sea, in which case the link between the Song and the psalmic context would lie in the words *neveh kodshekha*, 'thy holy habitation' (lines 23–4), assumed to allude to the Temple, and in the common assumption that the rescue at the Red Sea prefigures messianic redemption, including the Temple's restoration. It would also echo the argument in Psalm 149 that God's rescue will be violent.

It is clear that the Song reflects not only events in the Exodus but the speaker's survival in the present from the fact that Sephardim replace it on the morning of 9 Av with Moses' valedictory song from the end of the book of Deuteronomy.[164] These songs frame his career as leader and have different associations. The biblical prologue to Moses' final song suggests that it is to be reserved for times of great danger,[165] and it is indeed excluded on ordinary weekdays.

[159] See Gen. 17: 9–14.
[160] *Sidur avodat yisra'el*, 72–4.
[161] *Gen. Rabbah* 48: 2.
[162] See Rashi on Gen. 22: 1.
[163] Exod. 14: 30–15: 19, the last verse being narrative and optional.
[164] Deut. 32: 1–43; see *Sidur avodat yisra'el*, 73; Gaguine, *Keter shem tov*, v. 51–3; *Maḥzor vitry*, 265, pp. 226–7; Abraham Hayarhi of Lunel, *Sefer hamanhig*, 'Hilkhot tishah be'av', i. 297–8.
[165] Deut. 31: 19–21.

°Thus, God saved Israel on that day out of the hand of	*Ex.* 14,³⁰⁻¹
Miẓrayim and Israel saw *Miẓrayim* dead upon the sea shore;	*B'Br.* 58
Then Israel °realized the grand feat which God had	*B'Sn.* 95:
performed against *Miẓrayim*, so the people feared God, yea,	*Zo. Gn.* 52:
°they trusted in God and in Moses his servitor.	*Zo. Dt.* 285

°Then Moses and the children of Israel sang this song unto God; — *Ex.* 15,¹⁻¹⁹
they recited telling: — *Zo. Dt.* 285
I will sing unto God for he hath utterly triumphed—horse and — *B'Sn.* 91:
his rider °He hurled into the sea; °The Deity is both power and — *Dn.* 3,²¹
song unto me, yea, he is become salvation unto me—this is my — *Zo. Ex.* 55
Lord and °I will adorn him, the Lord of mine ancestor, so I will — *B'Sb.* 133:
exalt him! °God, man-of-war, 'Eternal' is his name. °Pharaoh's — *Md. Gn.* 3,¹
chariots and his army He cast into the sea, even his choice captains — *Ex.* 14,²⁸
are drowned in the *Suph* Sea, °The deeps covered them, they sank — *Ps.* 104,⁶
into the °fathoms as a stone.—Thy right, o God, is magnificent in — *Mi.* 7,¹⁹
power, thy right, God, hath demolished °the enemy! In the — *Zo. Lv.* 24
grandeur of thy supremacy thou overthrowest °the upstarts against — *Dt.* 33,¹¹
thee, °thou sendest forth thy wrath, it consumes them like stubble; — *Ps.* 18,⁹
Through a gust of thine exasperation were the waters piled up, the — *Mta. Ex.* 15
flow stood °upright as a heap, the depths were congealed in the core — *Ps.* 33,⁷
of the sea. The enemy said: 'I will pursue, I will overtake, °I will — *Jg.* 5,³⁰
divide the spoil, °my lust shall have its fill of them, I shall draw my — *Jg.* 5,²¹
sword, my hand shall °utterly destroy them.'—Thou didst exhale — *I Sm.* 2,¹
with thy breath, the sea covered them, they sank like lead in — *Ps.* 93,⁴
°torrential waters. °Who is alike to thee, God, among the powers?— — *Zo. Lv.* 94
Who is alike to thee?—magnificent in holiness, °awesome in — *Zph.* 2,¹¹
praises, performing wondrously! °Thou didst outstretch thy right, — *Is.* 31,³
the earth swallowed them; °Thou in thy loving-kindness didst — *Md. Nu.* 12,¹⁰/¹⁴
guide this People whom thou hadst redeemed, thou didst °conduct — *Ku.* 4,³
them with thy fortitude unto thy °holy habitation. Peoples heard, — *Jr.* 31,²²
they trembled, pangs seized °the inhabitants of Philistia, °Then — *Is.* 14,³¹
were the chiefs of Edom affrighted, the mighty of Moab were — *Zo. Ex.* 49,184
seized with trembling, °all the inhabitants of Canaan did melt — *Js.* 2,⁹
away; °Terror and dread fall upon them, by the grandeur of thine — *Zo. Ex.* 59:
arm they are °stilled as a stone—till thy People pass, o God, till they — *Hb.* 2,¹⁹

57. The Song of the Sea (*Vayosha* and *Shirat hayam*)

וַיּוֹשַׁע יְהוָה בַּיּוֹם הַהוּא אֶת־יִשְׂרָאֵל מִיַּד מִצְרָיִם וַיַּרְא

יִשְׂרָאֵל אֶת־מִצְרַיִם מֵת עַל־שְׂפַת הַיָּם: וַיַּרְא יִשְׂרָאֵל

אֶת־הַיָּד הַגְּדֹלָה אֲשֶׁר עָשָׂה יְהוָה בְּמִצְרַיִם וַיִּירְאוּ הָעָם

אֶת־יְהוָה וַיַּאֲמִינוּ בַּיהוָה וּבְמֹשֶׁה עַבְדּוֹ:

אָז יָשִׁיר־מֹשֶׁה וּבְנֵי יִשְׂרָאֵל אֶת־הַשִּׁירָה הַזֹּאת לַיהוָה וַיֹּאמְרוּ

לֵאמֹר   אָשִׁירָה לַיהוָה כִּי־גָאֹה גָּאָה סוּס

וְרֹכְבוֹ רָמָה בַיָּם: עָזִּי וְזִמְרָת יָהּ וַיְהִי־לִי

לִישׁוּעָה   זֶה אֵלִי וְאַנְוֵהוּ   אֱלֹהֵי

אָבִי וַאֲרֹמְמֶנְהוּ:   יְהוָה אִישׁ מִלְחָמָה יְהוָה

שְׁמוֹ:   מַרְכְּבֹת פַּרְעֹה וְחֵילוֹ יָרָה בַיָּם   וּמִבְחַר

שָׁלִשָׁיו טֻבְּעוּ בְיַם־סוּף: תְּהֹמֹת יְכַסְיֻמוּ יָרְדוּ בִמְצוֹלֹת כְּמוֹ־

אָבֶן: יְמִינְךָ יְהוָה נֶאְדָּרִי בַּכֹּחַ   יְמִינְךָ

יְהוָה תִּרְעַץ אוֹיֵב: וּבְרֹב גְּאוֹנְךָ תַּהֲרֹס

קָמֶיךָ   תְּשַׁלַּח חֲרֹנְךָ יֹאכְלֵמוֹ כַּקַּשׁ:   וּבְרוּחַ

אַפֶּיךָ נֶעֶרְמוּ מַיִם   נִצְּבוּ כְמוֹ־נֵד

נֹזְלִים   קָפְאוּ תְהֹמֹת בְּלֶב־יָם: אָמַר

אוֹיֵב אֶרְדֹּף אַשִּׂיג   אֲחַלֵּק שָׁלָל תִּמְלָאֵמוֹ

נַפְשִׁי   אָרִיק חַרְבִּי תּוֹרִישֵׁמוֹ יָדִי: נָשַׁפְתָּ

בְרוּחֲךָ כִּסָּמוֹ יָם   צָלֲלוּ כַּעוֹפֶרֶת בְּמַיִם

אַדִּירִים: מִי־כָמֹכָה בָּאֵלִם יְהוָה   מִי

כָּמֹכָה נֶאְדָּר בַּקֹּדֶשׁ   נוֹרָא תְהִלֹּת עֹשֵׂה

פֶלֶא: נָטִיתָ יְמִינְךָ תִּבְלָעֵמוֹ אָרֶץ: נָחִיתָ

בְחַסְדְּךָ עַם־זוּ גָּאָלְתָּ   נֵהַלְתָּ בְעָזְּךָ אֶל־נְוֵה

קָדְשֶׁךָ:   שָׁמְעוּ עַמִּים יִרְגָּזוּן   חִיל

אָחַז יֹשְׁבֵי פְּלָשֶׁת: אָז נִבְהֲלוּ אַלּוּפֵי

אֱדוֹם   אֵילֵי מוֹאָב יֹאחֲזֵמוֹ רָעַד   נָמֹגוּ

כֹּל יֹשְׁבֵי כְנָעַן: תִּפֹּל עֲלֵיהֶם אֵימָתָה

°pass, this People which thou hast gotten. Thou wilt bring them,	*B'So.* 36
yea, °wilt plant them upon the mount of thine inheritance, upon the	*Msh. Sn.* 10,[1]
°foundation which thou, God, °hast set for thee as thy residence,	*Y'Br.* 4,[5]
in the sanctuary, Lord, which thy hands have established—°God	*B'Br.* 33
shall reign for ever and aye—God shall reign for ever and aye!	*B'Er.* 54

°Thus, when the cavalry of Pharaoh, with his chariots and his riders,	*Ex.* 15,[10]
rushed into the sea, °then God caused the sea-waters to recoil upon	*Ex.* 18,[11]
them, while the Children of Israel walked on °dry land in the midst of	*Ps.* 95,[5]
the sea.	

57 (*cont.*)

This Song, like the previous text, is non-Davidic, but it is dissimilar in that it is associated only tangentially with the Temple. It is a latecomer to this point in the liturgy, commentators noting that talmudic sources refer to its recital only on sabbath afternoon and that Maimonides included it elsewhere in the morning liturgy.[166] Scholars have periodically emphasized its inappropriateness at this point,[167] and seek to justify its inclusion by arguing that its eighteen verses and references to God allude to the eighteen references to God in the Shema (eleven to the Tetragrammaton and seven to 'Lord') and to the original number of blessings in the Amidah.[168] Baer and the editors of the edition used here appear to regard the correspondence between the number of verses and the blessings in the Amidah as important enough to include an additional verse of the Song in small type (line 33), perhaps to indicate that it is optional, in order to bring the number of verses to nineteen, the present number of Amidah blessings.[169] Commentators have also noted the presence of ten references to the Tetragrammaton, the name associated with divine mercy. The Israelites had just escaped from slavery and survived drowning, suggesting that previous prayers might have been effective. Other commentators note that the Song supplies all the terms of praise used in the closing blessing of Pesukei Dezimra, but since this had been argued for the previous two passages as well, they may have had misgivings

---

[166] Natronai Gaon, in the mid 9th century, reported its reading as a custom, but did not recommend it. See Elbogen, *Liturgy*, 75–6; Hoffman, *Canonization of the Synagogue Service*, 130–1. BT *RH* 31*a*; Maimonides, *Mishneh Torah: The Book of Adoration*, 'On Prayer', 7: 13, fo. 106*a*.

[167] For 20th-century misgivings, see E. Munk, *World of Prayer*, i. 83.

[168] Ibid. 84–5; *Mekhilta derabi shimon bar yoḥai*, Exod. 15: 19, p. 70.

[169] See *Sidur avodat yisra'el*, 74; *Mekhilta derabi shimon bar yoḥai*, 70 n. *shin*. *Soferim* 12: 11 assumes this verse forms part of the Song.

עַד־ בְּגֹדֶל זְרוֹעֲךָ יִדְּמוּ כָּאָבֶן וָפַחַד 28

עַד־יַעֲבֹר עַמְּךָ יְיָ עַד־יַעֲבֹר עַם זוּ 29

מָכוֹן תְּבִאֵמוֹ וְתִטָּעֵמוֹ בְּהַר נַחֲלָתְךָ קָנִיתָ: 30

מִקְּדָשׁ אֲדֹנָי כּוֹנְנוּ לְשִׁבְתְּךָ פָּעַלְתָּ יְיָ 31

יְיָ יְיָ ׀ יִמְלֹךְ לְעֹלָם וָעֶד: יָדֶיךָ: 32

כִּי בָא סוּס פַּרְעֹה בְּרִכְבּוֹ וּבְפָרָשָׁיו בַּיָּם וַיָּשֶׁב יְיָ עֲלֵהֶם יִמְלֹךְ לְעֹלָם וָעֶד: 33
אֶת מֵי הַיָּם וּבְנֵי יִשְׂרָאֵל הָלְכוּ בַיַּבָּשָׁה בְּתוֹךְ הַיָּם:

about all three.[170] Such numerical and other details miss essential elements of what the Song actually says, however.

The major departure is that the Song puts the theme of warfare—a theme that was introduced apparently incidentally in Psalm 149 (Extract 52, lines 5–8)—centre stage. That psalm entered the liturgy when the last six psalms were included as a way of ensuring that 'Hallel'—interpreted as the biblical book of Psalms—was 'completed' each morning. Here, however, the military option was included for its own sake, suggesting that the liturgical editors had overcome their ambivalence about triumphalism. Unease about this option is evident from the omission of the present Song from the Haggadah recited on Passover eve, a service in which it would otherwise be expected to appear. That liturgy consequently focuses more on survival than on vengeance, a theme also clear from the abbreviation of Hallel on that festival, omitting the psalms referring to past tribulations. Midrashic texts echo this hesitation to rejoice at victory, reporting how God silenced angels who wished to join the Israelites in song by telling them that the Egyptians too were his creatures,[171] although omitting the Song on the first days of Passover can be seen as an acknowledgement that the Israelites arrived at the sea only on the seventh day of the festival, when it is indeed recited in the synagogue. Its inclusion here suggests that survival is a daily miracle, comparable to that enjoyed by the Israelites at the Red Sea. The speaker's joy is suggested by the lack of references to sin, punishment, or the conditional nature

[170] Jacob ben Asher, *Arba'ah turim*, 'Oraḥ ḥayim' 51; Abudarham, *Abudarham hashalem*, 63.

[171] BT *Meg.* 10b and BT *San.* 39b quote God referring to the Egyptians as 'the work of my hands'; but it is clear from *Exod. Rabbah* 23: 7 and *Midrash tanḥuma* (Buber), 'Beshalaḥ' 13, that in an alternative (and, according to Raphael Loewe (pers. comm.), earlier) tradition the danger to the Israelites was the reason the angels were silenced and that concern for the Egyptians was not being shown.

of rescue, and by the exclusive use of the Tetragrammaton, associated with God's
mercy, to refer to the Deity. Triumphalism at the crossing of the Red Sea is
midrashically qualified by the remark that the Israelites were saved only because
they were prepared to step into the sea even before it had begun to be divided;
this implies that the speaker should now show similar fearlessness in the face of
danger.[172] The association between fearlessness and martyrdom may have helped
inspire the links between the Song and circumcision noted earlier. Ambivalence
about triumphalism inspired the decision to transliterate the term usually translated 'Egypt' as *mitsrayim*, in Extract 56, line 9 above and in lines 2–3 here,
thereby avoiding associations between the Exodus and contemporary Egypt. The
decision to transliterate *suf* in the same line of the translation and in line 11,
rather than to translate it as 'Red [or better 'Reed'] Sea', reflects the uncertainty
of the identification.

The problematic nature of everyday life is acknowledged in the Song's prose
prologue (lines 3–4) by the reference to the Israelites' 'fear' of God, a term
implying not only love and awe, but 'aversion'. This idea (never expressed as
such in rabbinic thought) might arise from the realization that the Israelite slavery was predicted to Abraham as part of the covenantal agreement, a notion
related to the Akedah discussed earlier. Rabbinic commentators are unlikely to
have expressed fear of God's strength (line 9) against the nations in the Promised
Land (lines 24–7), suggesting that there are ominous undertones to what is said
here. The reference to the earth swallowing the Egyptians (line 22) anticipates
the spies' negative reports of the Promised Land as one 'which eats up its inhabitants', and also alludes to the later death in the wilderness of the adult Israelites
who believed this report.[173] The Israelites indeed first broke their side of the
covenant just after crossing the Red Sea, thereby justifying their exile even
before they had entered the Land. The speaker, already aware of the reasons for
Jewish suffering in the times of David and Nehemiah, here glances at the tragic
episodes that preceded and accompanied the building of the Tabernacle. This
shrine, as well as the first and second Temples which succeeded it, is thus linked
to the synagogue in which the liturgical speaker reflects on the sources of suffering in the present.

The theological conflict about God's kindness also emerges in the reference in
the prose introduction to Moses as *eved*, meaning both 'servant' and 'slave'.
Neither Moses nor the speaker is a free agent, this suggests, although freedom in
the liturgy is generally understood as arising out of the service of God, and happiness is visualized in the form of the Temple 'service', or sacrificial cult. The
route towards the Temple's completion, glanced at in lines 30–1, is thus strewn
with suffering, undermining the positive associations of 'service'.

The speaker is now located simultaneously at several stages in the sacred
narrative, both before the Temple was built and after its destruction. Its building

---

[172] *Exod. Rabbah* 21: 10.   [173] Num. 13: 32.

is described here in the perfect tense, either implying certainty that it will take place[174] or that it is already in existence, an ambiguity that places the speaker both in the 'miniature sanctuary' of the synagogue and in a Temple recreated, if only virtually, by liturgical representations of its building and rituals. Rabbinic commentators similarly remarked on the ambiguity of the opening imperfect verb of the first line, *az yashir mosheh*, 'then Moses [and the children of Israel] sang' (line 5), possibly referring in a quasi-future tense to a song to be sung at the coming of the messiah. They regarded the reference to the Temple at the end of the Song as pointing to messianic times when God would truly 'reign for ever and aye' (line 32).[175] But the use of the imperfect tense in these closing words also suggested that the people lacked faith in God's power, as a result of which they were unworthy to enjoy his direct rule immediately after crossing the Red Sea. Had they used the perfect tense implying completion in line 32, a midrashic text asserts, 'no nation would have had power over them'.[176] The daily repetition of the Song thus serves as much to explain the continuation of exile as to provide a means for terminating it, its inclusion here even implicating the liturgy in the continuation of suffering. A parallel association emerges from a midrashic re-reading of the words *mi khamokhah ba'elim*, 'Who is like thee, God, among the powers?' (line 20). In this, *elim*, 'powers', is revocalized as *ilemim*, 'mutes', because the slavery and pursuit to the Red Sea suggested God's inaction.[177] This reading is supported by the next words in the Song, 'magnificent in holiness', in which 'holiness' might be read as 'different' or 'remote'.[178]

By the end of the Song, therefore, the speaker has more grounds to doubt the possibility of achieving happiness through regaining the Temple than at the conclusion of the previous liturgical sequence, Birkhot Hashahar (Extracts 40 and 42). Each of the promises offered by the Song implicitly ends in exile.

EXTRACT 58. The Conclusion of Pesukei Dezimra

These concluding four scriptural verses of Pesukei Dezimra offer a range of views on the coming of the messiah,[179] and echo the problematic use of tense in the preceding Song. The first three verses contain the word 'king', recalling the

[174] Gesenius, *Hebrew Grammar*, 312–13, para. *n*.

[175] Rashi on Exod. 15: 1, and BT *San.* 91*b*; Rashi on Exod. 15: 17.

[176] *Mekhilta derabi shimon bar yohai*, Exod. 15: 18, p. 70. The Israelites may have preferred the free will of humanity rather than to be promoted to the status of angels, implies Schwab in *Rav Schwab on Prayer*, 243–5, without exploring the idea further.

[177] BT *Git.* 56*b*; *Lekah tov*, i, Exod. 48*b*.

[178] Rashi on Lev. 19: 2. See Schwab, *Rav Schwab on Prayer*, 239–40, whose traditional response resembles that outlined here. Suffering, not necessarily attributed to punishment, must be borne in good spirit according to Caro, *Shulhan arukh*, 'Orah hayim' 222: 3, since it might be related to the hiding of God's face and the ideas around *androlemusiyah*.

[179] Ps. 22: 29; Obad. 1: 21; Zech. 14: 9; Deut. 6: 4.

°Indeed, sovereignty is God's—yea, all rulership among the	*Ps.* 22,²⁹
nations! °Then shall champions ascend Mount Zion to judge the	*Ob.* 1,²¹
Mount of Esau, and sovereignty shall be confirmed unto God. °Yea,	*Ze.* 14,⁹
God shall be sovereign over all the world—°in that day shall God	*Zo. Lv.* 7:
be oneness and his name oneness. As in thy *Torah* it is writ	*OT bic*
declaring: Hearken, o Israel!—God our Lord, God is oneness!	*Dt.* 6,⁴

58. The conclusion of Pesukei Dezimra (*Ki lashem hamelukhah*)

incomplete kingship in the last line of the Song and the divine attribute of severity that dominates the exile, thereby contrasting with the Tetragrammaton used
in the Song. The first verse is drawn from a scriptural description of the relief of
suffering, the second from an account of victory over Edom, the Israelites' traditional enemy and later a sobriquet both for Rome and for the Church, and the
third from a messianic vision of the resolution of conflict. The eventual 'unifying
of God's name' in this third verse (line 3), the classic prophecy of messianic rule,
is expressed in the same imperfect tense as the incriminating statement in lines
32–3 above. One talmudic rabbi reads it as a prediction that humans will then be
permitted to pronounce the Tetragrammaton as it is written, thereby perhaps
ensuring the dominance of mercy implied in the first line of the Shema (see the
discussion of Extract 31, line 1), which challenges the speaker to establish the
unity of the divine attributes.[180]

In this Ashkenazi rite these three verses are joined by a fourth, the opening
line of the Shema itself (line 4), which is sometimes regarded as having been
included to complete an anthology of citations from the Pentateuch, Prophets,
and Writings—the major subdivisions of the Bible—as in the study sequences
seen earlier.[181] Similar arrangements are found in the 'kingships' and other
verses in the Additional Service on Rosh Hashanah.[182] Here, however, it can be
seen to confirm the previous prophecy, although such a juxtaposition also
demonstrates the virtual impossibility of accurate study, since each line is
removed from its context and acquires new meanings through proximity to other
texts. One consequence of the juxtaposition is to show how the Shema, which
asserts God's unity in the timeless present as distinct from the imperfect tense of
the Song and of the previous verse, acknowledges that God's rule is indeed realized in the present. The speaker's survival may be the only evidence of this,
exemplifying how the problems of the day ahead are resolved by redefining the
timescale of redemption and unifying future hopes with present experience. The

[180] BT *Pes.* 50a.
[181] For Baer's more tentative inclusion see *Sidur avodat yisra'el*, 74. For its exclusion, see *Book of Prayer: Daily and Occasional Prayers*, 25.   [182] See *Service of the Synagogue: New Year*, 135–6.

כִּי לַיָי הַמְּלוּכָה וּמֹשֵׁל בַּגּוֹיִם: וְעָלוּ מוֹשִׁעִים בְּהַר צִיּוֹן 1

לִשְׁפֹּט אֶת־הַר עֵשָׂו וְהָיְתָה לַיָי הַמְּלוּכָה: וְהָיָה יְיָ לְמֶלֶךְ 2

עַל־כָּל־הָאָרֶץ בַּיּוֹם הַהוּא יִהְיֶה יְיָ אֶחָד וּשְׁמוֹ אֶחָד: 3

וּבְתוֹרָתְךָ כָּתוּב לֵאמֹר שְׁמַע יִשְׂרָאֵל יְיָ אֱלֹהֵינוּ יְיָ אֶחָד: 4

absence of the Temple and of the messiah, represented by the Song and through-out Pesukei Dezimra, can be resolved in the medium of citation, but the liturgy can only comment on the world, not change it.

EXTRACT 59. The Closing Blessing of Pesukei Dezimra

This closing blessing of Pesukei Dezimra, the counterpart to the introductory paragraph in Extract 43, does not need to begin with a blessing formula since it is a sequel to the opening one, making the entire sequence into a single pro-longed statement that needs only to begin and end with the formula. The symmetry of this arrangement is emphasized by the ending of the first paragraph with a form of the root *sh-v-ḥ*, 'praise', with which the present one begins.

At first sight this text seems to revert to the mode of praise encountered in the verses after the book of Psalms (Extract 54), which is where earlier forms of Pesukei Dezimra ended. It now appears anticlimactic, however, since it contains no overt references to the Temple, Exodus, Red Sea, or messianic promise implicit in the intervening Song of the Sea or its brief appendix. In addition it differs from the opening blessing of Pesukei Dezimra by merely stating that praise is appropriate, rather than actually expressing it. This could reflect that the rescue promised in Extract 43, lines 5–6, has been realized by the time the speaker reaches Extract 59, lines 5–6, so no longer needs to be requested, or that the issues raised earlier are still unresolved and must be avoided, perhaps by turning to the here and now of survival.

The logical dissonance between this and the previous texts is also reflected in the fact that the prayer-leader of Pesukei Dezimra now gives way to another for the statutory service, entailing a change of voice.[183] The practice of changing reader at the end of Pesukei Dezimra, presumably derived from a desire to share the leading of prayers among those present, may have been introduced at this

---

[183] David ben Shmuel Halevi, *Magen david*, on *Shulḥan arukh*, 'Oraḥ ḥayim' 53: 1. See Elbogen, *Jewish Liturgy*, 76, 406 n. 13.

°Praised be thy name, o our king, for ever, the almighty,	*Ps.*106,[47]
the sovereign, °grand and holy, in °heaven and on earth!—	*Jr.*10,[6]
indeed, unto thee, o God our Lord and Lord of our	*Gn.*14,[19]
ancestors, is befitting:—°song and praise, laud and	*Jr.*10,[7-16]
hymn, °permanence and dominion, triumph, grandeur, might,	*Ex.*15,[2]
psalmody and glory, holiness and sovereignty, °blessings	*I Cr.*16,[36]
and acknowledgements—henceforth and for evermore—	*Zo.Ex.*135
blest art thou God, almighty sovereign, °grand in praises,	*Dn.*12,[7]
Lord of °acknowledgements, master of marvels, who elects	*Msh.Br.*7,[3]
psalm-songs, sovereign, Lord, °the life of the worlds!	*Dn.*12,[7]

59. The closing blessing of Pesukei Dezimra (*Yishtabaḥ*)

point rather than at the end of Pesukei Dezimra proper, after the present blessing, in order to minimize the separation between this closing blessing and the beginning of the statutory morning service which follows it. An ideal of continuity between the liturgical sequences is in this way subordinated to the demand for discontinuity dictated by the need to involve more than one reader.

The change has a wider impact on the meaning,[184] suggesting the abandonment of the themes of the texts which precede this paragraph, as though the narrative has run out of steam. However, there is considerable continuity of subject matter. Commentators have identified oblique allusions to the Temple in the fifteen synonyms for praise in lines 3–5[185] and the same number of words in the closing blessing (lines 6–8), which were taken to refer to the fifteen steps leading from the Court of the Women to the Court of the Israelites. The first was an area to which all had access, while the second was for men only, enabling them to watch the rituals of the priests and Levites within. This suggests a counterflow to the liturgical movement away from the Temple and from the hope that it can be recreated, and implies the speaker's increasing proximity to the Temple service. The association of the fifteen stairs with the same number of psalmic 'songs of degrees', each chapter of which was said to be sung while the Levites stood on a different step, has similar associations, as does the fact that the Temple-based

---

[184] *My People's Prayer Book*, iii. 181–2, mentions medieval authorities that cite the JT as forbidding talk at this stage of the liturgy. This citation has not been located in the JT. Hoffman quotes 'a midrash' (source unspecified) that reinforces this prohibition on speech between the end of Pesukei Dezimra and the blessings of the Shema.   [185] Derived, it was argued, from Extracts 55–7.

יִשְׁתַּבַּח שִׁמְךָ לָעַד מַלְכֵּנוּ הָאֵל הַמֶּלֶךְ הַגָּדוֹל 1

וְהַקָּדוֹשׁ בַּשָּׁמַיִם וּבָאָרֶץ · כִּי לְךָ נָאֶה יְיָ אֱלֹהֵינוּ 2

וֵאלֹהֵי אֲבוֹתֵינוּ שִׁיר וּשְׁבָחָה הַלֵּל וְזִמְרָה עֹז 3

וּמֶמְשָׁלָה נֶצַח גְּדֻלָּה וּגְבוּרָה תְּהִלָּה וְתִפְאֶרֶת 4

קְדֻשָּׁה וּמַלְכוּת בְּרָכוֹת וְהוֹדָאוֹת מֵעַתָּה וְעַד־ 5

עוֹלָם: בָּרוּךְ אַתָּה יְיָ, אֵל מֶלֶךְ, גָּדוֹל בַּתִּשְׁבָּחוֹת, 6

אֵל הַהוֹדָאוֹת, אֲדוֹן הַנִּפְלָאוֹת, הַבּוֹחֵר בְּשִׁירֵי 7

זִמְרָה, מֶלֶךְ, אֵל, חֵי הָעוֹלָמִים: צדיק 8

priestly blessing also has fifteen words.[186] It is also the numerical value of the last syllable of *haleluyah*, related to the divine name associated with mercy and to the fact that Pesukei Dezimra is talmudically termed 'Hallel'.[187] The idea that Pesukei Dezimra consists of fifteen separate texts is not reflected in the present version.

Other examples of number symbolism in this paragraph include the five appearances of the word 'king' (*malkenu* and *malkhut* appear once each, and *melekh* three times), suggesting the difficulty of activating the divine attribute of mercy, and the five terms describing God in lines 1–2 (*malkenu ha'el hamelekh hagadol vehakadosh*), which pointedly omit the Tetragrammaton. The name of God referring to the attribute of judgement appears three times in the 'seal', however, outnumbering the Tetragrammaton in the blessing formula and returning the reader to the painful problems evoked by the double *amen* of Extract 54, lines 1 and 4.

These associations with the Temple nevertheless renew the link with the cult and therefore proximity to God, even though the liturgical goal of bringing the messiah has not succeeded. The paragraph accordingly reconstructs the Temple not by verbal performance, but by enacting elements of its symbolism in a literary mode. The recurring number fifteen represents rituals and their setting without describing them, as though the speaker is taking leave of the real Temple and

---

[186] Num. 6: 24–6; Mishnah *Mid.* 2: 5. Pss. 120–34, the 'songs of degrees', are recited in the Ashkenazi rite on sabbath afternoons between Shabat Bereshit and two weeks before Passover; Abudarham, *Abudarham hashalem*, 64–5; *Sidur avodat yisra'el*, 75.   [187] BT *Shab.* 118*b*.

internalizing it. Words have failed to affect reality but can generate a virtual reality in which the speaker enacts the benefits of survival.

The Temple thus lies in the future, or in a dimension of potentiality generated by the liturgical performance, represented here by the eclipsing of David, who was named in the opening blessing of the sequence (Extract 43, line 9) but has now vanished. Instead the language embodies his son Solomon, whose name is spelled out by the initial letters of the second to the fifth words in the first line of this passage, and is followed by the word 'the king'.[188] This title and the fact that the text is too early to bear an author's acrostic make it highly probable that it refers to David's son.[189] If David's absence from lines 7–8 derives from his failure to build the Temple, then the hidden nature of Solomon's name might recall the ultimate failure of his dynasty. Since his success in building the Temple is the speaker's only hope at this moment, it could have been thought improper to examine his career too closely.

The way in which Pesukei Dezimra took leave of Davidic material and turned instead to the books of Nehemiah and Exodus could similarly point to an awareness of David's and Solomon's flaws. But David is never wholly discredited, despite rabbinic misgivings about him. One talmudic text regards King Hezekiah, his descendant, as more virtuous and more suited to play a messianic role than he, but prefers David because of his songs.[190] Hezekiah's prayer before facing Sennacherib was cited once (Extract 33, line 4), but did not reappear, much as David himself has vanished from this paragraph.

The Temple's rebuilding, to which the entire liturgical project has been symbolically compared, is now apparently deferred, leaving the speaker in a synagogue which resembles Solomon's Temple most in its vulnerability. The loss of the immediate hope of the Temple's reconstruction is symbolized by a change of genre and subject matter, leaving a gap which, as at previous moments of transition, is filled by Kaddish.

EXTRACT 41. **Kaddish: The Half-Kaddish (lines 1–8)**

This Kaddish, the third of the morning, is indicated as before by a rubric and marks the end of Pesukei Dezimra, the last liturgical sequence examined in this book. It is known as a half-Kaddish, and consists of only the first two paragraphs, as though withholding the sense of an ending implicit in the rabbinical and mourners' versions of the text discussed above. It is employed to call worshippers to order, or to conclude one sequence and introduce another, both of which are the case here. But the very repetition suggests that the previous recitals were ineffective, not surprisingly in view of the declaration of the inefficacy of lan-

---

[188] Abudarham, *Abudarham hashalem*, 64; *Sidur avodat yisra'el*, 75.

[189] It appears early, in Amram Gaon, *Seder rav amram hashalem*, i. 178. But see Elbogen, *Jewish Liturgy*, 76.   [190] BT *San.* 94a.

guage with which the second paragraph ends. The synagogue therefore looks more than ever like the ruins of Jerusalem, and less like even a virtual Temple.

This concluding paragraph of the preliminary sequences of the morning liturgy, marking the end of this analysis, therefore leaves the speaker in exile, uncertain how to survive the declaration that words cannot adequately praise God. However, since previous paradoxes of this nature have been survived, the liturgical project is unlikely to have deteriorated into silence. Indeed, this conclusion introduces the climactic call to 'bless' God, overcoming the limitations of language and enabling the speaker to re-examine the grounds for pessimism and to note that the exiled individual's hope of survival lies precisely in survival itself.

PART III

CHAPTER ELEVEN

☙

The Liturgical Argument Encapsulated

Summarizing the Analysis of Birkhot Hashaḥar and Pesukei Dezimra

This analysis of Birkhot Hashaḥar and Pesukei Dezimra, the opening elements of the morning liturgy, has taken into account not only the words on the page but also their subtexts. Each educated worshipper's experience of the prayer-book is coloured, if only unconsciously, by an awareness of the original contexts of those scriptural and rabbinic citations out of which the liturgy is largely constructed. However extraneous these original contexts might seem, they provide a counter-text to the words on the page, and this is as much part of the liturgy as the superficial meaning.[1] The sources of embedded texts have for the most part been identified by commentators and are well documented, but their effect on the liturgy has never been systematically examined before.

Interpreting the effect of such embedded citations, allusions, and echoes is far from straightforward, however, since they are drawn from diverse genres and periods and interact not only with the surface meaning but with each other, demanding multidirectional decoding: vertical reading, which relates each citation to the surface meaning, and horizontal reading, which attempts to assess its impact on adjacent citations, at all their levels. The fact that the surface and subtextual meanings are often at odds with one another makes these composite texts especially difficult to summarize. In the opening passages of the liturgy, for instance, the surface meaning appears to blend petition, thanks, and study in a conventionally devotional way, while the multi-layered subtext analyses the problematic nature of divine promises to humans.

The resulting liturgical document can be understood as a whole only by assessing the status of each element in an intricate and often contradictory network of text and subtext. Wherever the speaker is unable to bridge the dissonances and extrapolate a meaning, however, it is necessary to accept not only that the composite text is ambivalent and fluid and that its meaning must constantly

---

[1] An obvious example of such an association is the linking of the Shema with the martyrdom of Rabbi Akiba, e.g. *Sifrei*, Deut., 'Va'etḥanan' 31–2, pp. 72*a*–73*b*; BT *Ber.* 61*b*; JT *Ber.* 9: 5.

be renegotiated, but that literary ambivalence may reflect the nature of the emotional experience being described. This is particularly the case in elegiac hymns related to 9 Av, in which, although the speaker occasionally feels that confusion is clearing and meaning is about to emerge, glimpses of coherence frequently lead to disappointment and to the need for still more revision. It is frustrating to be deprived of clear narrative direction, as the reader will have noted in the liturgical sequence examined here, but imposing a resolution would betray the complexity of the argument. The present analysis thus reflects the multivocal nature of the liturgy and illuminates the sometimes paradoxical directions in which it leads the speaker.

Clearly, since this analysis relates to only a small section of the daily morning service—approximately the first third—it might be argued that its conclusions are partial and apply neither to the entire morning service nor to the rest of the annual round and life-cycle. Why, after all, should so wide-ranging a text reveal a coherent point of view in its initial moments? As the introduction to this book suggests, however, the sample examined here shows a remarkable consistency in its exploration of the encounter between daily life and cultural and theological responses to reality, describing the uncertain feelings of an individual facing the day ahead. It weaves a sense of the imponderable and unexpected into its very texture.

Below I attempt to outline the argument of the liturgy as it has emerged in the course of this book. My analysis distinguishes two levels of meaning, the first broadly 'narrative', involving the physical and imaginative location of the speaker, and the second 'ideological', addressing the theological concepts deployed by the speaker. The liturgical text moves freely between these levels of discourse, showing how the speaker negotiates a path between the here and now of daily life and the 'there and then' of theological time and place.

Birkhot Hashahar

The Waking Moments

The first sequence of the liturgy, Birkhot Hashahar, begins when the speaker wakes and reopens the relationship with God that was abandoned during sleep. The opening words are discussed in Chapter 4. In the real world the speaker is in bed, but the imagined location shifts between Daniel emerging from the lions' den and the ruins of Jerusalem, seen through the eyes of the author of the book of Lamentations. In these narrative settings the body reflects on the return of the soul after its night spent elsewhere, playing out a reunification of entities analogous to creation itself. The use of Daniel or the voice of the Lamenter as a vehicle to compare waking to surviving death shows how liturgical editors intuitively interpret reality with the help of imaginary settings, generating multi-layered symbolic sequences. Implicit in this reading is the association of the waking world with the ruins of Jerusalem, suggesting that regaining consciousness is to be equated not with salvation, but with exile. Full redemption, in the form of the ultimate rebuilding of Jerusalem, must await the messianic age, in which suffering will have no place.

It is also left uncertain whether the speaker should gratefully thank God for having woken, or whether God is contractually bound to return the speaker's soul after the night and so has merely honoured his obligations. The question of contractual obligation also colours the discussion of the covenantal promise to redeem the Jews, which dominates the later sections of the liturgy.

The opening statement of the day therefore introduces several ideas that will be explored elsewhere in the morning.[2] These are reflected in the shifting settings of prayer (home and synagogue in reality, but Babylon or Jerusalem in the imagination) and in the fluctuating reliance on the precision of language (if scriptural language is so hard to pin down, how can one obey what it says?). The allusion to the Temple suggests that intimacy with God is possible only in that place of worship specifically requested by God, and not at home or in synagogue. The speaker will later dream of the Temple's reconstruction, generating the virtual reality of its presence through descriptions of the sacrificial service, and transforming the home and subsequently the synagogue into 'non-Temple' locations, symbolizing homelessness and insecurity. The liturgy paradoxically offers language as the sole means of communication, although it can express only its own inefficacy at best.

The speaker's association with Daniel, sentenced to die in a lions' den because he had insisted on praying to God, additionally suggests that prayer itself offers an opportunity for martyrdom. But since the absence of the Temple is itself a cause of God's remoteness and a reason for the delaying of redemption, the opening statement introduces ambivalence about the source of suffering that is to be found throughout the liturgy.

The Ritual Garments

The texts associated with *talit* and *tefilin* (discussed in Chapter 5) were intended to form the climax to daily dressing at home, but in the Schonfeld edition are inserted before the liturgy for dressing is recited in synagogue, close to the beginning of private worship. The reasons for this displacement are practical, but the separation of actual dressing from its symbolic completion, like the distinction between real and symbolic locations noted in the first chapter, emphasizes that in this case dressing is an act of 'putting on' culture. The speaker will continue to reconstruct the order of the liturgy, at least imaginatively, until dressing is completed, and the point at which these texts should be inserted is reached.

[2] These themes are outlined in Ch. 4 above, their introductory status being discussed in the last two paragraphs on p. 80.

It can be argued that the ritual garments represent the opacity of revelation and the difficulty of gaining access to its meaning, since the scriptural commands on which they are based could arguably have been read metaphorically rather than literally. So acute is the speaker's anxiety about realizing the words of Torah that they are represented concretely, in order to strengthen the likelihood that God will keep his covenantal promise to save his people.

While the *talit* emerges as a protective cloak, reversing the nakedness of Eden and representing the ingathering of the exiles, *tefilin* 'bind' the Torah to the speaker in the hope of reversing the exile caused by deserting the sacred text. Both garments enact the speaker's anxiety about misinterpreting Torah, but while the *talit* points to the end of exile, *tefilin* symbolize its inevitability. This is because the scrolls within the *tefilin* allude to Israel's status as God's 'firstborn', a dangerous relationship in view of the smiting of the Egyptian firstborn. The midrashic notion that God wears *tefilin* containing texts which praise Israel represents the hope that he will be 'bound' to his promise to redeem the speaker.

This multi-layered representation of the simultaneous closeness and remoteness of God echoes the shift from intimacy, implied by the opening second-person address in each blessing, to the estrangement conveyed by its third-person continuation. The movement from intimacy to estrangement and back again symbolically corresponds to the withholding of redemption and the eventual coming of the messianic age. Other texts relating to the ritual garments allude to biblical descriptions (echoed by midrashic ones) of God's relationship with Israel as marriage, divorce, and eventual reconciliation.

The Passage from Home to Synagogue

The speaker's departure from home (discussed in Chapter 6) symbolically re-enacts the exile, since the synagogue, instituted at some point following the fall of the first Temple, represents the difficulty of communicating with God. In narrative terms the speaker reverts to the moments before putting on the ritual garments, whose texts originally formed the climax of the next sequence.

The texts designed to accompany hand-washing and bodily functions are here dissociated from their physical setting and instead introduce the study of Torah, the only route to God in the absence of the Temple. The synagogue thereby becomes a place of learning, although these liturgical citations could be defined either as prayer or as study, blurring the boundaries between them. Even study is undermined by editorial departures from the sources, however, pointing again to the opacity of Torah. Exile, which results from the neglect of study, becomes inevitable.

The Dawn Blessings

The speaker now returns to real time, since the blessings over dressing (discussed in Chapter 7) culminated in those over the ritual garments, which have already been put on. But although the speaker is back at home, at least in terms of the imagination, this sequence in reality takes place in synagogue. The texts again double as prayer and study, but their prayerfulness is reduced by their removal from home, while their status as study-texts is undermined by departures from the sources. The fact that they seem to form a new opening to the day either discounts previous beginnings or confirms that the liturgy consists entirely of study, without necessary links to the present.

The idea implied here, that everyday dangers derive from God, including those which arise from putting God to the test (Extract 25, line 3), is perhaps impossible to express openly in a rabbinic context and is theologically so unsettling that the liturgy enacts an intellectual flight, moving abruptly into what appears to be a different genre.

Texts on the Human Condition

In the texts discussed in Chapter 8 the speaker is poised between home, where, at least in the imagination, dressing has been completed, and synagogue, where the liturgy is being recited. The dangers of the day seem to be traced to God, while study, the only route of escape, is subverted by departures from the sources and by the incompatibility of surface and subtextual meanings. Although the words on the page denigrate humans for their sinfulness and suggest that suffering is punitive, the subtext presents daily challenges as divine trials or opportunities for martyrdom. Yet God's glory would be best served, it is argued, if he were to keep his side of the covenant and save his people. Indeed, if human imperfections are God's work, the failure to keep the covenant cannot be entirely their fault.

The first line of the Shema addresses the delicate balance between the remote or punitive aspects of God and the protective ones. This text challenges the speaker to resolve the distinction and to accept the unity of experience, good or bad, but also encourages the subordination of God's judgemental attributes to those of his mercy and the rescue of the speaker, however unworthy. The sequence closes with a prophetic redemptive promise, as though challenging God to fulfil his side of the bargain.

The Temple Imagined

The citation at the end of the previous sequence apparently leads the speaker to imagine the Temple rebuilt, since the beginning of the sacrificial day is now described in detail in texts discussed in Chapter 9, paradoxically employing words to override the previously recognized inefficacy of language. Interpolations underline the transcendent inexhaustibility of Torah, while more study-texts about the Temple culminate in an enumeration of the exegetical tools for understanding Torah, implying again that words do not correspond to reality.

Two versions of Kaddish, essentially a doxology after concluding study, end this first sequence of the morning (Birkhot Hashaḥar), each discounting the power of language to achieve closeness to God. Their silence about daily dangers suggests that the speaker's survival may be the equivalent of rescue, as the first Kaddish is followed by a psalm originally used in the Temple, renewing the idea that Jerusalem may be in virtual existence and transforming the speaker's synagogue into the Temple's successor. The second Kaddish both subverts and reconfirms the previous one, leaving the speaker simultaneously in the Temple and in exile.

Pesukei Dezimra

A semi-public sequence, Pesukei Dezimra (discussed in Chapter 10), follows Birkhot Hashahar, and will introduce in turn the statutory morning liturgy, which lies outside the scope of this book.

At this point the speaker is located in reality in the synagogue, but imaginarily in the period before the building of the first Temple. The introductory passage, which opens the day once again as though each previous effort had failed, is followed by David's prayer celebrating the bringing of the Ark to Jerusalem. The fact that he was judged unworthy to build the Temple similarly disqualifies the speaker.

The last six chapters of the book of Psalms symbolically 'complete' David's Temple-building work, but incidentally also introduce the use of force as a possible solution to the problem of suffering. A text relating to the second Temple introduces the Israelites' song of celebration after crossing the Red Sea, a model of the speaker's own salvation. However, other citations renew awareness of the opacity of Torah, culminating in another recital of the first line of the Shema, the exemplar of obscurity.

The closing blessing of this sequence introduces an abbreviated Kaddish that returns the speaker to the reality of the synagogue and to the awareness that the imagined Temple and the possibility of redemption have evaporated. The synagogue, commonly referred to as a *mikdash me'at*, 'miniature sanctuary', may thus simultaneously represent a place of 'miniature redemption' and its absence.

ॐ

This abbreviated survey omits most of the shifts of perspective and of voice that give the liturgy its dizzying power and eloquence, but at least indicates the general direction of its argument. Presented conceptually, rather than in terms of liturgical development, it could be described roughly as follows. The primary tool for obtaining God's redemption is study of Torah, the divine plan for the making and running of the world, yet an intimate knowledge of Torah is almost unattainable because of the limitations of human perception. Knowledge of God and of the world, and therefore safety, are thus elusive. The original and presumably superior means of securing intimacy with God is the Temple ritual, the unique form of worship requested by him, which can now be recreated only imaginarily by means of verbal description. The study of biblical descriptions of the cult, however, is compromised by the same opacity that undermined previous attempts to study. The synagogue, as a place of words rather than of ritual, shares the same drawbacks of the verbal medium.

The exile resulting from this lack of intimacy with God is symbolically enacted daily by the speaker's departure from home and by the inability to overcome the 'silence' of the liturgical medium and the opacity of Torah. The synagogue is therefore both a symbol of exile and of the impossibility of surviving it without divine help. The speaker's only hope lies in the eventual triumph of God's attribute of mercy over that of justice, a state of perfection which is represented by imagining the Temple as already in existence. In the process the speaker adopts the role of the Temple-builder David, but in so doing also accepts his unruly emotional life and violence, both of which prevented him from completing the project he took on himself. Messianic salvation consequently seems as far off as ever.

Underlying this development of ideas is the unexpressed fear that the world is a place of disorder and indirection to which God seems either inattentive or antagonistic, even though the speaker's place seems to be defined by the sense of order implied by God's covenant with Israel. The liturgy sustains both points of view, presenting the ambivalence of the human condition with a unique vividness.

Liturgical editors and authors did not use conceptual language of the kind employed here and might have eschewed it had it been available, since the impressionistic tools they had at their disposal enabled them to achieve far more complex literary effects. With their help they could shift the argument sideways and back again, allowing it to advance and retreat in ways that resemble the ebb and flow of daily experience. This summary is thus misleading in that it makes over-explicit ideas that must remain multivalent if the subtle balance between faith and philosophy is to be maintained. Simple faith assumes that prayer has the power to reach God, while philosophy concludes that the liturgy is merely a monologue aspiring to dialogic status. Combining these views will enable the speaker to communicate an aspect of truth that is otherwise unreachable. The fear that individual prayers do not reach God is indeed part of even a believer's reading of the prayer-book, as can be seen from the liturgical focus on the absence of the Temple, the sole location in which it is believed that real communication can take place. The speaker with access only to the synagogue, the Temple's pale shadow, struggles to refine liturgical routes to God and to avert the dangers of the day ahead. Both approaches—belief and philosophy—are additionally coloured by an implied criticism of God for the non-fulfilment of the covenant, an idea that is the cornerstone of the theological protest embodied in the liturgy.

Recurring Themes in the Liturgy

Since this outline of the central ideas of the liturgy is based entirely on Birkhot Hashaḥar and Pesukei Dezimra, it might be assumed that subsequent elements of the morning service resolve the problems raised. The rest of the morning liturgy, however, explores similar themes, even though these are approached in different ways, and the climactic moment when the tensions unknot comes only at the end of the day.

A brief review will show how this denouement emerges out of successive variations on the ideas already outlined. Immediately after the Kaddish that concludes the preliminary sections analysed in this book, a call to prayer introduces the statutory core texts of the morning. The first of two texts following this call is a blessing known as Yotser, 'maker', after the keyword of its 'seal'. This forms yet another liturgical opening to the day and describes how God illuminates the world at daybreak. The second, known as Ahavah, 'love', after its opening word and the key term of the 'seal', describes how Torah illuminates the world spiritually, complementing the physical daylight of the previous blessing. This second blessing also asks for help in understanding revelation, implying that this transcends human comprehension. It thereby suggests that the exile and alienation which result from ignorance of Torah are inevitable aspects of the human condition.

The argument that revelation is beyond human understanding is confirmed by the Shema, the central credal statement that follows these blessings. The first of its three pentateuchal passages insists on the importance of study, but the fact that this is juxtaposed with other pentateuchal texts, all of which overlap in subject matter, paradoxically demonstrates how the liturgical manipulation of Scripture generates arguments not evident in the original settings.[3] Since the human mind cannot encompass the entire Torah at once and must focus on short passages or groups of words, distortion is inevitable, a truth paradoxically illustrated by the Shema, which both makes study possible by citing those biblical passages calling for Torah to be read, reread, and taught, and demonstrates the impossibility of this enterprise.[4] The problem of study lies chiefly in the way that removing a passage from its context silences the passages adjacent to it, thereby compounding the 'misreading'. This pattern of distortion seems almost to be celebrated in the Shema, for the resonances generated by the juxtaposition of the biblical passages it includes and the deprivileging of neighbouring ones by their exclusion demonstrate the multivocal nature of Torah.

Although selection and rejection are distorting, they do make it possible to

---

[3] The first paragraph consists of Deut. 6: 4–9.

[4] This idea is implicit in the midrashic recognition that the different wording of the sabbath law in the two versions of the Decalogue can be reconciled only by God. See BT *Shev.* 20*b* and the first verse of the sabbath-eve hymn, *Lekha dodi*.

recover implicit meanings. Yet to capture all such nuances one would have to encompass the whole of revelation and recombine its fragments in infinite variations. The penalty for failing to perform this impossible task, as the second paragraph of the Shema makes clear, is exile, precisely the state from which the speaker is seeking to obtain release.[5] Human suffering thus results from the very text that seems to describe how to avoid it.

The third paragraph of the Shema provides a suggestion of how to survive exile, however.[6] This is drawn from the pentateuchal account of how the wandering Israelites believed the ten spies who brought negative reports of the Holy Land and mourned the news that it was unconquerable. As a consequence, they were told that not they, but only their children, would be allowed to enter the Land. They themselves would die in the wilderness, pointing to the exiled speaker's similar need to become reconciled to landlessness. This paragraph resolves the problem of survival by recommending that the identity of each individual (male) Jew be marked by symbolic dress. The 'fringes' on their garments, the origin of those now on the *talit*, compensate for their lack of territory and ensure that Jewish identity will survive intact, enabling Jews to be saved again in a future Exodus. The three paragraphs of the Shema thus attribute the speaker's exile to the manipulation of revelation, while discovering hope in an example of the very manipulation to which exile can be attributed.

This theme of redemption is confirmed by the Ge'ulah blessing, the paragraph which follows the Shema, which seems to locate the speaker somewhere between the recollection of slavery and the Israelites' rescue at the Red Sea, echoing Moses' song of redemption as if salvation had indeed been attained. This is followed by the Amidah, the first two of whose nineteen blessings similarly describe divine promises as though they had been fulfilled. But the central group of blessings specific to weekdays, from the fourth to the sixteenth blessings, withdraw from this position. The fourth and fifth blessings renew the suggestion that the speaker lacks the ability to understand Torah and therefore to obtain redemption, while in the seventh the speaker implicitly lives in misery. In the tenth, fourteenth, and fifteenth blessings the speaker awaits salvation, while in the sixteenth the efficacy of prayer is doubted. The closing three blessings, common to all versions of the Amidah, revert to the earlier sense of fulfilment, however, with the seventeenth equating prayer and sacrificial service as though the absence of the Temple can be ignored. The eighteenth assumes that all is well, and the nineteenth that peace has been granted. The statutory core of the liturgy therefore concludes with what seems to be a feeling of renewed safety.

The sense of tranquillity is stripped away by Taḥanun, however, a supplementary penitential sequence that revisits and amplifies the elements expressing the greatest neediness of the opening sequences analysed in this book. The

---

[5] The second paragraph consists of Deut. 11: 13–21.

[6] The third paragraph consists of Num. 15: 37–41.

speaker, overwhelmed by the dangers of everyday life, calls repeatedly for mercy, juxtaposing scriptural texts in ways that compound the problem of incomprehension observed in the Shema. This sequence is extended on Mondays and Thursdays by a formal reading from a Torah scroll of the opening section of the weekly pericope for the coming sabbath. This enactment of part of the annual cyclic reading of Torah, the least manipulated form of study performed in synagogue, is the last and most emphatic attempt of the morning to internalize the meaning of revelation and to fulfil the demand that Torah be understood.

The morning liturgy concludes with more messianic petitions, including Aleinu and the six psalms originally recited daily in the Temple, as though the Jerusalem cult might have been recreated in the speaker's mind. Multiple repetitions of Kaddish suggest that rescue has still to take place, however, although it also seems to be assumed that the speaker's survival is itself implicit proof of the efficacy of prayer.

The core and conclusions of the morning service thus echo the themes identified in the opening sections of the liturgy, leaving the speaker poised between belief in and despair of the possibility of liturgical dialogue, between hope in the possibility of study and resignation at its opacity, and between fear of the coming day and elation at survival. The synagogue, blended metaphorically with the verbal image of the Temple rebuilt, realizes the narrative of exile.

A sense of relief and resolution emerges only towards nightfall, when the speaker's survival seems to indicate that the daily dangers are past, for the evening liturgy turns away from physical threats to the dangers of the night ahead and the fear of sleep. Typically, the Hashkivenu blessing before the evening Amidah describes the speaker's dread of the night, setting the scene once again for the opening statement of the day and the renewal of the daily cycle.

The evening liturgy departs from that of the morning, however, in that it seems to be assumed that intimacy with the Torah has been achieved. The evening version of the Ahavah blessing, unlike the morning version described above, implies that Torah has indeed been taught successfully. It is not made clear whether this is because the necessary help has been given and the petitions for help in study have in some sense been answered. But since study is explicitly linked in the Shema to longevity, it is possible that the speaker's survival at this moment is to be attributed to a successful approach to the source of creativity.

Sufficient intimacy with revelation to ensure the speaker's survival may in fact have been attained merely through contact with the liturgy's scriptural and rabbinic echoes, their multiple associations constituting an act of study unifying the real and heavenly worlds. The equation between revelation and experience of the real world is suggested by the midrashic comment that Abraham, who lived before textual revelation took place, was taught by 'his two kidneys', as though Torah in some sense emerged from his inner self simply by living.[7] If so, the

---

[7] *Gen. Rabbah* 61: 1.

liturgy will have been effective because it enabled the speaker to 'keep talking' scripturally and thereby to become reconciled to reality as it is reflected in scriptural narrative.

The idea that liturgical worship can be equated with study and that it helps the speaker overcome daily dangers is a rabbinic one, alluded to in a midrashic description of teachers and students of Torah as soldiers defending a city.[8] The military metaphor relates both to the cultural survival of Jews, the continuity of whose society is dependent on learning, and to their physical existence, which the speaker perceives as being dependent on Torah. The liturgical argument proposes that Jewish life both derives from and tends towards the study of Torah.

If the function of liturgical prayer is mainly or solely to engage the speaker in study, however, how is the speaker to understand liturgical texts, such as the central blessings of the Amidah, in which God is directly petitioned? In the introductory chapters I argued that the question of the efficacy of prayer is only rarely discussed in traditional Jewish settings because to do so would risk demoralizing the public by upsetting the delicate balance between the emotional and intellectual approaches to worship. But the paradoxical emphasis on the speaker's powerlessness and silence can also be resolved by attributing the speaker's survival to the equation between liturgical worship and study. The medieval philosophical view that prayer is efficacious mainly or even uniquely in the mind of the speaker approximates to the assumption underlying this book that the function of prayers is chiefly to influence the inner life of the speaker.

The effectiveness of worship may therefore be attributed to the way in which it expresses the refusal to admit failure over study, and gives the speaker access to the scriptural source of Israel's covenant with God via its scrutiny. But in doing so it also provides a way into controversial areas of thought that are rarely examined in their own terms. The best example of this is the evidence of God's apparent neglect of his agreement with Israel. The speaker believes that rescue is overdue, but, like Job, refuses to invent reasons for suffering that he knows to be undeserved. God cannot be conceived of as failing to keep his promise to deliver salvation, so liturgical editors were forced to consider the rationale for his inaction. One liturgical response is to imply that exile continues because humans are unworthy of salvation, but it is equally implied that inherent human failings make this continuation unjust. What is only ever implied in a rabbinic context, and never stated openly, is the view that the original promise to save may have been delivered in bad faith, though this idea is so thinly disguised in the literature in general that it may be considered almost normative.

This is particularly clear from the use of the term *androlemusiyah*, derived from the Greek for 'the theft of individuals', in early rabbinic literature. This was employed in Hebrew in the sense of 'lawlessness' and was applied to conditions which seemed to demand divine intervention, such as that before the

---

[8] *Pesikta derav kahana* 15: 5.

Flood. Rashi describes how this universal punishment swept away 'sexual impropriety and idolatry', but the loanword may suggest that people had abandoned the attempt to understand Torah in all its senses, including the desire to judge people or events accurately. Rabbinic sources note that chaos flourished in this case in part because God had 'turned away his face', however, a biblically based description of how God angrily mirrors human inattention by absenting himself and refraining from intervention. Problematically, God's indifference merely encouraged people's cruelty to each other, and as a consequence he himself became party to the suffering. This pattern of incitement by indifference was compounded when the Flood he sent to sweep evil away 'killed the good with the bad', thereby providing no incentive to virtue. This combination of human and divine indifference is perhaps the closest rabbinic writers come to describing the situation of the liturgical speaker in the sequences analysed in this book.[9]

If the present age is one of *androlemusiyah*, suffering may result either from the lawlessness which caused God to turn aside, from the indiscriminate destruction caused when he intervenes, or from both. Only another Flood is discounted, because of the biblical promise that this would never recur,[10] but otherwise the pattern of general suffering, irrespective of virtue, is similar. The tragic nature of this situation may be reflected in the midrashic description of how God weeps for the exile, as though the divine attribute of mercy is helpless before the attribute of justice.[11]

The speaker must now await the return either of divine mercy or of justice, and in the meantime can only 'keep talking' about Torah in precisely the way the liturgy makes possible. The hope that the suffering is neither punitive nor the result of indifference is reflected in another rabbinic concept: 'suffering caused by [divine] love'. This is used to refer to pain that is in some sense 'good' for the sufferer, even if it merely ensures that reward after death is maximized. But it is also recognized that its usefulness ends the moment the sufferer no longer desires to study or to worship, the two activities that ensure engagement with God and Torah.[12] This proviso suggests that the liturgy, which itself approximates to study, can be defined as a tool for keeping the channels of communication open between God, Torah, and the world, even though the speaker is suffering. Stopping prayer and study would cut off this conduit of communication, and would also suggest that suffering results from God's inattention.

Awareness of human helplessness and incomprehension in the face of God's power is implicit in the rabbinic description of God as 'discerner, judge, witness, and complainant'.[13] This citation, from the popular and familiar mishnaic tractate *Pirkei avot*, recited in the sabbath afternoon liturgy during the summer months, compares human relations with God to a law-court in which the peti-

---

[9] See Ch. 4 n. 60.   [10] Gen. 9: 15.
[11] *Tana debei eliyahu*, ch. 30, p. 154, trans. Braude and Kapstein, pp. 334–6.
[12] BT *Ber.* 5*b*.   [13] Mishnah *Avot* 4: 29.

tioner has no voice and in which any attempt to accuse God of neglecting to fulfil the covenant would fail, leaving the accused speaker no chance of escape. In
view of the daily challenges faced by the speaker, this amounts to an indictment
of divine justice and effectively places God in the role of defendant.[14]

The idea that God's conduct can be assessed in the liturgy in legal terms has
been suggested by Joseph Heinemann, who noted law-court motifs of various
kinds in the liturgy[15] and in biblical and midrashic sources.[16] He defines as 'law-
court' prayers those which enumerate facts that an omniscient being would already know, and which include introductory formulas of deposition, such as that
with which the morning liturgy opens, or avowals of guilt.[17] Heinemann distinguishes these from texts which merely employ the tone of a 'servant before his
master'.[18] He regards this vein as so prevalent that even the praise of God's positive attributes may be interpreted as an implicit challenge to his justice, and also
notes the prayer-book's occasional 'bitter expression of grievance and . . . accusation', and its 'importunity, even impertinence towards God',[19] quoting a talmudic prayer that explicitly demands that God keep his side of the covenant.[20]
But his argument that prayers for times of distress tend to be particularly accusa-
tory in tone[21] may need to be revised in the light of the conclusion reached here
that the liturgical speaker lives each day as though in crisis.

Theological challenges of the kind noted here have been examined by Anson
Laytner, who argues that they are expressed more clearly in midrashic than in
liturgical texts. He attributes this to the idea that, while midrash is accessible
mainly to scholars, the prayer-book is a popular genre available to all, so it must
avoid promoting despondency.[22] He does not recognize the subversive undercurrents of the liturgy or acknowledge that the scholarly neglect of liturgical
meaning might be a fruitless defence against engaging with issues too painful to
contemplate. But he does describe how liturgical speakers like 'quoting God's
words back to him', 'using arguments that had been successful in the past', or
citing the 'merit of the ancestors' in order to direct accusation.[23] The present
analysis suggests that raw protest does emerge in liturgical texts, however, and
not only in poetic works.[24]

Readers in our post-Holocaust times will find many of the themes of the traditional liturgy outlined here familiar, and may even discover that its treatment of

---

[14] 'The very term *tefilah* ['prayer'] apparently implies a forensic metaphor. *Lefalel* in the *hitpa'el*
("pretend to judge") has the petitioner projecting himself into the position of arbitrating between
himself, *qua* petitioner, and God *qua* the other party to the suit' (Raphael Loewe, pers. comm.). See
Ben Yehuda, *Dictionary*, x. 4955–6, and Elbogen, *Jewish Liturgy*, 6.

[15] Heinemann, *Prayer in the Talmud*, 193–217.   [16] Ibid. 193, 199–200, 202, 206–8 n. 11.

[17] Ibid. 196–7 n. 6, 204; and see Extracts 1; 17, line 3; 28.

[18] Heinemann, *Prayer in the Talmud*, 204.   [19] Ibid. 195, 200, 202.

[20] Ibid. 199, 211 no. 12, citing BT *Sot.* 39*a–b*.   [21] Ibid. 198, 205.

[22] Laytner, *Arguing with God*, 110.   [23] Ibid. 117–24.   [24] Ibid. 132–76.

the themes of mourning, loss, reconciliation, and violence can contribute to contemporary debate. Tragically, the liturgical rejection of the use of force as a political solution still seems novel, one area in which the liturgy is in advance of much current debate.

CHAPTER TWELVE

❦

Other Versions, Other Readings

T O WHAT EXTENT are the conclusions drawn here specific to the particular
version of the liturgy studied in this book? Differences have been mentioned
between this and other rites, and attention drawn to variations of meaning resulting from even minor divergences. But do those versions present such different
messages that the conclusions reached in this book are called into question?

This chapter will examine the introductory sequences of four versions current
in the English-speaking world, and will conclude that there is in fact a remarkable degree of consistency of themes across rites. This supports the validity of the
interpretation offered here, and also the argument that critical reticence about
the liturgy reflects an unspoken awareness of its theological challenges. One of
the parallel rites examined here—the Sephardi one—even shows a remarkable
enrichment of the arguments identified in the version analysed here. This seems
not to have been noted before and underlines the intelligence and insight of the
liturgical editors.

The first version to be examined here, the Sephardi prayer-book, was a source
of variants appearing in branches of the Ashkenazi rite influenced by the hasidic
movement.[1] I have chosen it in preference to the far more widely used hasidic
rite since it presents more radical differences, highlighting liturgical divergence
and, as has been said, displaying real originality of approach. The second is an
east European variant of the west European Ashkenazi rite examined in the body
of the book, showing how variations survive within similar traditions. The last
examples are British progressive revisions, selected to illustrate trends within a
complex and developing field. Similar results would emerge if a range of
American versions were to be examined.

Only the more obvious departures from the version examined in this book can
be discussed here, even though this is an imperfect approach. Messages are generated by the interaction of all elements and not just a selection, so a full picture
cannot emerge from a survey which fails to take each element into account.
However, even a short review will show whether there is a broad consistency of
argument across these representative rites. Nor will this survey discuss the history of each version, mainly because no traditional liturgy can claim greater
'authenticity' than any other, at least in terms of its meaning to those who use it.

---

[1] Jacobs, *Hasidic Prayer*, 36–9; Reif, *Judaism and Hebrew Prayer*, 253–4. It also influenced the
liturgies of the British Reform movement.

Progressive liturgies are an exception to this principle since they are generally of known date and editorship, and the criteria employed in their composition are usually outlined in introductions or related literature. The consistency with which these principles are applied will be evident to all, although the consequences of doing so will become clear only with closer examination. Their revision every few decades suggests that they should be seen as accommodations with, or interpretations of, traditional liturgies, rather than as versions in their own right. The two examples chosen here, which happen to be British but, as has been said, reflect editorial principles also deployed in the United States, will be examined to see whether the traditional reticence about liturgical messages has prevented editors from recognizing what these might be, or has succeeded in suppressing even the expectation that such messages might be present.

A Sephardi Version

The edition surveyed here is that of the British community of Spanish and Portuguese Jews, or Western Sephardim, who were expelled from what is known in Hebrew as *sefarad*, 'Spain' or the Iberian Peninsula, and eventually arrived in places such as Amsterdam, London, and New York, bringing with them a liturgy traceable to pre-exilic Castilian rites.[2] The group of liturgies to which the London version belongs should not be confused with *minhag edot hamizrah*, the Oriental rites that are frequently described as Sephardi, but which developed in Muslim lands rather than in the Christian West. Popular translated editions of Oriental versions with explanatory notes reflect a subsequent trend towards mystic elaboration also seen in the east European Ashkenazi rite which will be examined later.[3] Neither the Sephardi nor the Oriental version should be mistaken for the hasidic rite usually named *nusaḥ sefarad*, which is a predominantly Ashkenazi version with some Sephardi characteristics.

The present Sephardi liturgy begins the liturgical day with the opening statement on waking, the washing of hands, and the excretion prayer, followed by the blessing over the small four-cornered garment worn under the shirt and verses relating to the passage to synagogue. All are familiar from our own version, but are grouped somewhat differently here.[4] In addition there is no prolonged transition between home and synagogue, and the clear rubrics prescribing certain psalmic verses for 'entering the synagogue' remove what in our version is a source of constructive ambiguity. The ritual garments are here put on before

[2] A recent British edition is *Book of Prayer: Daily and Occasional Prayers*; a related American version is *Book of Prayer According to the Custom of the Spanish and Portuguese Jews* (ed. D. De Sola Pool). For its pre-exilic links, see Moses Gaster's introduction to *Book of Prayer: Daily and Occasional Prayers*, p. xxiv.   [3] *Orot Sephardic Weekday Siddur*.

[4] In our version these appear in Extracts 1, 16, 17, 2, and 11, lines 1–2 (followed by Ps. 5: 9, to be said on leaving the synagogue, which does not appear in our version).

prayer begins, immediately after arriving in the synagogue, and are accompanied by the blessings alone. The garments therefore lack the meditations and verses which in our version contributed themes such as Eden, the breakdown of relations, and eventual reconciliation between God and Israel.[5] Also absent are the verses tracing the passage from the outside world into the community and the credal poems Yigdal and Adon Olam, which explored the ideas of language and God's remoteness. These themes are merely implicit in the Sephardi rite and are therefore in danger of being missed.

Birkhot Hashahar and Pesukei Dezimra, the sections covered in our analysis, are known collectively by Sephardim as *zemirot*, 'songs'. They are read in synagogue and are distinguished from the preliminary material by a heading identifying them as the 'Morning Service'. Zemirot opens with the talmudic meditation on waking, which in our version is a study portion, but which here occupies the introductory role assumed in its talmudic source (Extract 21). This is followed by the waking blessings, again as they appear in the talmudic source, although in our version they are positioned later in the liturgy and function at least partly as study-texts. The fact that the three negative blessings appear towards the end of the sequence rather than close to the beginning,[6] however, suggests that they address the speaker's awareness of social difference rather than, as in our version, the wider issues of why prayer is appropriate and who the speaker is or may become. The morning blessings conclude with the same pair of talmudic prayers for daily protection as in our version (Extracts 25 and 26), but the sequence in which the Ashkenazi speaker seeks intellectual and emotional refuge appears later and has a different function here.

The Sephardi editors now turn to the blessings over Torah, which are followed by an act of study, making this the first theme of the day after the waking sequence (Extract 18). Study is thus given more prominence and realism than in our version, where the Torah blessings follow the excretion text (Extract 17) and are thus disengaged from reality and themselves transformed into a study-text. The first Torah-study blessing omits the reference to 'engaging with Torah', which was read as evidence of a 'struggle' with the meaning of revelation, and describes instead how the speaker has been commanded 'concerning the words of Torah'. Sephardi editors seem either less troubled than their Ashkenazi counterparts regarding the possibility of comprehending Torah and of distinguishing between prayer and study, or more intent on avoiding theological controversy in this connection.

Any suspicion of reticence about theological paradoxes is transformed after the blessings over Torah, however, for Sephardi thinkers use the liturgy at this

[5] These appear in our version in Extracts 4 and 8, lines 1–2. The second *tefilin* blessing, Extract 8, lines 3–4, is prescribed for when an interruption has taken place.

[6] In our version these blessings are in Extracts 22 and 24, while in the Sephardi version the negative ones (our Extract 23), appear after our Extract 24, line 9.

point to explore controversial ideas in daring ways. The first text after the Torah blessings is the biblical priestly blessing (Extract 19), here supplemented by four framing pentateuchal verses designed to identify it as an act of study rather than a re-enactment of a Temple-based priestly ritual. In the Ashkenazi model this pentateuchal blessing is followed by a rabbinic text, as though this were the first in an anthology of biblical and rabbinic study-texts. Sephardi editors delay the rabbinic study-text and insert the pentateuchal narrative of the Akedah, preceded by a meditation.[7] This meditation is abridged and adapted from a longer discussion of that biblical passage which appears in the Rosh Hashanah liturgy, where the Binding is a central symbol.[8] The biblical text of the Akedah is then read, followed by another extract from the same meditation, supplemented by pentateuchal and prophetic citations exploring the implications of the Binding.

This liturgical unit, consisting of the Binding flanked by meditations, could be mistaken as an interpolation that merely disrupts the anthology begun by the pentateuchal priestly blessing and continued with rabbinic readings. If viewed in this way, it might be argued that the Binding theme had to be included near the beginning of the liturgy because it was midrashically claimed that Abraham founded morning worship when he 'rose early' to take Isaac to Moriah, and perhaps more incidentally because its themes will be relevant to the later discussion of suffering (Extract 29, lines 1–3). If the emphasis was indeed on including it early, then it could have been inserted here simply because the editors felt that the pentateuchal stage of a study anthology would be an appropriate location. This line of reasoning seems to have led some Ashkenazi editors to include similar meditations and the Binding narrative early in the day, although in a different place, as will be seen later. The Sephardim who included these texts here apparently had other motivations, however, and seem to have been concerned with comparing biblical blessings and investigating the meaning of blessings as such. Since this reading seems not to have been noted before, it will be outlined in some detail.[9]

The priestly blessing is a positive statement, with each clause featuring the Tetragrammaton, associated with divine mercy. As mentioned in the analysis above, the blessing is suited to the beginning of the liturgical day because of its association with the completion of the Tabernacle and the beginning of worship there; it is employed elsewhere to inaugurate holy time, for instance by being read on the eve of sabbath as a parental blessing for children.

The Binding of Isaac juxtaposed with it here seems to have been chosen not only for what is regarded as the major theme of the near-sacrifice of Isaac—the

---

[7] Gen. 22: 1–19.

[8] It appears there in the Amidah for Musaf, in the course of the *zikhronot* blessing. This daily Akedah sequence appears in *Book of Prayer: Daily and Occasional Prayers*, 4–6.

[9] It came to mind while I was leading the service at Bevis Marks synagogue, London, on Shemini Atseret 5763 (2002), in a moment of 'reverie' of the kind discussed in the first part of this book.

idea of martyrdom—but because it similarly contains a climactic blessing. This is not to discount the theme of suffering from this context, since several blessing-texts involving Abraham, or even other patriarchs, could have been selected but were not. However, its relevance lies in the complexity of real life that might culminate in a blessing such as the one at the end of the Akedah. It is therefore precisely the suffering of Abraham and Isaac that seems to have determined its location here. The speaker's fears for the day ahead immediately preceded the blessings over Torah study, and clearly lie behind the choice of the present pair of pentateuchal blessing texts.

Moreover, the priestly and Abrahamic blessings are linked not only by their early-morning origins and by theme but also by location, since Mount Moriah, where the Binding took place, was later the site of the Temple in which the priestly blessing was recited. It is because this now lies in ruins that the speaker must resort to the spoken word, aligning the ruins of the Temple and the speaker's present environment. The threefold wording of each blessing is also similar, for like the priestly blessing, the climactic blessing of the Akedah—the emphatic promise that 'I will surely bless you'—includes the verb 'bless' twice, and then closes with the statement that 'through your seed shall all the nations of the earth be blessed', which contains it once more.[10] The Akedah may thus even be editorially related to the priestly blessing, apparently being based on the same underlying model.

The liturgical juxtaposition of these blessings also draws attention to the way they deploy the divine names, since the Tetragrammaton dominates the priestly blessing, emphasizing the attribute of mercy, while the Binding narrative begins by referring to the divinity as *elohim*, the name associated with judgement. Abraham, at the beginning of the Akedah, indeed experiences not mercy, but an apparent attempt to destroy him and his hopes for descendants.[11] Yet when an angel 'of God' intervenes to prevent him from killing his son, the other divine name, the Tetragrammaton denoting mercy, appears, remaining dominant even when Abraham is praised by the angel associated with the Tetragrammaton for showing how he 'fears God', identified by the name of judgement. The disposition of divine names was noted by medieval commentators,[12] and described as evidence that the aspects of God are being contrasted in this narrative. According to this reading, Abraham was blessed in God's merciful and immanent guise only after he had acknowledged God's regal and transcendent character. This threefold blessing after the Akedah thus contrasts strongly with the unqualified completeness of the 'keeping', 'shining', 'grace', and 'peace' promised in the priestly

[10] Gen. 22: 17–18.

[11] See e.g. Rashi on Gen. 22: 2 for the impact of the command on Abraham. An *agadah* in BT *San.* 89*b*, which attributes the idea of the trial to Satan, tacitly acknowledges the intolerable nature of what Abraham was instructed to do.

[12] The change of divine name in mid-narrative is noted by Nahmanides in his notes on Gen. 22: 12. See the discussion in Spiegel, *The Last Trial*, 121–2.

blessing. In the priestly version Jews are the recipients of a blessing in which they themselves play no part, while in that delivered to Abraham they are challenged to emulate Abraham's discovery of the dual nature of God's relationship to the world. In this, the speaker is given a narrative context for the ideas implicit in the first line of the Shema (Extract 31, line 1), in which the names related to mercy and justice are similarly juxtaposed, the former appearing twice and flanking the latter as though to outweigh it. That line might have been the model for the editorial decision here to twin the priestly blessing, which contains only the Tetragrammaton, with the Binding, in which the name of judgement appears first, before giving way to the Tetragrammaton. These blessings, when read sequentially as they are here, reproduce the idea of the Shema and show how it can be enacted.

The thesis proposed by the Shema and by these blessings suggests that the speaker, like Abraham, must defer gratification or even forgo it in the certainty that others will eventually enjoy the 'victory over their enemies' promised to Abraham. In the liturgical present, therefore, the speaker journeys towards Moriah, differing from Abraham mainly by knowing that this particular episode ended without a tragedy.

The present reading of this liturgical juxtaposition of familiar biblical texts is confirmed by the meditation and scriptural verses that follow, for the meditation explicitly contrasts the characteristics reflected in divine names, citing Abraham's 'mercy' for Isaac as a reason for God to ensure that his 'mercy' overcomes his 'anger'.[13] What kind of 'anger' may have prompted the command to sacrifice Isaac is unclear, but the word itself suggests that the speaker's present sufferings are punitive. The fact that God is asked to 'return from [literally 'repent of'] his anger towards his people, city, land, and heritage' implies that divine alienation can be ended only by the resurgence of mercy, although how this is to be effected is not explained.[14]

Several scriptural verses are then cited, as though to encourage or even compel God to honour his promise. In their original context the first three conclude the first of two pentateuchal descriptions of exile resulting from the neglect of Torah.[15] But that exile, accompanied by the breakdown of natural law and the apparent dissolution of the relationship between God and Israel, will come to an end only because of divine mercy, it is implied, much like the suffering related to *androlemusiyah* discussed above. The fourth, fifth, and sixth verses are drawn from the coda to the second pentateuchal description of disaster and rescue and again describe a return to favour, similarly blurring the boundaries between punitive and gratuitous suffering. A rabbinic reading of this verse regards the statements that God will '*bring* you back' and that '*he* will return' as evidence that

---

[13] See the discussion of this theme in Spiegel, *The Last Trial*, 88–95.

[14] The fullest descriptions of punitive anger are in Lev. 26 and Deut. 28.

[15] Lev. 26: 42, 44–5.

he himself had been with the people in exile, implying that he not only causes suffering but is, in a sense, its victim. The theme emerges again in Isaiah 63: 9, included later in this group of verses, which implies that God himself has accompanied the people into exile and redeems himself in rescuing them, an idea rarely made explicit in rabbinic thought. This is one of its major textual sources.[16] Juxtaposing these six verses with the Akedah, however, implies that Abraham's trial might have resulted merely from divine turning aside or even have been gratuitous, like the Israelites' slavery in Egypt predicted to Abraham.[17] The Akedah implicitly adds, however, that divine mercy may arise as a result of human acceptance of suffering. If so, the speaker has no alternative but to await the return of mercy.

The remaining verses are prophetic in origin, the seventh referring to rescue in the morning and the eighth to rescue, but without reference to time.[18] But the ninth, more radically, alludes to the way in which the ambiguity of scriptural writing might be a source of human alienation from God, a theme that dominates the Ashkenazi liturgy but has not yet been encountered in the present version. It appears now because of the inclusion of one of two alternative versions of a single scriptural word, one of a number of such variants. The first alternative is a *ketiv*, the 'written [form]' of a word normally printed in the main text of Hebrew bibles. The other is a *keri*, 'read [form]', which, although usually relegated to the margin, is the version that the reader is to understand.[19] The present variant is significant since it affects the meaning of a Hebrew word which spelled in one way means 'not' and in the other way 'his'. This modification, which appears elsewhere in the Bible, here reverses the plain meaning of the phrase, as though copyists were embarrassed at what it appeared to be saying.[20] The 'written' version of this verse says that 'in all their [the Israelites'] sufferings he [God] was not afflicted', while the marginal variant, which the speaker is to regard as the true meaning, implies that God himself suffered from the exile, and therefore that he, possibly together with the Israelites, was later rescued by an angel. This more authoritative marginal version is what appears in the liturgy, and can be interpreted in a way that has far-reaching theological implications. If the relationship between God and Israel described here is compared to that between Abraham and Isaac at the Akedah, it would follow that God needs to be 'rescued' from his role as judge, casting him less as Abraham's tester than as his companion. This altered and effectively subordinate role would account for the intervention of an angel, acting on behalf of God's own attribute of divine mercy.

Implicit in this sequence of the Sephardi liturgy is the idea that God's aspect of mercy, like Abraham at the Akedah, dreads the power of the attribute of

---

[16] Deut. 30: 3–5, and see Rashi on Deut. 30: 3, citing BT *Meg.* 29*a*.

[17] Gen. 15: 13–14.   [18] Isa. 33: 2, Jer. 30: 7.   [19] Isa. 63: 9.

[20] See David Kimhi (Radak), Abraham Ibn Ezra, and Joseph Kaspi on this verse, and n. 16 above.

judgement and has reason to regret its own inaction. This notion, hinted at in other biblical and rabbinic texts, is highlighted here to suggest that God not only causes suffering but is its victim. The variant also implies that suffering can be attributed to the failure of study that results from textual uncertainty, as was noted earlier in this book, bringing the inevitability of suffering centre-stage.

The tenth and eleventh verses in the anthology are adjacent to each other in their source-text, but in another liturgical context they follow an echo of the attributes of divine mercy listed in the book of Exodus. These are frequently cited during the penitential days in the autumn, when the narrative of the Akedah is also a major theme.[21] The biblical context also refers to other rescues, suggesting that the attribute of mercy might be about to bring salvation once again, this time to the speaker. The twelfth and last verse in the anthology describes the return to the homeland and the restoration of the sacrificial order, referring to the Temple as a 'house of prayer' and stating that 'my house shall be called a house of prayer for all nations'.[22] These statements appear at first sight to refer to the Temple, but the second could be taken to mean that 'I dwell in each house of prayer', in which case it would relate to the synagogue or home in which the present words are pronounced. This would symbolically blur the speaker's location and the Temple Mount, the site both of the priestly blessing and of the Akedah. The Sephardi editors of this verse anthology thereby substitute the reality of the Temple for the Temple-like aspects of each place of prayer, incidentally emphasizing the ideological over any physical aspects of the Temple.

The Akedah sequence as a whole, therefore, including the introductory meditation, main narrative, and concluding verses, makes explicit a view of suffering found more obliquely in the Ashkenazi version. It acknowledges that the speaker's suffering is humanly incomprehensible, but argues that it is part of the divine scheme and that rescue can indeed be hoped for. The last verse even equates present survival to messianic rescue.

The success of the Sephardi editors in arguing this complex idea with the minimum means is matched by their skill in integrating it into the longer liturgical narrative. The Binding and its meditations are followed by a version of the composite mishnaic and talmudic texts on study found in our version (Extract 20), but this is handled not purely as a continuation of the text anthology in the Ashkenazi rite, but as part of the developing debate. In our version this passage precedes the waking prayer and morning blessings, which seem to be poised between the status of study-texts and prayers, while in the Sephardi version they

---

[21] Mic. 7: 18–20. In the Sephardi and Ashkenazi rites these verses are recited on the Day of Atonement at the end of the book of Jonah, the prophetic reading for the afternoon service, which ends with an expression of divine mercy. The thirteen attributes of God's mercy from Exod. 34: 6–7 are repeated on the Day of Atonement twenty-six times in the Sephardi liturgy, echoing the numerical value of the letters of the Tetragrammaton, the divine name associated with mercy. The readings are numbered in Hebrew in *Book of Prayer: Day of Atonement*, 29 and 267, for the first and last of these.   [22] Isa. 56: 7.

are prayers in real time. For the Sephardi liturgy now to revert to the study sequence left off before the Akedah would be understandable if somewhat maladroit, even though its closing line praises study in a way which might refer back to the complexity recognized in the verse collection after the Binding narrative.

In fact this listing of virtues is closely linked to the Akedah sequence, because it is possible to read each clause as a description of a form of ideal behaviour which Abraham at some time transgressed. The Ashkenazi version includes virtues which the Sephardi one does not, such as the duty to accompany brides, escort the dead, and, ambiguously, to 'attend to prayer', which relate less directly to Abraham's life than those in the Sephardi inventory. The Sephardi editors' listing seems pointedly relevant. The first virtue is honouring one's parents, which Isaac indeed did at the Akedah, but which Abraham did not, by deserting his childhood home on leaving for the Promised Land. Abraham's proverbial kindness,[23] which led him to plead for Sodom and Gomorrah and to welcome angels to his tent, inspired him neither to act on his misgivings about banishing Hagar and Ishmael nor to intervene for his son.[24] Ishmael, banished into the desert where he almost died of thirst, was neither visited nor offered hospitality by Abraham. Abraham's 'rising early', understood midrashically as a reference to morning prayer, equally alludes to the suffering he almost inflicted at the Akedah. He promoted good marital relations between himself and Sarah, but not with Hagar, and Sarah's death after the Akedah, perhaps due to shock, was also the result of his actions.[25] This listing of virtues therefore pinpoints Abraham's shortcomings, illustrating the compromises he was obliged to make in the course of the Binding and its related narratives. It incidentally implicates the speaker who is aligned with him and perhaps even God, whose suffering is itself alluded to in the ninth verse. The need to understand how these ethically questionable actions might have been avoided, or how they can emerge inevitably from the compromises inherent in human life, points directly to the need to study in its widest sense. Torah, as has been seen, is both a key to the often ambiguous and ambivalent workings of the world and inaccessible to even the most rigorous intellectual scrutiny.

The Sephardi liturgy here presents the speaker with a complex confection of ideas: an investigation of Jewish chosenness, of the character of God, of the nature of experience, and of the texture of understanding. By implicitly defining pain as a trial inimical to the divine attribute of mercy, the speaker is placed in Abraham's position at the Akedah and between the impact of the contrasting divine attributes. This throws light on the request in the closing paragraph of the blessings near the beginning of the Sephardi liturgy that the speaker should not be brought into 'temptation',[26] which should be read not as a petition to be saved

---

[23] BT *Ket.* 8*b*, and Rashi's comment.   [24] Gen. 21.   [25] See Rashi on Gen. 23: 2.

[26] In our version in Extract 25, line 3, and in *Book of Prayer: Daily and Occasional Prayers*, 3, shortly before the Torah blessings.

from being seduced into sinning but as a request to be spared a trial of the kind imposed on Abraham. So devastating was that trial that the priestly blessing looks almost like an ironic introduction to it, at least until the speaker learns that both divine names, that of justice and that of mercy, are sources of blessing, and that neither can be dispensed with if the truly universal blessing represented by the acceptance of life is to be attained. The speaker must find a way to reconcile the names and to discover the well-being and unhappiness they denote, but can do so only by means of the climactic item in the rabbinic listing of virtues—the study of Torah—itself exemplified by the present liturgical sequence. Study is thereby shown to require an engagement with the nature of experience as such.

After this editorial tour de force, the Sephardi liturgy turns to the sequence that in our version enacts a flight into study, away from the inevitability of suffering inspired by the two petitions that followed the morning blessings (Extracts 27–33). Here, however, the flight may be from the implications of the Akedah sequence examined above.

The call for integrity in private matters is expanded in the Sephardi liturgy to include public relations, suggesting a more integrated view of life than in our version, where this dimension appears only in the closing blessing (Extract 32, line 5). Integrity also appears to refer primarily to human relations in our version, whereas here, because of the context, it extends to the theological difficulties raised by human suffering and implicitly proposes solidarity in the face of the incomprehensibility of suffering. The penultimate word of the opening sentence, translated 'rise early', alludes to the Akedah and helps explain why that narrative was inserted here.[27] The theme of the next paragraph, human weakness, implicitly reviews the terms of the covenant and culminates in the challenge presented by the recital of the first line of the Shema (Extract 31, line 1). The passage concludes with the prophetic promise of eventual ingathering, which, in the Ashkenazi version, seems to bring the cult into virtual existence in a way which is reflected in sacrificial readings that appear to reverse the present exile.

The Sephardi version, however, interpolates before the sacrificial sequence a passage that excludes the possibility of the Temple having been brought into existence, for the same prophetic citation is followed by a petition asking for a restoration that has clearly yet to occur. This transforms the sacrificial readings into study-texts, while in the Ashkenazi rite they seemed inspired by an almost magical trust in nostalgia, hope, and contact with God's chosen form of worship. This Sephardi sense of realism is subverted in the Oriental version, however, where Psalm 67, printed in the shape of a seven-branched candelabrum, is inserted after the sacrificial readings and before the introductory blessing of Pesukei Dezimra. This common mystical device is accompanied in one annotated edition by a note comparing its recital to lighting the *menorah* in the rebuilt

[27] Gen. 22: 3.

Temple, thereby bringing the Temple into the here and now even more explicitly than in the Ashkenazi version.[28]

The sacrificial readings open with the pentateuchal description of the weekday offerings included in our version, but lacking the non-sacrificial interpolations that challenge their reality.[29] The Sephardi version is augmented by several supplements, one of them a pentateuchal citation about incense, identifying its ingredients and specifying that it is to be offered in the morning, the time of this liturgical reading.[30] The talmudic passages that follow, giving more details of the ingredients of incense and emphasizing that errors in its preparation are punishable by death, are all from the same talmudic folio but appear there in a different order, thereby contributing to the debate on suffering.[31] The sequence concludes with the statement that urine is 'not decent to bring into the Temple', followed by the prophetic petition (also present in the Ashkenazi version) that the offerings will be 'pleasant to God'.[32] The talmudic checklist of the Temple ritual sequence that follows has the effect of maximizing its realism.[33]

There follows the interpolated mystic poem encountered in our version, acknowledging the impossibility of recreating the Temple, accompanied by the one-line response suggesting it is a name of God (Extract 37). But next comes a prayer that does not appear in our version and which points out the logical difficulty of assuming that the sacrificial readings adequately replace sacrifice,[34] including a citation from the book of Hosea that identifies how this may be achieved.[35] There is also the verse from Leviticus that appears to refer to the slaughtering of animals on the 'north side' of the altar, but which is midrashically read as a reference to the merit gained by the Akedah (Extract 35).

Since this interpretation implicitly discounts the literal meaning of biblical language, however, the presence of this verse undermines the mishnaic description of the location of sacrifice, the aspect of the cult most difficult to recover, that also follows in our version (Extract 38). The intellectual distance between the speaker and this Temple description is increased by the listing of exegetical rules that follows, although the study anthology concludes with a brief petition for the Temple's rebuilding (Extract 39). An awareness of the loss of the Temple is thereby liturgically twinned with a demonstration of the near-impossibility of attaining a complete understanding of the Torah, written or oral.

The first section of the morning liturgy ends here with a rabbinic Kaddish, as in our version (after Extract 40). However, the blessing that formally opens Pesukei Dezimra is delayed by a number of psalms that do not seem to have been regarded as fully belonging to that section. The clear break produced in the

---

[28] *Orot Sephardic Weekday Siddur*, 94–5.

[29] Extract 34; Num. 28: 9–10.

[30] Exod. 30: 7–8, 34–6.

[31] BT *Ker.* 6a–b; JT *Yoma* 4: 5; see the note in *Tselota di'avraham*, i. 93.

[32] Mal. 3: 4, Extract 36, lines 3–4.

[33] BT *Yoma* 33a.

[34] See the note in *Tselota di'avraham*, i. 104.

[35] Hos. 14: 3.

Ashkenazi rite by the interpolation of Psalm 30 and the two versions of Kaddish that flank it only appears later.

The first three texts preceding the introductory blessing in the Sephardi rite are David's song on the arrival of the Ark in Jerusalem, the first of the psalmic verse anthologies, and Psalm 30, ostensibly related to the dedication of David's 'house' (Extracts 44, 45, and 42). Psalm 103, which follows these and appears in no weekly Ashkenazi service, is a circular text, the first words recurring at the end. It emphasizes God's forgiveness and mercy by echoing the thirteen attributes of divine mercy first announced after the episode of the Golden Calf.[36] In addition, comparing divine–human relations with those between fathers and sons may allude to the Akedah and to the appended verse implying that God may 'suffer' with his people, thereby concluding that survival depends on divine mercy. Circularity is also a quality of the argument of which it is part, the concluding angelic chorus even resembling the call to prayer that follows the sequences examined in this book, as though the present psalm enacts the speaker's arrival at the threshold of statutory prayer. The next non-biblical line expressing God's timelessness is sung twice antiphonally by prayer-leader and speaker, again as though beginning the day with a declaration of God's eternity and setting the scene for the call to prayer.[37] Another sign of arrival is the following prophetic statement of God's eventual rule, simultaneously predicting its arrival and accepting its remoteness, which appears at the end of Pesukei Dezimra in our version.[38] This is followed by an ingathering promise and blessing from the end of a psalmic book[39] and the closing words of the whole book of Psalms, as though this entire sequence from Psalm 103 onwards were a version of Pesukei Dezimra. If this is its function it is a powerful liturgical unit, parallel to, but unlike, those in our edition.

If so, it would explain why the next text, Psalm 19, seems to begin the day again,[40] by comparing daybreak to Creation and focusing on the origin of light, much as does the first blessing of the statutory service, which lies outside the scope of this book. It also alludes to the primacy of Torah and the near-inevitability of misunderstanding its language, and since its last words, asking for the acceptance of prayer, recur at the end of each Amidah it seems to conclude the liturgical unit.

There follows the introductory blessing of Pesukei Dezimra (Extract 43), which in the Sephardi ritual introduces only the main psalmic sequences. The fact that it is preceded by a number of Davidic texts detracts from its introductory role in our version, implicitly demoting the preceding Davidic writings to

---

[36] Exod. 34: 6–7.

[37] This composite line appears in our version in Extract 47, lines 7–8.

[38] Zech. 14: 9, cited in Extract 58, lines 2–3.   [39] Ps. 106: 47–8.

[40] Ps. 19 is the first of a sequence of psalms interpolated in our version on sabbath after Ps. 100, before the second psalmic anthology in Extract 47, itself a prelude to Pss. 145–50. This sequence falls outside the ambit of the present book.

study-texts. But its reduced status is counteracted by the length of the Sephardi version, which lists the human failings that God is said to lack, thereby pointing to the view that he possesses them, since denial is itself a form of suggestion.

The first Davidic text after the blessing is Psalm 100, followed by the second psalmic verse anthology as in our version, its separation from the previous one suggesting a distinctive role (Extracts 46 and 47). Thereafter the service is almost identical to our version, spanning Psalm 145 to the end of the book of Psalms, followed by the selection of concluding verses, David's song on surrendering his work to Solomon, the prayer relating to the second Temple, the Song of the Sea, and its concluding verses. The last item lacks the opening line of the Shema, which usefully recalled the near-impossibility of understanding Torah and the nature of God, and which returned the speaker to the range of ideas implicit in the opening statement of the liturgy. The sequence ends with the concluding blessing of Pesukei Dezimra and a short Kaddish, as in the Ashkenazi version (Extracts 48–59).

The differences between the opening sequences of the Sephardi and Ashkenazi liturgies therefore suggest that their core themes are identical, despite shifts in emphasis and pace of exposition and the presence of two sequences that stand out for their theological richness and narrative coherence.

Other Ashkenazi Trends

The edition of the Ashkenazi liturgy analysed in this book is based on Baer's *Sidur avodat yisra'el*, the magisterial publication that influenced many west European prayer-books. Its freedom from mystical additions and the awareness of historical development reflected in its meticulous commentary also provided a model for the edition used in constituent synagogues of the United Synagogue in Great Britain since 1890, translated by Simeon Singer, and its companion volume by Israel Abrahams. Differences between Baer's version and the one studied here have been noted in the course of the analysis, Baer himself mentioning variations in notes or in rubrics. But these divergences are worth summarizing.

The opening statement of the day appears not at the head of the liturgy, but earlier, in small type on the first page of the thirty-two-page prose introductory section, as one of a number of private meditations. As has been noted, it appears to have entered the normative western service only gradually. The liturgical day thus begins not at home, but with the passage to synagogue, which is accompanied by the same texts as in our version, despite different rubrics, as noted in the analysis. In addition the ritual garments appear before the introductory blessing of Pesukei Dezimra, rather than near the beginning as in our prayer-book (Extracts 11–13). The arrival in synagogue is followed by two verse meditations, neither of which appears in our version, marked off by printed rules. The first is a

poem by Solomon Ibn Gabirol for the early morning, reflecting on the inefficacy of prayer,[41] and the second, with the authorial acrostic 'Hayim', is a study
of hopelessness and dependence on God's mercy, introducing themes to be
explored later.

The morning service proper, identified by a main heading and a shift to a
larger font, begins with Adon Olam (the verse creed Yigdal being relegated to the
end of the morning service), and continues as in our version from the blessing
over hand-washing until the beginning of the sacrificial sequence (Extracts
15–33). There a rubric points to regional variations within the Ashkenazi tradition and offers a choice of rituals, producing a fuller sequence than in our own,
including several overlaps with the Sephardi rite examined above. This begins
with a pentateuchal description of the laver in the Temple court and continues
with the ritual of daily offerings which does appear in our version, as well as the
verse from Leviticus that alludes to the Binding of Isaac.[42] There next appears a
prose introduction to the pentateuchal description of the incense offerings and
the passage itself,[43] followed by a talmudic description appearing in the Sephardi
version reviewed above, but absent from our edition.[44] The survey of incense
offerings appears in smaller type, and Baer is silent about it in his otherwise comprehensive commentary, as though he regarded it as of secondary importance and
was reluctant to accept liturgical change of this kind. The incense material is followed by Extracts 36–7, the interpolated verses and medieval poem as in our version, after which Baer's liturgy corresponds to our own. A still more expansive
version of the sacrificial descriptions appears in the version examined below.

Baer's influence has waned in some later editions of the Ashkenazi liturgy,
such as that which replaced Singer's work in 1990,[45] which draws on traditions
from eastern Europe that have remained dominant in the United States, for
example in Philip Birnbaum's *Daily Prayer Book* and Nosson Scherman's *The
Complete Artscroll Siddur*, the latter in particular a staple text on both sides of the
Atlantic.[46] It is also evident in Shelomoh Tal's *Sidur rinat yisra'el*, a standard
Israeli edition. Baer looked over his shoulder at such trends, as can be seen from
the additional sacrificial material he included in smaller type, but that tradition
has now increased in dominance. For similar reasons the Ashkenazi rite has
recently been coloured, via hasidism, by the Sephardi rite.

The next edition to be reviewed is *The Complete Artscroll Siddur*, edited by
Nosson Scherman, which reflects in part the expansion of the western Ashkenazi

---

[41] For an analysis of the theological implications see Scheindlin, *The Gazelle*, 170–5.

[42] Exod. 30: 17–21; Lev. 1: 11; in our version in Extracts 34–5.

[43] Exod. 30: 34–6, 7–8.

[44] The prayer-book version of these paragraphs resembles, but in the second part differs considerably from, BT *Ker.* 6a and JT *Yoma* 5: 4. See *Tselota di'avraham*, i. 92–102.

[45] *Authorised Daily Prayer Book* (Jakobovits).

[46] Birnbaum's popularity, and his dependence on the east European traditions followed by
Elijah of Vilna, are acknowledged in *My People's Prayer Book*, v. 45.

liturgy acknowledged by Baer, and in part the survival of east European trends in North America. The English translation and homiletic commentary are designed for a popular readership.

In this version the day begins at home with the statement on waking (Extract 1), but this is followed by a psalmic verse containing the Tetragrammaton, even though this cannot be pronounced, even in its euphemistic form, before the hands have been washed. A rubric explains that the hands have indeed been washed by this point, although as no blessing is prescribed it is to be assumed that none is to be recited for this washing. There next appears the statement of praise used in our version in response to the first line of the Shema and for cancelling a blessing recited unnecessarily, presumably in acknowledgement of the divine name contained in the verse.[47] The verse itself stresses the importance of study, but its precise ritual function remains unclear, since the same information is conveyed by the Torah blessings that appear later.

This arrangement of texts is surprising because the opening statement of the day was introduced specifically to replace a talmudic waking prayer which contained the name of God and therefore could not be recited until the hands had been washed (Extract 21). Since the hands appear to have been washed by now, however, both the blessing and the waking prayer could be recited, but are not. It is possible that these are being reserved for recital in synagogue, and that this is why this psalmic verse was introduced as a substitute for the washing blessing, even though the psalmic verse itself contains a divine name which has to be cancelled by the formula appended to it. The present arrangement may also be a vestige of a larger group of mystically inspired early-morning readings, which would have provided a theological context for what remains.

The blessings over the *arba kanfot*, *talit*, and *tefilin* follow immediately, as they do in our version (Extracts 2–10), but with interpolated citations and meditations that expand their associations.[48] After the blessing over *arba kanfot* appears the meditation that in our version concludes putting on the *talit*, presumably since this is the earliest possible moment for its recital (Extract 6). The meditations before the blessing over the *talit* are preceded by the first two verses of Psalm 104, appropriate to the morning since it resembles the circular Psalm 103 included in the Sephardi liturgy before the introductory blessing of Pesukei Dezimra. Psalm 104 is otherwise reserved in the Ashkenazi tradition for sabbath afternoons during the winter months, as a prelude to the fifteen 'Songs of Degrees', Psalms 120–34, associated with the fifteen steps leading up to the court of the Israelites in the Temple and therefore with the beginning of worship in the Temple. The psalm's preoccupation with creation and God's mastery over it relates it to the speaker's sense of wonder at regaining consciousness. But this particular verse refers to the created world as God's 'garment', associating the

---

[47] The verse is Ps. 111: 10. The line that follows it appears in our version in Extract 8, line 5, and Extract 5, line 2.   [48] See *Otsar hatefilot*, 42*b*–45*a*.

talit with the cosmos in a way that invites comparison between the speaker and God, an anthropomorphism which may well have offended Baer's non-mystical tendencies. The editor himself may have been aware of this objection, for he prescribed the verse not for the moment of putting on the *talit*, but for when the fringes are checked, just before reciting the blessing over the *talit*, by draping the folded garment over the left shoulder with the fringes in front, so that they can be examined.

The meditation that follows, which focuses on the idea that the 'unity' of God's name has potentially messianic implications, is of a genre known as a *yihud*, 'unity'. It is characteristic of Lurianic and later kabbalistic thought and points to the need to unify the letters of the Tetragrammaton, which, in a non-kabbalistic context, may be read as the need to reconcile the divine names. This is followed by a different version of the meditation before putting on the *talit* included in our version (Extract 3), referring not only to the Garden of Eden, as does our version, but to physical aspects of the garment, much as does Isaiah Horowitz's meditation before *tefilin* in our version (Extract 7). Unlike the meditation in our version, this identifies biblical verses containing the word *kanaf*, which in the context of *talit* means 'corner', but elsewhere often 'wing', both readings relating to God's protectiveness. These multiple meanings are usefully made explicit here. The *talit* blessing and psalmic verses are the same as in our version (Extracts 4–6).

The *tefilin* meditations echo those of the *talit* and consist of a *yihud* and Horowitz's paragraph (Extract 7), followed by the blessings as in our version (Extract 8). But before the three verses from the book of Hosea (Extract 9) appear four sentences, corresponding in number to the texts in the *tefilin* and alluding to attributes in the sefirotic tree, presumably linked to the threefold winding of the strap onto the middle finger. This, in addition to the seven turns around the arm, completes a *sefirah* of ten circuits.[49] This rite also includes in full the two texts which appear in the *tefilin* besides the first two paragraphs of the Shema,[50] whose absence from our version was attributed to the problematic issues they raise. They are nonetheless tacitly present by being noted in Horowitz's introductory meditation, so their citation here has no additional impact on the liturgical narrative.

The transition to the synagogue is handled more briefly than in our version or in Baer's, for it includes only the group of verses beginning with the citation from Balaam's failed 'curse' (Extract 12) and lacks the scriptural citations alluding to arriving at and entering the building, as well as the verse anthologies culminating in the beginning of prayer (Extracts 11 and 13). These are surprising omissions from an edition with otherwise inclusive tendencies.

The poetic introductions to prayer are reversed in order, Adon Olam preced-

---

[49] Discussed in *Tselota di'avraham*, i. 26 and outlined in *My People's Prayer Book*, v. 80.

[50] Exod. 13: 1–10, 11–16, which do appear in *Otsar hatefilot*, 44*b*–45*a*.

ing Yigdal (Extracts 15 and 14), presumably so that the theme of waking appears before credal issues. Thereafter the liturgy matches our version until the end of the petitions for protection from daily dangers (Extract 26). In our version these lead the speaker into the theological cul-de-sac from which the interpolation on integrity offers escape. Here, however, a version of the Sephardi Akedah sequence has been inserted, with the same opening meditation and an abbreviated closing one, but without the suggestive verse sequence. A rubric confines these framing meditations to sabbath, leaving the biblical passage unexplained on weekdays.

As was mentioned above in the discussion of the Akedah's role in the Sephardi rite, the Ashkenazi editors seem to have included it at this particular point to illuminate the theme of suffering in the preceding paragraph, to set the scene for the flight from the inevitability of suffering in the following sequence, or to echo the previous petition not to be subjected to a trial (Extract 25, line 3).[51] They might equally have intended to employ Abraham's obedience as a bargaining point for enlisting God's help in protecting the patriarch's descendants, to allude to the instruction to 'rise early' in a subsequent paragraph, linking Abraham's preparations to morning prayers (Extract 29, lines 1–2), or even to equate Abraham's suffering with that of the speaker. It also resonates with the following sequence on integrity, which similarly emphasizes obedience and fear. But if so, its location here reflects a misunderstanding of the complex interactions in the Sephardi liturgy between the Akedah, the priestly blessing, and the mishnaic coda, missing the themes of the difficulty of study and of reconciling the dual aspects of God. Since brief allusion is sufficient to identify the relevance of the Akedah, the inclusion of the full text, as here, adds nothing, and even threatens to distract from the undercurrents of the argument. It probably reflects an editorial misunderstanding of the Sephardi version.

Its addition here is part of a pattern of ad hoc expansion in this edition, for elsewhere too the editors tend to enlarge on allusions, often with little impact. A similar example, besides the inclusion here of the two non-Shema texts in the *tefilin*, is that of the whole first paragraph of the Shema in the early morning, instead of just the opening line as in our version. This expansion again detracts from the clarity of the argument, which is to explain the need to unify God's names mentioned in the first line.[52]

The passages after the Shema are identical to our version, but only until the sacrificial sequence (Extract 33, lines 9–11). The sacrificial readings, after the introductory prophetic citation, approximate to those that Baer included in smaller type as a gesture towards the east European tradition. They open with the description of the laver in which the priests washed before they began their

---

[51] In our version in Extract 27. The arrangement is again the same as in *Otsar hatefilot*, 65b–66b.   [52] In Extract 27. This paragraph does not appear in *Otsar hatefilot*.

daily work,[53] but continue with one describing the gathering of the previous
day's altar-ashes, which does not appear in Baer.[54] These are followed by a petition for forgiveness and the rebuilding of the Temple, reflecting the circularity of
the attempt to pray in the absence of the Temple,[55] which is followed in turn by
the account of the daily *tamid* included in our version and the verse from
Leviticus in need of midrashic interpretation (Extracts 34 and 35). A short meditation requesting that the recital of sacrifices be regarded as equivalent to their
performance follows, similar to that in the Sephardi liturgy,[56] introducing additional biblical and talmudic passages on the preparation of incense that appear in
Baer as well as the Sephardi version.[57]

The interpolated scriptural verses mourning the absence of the Temple are
also included in our version (Extract 36), but here they are followed not by the
mystic poem that seemed to resolve the mourning over its loss, but by a talmudic
passage, also present in the Sephardi version, concerned with the correct
sequence of rituals. Next appears the medieval poem that in our version is introduced by the scriptural verses above,[58] followed by a petition, noted in the
Sephardi rite and similar to one preceding the incense texts above, which equates
the recital of sacrificial texts to their performance, a theme merely implied in our
own version.[59] The rest of the sequence conforms to our version, consisting of
the mishnaic chapter discussing the location of sacrifices in the Temple, as
appears in all rites (Extract 38), the quasi-talmudic listing of exegetical techniques that challenges the speaker to understand the sacrificial sequence non-
literally, and the concluding petition for the rebuilding of the Temple (Extracts
39 and 40).

This elaboration of the sacrificial sequence underlines the physical reality
of the rituals, including several ceremonies performed by priests alone, as though
the speaker should visualize even those aspects of the cult which non-priests
would normally not have seen. Drawing attention to the precise location of
the cultic rituals thus focuses on the dimension most remote from the exiled
speaker's experience, but makes the Temple available to the senses in a way that
democratizes it, echoing the transfer of Jewish cult from a priestly-run Temple to
a lay-led synagogue.

The remaining preliminaries before the morning service are the same as in
our version, except for the addition of a kabbalistic meditation before the introductory blessing of Pesukei Dezimra.[60]

---

[53] Exod. 30: 17–21.   [54] Lev. 6: 1–6.

[55] It appears also in the Sephardi version discussed above, and its origins are discussed in *Tselota
di'avraham*, i. 87.   [56] Both meditations appear in *Otsar hatefilot*, 72b and 73b.

[57] Exod. 30: 34–6, 7–8; BT *Ker.* 6a–b; JT *Yoma* 4: 5; see *Otsar hatefilot*, 73b–75b.

[58] BT *Yoma* 33a; also in *Otsar hatefilot*, 76b–77a.

[59] Its origins are discussed in *Tselota di'avraham*, i. 104.

[60] In our version before Extract 43, discussed in *Tselota di'avraham*, i. 160.

In general, therefore, this version includes more meditative material around the *talit* and *tefilin* than our own and weakens the comparison between the departure from home and the exile from Jerusalem by omitting verse sequences around the passage from home to synagogue. But it reflects the reality of Temple worship more sharply than our version, although including the full versions of the Akedah narrative, the first paragraph of the Shema, and the non-Shema texts from the *tefilin* reduces the suggestive power of what is already implicit. This version therefore again confirms the accuracy of the liturgical message outlined here, like the Sephardi version described above, but demonstrates how it can be weakened by indiscriminate augmentation.

Progressive Developments

Progressive liturgies have appeared in numerous revised editions since the early nineteenth century, in response to demands for shorter and more decorous services and for the removal of unfashionable theological themes, such as petitions for the rebuilding of the Temple and expressions of Jewish particularism, including the ingathering to the Holy Land.[61] Abbreviating the liturgy in this way does not necessarily shorten the time required to perform services, however, since progressive congregations recite texts reverentially and partly in unison rather than mantrically, as traditional Jews tend to do. If the traditional liturgy were read at such a pace it would indeed be prohibitively long. Apart from removing unfashionable material, however, progressive editors tend to reorganize the remaining elements, often doing so without regard to the underlying messages of the texts involved. Declaring certain texts to be optional makes it necessary to interrupt services with announcements of page-references, with the added effect of transforming a prayer-leader from one who merely paces the recital to one who defines its content, thereby undermining the speaker's independence as a participant and reducing opportunities for entering into reverie.

The removal of certain categories of material also has radical unintended effects on the overall meaning of the liturgy: excising the Temple material, for instance, prevents the liturgical vehicle from being used to discuss homelessness and daily danger. Other losses include the underlying ambivalence over study or prayer noted in this analysis, anxiety over the human ability to comprehend Torah, the debate over God's involvement in suffering, the hesitant consideration and final rejection of the option of force, and the comparison of the speaker to David, the failed Temple-builder. As a result, the speaker in progressive liturgies tends to address God in the expectation of being heard, without considering the theological problems associated with prayer or the philosophical doubts about the power of language that loom large in traditional versions.

---

[61] For a historical study of European Progressive prayer-books, see Petuchowski, *Prayerbook Reform in Europe*.

It might be argued that the intellectual freedoms offered by traditional liturgies are available only to the most learned users, but such learning may not be possessed by the majority of traditional users, who are consequently able to recover meaning only because regular use and mantric performance styles enable them to enter into the kind of reverie discussed in Chapter 2 of this book. It must therefore be asked whether the benefits of added clarity in some progressive liturgies adequately compensate for the loss of the potential for recovering complex meanings.

An edition of the British Reform movement's prayer-book in preparation at the time of writing will provide only one rather than six different versions of the sabbath morning service, reducing opportunities for prayer-leaders' intervention in the structure of services and returning in other respects to a more traditional liturgical structure.

There follow surveys of two of the more common progressive liturgies in use in Britain.

The British Reform Version

The seventh edition of the British Reform prayer-book, or at least its version of the weekday morning liturgy, reveals some of the strengths and limitations of the eclectic approach taken by progressive liturgical editors.[62] The day opens with familiar texts around the *talit*, including the psalmic verses (Psalm 104: 1–2) that appeared in the Artscroll version and the meditation and blessing in our version. However, it unaccountably omits the concluding psalmic verses that so extended the garment's implications (Extracts 3 and 4). This omission is curious since the corresponding verses for the *tefilin* are included. The texts for the *tefilin* lack only the closing meditation that reflects anxieties concerning the understanding of Torah (Extracts 7–9).

A rubric then invites the speaker to choose either Yigdal or Adon Olam, although only the second is fully relevant here, since it relates to daily creation and the problems of perception. There follows the talmudic waking prayer, from which the reference to resurrection has been removed, thereby transforming it into a prayer almost entirely about sleep. The morning blessings that follow appear without the negative formulations,[63] and these are followed by the appeal for integrity that in our version introduces the theme of human weakness (Extract 27). Then comes the petition for protection from daily danger, which in our version follows the morning blessings and precedes the discussion of human worth (Extract 25), and next the Sephardi version of the paragraph that in our version follows the call for integrity and its continuation (Extract 28). This rearrangement of the early-morning liturgy illustrates how it can be abbreviated without major loss of meaning.

---

[62] *Forms of Prayer for Jewish Worship.*

[63] The abridged material is drawn from our Extract 21 and Extract 24, lines 3–4, 6–7, 9–12.

The editorial interventions in the next section are more radical, for only the first of the three blessings over Torah, that alluding to struggle, is retained (Extract 18, lines 1–2). This introduces not an act of study, however, but the closing Davidic text of the traditional Pesukei Dezimra, in which David hands over the building materials of the Temple to his son Solomon, which is then followed by the Nehemiah text related to the second Temple, thereby divorcing the idea of study from the critique of the opacity of Torah and its theological consequences. The Nehemiah text is augmented by a clause appearing only in the Sephardi version, linking the passage to the theme of blessing in the call to prayer that follows this sequence.[64] This unfamiliar blend of study and praise is then followed by the declamation of God's timeless kingship, which features inconspicuously in our rite, but in the Sephardi liturgy seems to conclude a version of Pesukei Dezimra (Extract 47, lines 7–8). The verses attached to that verse by Sephardim appear next, including the messianic statement from Zechariah 14: 9 and the last verse of the book of Psalms; these conclude the preliminary sequence of the morning in this rite, except for an abridged version of the Sephardi closing blessing (Extract 59), even though the opening blessing of the liturgical unit is absent from this version.

The editorial decision to emphasize texts around the ritual garments rather than major liturgical markers tends, therefore, to blur the distinction between the two sequences and to silence several themes central to the liturgical depiction of human experience losing some major implicit themes. It should be mentioned, however, that the editors of this version were working within parameters set by earlier editions, and were far from free in the choices they made.

The British Liberal Version

The version of the weekday morning service in the British Liberal movement's *Siddur Lev Chadash* contrasts with the Reform version in several respects. It begins with the entry into synagogue as in our rite (Extract 12), followed by the poem by Solomon Ibn Gabirol that appeared as an optional reading in Baer's edition. It may have been selected here for its melody, much as Yigdal and Adon Olam probably were in our version, but since it implies the impossibility of prayer and the absence of free will it is courageous to have included it here.[65] There follows the Creation narrative from the book of Genesis, a text absent from traditional liturgies, but here divided into daily readings throughout the week. This completes the first sequence of the morning, entitled Birkhot Hashahar even though it contains no blessing. It also lacks the traditional themes of study, fear of the day ahead, and exile. Paradoxically, since this progressive liturgy is keen to distance itself from Temple practice, the daily reading of Creation is

---

[64] Extract 55 and, after the addition of the previous clause from Neh. 9: 5, Extract 56, lines 1–4.

[65] *Sidur avodat yisra'el*, 34; for an analysis of its meaning see Scheindlin, *The Gazelle*, 170–5.

associated in early rabbinic writings mainly with priests unable to travel to Jerusalem to officiate in the cult, doubtless an unintended association.[66]

The second sequence of the morning opens with an abbreviated version of the introductory blessing of Pesukei Dezimra (Extract 43), followed again by texts for each day of the week. These are, appropriately, psalms, but while that for Sunday was chosen from the mishnaic inventory of those to be read daily in the Temple, the others were not.[67] This forms the core of Pesukei Dezimra, which closes with a version of the concluding blessing for this liturgical unit that appears in our rite (Extract 59).

The editors of this prayer-book thus set out to retain the structure of the traditional liturgy, even though they took a more radical view of its contents than did those who compiled the Reform version. Although it usefully introduces texts specific to each day, thereby providing variety with the minimum of intervention by prayer-leaders and of consequent disruption to reverie, the disappearance of so much multi-layered material—such as the themes of study and the Temple, with their undercurrents of theological paradox—leaves little to remind one of the density and depth of traditional liturgies.

౷

This book ends on a note of caution. Abridging the liturgy may appear to maximize its clarity but, as can be seen from this discussion, in many cases it also risks impoverishing it. The lack of thematic transparency in traditional versions is generally due not to editorial oversight, this book suggests, but to an awareness that some subjects can be approached only in symbolically dense ways and, in the case of the feeling of being overwhelmed by reality, by imitatively echoing the chaos of experience.[68] The extent to which this is the case has become clear only as a result of the present study. The belatedness of this awareness is largely the result of the way in which traditional scholars have tended to underplay liturgical exegesis. This is due to their understanding, which they preferred not to declare openly, that traditional liturgies express ideas which can be presented in no other way. Perhaps uniquely in the Jewish tradition, the liturgy is a text with which each individual must come to terms on his or her own.

---

[66] Mishnah *Ta'an.* 4: 2–3.   [67] Ps. 24, see Mishnah *Tam.* 7: 4.

[68] See also Miller, 'The Limits of Change'.

APPENDIX

❧

Ritual Objects Used in Prayer

❧

Photographs by
RUTHIE MORRIS MA FRPS

Captions by
JEREMY SCHONFIELD

1. Vessel used for ritual hand-washing

The first ritual of the morning is to pour water over the right and left hands alternately three times, ideally using a two-handled vessel such as this, known as a *keli* (see discussion of Extract 16). The handles ensure that a clean hand does not touch a surface touched by an unwashed hand. Since people perform ritual hand-washing at various other times, such as before meals, after using the toilet, or on leaving a cemetery, two-handled hand-washing vessels are commonly available in Jewish homes and public places. They may be made from different materials, ranging from the luxurious (ornate engraved silver) to the rudimentary (plastic). This particular example, made in the 1990s by a Polish Jewish craftsman living in Israel, is hammered out of sheet brass.

2. The *arba kanfot*—the four-cornered undergarment

This lightweight poncho-like garment, known as *arba kanfot*, literally 'four corners', is worn to enable fulfilment of the biblical injunction to attach 'fringes to the corners of your garments' (Num. 15: 38), even though most garments no longer have four corners. Traditionally it is worn by males over the age of 3, either as an undergarment or, in some hasidic traditions, over the shirt, though today some women wear it too.

The most important element of this garment is the four fringes, or *tsitsiyot*. Most commonly, these are made by looping four thin woollen cords through a corner of the garment and knotting them twice. One longer cord is then bound seven times round the others, and all four knotted again. The cord is bound a further eight, eleven, and thirteen times, each group separated by a double knot, leaving the remainder of the eight cords free. The number symbolism is discussed in the context of Extracts 2–6.

This particular example, with black stripes similar to those on a *talit* (see Plate 3), is large enough for the fringes to be worn visibly, hanging outside the shirt and down each leg, even if the garment itself is concealed beneath the shirt. Some people wear smaller ones and keep the fringes inside their clothes. The garment and the blessing recited when putting it on are discussed in the context of Extract 2.

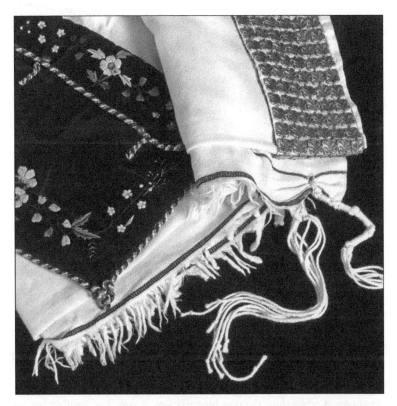

3. The *talit*—a four-cornered prayer-shawl—and decorative bag

The *talit* has here been folded to show its fine *atarah*, literally 'crown', or collar, of linked silver plates, made in the nineteenth century and favoured by an older generation of rabbis. Ashkenazi *talitot* like this are traditionally made of wool and have black stripes, a design going back to antiquity. They are large enough to cover much of the body. On the most solemn days of the year—Rosh Hashanah and Yom Kippur—some people wear all-white ones as a sign of repentance. Some Sephardi Jewish traditions prefer lighter-weight silk *talitot*, frequently with light blue stripes, a design adopted by many Progressive communities. The *talit* is traditionally worn during morning prayers by males (in some traditions, only married males), and in Progressive communities sometimes also by women. As with the *arba kanfot*, the most important element of the *talit*, whatever its size or design, is the ritually knotted fringe (*tsitsit*) at each corner, two of which can be seen here.

This particular *talit* belonged to Rabbi Dr Solomon Schonfeld, on whose edition of the prayer-book this publication is based. It is shown here together with an embroidered velvet bag in which it can be kept when not in use.

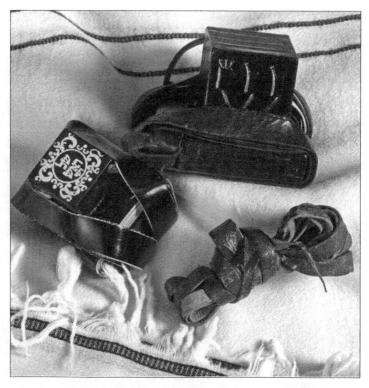

4. A selection of *tefilin*

These examples of *tefilin* show the possible variations in size. The smallest box seen here (12 mm across) dates from the nineteenth century and is western Sephardi in origin, while the largest (42 mm) is early twentieth-century from eastern Europe. The one on the left is new and is relatively small, for convenience when travelling.

The boxes on the right show Hebrew letters in relief on two sides. The faintly visible lines on the top correspond to the separate compartments inside for the four scrolls. The ornamental cover on the left is inscribed *shel rosh*, 'for the head'. The *tefilin* for the hand have no letters on them and also lack compartment-lines, since the four texts inside the boxes are written on a single scroll. Their symbolism is discussed in the context of Extracts 7–10.

The letter *shin*—the initial letter of Shema, the central credal prayer, which is written on a scroll inside the box—is embossed on both sides of the box . However, the shape on each side is different. On the right-hand side (from the point of view of the wearer) it has its usual three ascending arms, as can be seen on the largest box. On the left-hand side it has four arms—the only context in which it appears thus—as can be seen from the small-est box. Possible reasons for this are discussed in the context of Extract 9.

When the *tefilin* are not in use, the straps by which they are attached are wrapped around the boxes, and the *tefilin* themselves are kept in a decorative velvet or silk bag similar to that for the *talit*.

5. Inside view of *tefilin* for the head

An unusual view of *tefilin shel rosh*, 'for the head', with the box opened to show the scrolls in position. It is opened in this way once in seven years, so that the lettering of the scrolls can be checked for deterioration. The box is hand-made of thick parchment, dampened and stretched around a mould of the required shape. The base is reinforced by cuts of parchment, as seen here. The box for the head contains four compartments, one for each text, the scrolls being arranged in the order of their appearance in the Torah. Each scroll is folded, protected by a slip of parchment, and bound with an animal hair before the box is closed. The end of each hair projects outside the box through the aperture just visible at the top of the left-hand compartment, and emerges just between the container and the base. The symbolism is discussed in the context of Extract 7.

The leather strap that passes round the head and holds the box in position passes across the lower part of the picture. When the lid, visible below the box, is sewn to the base of the box, the strap will pass through the loop formed by the hinge. The twelve holes for sewing the box closed can be seen round its base, and three of the corresponding ones on the lid are visible at the foot of the picture.

6. A parchment scroll of the Shema, of the kind contained in *tefilin*

The opening words of a *tefilin* scroll, 40 mm high, containing the first paragraph of the Shema. The nineteenth-century scribe who produced this knew his work would never be seen, but he nevertheless wrote the text as beautifully as if it had been intended for display. The scribe would himself have prepared quills from goose feathers and have made his own ink, and the same techniques are still used today.

The opening words of the Shema, *Shema yisra'el*, 'Hear, O Israel', seen at the top right, are discussed in the context of Extract 31. The three ascenders of the initial letter can be compared with the three and four to be seen in Plates 4 and 7.

The scribe made four prick-marks in each margin of the parchment for ruling horizontal lines to guide his writing. Those in the right-hand margin can be seen here. The rules, which are almost invisible, run above the letters, rather than below, and the writing 'hangs' from them, rather than standing on them as is usual in writing the Latin alphabet.

The silver pointer shown here is of the kind used when reading from a Torah scroll, to protect the writing from being worn by repeated touching. It has been positioned here to obscure the Tetragrammaton, the sacred four-lettered name of God that Jews never pronounce and avoid writing except for sacred ritual purposes, so as not to 'take God's name in vain'. Other than for ritual purposes such as this, it is usually written in full only in copies of the Hebrew Bible. In prayer-books, including the one employed here, it is conventionally represented by a double *yod*. An example of this abbreviation can be seen in Extract 31.

Several of the letters in this scroll have stalk-like 'crowns' over them, known as *tagin*, which, although they appear merely decorative, are regarded as having esoteric significance. Rabbi Akiva, who lived in the second century CE, was said to have derived 'heaps and heaps of laws' from such crowns.

7. A detail of the outside of *tefilin* for the head

This shows the left-hand side of *tefilin shel rosh*, measuring 44 mm across and showing the four-armed letter *shin* embossed in the leather. Its shapely form, complete with elegant *tagin*, or 'crowns', is of a scribal quality rarely attained since the Second World War. The right-hand side of the box, shown in Plate 4, has a normal three-ascender *shin*.

The *shin* seen here is Ashkenazi in form, with a pointed base. On Sephardi *tefilin* the letter has a broader base, sloping down towards the left, reflecting a different scribal tradition. Other distinctive types of *tefilin* exist, but the differences are too complex to be discussed here.

The outside of each box is coated in scribal ink, leaving only the base uncoloured. This pair of *tefilin* has clearly seen much use, since the ink has been touched up a number of times.

8. A *talit* and *tefilin* in use

An Ashkenazi *talit*, a large rectangular garment of fine wool, often with black stripes, is shown here worn over the head, rather than, as is more usual, merely over the shoulders. This is a way both of avoiding visual distractions and of indicating that one does not wish to be disturbed, a useful signal in a synagogue where some might be studying or engaged in conversation while others worship. The edges of the *talit* are seen here hitched over the shoulders, so that the fringes do not trail on the ground.

The *tefilin* for the head are positioned above the hairline, held in place by a strap.

The prayer-book being used here contains only the Hebrew text, without translation or notes. The Jewish tradition of prayer without commentary is discussed in Chapters 1 and 2.

The author is shown here wearing *tefilin* made in the early twentieth century for his grandfather, Rabbi Dr Victor Schönfeld, and which now belong to his own son, the fourth generation to use them.

9. A *talit* and *tefilin* in use, showing the arrangement of straps

The *talit* is shown worn conventionally over the shoulders, rather than over the head.

The *tefilin shel rosh* is secured by a strap knotted at the nape of the neck, the loose ends hanging down the front of the body.

The box of the *tefilin shel yad* is bound to the left upper arm, pointing slightly inwards towards the body, with the strap wound seven times round the forearm. The strap is next passed three times around the middle finger (while reciting the marriage promises in Hos. 2: 21–2), and finally three times round the hand, forming the letter *shin*, the initial letter of the word Shema. This letter—together with the *dalet*-shaped knot at the back of the head and a *yod*-shaped knot beside the box for the hand—spells Shadai, one of the names of God. The symbolism is discussed in the context of Extract 9.

Sephardim wind the strap round the arm in the opposite direction and arrange it differently on the hand.

The two front *tsitsit* are shown here being held in the right hand during the recital of *Barukh she'amar* (Extract 43). At the end of that paragraph they are kissed before being released.

Bibliography

ਝ

Versions of the Prayer-Book

AMRAM GAON, *Seder rav amram hashalem*, ed. Arieh Lev Frumkin, 2 vols. (Jerusalem, 1912).

Artscroll. See *The Complete Artscroll Siddur*

Authorised Daily Prayer Book, ed. Joseph H. Hertz, 3 vols. (London, 1942–5; published in 1 vol., London, 1946).

Authorised Daily Prayer Book, ed. Simeon Singer (London, 1890).

Authorised Daily Prayer Book of the United Hebrew Congregations of the Commonwealth: Centenary Edition, ed. Immanuel Jakobovits (London, 1990).

Authorised Kinot for the Ninth of Av, ed. Abraham Rosenfeld (London, 1965).

BAER, SELIGMANN. See *Sidur avodat yisra'el*

BIRNBAUM, PHILIP. See *Daily Prayer Book*

Book of Prayer According to the Custom of the Spanish and Portuguese Jews, ed. David De Sola Pool (New York, 1941).

Book of Prayer of the Spanish and Portuguese Jews' Congregation, London, ed. Solomon Gaon: *Daily and Occasional Prayers* (London, 1958); *Day of Atonement Service* (London, 1969); *New Year Service* (London, 1971).

The Complete Artscroll Siddur, ed. Nosson Scherman (New York, 1984).

Daily Prayer Book, ed. Philip Birnbaum (New York, 1949).

DE SOLA, D. A. See *The Festival Prayers*; *Seder hatefilot. Forms of Prayer*

DE SOLA POOL, DAVID. See *Book of Prayer According to the Custom of the Spanish and Portuguese Jews*

EMDEN, JACOB, *Amudei shamayim* [*Sidur haya'avets*], 2 vols. (Altona, 1745–8); ed. J. S. H. Weinfeld (Jerusalem, 1993).

The Festival Prayers According to the Custom of the German and Polish Jews, ed. D. A. De Sola, 6 vols. (London, 1860).

Festival Prayers According to the Custom of the German and Polish Jews, ed. David Levi, 6 vols. (London, 1794–6).

Forms of Prayer for Jewish Worship: Daily, Sabbath and Occasional Prayers (London, 1977).

GAON, SOLOMON. See *Book of Prayer*

GORDON, ARIEH-LEV. See *Sidur otsar hatefilot*

HEIDENHEIM, WOLF. See *Sefat emet*; *Sefer kerovot hu mahazor*

HERTZ, JOSEPH H. See *Authorised Daily Prayer Book*, ed. Joseph H. Hertz

HOFFMAN, LAWRENCE. See *My People's Prayer Book*

HOROWITZ, ISAIAH, *Sidur hashelah hashalem: sha'ar hashamayim* (Amsterdam, 1717; new edn., 3 vols., Jerusalem, 1977).

Israels Gebete, ed. Samson Raphael Hirsch (Frankfurt am Main, 1906).

JAKOBOVITS, IMMANUEL. See *Authorised Daily Prayer Book of the United Hebrew Congregations*

Kol-bo. See *Sidur umaḥazor kol-bo*

KOOK, ABRAHAM. See *Seder tefilot im olat re'iyah*

Korban aharon, ed. Aaron ben Yehiel Halevi of Mikhailishok, 2 vols. (Slavuta, 1823).

LEVI, DAVID. See *Festival Prayers*; *Seder tefilot*

Maḥazor leyamim nora'im [*Rosh hashanah*], ed. Daniel Goldschmidt (Jerusalem, 1970).

My People's Prayer Book: Traditional Prayers, Modern Commentaries, ed. Lawrence Hoffman, 7 vols. (Woodstock, Vt., 1997–); vol. i: *The Sh'ma and its Blessings*; vol. ii: *The Amidah*; vol. iii: *P'sukei D'zimrah*; vol. iv: *Seder K'riat Hatorah*; vol. v: *Birkhot Hashachar*; vol. vi: *Tachanun and Concluding Prayers*; vol. vii: *Shabbat at Home*; vol. viii: *Kabbalat Shabbat*.

Nehora hashalem, ed. Aaron ben Yehiel Halevi of Mikhailishok (Slavuta, 1819; Vilna, 1840).

Olat re'iyah. See *Seder tefilot im olat re'iyah*

Or Hadash: A Commentary on Siddur Sim Shalom for Sabbath and Festivals, ed. Reuven Hammer (New York, 2003).

The Orot Sephardic Weekday Siddur, ed. Eliezer Toledano (Lakewood, NJ, 1994).

Otsar hatefilot. See *Sidur otsar hatefilot*

Pirkei Avot: The Sayings of the Fathers—Also the Sabbath Minchah *Service with an Orthodox English Translation and a Lineal Set of References*, ed. Solomon Schonfeld (London, 1969).

Routledge *maḥazor*. See *Service of the Synagogue*

SA'ADIAH GAON, *Sidur rav sa'adiah gaon*, ed. I. Davidson, S. Assaf, and B. I. Joel (Jerusalem, 1941; 5th edn., 1985).

SCHONFELD, SOLOMON. See *Pirkei Avot*; *Sidur metsuyan*

Seder hatefilot, ed. B. Meyers and A. Alexander (London, 1770).

Seder hatefilot. Forms of Prayer According to the Custom of the Spanish and Portuguese Jews, ed. D. A. De Sola, 5 vols. (London, 1836–8).

Seder tefilot. The Form of Prayers According to the Custom of the Spanish and Portuguese Jews, ed. David Levi, 6 vols. (London, 1789–93).

Seder tefilot im olat re'iyah, ed. Abraham Kook, 2 vols. (Jerusalem, 1939; repr. 1985).

Sefat emet, ed. Wolf Heidenheim (Rödelheim, 1806).

Sefer kerovot hu maḥazor, ed. Wolf Heidenheim, 9 vols. (Rödelheim, 1800–5); 9th vol., *Maḥazor lehag hashavuot* (1805).

Service of the Synagogue, ed. Arthur Davis and Herbert Adler: *New Year* (London, 1906); *Passover* (London, 1908); *Day of Atonement*, 2 vols. (London, 1944); *Pentecost* (14th edn., London, 1954).

Siddur Lev Chadash, Union of Liberal and Progressive Synagogues (London, 1995).

Sidur avodat halevavot, ed. Wolf Ze'ev Jawitz (Berlin, 1922; repr. Jerusalem, 1966).

Sidur avodat yisra'el, ed. Seligmann Baer (Rödelheim, 1868; repr. Berlin, 1937).

Sidur metsuyan: The Standard Siddur-Prayer Book with an Orthodox English Translation and a *Lineal Set of References*, ed. Solomon Schonfeld (London, 1973; repr. 1974, 1976).

Sidur otsar hatefilot, ed. Arieh-Lev Gordon (Vilna, 1914).

Sidur rinat yisra'el, ed. Shelomoh Tal (Jerusalem, 1972).

Sidur tefilah lemosheh, ed. A. S. Lupinski and Z. Weinreb, 3 vols. (Jerusalem, 2001).

Sidur umaḥazor kol-bo, 4 vols. (Vilna, 1904).

Singer's Siddur. See *Authorised Daily Prayer Book*, ed. Simeon Singer

SOLOMON OF WORMS, *Sidur rabenu shelomoh migarmaisa*, ed. Moses Hirschler (Jerusalem, 1971).

Tselota di'avraham, ed. Jacob Werdiger (vols. i–ii: Tel Aviv, 1963; vols. iii–v: Jerusalem, 1991–3).

General Bibliography

ABOAB, ISAAC, *Menorat hamaor*, ed. J. P. Horeb (Jerusalem, 1961).

ABRAHAM BEN ISAAC, *Sefer ha'eshkol*, ed. S. Albeck (Berlin, 1933; repr. Jerusalem, 1984).

ABRAHAM HAYARHI OF LUNEL, *Sefer hamanhig*, ed. Y. Raphael, 2 vols. (Jerusalem, 1978).

ABRAHAMS, ISRAEL, *Companion to the Daily Prayer Book* (London, 1922).

ABRAHAMS, ISRAEL, 'Belief', *Encyclopaedia Judaica* (Jerusalem, 1971), iv. 429–36.

ABUDARHAM, DAVID, *Abudarham hashalem* (Jerusalem, 1963).

AGNON, SHMUEL YOSEF, *Days of Awe*, trans. M. T. Galpert and J. Sloan, introd. Judah Goldin (New York, 1965).

ALBO, JOSEPH, *Sefer ha'ikarim*, trans. Isaac Husik, 5 vols. (Philadelphia, Pa., 1946).

ALFASI, ISAAC, *Hilkhot rav alfas*, 5 vols. (Vilna, 1907).

ALTER, ROBERT, *The Art of Biblical Narrative* (London, 1981).

—— *The World of Biblical Literature* (London, 1992).

—— and FRANK KERMODE (eds.), *The Literary Guide to the Bible* (London, 1987).

ANDERSON, WILLIAM, *The Rise of the Gothic* (London, 1985).

ANON., 'Ana bekho'aḥ', *Encyclopaedia Judaica* (Jerusalem, 1971), iii, cols. 25–6.

ASSAF, S., and E. URBACH, 'Agadah', *Ha'entsiklopediyah ha'ivrit*, vol. i (Jerusalem, 1954), 353–65.

AUERBACH, ERICH, *Mimesis: The Representation of Reality in Western Literature* (Princeton, NJ, 1953).

Avot derabi natan, ed. Solomon Schechter (Vienna, 1887).

AZULAI, HAYIM JOSEPH DAVID, *Shem hagedolim* (Vienna, 1864).

Babylonian Talmud, 26 vols. (Vilna, 1894).

The Babylonian Talmud Translated into English with Notes, Glossary and Indices under the Editorship of Rabbi Dr I. Epstein, 18 vols. (London, 1935–52; repr. 1978).

BARTHES, ROLAND, 'The Death of the Author', in David Lodge (ed.), *Modern Criticism and Theory* (London, 1988), 167–72.

BEIT-ARIE, MALACHI, 'The Affinity between Early Hebrew Printing and

Manuscripts' (Heb.), in M. Nadav and J. Rothschild (eds.), *Essays and Studies in Librarianship Presented to C. D. Wormann* (Jerusalem, 1975), 27–39, 113.

Beit hamidrash, ed. Adolph Jellinek, 2 vols. (repr. Jerusalem, 1967).

BENISCH, PEARL, *Carry Me in Your Heart: The Life and Legacy of Sarah Schenirer* (Jerusalem, 2002).

BENJACOB, I., *Otsar hasefarim* (Vilna, 1880).

BEN-SASSON, H. H., 'Maimonidean Controversy', *Encyclopaedia Judaica* (Jerusalem, 1971), xi. 745–54.

BEN YEHUDA, ELIEZER, *A Complete Dictionary of Ancient and Modern Hebrew*, 16 vols. (Berlin, Jerusalem, 1910–59).

BERLINER, ABRAHAM, *Randbemerkungen zum Täglichen Gebetbuch (Siddur)*, 2 vols. (Berlin, 1909, 1912).

BLAKE, WILLIAM, *The Complete Poems*, ed. W. H. Stevenson and David Erdman (London, 1971).

BLANK, DEBRA REED, 'Some Considerations Underlying Jewish Liturgical Revisions', *CCAR Journal*, 50/1 (Winter 2003), 11–20.

BLOOM, HAROLD, *The Anxiety of Influence* (Oxford, 1973).

BLUMENTHAL, DAVID, *Facing the Abusing God* (Louisville, Ky., 1993).

BOYARIN, DANIEL, *Intertextuality and the Reading of Midrash* (Bloomington, Ind., 1990).

—— 'The Song of Songs: Lock or Key? Intertextuality, Allegory and Midrash', in Regina Schwartz (ed.), *The Book and the Text* (Oxford, 1990), 214–30.

BRUNS, GERALD, 'The Hermeneutics of Midrash', in Regina Schwartz (ed.), *The Book and the Text* (Oxford, 1990), 189–213.

—— 'Midrash and Allegory: The Beginnings of Scriptural Interpretation', in Robert Alter and Frank Kermode (eds.), *The Literary Guide to the Bible* (London, 1987), 625–46.

BURN, A. R., *The Pelican History of Greece* (Harmondsworth, 1965).

CALMAN, MARIANNE, *The Carrière of Carpentras* (Oxford, 1984).

CARLEBACH, ALEXANDER, 'Aaron of Pesaro', *Encyclopaedia Judaica* (Jerusalem, 1971), ii. 22.

CARMI, TED (ed.), *The Penguin Book of Hebrew Verse* (Harmondsworth, 1981).

CARO, JOSEPH, *Beit yosef*, commentary on Jacob ben Asher, *Arba'ah turim*.

—— *Shulḥan arukh*, 'Oraḥ ḥayim', 2 vols. (Lemberg, 1876).

COHEN, HAYIM, 'Talion', *Encyclopaedia Judaica* (Jerusalem, 1971), xv. 471–2.

COHN, GABRIEL, and HAROLD FISCH (eds.), *Prayer in Judaism: Continuity and Change* (Northvale, NJ, 1996).

DAICHES, SAMUEL, *Babylonian Oil Magic in the Talmud and the Later Jewish Literature* (London, 1913).

DAMROSCH, DAVID, *The Narrative Covenant* (Ithaca, NY, 1987).

DANBY, HERBERT, *The Mishnah* (Oxford, 1933).

DAVIDSON, ISRAEL, *Thesaurus of Medieval Hebrew Poetry* [Otsar hashirah vehapiyut], 4 vols. + supplement (New York, 1925–38).

DEMBITZ, LEWIS, *Jewish Services in Synagogue and Home* (Philadelphia, Pa., 1898).

DOUGLAS, MARY, *Leviticus as Literature* (Oxford, 1999).

ELBOGEN, ISMAR, *Jewish Liturgy: A Comprehensive History*, trans. Raymond Scheindlin (New York, 1993).

ELEAZAR OF WORMS, *Sefer haroke'aḥ* (Jerusalem, 1966).

EMANUEL, MOSHE, *Tefillin: The Inside Story* (Jerusalem, 1995).

Encyclopaedia Judaica, 16 vols. (Jerusalem, 1971).

EPSTEIN, BARUKH, *Barukh she'amar* (Tel Aviv, 1968).

EPSTEIN, YEHIEL MIKHEL, *Kitsur shenei luḥot haberit* (Warsaw, 1874).

FALK, JACOB JOSHUA BEN TSEVI HIRSH, *Penei yehoshua* (Warsaw, 1868).

FISH, STANLEY, 'Interpreting the *Variorum*', in David Lodge (ed.), *Modern Criticism and Theory* (London, 1988), 311–46.

FISHBANE, MICHAEL, 'Inner Biblical Exegesis: Types and Strategies of Interpretation in Ancient Israel', in Geoffrey Hartman and Sanford Budick (eds.), *Midrash and Literature* (New Haven, Conn., 1986), 19–37.

——(ed.), *The Midrashic Imagination* (New York, 1993).

FISHMAN, ISIDORE, *The History of Jewish Education in Central Europe* (London, 1944).

FLEISCHER, EZRA, *Tefilah uminhagei tefilah arts-yisra'eliyim bitekufat hagenizah* (Jerusalem, 1988).

FOX, MARVIN, 'Prayer in the Thought of Maimonides', in Gabriel Cohn and Harold Fisch (eds.), *Prayer in Judaism: Continuity and Change* (Northvale, NJ, 1996), 119–41.

FREEHOF, SOLOMON, 'The Structure of the Birchos Hashachar', *HUCA* 22/3 (1950–1), 339–54.

FREUD, SIGMUND, *Moses and Monotheism*, in James Strachey (ed.), *The Standard Edition of the Complete Psychological Works of Sigmund Freud*, vol. xxiii (London, 1964), 1–137.

FRIEDMAN, NATHAN TSEVI, *Otsar harabanim* (Benei Berak, [1975]).

FÜRST, JULIUS, *Bibliotheca Judaica*, 3 vols. (Leipzig, 1863).

GAGUINE, SHEMTOB, *Keter shem tov* (vols. i–ii: Kėdainiai, 1934; vol. iii: London, 1948; vols. iv–v: London, 1954; vol. vi: London, 1955).

GANZFRIED, SOLOMON, supercommentary on Jacob Lorbeerbaum, *Derekh haḥayim* (Vienna, 1839).

GASTER, THEODOR, 'Modernizing the Jewish Prayerbook', *Commentary*, 17 (1954), 352–60.

GENETTE, GÉRARD, 'Structuralism and Literary Criticism', in David Lodge (ed.), *Modern Criticism and Theory* (London, 1988), 63–78.

GESENIUS, WILHELM, *Handwoerterbuch ueber das Alte Testament* (Leipzig, 1921).

——*Hebrew Grammar* (Oxford, 1910).

GINZBERG, LOUIS, *The Legends of the Jews*, 7 vols. (Philadelphia, Pa., 1909–38).

GLATZER, NAHUM (ed.), *Franz Rosenzweig: His Life and Thought* (New York, 1972).

GOLDIN, JUDAH, *The Fathers According to Rabbi Nathan* (New Haven, Conn., 1955).

GOLDSCHMIDT, DANIEL, 'Prayer Books', *Encyclopaedia Judaica* (Jerusalem, 1971), xiii. 985–94.

GOLINKIN, DAVID, 'May Women Wear Tefillin?', *Conservative Judaism*, 50 (1997), 3–18.

GORDIS, ROBERT, *Koheleth: The Man and his World: A Study of Ecclesiastes* (New York, 1968).

GOTTLIEB, EFRAIM, 'Gerondi, Jacob ben Sheshet', *Encyclopaedia Judaica* (Jerusalem, 1971), vii. 507–8.

GREEN, ARTHUR, *Tormented Master: The Life of Rabbi Nahman of Bratslav* (Woodstock, Vt., 1992).

——(ed.), *Jewish Spirituality*, 2 vols. (London, 1986, 1987).

GROSSMAN, AVRAHAM, *Pious and Rebellious: Jewish Women in Europe in the Middle Ages* [Ḥasidot umoredot: nashim yehudiyot be'eiropah biyemei habeinayim] (Jerusalem, 2001).

GRUENWALD, ITHAMAR, *Apocalyptic and Merkavah Mysticism* (Leiden, 1980).

HALEVI, JUDAH, *Kitab al Khazari*, trans. Hartwig Hirschfeld (London, 1905).

—— *Sefer hakuzari* (Pressburg, 1860).

HAMMER, REUVEN, *Entering Jewish Prayer: A Guide to Personal Devotion and the Worship Service* (New York, 1994).

HARDY, THOMAS, *The Return of the Native* (London, 1961).

HARLOW, JULES, *Pray Tell: A Hadassah Guide to Jewish Prayer* (Woodstock, Vt., 2003).

HARTMAN, DAVID, 'Prayer and Religious Consciousness: An Analysis of Jewish Prayer in the Works of Joseph B. Soloveitchik, Yeshayahu Leibowitz, and Abraham Joshua Heschel', *Modern Judaism*, 23/2 (2003), 105–25.

HARTMAN, GEOFFREY, and SANFORD BUDICK (eds.), *Midrash and Literature* (New Haven, Conn., 1986).

HAUT, IRWIN H., 'Are Women Obligated to Pray?', in Susan Grossman and Rivka Haut (eds.), *Daughters of the King: Women and the Synagogue* (Philadelphia, Pa., 1992), 89–101.

HAYMAN, PETER, 'Some Observations on Sefer Yesira: 2. The Temple at the Centre of the Universe', *Journal of Jewish Studies*, 37 (1986), 176–82.

HAYS, RICHARD, *Echoes of Scripture in the Letters of Paul* (New Haven, Conn., 1989).

HEILMAN, SAMUEL, *The People of the Book: Drama, Fellowship and Religion* (Chicago, 1983; 2nd edn. New Brunswick, NJ, 2002).

—— *Synagogue Life: A Study in Symbolic Interaction* (Chicago, 1976).

HEINEMANN, JOSEPH, 'The Fixed and the Fluid in Jewish Prayer', in Gabriel Cohn and Harold Fisch (eds.), *Prayer in Judaism: Continuity and Change* (Northvale, NJ, 1996), 45–52.

——'The Nature of the Aggadah', in Geoffrey Hartman and Sanford Budick (eds.), *Midrash and Literature* (New Haven, Conn., 1986), 41–55.

—— *Prayer in the Talmud*, trans. from the Hebrew by Richard Sarason (Berlin and New York, 1977).

HENDERSON, GEORGE, *Chartres* (Harmondsworth, 1968).

HERFORD, ROBERT TRAVERS, *Pirke Aboth* (New York, 1930).

HERTZ, J. H. (ed.), *The Pentateuch and Haftorahs*, 5 vols. (Oxford, 1929–36; in 1 vol. London, 1937).

HINCHELWOOD, ROBERT, *A Dictionary of Kleinian Thought* (London, 1991).

HIRSCH, SAMSON RAPHAEL, *Horeb: A Philosophy of Jewish Laws and Observances*, trans. Isidore Grunfeld, 2 vols. (London, 1962).

—— *The Pentateuch Translated and Explained*, trans. Isaac Levy, 5 vols. (London, 1962).

HOFFMAN, LAWRENCE, *The Art of Public Prayer* (Woodstock, Vt., 1988).

—— *The Canonization of the Synagogue Service* (Notre Dame, Ind., 1979).

HOFFMANN, DAVID, *Das Buch Leviticus uebersetzt und erklaert* (Berlin, 1905).

HOLLANDER, JOHN, *The Figure of Echo: A Mode of Allusion in Milton* (Berkeley, Calif., 1981).

HORBURY, WILLIAM, 'The Cult of Christ and the Cult of the Saints', *New Testament Studies*, 44 (1998), 444–69.

HOROWITZ, ISAIAH, *Shenei luhot haberit* (Amsterdam, 1649).

HOROWITZ, YEHOSHUA, 'Hanokh Zundel ben Joseph', *Encyclopaedia Judaica* (Jerusalem, 1971), vii. 1277.

IBN GABIROL, SOLOMON, *Shirei hakodesh lerabi shelomoh ibn gabirol*, ed. Dov Jarden, 2 vols. (Jerusalem, 1971).

IDEL, MOSHE, 'Midrashic versus Other Forms of Jewish Hermeneutics: Some Comparative Reflections', in Michael Fishbane (ed.), *The Midrashic Imagination* (New York, 1993), 45–58.

IDELSOHN, A. Z., *Jewish Liturgy and its Development* (New York, 1967).

ILAN, TAL, *Jewish Women in Greco-Roman Palestine: An Inquiry into Image and Status* (Tübingen, 1995).

—— *Mine and Yours Are Hers: Retrieving Women's History from Rabbinic Literature* (Leiden, 1997).

IMMANUEL OF ROME, *Mahbarot imanu'el haromi*, ed. Dov Jarden, 2 vols. (Jerusalem, 1957).

ISAAC BEN MOSES OF VIENNA, *Or zarua* (Jerusalem, n.d.).

ISER, WOLFGANG, *The Act of Reading: A Theory of Aesthetic Response* (Baltimore, Md., 1978).

—— 'The Reading Process: A Phenomenological Approach', in David Lodge (ed.), *Modern Criticism and Theory* (London, 1988), 212–28.

ISRAEL ME'IR HAKOHEN, *Mishnah berurah*, 6 vols. (Piotrków, 1891–1907).

JACOB BEN ASHER, *Arba'ah turim*, 7 vols. (Vilna, 1900).

JACOBS, LOUIS, *Hasidic Prayer* (London, 1972).

—— *Jewish Prayer* (London, 1962).

—— *A Jewish Theology* (London, 1973).

—— *Principles of the Jewish Faith* (London, 1964).

JACOBSON, B. S., *Netiv binah*, vol. i (Tel Aviv, 1964); trans. as *Meditations on the Siddur* (Tel Aviv, 1978) and *The Weekday Siddur* (Tel Aviv, 1978).

JASTROW, MARCUS, *A Dictionary of the Targumim, the Talmud Babli and Yerushalmi, and the Midrashic Literature* (Berlin, 1926).

JELLINEK, ADOLF, *Beit hamidrash*, 6 vols. (Leipzig, 1853–78).

Jerusalem Talmud, 2 vols. (Berlin, 1929).

The Jewish Encyclopedia, 12 vols. (New York, 1901–7).

JOSIPOVICI, GABRIEL, *The Book of God* (New Haven, Conn., 1988).

JUDAH BEN SAMUEL HEHASID, *Perushei sidur hatefilah laroke'ah*, ed. Moses Hirschler, 2 vols. (Jerusalem, 1992).

JUDAH BEN YAKAR, *Perush hatefilot vehaberakhot*, ed. S. Yerushalmi (Jerusalem, 1968; expanded edn. 1979).

JUDAH LOEW BEN BEZALEL, *Netivot olam* (Jerusalem, 1972).

KADISH, SETH, *Kavvana: Directing the Heart in Jewish Prayer* (Northvale, NJ, 1997).

KAGAN, ISRAEL ME'IR HAKOHEN, *Mishnah berurah*, 6 vols. (Piotrków and Warsaw, 1891–1921).

KAHANA, ABRAHAM, *Sefer hahasidut* (Warsaw, 1922).

KAHN, YOEL, and DANIEL LANDES, 'On Gentiles, Slaves, and Women: The Blessings "Who Did Not Make Me"', in L. Hoffman (ed.), *My People's Prayer Book*, vol. v (Woodstock, Vt., 2001), 17–34.

KANT, IMMANUEL, *Religion within the Limits of Reason Alone*, trans. T. M. Greene and H. H. Hudson (New York, 1960).

KASHER, MENACHEM (ed.), *Hagadah shelemah* (Jerusalem, 1956).

—— *Torah shelemah*, 45 vols. (Jerusalem, New York 1927–).

KATZENELLENBOGEN, MORDECHAI LEIB (ed.), *Hagadah shel pesah: torat hayim* (Jerusalem, 1998).

KEATS, JOHN, *The Letters of John Keats, 1814–1821*, ed. H. E. Rollins, 2 vols. (Cambridge, 1958).

KELLNER, MENACHEM, *Must a Jew Believe Anything?* (London, 1999).

KERMODE, FRANK, *The Genesis of Secrecy* (London, 1979).

KIMELMAN, REUVEN, 'A Prolegomena to *Lekhah Dodi* and *Kabalat Shabat*' (Heb.), in Aviezer Ravitzky (ed.), *Jerusalem Studies in Jewish Thought*, 14 (Jerusalem, 1998), pp. xx–xxii, 393–454.

—— 'Psalm 145: Theme, Structure, and Impact', *Journal of Biblical Literature*, 113 (1994), 37–58.

KITTEL, RUDOLF (ed.), *Biblia Hebraica* (Leipzig, 1909).

KLATZKIN, JACOB, *Otsar munahim filosofi'im*, 4 vols. (Leipzig, 1928).

KRAEMER, DAVID, *Responses to Suffering in Classical Rabbinic Literature* (Oxford, 1995).

KRAUSS, SAMUEL, *Griechische and lateinische Lehnwörter im Talmud, Midrasch and Targum*, 2 vols. (Berlin, 1899).

—— 'The Jewish Rite of Covering the Head', *HUCA* 19 (1946), 121–68.

KUGEL, JAMES, *The Idea of Biblical Poetry: Parallelism and its History* (New Haven, Conn., 1981).

—— 'Two Introductions to Midrash', in Geoffrey Hartman and Sanford Budick (eds.), *Midrash and Literature* (Ne Haven, Conn., 1986), 77–103.

KUPFER, EPHRAIM, 'Jacob Lorbeerbaum', *Encyclopaedia Judaica* (Jerusalem, 1971), xi. 492–3.

LAMM, NORMAN (ed.), *The Religious Thought of Hasidism: Text and Commentary* (New York, 1999).

LANDES, DANIEL, 'The Halakhah of Waking Up', in Lawrence Hoffman (ed.), *My People's Prayer Book* (Woodstock, Vt., 2001), v. 35–42.

LANGER, RUTH, *To Worship God Properly* (Cincinnati, Ohio, 1999).

LAYTNER, ANSON, *Arguing with God: A Jewish Tradition* (Northvale, NJ, 1990).

LEIBOWITZ, YESHAYAHU, *Judaism, Human Values, and the Jewish State* (Cambridge, Mass., 1992).

Lekaḥ tov, ed. Solomon Buber, 2 vols. (Vilna, 1884).

LEVENE, ABRAHAM, *The Early Syrian Fathers on Genesis* (London, 1951).

LEVINE, YAEL, 'Women who Composed Prayers for the Public: A Historical Study' (Heb.), in Joseph Tabory (ed.), *Kenishta: Studies in the Synagogue World* (Tel Aviv, 2003), ii. 89–97.

LEVINGER, JACOB, 'Solomon Ganzfried', *Encyclopaedia Judaica* (Jerusalem, 1971), vii. 313–15.

LEVY, BARRY, *Fixing God's Torah: The Accuracy of Jewish Law* (New York, 2001).

LEVY, ELIEZER, *Yesodot hatefilah* (Tel Aviv, 1961).

LEWIN, DANIEL, *A Jewish Geneology* [*sic*]*: The Lewin–Steinberger Saga* (Great Neck, NY, 1993).

LIEBER, DAVID, 'Census', *Encyclopaedia Judaica* (Jerusalem, 1971), v. 281–3.

LIEBREICH, LEON, 'The Compilation of the Pesuke de-Zimra', *Proceedings of the American Academy for Jewish Research*, 18 (1948–9), 255–67.

—— 'The Impact of Nehemiah 9: 5–37 on the Liturgy of the Synagogue', *HUCA* 32 (1961), 227–37.

LITTMAN, LOUIS, 'The Littman Library of Jewish Civilization', *Jewish Historical Studies: Transactions of the Jewish Historical Society of England*, 29 (1988), 311–25.

LODGE, DAVID (ed.), *Modern Criticism and Theory* (London, 1988).

LOEB, ISIDORE, 'Les Dix-huit bénédictions', *Revue des Études Juives*, 19 (1889), 17–40.

LOEWE, HERBERT, *Mosaic Revelation*, Presidential Lecture to the Society for Old Testament Study, 5 (London, 1939).

LOEWE, RAPHAEL, 'Akdamuth: A Liturgical Fossil', *The Jewish Outlook* (May 1947), 3.

—— 'Ark, Archaicism and Misappropriation', in Ada Rapoport-Albert and Gillian Greenberg (eds.), *Biblical Hebrews, Biblical Texts* (Sheffield, 2001), 113–45.

—— 'The Bible in Medieval Hebrew Poetry', in J. A. Emerton and Stefan Reif (eds.), *Interpreting the Hebrew Bible: Essays in Honour of E. I. J. Rosenthal* (Cambridge, 1982), 133–55.

—— 'Hebrew Linguistics', in Giulio Lepschy, *History of Linguistics*, i: *The Eastern Traditions of Linguistics* (London, 1994), 97–163.

—— *Ibn Gabirol* (London, 1989).

—— 'Jerome's Rendering of *Olam*', *HUCA* 22 (1949), 265–306.

—— 'The Jewish Midrashim and Patristic and Scholastic Exegesis of the Bible', *Studia Patristica*, 1 (1957), 492–515.

—— 'The "Plain" Meaning of Scripture in Early Jewish Exegesis', *Papers of the Institute of Jewish Studies*, 1 (1964), 140–85.

—— *The Position of Women in Judaism* (London, 1966).

LOEWE, RAPHAEL (ed.), *The Rylands Haggadah* (London, 1988).

LORBEERBAUM, JACOB, *Derekh haḥayim* (Żółkiew, 1828).

Maḥzor vitry, ed. S. Hurwitz (2nd edn., Nuremberg, 1923).

MAIMONIDES, MOSES, *The Code of Maimonides, Book 8: Book of the Temple Service*, trans. Mendel Lewittes (New Haven, Conn., 1957).

—— *The Code of Maimonides, Book 14: The Book of Judges*, trans. A. M. Hershman (New Haven, Conn., 1963).

—— *The Guide of the Perplexed*, trans. Shlomo Pines (Chicago, 1963).

—— *Mishneh torah*, ed. Samuel Rubinstein, 17 vols. (Jerusalem, 1958–62).

—— *Mishneh Torah: The Book of Adoration*, trans. Moses Hyamson (Jerusalem, 1962).

—— *Mishneh Torah: The Book of Knowledge by Maimonides*, trans. Moses Hyamson (new corrected edn., Jerusalem, 1981).

MALBIM, MEIR LEVUSH, *Mikra'ei kodesh*, 11 vols. (Vilna, 1891).

MANDELKERN, SOLOMON, *Veteris Testamenti Concordantiae* (Tel Aviv, 1978).

MARCUS, IVAN, 'The Devotional Ideals of Ashkenazic Pietism', in Arthur Green (ed.), *Jewish Spirituality* (London, 1986), i. 356–66.

MARMORSTEIN, ARTHUR, *The Old Rabbinic Doctrine of God*, i: *The Names and Attributes of God* (Oxford, 1927).

Mekhilta derabi shimon bar yoḥai, ed. D. Hoffmann (Frankfurt am Main, 1905).

Mekhilta derabi yishma'el, ed. and trans. Jacob Lauterbach, 3 vols. (Philadelphia, Pa., 1933–5).

MENN, ESTHER, 'Praying King and Sanctuary of Prayer, Part 2: David's Deferment and the Temple's Dedication in Rabbinic Psalms Commentary (Midrash Tehillim)', *Journal of Jewish Studies*, 53 (2002), 298–323.

MEYER, MICHAEL, '"How Awesome Is This Place!" The Reconceptualisation of the Synagogue in Nineteenth-Century Germany', *Leo Baeck Institute Yearbook*, 41 (1996), 51–63.

Midrash agadah, ed. Salomon Buber (Vienna, 1894).

Midrash mishlei, ed. Salomon Buber (Vilna, 1893).

The Midrash on Psalms, trans. William Braude, 2 vols. (New Haven, Conn., 1959).

Midrash rabah, 2 vols. (Vilna, 1894).

The Midrash Rabbah: Translated into English with Notes, Glossary, and Indices, ed. H. Freedman and M. Simon, 5 vols. (London, 1977).

Midrash tanḥuma (Warsaw, n.d.).

Midrash tanḥuma hakadum vehayashan, ed. Salomon Buber (repr. Jerusalem, n.d.).

Midrash tehilim, ed. Salomon Buber, 2 vols. (Vilna, 1891).

MILLER, ALAN W., 'The Limits of Change in Judaism: Reshaping Liturgy', *Conservative Judaism*, 41/2 (1988–9), 21–8.

MILLGRAM, ABRAHAM, *Jewish Worship* (Philadelphia, Pa., 1971).

The Minor Tractates of the Talmud, ed. A. Cohen (London, 1965).

Mishnah, 12 vols. (Vilna; repr. New York, n.d.).

MITCHELL, JULIET, 'Femininity, Narrative and Psychoanalysis', in David Lodge (ed.), *Modern Criticism and Theory* (London, 1988), 426–30.

MONTEFIORE, CLAUDE, and HERBERT LOEWE (eds.), *A Rabbinic Anthology* (London, 1938).

MOSES BEN MAKHIR, *Seder hayom* (Warsaw, 1871).

MOSES OF PREMYSL, *Mateh mosheh*, ed. M. Knoblowicz (London, 1958).

MUNK, ELIE, *The World of Prayer*, trans. Henry Biberfeld and Leonard Oschry, 2 vols. (New York, 1954 (repr. 1961); 1963).

MUNK, MICHAEL, *The Wisdom in the Hebrew Alphabet* (New York, 1983).

NAHMAN OF BRATZLAV, *Likutei moharan*, 2 vols. (Jerusalem, 1993).

NEUSNER, JACOB et al. (eds.), *The Encyclopaedia of Judaism*, 3 vols. (Leiden, 2000).

NEWMAN, LOUIS, *The Hasidic Anthology* (New York, 1934).

NICHOLSON, ERNEST, *The Pentateuch in the Twentieth Century: The Legacy of Julius Wellhausen* (Oxford, 1998).

NULMAN, MACY, *The Encyclopedia of Jewish Prayer* (New York, 1993).

Otsar midrashim, ed. J. D. Eisenstein, 2 vols., through-paginated (New York, 1915).

OZ, AMOS, *The Story Begins: Essays in Literature* (London, 1999).

PARSONS, MICHAEL, *The Dove that Returns, the Dove that Vanishes: Paradox and Creativity in Psychoanalysis* (London, 2000).

Pesikta de-Rab Kahana, trans. William Braude and Israel Kapstein (London, 1975).

Pesikta derav kahana, ed. Salomon Buber (Lyck, 1868).

Pesikta rabati, ed. M. Friedmann (Vienna, 1880).

Pesikta Rabbati, trans. William Braude, 2 vols. (New Haven, Conn., 1968).

PETUCHOWSKI, JAKOB, 'Modern Misunderstandings of an Ancient Benediction', in J. Petuchowski and E. Fleischer (eds.), *Studies in Aggadah, Targum and Jewish Liturgy in Memory of Joseph Heinemann* (Jerusalem, 1981), 45–54.

——*Prayerbook Reform in Europe: The Liturgy of European Liberal and Reform Judaism* (New York, 1968).

——*Theology and Poetry* (London, 1978).

——(ed.), *Understanding Jewish Prayer* (New York, 1972).

PICKSTOCK, CATHERINE, *After Writing: On the Liturgical Consummation of Philosophy* (Oxford, 1998).

Pirke de Rabbi Eliezer, trans. Gerald Friedlander (London, 1916).

Pirkei derabi eli'ezer (Warsaw, 1852).

POLZIN, ROBERT, *Moses and the Deuteronomist* (Bloomington, Ind., 1980).

PROUST, MARCEL, *A la recherche du temps perdu*, 3 vols. (Paris, 1955).

——*Remembrance of Things Past*, vol. i: *Swann's Way*, trans. C. K. Scott Moncrieff, 2 vols. (London, 1964).

RABINOWITZ, LOUIS, 'Psalms, Book of', *Encyclopaedia Judaica* (Jerusalem, 1971), xiii. 1303–34.

RACKMAN, EMMANUEL, MICHAEL BROYDE, and AMY LYNNE FISHKIN, 'Halakhah, Law in Judaism', in Jacob Neusner et al. (eds.), *The Encyclopaedia of Judaism* (Leiden, 2000), i. 340–50.

RAPPAPORT, ROY, *Ecology, Meaning, and Religion* (Richmond, Calif., 1979).

RASHI, *Pentateuch with Rashi's Commentary*, trans. M. Rosenbaum and M. Silvermann, 5 vols. (London, 1929–34).

REIF, STEFAN, 'The Early Liturgy of the Synagogue', in W. Horbury, W. D. Davies, and J. Sturdy (eds.), *The Cambridge History of Judaism*, vol. iii (Cambridge, 1999), 326–57.

—— 'Jewish Liturgical Research: Past, Present, and Future', *Journal of Jewish Studies*, 34 (1983), 161–70.

—— *Judaism and Hebrew Prayer* (Cambridge, 1993).

RIMMON-KENAN, SHLOMITH, *Narrative Fiction: Contemporary Poetics* (London, 1983).

ROEMER, MICHAEL, *Telling Stories: Postmodernism and the Invalidation of Traditional Narrative* (London, 1995).

ROITMAN, BETTY, 'Sacred Language and Open Text', in Geoffrey Hartman and Sanford Budick (eds.), *Midrash and Literature* (New Haven, Conn., 1986), 159–75.

ROSENBERG, SHALOM, 'Prayer and Jewish Thought: Approaches and Problems (A Survey)', in Gabriel Cohn and Harold Fisch (eds.), *Prayer in Judaism: Continuity and Change* (Northvale, NJ, 1996), 69–107.

ROTH, CECIL, *Magna Bibliotheca Anglo-Judaica* (London, 1937).

ROTH, LEON, *Judaism: A Portrait* (London, 1960).

RYCROFT, CHARLES, *A Critical Dictionary of Psychoanalysis* (Harmondsworth, 1979).

SA'ADIAH GAON, *The Book of Beliefs and Opinions*, trans. Samuel Rosenblatt (New Haven, Conn., 1948).

SAFRAI, HANNAH, 'Women and the Ancient Synagogue', in Susan Grossman and Rivka Haut (eds.), *Daughters of the King: Women and the Synagogue* (Philadelphia, Pa., 1992), 39–49.

SAFRAI, SHMUEL, 'Ishmael ben Elisha', *Encyclopaedia Judaica* (Jerusalem, 1971), ix. 83–6.

SAID, EDWARD, *Beginnings: Intentions and Methods* (London, 1978).

SARAH, ELIZABETH TIKVAH, 'Meditations for *Tallit* and *T'fillin*', in Sylvia Rothschild and Sybil Sheridan (eds.), *Taking up the Timbrel: The Challenge of Creating Ritual for Jewish Women Today* (London, 2000), 33–6.

SCHÄFER, PETER, 'Gershom Scholem Reconsidered: The Aim and Purpose of Early Jewish Mysticism', *The Twelfth Sacks Lecture Delivered on 29th May 1985* (Oxford, 1986).

SCHALLER, JOSEPH, 'Performative Language Theory: An Exercise in the Analysis of Ritual', *Worship*, 62 (1988), 415–32.

SCHECHTER, SOLOMON, *Some Aspects of Rabbinic Theology* (New York, 1909).

—— *Studies in Judaism* (London, 1896).

SCHEINDLIN, RAYMOND, *The Gazelle: Medieval Hebrew Poems on God, Israel, and the Soul* (Philadelphia, Pa., 1991).

SCHLEIERMACHER, FRIEDRICH, *Predigten* (Berlin, 1806).

SCHOLEM, GERSHOM, *Jewish Gnosticism, Merkabah Mysticism, and Talmudic Tradition* (New York, 1965).

—— *Kabbalah* (Jerusalem, 1974).

—— *Major Trends in Jewish Mysticism* (London, 1955).

—— *Origins of the Kabbalah* (Princeton, NJ, 1987).

SCHONFELD, SOLOMON, *Jewish Religious Education* (London, 1943).

SCHONFIELD, JEREMY, 'Zion: The Fundamentals of a Misreading', *European Judaism*, 34 (2001), 70–84.

——(ed.), *The Barcelona Haggadah* (London, 1992).

SCHWAB, SHIMON, *Rav Schwab on Prayer* (New York, 2001).

SCHWARTZ, REGINA (ed.), *The Book and the Text: The Bible and Literary Theory* (Oxford, 1990).

SCHWEID, ELIEZER, 'Kedushah', *Encyclopaedia Judaica* (Jerusalem, 1971), x. 866–75.

——'Prayer in the Thought of Yehudah Halevi', in Gabriel Cohn and Harold Fisch (eds.), *Prayer in Judaism: Continuity and Change* (Northvale, NJ, 1996), 109–17.

Seder olam rabah, ed. B. Ratner (repr. Jerusalem, 1987).

SED-RAJNA, GABRIELLE (ed.), *Azriel de Gérone: Commentaire sur la liturgie quotidienne, introduction, traduction annotée et glossaire des termes techniques* (Leiden, 1974).

Sefer haroke'aḥ (Jerusalem, 1966).

SEGAL, J. B., *The Hebrew Passover from the Earliest Times to AD 70* (Oxford, 1963).

SHAPIRA, NATHAN BEN DAVID REUBEN TEVELE, *Metsat shimurim* (Venice, 1665; Jerusalem, 2001).

SHERWIN, BYRON, *Mystical Theology and Social Dissent: The Life and Works of Judah Loew of Prague* (London, 1982).

SHERWOOD, YVONNE, *A Biblical Text and its Afterlives* (Cambridge, 2000).

——*The Prostitute and the Prophet* (Sheffield, 1996).

SHKLOVSKY, VICTOR, 'Art as Technique', in David Lodge (ed.), *Modern Criticism and Theory* (London, 1988), 16–30.

Shulḥan arukh. See Caro, Joseph

Sifra (New York, n.d.).

Sifrei debei rab, ed. M. Friedmann (Vienna, 1864).

SILVER, DANIEL JEREMY, *Maimonidean Criticism and the Maimonidean Controversy, 1180–1240* (Leiden, 1965).

SIMON, ERNST, 'On the Meaning of Prayer', in Jakob Petuchowski (ed.), *Understanding Jewish Prayer* (New York, 1972), 100–11.

SIMON, URIEL, *Four Approaches to the Book of Psalms* (New York, 1991).

——'Teaching *Siddur* to Enhance Devotion in Prayer', in Gabriel Cohn and Harold Fisch (eds.), *Prayer in Judaism: Continuity and Change* (Northvale, NJ, 1996), 189–97.

SIRAT, COLETTE, *A History of Jewish Philosophy in the Middle Ages* (Cambridge, 1985).

SLUTSKY, YEHUDA, 'Romm', *Encyclopaedia Judaica* (Jerusalem, 1971), xiv. 255–6.

SMIRNOV, ANDREY, 'The Universe as a Phenomenon of Language: Sa'adiah Gaon's Commentary to the *Book of Creation*', in Raphael Jospe (ed.), *Paradigms in Jewish Philosophy* (London, 1997), 87–111.

SOPHOCLES, *The Theban Plays*, trans. E. F. Watling (Harmondsworth, 1947).

SPIEGEL, SHALOM, *The Last Trial* (New York, 1979).

STEINER, GEORGE, *Real Presences* (Chicago, 1989).

STEMBERGER, GÜNTER, *Introduction to the Talmud and Midrash* (Edinburgh, 1996).

STERN, DAVID, *Midrash and Theory: Ancient Jewish Exegesis and Contemporary Literary Studies* (Evanston, Ill., 1996).

TABORY, JOSEPH, 'The Benedictions of Self-Identity and the Changing Status of Women and of Orthodoxy', in id. (ed.), *Kenishta: Studies of the Synagogue World* (Tel Aviv, 2001), i. 121–38.

——'Prayer and *Halakhah*', in Gabriel Cohn and Harold Fisch (eds.), *Prayer in Judaism: Continuity and Change* (Northvale, NJ, 1996), 53–68.

——(ed.), *Kenishta: Studies of the Synagogue World*, 2 vols. (Tel Aviv, 2001, 2003).

TAITZ, EMILY, 'Women's Voices, Women's Prayers: Women in European Synagogues of the Middle Ages', in Susan Grossman and Rivka Haut (eds.), *Daughters of the King: Women and the Synagogue* (Philadelphia, Pa., 1992), 59–71.

TALMAGE, FRANK, 'Apples of Gold: The Inner Meaning of Sacred Texts in Medieval Judaism', in Arthur Green (ed.), *Jewish Spirituality*, (London, 1986), i. 313–55.

Talmudic Encyclopaedia [Entsiklopediyah talmudit], 25 vols. (Jerusalem, 1947–).

Tana debei eliyahu, ed. M. Friedmann (Vienna, 1902).

Tanna debe Eliyyahu, trans. William Braude and Israel Kapstein (Philadelphia, Pa., 1981).

TEMKIN, SEFTON, 'Wolf Heidenheim', *Encyclopaedia Judaica* (Jerusalem, 1971), viii. 258–9.

TISHBY, ISAIAH, *Mishnat hazohar*, 2 vols. (Jerusalem, 1971–4).

—— *Wisdom of the Zohar*, trans. David Goldstein, 3 vols. (Oxford, 1989).

TOMPKINS, JANE (ed.), *Reader-Response Criticism: From Formalism to Post-structuralism* (Baltimore, Md., 1980).

Torat hayim [Pentateuch with medieval commentaries], 5 vols. (Jerusalem, 1986–93).

Tosefta [in edn. of Babylonian Talmud] (Vilna, 1907).

UFFENHEIMER, RIVKA SCHATZ, *Hasidism as Mysticism: Quietistic Elements in Eighteenth Century Hasidic Thought* (Princeton, NJ, 1993).

URBACH, EPHRAIM, *The Sages*, trans. from the Hebrew by Israel Abrahams, 2 vols. (Jerusalem, 1987).

WEINBERGER, LEON, *Jewish Hymnography: A Literary History* (London, 1998).

WEISS, AVRAHAM, *Women at Prayer: A Halakhic Analysis of Women's Prayer Groups* (Hoboken, NJ, 1990).

WEITZMAN, MICHAEL, 'The Origin of the "Qaddish"', in Nicholas de Lange (ed.), *Hebrew Scholarship and the Medieval World* (Cambridge, 2001), 131–7.

WERTHEIMER, SOLOMON (ed.), *Batei midrashot*, 2 vols., 2nd edn. (Jerusalem, 1989).

WHITE, HAYDEN, *Tropics of Discourse: Essays in Cultural Criticism* (Baltimore, Md., 1978).

WIESELTIER, LEON, *Kaddish* (New York, 1998).

WILLETT, JOHN, *The Theatre of Bertolt Brecht: A Study from Eight Aspects* (London, 1977).

WIMSATT, W. K., and MONROE BEARDSLEY, *The Verbal Icon: Studies in the Meaning of Poetry* (Lexington, Ky., 1954).

WRIGHT, ALEXANDRA, 'Speech—the Ultimate Healer', *Manna*, 12 (1986), 19.

Yalkut shimoni (Berlin, 1926).

YANNAI, *The Liturgical Poems of Rabbi Yannai*, ed. Z. M. Rabinovitz, 2 vols. (Jerusalem, 1985).

ZAHAVY, TZVEE, 'A New Approach to Early Jewish Prayer', in M. B. Bokser (ed.), *History of Judaism: The Next Ten Years* (Chico, Calif., 1980), 45–60.

ZANGWILL, ISRAEL, *Children of the Ghetto* (London, 1892).

ZEDEKIAH BEN ABRAHAM, *Shibolei haleket*, ed. Solomon Buber (Vilna, 1887).

ZIMMELS, H. J., *Ashkenazim and Sephardim: Their Relations, Differences and Problems as Reflected in the Rabbinical Responsa* (London, 1958).

Zohar, 3 vols. (Vilna, n.d.).

Zohar, trans. M. Simon, H. Sperling, and P. P. Levertoff, 5 vols. (London, 1934).

ZORNBERG, AVIVAH GOTTLIEB, *The Beginning of Desire: Reflections on Genesis* (New York, 1995).

ZUNZ, LEOPOLD, *Die Ritus des synagogalen Gottesdienstes* (Berlin, 1859).

Index of Biblical and Rabbinic References

🙟

Rashi (cont.):

Gen. 26: 20 — 141 n.
Gen. 28: 17 — 207 n.
Exod. 14: 4 — 236 n.
Exod. 15: 1 — 301 n.
Exod. 15: 17 — 301 n.
Exod. 17: 11 — 36 n.
Exod. 20: 1 — 141 n.
Exod. 22: 25 — 75 n.
Exod. 33: 23 — 101 n.
Exod. 34: 1 — 91 n.
Exod. 34: 6–7 — 228 n.
Lev. 19: 2 — 301 n.
Num. 3: 1 — 143 n.
Num. 8: 2 — 45 n.
Num. 15: 39 — 93 n.
Num. 15: 41 — 90 n.
Num. 16: 1 — 215 n.
Num. 19: 2 — 26 n., 55 n., 83 n.
Num. 21: 8 — 36 n.
Num. 24: 5 — 114 n.
Deut. 6: 7 — 46 n.
Deut. 22: 12 — 90 n.
Deut. 30: 3 — 331 n.
2 Sam. 24: 1 — 258 n.
Ps. 30: 1 — 242 n.
Prov. 20: 17 — 143 n.
Eccles. 3: 21 — 181 n.
Eccles. 12: 3 — 243 n.
Isa. 49: 8 — 159 n.
Dan. 6: 8 — 74 n., 77 n.

MEDIEVAL COMMENTARIES ON THE TALMUD, AND TOSAFOT

Rashi on the Babylonian Talmud

Ber. 11b — 138 n.
Shab. 118b — 249 n., 264 n.
Ket. 8b — 333 n.
BB 123a — 246 n.
San. 91b — 301 n.
Zev. 46b–47a — 24 n.
Ḥul. 12b–13a — 24 n.

Tosafot

Berakhot
11b — 145 n.
46a — 142 n.

Kidushin
30a — 145 n.

Sanhedrin
24a — 206 n.

MAIMONIDES

Guide of the Perplexed
1: 59 — 237 n.
3: 26 — 209 n.
3: 32, 36, 44, 51 — 34 n., 209 n.
3: 45–6 — 34 n.

Mishneh torah
Sefer hamada
'Hilkhot teshuvah' (Laws of Repentance)
3: 13 — 201 n.

Sefer ahavah
'Hilkhot keriat shema' (Laws of Reading the Shema) — 23 n.
'Hilkhot tefilah uvirkhat kohanim' (Laws of Prayer)
1–10 — 23 n.
1: 4 — 4 n.
2 (Seder tefilot lekol hashanah) — 23 n.
4: 15–16 — 22 n.
7: 3 — 150 n.
7: 9 — 82 n.
7: 10 — 142 n.
7: 12 — 272 n.
7: 13 — 298 n.
Seder tefilot kol hashanah — 23 n.

Sefer avodah
'Hilkhot me'ilah' (Laws Concerning Trespass)
8: 8 — 207 n.

Sefer shofetim
'Hilkhot melakhim umilḥamoteihem' (Laws of Kings and their Wars)
11–12 — 84 n.
11: 1 — 209 n.

JACOB BEN ASHER

Arba'ah turim, 'Oraḥ ḥayim'
46–149 — 23 n.
46 — 9 n., 161 n., 174 n., 189 n., 194 n.
48–50 — 208 n.
50 — 21 n., 225 n.
51 — 276 n., 285 n., 289 n., 299 n.
56 — 235 n., 236 n.
116 — 116 n.

JOSEPH CARO

Beit yosef, 'Oraḥ ḥayim'
46 — 173 n.
50 — 225 n.

Shulḥan arukh, 'Oraḥ ḥayim'
4 — 131 n.
4: 18, 23 — 132 n.
17: 2 — 84 n.
30: 1 — 82 n.
46: 2 — 82 n.
46: 4 — 159 n.
47: 1 — 141 n.
50 — 221 n., 226 n.
51 — 256 n., 268 n.
62: 2 — 25 n.

Index of Subjects and Names

Index of Subjects and Names

Lamentations, book of:
  fear of loss in 80
  idea of exile 109
  opening of 43, 218, 245
  personification of city 208
  personification of Israel 218
  quoted in opening statement of the day 109,
    200, 312
  views of God 60–1
Landes, Daniel 62
language:
  angelic 103, 178, 193, 336
  Aramaic 59, 230, 238
  centrality of, in liturgy 80
  effectiveness of 230
  God's 56–7, 211, 250–1, 253, 255
  Hebrew 19, 23–4, 26, 34, 59, 238, 294
  human 250–1
  ineffectiveness of 123, 212, 250, 272, 306–7,
    315
  power to transform reality 207, 210–11
  rabbinic relationship to 210, 226–7
  vernacular 24
Laytner, Anson 323
lehaniyaḥ tefilin 103–5
lehitatef batsitsit 90–1
Leibowitz, Yeshayahu 36
Lekhah Dodi 42, 318 n.
Le'olam yehe adam yere shamayim 171–6
Lefikhakh anaḥnu ḥayavim lehodot lekha 185–8
Levi 246
Levi, David 16
Levi ben Gershon 5 n.
Levites 45
Leviticus 212–13, 219, 220, 335, 338, 342
liturgy:
  approaches to reading 54–8
  as a literary genre 47–51
  Ashkenazi 10, 69, 173, 188, 219, 244, 262,
    302, 325, 331, 332–3, 334–5, 337–43
  commentaries on 6–7, 11–19
  detachment factor 30–2
  difficulty factor 29–30
  eastern Ashkenazi 28, 326
  editions of 11–19
  evening 320
  failure to study 22, 26, 29, 30, 37, 44
  gaps in 55–7, 58–60, 123
  hasidic 28, 326
  historical approach to 21, 30
  'ideal reader' of 38–44

Liberal 345–6
  mantric approach to 7–8, 10, 32
  multiple versions of 26–9
  narrative of 5–7, 58–62
  oriental 326, 334
  origins 51
  performance 22–6, 38–9, 47–51
  philosophical factor 32–8, 317
  prayer-leader 25, 83, 238, 250
  progressive movements 343–6
  recurring themes in 318–24
  Reform 344–5
  relationship with study 320–1
  repetition in 59, 62–3, 229
  responses 25–6
  role in Jewish thought 4
  Sephardi, *see* Sephardi rite
  structure 19–21
  study of 4–5, 10, 12, 15, 26, 37–8, 44
  theatre and 48–51
  translations of 11–19
  western Ashkenazi 325, 338–9
Lorbeerbaum, Jacob 13, 16, 48
Lupinski, A. S. 18
Lurianic thought:
  hymn 141
  influence 69, 90, 214, 239
  liturgists 273
  on God's name 340
  tsimtsum 35

M

Maharal, *see* Judah Loew ben Bezalel
Mah yakar ḥasdekha 90–3
Mah tovu ohaleikha 112–17
Maimonides, Moses:
  commentary on Mishnah 11
  laws of prayer 23
  Maimonidean controversy 32, 34, 125–6
  on sacrifice 209
  on silence as worship 237
  on Song of the Sea 298
  on waking prayer 150
  Sefer ahavah 23
  thirteen articles of faith 123, 126
Malachi 143, 214, 229
Ma'oz Tsur 29
martyrdom:
  Akedah allusion 173, 328–9
  Akiba's 174–5, 177, 228, 311 n.
  challenge to 192–6
  identification with bereavement 245

Printed and bound by CPI Group (UK) Ltd, Croydon, CR0 4YY

09/06/2025

14685820-0005